MULTITUDE
Cross-Cultural Readings for Writers

MULTITUDE

Cross-Cultural Readings for Writers

SECOND EDITION

Chitra Divakaruni

Foothill College

THE McGRAW-HILL COMPANIES, INC.

New York   St. Louis   San Francisco   Auckland   Bogotá   Caracas   Lisbon
London   Madrid   Mexico City   Milan   Montreal   New Delhi
San Juan   Singapore   Sydney   Tokyo   Toronto

McGraw-Hill

A Division of The McGraw·Hill Companies

MULTITUDE

Cross-Cultural Readings for Writers

This book is printed on acid-free paper.

1 2 3 4 5 6 7 8 9 0   FGR   FGR   9 0 9 8 7 6

ISBN 0-07-017086-X

This book was set in Galliard by The Clarinda Company.
The editors were Tim Julet and Laura Lynch;
the production supervisor was Louise Karam.
The cover was designed by Karen K. Quigley.
The photo editor was Natalia Yamrom.
Project supervision was done by The Total Book.
Quebecor Printing/Fairfield was printer and binder.

Credits for Part-Opening Photographs

Part One	Edward P. Lincoln/Photo Researchers
Part Two	David M. Grossman/Photo Researchers
Part Three	Joel Gordon
Part Four	Chester Higgins, Jr./Photo Researchers
Part Five	Spencer Grant/Stock, Boston
Part Six	Marilyn Humphries/Impact Visuals
Part Seven	Sandra Weiner/The Image Works
Part Eight	Joel Gordon
Part Nine	Eugene Richards/Magnum
Part Ten	Joel Gordon

Library of Congress Cataloging-in-Publication Data

Divakaruni, Chitra, (date).
    Multitude: cross-cultural readings for writers/Chitra
Divakaruni. — 2d ed.
        p.   cm.
    Includes index.
    ISBN 0-07-017086-X
    1. Readers—Social sciences.   2. Pluralism (Social sciences)—
Problems, exercises, etc.   3. Culture—Problems, exercises, etc.
4. English language—Rhetoric.   5. College readers.   I. Title.
[PE1127.S6D58   1997]
808'.0427—dc20
                                                96-2699

http://www.mhcollege.com

ABOUT THE EDITOR

Originally from India, Chitra B. Divakaruni has a Ph.D. in English from the University of California at Berkeley. She lives with her husband Murthy and son Anand in the San Francisco Bay Area and teaches English and creative writing at Foothill College, where she is a director of the annual multicultural creative writing conference. Dr. Divakaruni's poems have appeared in publications such as *The Beloit Poetry Journal, Chelsea, The Colorado Review, Ms.*, and *The Threepenny Review*. She has also published three books of poetry—*Dark Like the River, The Reason for Nasturtiums,* and *Black Candle*—and has been nominated twice for the Pushcart Prize. She has also received a Gerbode Foundation Award. Actively involved in women's issues, she is a volunteer for the Mid Peninsula Support Network Women's Shelter and the coordinator of MAITRI, a Bay Area help line for south Asian women.

PHOTO CREDIT: DHRUVA BANERJEE

For my teachers and my students

CONTENTS

PART NINE
The Uses of Entertainment   471

PART TEN
Our Sameness, Our Difference

LIST OF SELECTIONS BY RHETORICAL MODE

Note: Selections using more than one rhetorical mode are listed under each pertinent category. Fiction and poetry are listed separately. Some selections have a unique character and thus are not listed under any of these categories.

Narration

Description

Comparison and Contrast

Cause and Effect

Illustration

Process

Classification

Analysis

Argumentation

Fiction and Poetry

PREFACE

Like the first edition of *Multitude*, this second edition, designed for use in first year college composition classes, is a thematically arranged collection of readings with a multicultural focus that broadens our awareness of diversity and allows us to take pride in our many heritages. The growing numbers of multicultural texts on the market today affirm the importance of teaching reading and writing from this perspective. A particular strength of *Multitude* is that it approaches the theme of diversity joyfully, balancing serious or tragic readings with positive, life-affirming ones which assert the common humanity we all share.

Distinctive Features of the Text

The following features of this edition of *Multitude* deserve special mention:

- Ten thematic parts, moving from the personal to the social, and the relatively simple to the increasingly complex, on topics easy for students to relate to
- Readings (approximately 40% new) from many cultures—from within the U.S. and from other countries—to provide contrasting perspectives which help us examine ourselves more closely and understand ourselves better
- Readings of varying lengths and levels of difficulty to suit the needs of different types of students
- Readings that span the different rhetorical modes and genres
- Added emphasis on non-fiction and argumentation
- A good mix of classic readings known to work well in the classroom and recently published work dealing with contemporary issues
- New writing by established authors
- Companion pieces that explore different facets of the same issue and argue different sides of a question
- Student essays that use various rhetorical modes, from narration and description to argument and literary analysis, and that inspire students in a number of ways
- An extensive teaching apparatus with each selection including Prereading activities geared to different learning styles, Biographical Notes to aid the students' understanding of the writer's background, Analysis questions to check the students' grasp of the text, and Writing Assignments that make strong reading/writing connections and challenge students to think critically and read widely
- New Collaborative Learning exercises to develop the skill of working and learning together

- Expanded Synthesis questions at the end of each chapter to help students connect up different readings and understand each in the context of the others
- An updated Instructors' Manual with teaching strategies, discussion ideas, modeling assignments and some sample responses

Acknowledgments

I would like to thank the many, many people who have helped me improve this book, though I can express my gratitude to only a few by name.

McGraw-Hill and I would like to thank the following reviewers (of both the first and second editions of *Multitude*) for their many helpful comments and suggestions: Ken Autry, Francis Marion College; Margaret Bedrosian, University of California-Davis; Marian Calabrese, Sacred Heart University; Beverly Conner, University of Puget Sound; Tamara S. Cornelison, La Salle University; Janet Erickson, University of Illinois; Joan Gilson, University of Missouri at Kansas City; Suhail Hanna, Geneva College; Anna Katsavos, Nassau Community College; René Martin, Miami-Dade Community College, South; Lyle Morgan, II, Pittsburg State University; Sarah-Hope Parmeter, University of California at Santa Cruz; Michele Peterson, Santa Barbara City College; Richard Prystowski, Irvine Valley College; Christie Rubio, American River College; Jonathan Smith, University of Michigan-Dearborn; Linda J. Strom, Youngstown State University; Ron Taylor, Santa Rosa Junior College; and Jacqueline S. Wilson, Western Illinois University.

My thanks to my friends Marjorie and Jon Ford for their continuing support, encouragement and feedback. To my colleagues at Foothill College, especially Scott Lankford, Nancy Gill, Kurt Gravenhorst and Denny Berthiaume for helping me find effective readings and student papers. To Karen Gillette in the library for helping me locate elusive essays, and to Kathy Fransham in the Teaching Resource Center for helping with word processing problems. And especially to all the students at Foothill College who enthusiastically tried out the reading and writing assignments and told me which ones worked best for them.

At McGraw-Hill I would like to thank my editors Tim Julet and Laura Lynch for their astute suggestions, and Lesley Denton, Marketing Manager, for letting people know of the book.

And finally, my deepest thanks to my family: my husband Murthy, my mother Tatini Banerjee, my mother-in-law Sita Divakaruni, and my little ones, Anand and Abhay, for their loving encouragement and patience, without which this book would not have been possible.

CHITRA B. DIVAKARUNI

MULTITUDE
Cross-Cultural Readings for Writers

PART ONE

How It All Began

SELECTIONS IN PART ONE

PART 1: INTRODUCTION

*T*he subject of origins is fascinating for us all, no matter what culture we come from. As children, we start asking questions which often stay with us through our adult lives: How did the world come about? How did the human race begin? It is unlikely that any of these questions has a single definitive answer; yet if we are to make sense of the complex world in which we live and interact with others—if we are even to survive—some sort of answer must be attempted. Therefore, religions and philosophies through the ages have given us many versions of our origins—some presented simply as myths or tales, and some presented as divine revelation. In either case, each version is affected by the culture and time out of which it rises, as can be seen in selections 1, 2, and 3: the Eskimo creation myth and the excerpts from Plato's *Symposium* and from the Bible. And yet we can also see that there is something timeless and universal about these selections, something they possess in common that touches us no matter how our heritage and beliefs may differ from those of their authors.

From questions about the origin of our species, we move to questions more clearly focused on our own racial and historical heritage: Where did my people come from? How did we get here, and why did we come? What was this country like when we arrived? How were we treated? The immense range of possible answers is hinted at by selections as varied as Christopher Columbus's "Letter" (selection 4), Mary Antin's "The Promised Land" (selection 5), and Hongo's "America Singing" (selection 6). Where Columbus takes possession of the lands he sees, renaming them so that they echo the lands he has left behind, Antin's experience is a metaphoric birth into a new life, at once strange, frightening, and exhilarating. And Hongo's immigrants, many of whom have come to America to save their lives, form a "new republic of exchange" at turns admired and feared by those whom Hongo ironically terms the "real Americans."

Ultimately we come to that aspect of origins which is closest to us and which has attracted the attention of many writers irrespective of place and time: Who am I? How did *my* life begin? What happened in my early years to make me the person I am today? Three authors in Part One explore different facets of this intimate experience. Mei Mei Berssenbrugge (selection 8) looks at the moment of her birth, uniquely colored by the dynamics of her Asian family. Frederick Douglass (selection 7) intertwines personal reality with social reality and gives us a penetrating glimpse into the life of a slave child in the early 1800s. And the student essay by Mary Peterson uses research to analyze the tremendous obstacles Douglass had to overcome in order to achieve his rare success, thus providing one more way of approaching the complex, ever-fascinating subject of how it all began.

1

PREREADING ACTIVITY

Before reading selection 1, think back to stories from your culture which you heard or read, as you were growing up, that attempted to explain the creation of the world. Write down the story you remember most distinctly.

The Time When There Were No People on the Earth Plain

Bering Strait Eskimo Creation Myth

The Bering Strait Eskimos are among the Alaskan Eskimos. They do not, however, call themselves Eskimos, which is a name given to them by the Algonquin Indians and means "eaters of raw meat." Their name for themselves is Inuit, or "real people," a term that throws interesting light on their creation myth (which was recorded around the turn of the century). Although they are descendents of the Old Bering Sea Eskimos (300 B.C.–A.D. 500) and racially distinct from Native Americans (American Indians), selection 1 has many similarities with Native American myths, including an animistic religion. Surprisingly, there are almost no indications in the myth that the Bering Strait Eskimos are primarily hunters of maritime mammals.

*I*t was in the time when there were no people on the earth plain. During four days the first man lay coiled up in the pod of a beach-pea. On the fifth day he stretched out his feet and burst the pod, falling to the ground, where he stood up, a full-grown man. He looked about him, and then moved his hands and arms, his neck and legs, and examined himself curiously. Looking back, he saw the pod from which he had fallen, still hanging to the vine, with a hole in the lower end, out of which he had dropped. Then he looked about him again and saw that he was getting farther away from his starting place, and that the ground moved up and down under his feet and seemed very soft. After a while he had an unpleasant feeling in his stomach, and he stooped down to take some water into his mouth from a small pool at his feet. The water ran down into his stomach and he felt better. When he looked up again he saw approaching, with a waving motion, a dark object which came on until just in front of him, when it stopped, and, standing on the ground, looked at him. This was a raven, and, as soon as it stopped, it raised one of its wings, pushed up its beak, like a mask, to the top of its head, and changed at once into a man. Before he raised his mask Raven had

1

stared at the man, and after it was raised he stared more than ever, moving about from side to side to obtain a better view. At last he said: "What are you? Whence did you come? I have never seen anything like you." Then Raven looked at Man, and was still more surprised to find that this strange new being was so much like himself in shape.

Then he told Man to walk away a few steps, and in astonishment exclaimed again: "When did you come? I have never seen anything like you before." To this Man replied: "I came from the pea-pod." And he pointed to the plant from which he came. "Ah!" exclaimed Raven, "I made that vine, but did not know that anything like you would ever come from it. Come with me to the high ground over there; this ground I made later, and it is still soft and thin, but it is thicker and harder there."

In a short time they came to the higher land, which was firm under their feet. Then Raven asked Man if he had eaten anything. The latter answered that he had taken some soft stuff into him at one of the pools. "Ah!" said Raven, "you drank some water. Now wait for me here."

Then he drew down the mask over his face, changing again into a bird, and flew far up into the sky where he disappeared. Man waited where he had been left until the fourth day, when Raven returned, bringing four berries in his claws. Pushing up his mask, Raven became a man again and held out two salmonberries and two hearthberries, saying, "Here is what I have made for you to eat. I also wish them to be plentiful over the earth. Now eat them." Man took the berries and placed them in his mouth one after the other and they satisfied his hunger, which had made him feel uncomfortable. Raven then led Man to a small creek near by and left him while he went to the water's edge and molded a couple of pieces of clay into the form of a pair of mountain sheep, which he held in his hand, and when they became dry he called Man to show him what he had done. Man thought they were very pretty, and Raven told him to close his eyes. As soon as Man's eyes were closed Raven drew down his mask and waved his wings four times over the images, when they became endowed with life and bounded away as full-grown mountain sheep. Raven then raised his mask and told Man to look. When Man saw the sheep moving away, full of life, he cried out with pleasure. Seeing how pleased Man was, Raven said, "If these animals are numerous, perhaps people will wish very much to get them." And Man said he thought they would. "Well," said Raven, "it will be better for them to have their home among the high cliffs, so that every one can not kill them, and there only shall they be found."

Then Raven made two animals of clay which he endowed with life as before, but as they were dry only in spots when they were given life, they remained brown and white, and so originated the tame reindeer with mottled coat. Man thought these were very handsome, and Raven told him that they would be very scarce. In the same way a pair of wild reindeer were made and permitted to get dry and white only on their bellies, then they were given life; in consequence, to this day the belly of the wild reindeer is the only white part about it. Raven told Man that these animals would be very common, and people would kill many of them.

"You will be very lonely by yourself," said Raven. "I will make you a companion." He then went to a spot some distance from where he had made the animals, and looking now and then at Man, made an image very much like him. Then he fastened a lot of fine water grass on the back of the head for hair, and after the image had dried in his hands, he waved his wings over it as before and a beautiful young woman arose and stood beside Man. "There," cried Raven, "is a companion for you," and he led them back to a small knoll near by.

In those days there were no mountains far or near, and the sun never ceased shining brightly; no rain ever fell and no winds blew. When they came to the knoll, Raven showed the pair how to make a bed in the dry moss, and they slept there very warmly; Raven drew down his mask and slept nearby in the form of a bird. Waking before the others, Raven went back to the creek and made a pair each of sticklebacks, graylings, and blackfish. When these were swimming about in the water, he called Man to see them. When the latter looked at them and saw the sticklebacks swim up the stream with a wriggling motion he was so surprised that he raised his hand suddenly and the fish darted away. Raven then showed him the graylings and told him that they would be found in clear mountain streams, while the sticklebacks would live along the seacoast and that both would be good for food. Next the shrew-mouse was made, Raven saying that it would not be good for food but would enliven the ground and prevent it from seeming barren and cheerless.

In this way Raven continued for several days making birds, fishes, and animals, showing them to Man, and explaining their uses.

QUESTIONS FOR CRITICAL READING, THINKING, DISCUSSION, AND WRITING

Analyzing Content and Technique

1. Who is the "creator" in this myth? What surprising characteristics does he possess?
2. Analyze the relationship between human beings and the other creatures that inhabit the earth plain. What underlying world vision is indicated by this relationship?
3. Discuss the tone of this piece. What stylistic details help to create this tone? How is this piece (an oral tale) different from a formally written piece?
4. Explain the implied message or main idea of the piece. What is its purpose?

Collaborative Activity

Selection 1 presents us with the picture of a perfect world, a utopia. As a group, examine the most important elements of this world. Now have group members brainstorm for a few minutes to create a list of elements they would want in *their* utopia. How is your utopia similar to, or different from, the one in the Eskimo myth?

Making Connections

1. Often the narrative perspective of a story can affect its structure, focus, and atmosphere greatly. Rewrite this myth, which is written in an omniscient third person, from a different perspective, maybe that of man, or maybe that of one of the other animals. Examine what you have written, comparing it to the original myth. How it is different?

2. Read one or two other Native American myths, such as those dealing with Coyote or Spider Woman. Write an essay in which you analyze important elements which these myths have in common and which indicate to you some of the values of the culture they come from.

2

PREREADING ACTIVITY

Before reading selection 2, sprint write for five minutes about what you know of the origins of human beings. Are you familiar with more than one theory or belief? Which do you believe in? Why?

On Love, from "Symposium"

PLATO

Plato (c. 428–348 B.C.)—the most eminent student of Socrates and in turn the teacher of Aristotle—created many of the philosophical ideas and terms that make up the core of western civilization. Inspired by Socrates, he gave up the chance of pursuing a powerful political career to found the Academy—the first western university—and devoted his life to philosophical inquiry. He wrote over twenty volumes in which he recorded the conversations of Socrates with his students and friends.

Well then, Eryximachus, Aristophanes began, I propose, as you 1 suggested, to take quite a different line from you and Pausanias. I am convinced that mankind has never had any conception of the power of Love, for if we had known him as he really is, surely we should have raised the mightiest temples and altars, and offered the most splendid sacrifices, in his honor, and not—as in fact we do—have utterly neglected him. Yet he of all the gods has the best title to our service, for he, more than all the rest, is the friend of man; he is our great ally, and it is he that cures us of those ills whose relief opens the way to man's highest happiness. And so, gentlemen, I will do my best to acquaint you with the power of Love, and you in your turn shall pass the lesson on.

First of all I must explain the real nature of man, and the change which it 2 has undergone—for in the beginning we were nothing like we are now. For one thing, the race was divided into three; that is to say, besides the two sexes, male and female, which we have at present, there was a third which partook of the nature of both, and for which we still have a name, though the creature itself is forgotten. For though "hermaphrodite" is only used nowadays as a term of contempt, there really was a man-woman in those days, a being which was half male and half female.

Source: *The Collected Dialogues of Plato*, ed. Edith Hamilton and Huntington Cairns, Bollingen Series LXXI. Copyright © 1961, renewed 1989 by Princeton University Press. Excerpts from *Symposium*, trans. Michael Joyce. Reprinted by permission of Princeton University Press.

And secondly, gentlemen, each of these beings was globular in shape, with rounded back and sides, four arms and four legs, and two faces, both the same, on a cylindrical neck, and one head, with one face one side and one the other, and four ears, and two lots of privates, and all the other parts to match. They walked erect, as we do ourselves, backward or forward, whichever they pleased, but when they broke into a run they simply stuck their legs straight out and went whirling round and round like a clown turning cartwheels. And since they had eight legs, if you count their arms as well, you can imagine that they went bowling along at a pretty good speed.

The three sexes, I may say, arose as follows. The males were descended from the Sun, the females from the Earth, and the hermaphrodites from the Moon, which partakes of either sex, and they were round and they *went* round, because they took after their parents. And such, gentlemen, were their strength and energy, and such their arrogance, that they actually tried—like Ephialtes and Otus in Homer—to scale the heights of heaven and set upon the gods.

At this Zeus took counsel with the other gods as to what was to be done. They found themselves in rather an awkward position; they didn't want to blast them out of existence with thunderbolts as they did the giants, because that would be saying good-bye to all their offerings and devotions, but at the same time they couldn't let them get altogether out of hand. At last, however, after racking his brains, Zeus offered a solution.

I think I can see my way, he said, to put an end to this disturbance by weakening these people without destroying them. What I propose to do is to cut them all in half, thus killing two birds with one stone, for each one will be only half as strong, and there'll be twice as many of them, which will suit us very nicely. They can walk about, upright, on their two legs, and if, said Zeus, I have any more trouble with them, I shall split them up again, and they'll have to hop about on one.

So saying, he cut them all in half just as you or I might chop up sorb apples for pickling, or slice an egg with a hair. And as each half was ready he told Apollo to turn its face, with the half-neck that was left, toward the side that was cut away—thinking that the sight of such a gash might frighten it into keeping quiet—and then to heal the whole thing up. So Apollo turned their faces back to front, and, pulling in the skin all the way round, he stretched it over what we now call the belly—like those bags you pull together with a string—and tied up the one remaining opening so as to form what we call the navel. As for the creases that were left, he smoothed most of them away, finishing off the chest with the sort of tool a cobbler uses to smooth down the leather on the last, but he left a few puckers round about the belly and the navel, to remind us of what we suffered long ago.

Now, when the work of bisection was complete it left each half with a desperate yearning for the other, and they ran together and flung their arms around each other's necks, and asked for nothing better than to be rolled into one. So much so, that they began to die of hunger and general inertia, for neither would do anything without the other. And whenever one half was left alone by the death of its mate, it wandered about questing and clasping in the hope of finding a spare half-woman—or a whole woman, as we should call her nowadays—or half a man. And so the race was dying out.

Fortunately, however, Zeus felt so sorry for them that he devised another 9 scheme. He moved their privates round to the front, for of course they had originally been on the outside—which was now the back—and they had begotten and conceived not upon each other, but, like the grasshoppers, upon the earth. So now, as I say, he moved their members round to the front and made them propagate among themselves, the male begetting upon the female—the idea being that if, in all these clippings and claspings, a man should chance upon a woman, conception would take place and the race would be continued, while if man should conjugate with man, he might at least obtain such satisfaction as would allow him to turn his attention and his energies to the everyday affairs of life. So you see, gentlemen, how far back we can trace our innate love for one another, and how this love is always trying to reintegrate our former nature, to make two into one, and to bridge the gulf between one human being and another.

And so, gentlemen, we are all like pieces of the coins that children break in 10 half for keepsakes—making two out of one, like the flatfish—and each of us is forever seeking the half that will tally with himself. The man who is a slice of the hermaphrodite sex, as it was called, will naturally be attracted by women—the adulterer, for instance—and women who run after men are of similar descent—as, for instance, the unfaithful wife. But the woman who is a slice of the original female is attracted by women rather than by men—in fact she is a Lesbian—while men who are slices of the male are followers of the male, and show their masculinity throughout their boyhood by the way they make friends with men, and the delight they take in lying beside them and being taken in their arms. And these are the most hopeful of the nation's youth, for theirs is the most virile constitution.

I know there are some people who call them shameless, but they are wrong. 11 It is not immodesty that leads them to such pleasures, but daring, fortitude, and masculinity—the very virtues that they recognize and welcome in their lovers—which is proved by the fact that in after years they are the only men who show any real manliness in public life. And so, when they themselves have come to manhood, their love in turn is lavished upon boys. They have no natural inclination to marry and beget children. Indeed, they only do so in deference to the usage of society, for they would just as soon renounce marriage altogether and spend their lives with one another.

Such a man, then, gentlemen, is of an amorous disposition, and gives 12 his love to boys, always clinging to his like. And so, when this boy lover—or any lover, for that matter—is fortunate enough to meet his other half, they are both so intoxicated with affection, with friendship, and with love, that they cannot bear to let each other out of sight for a single instant. It is such reunions as these that impel men to spend their lives together, although they may be hard put to it to say what they really want with one another, and indeed, the purely sexual pleasures of their friendship could hardly account for the huge delight they take in one another's company. The fact is that both their souls are longing for a something else—a something to which they can neither of them put a name, and which they can only give an inkling of in cryptic sayings and prophetic riddles.

Now, supposing Hephaestus were to come and stand over them with his tool bag as they lay there side by side, and suppose he were to ask, Tell me, my dear creatures, what do you really want with one another? [13]

And suppose they didn't know what to say, and he went on, How would you like to be rolled into one, so that you could always be together, day and night, and never be parted again? Because if that's what you want, I can easily weld you together, and then you can live your two lives in one, and, when the time comes, you can die a common death and still be two-in-one in the lower world. Now, what do you say? Is that what you'd like me to do? And would you be happy if I did? [14]

We may be sure, gentlemen, that no lover on earth would dream of refusing such an offer, for not one of them could imagine a happier fate. Indeed, they would be convinced that this was just what they'd been waiting for—to be merged, that is, into an utter oneness with the beloved. [15]

And so all this to-do is a relic of that original state of ours, when we were whole, and now, when we are longing for and following after that primeval wholeness, we say we are in love. For there was a time, I repeat, when we were one, but now, for our sins, God has scattered us abroad, as the Spartans scattered the Arcadians. Moreover, gentlemen, there is every reason to fear that, if we neglect the worship of the gods, they will split us up again, and then we shall have to go about with our noses sawed asunder, part and counterpart, like the basso-relievos on the tombstones. And therefore it is our duty one and all to inspire our friends with reverence and piety, for so we may ensure our safety and attain that blessed union by enlisting in the army of Love and marching beneath his banners. [16]

For Love must never be withstood—if we do, we incur the displeasure of the gods. But if we cling to him in friendship and reconciliation, we shall be among the happy few to whom it is given in these latter days to meet their other halves. Now, I don't want any coarse remarks from Eryximachus. I don't mean Pausanias and Agathon, though for all I know they may be among the lucky ones, and both be sections of the male. But what I am trying to say is this—that the happiness of the whole human race, women no less than men, is to be found in the consummation of our love, and in the healing of our disseevered nature by finding each his proper mate. And if this be a counsel of perfection, then we must do what, in our present circumstances, is next best, and bestow our love upon the natures most congenial to our own. [17]

And so I say that Love, the god who brings all this to pass, is worthy of our hymns, for his is the inestimable and present service of conducting us to our true affinities, and it is he that offers this great hope for the future—that, if we do not fail in reverence to the gods, he will one day heal us and restore us to our old estate, and establish us in joy and blessedness. [18]

Such, Eryximachus, is my discourse on Love—as different as could be from yours. And now I must ask you again. Will you please refrain from making fun of it, and let us hear what all the others have to say—or rather, the other two, for I see there's no one left but Agathon and Socrates. [19]

QUESTIONS FOR CRITICAL READING, THINKING, DISCUSSION, AND WRITING

Analyzing Content and Technique

1. According to Aristophanes, what is the original nature of humans? What causes them to undergo a change?
2. Describe the "creators" (gods) as they are presented in selection 2. What distinguishes them from other "creators" that you have come across in your reading? What is their relationship with humans?
3. Based on this selection, what can you deduce about attitudes in the Greek culture toward homosexuals?
4. This selection is supposed to have taken place at a "symposium," an after-dinner party for drinking and conversation. How is that indicated in its tone? How seriously are we to take the argument? What symbolic truths appear below the fiction?

Collaborative Activity

As a group, research one aspect of Greek culture, or a Greek concept, or an allusion to Greek history that appears in the excerpt (the hermaphrodite, Zeus, the god of Love, the symposium, the Spartans and Arcadians, etc.). Make a brief presentation of your findings to the class.

Making Connections

1. Plato gives some mythical reasons why people need each other. Write an essay in which you examine some practical and psychological reasons for such a need, which seems to have existed since the beginning of the human race.
2. In addition to being interested in the beginnings of the world, human beings have always been interested in supernatural or divine beings who "rule" the world and thus have created many stories about these divinities. As selections 1, 2, and 3 reveal, portrayals of supernatural beings differ from culture to culture. Write an essay examining how far our notions of the divine are influenced by our culture.

3

Before reading selection 3, write briefly about what your religion or culture considers the ideal relationship between men and women. Do you know any stories or myths that illustrate this?

Genesis, Chapters 1, 2, and 3: The Creation and the Fall

FROM THE KING JAMES VERSION OF THE BIBLE

The King James Version of the Bible, one of the best known, was translated in England between 1604 and 1611 by forty-seven scholars appointed by James I. It is considered to be of superior literary merit and is also quite faithful to the original languages of the Bible—Hebrew and Greek. In the Old Testament, from which this excerpt is taken, the translators made a special effort to imitate the rhythm and style of the Hebrew text, though they preserved the forms of proper names commonly used in England at the time. The King James Bible was very successful in popularizing the Scriptures.

The Creation

Chapter 1

1 In the beginning God created the heaven and the earth.

2 And the earth was without form, and void; and darkness was upon the face of the deep. And the Spirit of God moved upon the face of the waters.

3 And God said, Let there be light, and there was light.

4 And God saw the light, that *it was* good: and God divided the light from the darkness.

5 And God called the light Day, and the darkness he called Night. And the evening and the morning were the first day.

6 And God said, Let there be a firmament in the midst of the waters, and let it divide the waters from the waters.

7 And God made the firmament, and divided the waters which *were* under the firmament from the waters which *were* above the firmament: and it was so.

8 And God called the firmament Heaven. And the evening and the morning were the second day.

9 And God said, Let the waters under the heaven be gathered together unto one place, and let the dry *land* appear: and it was so.

10 And God called the dry *land* Earth; and the gathering together of the waters called he Seas: and God saw that *it was* good.

11 And God said, Let the earth bring forth grass, the herb yielding seed, *and* the fruit tree yielding fruit after his kind, whose seed *is* in itself, upon the earth: and it was so.

12 And the earth brought forth grass, *and* herb yielding seed after his kind, and the tree yielding fruit, whose seed *was* in itself, after his kind: and God saw that *it was* good.

13 And the evening and the morning were the third day.

14 And God said, Let there be lights in the firmament of the heaven to divide the day from the night; and let them be for signs, and for seasons, and for days, and years:

15 And let them be for lights in the firmament of the heaven to give light upon the earth: and it was so.

16 And God made two great lights; the greater light to rule the day, and the lesser light to rule the night: *he made* the stars also.

17 And God set them in the firmament of the heaven to give light upon the earth.

18 And to rule over the day and over the night, and to divide the light from the darkness: and God saw that *it was* good.

19 And the evening and the morning were the fourth day.

20 And God said, Let the waters bring forth abundantly the moving creature that hath life, and fowl *that* may fly above the earth in the open firmament of heaven.

21 And God created great whales, and every living creature that moveth, which the waters brought forth abundantly, after their kind, and every winged fowl after his kind: and God saw that *it was* good.

22 And God blessed them, saying, Be fruitful, and multiply, and fill the waters in the seas, and let fowl multiply in the earth.

23 And the evening and the morning were the fifth day.

24 And God said, Let the earth bring forth the living creature after his kind, cattle, and creeping thing, and beast of the earth after his kind: and it was so.

25 And God made the beast of the earth after his kind, and cattle after their kind, and every thing that creepeth upon the earth after his kind: and God saw that *it was* good.

26 And God said, Let us make man in our image, after our likeness: and let them have dominion over the fish of the sea, and over the fowl of the air, and over the cattle, and over all the earth, and over every creeping thing that creepeth upon the earth.

27 So God created man in his *own* image, in the image of God created he him; male and female created he them.

28 And God blessed them, and God said unto them, Be fruitful, and multiply, and replenish the earth, and subdue it: and have dominion over the fish of the sea, and over the fowl of the air, and over every living thing that moveth upon the earth.

29 And God said, Behold, I have given you every herb bearing seed, which *is* upon the face of all the earth, and every tree, in the which *is* the fruit of a tree yielding seed; to you it shall be for meat.

30 And to every beast of the earth, and to every fowl of the air, and to every thing that creepeth upon the earth, wherein *there is* life, *I have given* every green herb for meat: and it was so.

31 And God saw every thing that he had made, and, behold, *it was* very good. And the evening and the morning were the sixth day.

Chapter 2

1 Thus the heavens and the earth were finished, and all the host of them.

2 And on the seventh day God ended his work which he had made; and he rested on the seventh day from all his work which he had made.

3 And God blessed the seventh day, and sanctified it: because that in it he had rested from all his work which God created and made.

4 These *are* the generations of the heavens and of the earth when they were created, in the day that the LORD God made the earth and the heavens,

5 And every plant of the field before it was in the earth, and every herb of the field before it grew: for the LORD God had not caused it to rain upon the earth, and *there was* not a man to till the ground.

6 But there went up a mist from the earth, and watered the whole face of the ground.

7 And the LORD God formed man *of* the dust of the ground, and breathed into his nostrils the breath of life; and man became a living soul.

8 And the LORD God planted a garden eastward in Eden; and there he put the man whom he had formed.

9 And out of the ground made the LORD God to grow every tree that is pleasant to the sight, and good for food; the tree of life also in the midst of the garden, and the tree of knowledge of good and evil.

10 And a river went out of Eden to water the garden; and from thence it was parted, and became into four heads.

11 The name of the first *is* Pison: that *is* it which compasseth the whole land of Havilah, where *there is* gold;

12 And the gold of that land *is* good: there *is* bdellium and the onyx stone.

13 And the name of the second river *is* Gihon: the same *is* it that compasseth the whole land of Ethiopia.

14 And the name of the third river *is* Hiddekel: that *is* it which goeth toward the east of Assyria. And the fourth river *is* Euphrates.

15 And the LORD God took the man, and put him into the garden of Eden to dress it and to keep it.

16 And the LORD God commanded the man, saying, Of every tree of the garden thou mayest freely eat:

17 But of the tree of knowledge of good and evil, thou shalt not eat of it: for in the day that thou eatest thereof thou shalt surely die.

18 And the L<small>ORD</small> God said, *It is* not good that the man should be alone; I will make him an help meet for him.

19 And out of the ground the L<small>ORD</small> God formed every beast of the field, and every fowl of the air; and brought *them* unto Adam to see what he would call them: and whatsoever Adam called every living creature, that *was* the name thereof.

20 And Adam gave names to all cattle, and to the fowl of the air, and to every beast of the field; but for Adam there was not found an help meet for him.

21 And the L<small>ORD</small> God caused a deep sleep to fall upon Adam, and he slept: and he took one of his ribs, and closed up the flesh instead thereof;

22 And the rib, which the L<small>ORD</small> God had taken from man, made he a woman, and brought her unto the man.

23 And Adam said, This *is* now bone of my bones, and flesh of my flesh: she shall be called Woman, because she was taken out of Man.

24 Therefore shall a man leave his father and his mother, and shall cleave unto his wife: and they shall be one flesh.

25 And they were both naked, the man and his wife, and were not ashamed.

The Fall

Chapter 3

1 Now the serpent was more subtil than any beast of the field which the L<small>ORD</small> God had made. And he said unto the woman, Yea, hath God said, Ye shall not eat of every tree of the garden?

2 And the woman said unto the serpent, We may eat of the fruit of the trees of the garden:

3 But of the fruit of the tree which *is* in the midst of the garden, God hath said, Ye shall not eat of it, neither shall ye touch it, lest ye die.

4 And the serpent said unto the woman, Ye shall not surely die:

5 For God doth know that in the day ye eat thereof, then your eyes shall be opened, and ye shall be as gods, knowing good and evil.

6 And when the woman saw that the tree *was* good for food, and that it *was* pleasant to the eyes, and a tree to be desired to make *one* wise, she took of the fruit thereof, and did eat, and gave also unto her husband with her; and he did eat.

7 And the eyes of them both were opened, and they knew that they *were* naked; and they sewed fig leaves together, and made themselves aprons.

8 And they heard the voice of the L<small>ORD</small> God walking in the garden in the cool of the day: and Adam and his wife hid themselves from the presence of the L<small>ORD</small> God amongst the trees of the garden.

9 And the L<small>ORD</small> God called unto Adam, and said unto him, Where *art* thou?

10 And he said, I heard thy voice in the garden, and I was afraid, because I *was* naked; and I hid myself.

11 And he said, Who told thee that thou *wast* naked? Hast thou eaten of the tree, whereof I commanded thee that thou shouldest not eat?

12 And the man said, The woman whom thou gavest *to be* with me, she gave me of the tree, and I did eat.

13 And the LORD God said unto the woman, What *is* this *that* thou hast done? And the woman said, The serpent beguiled me, and I did eat.

14 And the LORD God said unto the serpent, Because thou hast done this, thou *art* cursed above all cattle, and above every beast of the field; upon thy belly shalt thou go, and dust shalt thou eat all the days of thy life:

15 And I will put enmity between thee and the woman, and between thy seed and her seed; it shall bruise thy head, and thou shalt bruise his heel.

16 Unto the woman he said, I will greatly multiply thy sorrow and thy conception; in sorrow thou shalt bring forth children; and thy desire *shall be* to thy husband, and he shall rule over thee.

17 And unto Adam he said, Because thou hast hearkened unto the voice of thy wife, and hast eaten of the tree, of which I commanded thee, saying, Thou shalt not eat of it: cursed *is* the ground for thy sake; in sorrow shalt thou eat *of* it all the days of thy life;

18 Thorns also and thistles shall it bring forth to thee; and thou shalt eat the herb of the field;

19 In the sweat of thy face shalt thou eat bread, till thou return unto the ground; for out of it wast thou taken: for dust thou *art*, and unto dust shalt thou return.

20 And Adam called his wife's name Eve; because she was the mother of all living.

21 Unto Adam also and to his wife did the LORD God make coats of skins, and clothed them.

22 And the LORD God said, Behold, the man is become as one of us, to know good and evil: and now, lest he put forth his hand, and take also of the tree of life, and eat, and live for ever:

23 Therefore the LORD God sent him forth from the garden of Eden, to till the ground from whence he was taken.

24 So he drove out the man; and he placed at the east of the garden of Eden Cherubims, and a flaming sword which turned every way, to keep the way of the tree of life.

QUESTIONS FOR CRITICAL READING, THINKING, DISCUSSION, AND WRITING

Analyzing Content and Technique

1. Examine the nature of the "creator" in selection 3. How is he similar to the "creators" envisioned in other cultures? (You might wish to read selections 1 and 2 before you answer this.)
2. Analyze the relationship between human beings and the other creatures that inhabit the world. What hierarchy does this imply? Identify the dangers inherent in such a hierarchy.
3. What is man created out of? In what way is this symbolic?
4. What is woman created out of? In what way is this symbolic?
5. Examine the concept of the "fall" of humankind. What are its causes?
6. What does the myth indicate about human nature?

Collaborative Activity

As a group, research and find two or three biblical references to man-woman relationships. Discuss, comparing them to the one depicted in this creation excerpt. What conclusions can you draw about the expectations and goals in these relationships? What is the group's attitude to these expectations?

Making Connections

1. Compare the biblical tale of creation with that presented in the Eskimo myth and write an essay in which you examine their similarities and differences. Some aspects to take into account are: the nature of the creators, the nature of the first man, the relationship between the first man and woman, the relationship between the creator and his creations, and the moral values and taboos implied in the two stories. You may want to make this an argumentative essay by evaluating the merits of each story, indicating which one you prefer and why.

2. Compare the biblical account of creation with the scientific theory of human evolution. The differences are obvious, but can you discover ways in which they may be saying the same things?

Letter Describing the Results of His First Voyage

CHRISTOPHER COLUMBUS

Christopher Columbus (1451?–1506) is the famous Italian Renaissance explorer who sailed to the New World in the service of Spain with the mission of finding an alternative route to India. He is credited with "discovering" America in 1492.

Sir: Since I know that you will be pleased at the great victory with which Our Lord has crowned my voyage, I write this to you, from which you will learn how in thirty-three days I passed from the Canary Islands to the Indies, with the fleet which the most illustrious King and Queen, our Sovereigns, gave to me. There I found very many islands, filled with innumerable people, and I have taken possession of them all for their Highnesses, done by proclamation and with the royal standard unfurled, and no opposition was offered to me.

To the first island which I found I gave the name "San Salvador," in remembrance of the Divine Majesty, Who had marvellously bestowed all this; the Indians call it "Guanahani." To the second, I gave the name the island of "Santa Maria de Concepcion," to the third, "Fernandina," to the fourth, "Isabella," to the fifth island, "Juana," and so each received from me a new name.

When I came to Juana, I followed its coast to the westward, and I found it to be so extensive that I thought that it must be the mainland, the province of Cathay. And since there were neither towns nor villages on the seashore, but small hamlets only, with the people of which I could not have speech because they all fled immediately, I went forward on the same course, thinking that I could not fail to find great cities or towns. At the end of many leagues, seeing that there was no change and that the coast was bearing me northwards, which I wished to avoid, since winter was already approaching and I proposed to make

Source: From *Journals and Other Documents in the Life of Christopher Columbus* by Samuel Eliot Morrison, 1963.

from it to the south, and as, moreover, the wind was carrying me forward, I determined not to wait for a change in the weather and retraced my path as far as a remarkable harbour known to me. From that point, I sent two men inland to learn if there were a king or great cities. They travelled three days' journey, finding an infinity of small hamlets and people without number, but nothing of importance. For this reason, they returned.

I understood sufficiently from other Indians, whom I had already taken, 4 that this land was nothing but an island, and I therefore followed its coast eastward for one hundred and seven leagues to the point where it ended. From that point, I saw another island, distant about eighteen leagues from the first, to the east, and to it I at once gave the name "Española." I went there and followed its northern coast, as I had followed that of Juana, to the eastward for one hundred and eighty-eight great leagues in a straight line. This island and all the others are very fertile to a limitless degree, and this island is extremely so. In it there are many harbours on the coast of the sea, beyond comparison with others that I know in Christendom, and many rivers, good and large, which is marvellous. Its lands are high; there are in it many sierras and very lofty mountains, beyond comparison with that of Tenerife. All are most beautiful, of a thousand shapes; all are accessible and are filled with trees of a thousand kinds and tall, so that they seem to touch the sky. I am told that they never lose their foliage, and this I can believe, for I saw them as green and lovely as they are in Spain in May, and some of them were flowering, some bearing fruit, and some at another stage, according to their nature. The nightingale was singing and other birds of a thousand kinds, in the month of November, there where I went. There are six or eight kinds of palm, which are a wonder to behold on account of their beautiful variety, but so are the other trees and fruits and plants. In it are marvellous pine groves; there are very wide and fertile plains, and there is honey; and there are birds of many kinds and fruits in great diversity. In the interior, there are mines of metals, and the population is without number.

Española is a marvel. The sierras and the mountains, the plains, the 5 champaigns, are so lovely and so rich for planting and sowing, for breeding cattle of every kind, for building towns and villages. The harbours of the sea here are such as cannot be believed to exist unless they have been seen, and so with the rivers, many and great, and of good water, the majority of which contain gold. In the trees, fruits and plants, there is a great difference from those of Juana. In this island, there are many spices and great mines of gold and of other metals.

The people of this island and of all the other islands which I have found and 6 of which I have information, all go naked, men and women, as their mothers bore them, although some of the women cover a single place with the leaf of a plant or with a net of cotton which they make for the purpose. They have no iron or steel or weapons, nor are they fitted to use them. This is not because they are not well built and of handsome stature, but because they are very marvellously timorous. They have no other arms than spears made of canes, cut in seeding time, to the ends of which they fix a small sharpened stick. Of these they do not dare to make use, for many times it has happened that I have sent ashore two or three men to some town to have speech with them, and countless people have come out to them, and as soon as they have seen my men approaching, they have fled, a father not even waiting for his son. This is not because ill has been done to any one of them; on the contrary, at every place where I have been and have been able to have speech with them, I have given to them of that which I had, such as cloth and many other things, receiving nothing in exchange. But so they are, incurably timid. It is true that, after they have been reassured and have lost this fear, they are so guileless and so generous with all that they possess, that no one would believe it who has not seen it. They refuse nothing that they possess, if it be asked of them; on the contrary, they invite any one to share it and display as much love as if they would give their hearts. They are content with whatever trifle of whatever kind that may be given to them, whether it be of value or valueless. I forbade that they should be given things so worthless as fragments of broken crockery, scraps of broken glass and lace tips, although when they were able to get them, they fancied that they possessed the best jewel in the world. So it was found that for a thong a sailor received gold to the weight of two and a half castellanos, and others received much more for other things which were worth less. As for new blancas, for them they would give everything which they had, although it might be two or three castellanos' weight of gold or an arroba or two of spun cotton. They took even the pieces of the broken hoops of the wine barrels and, like savages, gave what they had, so that it seemed to me to be wrong and I forbade it. I gave them a thousand handsome good things, which I had brought, in order that they might conceive affection for us and, more than that, might become Christians and be inclined to the love and service of Your Highnesses and of the whole Castilian nation, and strive to collect and give us of the things which they have in abundance and which are necessary to us.

They do not hold any creed nor are they idolaters; but they all believe that [7] power and good are in the heavens and were very firmly convinced that I, with these ships and men, came from the heavens, and in this belief they everywhere received me after they had mastered their fear. This belief is not the result of ignorance, for they are, on the contrary, of a very acute intelligence and they are men who navigate all those seas, so that it is amazing how good an account they give of everything. It is because they have never seen people clothed or ships of such a kind.

As soon as I arrived in the Indies, in the first island which I found, I took [8] some of the natives by force, in order that they might learn and might give me information of whatever there is in these parts. And so it was that they soon understood us, and we them, either by speech or signs, and they have been very serviceable. At present, those I bring with me are still of the opinion that I come from Heaven, for all the intercourse which they have had with me. They were the first to announce this wherever I went, and the others went running from house to house, and to the neighbouring towns, with loud cries of, "Come! Come! See the men from Heaven!" So all came, men and women alike, when their minds were set at rest concerning us, not one, small or great, remaining behind, and they all brought something to eat and drink, which they gave with extraordinary affection.

In all the islands, they have very many canoes, which are like rowing fustas, [9] some larger and some smaller; some are greater than a fusta of eighteen benches. They are not so broad, because they are made of a single log of wood, but a fusta would not keep up with them in rowing, since their speed is an incredible thing. In these they navigate among all those islands, which are innumerable, and carry their goods. I have seen one of these canoes with seventy or eighty men in it, each one with his paddle.

In all these islands, I saw no great diversity in the appearance of the people or in their manners and language. On the contrary, they all understand one another, which is a very curious thing, on account of which I hope that their Highnesses will determine upon their conversion to our holy faith, towards which they are very inclined. 10

I have already said how I went one hundred and seven leagues in a straight line from west to east along the seashore of the island of Juana, and as a result of this voyage I can say that this island is larger than England and Scotland together, for, beyond these one hundred and seven leagues, there remain to the westward two provinces to which I have not gone. One of these provinces they call "Avan," and there people are born with tails. These provinces cannot have a length of less than fifty or sixty leagues, as I could understand from those Indians whom I have and who know all the islands. 11

The other island, Española, has a circumference greater than all Spain from Collioure by the seacoast to Fuenterabia in Vizcaya, for I voyaged along one side for one hundred and eighty-eight great leagues in a straight line from west to east. It is a land to be desired and, when seen, never to be left. I have taken possession of all for their Highnesses, and all are more richly endowed than I know how or am able to say, and I hold all for their Highnesses, so that they may dispose of them as they do of the kingdoms of Castile and as absolutely. But especially, in this Española, in the situation most convenient and in the best position for the mines of gold and for all trade as well with the mainland here as with that there, belonging to the Grand Khan, where will be great trade and profit, I have taken possession of a large town, to which I gave the name "Villa de Navidad," and in it I have made fortifications and a fort, which will now by this time be entirely completed. In it I have left enough men for such a purpose with arms and artillery and provisions for more than a year, and a fusta, and one, a master of all seacraft, to build others, and I have established great friendship with the king of that land, so much so, that he was proud to call me "brother" and to treat me as such. And even were he to change his attitude to one of hostility towards these men, he and his do not know what arms are. They go naked, as I have already said, and they are the most timorous people in the world, so that the men whom I have left there alone would suffice to destroy all that land, and the island is without danger for their persons, if they know how to govern themselves. 12

In all these islands, it seems to me that all men are content with one woman, and to their chief or king they give as many as twenty. It appears to me that the women work more than do the men. I have not been able to learn if they hold private property; it seemed to me to be that all took a share in whatever any one had, especially of eatable things. 13

In these islands I have so far found no human monstrosities, as many expected, but on the contrary the whole population is very well formed, nor are 14 they negroes as in Guinea, but their hair is flowing and they are not born where there is intense force in the rays of the sun. It is true that the sun there has great power, although it is distant from the equinoctial line twenty-six degrees. In these islands, where there are high mountains, the cold was severe this winter, but they endure it, being used to it and with the help of meats which they consume with many and extremely hot spices. Thus I have found no monsters, nor had a report of any, except in an island "Carib," which is the second at the coming into the Indies, and which is inhabited by a people who are regarded in all the islands as very fierce and who eat human flesh. They have many canoes with which they range through all the islands of India and pillage and take whatever they can. They are no more malformed than are the others, except that they have the custom of wearing their hair long like women, and they use bows and arrows of the same cane stems, with a small piece of wood at the end, owing to their lack of iron which they do not possess. They are ferocious among these other people who are cowardly to an excessive degree, but I make no more account of them than of the rest. These are they who have intercourse with the women of "Matinino," which is the first island met on the way from Spain to the Indies, in which there is not a man. These women engage in no feminine occupation, but use bows and arrows of cane, like those already mentioned, and they arm and protect themselves with plates of copper, of which they have much.

In another island, which they assure me is larger than Española, the people 15 have no hair. In it there is incalculable gold, and from it and from the other islands I bring with me Indians as evidence.

In conclusion, to speak only of what has been accomplished on this voyage, 16 which was so hasty, their Highnesses can see that I will give them as much gold as they may need, if their Highnesses will render me very slight assistance; presently, I will give them spices and cotton, as much as their Highnesses shall command; and mastic, as much as they shall order to be shipped and which, up to now, has been found only in Greece, in the island of Chios, and the Seignory sells it for what it pleases; and aloe, as much as they shall order to be shipped; and slaves, as many as they shall order, and who will be from the idolaters. I believe also that I have found rhubarb and cinnamon, and I shall find a thousand other things of value, which the people whom I have left there will have discovered, for I have not delayed at any point, so far as the wind allowed me to sail, except in the town of Navidad, in order to leave it secured and well established, and in truth I should have done much more if the ships had served me as reason demanded.

This is enough. And thus the eternal God, Our Lord, gives to all those who 17 walk in His way triumph over things which appear to be impossible, and this was notably one. For, although men have talked or have written of these lands, all was conjectural, without ocular evidence, but amounted only to this, that those who heard for the most part listened and judged rather by hearsay than from even a small something tangible. So that, since Our Redeemer has given the victory to our most illustrious King and Queen, and to their renowned kingdoms, in so great a matter, for this all Christendom ought to feel delight and make great feasts and give solemn thanks to the Holy Trinity, with many solemn prayers for the great exaltation which they shall have in the turning of so many peoples to our holy faith, and afterwards for the temporal benefits, because not only Spain but all Christendom will have hence refreshment and gain.

QUESTIONS FOR CRITICAL READING, THINKING, DISCUSSION, AND WRITING

Analyzing Content and Technique

1. How is Columbus's act of renaming the islands symbolic? What does it indicate about his attitude? How does it foreshadow his later actions?
2. Evaluate Columbus's statement in paragraph 3 that his men found "an infinity of small hamlets and people without number, but nothing of importance." How might this be ironic? What does it reveal of his values and goals?
3. Examine Columbus's assessment of the character of the Indians. How well do you think he understands them? Find examples from the text to support your answer.
4. What is the purpose of this letter? Which details in it are central to achieving this purpose? Is it adequately persuasive? Why or why not?

Collaborative Activity

As a group, research the voyages of Columbus, focusing especially on the treatment of the Indians by the Spaniards. What do other sources reveal about these voyages that is not present in this letter? Did you find any evidence that contradicts what Columbus states? Write a brief collaborative report about the major effects of Columbus's discovery on the native populations.

Making Connections

1. Columbus's voyage forms an important landmark in the history of colonization. Write a research essay in which you examine one aspect of colonization that you find interesting—perhaps the reasons for its beginnings, or perhaps a particular world-view it promoted, or perhaps a particular effect it had, either on the colonizers or on the colonized. Be sure to narrow down your thesis significantly so that you can discuss your ideas in depth and present adequate support.
2. Write a letter to Columbus in which you respond to the main points he makes about his voyage and goals. Your letter can be in your own voice, written from the perspective of a twentieth-century American, or in the voice of some historical person who is a contemporary of Columbus. (In the latter case, you will need to do some research on fifteenth-century Italy, or the Spanish court.) Clarify your opinion of Columbus through specific references to his letter and through strong arguments of your own.

5

PREREADING ACTIVITY

Write about an experience of your own of moving to a new country, city, or neighborhood. What differences in culture or lifestyle did you encounter? If you have never actually moved, imagine such an experience and write about the emotions, both positive and negative, you think you might have felt.

The Promised Land

MARY ANTIN

Mary Antin (1881–1949) was born in czarist Russia. Her family immigrated to the United States early in her childhood to escape anti-Semitic oppression. Selection 5 is from Antin's autobiography, *The Promised Land*.

*A*nybody who knows Boston knows that the West and North Ends 1 are the wrong ends of that city. They form the tenement district, or, in the newer phrase, the slums of Boston. Anybody who is acquainted with the slums of any American metropolis knows that that is the quarter where poor immigrants foregather, to live, for the most part, as unkempt, half-washed, toiling, unaspiring foreigners; pitiful in the eyes of social missionaries, the despair of boards of health, the hope of ward politicians, the touchstone of American democracy. The well-versed metropolitan knows the slums as a sort of house of detention for poor aliens, where they live on probation till they can show a certificate of good citizenship.

He may know all this and yet not guess how Wall Street, in the West End, 2 appears in the eyes of a little immigrant from Polotzk. What would the sophisticated sight-seer say about Union Place, off Wall Street, where my new home waited for me? He would say that it is no place at all, but a short box of an alley. Two rows of three-story tenements are its sides, a stingy strip of sky is its lid, a littered pavement is the floor, and a narrow mouth its exit.

But I saw a very different picture on my introduction to Union Place. I saw 3 two imposing rows of brick buildings, loftier than any dwelling I had ever lived in. Brick was even on the ground for me to tread on, instead of common earth or boards. Many friendly windows stood open, filled with uncovered heads of women and children. I thought the people were interested in us, which was very neighborly. I looked up to the topmost row of windows, and my eyes were filled with the May blue of an American sky!

In our days of affluence in Russia we had been accustomed to upholstered 4 parlors, embroidered linen, silver spoons and candlesticks, goblets of gold, kitchen shelves shining with copper and brass. We had featherbeds heaped halfway to the ceiling; we had clothes presses dusky with velvet and silk and fine woollen. The three small rooms into which my father now ushered us, up one flight of stairs, contained only the necessary beds, with lean mattresses; a few wooden chairs; a table or two; a mysterious iron structure, which later turned out to be a stove; a couple of unornamental kerosene lamps; and a scanty array of cooking-utensils and crockery. And yet we were all impressed with our new home and its furniture. It was not only because we had just passed through our seven lean years, cooking in earthen vessels, eating black bread on holidays and wearing cotton; it was chiefly because these wooden chairs and tin pans were American chairs and pans that they shone glorious in our eyes. And if there was anything lacking for comfort or decoration we expected it to be presently supplied—at least, we children did. Perhaps my mother alone, of us newcomers, appreciated the shabbiness of the little apartment, and realized that for her there was as yet no laying down of the burden of poverty.

Our initiation into American ways began with the first step on the new 5 soil. My father found occasion to instruct or correct us even on the way from the pier to Wall Street, which journey we made crowded together in a rickety cab. He told us not to lean out of the windows, not to point, and explained the word "greenhorn." We did not want to be "greenhorns," and gave the strictest attention to my father's instructions. I do not know when my parents found opportunity to review together the history of Polotzk in the three years past, for we children had no patience with the subject; my mother's narrative was constantly interrupted by irrelevant questions, interjections, and explanations.

The first meal was an object lesson of much variety. My father produced 6 several kinds of food, ready to eat, without any cooking, from little tin cans that had printing all over them. He attempted to introduce us to a queer, slippery kind of fruit, which he called "banana," but had to give it up for the time being. After the meal, he had better luck with a curious piece of furniture on runners, which he called "rocking-chair." There were five of us newcomers, and we found five different ways of getting into the American machine of perpetual motion, and as many ways of getting out of it. One born and bred to the use of a rocking-chair cannot imagine how ludicrous people can make themselves when attempting to use it for the first time. We laughed immoderately over our various experiments with the novelty, which was a wholesome way of letting off steam after the unusual excitement of the day.

In our flat we did not think of such a thing as storing the coal in the 7 bathtub. There was no bathtub. So in the evening of the first day my father conducted us to the public baths. As we moved along in a little procession, I was delighted with the illumination of the streets. So many lamps, and they burned until morning, my father said, and so people did not need to carry lanterns. In America, then, everything was free, as we had heard in Russia. Light was free; the streets were as bright as a synagogue on a holy day. Music was free; we had been serenaded, to our gaping delight, by a brass band of many pieces, soon after our installation on Union Place.

Education was free. That subject my father had written about repeatedly, as 8 comprising his chief hope for us children, the essence of American opportunity, the treasure that no thief could touch, not even misfortune or poverty. It was the one thing that he was able to promise us when he sent for us; surer, safer than bread or shelter. On our second day I was thrilled with the realization of what this freedom of education meant. A little girl from across the alley came and offered to conduct us to school. My father was out, but we five between us had a few words of English by this time. We knew the word school. We understood. This child, who had never seen us till yesterday, who could not pronounce our names, who was not much better dressed than we, was able to offer us the freedom of the schools of Boston! No application made, no questions asked, no examinations, rulings, exclusions; no machinations, no fees. The doors stood open for every one of us. The smallest child could show us the way.

This incident impressed me more than anything I had heard in advance of 9 the freedom of education in America. It was a concrete proof—almost the thing itself. One had to experience it to understand it.

It was a great disappointment to be told by my father that we were not to 10 enter upon our school career at once. It was too near the end of the term, he said, and we were going to move to Crescent Beach in a week or so. We had to wait until the opening of the schools in September. What a loss of precious time—from May till September?

Not that the time was really lost. Even the interval on Union Place was 11 crowded with lessons and experiences. We had to visit the stores and be dressed from head to foot in American clothing; we had to learn the mysteries of the iron stove, the washboard, and the speaking-tube; we had to learn to trade with the fruit peddler through the window, and not to be afraid of the policeman; and, above all, we had to learn English.

The kind people who assisted us in these important matters form a group 12 by themselves in the gallery of my friends. If I had never seen them from those early days till now, I should still have remembered them with gratitude. When I enumerate the long list of my American teachers, I must begin with those who came to us on Wall Street and taught us our first steps. To my mother, in her perplexity over the cookstove, the woman who showed her how to make the fire was an angel of deliverance. A fairy godmother to us children was she who led us to a wonderful country called "uptown," where, in a dazzlingly beautiful palace called a "department store," we exchanged our hateful homemade European costumes, which pointed us out as "greenhorns" to the children on the street, for real American machine-made garments, and issued forth glorified in each other's eyes.

With our despised immigrant clothing we shed also our impossible Hebrew 13 names. A committee of our friends, several years ahead of us in American experience, put their heads together and concocted American names for us all. Those of our real names that had no pleasing American equivalents they ruthlessly discarded, content if they retained the initials. My mother, possessing a name that was not easily translatable, was punished with the undignified nickname of Annie. Fetchke, Joseph, and Deborah issued as Frieda, Joseph, and Dora, respectively. As for poor me, I was simply cheated. The name they gave me was hardly new. My Hebrew name being Maryashe in full, Mashke for short, Russianized into Marya *(Mar-ya)*, my friends said that it would hold good in English as *Mary:* which was very disappointing, as I longed to possess a strange-sounding American name like the others.

I am forgetting the consolation I had, in this matter of names, from the use ₁₄ of my surname, which I have had no occasion to mention until now. I found on my arrival that my father was "Mr. Antin" on the slightest provocation, and not, as in Polotzk, on state occasions alone. And so I was "Mary Antin," and I felt very important to answer to such a dignified title. It was just like America that even plain people should wear their surnames on week days.

As a family we were so diligent under instruction, so adaptable, and so ₁₅ clever in hiding our deficiencies, that when we made the journey to Crescent Beach, in the wake of our small wagon-load of household goods, my father had very little occasion to admonish us on the way, and I am sure he was not ashamed of us. So much we had achieved toward our Americanization during the two weeks since our landing.

QUESTIONS FOR CRITICAL READING, THINKING, DISCUSSION, AND WRITING

Analyzing Content and Technique

1. How would the "well-versed metropolitan" regard the neighborhood into which the Antin family moved? How did the writer view it? What accounts for the difference?
2. What do we learn of Antin's life before she came to America? What hints are we given about the family's future?
3. Which of America's "freedoms" impresses Antin the most? Why is this so important to her? Do you agree with her evaluation? Explain.
4. How does the family go about the process of Americanization in the first two weeks? What is significant or symbolic about their actions? What do we understand of the needs and desires of immigrants from looking at them?
5. At several points, the author uses quotation marks around words. Why? What effect does this have on the reader?

Collaborative Activity

As a group, research the historical background Antin briefly alludes to in paragraph 4. Why did her family, and many like them, leave Russia? Write a collaborative letter to Antin commenting on what you discovered.

Making Connections

1. Write an essay examining the changes undergone by an immigrant as he or she begins life in a new culture. You may describe a personal experience, as Antin does, involving yourself or a close friend or relative. If you do not know any immigrants, make this a research essay, gathering information about a particular group of immigrants from historically and sociologically accurate books and films. Make sure, in either case, that your essay has a strong thesis that leaves the reader with an increased understanding of the process of acculturation.

2. Many of the selections in this book deal with the importance of names: the name itself, the act of being named, who does the naming, and the attitude behind the name. Names are an intrinsic part of our origins. Write an essay examining your own name, your feelings about it, and the process of naming in your culture. Some aspects to consider: the background of your name; the person, if any, after whom you were named; the meaning and cultural significance of your name; and any experiences in which your name was changed or distorted—with the reasons behind the change or distortion.

6

PREREADING ACTIVITY

Go to a public place you often visit—a market, a mall, a concert hall, the lobby of a movie theater, a church or temple, a busy downtown corner, or some other venue—and observe the people there. What can you discern of their racial or ethnic background? How much assimilation do you notice? How does it make you feel?

America Singing: An Address to the Newly Arrived Peoples

GARRETT HONGO

Born in Hawaii, Garrett Hongo lives in Eugene, Oregon, where he teaches Creative Writing at the University of Oregon. A writer of poetry, memoir, and drama, he has won a Lamont Award and has edited the Asian American collections *The Open Boat: Poems from Asian America* and *Under Western Eyes: Personal Essays from Asian America*. His own books include *Yellow Light, The River of Heaven,* and *Volcano: A Memoir of Hawaii*. This selection was first published in *Parnassus*, 1992.

Maybe you've seen the sign
On old Sepulveda. Tai Song,
Cantonese Cuisine, *on your way*
to or from the L.A. airport.

                       Greg Pape

I've never been in Peking, or in the Summer
   Palace,
nor stood on the Great Stone Boat to watch
the rain begin on Kuen Ming Lake, the
   picnickers
running away in the grass.
But I love to hear it sung. . . .

                       Li-Young Lee

I hear America singing, the varied carols I
   hear. . . .

                       Walt Whitman

I'm fascinated and thrilled that there has been such a surge in new ₁
immigration from across the Pacific these past few years, that, as a country, we are
again in the process of being renewed and reformed by the New Americans from
Asia and elsewhere. These newly arrived peoples, I know, come not so much from
Japan and Okinawa and Guangdong as did the ancestors of we third- and fourth-
generation Asian Americans, but rather they are now coming, in increasing
numbers, from Taiwan, Hong Kong, Korea, Southeast Asia, Tonga, Fiji, Samoa,
the Caribbean, Central America, and the Philippines. Their presence has charged
our society with energy and change.

When I visit California now, and walk about in the resurgent downtowns of ₂
San Jose and Santa Ana, I pass Vietnamese markets, Korean grocery stores, and
restaurants for every kind of Pacific/Asian cuisine. When I was teaching at the
University of Houston in 1988, I did most of my shopping in a huge super-
supermarket run by Chinese for almost every Asian ethnicity—there was a Korean
section, a section for Japanese foods (*nap-pa* cabbage, *daikon*, *kamaboko* fishcakes
and *Kal-Pis* in the coolers), racks and racks of Chinese condiments like chili oil
and oyster and plum sauces. I saw what I've always loved seeing—bins full of
bean threads, bags of sesame seeds in various grades, cellophaned flats of dried
seaweed, cans of black beans and bamboo shoots, fifty-pound bags of rice. The
smells were gorgeous. The market was on its own little complex of shops—a big
parking lot ringed with little storefronts for a travel agency, an optometrist, a
records and tapes store, a bookstore, a coffee and *dim sum* shop, a casual
restaurant, and a movie theater that showed *chop-sockie* Saturday matinees, mildly
lurid *cheongsam* romances weekend nights, and serials all week long.

I was taken there by one of my master's students, Edmund Chang—a graduate ₃
of Tufts in Boston, who was born in Taiwan, who had grown up in Malta and Libya,
who went to high school in New Jersey, and who had just become an American
citizen the year before. He wanted to show me where to buy rice. We went with my
two small sons, themselves half-Asian, who loved the sweet rice candies but wrinkled
their noses at the carded, yellow circles of sliced, seal-wrapped octopus hanging on
hooks near the check stand. And me—I loved the goddamn place. I loved the feeling
of the throng of new peoples swirling around me. I loved the feeling that I was in a
vortex of cultures, a new republic of exchange—the thrilled, New Americans all
around me. I heard a new chorus—it was America singing.

When I left Houston in 1989, I got my car ready by getting it detailed. I didn't ₄
know if I was going to sell it or drive it to the West Coast where I was going to take a
new job. I took it to a detail shop I'd noticed while driving by one day. The guy there
was a young hot shot, a sassy white dude who could do everything—I knew it and he
knew I knew it. I liked him. He had Benzes, Beamers, even a Maserati in his shop.
There was a Volvo being vacuumed and shined up when I drove in. He gave me a
guarantee and a good price. This was the place, I thought.

We made the deal and I handed the pup my keys. He leaned out of the little ₅
waiting room and yelled over to one of his employees inside the garage, busy
shammying down a slick, black Riviera. The pup called him "Juan-Oh!"—a
wiseass joke. Juan was a handsome, Native American-looking guy with thick,
crow-black hair who was to drive me home in the shop car. He and I climbed

into a Jeep Cherokee, freshly shined and, inside, its plastic wiped down with Armor-All. We rode together in silence for a while, then, typically American, I'd stood about as much of it as I could, so I struck up a conversation.

"Where are you from?" I asked, typically blunt. His hair was jet-black, his 6 skin rich and brown like stained Hawaiian *koa* wood. He held himself stiffly, and shifted gears with precision. He had the posture and build of a Navajo, I thought.

"El Salvador," he said to me, and turned his face to show me his grin. 7

"Oh," I said, surprised. In an instant, I felt redundant for being nosey. But 8 I was curious too. "Are you here to save your life?" I said.

He told me *yes, mine and my mother's, my wife's, my children's.* "We all 9 come," he said. There was silence again as we moved through traffic into the little university village near where I lived. I wanted to give him something.

"Do you know the phrase," I said, "El Pueblo Unído, Jamás Será 10 Vencido?" I learned it from my Chilean friends who fled the murders after the coup of General Pinochet. It meant, "Our country, united, can never be defeated" and was a slogan used to rally the various splinter groups of the Latin American Left into unified coalitions. Hundreds of thousands chanted this as they marched in demonstrations through the streets of Santiago in support of the democracy of Salvador Allende, the doctor and Socialist who was the elected President of Chile and who was deposed and murdered by his own military and, it is frequently said, with some assistance from our CIA.

The El Salvadoran man next to me turned and grinned again, "Yes, sir. I 11 know this saying. It is full of heart. We in El Salvador say it too, though we die for it."

What was chilling was his modesty, his resolve. Riding through Houston in 12 that car, we were both humbled by the histories we carried and invoked.

Some folks—a lot white Americans who fear people like us, who fear the 13 oncoming change as weak, inner-reef swimmers fear the largest swells at sea beyond the reef—look to our renewed cities with anger and pessimism, consider them now as *terra incognita,* lands where monsters dwell and where they are no longer safe or welcome. Many of the people I talk with in so-called educated circles feel that the inner cities, the ghettoes, are a demilitarized zone to them, an unknown, an X or Mysterious Island where others belong, but not them, not the real Americans.

•

I remember a time—it was some years ago, in '82 or so—I invited another poet 14 out to lunch. He is older than me by a generation or so, a teacher of mine in a way, one who was part of the '60s shift away from formal verse towards freer, more popularly accessible forms. I revered him a little and wanted to be his friend. He'd just moved to the suburbs east of Los Angeles, had a new job teaching at a private college there and, as one who had grown up very eastern in Philadelphia, was missing cities and their splendors. I called him up and offered to show him L.A.'s Chinatown, take him for *dim-sum* at the Jade Gardens, my current favorite, and then to an afternoon movie downtown or something. We made the date and met at some designated corner of the city that weekend.

Dim-sum started out fine. He marvelled at the variety, at the tastes, at the 15
throng of Asians all around us at round tables, the dozen or so carts like street
vendors making their way around the huge upstairs hall of the restaurant. He
said, "Oh, this is wonderful. Oh, this is better than Philly. Oh, how has the world
kept this a secret from me?" He, in exchange, told me about how he met Ezra
Pound, the great and politically strange poet of High Modernism. He told me
about the revolution against formal metrics during the '60s and the wave of
interest in open forms, primitive and international poetries, and social justice. He
believed in social justice. He might have joined the black and white Freedom
Riders who rode together on the buses to integrate the South if he could've, but
he was too young then, he said.

But there were things about him which were enormously troubling. At the 16
same time as I enjoyed his stories of his apprenticeship in the afterglow of
Modernism, the generous accounts of his time scuffling up the literary ladder and
finding his rung on it, I was disturbed by his other anecdotes, his ample scorn for
other poets of his generation, and his complaints. He talked incessantly about a
rival, another poet he'd once been close to, but with whom he'd had a severe
falling-out. He spent an entire course of *dim-sum* bashing the other man's
reputation, debunking a seriously arrived at politics as fraudulent, ridiculing his
rival's lack of skill at "true" poetry, which was metric and lovely and free of
politics. It was hard for me to listen to as, to me, ephebe in the art, both men
were genuine heroes. He then recanted much of his own work at mid-career,
done during the '60s when the two poets had been friends, calling his own
poetry of that time—the poetry which I admired so much and had inspired me to
seek him out—"sentimental, misguided and stupid—*another man's poems.*" I
poured tea for him in a small porcelain cup decorated with dragons, and he
leaned towards me and said, "I didn't know what I was doing. I was on dope all
the time and chasing girls and nirvana. I thought life was a circus and I wasn't
serious."

We paid the check—a small amount, five dollars each, another miracle—and 17
rode a bus to a downtown theater, the old Orpheum, a once-lavish Fox palace
gone the route of decay and semi-abandonment. Yet, miraculously, it was open
and showing a Richard Pryor comedy for the four o'clock matinee late that
afternoon. We went. My friend marvelled at the ornate appointments and plush
chairs inside. He reminisced about his childhood in Philly. He laughed
uproariously at the jokes, the sight gags, the crazy, convoluted plot that ended
everything in a long chase scene. I relaxed and hoped the bitterness in him had
been dispersed by our good time. We left the place euphoric, and, junior that I
was, I was pleased I'd pleased him.

Outside, the city had turned dark while we were inside. The sidewalks, 18
moderately trafficked when we entered, were now thronged with Friday-night
cruisers, crowds of the poor and hustling. Buses and dirty cars jammed the
streets. We heard rap music from a huge stereo boombox a passerby shouldered
like a cargo sack as he sauntered before us. Like the calliope music of a carousel
thrashing tidelike together with a Ferris wheel's countersongs and squeals from its
riders, we heard disco pouring from the electronics store next door mingling with

the car horns of traffic noise and hubbub from the passing crowd. A hawker in a red tuxedo and frilly dress shirt announced in Spanish that a ticket dance was fixing to start in the basement room below the movie theater. The New Americans surrounded us—Jamaicans in shiny polyester disco shirts, Cubanos and Puerto Ricans, El Salvadorans, blacks from Watts and Compton and Inglewood, Chicanos from Whittier and East L.A. They were a processional of *penitentes.* The feeling was grand and powerful and strong. I felt the beat and wanted to dance.

My friend was terrified. A paranoid, he had panicked, running out to the [19] street and hailing a bus down, making it stop, banging on the pneumatic door until the driver hissed it open. He stared blankly for a moment and then recoiled at all the Asian, black, and Hispanic faces he saw filling up the bus when he started to get on. It seemed to me, stupefied on the sidewalk behind him, that he fell backwards off the bus as he fled back to me, shouting. He pushed past me and ran for the street corner where he may have seen a taxi cruise by.

I let him go. There was more than a generation of difference between us. [20] He had refuted all that I had loved about him. I recognized, finally, that he suffered from the Lethelike, irrational wish, in poetry and in his concept of civilization, for an unblemished purity that can only be accomplished in death— that lavish extinguishment of desire and differences. There was in him a tremendous fear that may have begun, innocently, as mild cultural disdain, a kind of antipathy-budding-into-intolerance, which had eventually metathesized into a powerful Kurtz-like horror for those of us who come from struggle in the Heart of Darkness and want to help shape and belong to the New America. The general term is racism. And it grows strangely.

I remember one of my professors in graduate school—a place I still refer [21] to as "Apartheid Tech"—sidling up to me at an afternoon reception and jostling me in a friendly way. I turned and he was beaming a little, clearly drunken from sampling the ample supply of reception chardonnay (though we were a state school, there was always money for things). "Hey, Hahngo," he said, punching my shoulder, chummily macho. The happy people in the room around us were oblivious, abuzz with their own excited chatter, our mentors in sensible shoes and tweeds mixing with graduate students. I overheard someone tittivating on the lyrics to John Lennon's tunes, comparing them to Spenser's *Amoretti.*

"Hey, Hahngo," said my professor, "I hear you've got an interest in *Gook* [22] Lit!" I felt the skin on my face freeze. I was stunned. I couldn't tell what he meant. "You know, that *minority* stuff," he continued. He mistook my shock for incomprehension. "I'm glad there's finally someone around here to cover it, fend off the Mongol hordes." He gestured with his plastic wineglass to the universe. He clapped me on the shoulder, turned away, and ambled over to the tray of cheeses and grapes. The room with its plateglass windows opening to a view of California eucalyptus and blooming jacarandas gyred around me as if my place in it were the mirrors of a circus carousel. I was fixed to the earth, speechless. And sickened.

I look upon the newly arrived peoples—Hispanics, Carribs, Asians and [23] Pacific Islanders, refugees and refuseniks from Europe, our new inhabitants of the inner cities, a new middle class renovating and swelling the suburban satellites around our cities, our new workers in the farm belts—with great hope and expectation. I know they are what my father was when he arrived in Los Angeles from Hawai`i thirty years ago. I know they are what my great-grandfathers were when they arrived, tanned and thinned by seasickness and lousy food, crossing over the long gangplank of the Immigration Station at Honolulu Bay over a hundred years ago. My grandfathers were the immigrant poor who were rich in hope and expectation. They would give their bodies and their spirit to make a place for their children in this new land. They would give us their singing, a small legacy of pain and sacrifice, and they would give us some of their courage.

·

I rode from the Upper East Side of Manhattan once, leaving early for a plane *24* back to Hawai`i or Houston or Missouri or wherever it was I was teaching or fleeing from teaching that year. My driver, a guy I simply hailed down as I stood on the street corner in front of my hotel that morning, turned out to be an elderly man from Greece. Other times the man was from Russia or Jamaica or Korea or Rumania. They each have a story. The Greek's was this: I glanced down at the identification shield hanging down from the visor over the passenger's seat in front, and I noticed his was a long, lavish name like Popoladopolous. "Mr. Popoladopolous," I began, "I am guessing you are a Greek. Can you guess where I am from?" It is one of my favorite games when I travel. The night clerk from Poland stationed at the front desk of my hotel guessed Singapore. The Egyptian cardiac surgeon who wanted to buy my freshly detailed car in Houston guessed China or Taiwan.

"You are right," my Greek driver said, "But you have the advantage over *25* me—you know my name."

"I am Hohngo," I said, giving it the Japanese pronunciation, as I would *26* back home in Hawai`i. On the Mainland, in "America," I give in and pronounce it "Hahngo," attuning myself to the dominant accent that calls my Senator Daniel Inouye, officially, "Inui."

"Oh," Popoladopolous said, "You are a complicated man. You are an *27* American from California or Los Angeles, and you are Oriental. Your father maybe came from Japan?"

"Very good," I said. "You are almost perfectly right. I am from Hawai`i, *28* and, yes, my *great-grandfather* came from Japan."

The traffic was intense. We ran into the infamous Manhattan gridlock as we *29* crossed towards the East River and one of the bridges. I asked him what he was doing in America. He told me he had been an attorney in Greece, a prominent man of his city, with a family—a wife and several daughters. Then the Colonels took over. "Do you know the Colonels?" he asked me.

I knew that there had been the terrible conflict between the different factions *30* in Greece. The Costa-Gavras film *Z* is about that. The books *When a Tree Sings* and *Eleni* by my friends Stratis Haviaris and Nicholas Gage tell both sides of a tough story. I remembered the headlines about Greece when I was a teenager in Los Angeles, the exile of the king, the military dictatorship, the protest of the oppression by film star Melina Mercouri. I thought of the poet Yannis Ritsos and how he had lived long in exile. "Yes," I said, "I know the Colonels."

"I was an attorney in Greece, in Athens, a dirty but beautiful city. I was a leader and supported the wrong side. I came to America. I brought my family. My daughter, she is grown now, and she is next week taking the New York bar examination. She will be a lawyer as well. Here, let me show you. Come with me." 31

Popoladopolous jumped out of the taxi and motioned for me to do the same. The traffic was still locked around us. He went to the back of the car and lifted the battered trunk lid. There was a suitcase inside of it made of leather, badly scuffed. He opened it. There were clothes, books, a loose-leaf binder. He grabbed a small parcel. Inside where photographs and a certificate. 32

"See?" he said, pointing and holding up a snapshot, "Here is my daughter in red and my nieces and myself in the back." I saw buxom girls in party dresses and heavy makeup and Mr. Popoladopolous in a grey suit standing behind them. "This is her graduation party from Hofstra School of Law. We take her to the restaurant of my son-in-law." He shared his pride with me. Then he flipped through more photographs—his house in Queens, his old house in Athens, snaps of an island holiday on Eretria many years ago—and, finally, he held up the certificate I'd noticed, wrapped in yellowing plastic. 33

"To be an attorney," he said, "This is my diploma from Greece." For an instant, he held it up over our heads like a chalice and then handed it to me "So, you see," he said, "I am telling truth to you." I saw it was smallish, only 5″ x 7″ or so, but there were seals and signatures on it. I nodded yes, I believed him. "But why do you not practice here," I asked, though I knew the answer. It was ritual. "This is not possible," he said, brusquely. He could not return to law school, study for the bar, begin again as a clerk, then associate, and so on. "I must work for my family, bring them, feed them, send my daughters to school. Give them my future. I drive cab, make money. The house in Queens. We are Americans now. Greece is the past. I am lonely for it, but here I live." 34

The traffic loosened around us. We got back in his cab and sped away to La Guardia, feeling our common resolve. 35

•

Some years ago, on the way to Hawai`i on a leave from Missouri, I stopped over in Los Angeles to give some poetry readings. It was winter, January in southern California, and the great beauty of the place was in the snow-lined ridges of Angeles Crest and the San Gabriel Mountains, a stunning natural backdrop to the city that swarmed around us in its infinite patterns of distraction. You could be driving from the south up the Harbor Freeway, and the mountains would be constantly before you, blue behemoths splashed and lichened with snow. This time of year, the air was clear as summer in the Arctic, and visibility stretched from the pier at Long Beach to the Hale Telescope at the Cal Tech Observatory on the ridgeline above the city. 36

One morning, I gave a reading to a teenage audience at Alhambra High School, a place just east of Pasadena tucked in one of the canyon valleys against the San Gabriels. I drove up from the south where I was staying and parked my 37 rented car on the street under an enormous palm tree next to a warehouse a few blocks from the school. I liked Alhambra. It was an older section of the metropolis, built up during the forties and fifties and the aircraft boom, the scale and vintage of the streets and buildings seeming to come straight out of a Raymond Chandler novel. I noticed small custom garages, a coin shop, bakeries, a few restaurants and diners, and one place with that classic extravagance of neon, stainless steel, asphalt and glass that meant a drive-in.

The day's event was sponsored by California State University, Los Angeles, an idea thought up by Carl Selkin—Director of the Poetry Center there and my host—as part of an outreach program by the university to the communities nearby, gone largely "ethnic." It was an experiment run as part of the celebration around Dr. Martin Luther King's birthday. At Cal State the day before, Selkin had explained that the poet on their faculty had not been interested in doing this, had found it impossible to reach an audience he deemed "largely illiterate." But the high school English teachers—many of them graduates of CSU's excellent education program—were thrilled with the idea. Two of them had studied with Zbigniew Herbert, the great Polish poet who had once taught at CSU in the '60s. They wanted me to come, so I agreed.

I was put in a large science classroom. I sat in front of a huge desk with a sink on one end and a kind of projector that looked like a clunky, off-scale microscope on the other. The teachers told me I would read to an assembly made up largely of Asians and whites—about a hundred students, most of them juniors and seniors. The Asians were a mixture of Chinese and Southeast Asians, they told me, some of them Vietnamese, some Cambodians, a lot of them from Hong Kong too. Some four or five English classes were put together to make up the audience, and the students trooped in and took their seats, the whites giggling and self-conscious, the Asians largely silent.

I read my poems about the inner city and my poems about Hawai'i, about my leaving there as a child, returning to it many years later as an adult, a poet, and seeking out the old places, the plantation lands, the sugar mills, the cane field and graveyard where I might have played as a child, the rough seashore which was like kin. I read a long poem about walking through the old Japanese cemetery in Kahuku on the plantation. I told them how it was placed on a promontory overlooking the sea, on a sandy point jutting into the ocean. I told them how we Japanese and Filipinos and Chinese put our cemeteries there because it was the land given to us by the growers, who needed the good land, the land that was arable, for growing the sugar cane and the pineapple. But what we didn't know, what the growers didn't know, was that the sea would come and take our dead from us then, in the periodic raids of rips and tidal waves from a swelling ocean. The Hawaiians knew this and took the bones of their dead to the high ground, to caves on the cliffs and rock mounds on the rainy plateau above the shelves of land between the sea and windward mountains. But we immigrants, we newly arrived laborers, placed generation after generation in the sand by the sea.

A *tsunami* came in 1946 and took over half of our dead in one night. "Bones and tombstones/up and down the beach," my poem said. I told them of walking over the patchy carpeting of temple moss "yellowing in the saline earth," the stinging sand clouds kicked up by the tough, onshore wind, I recalled a story of a murder committed out of outrage and shame—it was an act of victimage committed *within* the community—and paid homage to it as part of my past. It was to the journey I paid homage, the quest and travail of it from an Asian past to our American present. And it was to its remembrance—as shame and pride—that the poem was dedicated.

When I finished, I looked up. In the back rows was a Chinese girl, or maybe she was Vietnamese, dressed in a plain white school shirt and dark woolen skirt. Her hair was long and hung in two thick braids against her ears and jaw. Her eyes were shining. She wept, staring at me as if I were a statue. I averted my own eyes, glancing quickly across the row and throughout the assembly, and saw others weeping too, wiping their faces. Some were embarrassed and gazed down at the floor or at their shoes. A few teachers nodded. I don't remember any one smiling. Nothing like it had ever happened to me before. There was a feeling in the room and a momentary, heavy silence. I was surprised and a little unsettled by it.

The assembly broke up, a teacher standing and thanking everyone, gesturing towards me and calling for more applause. The classes began filing out, and I remember beginning to think about what to do for lunch. I dismissed the thought of the drive-in immediately. An Asian girl came up and asked me to sign her *Pee-Chee*.[1] Then another had me sign a napkin. A few more had xeroxes of my poems. I signed them all. A boy with acne and hair cut close to his temples but thick with pomade at the top—it was a style then coming into fashion with urban rappers—asked if I'd be reading for "adults" anytime that week. He wanted his parents to hear me too. I phlumphered something about the Pacific-Asia Museum that Saturday.

I had lunch with the teachers. They took me to the cafeteria, and we sat at the long bench-tables I remember from my public school days. Over fish sticks or breaded veal and tapioca pudding, we talked poetry and the new Asian students. A youngish man dressed in brown tweeds then spoke. He had a light brown beard, neatly trimmed.

"I've never seen them respond like that," he said, "Never seen them act so openly, show emotion like that before. You really connected."

I was learning something, something new and strong. These children with so much passion, so much raw affection, were teaching me that I had an audience, that my experience and sensibility spoke for their experiences, that I could address a world of others like myself, of Asians newly arrived, of peoples wanting to make America their place too. Up until then, I'd pretty much felt embattled as an artist and took it as part of my identity. I saw myself as an individual presence up against cultural indifference or mild hostility, particularly because my subject—the history of Japanese in America—was something I thought few cared hearing about. Except for some wonderful exceptions—and most of these among my fellow poets—it had been so while in college, and even more so in graduate school. I'd felt that, even if I was allowed a place in academe

---

[1]A notebook.

or the literary world, it would be on sufferance, that no one was *intrinsically* interested in my obsession, my passions. I thought of America as an establishment aloof from me. But after that assembly under Los Angeles mountains, signing the *Pee-Chees* and napkins and xeroxes those teenage students had of my poems, I sensed that I was beginning to belong to something, to join a throng of voices in need of their own singing.

When Walt Whitman, the great American poet of the nineteenth century, 47 wrote his poems of robust American optimism, full of the democratic spirit and lust for challenges and union jobs, he shouted "I Hear America Singing!" and announced a theme that characterized more than a century of our history. Well, I look upon all of us here, now—we, the New Americans, among newly arrived peoples with their boat trails of memories from across the oceans, and, I think, I Hear America Singing too.

QUESTIONS FOR CRITICAL READING, THINKING, DISCUSSION, AND WRITING

Analyzing Content and Technique

1. Why does Hongo enjoy the Chinese "super-super-market?" What does it symbolize for him?
2. Analyze what Hongo learns from his encounter with the El Salvadoran. Explain his statement in paragraph 12, "we were both humbled by the histories we carried and invoked." What history might Hongo be thinking of in terms of his own Japanese American heritage?
3. Summarize paragraph 13. Do you agree with Hongo's evaluation of the attitude of many white Americans toward the new immigrants? Support your opinion with an example from your own observation or experience.
4. Why is Hongo disappointed by the older poet he had revered as a young man? Examine his analysis of his character in paragraph 20. Based on the information you are given in the essay, how accurate does it seem to you? Explain.
5. Discuss Hongo's conversation with the Greek taxi driver. How is it significant? What new insights does the reader gain from this section of the essay?
6. Why is Hongo's poetry reading at the Los Angeles high school meaningful to him? What does he learn there that destroys one of his negative preconceptions?

Collaborative Activity

Have each group member do library research to find a poem or prose piece which, like Hongo's essay, uses one or more epigraphs. As a group, discuss these pieces, including Hongo's essay. Why are epigraphs used? What do they add to our understanding of a work? Might they have any drawbacks?

Making Connections

1. In his essay, Hongo writes of one of the main reasons people immigrate to the United States—to save their lives. What are some groups that have immigrated to this country in the last forty years primarily for this reason? Choosing one of them, write a research paper

on the causes that led them to find sanctuary in America, and the kinds of problems they experienced in transit.

2. There are many reasons, in addition to the one discussed above, why people wish to immigrate to the United States. What, according to you, are the most important of these other reasons? Write an essay in which you analyze these reasons and formulate an opinion about whether America should or should not allow entry to these kinds of immigrants. Be sure to present specific supporting material.

Before reading selection 7, list several incidents from your childhood that gave you a sense of yourself, your family, and your heritage. Choose the one that you remember best and, using the technique of clustering, write down the most significant details associated with it.

My Early Years

FREDERICK DOUGLASS

Born into slavery in the southern United States, Frederick Douglass (1817?–1895) escaped to the north at age twenty-one. Self-educated, he became one of the most eloquent writers and orators of his time. He was a leader of the abolitionist movement and founded and edited the *North Star* and *Douglass' Monthly*. He served as a United States marshal and a consul general to Haiti. Selection 7 is taken from his memoirs, *The Life and Times of Frederick Douglass*.

Chapter 1

I was born in Tuckahoe, near Hillsborough, and about twelve miles 1 from Easton, in Talbot county, Maryland. I have no accurate knowledge of my age, never having seen any authentic record containing it. By far the larger part of the slaves know as little of their ages as horses know of theirs, and it is the wish of most masters within my knowledge to keep their slaves thus ignorant. I do not remember to have ever met a slave who could tell of his birthday. They seldom come nearer to it than planting-time, harvest-time, cherry-time, spring-time, or fall-time. A want of information concerning my own was a source of unhappiness to me even during childhood. The white children could tell their ages. I could not tell why I ought to be deprived of the same privilege. I was not allowed to make any inquiries of my master concerning it. He deemed all such inquiries on the part of a slave improper and impertinent, and evidence of a restless spirit. The nearest estimate I can give makes me now between twenty-seven and twenty-eight years of age. I come to this, from hearing my master say, some time during 1835, I was about seventeen years old.

My mother was named Harriet Bailey. She was the daughter of Isaac and 2 Betsey Bailey, both colored, and quite dark. My mother was of a darker complexion than either my grandmother or grandfather.

My father was a white man. He was admitted to be such by all I ever heard 3 speak of my parentage. The opinion was also whispered that my master was my father; but of the correctness of this opinion, I know nothing; the means of knowing was withheld from me. My mother and I were separated when I was but an infant—before I knew her as my mother. It is a common custom, in the part of Maryland from which I ran away, to part children from their mothers at a very early age. Frequently, before the child has reached its twelfth month, its mother is taken from it, and hired out on some farm a considerable distance off, and the child is placed under the care of an old woman, too old for field labor. For what this separation is done, I do not know, unless it be to hinder the development of the child's affection toward its mother, and to blunt and destroy the natural affection of the mother for the child. This is the inevitable result.

I never saw my mother, to know her as such, more than four or five times in my life; and each of these times was very short in duration, and at night. She was hired by a Mr. Stewart, who lived about twelve miles from my home. She made her journeys to see me in the night, travelling the whole distance on foot, after the performance of her day's work. She was a field hand, and a whipping is the penalty of not being in the field at sunrise, unless a slave has special permission from his or her master to the contrary—a permission which they seldom get, and one that gives to him that gives it the proud name of being a kind master. I do not recollect of ever seeing my mother by the light of day. She was with me in the night. She would lie down with me, and get me to sleep, but long before I waked she was gone. Very little communication ever took place between us. Death soon ended what little we could have while she lived, and with it her hardships and suffering. She died when I was about seven years old, on one of my master's farms, near Lee's Mill. I was not allowed to be present during her illness, at her death, or burial. She was gone long before I knew any thing about it. Never having enjoyed, to any considerable extent, her soothing presence, her tender and watchful care, I received the tidings of her death with much the same emotions I should have probably felt at the death of a stranger.

Called thus suddenly away, she left me without the slightest intimation of who my father was. The whisper that my master was my father, may or may not be true; and, true or false, it is of but little consequence to my purpose whilst the fact remains, in all its glaring odiousness, that slaveholders have ordained, and by law established, that the children of slave women shall in all cases follow the condition of their mothers; and this is done too obviously to administer to their own lusts, and make a gratification of their wicked desires profitable as well as pleasurable; for by this cunning arrangement, the slaveholder, in cases not a few, sustains to his slaves the double relation of master and father.

I know of such cases; and it is worthy of remark that such slaves invariably suffer greater hardships, and have more to contend with, than others. They are, in the first place, a constant offence to their mistress. She is ever disposed to find fault with them; they can seldom do any thing to please her; she is never better pleased than when she sees them under the lash, especially when she suspects her husband of showing to his mulatto children favors which he withholds from his black slaves. The master is frequently compelled to sell this class of his slaves, out of deference to the feelings of his white wife; and, cruel as the deed may strike any one to be, for a man to sell his own children to human flesh-mongers, it is often the dictate of humanity for him to do so; for, unless he does this, he must not only whip them himself, but must stand by and see one white son tie up his brother, of but few shades darker complexion than himself, and ply the gory lash to his naked back; and if he lisp one word of disapproval, it is set down to his parental partiality, and only makes a bad matter worse, both for himself and the slave whom he would protect and defend.

Every year brings with it multitudes of this class of slaves. It was doubtless in consequence of a knowledge of this fact, that one great statesman of the south predicted the downfall of slavery by the inevitable laws of population. Whether this prophecy is ever fulfilled or not, it is nevertheless plain that a very different-looking class of people are springing up at the south, and are now held in slavery, from those originally brought to this country from Africa; and if their increase will do no other good, it will do away the force of the argument, that God cursed Ham, and therefore American slavery is right. If the lineal descendants of Ham are alone to be scripturally enslaved, it is certain that slavery at the south must soon become unscriptural; for thousands are ushered into the world, annually, who, like myself, owe their existence to white fathers, and those fathers most frequently their own masters.

I have had two masters. My first master's name was Anthony. I do not remember his first name. He was generally called Captain Anthony—a title which, I presume, he acquired by sailing a craft on the Chesapeake Bay. He was not considered a rich slaveholder. He owned two or three farms, and about thirty slaves. His farms and slaves were under the care of an overseer. The overseer's name was Plummer. Mr. Plummer was a miserable drunkard, a profane swearer, and a savage monster. He always went armed with a cowskin and a heavy cudgel. I have known him to cut and slash the women's heads so horribly, that even master would be enraged at his cruelty, and would threaten to whip him if he did not mind himself. Master, however, was not a humane slaveholder. It required extraordinary barbarity on the part of an overseer to affect him. He was a cruel man, hardened by a long life of slaveholding. He would at times seem to take great pleasure in whipping a slave. I have often been awakened at the dawn of day by the most heart-rending shrieks of an own aunt of mine, whom he used to tie up to a joist, and whip upon her naked back till she was literally covered with blood. No words, no tears, no prayers, from his gory victim, seemed to move his iron heart from its bloody purpose. The louder she screamed, the harder he whipped; and where the blood ran fastest, there he whipped longest. He would whip her to make her scream, and whip her to make her hush; and not until overcome by fatigue, would he cease to swing the blood-clotted cowskin. I remember the first time I ever witnessed this horrible exhibition. I was quite a child, but I well remember it. I never shall forget it whilst I remember any thing. It was the first of a long series of such outrages, of which I was doomed to be a witness and a participant. It struck me with awful force. It was the blood-stained gate, the entrance to the hell of slavery, through which I was about to pass. It was a most terrible spectacle. I wish I could commit to paper the feelings with which I beheld it.

This occurrence took place very soon after I went to live with my old master, and under the following circumstances. Aunt Hester went out one night,—where or for what I do not know,—and happened to be absent when my master desired her presence. He had ordered her not to go out evenings, and warned her that she must never let him catch her in company with a young man, who was paying attention to her belonging to Colonel Lloyd. The young man's name was Ned Roberts, generally called Lloyd's Ned. Why master was so careful of her, may be safely left to conjecture. She was a woman of noble form, and of graceful proportions, having very few equals, and fewer superiors, in personal appearance, among the colored or white women of our neighborhood. 9

Aunt Hester had not only disobeyed his orders in going out, but had been found in company with Lloyd's Ned; which circumstance, I found, from what he said while whipping her, was the chief offence. Had he been a man of pure morals himself, he might have been thought interested in protecting the innocence of my aunt; but those who knew him will not suspect him of any such virtue. Before he commenced whipping Aunt Hester, he took her into the kitchen, and stripped her from neck to waist, leaving her neck, shoulders, and back, entirely naked. He then told her to cross her hands, calling her at the same time a d——d b——h. After crossing her hands, he tied them with a strong rope, and led her to a stool under a large hook in the joist, put in for the purpose. He made her get upon the stool, and tied her hands to the hook. She now stood fair for his infernal purpose. Her arms were stretched up at their full length, so that she stood upon the ends of her toes. He then said to her, "Now, you d——d b——h, I'll learn you how to disobey my orders!" and after rolling up his sleeves, he commenced to lay on the heavy cowskin, and soon the warm, red blood (amid heart-rending shrieks from her, and horrid oaths from him) came dripping to the floor. I was so terrified and horror-stricken at the sight, that I hid myself in a closet, and dared not venture out till long after the bloody transaction was over. I expected it would be my turn next. It was all new to me. I had never seen any thing like it before. I had always lived with my grandmother on the outskirts of the plantation, where she was put to raise the children of the younger women. I had therefore been, until now, out of the way of the bloody scenes that often occurred on the plantation. 10

Chapter II

My master's family consisted of two sons, Andrew and Richard; one daughter, Lucretia, and her husband, Captain Thomas Auld. They lived in one house, upon the home plantation of Colonel Edward Lloyd. My master was Colonel Lloyd's clerk and superintendent. He was what might be called the overseer of the overseers. I spent two years of childhood on this plantation in my old master's family. It was here that I witnessed the bloody transaction recorded in the first chapter; and as I received my first impressions of slavery on this plantation, I will give some description of it, and of slavery as it there existed. The plantation is about twelve miles north of Easton, in Talbot county, and is situated on the border of Miles River. The principal products raised upon it were tobacco, corn, and wheat. These were raised in great abundance; so that, with the 11 products of this and the other farms belonging to him, he was able to keep in almost constant employment a large sloop, in carrying them to market at Baltimore. This sloop was named Sally Lloyd, in honor of one of the colonel's daughters. My master's son-in-law, Captain Auld, was master of the vessel; she was otherwise manned by the colonel's own slaves. Their names were Peter, Isaac, Rich, and Jake. These were esteemed very highly by the other slaves, and looked upon as the privileged ones of the plantation; for it was no small affair, in the eyes of the slaves, to be allowed to see Baltimore.

Colonel Lloyd kept from three to four hundred slaves on his home 12 plantation, and owned a large number more on the neighboring farms belonging to him. The names of the farms nearest to the home plantation were Wye Town and New Design. "Wye Town" was under the overseership of a man named Noah Willis. New Design was under the overseership of a Mr. Townsend. The overseers of these, and all the rest of the farms, numbering over twenty, received advice and direction from the managers of the home plantation. This was the great business place. It was the seat of government for the whole twenty farms. All disputes among the overseers were settled here. If a slave was convicted of any high misdemeanor, became unmanageable, or evinced a determination to run away, he was brought immediately here, severely whipped, put on board the sloop, carried to Baltimore, and sold to Austin Woolfolk, or some other slave-trader, as a warning to the slaves remaining.

Here, too, the slaves of all the other farms received their monthly allowance 13 of food, and their yearly clothing. The men and women slaves received, as their monthly allowance of food, eight pounds of pork, or its equivalent in fish, and one bushel of corn meal. Their yearly clothing consisted of two coarse linen shirts, one pair of linen trousers, like the shirts, one jacket, one pair of trousers for winter, made of coarse negro cloth, one pair of stockings, and one pair of shoes; the whole of which could not have cost more than seven dollars. The allowance of the slave children was given to their mothers, or the old women having the care of them. The children unable to work in the field had neither shoes, stockings, jackets, nor trousers, given to them; their clothing consisted of two coarse linen shirts per year. When these failed them, they went naked until the next allowance-day. Children from seven to ten years old, of both sexes, almost naked, might be seen at all seasons of the year.

There were no beds given the slaves, unless one coarse blanket be 14 considered such, and none but the men and women had these. This, however, is not considered a very great privation. They find less difficulty from the want of beds, than from the want of time to sleep; for when their day's work in the field is done, the most of them having their washing, mending, and cooking to do, and having few or none of the ordinary facilities for doing either of these, very many of their sleeping hours are consumed in preparing for the field the coming day; and when this is done, old and young, male and female, married and single, drop down side by side, on one common bed,—the cold, damp floor,—each covering himself or herself with their miserable blankets; and here they sleep till they are summoned to the field by the driver's horn. At the sound of this, all must rise, and be off to the field. There must be no halting; every one must be at his or her post; and woe betides them who hear not this morning summons to the field; for if they are not awakened by the sense of hearing, they are by the sense of feeling: no age nor sex finds any favor. Mr. Severe, the overseer, used to stand by the door of the quarter, armed with a large hickory stick and heavy cowskin, ready to whip any one who was so unfortunate as not to hear, or, from any other cause, was prevented from being ready to start for the field at the sound of the horn.

Mr. Severe was rightly named: he was a cruel man. I have seen him whip a 15 woman, causing the blood to run half an hour at the time; and this, too, in the midst of her crying children, pleading for their mother's release. He seemed to take pleasure in manifesting his fiendish barbarity. Added to his cruelty, he was a profane swearer. It was enough to chill the blood and stiffen the hair of an ordinary man to hear him talk. Scarce a sentence escaped him but that was commenced or concluded by some horrid oath. The field was the place to witness his cruelty and profanity. His presence made it both the field of blood and of blasphemy. From the rising till the going down of the sun, he was cursing, raving, cutting, and slashing among the slaves of the field, in the most frightful manner. His career was short. He died very soon after I went to Colonel Lloyd's; and he died as he lived, uttering, with his dying groans, bitter curses and horrid oaths. His death was regarded by the slaves as the result of a merciful providence.

Mr. Severe's place was filled by a Mr. Hopkins. He was a very different man. 16 He was less cruel, less profane, and made less noise, than Mr. Severe. His course was characterized by no extraordinary demonstrations of cruelty. He whipped, but seemed to take no pleasure in it. He was called by the slaves a good overseer.

The home plantation of Colonel Lloyd wore the appearance of a country 17 village. All the mechanical operations for all the farms were performed here. The shoemaking and mending, the blacksmithing, cartwrighting, coopering, weaving, and grain-grinding, were all performed by the slaves on the home plantation. The whole place wore a business-like aspect very unlike the neighboring farms. The number of houses, too, conspired to give it advantage over the neighboring farms. It was called by the slaves the *Great House Farm.* Few privileges were esteemed higher, by the slaves of the out-farms, than that of being selected to do errands at the Great House Farm. It was associated in their minds with greatness. A representative could not be prouder of his election to a seat in the American Congress, than a slave on one of the out-farms would be of his election to do errands at the Great House Farm. They regarded it as evidence of great confidence reposed in them by their overseers; and it was on this account, as well as a constant desire to be out of the field from under the driver's lash, that they esteemed it a high privilege, one worth careful living for. He was called the smartest and most trusty fellow, who had this honor conferred upon him the most frequently. The competitors for this office sought as diligently to please their overseers, as the office-seekers in the political parties seek to please and deceive the people. The same traits of character might be seen in Colonel Lloyd's slaves, as are seen in the slaves of the political parties.

The slaves selected to go to the Great House Farm, for the monthly 18 allowance for themselves and their fellow-slaves, were peculiarly enthusiastic. While on their way, they would make the dense old woods, for miles around, reverberate with their wild songs, revealing at once the highest joy and the deepest sadness. They would compose and sing as they went along, consulting neither time nor tune. The thought that came up, came out—if not in the word, in the sound;—and as frequently in the one as in the other. They would sometimes sing the most pathetic sentiment in the most rapturous tone, and the most rapturous sentiment in the most pathetic tone. Into all of their songs they would manage to weave something of the Great House Farm. Especially would they do this, when leaving home. They would then sing most exultingly the following words:—

> "I am going away to the Great House Farm!
> O, yea! O, yea! O!"

This they would sing, as a chorus, to words which to many would seem unmeaning jargon, but which, nevertheless, were full of meaning to themselves. I have sometimes thought that the mere hearing of those songs would do more to impress some minds with the horrible character of slavery, than the reading of whole volumes of philosophy on the subject could do.

I did not, when a slave, understand the deep meaning of those rude and apparently incoherent songs. I was myself within the circle; so that I neither saw nor heard as those without might see and hear. They told a tale of woe which was then altogether beyond my feeble comprehension; they were tones loud, long, and deep; they breathed the prayer and complaint of souls boiling over with the bitterest anguish. Every tone was a testimony against slavery, and a prayer to God for deliverance from chains. The hearing of those wild notes always depressed my spirit, and filled me with ineffable sadness. I have frequently found myself in tears while hearing them. The mere recurrence to those songs, even now, afflicts me; and while I am writing these lines, an expression of feeling has already found its way down my cheek. To those songs I trace my first glimmering conception of the dehumanizing character of slavery. I can never get rid of that conception. Those songs still follow me, to deepen my hatred of slavery, and quicken my sympathies for my brethren in bonds. If any one wishes to be impressed with the soul-killing effects of slavery, let him go to Colonel Lloyd's plantation, and, on allowance-day, place himself in the deep pine woods, and there let him, in silence, analyze the sounds that shall pass through the chambers of his soul,—and if he is not thus impressed, it will only be because "there is no flesh in his obdurate heart." [19]

I have often been utterly astonished, since I came to the north, to find persons who could speak of the singing, among slaves, as evidence of their contentment and happiness. It is impossible to conceive of a greater mistake. Slaves sing most when they are most unhappy. The songs of the slave represent the sorrows of his heart; and he is relieved by them, only as an aching heart is relieved by its tears. At least, such is my experience. I have often sung to drown my sorrow, but seldom to express my happiness. Crying for joy, and singing for joy, were alike uncommon to me while in the jaws of slavery. The singing of a man cast away upon a desolate island might be as appropriately considered as evidence of contentment and happiness, as the singing of a slave; the songs of the one and of the other are prompted by the same emotion. [20]

QUESTIONS FOR CRITICAL READING, THINKING, DISCUSSION, AND WRITING

Analyzing Content and Technique

1. Frederick Douglass's childhood is haunted by information that is withheld from him. What is this information, why is it withheld, and what effect does it have on Douglass, both as a child and as a man?
2. Describe the relationship between Douglass and his mother. From the evidence it provides, what conclusions can you draw about the attitudes of owners toward slaves?
3. Explain the statement Douglass makes about the condition of the mulatto slaves. How does he use this as an argument against people who are trying to justify slavery? Does he convince you? Why or why not? Are there other arguments you can add to his?
4. Douglass gives us a graphic description of the whipping of his aunt. Which aspect of the incident do you find most shocking? Why?
5. Describe the living conditions of Colonel Lloyd's slaves. What ironic elements can you discern in their behavior and attitudes? How does Douglass interpret the songs they sing?
6. In this selection, in addition to narration, Douglass uses several other rhetorical modes such as description, illustration, and argumentation. Identify where they occur and evaluate their effectiveness.

Collaborative Activity

In this excerpt Douglass describes the songs sung by the slaves as more expressive of "the horrible character of slavery than . . . whole volumes of philosophy on the subject." Discuss, as a group, the special power songs have to move the human heart. Have members provide examples of songs which brought particular issues, ideas, problems, or historical situations alive for them. Summarize your discussion in a collaborative paragraph.

Making Connections

1. Write an essay analyzing Douglass's implied thesis about slavery. What kinds of support has he used to prove his point? Evaluate them and discuss which ones you find most powerful.
2. The bringing over of a people from Africa to be sold as slaves in America began a chain of events that changed American society in many significant ways. Write an essay examining one important social condition or situation that exists today as a result of this, and relating this condition or situation (where possible) to Douglass's description of the lives of the early slaves. (You might need to do some research before you write this essay.)

8

PREREADING ACTIVITY

Other than your parents, who influenced your early years? Freewrite for ten minutes about all the people you remember as being important to your childhood, putting down as many memory details as you can.

Chronicle

MEI-MEI BERSSENBRUGGE

Mei-Mei Berssenbrugge (1947–) is Chinese American. She was born in Beijing, grew up in Massachusetts, and now lives in New Mexico. Her books include *The Heat Bird* and *Empathy*.

I was born the year of the loon
in a great commotion. My mother—
who used to pack $500 cash
in the shoulders of her fur gambling coat,
who had always considered herself
the family's "First Son"—   5
took one look at me
and lit out
on a vacation to Sumatra.
Her brother purchased my baby clothes;   10
I've seen them, little clown suits
of silk and color.

Each day
my Chinese grandmother bathed me
with elaboration in an iron tub;
amahs waiting in line   15
with sterilized water and towels
clucked and smiled
and rushed about the tall stone room
in tiny slippers.   20

Source: "Chronicle" by Mei-Mei Berssenbrugge first appeared in *The Forbidden Stitch: An Asian American Women's Anthology,* © Calyx Books, editors Shirley Geok-Lin Lim, Mayami Tsutakawa. Reprinted by permission of the publishers.

After my grandfather
accustomed himself
to this betrayal by First Son,
he would take me in his arms,
walk with me   25
by the plum trees, cherries, persimmons;
he showed me the stiff robes
of my ancestors and their drafty hall,
the long beards of his learned old friends,
and his crickets.   30

Grandfather talked to me, taught me.
At two months, my mother tells me,
I could sniff for flowers,
stab my small hand upwards to moon.
Even today I get proud   35
when I remember
this all took place in Chinese.

QUESTIONS FOR CRITICAL READING, THINKING, DISCUSSION, AND WRITING

Analyzing Content and Technique

1. In many ways poetry works differently from prose, relying on images, symbols, hints, and implications to make its points. Taking this into account, create a brief character sketch of the narrator's mother. Why do you think the mother leaves for Sumatra as soon as the baby is born?

2. How does the mother's absence affect the relationship between the child and the other members of the family? What are some of the effects on the child?

3. What glimpses are we given of Chinese values and lifestyles? Which images bring these out most clearly?

4. Analyze the word "betrayal" in the third stanza. Why does the writer use this word? Which cultural values are implied through it?

5. The last stanza provides us with some suprising information. What is it? Based on this, what can you deduce about changes in the narrator's life as she grew up? Why does she end the poem the way she does?

Collaborative Activity

Write the word "childhood" in the center of a large sheet of paper and do a group clustering exercise around it, with members contributing descriptive words or phrases that evoke a sense of that time for them. Discuss the ideas and emotions that come up. At the end of the activity, all the groups should put up their sheets on walls or boards so that the class can examine them.

Making Connections

1. Write an essay comparing the attitude to females portrayed in this piece with that brought out in Maxine Hong Kingston's "No Name Woman" in Part Three. How are the attitudes similar? How are they different? What facts about the writers' lives and circumstances might account for the similarities as well as the changes? (You may want to do some research on the writers before dealing with this last question.)

2. Write an essay looking back on your childhood and on the earliest cultural values that influenced and shaped you. Some aspects to consider: What were these values? Were they taught to you at home or elsewhere? Which persons or incidents brought them out most clearly? How did you feel about them? Were some of the values in conflict with each other?

9

PREREADING ACTIVITY

This essay was written as a response to an assignment that asked the student to consider the effect of slavery on any one sector of the society of that period. What other topics might this writer have chosen? Brainstorm to come up with a list.

Born without Light: The Effect of Slavery on African American Children (Student Essay)

MARY PETERSON

"We have as far as possible closed every avenue by which light may enter their minds. If we could extinguish the capacity to see the light our work would be completed."

Unknown Delegate, Virginia House of Delegates, 1828

*H*e was born in February of 1818, but he died without knowing 1
this. His ancestry was as rooted in America as that of many Anglo-Saxons, but he died without society's acceptance of this fact. He was born a slave in a time and a place where most white men considered slaves less than human. He died a famous American orator, U.S. Minister, Secretary of the Santo Domingo Commission, Recorder of Deeds in the District of Columbia, and United States Minister to Haiti. He was Frederick Douglass Augustus Washington Bailey, a great man whom we know today as Frederick Douglass.

When examining Frederick Douglass' life, we cannot help but admire his 2
rare and remarkable achievements. But it is only when we analyze his life against the backdrop of the atrocious conditions to which slave children of his day, himself included, were subjected—separation from family, brainwashing, and illiteracy enforced by punishment—that we can begin to gauge the immensity of these achievements.

The first fact that we notice about Douglass' early life was his lack of family 3
bonds. He was separated from his mother, Harriet Bailey, when he was an infant. Research on his life does not explain the reason for their separation. Although she lived on a nearby plantation, he only saw his mother a few times in his life. Whether she could have visited more often and chose not to, or whether she was prevented from seeing him more frequently, nobody knows. Unfortunately,

Source: Student essay reprinted by permission.

Harriet died when Douglass was only seven years old—without ever having an opportunity to develop a loving relationship with her son. When told of her death, Douglass "received the tidings . . . with much the same emotions [he] should have probably felt at the death of a stranger" (Douglass 23).

Douglass was raised by his grandmother, Betsy Bailey, with whom he had a close but brief relationship. In his autobiography, he speaks of her in warm, loving, and respectful terms. Apparently, Betsy played the role of "mother" for all of her grandchildren so that her daughters could labor in the fields of the Tuckahoe farms owned by Captain Aaron Anthony. As soon as they were old enough to assist with any chores, the children were summoned to Captain Anthony's home, Wye House, twelve miles away. And the time eventually came, at the age of six, for Douglass to move to the "Old Master's House." In August of 1824, he and his grandmother left their cabin and walked in the scorching heat to Wye House. But Douglass was unaware of the reason for their journey. At the house they were given much needed drinks of water, and soon the other children's laughter and gaiety drew the shy child into the yard. But his exuberance abruptly ended when one of the children ran out of the house yelling, "Fed, Fed! Grandmammy gone!" And, indeed, when he ran to the kitchen, she was not there. The person he loved and trusted above all others had left him without even a goodbye. He was shattered. Did she leave him in the only way she saw possible—the way of least torment at a parting that was inevitable? We will never know.

Douglass' situation was made worse by the fact that, like many slave children of the time, he did not know who his father was. His coloring was more fair than his mother's or grandmother's and he had a sun-tanned look that was referred to as "yellow," so it was rumored that his father was white, and quite possibly, his master. Although Douglass appeared to be a mulatto, "he was denied that legal status because he was never acknowledged by his father" (Preston 35). Whether or not Master Anthony was his father, we can only speculate, but it is clear that Douglass never had a father-figure to turn to.

As abhorrent as Douglass' situation was, being separated from one's parents and family was a common occurrence for children of slavery. They lived in constant fear of being sold, bartered, deeded, or gambled away. the traveler William Reynolds, who witnessed first-hand the barbarity of the slave trade, wrote in his journal about an auction of twenty-three slaves, focusing on one of the women being sold:

> She begged and implored her new master on her knees to buy her children also, but it had no effect, he would not do it. She then begged him to buy her little girl (about five years old) but all to no purpose, it was truly heart rendering to hear her cries when they were taking her away (Gutman 93).

Thomas James, a slave in upstate New York, was eight years old at the time his family was separated. His mother, who was hiding in the attic, was dragged out of the house and forced onto a horse. James never saw her again. Henry Brown remembered his mother telling him that slave children "were often taken by tyrants, just as, in autumn, 'leaves are stripped from the trees of the forest'"

(Webber 103). Harriet Tubman recalled that when she was a child, every time she saw a white man she was fearful of being taken away. Because she was taken from her parents at an early age, one ex-slave, Charlotte Burris, was quoted as saying, "I can't tell my age to save my life. You know when children are separated from their parents early, they don't know how old they are" (Gutman 29).

Such separations obviously caused very deep pain—socially and personally. 8 In his autobiography, Douglass states,

> A single word from the white man was enough—against all our wishes, prayers and entreaties—to sunder forever the dearest friends, dearest kindred, and strongest ties known to human beings (Douglass 60).

Most families were more comforted by the death of a family member than 9 the sale of one. According to some Virginia ex-slaves, "when your child dies you know where it is, but when he is sold away, you never know what may happen to him" (Gutman 193).

Douglass himself felt the long-term effects of the fear and insecurity at not 10 having family all his life. Long after he was free and successful, he was subject to terrifying nightmares of being dragged away from his grandmother and being sent aboard slave ships as part of a chain gang. He was also unable to trust deeply enough to establish a strong relationship with his wife Anna and sought solace in friendships with other women.

Because of the instability of not knowing if or when a family member 11 might be sold, all families were insecure—no matter how long they had been together. Even a "good" master might die, and how his estate was divided was purely up to the "vicissitudes of the business cycle" (Gutman 153). Slave parents were, thus, forced to prepare their children for a possible separation. Even very young children were taught the white man's habits and peculiarities. They learned how to work within his system, and what types of techniques to use when dealing with him. For their own security, from an early age they were taught to be fearful of the white man—to view every white man as an enemy and to learn to deceive him.

But the white man had his own ideas of what slave children should be 12 taught. Although many whites, regardless of their status, viewed physical labor as degrading, black children were taught that to "work as a slave was a privilege. They must, therefore, work with a happy contentment" (Webber 35). They were not allowed to talk to white people other than their masters or people their masters knew. Some slave children were even taught that they could not look upon "po' white children." One ex-slave recalled being told that the "stork brought the white babies to their mothers, but the slave children were all hatched out from buzzards' eggs" (Mellon 39). The tragedy is that she believed it. These teachings were crucial to the preservation of slavery—the institution upon which the slave holders' prosperity was based. They needed to keep the slaves believing that the "Negroid race" was inferior. Thus, their basic premise of handling and teaching slaves was to have them internalize the knowledge, attitudes, values, skills, and sensibilities of the "perfect servant."

This model slave would be: conscious of his own innate inferiority as a member of "the Negroid race"; overflowing with awe, respect, and childlike affection for the planter and his family, cheerfully mindful of the formalities of plantation etiquette and of the rules and regulations regarding slave behavior; firmly convinced of the morality of slavery and of the happy fortuity of his own slavehood, and that of his fellow slaves, in a plantation setting that represented, for "his kind," the best of all possible worlds (Webber 27).

Slave owners tried to instill these values into the children by keeping them 13 ignorant. They "closed every avenue by which light may enter their minds" (Gutman 27). Neither children nor adults were allowed to learn to read. Often, those who violated this "rule" were threatened with having their arms cut off. Some children actually saw their friends divested of a finger for attempting to learn to read because slaveholders feared that "learning would spoil the best nigger in the world" (Douglass 49). Douglass' autobiography describes in detail how difficult it was for him to overcome these obstacles, how often he was severely and cruelly disciplined for trying, and how, ultimately, with great tenacity, he managed to succeed.

It was this tenacity, along with courage, wisdom, and the keen perception he 14 applied to his reading, that enabled Douglass finally to move beyond the confines of slavery. When he was quite young, his logic led him to dispute what he was taught by the white slaveholders. While most children were told that God had crated white people to be masters and black people to be slaves, Douglass knew some black people that were not slaves. And he also knew some black people who were born free in their native country, Africa. He knew that some white people refused to own slaves. His ability to analyze what he saw helped him realize that slavery was invented by man, not God. "And what men could do, other men could undo" (Preston 80). This intelligence, coupled with resilience and perseverance, led him to challenge the doctrine of white supremacy and to become one of the greatest orators of his time.

Ironically, because of his intelligence and eloquence, many people refused 15 to believe that Douglass was from the background he claimed, or that he suffered as greatly as he describes in his autobiography. He was called "a white man trapped in a black man's skin." And his superior qualities were oftentimes attributed to his unknown white father. When, after the Civil War, Douglass went back to visit one of his old masters, he told him that "I always knew you were too smart to be a slave" (Preston 186).

For half a century, Frederick Douglass jabbed American consciousness. He 16 laid to rest the myth that Negroes were inferior. During the 1870s he was named assistant secretary of a commission that was to investigate the proposal that the Dominican Republic be annexed by the United States. And although he did not campaign for the office, he was nominated for vice-president by the Equal Rights Party. He was a presidential elector from New York as well as the official messenger to convey the state's election results to the President of the Senate. He was chosen as the president of the Freedmen's Bank, and he was appointed to the highest office ever held by a black, United States Marshal for the District of Columbia. But he did more than rise higher than any American black before him—he did it on white man's terms, in white man's territory, and in spite of the white man's obstacles. The slave boy from Tuckahoe Creek had pushed beyond his lowly beginnings, refused to have his mind extinguished, and had become the most honored black in American history. With great confidence and dignity, he had reclaimed his light.

BIBLIOGRAPHY

DOUGLASS, FREDERICK. *Narrative of the Life of Frederick Douglass, An American Slave.* New York: Penguin Books, 1968.

GUTMAN, HERBERT G. *The Black Family in Slavery and Freedom, 1750–1925.* New York: Vintage Books, 1976.

McFEELY, WILLIAM S. *Frederick Douglass.* New York: W. W. Norton & Company, 1991.

MELLON, JAMES. *Bullwhip Days: The Slaves Remember. An Oral History.* New York: Weidenfeld & Nicolson, 1988.

PRESTON, DICKSON J. *Young Frederick Douglass: The Maryland Years.* Maryland: John Hopkins University Press, 1980.

WEBBER, THOMAS L. *Deep Like the Rivers: Education in the Slave Quarter Community, 1831–1865.* Toronto: W. W. Norton & Company, Inc., 1978.

STRUCTURE, STRATEGY, AND SUGGESTION

1. Analyze the writer's introduction. How is it different from a regular introduction? What effect does it have on the reader? How else might the writer have begun the essay?
2. Where is the thesis of the essay placed? Is this an effective placement? Why or why not?
3. Do you think this essay is sufficiently supported with evidence? Examine the two different kinds of sources, primary and secondary, which the writer has used. What purpose does each kind serve? Give an example of each.
4. Of all the effects of slavery upon children which she has described, which do you think the writer considers the most harmful? How do you deduce this? Do you agree with her?
5. How, according to the writer, did Douglass continue to feel the effects of slavery even after he became an adult? What evidence does she provide?
6. Make a brief outline of the major points of this essay. From studying this outline, what do yo learn of the organizational strategy used by Peterson?
7. Write an essay in which you discuss the life of a person who overcame great odds to achieve success. This can be someone you know, or a fictional or historical personage. Your essay should not merely describe but analyze the difficulties faced by this person and should explain how he or she overcame them.

SYNTHESIS *Part One*

1. Several selections in Part One examine the importance of learning about one's origins. Do you believe in the importance of such an enterprise? What is to be gained from it? Are there any negative aspects to it? Write an essay in which you examine these issues.

2. Selections 1, 2, and 3, which give us three different creation stories, illustrate that mythic tales have been a matter of great interest and concern for almost every culture. Why? What part, if any, do these stories play in our lives today? If they are no longer a part of our lives, have we lost anything as a result? Write an essay on the role of myth in modern lives, in which you address some of the above questions.

3. "The Promised Land" and "America Singing" present us with several immigration experiences, but their focuses are often different. Which aspect of the immigrant experience does the first selection stress? Which ones are central to the second selection? Studying these selections and adding to them from your own experience and observation, write an essay in which you explore the pros and cons of the immigrant experience.

4. The experience of African Americans has been significantly different from that of other immigrants who have come to America. In what ways? Looking at Douglass's autobiography and perhaps some other outside sources, write an essay in which you delineate and analyze these differences, focusing particularly on the less obvious ones.

Bonds of Passion,
Bonds of Love

SELECTIONS IN PART TWO

PART 2: INTRODUCTION

*T*here have always been families. Biologically and emotionally, we could not have survived without them. And even though the family today may be very different from what our ancestors envisioned, it continues to fulfill basic human needs—a need to reach out and connect, a need to protect and nurture.

Although the family is a ubiquitous phenomenon, it comes in many forms. As Jane Howard and Jean Seligmann point out in "Families" (selection 10) and "Variations on a Theme" (selection 11), in today's society we have redefined the family so that it need not be a result of birth or marriage. Even when it does result from birth or marriage, the roles of family members can vary widely. We see this in the diverse portrayals of husbands and wives, parents (or grandparents) and children, by Ved Mehta (selection 13), Jeanne Wakatsuki Houston (selection 17), and Alberto Rios (selection 18). These writers give us insight into three different cultures—Indian, Japanese, and Hispanic—each of which has a somewhat different attitude toward how much independence is granted to family members and how much allegiance is expected from them. The writers also illustrate that within the same tradition there are often conflicting opinions, especially between generations, about what family roles should be, but that successful compromises may be possible.

The members of our family are the first people who give us a sense of confidence, who provide us with a secure atmosphere where we can learn who we are and what we are capable of achieving. We see this in Houston's "Beyond Manzanar" and Rios's "Nani." David Elkind's "Teenagers in Crisis" (selection 15) and Sue Horton's "Mothers, Sons and the Gangs" (selection 16), however, explore a darker side of this responsibility. Elkind demonstrates what happens when parental figures are too involved in their own fast-moving lives to pay attention to teenagers, and Horton examines the tragedies that may occur when children turn to the negative forces outside the family to gain a sense of self.

The family is a source of great joy and comfort, as we see in Gary Soto's "Finding a Wife" (selection 12), but it can also cause much anguish. The ties that bind us most closely are the ones that hurt the most when they are wrenched. Pain can be caused by the loss of loved ones as in "Mothers, Sons and the Gangs," along with guilt at not having been able to save them. Or it can be a result of no longer being able to communicate as well as one wishes, as in Rios's "Nani." It can lie below the surface even in "happy" families headed by benevolent dictators, as shown by Houston and Mehta.

Having accepted the fact that the family is a shifting, changing concept, one must then analyze the forces that help to shape it. Howard, Seligmann, and Ella Taylor (selection 14, "TV Families") examine this issue from different angles, delineating elements that may endanger the family, noting a growing flexibility in terms of legal rights of nontraditional families, and identifying stereotyped portrayals that might influence how we evaluate our own families.

The writers in Part Two explore and cross boundaries, expose taboos, and acknowledge pain. They encourage us to ask questions and to redefine the concept of family for ourselves, to choose out of the old and new cultures around us those elements which we find valuable. They free us from claustrophobic notions of what a "perfect" family should be, even as they illustrate that successful families do have certain qualities in common—qualities that we can learn and apply to our own situation. Overall, they leave us with a sense of hope for the future of the human race and a belief in the power of love to overcome—or at least help us through—the darkest moments of our lives.

10

PREREADING ACTIVITY

Before reading selection 10, formulate your own definition of a good family. What are some elements that it must possess?

Families

JANE HOWARD

Jane Howard (1935–) is a reporter, editor, and writer. She lives in Illinois and has taught at several universities. Her books include *Please Touch: A Guided Tour of the Human Potential Movement; Margaret Mead: A Life;* the autobiographical *A Different Woman;* and *Families,* from which selection 10 is taken.

*E*ach of us is born into one family not of our choosing. If we're 1 going to go around devising new ones, we might as well have the luxury of picking their members ourselves. Clever picking might result in new families whose benefits would surpass or at least equal those of the old. The new ones by definition cannot spawn us—as soon as they do that, they stop being new—but there is plenty they can do. I have seen them work wonders. As a member in reasonable standing of six or seven tribes in addition to the one I was born to, I have been trying to figure which earmarks are common to both kinds of families.

(1) Good families have a chief, or a heroine, or a founder—someone around 2 whom others cluster, whose achievements as the Yiddish word has it, let them *kvell,* and whose example spurs them on to like feats. Some blood dynasties produce such figures regularly; others languish for as many as five generations between demigods, wondering with each new pregnancy whether this, at last, might be the messianic baby who will redeem s. Look, is there not something gubernatorial about her footstep, or musica out the way he bangs with his spoon on his cup? All clans, of all kinds, need h a figure now and then. Sometimes clans based on water rather than bloo rbor several such personages at one time. The Bloomsbury Group in Lond six decades ago was not much hampered by its lack of a temporal history.

(2) Good families have a switchboard operator—someone like my mother 3
who cannot help but keep track of what all the others are up to, who plays
Houston Mission Control to everyone else's Apollo. This role, like the forego-
ing one, is assumed rather than assigned. Someone always volunteers for it. That
person often also has the instincts of an archivist, and feels driven to keep scrap-
books and photograph albums up to date, so that the clan can see proof of its
own continuity.

(3) Good families are much to all their members, but everything to none. 4
Good families are fortresses with many windows and doors to the outer world.
The blood clans I feel most drawn to were founded by parents who are nearly as
devoted to whatever it is they do outside as they are to each other and their children. Their curiosity and passion are contagious. Everybody, where they live, is
busy. Paint is spattered on eyeglasses. Mud lurks under fingernails. Person-to-
person calls come in the middle of the night from Tokyo and Brussels. Catchers'
mitts, ballet slippers, overdue library books and other signs of extrafamilial concerns are everywhere.

(4) Good families are hospitable. Knowing that hosts need guests as much 5
as guests need hosts, they are generous with honorary memberships for friends,
whom they urge to come early and often and to stay late. Such clans exude a vivid
sense of surrounding rings of relatives, neighbors, teachers, students and godpar-
ents, any of whom at any time might break or slide into the inner circle. Inside
that circle a wholesome, tacit emotional feudalism develops: you give me protection, I'll give you fealty. Such treaties begin with, but soon go far beyond, the
jolly exchange of pie at Thanksgiving for cake on birthdays. It means you can ask
me to supervise your children for the fortnight you will be in the hospital, and
that however inconvenient this might be for me, I shall manage to. It means I can
phone you on what for me is a dreary, wretched Sunday afternoon and for you
is the eve of a deadline, knowing you will tell me to come right over, if only
to watch you type. It means we need not dissemble. ("To yield to seeming,"
as Buber wrote, "is man's essential cowardice, to resist it is his essential courage
. . . one must at times pay dearly for life lived from the being, but it is never
too dear.")

(5) Good families deal squarely with direness. Pity the tribe that doesn't 6
have, and cherish, at least one flamboyant eccentric. Pity too the one that sup-
poses it can avoid for long the woes to which all flesh is heir. Lunacy, bankruptcy, suicide and other unthinkable fates sooner or later afflict the noblest of
clans with an undertow of gloom. Family life is a set of givens, someone once
told me, and it takes courage to see certain givens as blessings rather than as
curses. Contradictions and inconsistencies are givens, too. So is the war against
what the Oregon patriarch Kenneth Babbs calls malarkey. "There's always
malarkey lurking, bubbles in the cesspool, fetid bubbles that pop and smell. But
I don't put up with malarkey, between my stepkids and my natural ones or anywhere else in the family."

(6) Good families prize their rituals. Nothing welds a family more than these. Rituals are vital especially for clans without histories, because they evoke a past, imply a future, and hint at continuity. No line in the Seder service at Passover reassures more than the last: "Next year in Jerusalem!" A clan becomes more of a clan each time it gathers to observe a fixed ritual (Christmas, birthdays, Thanksgiving, and so on), grieve at a funeral (anyone may come to most funerals; those who do declare their tribalness), and devises a new rite of its own. Equinox breakfasts and all-white dinners can be at least as welding as Memorial Day parades. Several of us in the old *Life* magazine years used to meet for lunch every Pearl Harbor Day, preferably to eat some politically neutral fare like smorgasbord, to "forgive" our only ancestrally Japanese colleague Irene Kubota Neves. For that and other reasons we became, and remain, a sort of family.

"Rituals," a California friend of mine said, "aren't just externals and holidays. They are the performances of our lives. They are a kind of shorthand. They can't be decreed. My mother used to try to decree them. She'd make such a goddamn fuss over what we talked about at dinner, aiming at Topics of Common Interest, topics that celebrated our cohesion as a family. These performances were always hollow, because the phenomenology of the moment got sacrificed for the *idea* of the moment. Real rituals are discovered in retrospect. They emerge around constitutive moments, moments that only happen once, around whose memory meanings cluster. You don't choose those moments. They choose themselves." A lucky clan includes a born mythologizer, like my blood sister, who has the gift of apprehending such a moment when she sees it, and who cannot help but invent new rituals everywhere she goes.

(7) Good families are affectionate. This is of course a matter of style. I know clans whose members greet each other with gingerly handshakes or, in what pass for kisses, with hurried brushes of side jawbones, as if the object were to touch not the lips but the ear. I don't see how such people manage. "The tribe that does not hug," as someone who has been part of many *ad hoc* families recently wrote to me, "is no tribe at all. More and more I realize that everybody, regardless of age, needs to be hugged and comforted in a brotherly or sisterly way now and then. Preferably now."

(8) Good families have a sense of place, which these days is not achieved easily. As Susanne Langer wrote in 1957, "Most people have no home that is a symbol of their childhood, not even a definite memory of one place to serve that purpose . . . all the old symbols are gone." Once I asked a roomful of supper guests who, if anyone, felt any strong pull to any certain spot on the face of the earth. Everyone was silent, except for a visitor from Bavaria. The rest of us seemed to know all too well what Walker Percy means in *The Moviegoer* when he tells of the "genie-soul of the place which every place has or else is not a place [and which] wherever you go, you must meet and master or else be met and mastered." All that meeting and mastering saps plenty of strength. It also underscores our need for tribal bases of the sort which soaring real estate taxes and splintering families have made all but obsolete.

So what are we to do, those of us whose habit and pleasure and doom is 11
our tendency, as a Georgia lady put it, to "fly off at every other whipstitch?"
Think in terms of movable feasts, for a start. Live here, wherever here may be,
as if we were going to belong here for the rest of our lives. Learn to hallow
whatever ground we happen to stand on or land on. Like medieval knights
who took their tapestries along on Crusades, like modern Afghanis with their
yurts, we must pack such totems and icons as we can to make short-term quarters feel like home. Pillows, small rugs, watercolors can dispel much of the
chilling anonymity of a sublet apartment or motel room. When we can, we
should live in rooms with stoves or fireplaces or anyway candlelight. The
ancient saying still is true: Extinguished hearth, extinguished family. Round
tables help, too, and as a friend of mine once put it, so do "too many comfortable chairs, with surfaces to put feet on, arranged so as to encourage a maximum of eye contact." Such rooms inspire good talk, of which good clans can
never have enough.

(9) Good families, not just the blood kind, find some way to connect 12
with posterity. "To forge a link in the humble chain of being, encircling heirs to
ancestors," as Michael Novak has written, "is to walk within a circle of magic as
primitive as humans knew in caves." He is talking of course about babies, feeling them leap in wombs, giving them suck. Parenthood, however, is a state
which some miss by chance and others by design, and a vocation to which not
all are called. Some of us, like the novelist Richard P. Brickner, "look on as others name their children who in turn name their own lives, devising their own
flags from their parents' cloth." What are we who lack children to do? Build
houses? Plant trees? Write books or symphonies or laws? Perhaps, but even if we
do these things, there still should be children on the sidelines, if not at the center, of our lives. It is a sadly impoverished tribe that does not allow access to,
and make much of, some children. Not too much, of course: it has truly been
said that never in history have so many educated people devoted so much attention to so few children. Attention, in excess, can turn to fawning, which isn't
much better than neglect. Still, if we don't regularly see and talk to and laugh
with people who can expect to outlive us by twenty years or so, we had better
get busy and find some.

(10) Good families also honor their elders. The wider the age range, the 13
stronger the tribe. Jean-Paul Sartre and Margaret Mead, to name two spectacu-
larly confident former children, have both remarked on the central importance of
grandparents in their own early lives. Grandparents now are in much more abundant supply than they were a generation or two ago when old age was more rare.
If actual grandparents are not at hand, no family should have too hard a time
finding substitute ones to whom to give unfeigned homage. The Soviet Union's
enchantment with day care centers, I have heard, stems at least in part from the
state's eagerness to keep children away from their presumably subversive grandparents. Let that be a lesson to clans based on interest as well as to those based
on genes.

QUESTIONS FOR CRITICAL READING, THINKING, DISCUSSION, AND WRITING

Analyzing Content and Technique

1. What two kinds of families does Howard discuss in her opening paragraph? Point out the advantages of each kind.
2. Paraphrase the thesis of the essay. Where is it placed? Why? How far do you agree with this thesis? Explain your standpoint.
3. Howard gives us ten characteristics of good families. List these in what you consider their order of importance, which might be different from the order in which Howard listed them. Explain, with an example, why you chose the one you consider most important.
4. What does Howard mean when she asks the reader to "think in terms of moveable feasts"? How might this aspect of our modern lifestyle negatively affect family life? What solutions has Howard proposed?
5. Throughout the essay, Howard uses the rhetorical technique of repetition. Analyze the effect of this on the reader.
6. Who is the intended audience of this essay? How do you deduce this?

Collaborative Activity

Have each member of your group think of an additional quality, not mentioned by Howard, that he or she considers an integral part of a successful family. Each quality needs to be supported by a reason. Make a collaborative list of these qualities and reasons and present them to the class.

Making Connections

1. Write an essay about a family that you consider "good"—either your own or one you know well—comparing it with Howard's ideal family. What are the elements that make "your" family successful? What, if any, unique characteristics does it possess? Be sure to support your thesis with well-chosen examples and quotations, as Howard does.
2. Howard's essay suggests that successful families learn how to adapt to their surroundings. Identify some effective examples she provides of adaptability. Do you agree with her assumption? Write an essay expressing your opinion on this subject and supporting it with your own examples.

11

PREREADING ACTIVITY

Do you think the American family is changing in important ways? Briefly list the major ways in which you consider the American family to have changed or not changed in the last three or four decades.

Variations on a Theme

JEAN SELIGMANN

Born in New York, Jean Seligmann holds a degree from Bryn Mawr College and is a general editor covering health and lifestyle issues for *Newsweek*. In 1983 she wrote the first cover story on AIDS to be published by a national magazine. Since then she has received several awards for her coverage of stories related to the gay community. This essay appeared in *Newsweek* in 1990.

What's in a family? A mommy, a daddy, a couple of kids and maybe a grandma, right? Well, yes, but that's not the whole picture anymore. The family tree of American society is sending forth a variety of new and fast-growing branches. Gay and lesbian couples (with or without children) and unmarried heterosexual couples are now commonplace. What's surprising is not so much that these offshoots of the main trunk are flourishing but that the public seems more and more willing to recognize them as families. Earlier this year the Massachusetts Mutual Life Insurance Co. asked 1,200 randomly selected adults to define the word "family." Only 22 percent picked the legalistic definition: "A group of people related by blood, marriage or adoption." Almost three-quarters instead chose a much broader and more emotional description: "A group of people who love and care for each other." As usual, the American people are changing old perceptions much faster than the courts are. But in many parts of the country lawmakers are now finally catching up and validating the legitimacy of the nontraditional family. 1

Several landmark legal developments this year have greatly expanded the definition of what constitutes a family. In May, San Francisco's Board of Supervisors passed "domestic partnership" legislation recognizing homosexual and unmarried heterosexual couples as families. The ordinance, which was put on the ballot for a November referendum, defines domestic partners as "two people who have chosen to share one another's lives in an intimate and committed relationship of mutual caring." The law's intent was to extend to qualifying domestic 2 partners some of the benefits accorded married heterosexuals. Health benefits, property and life insurance, bereavement leave, and annuity and pension rights are all under consideration.

In July the New York State Court of Appeals ruled that a gay man whose 3 long-term lover had died qualified as family. The survivor was therefore entitled to assume the lease of his partner's rent-controlled Manhattan apartment. Similar state legislation and municipal ordinances are under consideration nationwide. Legislators, judges, and elected officials in Michigan, Wisconsin, Washington, Maryland, and the District of Columbia are forging efforts to reach an all-inclusive understanding of the family.

Some experts think it's no longer possible to define the family. "Family has 4 become a fluid concept," says Arthur Leonard, professor of law at New York Law School. Others fear recognizing domestic partnerships will undermine the sanctity of the heterosexual nuclear family, reducing it to a mere abstraction. But in fact most American households today don't consist of the "traditional" family (a mother and father living with their children under eighteen—or step-parents and stepchildren). Many are single-parent families; others are just plain singles. The courts are acting appropriately, says Leonard, who is also chairman of the New York City Bar Association's Committee on Sex and Law. "The law must follow society and reflect reality," he maintains.

Figures from the annual census reports underscore Leonard's argument. 5 Fewer than 27 percent of the nation's 91 million households in 1988 fit in the traditional model of a family. At the same time, the bureau has counted 1.6 million same-sex couples living together, up from 1.3 million in 1970, and 2.6 million opposite-sex couples sharing a household, up from just half a million in 1970. Reasons cited for these demographic changes include divorce, delayed marriage, and the growth of the gay-liberation movement. For now the Census Bureau still excludes most nontraditional arrangements from its "family" category. But Paul Glick, until 1981 the department's senior demographer, thinks the federal legal definition of family could broaden considerably in the next twenty years.

While gays are not the only beneficiaries of the new legislation, they, above 6 all others, have been most profoundly changed by increased social acceptance of alternative lifestyles. Galen Ellis, twenty-eight, and Elaine Askari, thirty-eight, have been a couple since 1986 and this year donned white tuxedos to celebrate their "commitment ceremony" before one hundred friends and family members in an Oakland, California, park. They exchanged vows and rings and cut a wedding cake. Ellis's mother attended the festivities, and Askari's father sent a wedding card. Since deciding they are a family, they've bought a house together and drafted a variety of legal forms designed to cement their relationship, including wills, powers of attorney, and other contracts. Soon they'd like to become parents, as so many other gay couples have done already.

According to Roberta Achtenberg, executive director of the National Cen- 7 ter for Lesbian Rights, there are more than two million gay mothers and fathers. Most of their children are from earlier, heterosexual relationships, but she estimates that some 5,000 to 10,000 lesbians have borne children after "coming out," and hundreds of gay and lesbian couples have adopted.

Among these nontraditional parents are Michael Pesce, thirty-five, and Jonathan Jarnig, thirty-six. Pesce, a social worker, and Jarnig, a maitre d' at a restaurant, live in a three-bedroom house in suburban Sacramento with their two kids, James, seven, and Carly, five. Parenthood was always a compelling goal for both men; they even discussed it on their second date seven years ago. "I didn't feel like a whole person without kids," recalls Jarnig. "I didn't feel it was right for gay people to be robbed of a sense of family." The couple, whom the kids call Dad and Poppa, are among fewer than a dozen gay couples in the United States who have been granted "joint adoption," which means both fathers have the same secure legal relationship to the children. 8

"Our values really are the same as those of our parents," says Jarnig. "We just happen to be two men." "We're really quite boring," adds Pesce. "Just homebodies. We're Ozzie and Harry." Their home is one with rules and structure: No playing in the living room, cleaning up the family room after play, and no candy. But it's also one with love and understanding for the children, who are Hispanic siblings. "It's important to tell them every night that they're valued and loved," says Pesce. 9

Cindy and Margie share a house on a quiet side street near Boston with their son, Jonah, who recently turned three. (Like several others in this story, they chose not to have their last names published.) Both professionals in their mid-thirties, they have been together for twelve years. Their decision to become "Mommy" and "Mama," as Jonah calls them, reflects societal changes that also affect single straight women seeking to become mothers. Medical advances have made donor insemination much safer from infection by AIDS and other sexually transmitted diseases, and activism by the feminist and gay women's movements has made it more widely available. 10

Despite the growing demand, many U.S. doctors still won't inseminate unmarried women. But there are some exceptions. "We opened our facility to accommodate women being turned away by sperm banks across the country," says Mary Lynn Hemphill of the Feminist Women's Health Center in Atlanta. Almost all FWHC clients are single; one third are lesbians. At Boston's Fenway Community Health Center, which expanded in 1983 to serve lesbians seeking to become mothers, the clientele is still mostly gay, with a growing straight minority. 11

Sperm donors at many facilities are drawn from college and graduate students, who earn about thirty-five dollars each time they "give." For the most part, that's the last connection they have with the children they sire this way, but a couple of programs now offer a "yes" option, in which the donor agrees to let his offspring get in touch with him once they reach the age of eighteen. 12

Donors are thoroughly screened for a family history of inherited diseases and also for current infections, especially for the HIV virus that causes AIDS. Indeed, the AIDS epidemic has made the use of fresh semen donations obsolete. In September New York became the first state to adopt protective regulations to prevent the transmission of AIDS through donor insemination. The new rulings require that a donor be tested twice during a six-month period for antibodies to the AIDS virus, before his frozen donation can be released and used. 13

Some insemination programs require donors to fill out a twenty-five page 14
questionnaire, mostly anticipating requests by recipients on topics like religious
and academic background, hobbies, and even receding hairlines. The would-be
mom can specify the race and physical characteristics of her baby's father; everyone, of course, wants good health and high intelligence. At most facilities, recipients can choose the baby's sex (since it is the sperm that determines gender). But
most women don't exercise the option.

In some states, insemination must be performed by a physician, but the 15
Fenway and other centers encourage women to bring the semen home and
inseminate themselves using a syringe or pipette. As with standard conception,
some women get pregnant on the first try; for others, it may take a dozen or
more attempts. At Fenway, the monthly cost for two vials of semen is $250.

Cindy and Margie, who had a private physician perform their insemination, 16
meet with a group of fifty Boston-area lesbian families at least four times a year—
including Mother's Day. Among their friends are Lorraine, forty-three, and
Linda, thirty-three, who gave birth to the couple's son, Andrew, nearly four years
ago. She tries to describe the boy's relationship with Lorraine, whom he calls
"Boppie." "There aren't words for it," she says. "Lorraine's not the same as a
father, but she's also not a mother." Lorraine would like to legalize her relationship to Andrew through "second-parent" adoption but doesn't care about labels.
"I can be 'Boppie' all his life," she says. In fact, the arrangement has worked out
so well that she and Linda hope to have another child by the same donor.

Most couples who are openly gay, with and without children, acknowledge 17
that they are still not universally accepted as families, and many have experienced
some form of rejection or discrimination. Pesce and Jarnig say their biggest disappointment is that their own parents have kept their distance. "My mother
lumps gay people together with child molesters," says Jarnig. "She's ashamed that
I'm gay and have children—her only grandchildren—and doesn't want to get
involved as a grandmother."

Linda and Lorraine worry about the effect of their nontraditional arrange- 18
ment on their son. For now, "we don't have people around us that don't accept
us as a family," says Linda, but she realizes that will inevitably change as Andrew
grows up. "When he's a teenager," she says, "if he doesn't want both of us to go
to some event, we won't go." Adds Lorraine: "We want to protect him but not
get outrageous about it. We want him to know we made choices that affected him
and that we tried to do it the right way."

Single Mothers by Choice

Lesbians aren't the only women taking advantage of donor insemination. A 19
growing number of unmarried moms are heterosexual but have decided they just
can't wait any longer for Mr. Right to show up. "When people hear about a woman
having a baby without a man, they still kind of scratch their heads," says Lisa
McDonnell of Boston's Fenway Community Health Center. During the next
decade the head scratching is likely to disappear, as illegitimacy continues to lose its
stigma and more women become economically independent. "Most of us wanted

to be married and have children in a more traditional way, but it just didn't work out," says Noel (not her real name), thirty-seven, a Boston-area classical musician and mother of a three-year-old daughter conceived through donor insemination. "Then we hit those age deadlines and we can either make the choice of having children on our own or never have the experience of having a family."

The typical single woman pursuing pregnancy is a middle-class professional [20] in her mid-thirties or older. Marilyn Levin, forty-five, trained as a psychotherapist, now spends her spare time leading workshops for the Boston chapter of Single Mothers by Choice. For Levin, like most women in her support group, putting motherhood before marriage came only after a long struggle. At thirty, she reports, she caught "baby fever," then got married and divorced without having a child. As the ticking of her biological clock grew louder, she launched a last-ditch effort to start a traditional family. "I tried therapy. I did the singles scene. I gave finding a relationship top priority. It was unproductive. Finally I said, 'That's it,' and went ahead on my own."

Levin's daughter, Cate Lara, was born two-and-a-half years ago; Levin's sis- [21] ter attended childbirth classes with her and was at the delivery. Initially, Levin says, her father was "worried about what society would think." Now, both her septuagenarian parents are very much involved with the new little relative. "It's probably lengthened their lives," she says.

Noel, who picked a Chinese sperm donor, often wonders about his genetic [22] contribution to her daughter. "At times I wish she looked a little bit more like me," she admits. "But other times I just think of how beautiful she is." Noel is convinced some of her daughter's personality traits come from the father. "She tends to be much more of a neatnik and much more orderly than I am," she says.

Susan (also a pseudonym), forty-one, is a registered nurse in a small town [23] in the Southwest. When she took stock at thirty-six of "possible life partners," her options seemed few. A year later she began inseminating and after five failed attempts became pregnant; her son is now two. Unlike Noel and Marilyn Levin, she knows almost no one who had done what she did. She and her son have been easily accepted, however, by the largely Hispanic community they live in. Though she sometimes feels isolated and thinks of moving, Susan has no regrets. "Donor insemination was the way to do it," she says. "I didn't want to just sort of use some man and not tell him. Besides there's no one I wanted to have as a father." She often speculates about the man who is her son's biological father. "It's interesting to wonder what the other half of his genes are, because people say he looks like me," she says. "But no one in my family has eyes that color."

For Susan, who now works just one day a week, many worries of single [24] motherhood have been mitigated by family money. Levin, on the other hand, had to return full time to her job as an administrator at the Massachusetts Department of Mental Health when Cate was still an infant. Now Cate attends a licensed family-day-care center, run by two women who take a small number of babies and toddlers into their homes. Levin says the other kids are a good substitute for siblings. Noel's parents pay for day-care costs, but her finances are always a worry.

All three moms realize their children will soon ask about their origins or the 25 absence of a father in the household. Levin plans to explain gradually. When her daughter is young, she says, "I'll tell her, 'Families are different. There are all kinds. Ours is the kind with just a mommy.' When she realizes that she had to have a father to be born, I will tell her that her father is a kind man who wanted to help me have her. We're grateful to him, but he's not involved in our life." At some point, Levin thinks Cate will have to grieve, and may be angry. "When she's a rebelling adolescent, she'll have an easy target."

Noel also believes her daughter may eventually feel hurt and angry. "You do 26 wonder about the psychological ramifications later on," she says. "We're at the forefront, so we don't know how it's going to affect the children. We're just going to have to do the best we can."

"Skip-Generation" Parents

An entirely different kind of nontraditional family is born when mothers 27 can't or won't take care of their children. Often it's Grandma who comes to the rescue. Five years ago Ruth Rench was looking forward to retirement. Her children had long since moved out of her house near Ft. Worth, and she was planning to travel, using the nest egg built up during twenty-five years with the local school system. That's when Rench's three-year-old granddaughter gave her some chilling news: She had been molested by one of her mother's male friends. It would not be the last time the girl was abused. Finally, Rench filed for custody.

Two years and twenty-five-thousand dollars later, Rench, now sixty-five, 28 finally won custody of her granddaughter, who is now eight. She has joined a nationwide groundswell of grandparents who are stepping in to raise their children's children. Rench and her granddaughter are one of ninety-five "skip-generation" families who belong to the Ft. Worth area chapter of Grandparents Raising Grandchildren (GRG).

According to family-court judges, social workers, and counselors, the skip- 29 generation phenomenon is often linked to drug and alcohol abuse. The affected parents cannot or should not assume responsibility for their children. But the problem is not limited to families of the inner city, or even to drug users. "Most of these grandparents are from good middle-class families who have never had to face anything like this before," says Ellen Hogan, forty-four. Hogan, who heads a fifty-five-member Houston GRG group, and her husband, Harold, are in the middle of a court battle with their twenty-three-year-old daughter over custody of their two grandchildren, ages one and four. "It's happening to blue-collar workers, white-collar workers, blacks, and whites," she says. "It's so widespread—it's happening all over."

Often frustrated by the expense and the legal hoops they must jump 30 through to gain custody of neglected or abused grandchildren, many grandparents stand by helplessly as the youngsters are shipped off to foster homes. Others simply take on the child-rearing burden without legal custody. They may start on an informal basis: watching the grandchildren for the weekend, or while the parents are at work. Gradually, the time the children spend with them is extended as the parents lose control of their lives through drugs, financial difficulties, or extreme self-absorption. This situation may go on for years until suddenly the mother decides she wants the child back—often in order to increase her welfare payments so she can buy drugs. "It often ends up in court," says one family counselor, "sometimes amicably, sometimes not."

Psychologists are just beginning to look at the long-term emotional effects skip-generation rearing has on children. California social worker Sylvie de Toledo has spent the last two years working with such families in programs she started at the Psychiatric Clinic for Youth in Long Beach and the Reiss-Davis Child Study Center in Los Angeles. Though skip-generation grandparents and parents suffer great emotional strain during these crises, it is the children who are at greatest risk. They often do poorly in school, defy authority, have problems making friends, and exhibit physical aggressiveness or feelings of isolation. "It is crucial that the children be helped to understand that they are blameless," de Toledo emphasizes.

Although these children are quite attached to their grandparents, she explains, "they have a profound sense of abandonment and loss and rejection by their parents. . . . They worry consciously and unconsciously that they may once again be abandoned." One of their greatest fears is that their grandparents may get sick or die, leaving them with no one else to turn to.

Quietly heroic grandmothers like Ruth Rench are sacrificing their own needs and plans to provide their "rescued" grandchildren with that precious sense of security and love that is every child's birthright. They are also struggling to keep their grandkids from perpetuating a dangerous cycle. "All I can do now is give her all the moral and spiritual training that she needs and hope that she doesn't grow up in the pattern she was born into," says Rench. "You've got to break that pattern somewhere. If you don't, we're all going down the drain."

QUESTIONS FOR CRITICAL READING, THINKING, DISCUSSION, AND WRITING

Analyzing Content and Technique

1. Consider the title. What "variations" has Seligmann presented to the reader? What is her attitude to these variations? How is her attitude indicated in the essay?
2. In paragraph 4, Arthur Leonard, a professor of law at New York Law School, comments that "the law must follow society and reflect reality." Explain the meaning of this statement and give an example from the text that illustrates this phenomenon. Do you agree with the statement? Give reasons.
3. List the major legal changes that have positively affected gay couples. What societal attitudes may be deduced from this? Analyze the kinds of problems that children of gay households may still have to face.
4. Describe the typical "single mother by choice." Why does she decide to become a single mother? How is she different from the other kind of single mother the section title hints at?
5. Explain the term "skip-generation parents." What are two major problems faced by these "parents"? Why do the children in this situation suffer?

6. What is the tone of this essay? How is it influenced by the kind of magazine Seligmann is writing for? What does the writer wish to accomplish by choosing this tone?

7. What rhetorical mode has the writer used throughout the article to support her points? Pick out a few examples of this mode and evaluate its effectiveness.

Collaborative Activity

As a group, discuss the families that you know most closely. How many of them are "traditional"? How many are "variations"? In your group, are there variations other than the ones Seligmann discusses? Based on your discussion, write a collaborative paragraph about the American family as you have experienced it.

Making Connections

1. Examine your own family, or that of a close friend. Were you brought up in a "traditional" household, or was your household a "variation"? What advantages and disadvantages did you experience as a result? Write an essay in which you balance the pros and cons of your family structure and analyze how these affected your development.

2. Choose one of the family categories Seligmann has presented in her article and research its development. Some questions you might ask are: When did it come into being? What was society's opinion about such a family at first? What changes have occurred? Does this kind of family still face prejudice? Support your essay with specific examples.

12

Do ten minutes of focused freewriting on the title. You might think about the following: What are the different ways in which one goes about finding a mate? What are some difficulties and pressures associated with the process? What are the rewards?

Finding a Wife

GARY SOTO

Born in the agricultural San Joaquin Valley in California, Gary Soto has written poetry, memoir, and fiction. He teaches English and Chicano Studies at U.C. Berkeley. His books include *Black Hair, The Elements of San Joaquin, Neighborhood Odes, Local News,* and *Small Faces* (1986), from which this selection is taken.

It's easy to find a wife, I told my students. Pick anybody, I said, and they chuckled and fidgeted in their chairs. I laughed a delayed laugh, feeling hearty and foolish as a pup among these young men who were in my house to talk poetry and books. We talked, occasionally making sense, and drank cup after cup of coffee until we were so wired we had to stand up and walk around the block to shake out our nerves.

When they left I tried to write a letter, grade papers, and finally nap on the couch. My mind kept turning to how simple it is to find a wife; that we can easily say after a brief two- or three-week courtship, "I want to marry you."

When I was twenty, in college and living on a street that was a row of broken apartment buildings, my brother and I returned to our apartment from a game of racquetball to sit in the living room and argue whether we should buy a quart of beer. We were college poor, living off the cheap blessings of rice, raisins, and eggs that I took from our mom's refrigerator when Rick called her into the back yard about a missing sock from his laundry—a ploy from the start.

"Rick, I only got a dollar," I told him. He slapped his thigh and told me to wake up. It was almost the end of the month. And he was right. In two days our paychecks from Zak's Car Wash would burn like good report cards in our pockets. So I gave in. I took the fifteen cents—a dime and five pennies—he had plucked from the ashtray of loose change in his bedroom, and went downstairs, across the street and the two blocks to Scott's Liquor. While I was returning home, swinging the quart of beer like a lantern, I saw the Japanese woman who was my neighbor, cracking walnuts on her front porch. I walked slowly so that she looked up, smiling. I smiled, said hello, and continued walking to the rhythm of her hammer rising and falling.

In the apartment I opened the beer and raised it like a chalice before we   5
measured it in glasses, each of us suspicious that the other would get more. I rattled sunflower seeds onto a plate, and we pinched fingersful, the beer in our hands cutting loose a curtain of bubbles. We were at a party with no music, no host, no girls. Our cat, Mensa, dawdled in, blinking from the dull smoke of a sleepy afternoon. She looked at us, and we looked at her. Rick flicked a seed at her and said, "That's what we need—a woman!"

I didn't say anything. I closed my eyes, legs shot out in a V from the couch,   6
and thought of that girl on the porch, the rise and fall of her hammer, and the walnuts cracking open like hearts.

I got up and peeked from our two-story window that looked out onto a   7
lawn and her apartment. No one. A wicker chair, potted plants, and a pile of old newspapers. I looked until she came out with a broom to clean up the shells. "Ah, my little witch," I thought, and raced my heart downstairs, but stopped short of her house because I didn't know what to say or do. I stayed behind the hedge that separated our yards and listened to her broom swish across the porch, then start up the walk to the curb. It was then that I started to walk casually from behind the hedge and, when she looked at me with a quick grin, I said a hearty hello and walked past her without stopping to talk. I made my way to the end of the block where I stood behind another hedge, feeling foolish. I should have said something. "Do you like walnuts," I could have said, or maybe, "Nice day to sweep, isn't it?"—anything that would have my mouth going.

I waited behind that hedge, troubled by my indecision. I started back up   8
the street and found her bending over a potted geranium, a jar of cloudy water in her hand. Lucky guy, I thought, to be fed by her.

I smiled as I passed, and she smiled back. I returned to the apartment and   9
my bedroom where I stared at my homework and occasionally looked out the window to see if she was busy on the porch. But she wasn't there. Only the wicker chair, the plants, the pile of newspapers.

The days passed, white as clouds. I passed her house so often that we began   10
to talk, sit together on the porch, and eventually snack on sandwiches that were thick as Bibles, with tumblers of milk to wash down her baked sweet bread flecked with tiny crushed walnuts.

After the first time I ate at her house, I hurried to the apartment to brag   11
about my lunch to my brother who was in the kitchen sprinkling raisins on his rice. Sandwiches, I screamed, milk, cold cuts, chocolate ice cream! I spoke about her cupboards, creaking like ships weighed down with a cargo of rich food, and about her, that woman who came up to my shoulder. I was in love and didn't know where to go from there.

As the weeks passed, still white as clouds, we saw more of each other. Then   12
it happened. On another Saturday, after browsing at a thrift shop among gooseneck lamps and couches as jolly as fat men, we went to the west side of Fresno for Mexican food—menudo for me and burritos for her, with two beers clunked down on our table. When we finished eating and were ready to go, I wiped my

mouth and plucked my sole five-dollar bill from my wallet as I walked to the cashier. It was all the big money I had. I paid and left the restaurant as if it were nothing, as if I spent such money every day. But inside I was thinking, "What am I going to do?"

Scared as I was, I took Carolyn's hand into mine as we walked to the car. I released it to open the door for her. We drove and drove, past thrift shops she longed to browse through, but I didn't want to stop because I was scared I would want to hold her hand again. After turning corners aimlessly, I drove back to her house where we sat together on the front porch, not touching. I was shivering, almost noticeably. But after a while, I did take her hand into mine and that space between us closed. We held hands, little tents opening and closing, and soon I nuzzled my face into her neck to find a place to kiss. 13

I married this one Carolyn Oda, a woman I found cracking walnuts on an afternoon. It was a chance meeting: I was walking past when she looked up to smile. It could have been somebody else, a girl drying persimmons on a line, or one hosing down her car, and I might have married another and been unhappy. But it was Carolyn, daughter of hard workers, whom I found cracking walnuts. She stirred them into dough that she shaped into loaves, baked in the oven, and set before me so that my mouth would keep talking in its search of the words to make me stay. 14

QUESTIONS FOR CRITICAL READING, THINKING, DISCUSSION, AND WRITING

Analyzing Content and Technique

1. Examine the introduction. What is its purpose? Paraphrase the thesis of the piece. Where is it placed?
2. How do you think the writer wants readers to take his assertion that it is easy to find a wife—literally or ironically? In his case, what did the process involve? Which parts were most difficult for him?
3. From the details given in the essay, write a brief character analysis of the young narrator.
4. What is the main point of paragraph 14? From it, what can you deduce of the writer's values and beliefs?
5. This writer, who is also a poet, often uses similes and metaphors to make a point. Create a list of these. What do they add to the tone and texture of this piece?

Collaborative Activity

Have each member of your group write a brief description of an ideal mate. Compare the descriptions. Which features do group members stress most? Are there any features that occur more than once? Write a collaborative paragraph summarizing your findings and present it to the class.

Making Connections

1. How far do you agree with Soto's views on the ease of finding a mate? Write a paper in which you take the opposite position, presenting all the difficulties of finding a suitable partner. In

addition to drawing on your own experience, interview a few people, married and single, of different financial and racial backgrounds.

2. Soto writes this essay from a male viewpoint. How would a woman go about looking for a mate? How difficult or easy would it be for her? Would she be looking for different qualities in a mate than a man would? What taboos might she face? Write an essay in which you examine this process, using specific examples to support your points.

Before reading selection 13, write about your own family. What are some elements you most appreciate about it? What are some qualities you feel are missing in your family relationships? Choose two or three good examples to support your points.

Pom's Engagement

VED MEHTA

Ved Mehta (1934–), blind since the age of three, has published more than a dozen books and a screenplay. Born in India, he was educated at the Arkansas State School for the Blind, at Pomona College in California, and at Harvard University. He is a staff writer for *The New Yorker*, in which many of his pieces have appeared.

*B*efore we moved to Lahore, Daddyji had gone to Mussoorie, a hill 1 station in the United Provinces, without telling us why he was going out of the Punjab. Now, several months after he made that trip, he gathered us around him in the drawing room at 11 Temple Road while Mamaji mysteriously hurried Sister Pom upstairs. He started talking as if we were all very small and he were conducting one of our "dinner-table-school" discussions. He said that by right and tradition the oldest daughter had to be given in marriage first, and that the ripe age for marriage was nineteen. He said that when a girl approached that age her parents, who had to take the initiative, made many inquiries and followed many leads. They investigated each young man and his family background, his relatives, his friends, his classmates, because it was important to know what kind of family the girl would be marrying into, what kind of company she would be expected to keep. If the girl's parents decided that a particular young man was suitable, then his people also had to make their investigations, but, however favorable their findings, their decision was unpredictable, because good, well-settled boys were in great demand and could afford to be choosy. All this took a lot of time. "That's why I said nothing to you children about why I went to Mussoorie," he concluded. "I went to see a young man for Pom. She's already nineteen."

We were stunned. We have never really faced the idea that Sister Pom might 2 get married and suddenly leave, I thought.

"We won't lose Pom, we'll get a new family member," Daddyji said, as if ₃ reading my thoughts.

Then all of us started talking at once. We wanted to know if Sister Pom had ₄ been told; if she'd agreed; whom she'd be marrying.

"Your mother has just taken Pom up to tell her," Daddyji said. "But she's ₅ a good girl. She will agree." He added, "The young man in question is twenty-eight years old. He's a dentist, and so has a profession."

"Did you get a dentist because Sister Pom has bad teeth?" Usha asked. Sis- ₆ ter Pom had always been held up to us as an example of someone who, as a child, had spurned greens and had therefore grown up with a mouthful of poor teeth.

Daddyji laughed. "I confess I didn't think of anyone's teeth when I chose ₇ the young man in question."

"What is he like?" I asked. "What are we to call him?" ₈

"He's a little bit on the short side, but he has a happy-go-lucky nature, like ₉ Nimi's. He doesn't drink, but, unfortunately, he does smoke. His father died at an early age of a heart attack, but he has a nice mother, who will not give Pom any trouble. It seems that everyone calls him Kakaji."

We all laughed. Kakaji, or "youngster," was what very small boys were ₁₀ called.

"That's what he must have been called when he was small, and the name ₁₁ stuck," Daddyji said.

In spite of myself, I pictured a boy smaller than I was and imagined him tak- ₁₂ ing Sister Pom away, and then I imagined her having to keep his pocket money, to arrange his clothes in the cupboards, to comb his hair. My mouth felt dry.

"What will Kakaji call Sister Pom?" I asked. ₁₃

"Pom, silly—what else?" Sister Umi said. ₁₄

Mamaji and Sister Pom walked into the room. Daddyji made a place for Sis- ₁₅ ter Pom next to him and said, "Now, now, now, no reason to cry. Is it to be yes?"

"Whatever you say," Sister Pom said in a small voice, between sobs. ₁₆

"Pom, how can you say that? You've never seen him," Sister Umi said. ₁₇

"Kakaji's uncle, Dr. Prakash Mehrotra, himself a dentist, has known our ₁₈ family from his student days in Lahore," Daddyji said. "As a student dentist, he used to be welcomed in Babuji's Shahalmi Gate house. He would come and go as he pleased. He has known for a long time what kind of people we are. He remembered seeing you, Pom, when we went to Mussoorie on holiday. He said yes immediately, and his approval seemed to be enough for Kakaji."

"You promised me you wouldn't cry again," Mamaji said to Sister Pom, ₁₉ patting her on the back, and then, to Daddyji, "She's agreed."

Daddyji said much else, sometimes talking just for the sake of talking, some- ₂₀ times laughing at us because we were sniffling, and all the time trying to make us believe that this was a happy occasion. First, Sister Umi took issue with him: parents had no business arranging marriages; if she were Pom she would run away. Then Sister Nimi: all her life she had heard him say to us children, "Think for yourself—be independent," and here he was not allowing Pom to think for herself. Brother Om took Daddyji's part: girls who didn't get married became a burden on their parents, and Daddyji had four daughters to marry off, and would be retiring in a few years. Sisters Nimi and Umi retorted: they hadn't gone to college to get married off, to have some young man following them around like a leech. Daddyji just laughed. I thought he was so wise, and right.

"Go and bless your big sister," Mamaji said, pushing me in the direction of   21
Sister Pom.

"I don't want to," I said. "I don't know him."   22

"What'll happen to Sister Pom's room?" Usha asked. She and Ashok didn't   23
have rooms of their own. They slept in Mamaji's room.

"Pom's room will remain empty, so that any time she likes she can come   24
and stay in her room with Kakaji," Daddyji said.

The thought that a man I never met would sleep in Pom's room with Sis-   25
ter Pom there made my heart race. A sob shook me. I ran outside.

The whole house seemed to be in an uproar. Mamaji was shouting at Gian   26
Chand, Gian Chand was shouting at the bearer, the bearer was shouting at the
sweeper. There were the sounds of the kitchen fire being stoked, of the drain
being washed out, of water running in bathrooms. From behind whichever
door I passed came the rustle of saris, salwars, and kemises. The house smelled
of fresh flowers, but it had a ghostly chill. I would climb to the landing of Sister Pom's room and thump down the stairs two at a time. Brother Om would
shout up at me, "Stop it!" Sister Umi would shout down at me, "Don't you
have anything better to do?" Sister Nimi would call to me from somewhere,
"You're giving Pom a headache." I wouldn't heed any of them. As soon as I
had thumped down, I would clatter to the top and thump my way down again.

Daddyji went past on the back veranda. "Who's coming with Kakaji?" I   27
asked. Kakaji was in Lahore to buy some dental equipment, and in a few minutes
he was expected for tea, to meet Sister Pom and the family.

"He's coming alone," Daddyji said, over his shoulder. "He's come from   28
very far away." I had somehow imagined that Kakaji would come with at least as
many people as we had in our family, because I had started thinking of the tea as
a kind of cricket match—the elevens facing off.

I followed Daddyji into the drawing room. "Will he come alone for his   29
wedding, too?"

"No. Then he'll come with the bridegroom's party."   30

We were joined by everyone except Mamaji and Sister Pom, who from the   31
moment we got the news of Sister Pom's marriage had become inseparable.

Gian Chand came in, the tea things rattling on his tray.   32

Later, I couldn't remember exactly how Kakaji had arrived, but I remember   33
noticing that his footfall was heavy, that his greeting was affectionate, and that his
voice seemed to float up with laughter. I don't know what I'd expected, but I
imagined that if I had been in his place I would have skulked in the *gulli,* and perhaps changed my mind and not entered at all.

"Better to have ventured and lost than never to have ventured at all," Dad-   34
dyji was saying to Kakaji about life's battles.

"Yes, Daddyji, just so," he said, with a little laugh. I had never heard any-   35
body outside our family call my father Daddyji. It sounded odd.

Sister Pom was sent for, and she came in with Mamaji. Her footsteps were   36
shy, and the rustle of her sari around her feet was slow, as if she felt too conscious
of the noise she was making just in walking. Daddyji made some complimentary
remark about the silver border on her sari, and told her to sit next to Kakaji.
Kakaji and Sister Pom exchanged a few words about a family group photograph
on the mantelpiece, and about her studies. There was the clink of china as Sister
Pom served Kakaji tea.

"Won't you have some tea yourself?" Kakaji asked Sister Pom.   37

Sister Pom's sari rustled over her shoulder as she turned to Daddyji.   38

"Kakaji, none of my children have ever tasted tea or coffee," Daddyji said.   39
"We consider both to be bad habits. My children have been brought up on hot
milk, and lately Pom has been taking a little ghi in her milk at bedtime, for health
reasons."

We all protested at Daddyji's broadcasting family matters.   40

Kakaji tactfully turned the conversation to a visit to Mussoorie that our fam-   41
ily was planning.

Mamaji offered him onion, potato, and cauliflower pakoras. He accepted,   42
remarking how hot and crisp they were.

"Where will Sister Pom live?" Usha asked.   43

"In the summer, my practice is in Mussoorie," Kakaji said, "but in the win-   44
ter it's in Dehra Dun."

It struck me for the first time that after Sister Pom got married people we   45
didn't know, people she didn't know, would become more important to her than
we were.

Kakaji had left without formally committing himself. Then, four days later,   46
when we were all sitting in the drawing room, a servant brought a letter to
Mamaji. She told us that it was from Kakaji's mother, and that it asked if Sister
Pom might be engaged to Kakaji. "She even wants to know if Pom can be married in April or May," Mamaji said excitedly. "How propitious! That'll be the fifth
wedding in the family in those two months." Cousins Prakash and Dev, Cousin
Pushpa (Bhaji Ganga Ram's adopted daughter), and Auntie Vimla were all due to
be married in Lahore then.

"You still have time to change your mind," Daddyji said to Sister Pom.   47
"What do you really think of him?"

Sister Pom wouldn't say anything.   48

"How do you expect her to know what her mind is when all that the two   49
talked about was a picture and her bachelor's exam in May?" Sister Umi
demanded. "Could she have fallen in love already?"

"Love, Umi, means something very different from 'falling in love,'" Dad-   50
dyji said. "It's not an act but a lifelong process. The best we can do as Pom's parents is to give her love every opportunity to grow."

"But doesn't your 'every opportunity' include knowing the person better   51
than over a cup of tea, or whatever?" Sister Umi persisted.

"Yes, of course it does. But what we are discussing here is a simple matter   52
of choice—not love," Daddyji said. "To know a person, to love a person, takes
years of living together."

"Do you mean, then, that knowing a person and loving a person are the 53 same thing?" Sister Umi asked.

"Not quite, but understanding and respect are essential to love, and that 54 cannot come from talking together, even over a period of days or months. That can come only in good time, through years of experience. It is only when Pom and Kakaji learn to consider each other's problems as one and the same that they will find love."

"But, Daddyji, look at the risk you're taking, the risk you're making Pom 55 take," Sister Nimi said.

"We are trying to minimize the risk as much as we can by finding Pom a 56 family that is like ours," Daddyji said. "Kakaji is a dentist, I am a doctor. His life and way of thinking will be similar to mine. We are from the same caste, and Kakaji's family originally came from the Punjab. They eat meat and eggs, and they take religion in their stride, and don't pray every day and go to temples, like Brahmans. Kakaji knows how I walk into a club and how I am greeted there. The atmosphere in Pom's new home will be very much the same as the atmosphere here. Now, if I were to give Pom in marriage to a Brahman he'd expect Pom to live as he did. That would really be gambling."

"Then what you're doing is perpetuating the caste system," Sister Nimi 57 said. She was the political rebel in the family. "You seem to presuppose that a Kshatriya should marry only a Kshatriya, that a Brahman should marry only a Brahman. I would just as soon marry a shopkeeper from the Bania caste or an Untouchable, and help to break down caste barriers."

"That day might come," Daddyji said. "But you will admit, Nimi, that by 58 doing that you'd be increasing the odds."

"But for a cause I believe in," Sister Nimi said. 59

"Yes, but that's a whole other issue," Daddyji said. 60

"Daddyji, you say that understanding and respect are necessary for love," 61 Sister Umi said. "I don't see why you would respect a person more because you lived with him and shared his problems."

"In our society, we think of understanding and respect as coming only 62 through sacrifice," Daddyji said.

"Then you're advocating the subservience of women," Sister Nimi said, "be- 63 cause it's not Kakaji who will be expected to sacrifice—it's Pom. That's not fair."

"And why do you think that Pom will learn to respect Kakaji because she 64 sacrifices for him?" Sister Umi said, pressing her point.

"No, Umi, it is the other way around," Daddyji said. "It is Kakaji who will 65 respect Pom because she sacrifices for him."

"But that doesn't mean that Pom will respect Kakaji," Sister Umi persisted. 66

"But if Kakaji is moved by Pom's sacrifices he will show more consideration 67 for her. He will grow to love her. I know in my own case I was moved to the depths to see Shanti suffer so because she was so ill-prepared to be my wife. It took me long enough—too long, I believe—to reach that understanding, perhaps because I had broken away from the old traditions and had given in to Western influences."

"So you admit that Pom will have to suffer for years," Sister Umi said. 68

"Perhaps," Daddyji said. "But all that time she will be striving for ultimate 69 happiness and love. Those are precious gifts that can only be cultivated in time."

"You haven't told us what this ultimate happiness is," Sister Umi said. "I 70 don't really understand it."

"It is a uniting of ideals and purposes, and a merging of them. This is the 71 tradition of our society, and it is the means we have adopted to make our marriages successful and beautiful. It works because we believe in the goodness of the individuals going into the marriage and rely on the strength of the sacred bond."

"But my ideal is to be independent," Sister Nimi said. "As you say, 'Think 72 for yourself.'"

"But often you have to choose among ideals," Daddyji said. "You may have 73 to choose between being independent and being married."

"But aren't you struck by the fact that all the suffering is going to be on 74 Pom's part? Shouldn't Kakaji be required to sacrifice for their happiness, too?" Sister Nimi said, reverting to the old theme.

"There has to be a start," Daddyji said. "Remember, in our tradition it's her 75 life that is joined with his; it is she who will forsake her past to build a new future with him. If both Pom and Kakaji were to be obstinate, were to compete with each other about who would sacrifice first, who would sacrifice more, what hope would there be of their ever getting on together, of their ever finding love?"

"Daddyji, you're evading the issue," Sister Nimi said. "Why shouldn't he 76 take the initiative in this business of sacrifice?"

"He would perhaps be expected to if Pom were working, too, as in the 77 West, and, though married, leading a whole different life from his. I suppose more than this I really can't say, and there may be some injustice in our system, at that. In the West, they go in for romantic love, which is unknown among us. I'm not sure that that method works any better than our method does."

Then Daddyji said to Sister Pom, "I have done my best. Even after you 78 marry Kakaji, my responsibility for you will not be over. I will always be there in the background if you should need me."

"I respect your judgment, Daddyji," Sister Pom said obediently. "I'll do 79 what you say."

Mamaji consulted Shambu Pandit. He compared the horoscopes of Sister 80 Pom and Kakaji and set the date of the marriage for the eleventh of May. . . . "That's just three days after she finishes her B.A. finals!" we cried. "When will she study? You are sacrificing her education to some silly superstition."

But Shambu Pandit would not be budged from the date. "I am only going 81 by the horoscopes of the couple," he said. "You might as well protest to the stars."

We appealed to Daddyji, but he said that he didn't want to interfere, 82 because such matters were up to Mamaji. That was as much as to say that Shambu Pandit's date was a settled thing.

I recall that at about that time there was an engagement ceremony. We all— 83 Daddyji, Mamaji, Sister Pom, many of our Mehta and Mehra relatives—sat cross-legged on the floor of the front veranda around Shambu Pandit. He recited the Gayatri Mantra, the simple prayer he used to tell us to say before we went to sleep, and made a thank offering of incense and ghi to a fire in a brazier, much as Mamaji did—behind Daddyji's back—when one of us was going on a trip or had recovered from a bout of illness. Servants passed around a platter heaped up with crumbly sweet balls. I heard Kakaji's sister, Billo, saying something to Sister Pom; she had just come from Dehra Dun bearing a sari, a veil, and the engagement ring for Sister Pom, after Romesh Chachaji, one of Daddyji's brothers, had gone to Dehra Dun bearing some money, a silver platter and silver bowls, and sweet-meats for Kakaji. It was the first time that I was able to think of Kakaji both as a remote and frightening dentist who was going to take Sister Pom away and as someone ordinary like us, who had his own family. At some point, Mamaji prod-ded me, and I scooted forward, crab fashion, to embrace Sister Pom. I felt her hand on my neck. It had something cold and metallic on it, which sent a shiver through me. I realized that she was wearing her engagement ring, and that until then Mamaji was the only one in our family who had worn a ring.

In the evening, the women relatives closeted themselves in the drawing room with Sister Pom for the engagement singsong. I crouched outside with my ear to the door. The door pulsated with the beat of a barrel drum. The pulse in my forehead throbbed in sympathy with the beat as I caught snatches of songs about bedsheets and henna, along with explosions of laughter, the songs them-selves rising and falling like the cooing of the doves that nested under the eaves of the veranda. I thought that a couple of years earlier I would have been playing somewhere outside on such an occasion, without knowing what I was missing, or been in the drawing room clapping and singing, but now I was crouching by the door like a thief, and was feeling ashamed even as I was captivated. ₈₄

QUESTIONS FOR CRITICAL READING, THINKING, DISCUSSION, AND WRITING

Analyzing Content and Technique

1. In what major ways does the Indian system of marriage differ from the western one? Analyze some of the important assumptions (about romance, about duty, about the importance of indi-vidual choice, and so forth) behind each system.
2. Analyze the character of the father in this selection. Would you consider him a good father? Why or why not? Choose at least two passages from the text to support your answer.
3. Analyze the character of Pom. What values do you think are important to her? In what way is she different from a contemporary American woman of her age? In what way is she different from her sisters?
4. Mehta's family experiences some conflict during the "arranging" of this marriage. Why? How is it resolved? Do you feel the resolution to be satisfactory? Do you think this conflict will recur in the near future?
5. This selection is full of sense details of all kinds except one. What is missing? Why? Choose a passage that you feel to be particularly effective and analyze how the writer has achieved his effect. From this passage, what conclusions can you draw about the effect of sense details on readers?

Collaborative Activity

Look back at the selection "Families." Have each group in the class choose one of the elements Howard discusses. Does this element play an important part in Mehta's family? Is there a different element that has taken its place? Make a collaborative presentation to the class based on your findings.

Making Connections

1. Write an essay analyzing the pros and cons of the Indian system of marriage as it appears in this excerpt. You may wish to do some library research to gain a more comprehensive picture of the society out of which this system comes. Some things to focus on are the roles of men and women, values such as filial obedience, the economics behind such marriages, and the percentage of success or failure.
2. Often when immigrants move to a different country, their customs and lifestyle undergo a transformation. But sometimes, faced by confusion and an excess of change, people hold on more tightly to their traditions. Analyze the Indian marriage system in the United States to see whether it has changed or remained the same. If possible, interview some Indian Americans or research Indian American papers and magazines to gather material for your essay.

Which is your favorite television show about families? What do you like about it? Explain why you enjoy it more than other shows about families.

TV Families

ELLA TAYLOR

Ella Taylor (1948–   ) was born in Israel. She was educated in England and in the United States, where she completed her Ph.D. at Brandeis University. She currently teaches cultural theory at the University of Washington. Her work has been published in *The New York Times,* the *Village Voice,* and the *Philadelphia Inquirer.* A slightly different version of this selection appears in her book *All in the Work-Family: Family and Workplace Imagery in Television.*

*F*ew contemporary forms of storytelling offer territory as fertile as   1
television for unearthing changing public ideas about family. The tube is at once the most truly popular and the most relentlessly familial entertainment medium we have. And our national culture is so thoroughly suffused with its images that you needn't ever have seen *The Cosby Show* or *All in the Family* or *Ozzie and Harriet* to know the outlines of what these TV institutions are about. Your kids, your parents, your friends and co-workers, or, failing these, other media will tell you even if you belong to that tiny group of perverse social isolates who proudly declare they don't own a television or that they watch only *Masterpiece Theatre* and wildlife documentaries. The shared experience of tele-history has become one of the major ways in which we locate ourselves in time, place, and generation, and at the heart of that history lies television's obsession—the family.

Domesticity was from the beginning built into the forms and structures of   2
television, primarily for the sound business reasons that have always guided programming policy. An early alliance between broadcasters and advertising sponsors installed television, as it had radio, in private homes as a domestic appliance, used to sell other appliances to audiences conceived as family units. With its small screen, "talking heads" format, and interior settings, television combines the looming proximity of film with the constraining space of the theater. It lends itself to the intimacy of character and relationship rather than to action, the routinized

Source: From *Prime Time Families* by Ella Taylor. Reprinted by permission of the author.

intimacy of domestic life rather than the melodramatic intensity of live theater or film. In all its genres—whether comedy or dramatic series, day or night-time soaps, TV movies, even news—the language and imagery of family break obsessively through its surface forms. Still, it is the episodic series, which fosters a gradual buildup of audience attachment to individual characters and primary relationships, that generates the fullest possibilities for a meditation on domestic themes. The situation comedy that TV inherited from radio and from vaudeville has evolved into a character comedy, more a continuous family chronicle than a conventionally plotted narrative, though it still provides the satisfaction of a weekly resolution that the soaps lack.

Over the years, television's changing commentary on family life has been by   3
turns reflective, utopian, dystopic, its mood now anxious, now euphoric, now redemptive. It articulates prevailing cultural attitudes—but these come filtered through the changing world views and daily routines of producers, network executives, and advertisers, and are filtered again through the varied perceptions of viewers.

To some degree the stance TV adopts toward social trends has been deter-   4
mined by ad hoc changes in the strategies used by the TV industry to attract audiences. The powers that be who decided, in the early fifties, to phase out ethnic sitcoms like *Amos and Andy, Life with Luigi,* and *The Goldbergs* and replace them with the upper-middle-class white coziness of *Leave It to Beaver* and *Ozzie and Harriet* may well have thought they were reproducing the typical American family, if not of the present, then certainly of the near future—just the people their advertisers wanted to reach. What they reproduced, in fact, was not the reality of most family lives, but a postwar ideology breezily forecasting a steady rate of economic growth that would produce sufficient abundance to eliminate the basis for class and ethnic conflict. The "end of ideology" would produce a vast middle-class consensus, with the family as the essential building block integrating the individual into a fundamentally benign social order. So the Nelsons and the Cleavers were both advertising—and embodying—the American Dream.

It's unlikely that such grand visions circulated at programming conferences   5
in the network entertainment divisions, or if they did they percolated through the more immediate, perceived imperatives of the market. From the beginning, producers and networks made their programming decisions with advertisers in mind. In the fifties that meant casting nets as wide as possible to deliver a "mass audience" of potential buyers for the explosion of consumer goods and services that poured off production lines. Fashioning a mass out of an enormous, heterogeneous, and highly mobile population meant, in practice, producing entertainment so bland that it would offend no one.

Out of this climate grew the motto of the successful network careerist,   6
"least objectionable programming," and it produced those least objectionable families, the Cleavers, the Nelsons, and the Andersons of *Father Knows Best*. The magically spotless kitchens of those least objectionable wives and mothers, June Cleaver, Harriet Nelson, and Margaret Anderson, came amply stocked with all

the latest consumer durables. Harriet promoted Listerine and other products on her own show, exhorting her viewers to become model consumers and, by extension, model families.

Taken together, these shows proposed family life as a zany, conflict-free 7 adventure. Past and future merged into an eternal present in which parents would love and respect each other and their children forever. The children would grow up, go to college, and take up lives identical in most essentials to those of their parents, only wealthier. (The sad fate of that dream is well expressed in an early 1980s TV movie in which the Beaver returns, a true child of his generation, jobless, divorced, and confused.) Even the working-class families, the Kramdens and the Rileys, and the upwardly mobile ones like Lucy and Ricky, embraced the rags-to-riches mythology and labored ceaselessly, through their get-rich-quick schemes, to attain the rewards and the life styles of the middle class.

. . . By the mid-sixties, the dream of a great harmonious middle-class 8 America was fraying at the edges, and the latent schisms of class, race, gender, and age erupted into open conflict. But programming executives, for all their declared sensitivity to changes in public mood, stubbornly went on *seeing*—and producing for—the masses they needed to draw advertising dollars. Throughout the sixties the industry continued to consolidate around blandly consensual family comedies like *The Donna Reed Show* and *My Three Sons,* or loony clans like *The Munsters* and *The Addams Family. The Beverly Hillbillies,* one of the most popular (and populist) shows of the decade, plonked a pre-industrial extended family down in big bad Los Angeles, extolling the virtues of unpretentious rural innocence at the same time as it poked fun at the double standards and snobbery of the urban *nouveaux riches. The Dick Van Dyke Show* extended the fifties dream of middle-class prosperity and harmony into the more sophisticated, urban/suburban style of John F. Kennedy's America. If TV news was preoccupied with urban unrest, an unstable economy, the escalating Vietnam War, and a generation of college kids rebelling against the values of their parents—the world of TV entertainment blithely pretended nothing was happening.

Until 1970, that is, when a decisive shift in network ratings policy reshaped 9 the industry's perceptions of its audience and created conditions more hospitable to the emergence of new kinds of family-oriented shows. Bob Wood, the incoming president of "top network" CBS, quickly realized that the network's most successful shows (*Gunsmoke, The Beverly Hillbillies,* and *Hee Haw*) appealed primarily to older, rural viewers and did less well in the big cities. Wood also saw that from the advertising sponsors' point of view, what mattered was less how many people tuned in than how much they earned and spent. So he turned his attention to the political attitudes of the younger, better educated, and more affluent urban viewers between the ages of 18 and 34 who, at least in the eyes of the media, were fast becoming cultural leaders. The new ratings game of "demographics" would break down the mass audience by age, gender, income, and other variables to isolate the most profitable markets for TV entertainment. Accordingly, scheduling became an elaborate strategic exercise whose purpose was no longer merely to reach the widest possible audience with any given show, but to group programs and commercials in time slots by the type of audience most likely to watch—and spend. The mass audience became a collection of specific "target" audiences.

It was, then, largely as a marketing device that the turbulence of the middle to late sixties, and the lively adversarial spirit and liberal politics of the generation coming of age during this period, found their way into television entertainment. The "age of relevance," as it's often called in TV histories, was ushered in by Norman Lear's *All in the Family,* which after a rocky start on CBS shot to number one in the ratings and reigned over the top three positions for much of the decade, spawning spinoffs and clones on all three networks as it went. The Bunkers (and in their wake, the George Jeffersons and Maude Findlays and the Ann Romanos of *One Day at a Time*) quarrelled and stormed and suffered their way through the 1970s, blazing a trail for the vast array of social problems that have since become the standard fare of television families.

In their early years the Bunkers remained resolutely intact as a family unit, confining their squabbles to highly formalized public issues of race, class, gender, and government corruption. But as the decade went on, the problems that plagued those close to them—menopause, infidelity, divorce, alcoholism, impotence, depression—became steadily more private in nature and drew closer to the Bunkers themselves. Family-show comedy was mixed more and more with drama as the issue became the painful fragility of marriage and the family unit; many episodes were barely identifiable as comedies. Finally Gloria and Meathead, true to their generation, moved to California and divorced, and with Edith's death both Archie and Gloria were left free to negotiate the vicissitudes of life after the nuclear family, on their own spinoff shows.

For the first half of the 1970s, *All in the Family* set the tone for the TV series; the vast majority of series with domestic settings offered their viewers troubled or fractured or "reconstituted" families. (Two striking exceptions were *The Waltons* and *Little House on the Prairie,* both intact-family dramas but set in a rural past sodden with romantic nostalgia.) These early seventies domestic dramas echoed an anxiety about the erosion of domestic life that was beginning to punctuate the rhetoric of politicians and policymakers, social scientists and therapists. From the more visible problems like wife or child abuse, divorce, or teenage pregnancy, to the less tangible areas of marital and generational conflict, social trouble was increasingly being defined as family trouble. The women's movement was raising bracing questions about the compatibility of traditional family forms with women's emancipation, and since women (because they buy things and stay home more than men) are television's most prized viewers, a "prime time feminism" of sorts developed with heart-warming rapidity. It was television's new single women—Mary Richards, Rhoda Morgenstern, Maude Findlay, Ann Romano—who cobbled together all kinds of interesting new family forms from the remnants of old families.

Archie Bunker's blustery authority was eroded week after week by the hip liberal pluralism of his daughter and son-in-law, while feminists rejoiced. Archie's fulminations against "hebes" and "coons" and "fags" amounted to a long bellow of pain from a man whose most cherished guidelines for living—family, country, authority—were being pried loose by the relentless rush of modernity. It's fitting that his worn chair, icon not only of an outmoded patriarchy but of a whole working class way of life, has ended up as a museum piece at the Smithsonian.

If TV's domestic hearth was becoming a repository for family anxiety, other, more benign images of family and community were surfacing in a subgenre also designed for the younger, upscale markets, the television workplace series. The success of *The Mary Tyler Moore Show* and *M*A*S*H* in CBS's Saturday night lineup early in the seventies led to a wave of shows with occupational settings like *Lou Grant, Taxi, Barney Miller, The Bob Newhart Show.* The emotional center of these shows was not work, not even the star, but the relationships between colleagues whose own family attachments were either severely attenuated or nonexistent. *M*A*S*H*'s medical team, the television producers of WJM in *The Mary Tyler Moore Show,* the detectives of *Barney Miller,* all these groups had the claustrophobic testiness and warm solidarity of the families we carry around as ideals in our heads. "You've been a family to me," cried tearful Mary Richards when WJM was shut down at the end of its seventh successful season. If the television workplace was offering a community that compensated for the ravaged instability of the domestic shows, it may also have been suggesting to a career-oriented generation that the opportunities for emotional engagement and support no longer lay in the family, but in the workplace.

American television is by nature faddish. The sheer volume of its ephemeral output; the fierce competition between the networks; their collective fear of the commercial threat from cable and pay TV, and of the power of home video and other new technologies to restructure viewing habits—all these constraints press into the routines of programming a demand for constant novelty with relatively little innovation. Even the most successful series usually last no longer than seven years which, some critics argue, suggests that changes in genre or style have little significance as indices of social trends. Fads, however, are more than whims; they're the staple diet of our culture, and fads with staying power can tell us much about the ways people respond to social change. As advertisers and broadcasters try to second-guess the public mood (a daunting project, even if a unitary Zeitgeist existed), they pay earnest attention to what they consider to be the mirrors of public concern, namely the media themselves. Television feeds off itself and other media, and in this way its images both echo and participate in the shaping of cultural trends. Buzz-words like "the sixties," "the me-decade," "yuppies," are casually threaded through the rhetoric of television and become enshrined in programming knowledge and routines. That makes them important, however short-lived.

By the 1980s, the craze for domestic comedies seemed to be tapering off and, in the wake of Reagan's massive victory at the polls, cultural diagnosticians at the networks were announcing a "shift to the right." . . . In fact, the "shift to the right" was expressing itself with greatest force on the American domestic front. If in the seventies the *family* had been acknowledged as the primary arena for the expression of social conflict, by the early 1980s it had become the focus of a fierce backlash, led by the religious right. The failure of many states to ratify the Equal Rights Amendment, the struggles over abortion rights and contraception for teenagers, the call for a "return to basic values" (less government intervention in family matters and a reassertion of parental authority over the young), all became major issues of public concern. Television leaped onto the ideological bandwagon not just in news and talk shows, but also in its entertainment themes. The made-for-TV movie in particular, with its solemn, sociological-therapeutic format, framed the "official" social problems of our day—rape, anorexia, mental illness, drug abuse, incest, divorce, homosexuality—and resolved them within the family.

But it is the sitcom, where the routines of everyday "normal" life are 17 rehearsed weekly, that works over and redefines the *meaning* of family. . . . The extraordinarily successful Thursday night lineup that catapulted NBC to the head of the network race begins in Family Hour with *Cosby* and *Family Ties*, which secure the mass audience, and, after children's bedtime, moves smoothly into the adult markets with the work-families of *Cheers, Night Court,* and *Hill Street Blues,* now bounced in favor of the glossier *L.A. Law:* in short, an advertiser's paradise.

Like *All in the Family, The Cosby Show* has attracted an enormous amount of 18 attention from critics and public interest groups, as well as a huge and devoted audience, but there the similarity ends. The robustly working-class Bunker household was never a model of consumer vitality, nor did it aspire to be. If Archie was dragged, kicking and screaming, into the seventies, the Huxtables embrace modernity with gusto. From grandparents to the disarmingly cute Rudy, this family is sexy and glamorous. Surrounded by the material evidence of their success, the Huxtables radiate wealth, health, energy, and up-to-the-minute style. *The Cosby Show* offers the same pleasures as a commercial, a parade of gleaming commodities and expensive designer clothing, unabashedly enjoyed by successful people. And Cosby himself is a talented promoter of the goods and services, from Jell-O to E.F. Hutton, that finance his series.

Given the troubled condition of many American families in the eighties, 19 *Cosby* must be palpably compensatory for many of its fans. Week after week, the show offers what family comedy in the fifties offered, and what most of us don't have, the continuity of orderly lives lived without major trauma or disturbance, stretching back into an identical past and reaching confidently forward into an identical future. Two generations of Huxtable men attended "Hillman College" and met their wives there, and although Cliff's eldest daughter chooses Princeton, the next goes for Hillman too.

But where the TV families of the fifties casually took harmony and order for 20 granted, the Huxtables work strenuously and self-consciously at showing us how well they get along. Not that much happens on *Cosby*. It's a virtually plotless chronicle of the small, quotidian details of family life, at the heart of which lies a moral etiquette of parenting and a developmental psychology of growing up. Every week provides family members, and us, with a Learning Experience and a lesson in social adjustment. Rudy's terrified playmate learns to love going to the dentist. Rudy learns to stop bossing her friends around. Theo learns not to embark on expensive projects he won't complete. Sandra and her boy friend learn to arbitrate their bickering over sex roles. Denise learns to cope with bad grades in college. Even Cliff and Clair, who despite high-powered careers as physician and lawyer respectively, have all the leisure in the world to spend "quality time" with their kids, teach each other parenting by discussion as well as by example. The show's endless rehearsal of mild domestic disorder and its resolution suggests a perfect family that *works*. The family that plays, sings, dances, and above all, communicates together, stays together.

Didacticism is nothing new in television entertainment. *All in the Family* 21 was stuffed with messages of all kinds, but on *Cosby,* moral and psychological instruction are rendered monolithic and indisputable. Unlike the Bunkers, for whom every problem became the occasion for an all-out war of ideas, no one ever screams at Huxtable Manor. True, beneath their beguiling mildness there lurks a casual hostility, in which everyone, Clair and Cliff included, trades insults and makes fun of everyone else. But there's no dissent, no real difference of opinion or belief, only vaguely malicious banter that quickly dissolves into sweet agreement, all part of the busy daily manufacture of consensus.

Undercutting the warm color and light, the jokey good humor and the 22 impeccable salutes to feminism, is a persistent authoritarianism. The tone is set by Cosby himself, whose prodigious charm overlays a subtle menace. If the pint-sized Rudy gets her laughs by aping the speech and manners of adults, Cliff gets his laughs—and his way—by turning into a giant child, and then slipping his kids or his wife their moral or psychological pills with a wordless, grimacing comic caper. A captivating child, undoubtedly, with his little vanities and his competitiveness, but he's also quietly coercive: Father knows best, or else. The cuddly, overgrown schoolboy becomes the amused onlooker and then the oracle, master of the strategic silence or the innocent question that lets one of his kids know they've said or done something dumb, or gives his wife to understand that her independence is slipping into bossiness. In Huxtable-speak, this is called "communicating." Cliff practices a thoroughly contemporary politics of strong leadership, managing potential conflicts with all the skill of a well-socialized corporate executive.

There's none of the generational warfare that rocked the Bunker household 23 every week. And this family doesn't *need* the openly authoritarian "tough love" that's cropping up more and more in recent TV movies, because parental authority has already been internalized. The kids put up a token display of playful resistance, then surrender happily to the divine right of parents whose easy knowledge of the difference between right and wrong irons out the inconvenient ambiguities of contemporary life. Indeed, since the Huxtables are a supremely "intact" nuclear family, those ambiguities rarely come up, or if they do, they occur outside the charmed circle and stay outside it. A teenage pregnancy, a drug problem, a worker laid off; occasionally one of the problems that bedevil most families hovers near, casts a brief shadow on the bright domestic light and then slinks away, intimidated by the fortress of Huxtable togetherness. Unlike the sitcoms of the fifties whose vision of the social terrain outside the family was as benign as that inside it, the "world outside" *Cosby* is downright perilous, to the limited degree that it exists at all.

The Huxtables have friends but no discernible neighborhood community, indeed no public life to speak of aside from their jobs, which seem to run on automatic pilot. They inhabit a visibly black world, whose blackness is hardly ever alluded to. "I'm not going to talk about social justice or racial harmony or peace, because you all know how I feel about them," intones the retiring President of Cliff's alma mater, and delivers a limp homily exhorting old alumnae to invite young alumnae to dinner, which earns him a standing ovation from old and young alike—all black. No wonder *The Cosby Show* is number one in the South African ratings. It is, as a Johannesburg television executive remarked complacently on the nightly Hollywood chat show *Entertainment Tonight* last year, not a show about race, but about "family values." [24]

Even *Family Ties* (the white obverse of *Cosby*), whose premise of ex-hippie parents with a pre-corporate, neoconservative son promises some refreshing friction, flattens genuine argument into the stifling warmth of domestic affection. The mild-mannered Keaton father, Stephen, is persuaded by an old friend from the campus Left to start a radical magazine. A difference of opinion leads to Stephen's being accused of copping out, but his wife Elyse assures him that "you're making a statement by the way you live your life and raise your children," suggesting not only that family integrity transcends politics, but that political affiliation is reducible to being nice to other people—especially your family. [25]

This is not to say that the articulation of family trouble so central to seventies television has disappeared from the small screen. Other sitcoms retain the preoccupation with "reconstituted" families, if in watered-down form. "Do I have to be a relative to be family?" a small boy asks his mother on *Who's the Boss?*, a role reversal comedy about two single parents (she the breadwinner, he the housekeeper) living together. "Not necessarily," his mother smiles down at him, "a family means people who share each other's lives and care about each other." An unexceptional definition, and also virtually meaningless; with the sting of divorce and family poverty removed, single parenthood and stepparenting turn into a romp, a permanent pajama party. Even *Kate and Allie*, which began as a witty comedy of divorce manners and a chronicle of the single life encountered second time around, has slipped into the parenting psychology mold, focusing more on the kids and teenagers' rites of passage than on the adults. Here we see television hedging its bets by nodding in the direction of radical changes in family form and structure, without really taking them on. And the "single woman" comedy so wildly popular in the seventies seems to have little resonance for the eighties; several new shows of this kind, including a new *Mary Tyler Moore Show*, were cancelled in short order. Christine Cagney of *Cagney and Lacey* alone survives as a prototype of the mature single woman, and even she must be balanced with her partner Marybeth Lacey, the harried working mother. [26]

If anything, the locus of family disharmony on TV these days seems to be the nighttime soaps, and nothing else on prime time matches the seething ambi- [27]

guities and flaring passions of these clans. On *Dynasty* this season, Blake Carring-ton struggles to contain his wife and his former wife (who collects younger men with a studied casualness only Joan Collins could bring off with a straight face); his son Stephen, whose sexual identity oscillates between gay and straight as the plot requires; his son Adam, who turns out not to be his son at all (so he adopts him); his niece Leslie, who has just discovered her lover is her brother; and, in a grand but wildly implausible burst of televisual affirmative action, his sister Dominique, who's black. Season after season, the soaps' elastic tribal boundaries expand and contract to admit or expel undiscovered relatives, bogus and genuine. But I suspect that soap audiences appropriate these shows in the high camp spirit in which they're offered. This is not "reality," which may be why soap stars invari-ably collapse into disclaiming giggles when interviewed about the characters they play.

Bill Cosby, in his rare interviews, *never* giggles. The actor takes his respon- 28 sibilities as an educator very seriously. *Newsweek* reported in 1984 that Cosby had commissioned a well-known black psychiatrist to review every *Cosby Show* script for authenticity. And the actor told the *Los Angeles Times* in 1985 that viewers loved the series because it showed that "the people in his house respect the par-ents and the parents respect the children and that there is a l-o-v-e generated in this house." Norman Lear in his heyday felt convinced that viewers loved *All in the Family* because it exposed bigotry and addressed "real life" problems. No one really knows much about audience responses to television, but there's probably always an asymmetry between producers' intentions and viewers' readings. It's equally plausible that Bunker fans were as engaged by the rage that imprinted itself on almost every episode of *All in the Family* as by its liberal politics.

Similarly, the Huxtable brand of patriarchal dominance may strike as reso- 29 nant a chord as the l-o-v-e Cosby cites—testified to by the success of his recent book *Fatherhood*, which topped the bestseller list in 1986. And if Cosby's child-like charm works, it may also be catering to what is most child-like in us, his audi-ence; namely the yearnings for a perfectly synchronized family, or community, that provides for the needs of all its members and regulates itself through a benevolent dictatorship, a family that always was as perfect as it is now, and always will be. That isn't merely infantile; it also signals the political retrenchment that comes from a cultural exhaustion, a weary inability to imagine new forms of com-munity, new ways of living.

In each successive television era, a particular congruence of marketing exi- 30 gencies and cultural trends has produced different portraits of the American fam-ily. In television, genre is always about eighty percent commerce. But in the 1970s, commerce made room for lively, innovative programming that interrupted the hitherto bland conventions of the TV family, giving us programming that above all didn't condescend to its audiences. The Bunkers were never a restful or reassuring family, but their battles, however strident, raised the possibility that there might be, might *have* to be more ways than one to conduct family life, that blood ties are not the only bonds of community, that divorce is a feature of modern life to be confronted, that women and men must find new ways of living together and raising children.

Today, the generous space that was opened up then for public discussion is once again being narrowed. With their eyes firmly fixed on the new mass audience, *The Cosby Show* and its clones are short-circuiting the quarrelsome gutsiness of seventies TV by burying their heads in the nostalgic sands of "traditional values" that never were. Public interest groups may be all smiles at the jolly harmony of these shows. But their obsession with engineering a spurious consensus returns us to the dullest kind of television, with its twin besetting sins, sentimentality and a profound horror of argument. 31

QUESTIONS FOR CRITICAL READING, THINKING, DISCUSSION, AND WRITING

Analyzing Content and Technique

1. Why, according to Taylor, has television been so concerned with depicting family life? Is this as true of television in the nineties?
2. Enumerate the main characteristics of the television families of the 1950s. What changes occurred in the 1960s? Why?
3. What did the television industry realize in the 1970s? How did this change the types of family shows being produced? Give examples.
4. Two shows that Taylor analyzes in her essay are *All in the Family* and *The Cosby Show*. What does she perceive as the main differences between these shows? From her descriptions, deduce which show she prefers and her reasons for doing so.
5. In her conclusion Taylor states, "Today, the generous space that was opened up then for public discussion is once again being narrowed . . . [to] sentimentality and a profound horror of argument." What evidence does she provide of this? Do you find her evidence adequate? Why or why not?

Collaborative Activity

Imagine you are a television production group about to design a new family show. Discuss what kinds of characters and issues you would like to put into this show. Brainstorm and create a list of situations you would dramatize. Why would these be good for bringing out the issues the group is interested in?

Making Connections

1. Write an essay in which you examine two or three current television shows about family life. What kinds of problems, issues, and social trends do they portray? How accurately have they managed to capture the situation of the American family today?
2. Write an essay comparing and contrasting your own family with one specific television family. Elements to consider might be: the roles played by various members, the kinds of problems that arise and the methods for solving them, and the influence of ethnicity in shaping family lifestyle.

15

PREREADING ACTIVITY

Write briefly about your own teenage years. What were (or are) some of the difficulties you faced (or are facing) as a teenager? What special elements make the
teenage years special? Briefly describe the teenage culture that you experienced.

Teenagers in Crisis

DAVID ELKIND

David Elkind (1931–) is a child and adolescent psychologist who has taught
across the nation at universities such as the University of California at Los Angeles,
the University of Denver, and Tufts University. His books include *A Sympathetic
Understanding of the Child*, *Mis-Education: Pre-Schoolers at Risk*, and *All Grown Up
and No Place to Go*, from which selection 15 is taken. A National Science Foundation fellow who lived in Geneva for some years, Elkind is well known for his writings
on the works of the Swiss psychologist Jean Piaget.

*T*here is no place for teenagers in American society today—not in our 1
homes, not in our schools, and not in society at large. This was not always the
case: barely a decade ago, teenagers had a clearly defined position in the social
structure. They were the "next generation," the "future leaders" of America.
Their intellectual, social, and moral development was considered important, and
therefore it was protected and nurtured. The teenager's occasional foibles and
excesses were excused as an expression of youthful spirit, a necessary Mardi Gras
before assuming adult responsibility and decorum. Teenagers thus received the
time needed to adapt to the remarkable transformations their bodies, minds, and
emotions were undergoing. Society recognized that the transition from childhood to adulthood was difficult and that young people needed time, support, and
guidance in this endeavor.

In today's rapidly changing society, teenagers have lost their once privileged 2
position. Instead, they have had a premature adulthood thrust upon them.
Teenagers now are expected to confront life and its challenges with the maturity
once expected only of the middle-aged, without any time for preparation. Many
adults are too busy retooling and retraining their own job skills to devote any
time to preparing the next generation of workers. And some parents are so

involved in reordering their own lives, managing a career, marriage, parenting, and leisure, that they have no time to give their teenagers; other parents simply cannot train a teenager for an adulthood they themselves have yet to attain fully. The media and merchandisers, too, no longer abide by the unwritten rule that teenagers are a privileged group who require special protection and nurturing. They now see teenagers as fair game for all the arts of persuasion and sexual innuendo once directed only to adult audiences and consumers. High schools, which were once the setting for a unique teenage culture and language, have become miniatures of the adult community. Theft, violence, sex, and substance abuse are now as common in the high schools as they are on the streets.

It is true, of course, that many parents and other adults are still committed 3 to giving teenagers the time, protection, and guidance they require to traverse this difficult period. But these well-meaning adults meet almost insurmountable barriers in today's society, and many feel powerless to provide the kind of guidance they believe teenagers need. For example, a mother of a teenager asked me recently what to do with her fourteen-year-old son who was staying up late to watch X-rated movies on cable television. I suggested that if she did not want him to see the movies, she should not permit him to do so and should give him her reasons for the prohibition. Her next question surprised me. She asked me what she should do if he watches them after she goes to bed. It was clear that the mother felt helpless to monitor her son's TV watching. For this youth, as for many others, premature adulthood is gained by default.

In today's society we seem unable to accept the fact of adolescence, that 4 there are young people in transition from childhood to adulthood who need adult guidance and direction. Rather, we assume the teenager is a kind of adult. Whether we confer premature adulthood upon teenagers because we are too caught up in our own lives to give them the time and attention they require or because we feel helpless to provide them with the safe world they need, the end result is the same: teenagers have no place in this society. They are not adults capable of carrying the adult responsibilities we confer upon them. And they are not children whose subservience to adults can be taken for granted. We expect them to be grown up in all those domains where we cannot or do not want to maintain control. But in other domains, such as attending school, we expect our teenagers to behave like obedient children.

Perhaps the best word to describe the predicament of today's teenagers is 5 "unplaced." Teenagers are not displaced in the sense of having been put in a position they did not choose to be in (a state sometimes called anomie). Nor are they misplaced in the sense of having been put in the wrong place (a state sometimes called alienation). Rather, they are unplaced in the sense that there is no place for a young person who needs a measured and controlled introduction to adulthood. In a rapidly changing society, when adults are struggling to adapt to a new social order, few adults are genuinely committed to helping teenagers attain a healthy adulthood. Young people are thus denied the special recognition and protection that society previously accorded their age group. The special stage belonging to teenagers has been excised from the life cycle, and teenagers have been given a pro forma adulthood, an adulthood with all of the responsibilities but few of the prerogatives. Young people today are quite literally all grown up with no place to go.

The imposition of premature adulthood upon today's teenagers affects them in two different but closely related ways. First, because teenagers need a protected period of time within which to construct a personal identity, the absence of that period impairs the formation of that all-important self-definition. Having a personal identity amounts to having an abiding sense of self that brings together, and gives meaning to, the teenager's past while at the same time giving him or her guidance and direction for the future. A secure sense of self, of personal identity, allows the young person to deal with both inner and outer demands with consistency and efficiency. This sense of self is thus one of the teenager's most important defenses against stress. By impairing his or her ability to construct a secure personal identity, today's society leaves the teenager more vulnerable and less competent to meet the challenges that are inevitable in life.

The second effect of premature adulthood is inordinate stress: teenagers today are subject to more stress than were teenagers in previous generations. This stress is of three types. First, teenagers are confronted with many more freedoms today than were available to past generations. Second, they are experiencing losses, to their basic sense of security and expectations for the future, that earlier generations did not encounter. And third, they must cope with the frustration of trying to prepare for their life's work in school settings that hinder rather than facilitate this goal. Any one of these new stresses would put a heavy burden on a young person; taken together, they make a formidable demand on the teenager's ability to adapt to new demands and new situations.

Contemporary American society has thus struck teenagers a double blow. It has rendered them more vulnerable to stress while at the same time exposing them to new and more powerful stresses than were ever faced by previous generations of adolescents. It is not surprising, then, to find that the number of stress-related problems among teenagers has more than trebled in the last decade and a half. Before we examine in more detail the predicament of today's teenagers, we need to look at some of the frightening statistics in order to understand both the seriousness and the magnitude of the problem.

A Generation under Stress

Substance abuse is now the leading cause of death among teenagers and accounts for more than ten thousand deaths each year. Although the use of drugs has leveled off after a threefold rise in the last decade and a half, alcohol use is becoming more widespread and is appearing among younger age groups. According to a recent survey of junior high school students, 65 percent of the thirteen-year-olds had used alcohol at least once that year, some 35 percent used it once a month, and 20 percent used it once a week. Thirty-five percent of the thirteen-year-olds queried said that it was fun and all right to get drunk. The National Institute on Alcohol Abuse and Alcoholism reports, conservatively, that 1.3 million teenagers between the ages of twelve and seventeen have serious drinking problems. According to a 1981 report from the Department of Health, Education and Welfare, more than three million youths nationwide have experienced problems at home, in school, or on the highways as a result of drinking.[1] In my own travels throughout this country I have found that it is commonplace for beer to be available at parties for twelve- and thirteen-year-olds. It is often provided by parents, who, relieved that the youngsters are not into drugs, appear to consider alcohol benign by comparison.

Sexual activity, at least among teenage girls, has more than tripled over the last two decades. In contrast to the 1960s, when only about 10 percent of teenage girls were sexually active, more than 50 percent are sexually active today. By the age of nineteen at least 70 percent of young women have had at least one sexual experience. Among young women who are sexually active, four out of ten will become pregnant before they leave their teens. Currently about 1.3 million teenagers become pregnant each year, and more than a third of them are choosing to have and to keep their babies.[2] Although young women may be able to conceive an infant, the pelvic girdle does not attain its full size until the age of seventeen or eighteen. This puts the young teenage mother and her infant at physical risk. The data also indicate that the infants of teenage mothers are more at risk for child abuse and for emotional problems than are the children of more mature mothers.

Suicide rates for teenagers have climbed at a fearful pace. Five thousand teenagers commit suicide each year, and for each of these suicides fifty to one hundred youngsters make an unsuccessful attempt.[3] Sex differences in mode of suicide are changing. Girls, who in the past resorted to pills and slashing their wrists, are now using the more violent means often employed by boys, namely, hanging and shooting. In addition, many "accidental" teenage deaths are regarded by experts as being, in part at least, suicidal.

Crime rates have increased dramatically among juveniles. For many children, crime is a regular part of their lives, in both the home and the school.

Every month, secondary schools experience 2.4 million thefts, almost 300,000 assaults and over 100,000 robberies. Criminal behavior starts early, usually in school, and peaks quickly. More 17 to 20 year old males are arrested for virtually every class of crime (including homicide) than males in any other age group. But the record of children under 10 (55,000 arrests in 1980) is itself sobering and it gets seven times worse by age 14.[4]

To these alarming statistics we must add that over one million children run away from home each year, and an indeterminate number of these are forced into prostitution or pornography, or both.[5]

These statistics define the gravity of the problems resulting from teenage stress. Now we need to examine some of the social changes that have taken place in this country and how they have led us to deny, ignore, or abdicate our responsibilities toward youth.

Social Change and Teenage Identity

It is generally agreed today, following the original work of the psychoanalyst Erik Erikson, that the primary task of the teenage years is to construct a sense of personal identity.[6] In Erikson's view, the teenager's task is to bring together all of the various and sometimes conflicting facets of self into a working whole that at once provides continuity with the past and focus and direction for the future. This sense of personal identity includes various roles (son or daughter, student, athlete, musician, artist, and so on), various traits and abilities (quiet, outgoing, timid, generous, high-strung), as well as the teenager's personal tableau of likes and dislikes, political and social attitudes, religious orientation, and much more.

It is clear from this description that the task of forming an identity is a difficult and complex one. It is not undertaken until the teen years in part because the young person has not accumulated all the necessary ingredients until this time, and in part because prior to adolescence young people lack the mental abilities required for the task. The late Jean Piaget demonstrated that it is not until the teen years that young people are capable of constructing theories.[7] And it is not unreasonable to characterize identity as a theory of oneself. Forming an identity, like building a theory, is a creative endeavor that takes much time and concentrated effort. That is why Erikson has suggested that teenagers either make or find a "moratorium," a period of time for themselves during which they can engage in the task of identity formation.

In the past, a clearly demarcated period of development, called adolescence, gave young people the needed respite before assuming adult responsibility and decision making. But this period is no longer available. The current generation of young people is being denied the time needed to put together a workable theory of self. The issue, it should be said, is not one of leisure or free time. Many teenagers today have that. Rather, what is lacking is *pressure-free* time, time that is free of the burdens designated properly for adults. Even at their leisure teenagers carry with them the adult expectation that they will behave as if they were already fully grown and mature. It is because young people today carry with them, and are often preoccupied by, adult issues that they do not have the time to deal with properly teenage concerns, namely, the construction of a personal definition of self.

It is not only time that is missing. Teenagers also need a clearly defined value system against which to test other values and discover their own. But when the important adults in their lives don't know what their own values are and are not sure what is right and what is wrong, what is good and what is bad, the teenagers' task is even more difficult and more time-consuming. The process of constructing an identity is adversely affected because neither the proper time nor the proper ingredients are available. Let us consider how the very process of identity formation is affected by the teenager's being "unplaced" in the society.

Social Change and Parenting

In the last thirty years our society has undergone more change, at a faster rate, than during any other period. We are now moving rapidly from an industrial to a postindustrial or information society:

> Twenty-five years ago, the nation's work force was about equally divided between white-collar and blue-collar jobs, between goods and service industries. There are now more people employed full time in our colleges and universities than are

employed in agriculture. In 1981, white-collar jobs outnumbered blue-collar jobs by three to two. And the number of people employed by U.S. Steel is smaller than the number of employees at McDonald's.[8]

The nature of the work force has changed as well. Over half of the twenty-five million women with children in the United States are working outside the home, compared with 20 percent in 1950.

Although the changes relating to work are significant, even greater changes 20 have come about in our values and social philosophy. Daniel Yankelovich has likened this shift to the major changes in the earth's crust as a result of shifts of the tectonic plates deep in the earth's interior. Yankelovich argues that we are rapidly moving away from the "social role" orientation that once dominated American society.[9] He describes the old "social role" (give-and-take) philosophy this way:

> I give hard work, loyalty and steadfastness, I swallow my frustrations and suppress my impulse to do what I would enjoy, and do what is expected of me instead. I do not put myself first; I put the needs of others ahead of my own. I give a lot, but what I get in return is worth it. I receive an ever growing standard of living, and a family life with a devoted spouse and decent kids. Our children will take care of us in our old age if we really need it, which thank goodness we will not. I have a nice home, a good job, the respect of my friends and neighbors, a sense of accomplishment at having made something of my life. Last but not least, as an American I am proud to be a citizen of the finest country in the world.[10]

That is the philosophy most of today's parents grew up with, and it is the 21 one most adults today recognize as familiar and generally their own. But over the last twenty years a new philosophy has emerged to vie with the older social role orientation. This new philosophy has been variously called the "culture of narcissism" or the "me generation" or more kindly by Yankelovich as a "search for self-fulfillment." According to numerous surveys by Yankelovich and others, this new philosophy now fully pervades our society:

> By the late seventies . . . seven out of ten Americans (72 percent) [were] spending a great deal of time thinking about themselves and their inner lives, this in a nation once notorious for its impatience with inwardness. The rage for self-fulfillment . . . has now spread to virtually the entire U.S. population.[11]

The changes we are undergoing today in American society have been 22 described in somewhat different terms by John Naisbitt in his book *Megatrends*.[12] He argues that the "basic building block of the society is shifting from the family to the individual" and that we are changing from a "fixed option" to a "multiple option" society. Choices in the basic areas of family and work have exploded into a multitude of highly individual arrangements and life-styles. And the basic idea of a multiple option society has spilled over into other important areas of our lives: religion, the arts, music, food, entertainment, and, finally, the extent to which cultural, ethnic, and racial diversity are now celebrated in the United States. Both Yankelovich and Naisbitt suggest that there are many pluses and minuses to the new self-fulfillment philosophy, just as there were for the social role orientation. Moreover, it may be, as Naisbitt suggests, that an individual-oriented social philosophy is better suited than a role-oriented social philosophy to the requirements of an information society.

However that may be, the important point here is not that one philosophy is good and the other is bad, but rather that we as adults and parents are caught in the crossfire of these two social philosophies. Sexual values are a case in point. As parents and adults, we have the values we learned as children; as members of a modern society, we recognize that values have changed and a new set of values is followed. The conflict arises when we as adults must confront the new values rather than merely tolerate them. Recently a father admitted to me that his daughter is living with a man. The father grew up when I did, and at that time a young woman who lived with a man would most probably be disowned by her family. But such behavior is the norm today, and though the father may feel deeply that what his daughter is doing is wrong, the contemporary value system supports it. After all, isn't everyone else doing it? This father must now cope with two conflicting value systems—his own and his daughter's.

Parents who, like this father, would like to protect and shield their offspring feel overwhelmed by the pressure to accept the new social code. If they openly challenge the new values, they are sure to be labeled, and dismissed, as old-fashioned and stuffy. Ellen Goodman put the dilemma of the committed parent in a time of changing values this way:

> I belong to a whole generation of people who grew up under traditional rules about sex. We heard all about the rights and wrongs, shoulds and shouldn'ts, do's and don'ts. As adults we have lived through a time when all these rules were questioned, when people were set "free" to discover their own sexuality and their own definition of morality. Whether we observed this change from the outside or were part of it, we were nevertheless affected by it. Now, with all of our ambivalence and confusion, we are the new generation of parents raising the next generation of adults. Our agenda is a complicated one, because we do not want to be the new guardians of sexual repression. Nor are we willing to define sexual freedom as the children's right to do it. We are equally uncomfortable with notions that sex is evil and sex is groovy.[13]

In times of rapid social change, even committed parents are confused about what limits to set and what values to advocate and to enforce. For us adults this is a time to give serious thought to our values and principles, just as it is a time to struggle for greater tolerance. Ironically, our responses may only make matters worse for teenagers. Caught between two value systems, parents become ambivalent, and teenagers perceive their ambivalence as license. Failing to act, we force our teenagers to do so, before they are ready. Because we are reluctant to take a firm stand, we deny teenagers the benefit of our parental concern and we impel them into premature adulthood. We say, honestly, "I don't know," but teenagers hear, "They don't care."

Parents who are themselves awash in the tide of social change and are looking for self-fulfillment may have a different reaction to the teenager. A parent going through a "midlife" crisis may be too self-absorbed with his or her own voyage of personal discovery to appreciate fully and support the needs of a teenage son or daughter. Similarly, parents who are undergoing a divorce (as more than one million couples a year do) may be too caught up in the turbulence of their own lives to be of much help to a teenager with his or her own kind of life change. Other parents, who may be learning new job skills such as those involved in using computers, may look upon teenagers as having the advantage. Such parents may feel that the teenager has more knowledge and technological sophistication than they have and therefore that teenagers have it made. It may be hard for these parents to see the teenager's need for a special time and for support and guidance.

Still other parents and adults find the pace of social change too much to take and are overwhelmed by it. While their mates may have found the new social philosophy liberating and challenging, they find it frightening and isolating. If divorce comes, they feel adrift and alone, lost in a world they did not bargain for and do not want to participate in. It is a great temptation for these parents to reverse roles and look to their teenagers for support and guidance. Here again, the impact of social change is to deny the teenager the time and freedom to be a teenager in order to prepare for adulthood; the teenager is rushed from childhood to adulthood in order to meet the needs of a troubled parent.

Rapid social change, particularly from one social philosophy to another, inevitably affects parental attitudes toward teenagers. Although different parents are affected in different ways, the end result is always the same. For one reason or another, in one way or another, teenagers are denied the protection, guidance, and instruction they desperately need in order to mature. As we shall see in later chapters, it is not only parents but society as a whole that is unplacing teenagers. Perhaps this is why Hermann Hesse in *Steppenwolf* described the plight of youth caught between social philosophies in this way:

> Every age, every culture, every custom and tradition has its own character, its own weaknesses and its own strength, its beauties and ugliness; accepts certain sufferings as matters of course, puts up patiently with certain evils. Human life is reduced to real suffering, to real hell only when two ages, two cultures and religions overlap. . . . Now there are times when a whole generation is caught in this way between two ages, two modes of life with the consequence that it loses all power to understand itself, and has no standard, no security, no simple acquiescence.[14]

If we put Hesse's last sentence in contemporary terms, we would say that youths caught between two cultures have a weak sense of identity (no standard, no security) and self-definition and are thus more vulnerable to stress. Clearly our situation today is not unique; there have been comparable periods in history. But that does not make our present situation any more tolerable. Today's teenager must struggle to achieve a sense of self, a sense of personal identity, if she or he is going to go on to build a full life as a mature and complete adult. But by bestowing a premature mantle of adulthood upon teenagers, we as parents and adults impair the formation of their sense of identity and render them more vulnerable to stress. We thus endanger their future and society's as well.

NOTES

1. N. Cobb, "Who's Getting High on What?" *Boston Globe,* October 10, 1982.
2. M. Zelnick and J. Kantner, "Sexuality, Contraception, and Pregnancy among Young Unwed Females in the United States," *Research Reports,* Commission on Population Growth and the American Future, vol. 1 (Washington, D.C.: Government Printing Office, 1980).
3. C. L. Tishler, "Adolescent Suicide: Prevention, Practice and Treatment," *Feelings and Their Medical Significance* 23, no. 6 (November–December 1981).
4. C. Murphy, "Kids Today," *Wilson Quarterly,* Autumn 1982.
5. "Shelters and Streets Draw Throw-away Kids," *New York Times,* June 3, 1983.
6. E. Erikson, *Childhood and Society* (New York: Norton, 1950).
7. Piaget, *The Psychology of Intelligence* (London: Routledge & Kegan Paul, 1950).
8. E. L. Boyer, *Highschool* (New York: Harper & Row, 1983), p. 4.
9. D. Yankelovich, *New Rules* (New York: Bantam, 1981).
10. Ibid., p. 7.
11. Ibid., p. 3.
12. Naisbitt, *Megatrends* (New York: Warner, 1982).
13. E. Goodman, "The Turmoil of Teenage Sexuality," *Ms.,* July 1983, pp. 37–41.
14. H. Hesse, *Steppenwolf* (New York: Rinehart, 1963), p. 24.

QUESTIONS FOR CRITICAL READING, THINKING, DISCUSSION, AND WRITING

Analyzing Content and Technique

1. Elkind states (paragraph 2) that in today's society teenagers have lost their "privileged position." What kind of privilege is he writing of? Evaluate the evidence he provides to support his statement.
2. What are the results of imposing "premature adulthood" on teenagers (paragraphs 6–8)? How has the writer organized these results?
3. Examine the section titled "A Generation under Stress" (starting at paragraph 9). What is Elkind's main point here? What kinds of support has he used to convince his reader? Pick out one that you find particularly powerful and explain why.
4. What major change in our values and social philosophy does Elkind blame for the teenage crisis? Do you agree with his viewpoint? Why or why not? Are there other important reasons for the problems faced by teenagers?
5. Explain further Hesse's statement (paragraph 28) that "human life is reduced to real suffering, to real hell only when two ages, two cultures and religions overlap." What, according to Elkind, are the results of this? Based on your experiences, would you agree with Elkind and Hesse?

Collaborative Activity

Discuss Elkind's premise that a major problem facing teenagers today is that they are burdened too soon with adult responsibilities. How far do group members agree with this? Could adult responsibilities have positive effects on a teenager's life? Under what circumstances? Make a collaborative presentation to the class in which you talk about one positive and one negative effect of responsibility on teenagers, supporting your ideas with examples.

Making Connections

1. Much is being written today about the problems faced by teenagers. In your opinion, is the plight of teenagers today worse than that a generation ago? Is it better? Would your answer be different depending on the ethnic identity of the teenagers you are considering? Conduct an interview with a person of your parents' generation, incorporate some library research, and write an essay in which you discuss your findings.
2. Elkind declares that we are moving from a society oriented toward "social roles" to a society concerned primarily with a "search for self-fulfillment." Write an essay defining the two societies and the effects they have on teenagers. You may choose examples from Elkind's essay as well as from your own experience.

PREREADING ACTIVITY

Write a journal entry on the title of the essay. Some questions you might consider are: What do you think the essay will discuss? What kinds of mothers do you think it will portray? What will be their emotions about their sons who are involved in gangs? What will be the attitudes of the sons toward their mothers?

Mothers, Sons and the Gangs

SUE HORTON

Sue Horton is an investigative reporter who writes for the *Los Angeles Times,* in which this piece appeared in 1992.

On the side of a market in East Los Angeles is a roughly done mural, painted by gang members from the Lil' Valley Barrio. The untrained artists did the wall to honor homeboys who met violent deaths on the streets. Two blocks away, the same gang painted another mural, this one depicting the mothers of slain gang members. But, when earthquake repairs were made on the small store that held the mural, the painting was covered over. The mothers are forgotten.

To many mothers of gang members, all across Southern California, the obliterated mural could be taken as an appropriate symbol of their lives. They are, they feel, almost invisible, ignored by many of the law-enforcement agencies and institutions set up to deal with their sons. These women feel isolated, frustrated and angry. "I am tired of people assuming I must be a bad person because my son is a Crip," says a mother who lives in South-Central L.A. "I love my son and have cared for him just like any other mother. Maybe I wasn't perfect, but what mother is?"

Lately, however, some of the officials most involved in dealing with local street gangs have come to realize that to blame a gang member's family and upbringing is to grossly oversimplify the problem. "There is no typical profile of a gang parent," says Jim Galipeau, a Los Angeles County probation officer who works exclusively with gang kids and their families in South-Central Los Angeles. "I have one mother who owns a 12-unit complex, and on the other end of the spectrum is a mom who's a cocaine addict and a prostitute. Mostly it's a one-parent family and the mom making the money, but there are working families

Source: "Mothers, Sons and the Gangs" by Sue Horton, editor-in-chief of the LA Weekly.

with nice homes and gardeners. These parents just happen to live where the gangs are a way of life and their kids become involved."

In many parts of Southern California where street gangs flourish, dropout 4 rates from neighborhood high schools are as high as 35%. A significant proportion of the families in South-Central and East L.A. are living below the poverty level. Drug use and violent crime are rampant. And opportunities for jobs, education and recreation are limited. It's a setting, authorities say, that causes youths to turn to gangs regardless of their upbringing. "For a lot of these kids," says one LAPD officer, "the gang is about the only happening thing in the neighborhood."

Gangs and gang violence have become subjects of great interest and concern for all of Southern California. Law-enforcement agencies are expending enormous resources in their fight against gang-related crime. But, for the mothers of the targets of this law-enforcement effort, the problem is far more immediate than newspaper headlines and stories on TV news. The problem is family.

And now, some police departments are beginning to realize that mothers, 6 instead of being viewed as part of the problem, should be enlisted to help search for solutions.

Capt. Jack Blair of the Pomona Police Department leads weekly gang-truce 7 meetings attended by parents, gang members and local clergy. In the course of his year-long involvement with the Pomona program, he has become convinced that "parents are the key to [solving] the whole problem." At his meetings, and at other meetings of parents around the county, Blair believes that parents have begun to make a difference. "Once the parents unite and form groups, talking to each other and sharing information, that is threatening to the gang members. They want anonymity. They don't want their tactics or activities talked about with parents of rival gangs. When the moms are saying, 'Hey, don't go over to this neighborhood,' or 'I know that you went over to that neighborhood,' there is a certain amount of sport removed."

"Ours is not a program to turn your kid in. We don't ask parents to be 8 informants on their child. But the moms realize what an effect they can have on the kids," Blair says. "The kids may go out gang-banging at night, but eventually they have to go back home and eat the dinner their mom's prepared. Even though they might exhibit some of the machismo characteristics, there is still concern on how they are impacting their family."

"Just because you shoot someone," Galipeau adds, "it doesn't mean that 9 you don't love your mother."

Still, even as outsiders begin to recognize the contributions they can make, 10 mothers of gang members face constant fear and worry. They feel overwhelming guilt, asking themselves again and again where they've failed as parents. And they have to deal with the scorn of a society that holds them in some measure responsible for the actions of their sons.

Although these mothers of gang members live in divergent parts of the city 11 and come from a variety of cultures, they share similar pains. These are some of their stores.

Teresa Rodriguez

Fear: Her Son Lived and the Family Became the Target   Teresa Rodriguez [12] spends her Friday nights cowering in a back bedroom of the tiny stucco house she shares with her husband and eight children in a west Pomona barrio. The living room, she knows from experience, is simply not safe.

During the past two years, most often on Fridays, Rodriguez's home has [13] been shot up half a dozen times, and one night recently when her husband came home late from work, someone shot at him. The family's car and house still bear bullet holes.

The problems all started two years ago, when Rodriguez's youngest son was [14] 13. Unbeknown to his mother, he had become a member of a small Pomona gang, Sur 13. One day when he and several other Sur 13 members were out walking, a car full of rival gang members passed by. "Which barrio are you from?" the other gang demanded to know. Most of the Sur 13 boys didn't answer; Rodriguez's son did. Upon hearing the hated neighborhood name spoken aloud, one of the boys in the car leaned out the window with a gun and pulled the trigger.

Rodriguez didn't know for several hours that her son had been shot. "His [15] friends took him to the hospital and left him there. They couldn't find the courage to tell me," she said recently through an interpreter. Finally, one of the neighborhood kids came to the door and told Rodriguez what had happened. She was stunned. Having come to the United States from Mexico in 1973, she was still timid and uncertain about the culture here. "I had no idea any of my sons was in a gang until that day," she said.

The bullet had lodged near the 13-year-old's heart but hadn't damaged any [16] internal organs. "The doctor told me we were very, very lucky," Rodriguez recalls. Her son recovered, but Rodriguez's life was irreversibly changed.

Because the boy claimed his neighborhood with so much bravado on the [17] day he was shot, he has become a target for the rival gang, which now sees the boy as Sur 13's most visible member. "Whenever there is a problem, they come after him," his mother says. "The problem is no longer just on him; it is on the house."

Immediately after the shooting, Rodriguez was too grateful that her son was [18] alive to reprimand him. But events soon prompted her to take action. Shortly after the boy returned to school, Rodriguez was summoned by the principal. Four members of the rival gang had been circling the campus all day waiting for her son. The school couldn't take that sort of disruption, so officials were asking the boy to leave and attend continuation school. "My older son told me that if I didn't get [his brother] away from here, he'd be killed," Rodriguez says. "He is looked on as a particular enemy now."

Rodriguez says she knew she would have to talk to the boy, as her husband [19] had always left rearing the children to her. But getting her son to listen proved difficult. "I said to him, 'You're going to get killed,' but he just said, 'I don't care.' He is very rebellious."

This year he is enrolled in a Pomona program for gang members who are at [20] risk in other schools. He continues to dress like and act the part of a Sur 13, although he no longer hangs out on the street. "I finally told him that if he went out, I would send him to live in Mexico," Rodriguez says. "He doesn't want that, so he stays inside."

The shooting, says Rodriguez, has had some positive effects. For one thing, 21 she acknowledged that all three of her older sons were in the gang. "Looking back now, I remember that when they were 9 years old they started wearing khakis and white T-shirts. They started coming home later and later," Rodriguez says. One son had a size 32 waist, but he had his mother buy him size 42 pants. "I didn't know these were gang clothes. Now I do.

"My 16-year-old threw away his *cholo* clothes right when he heard about his 22 brother," she says. "He hasn't been with the gang since then. The two older boys are very repentant, but it is hard to step away from their pasts."

Rodriguez has begun attending meetings of the Pomona chapter of Con- 23 cerned Parents, a group working to stop gang violence, and is hopeful for the first time that something can be done to prevent recurrences of the kind of gang activity that nearly killed her son. "Communication between parents, police and the church is very important. Together we can solve the problem. We can't do it alone."

Still, Rodriguez dreads Friday nights. On her front door, where a thick 24 board has replaced a window shot out by a gang, she has posted a small picture of Jesus on the cross. "The only thing I can do about the shooting is put it in his hands," she says, gesturing toward the picture. "He's the only one who can take care of me."

Maggie Garcia

Acceptance: Mean Streets, But the Neighborhood Is Still Everything A few 25 blocks from the Rodriguez house, in another Pomona barrio, Maggie Garcia doesn't really see her youngest son as a gang member. He is just, she says, very loyal to his friends and his neighborhood.

Loyalty to the Cherryville barrio in Pomona where she lives is something 26 Garcia understands completely: "I was raised in the house next door to the one in which I raised my kids. Two of my sisters and one of my brothers live in the neighborhood, too." Maggie Garcia's whole life, she says, is wrapped up in the few blocks radiating from her house. "Here in the neighborhood, it is family."

Garcia realizes that her youngest son has taken his feelings for his barrio a 27 little far on occasion. Last September, when the boy had just turned 14, he got into a fight at school. "He claimed his neighborhood, and the other boy claimed his neighborhood, and all of a sudden they are fighting for two gangs."

After the fight, he was expelled and sent to a local continuation school. 28 "The principal at his old school was upset because my son said, 'I'd die for my neighborhood.' If he'd said, 'I'd die for my country,' the principal probably would have given him a medal."

Garcia worried about her son at the continuation school. Because it drew 29 students from the whole Pomona school district, her son was in constant contact with boys from rival gangs. "One day, two boys from Twelfth Street [another

Pomona gang] laid in wait for my son. He came home all bloody and with bruises," Garcia recalls. "I told him you're not going back to school. You could be killed."

Garcia knew that inter-neighborhood conflicts could be deadly in the Pomona barrios: Three nephews and three of her nieces' boyfriends had been killed by rival gang members. She told her son that if he was out late with his cousins, he wasn't to walk home on the streets but should instead cut through neighbors' back yards. When he goes out the door, Garcia blesses him in hopes that God will protect him out on the streets. But there is only so much, she feels, that she can do. "I've tried to talk to him," she says. "Some people think I should forbid him from being with his friends, but that would be like his telling me, 'Mom, I don't want you hanging out with your best friends in this neighborhood.' It's such a small neighborhood, there are only a few boys my son has here. If he didn't hang out with them, he wouldn't have any friends." [30]

"I see it this way," she says. "Nowadays you have to protect yourself as much as possible, and the friends help protect. The Bible says when you are slapped you turn the other cheek, but you don't do that around here because they will shoot you if you're not looking. Children in any neighborhood have to be aware and have eyes in the back of their heads or they will be dead. They are streetwise. I've taught them to be that way. I feel that when a child is running with three or four of his friends it's better than being alone." [31]

So instead of forbidding her son to associate with the gang, Garcia says, she has taken a more moderate line. "I tell him you can live in the fire, but you don't have to let yourself get burned. You've got to learn to live outside, but when you see something about to go down, you have to get out of there." [32]

In early August, it became apparent that Garcia's youngest son hadn't absorbed the lessons his mother was trying to teach him. After coming home late one night, the boy went back out into the neighborhood. What happened next is in dispute, but in the end he was arrested and charged with an armed robbery that took place a few blocks from his house. Garcia insists that her son was simply in the wrong place at the wrong time. After being held at Los Padrinos Juvenile Hall in Downey, he was released into his mother's custody and is attending school through a Pomona program for gang members who are at risk in other schools. His case will be reviewed by a judge in December. [33]

"My older son has gotten very angry at my younger son," Garcia says. "He tells [his brother], 'You know, if they kill you, your friends will go to your Rosary and they'll go to your funeral. Then they'll have a party and forget you.' But my younger son doesn't see it that way. He sort of says, 'Here today, gone tomorrow—so what?' " [34]

Gayle Thomas Kary

Death: Just When She Thought She'd Beaten the Odds Fifteen-year-old Jamee Kary hadn't been active in the Five Deuce Broadway Crips in recent months. But that didn't matter to a car full of the rival Blood gang members who spotted the boy crossing West 27th Street on the night of Sept. 10. The Bloods [35] called the boy to their car. Words were exchanged. The Bloods began to drive off, but then stopped and got out of their car. Jamee tried to run, but he was shot in the face before he could reach cover. He died within minutes.

Gayle Thomas Kary had worried frantically about Jamee, her middle son, for more than two years before his death. His problems, she feels, started four years ago when tight finances forced her to move from Long Beach to a family-owned house in South-Central Los Angeles half a block from the Harbor Freeway. In the old neighborhood, there had been so much for an adolescent boy to do. There were youth centers and year-round organized sports. In the new neighborhood, there was only the gang. 36

Because Jamee had a slight learning disability, school had always been difficult for him, but he had always had friends. A charming boy with a quick smile and easy affability, Jamee fit right into the new neighborhood. By the time he was 13, he had fit right into the gang. 37

Kary could tell from her son's style of dress and friends that he had become a gang member. And she was very worried. A data-entry operator with a full-time job and a steady life style, Kary had always believed that if she set a good example and enforced limits, her sons would turn out well. Her oldest son, now 20, had always met his mother's expectations. But Jamee seemed torn. At home he was respectful and loving, but out on the streets, he seemed like a different boy. "He knew that he was loved at home," Kary says, sitting in the immaculate California bungalow she shares with her sons. "But he somehow felt the need to be out there with those boys and not be considered a wimp." 38

One day during the summer of 1986, when Jamee was 13, his mother found him cutting up soap to look like cocaine. Kary was horrified that the boy found the drug culture so appealing. Within weeks, she sent Jamee off to stay with his father, a Louisiana minister, hoping that a change of environment would divert Jamee from trouble. Three weeks later, his father sent him back, saying he couldn't control the boy. 39

Later that summer, Jamee stole his mother's car one evening. He was stopped by police for driving the wrong way on a one-way street. But the police just gave the boy a traffic citation and told him to lock up the car and go home. When Kary heard about the incident, she was outraged. She bundled Jamee into the car, drove to the police station, and asked the police there to arrest her son. "I needed help in dealing with my son, but they just said, 'There's nothing we can do.'" Kary says, a bitter sorrow apparent in her voice. 40

In the months that followed, Jamee was increasingly out of control. Kary had always expected her sons to abide by certain household rules if they wanted to live under her roof. Jamee was required to attend school and do his homework, to keep his room clean, to wash his clothes, to wash dishes on alternate days and to feed the dogs. It was not too much to ask, Kary felt. 41

Jamee, by the fall of his 14th year, felt differently. "Jamee started seeing these guys out there who were wearing expensive clothes and they didn't have to go to school or do chores or ask their parents for money," Kary recalls. Unwilling to meet his mother's demands, Jamee began running away from home for short periods of time to live with members of the Five Deuce Broadway Crips. By 42 this time, his mother knew from other kids in the neighborhood, her son was also selling drugs.

During his times away from home, Kary tried to keep tabs on him. "I always knew where he was and that he was safe," Kary says. "He'd sneak over and try to get his brothers to get him a clean set of clothes." Eventually, Jamee would tire of life on the streets and return home. "He'd always promise to toe the line," Kary says. "He'd say he had changed. He knew my rules were the same." [43]

When her son was at home, Kary tried to reason with him. "I told him that kind of life could lead to no good," Kary says with tears in her eyes. "I told him that a fast life goes fast." She warned him, she says, that he could be arrested or killed. "He would just tell me he wouldn't get busted because he could run faster than the police. He told me nobody would kill him because he didn't do any bad drug deals." [44]

In the spring of 1987, Jamee was arrested for possession of cocaine with intent to sell. The arrest was a relief for his mother, who hoped that at last her son would be in the hands of people who could help him. But when the time came for Jamee's sentencing, Kary was once again disappointed. "They wanted to give him probation. The conditions were things like he had to be in by 10 and stop associating with gang members. I told them I'd been trying to get him to do those things and he wouldn't. There was no way he was going to do them now, either. I said I wouldn't take him," Kary recalls. [45]

Instead, the court sentenced Jamee to juvenile hall and later to a youth camp. After five months, Jamee returned home. At first he seemed to be less involved with the gang, but he soon returned to his old ways. There was just one difference now: Jamee had been assigned to probation officer Jim Galipeau, who seemed to really care about the boy. Galipeau also listened to Kary's concerns. [46]

"I called Mr. Galipeau and said Jamee was in trouble again. He told me to keep a record of what he was doing and when," Kary recalls. Thankful for something to do, Kary kept detailed notes on her son's transgressions, hoping to build a case for revoking Jamee's probation. But before she could do that, Galipeau had a heart-to-heart talk with her son. "Jamee told Mr. Galipeau he was tired of life on the streets," Kary says. "He got tired of the police swooping up the street and having to run and not knowing where he was going to sleep." At his probation officer's suggestion, Jamee agreed to request placement in a county-run youth facility to get away from his life in Los Angeles. [47]

By last summer, Jamee was doing beautifully. "I knew I still had to take it one day at a time," his mother says, "but he really seemed to have changed. It was like he was the child I used to know. He wouldn't even go up to Broadway [where the gang liked to hang out]. The friends he associated with were not gang members." [48]

Jamee arrived home for his last weekend furlough on Friday, Sept. 9. On Saturday evening, he asked his mother if he could go with a friend to pick up another fellow and get something to eat. She readily agreed. An hour and a half later, a neighbor came to the door with the news that Jamee had been shot on 27th Street. [49]

Kary raced to the scene, where she saw police had cordoned off a large area. 50 "I saw that yellow police rope, and I knew right then my son was dead." Kary recalls. But police at the scene refused to let her see whether the victim was her son, and after pleading to no avail for information, Kary was finally persuaded to go home and wait. Several hours later, the police called and asked Kary's oldest son to go and identify photographs. Kary finally knew for sure. Her 15-year-old son was dead.

After Jamee's killing, Kary continued to learn what it was like to have a 51 gang member for a son. She wanted to have the funeral service at her own church, but neighbors dissuaded her. "They told me there was a rival gang over there. They said, 'You can't have it there or there'll be troubles,'" Kary says. She also realized with shock that colors, particularly Crip blue, had taken on a new meaning in her life. "All those years that blue stood for boys, and I couldn't let my boy wear blue at his funeral or have the programs printed in blue," Kary says. She had originally planned to wear her nicest dress to the services, but then she realized that it, too, was blue. "A friend told me, 'You can't wear that or you'll be sitting there looking the queen Crip mother,'" Kary says.

Kary worried about how the Five Deuce Broadways would behave at her 52 son's funeral. But that, she says, turned out to be a pleasant surprise. Several days after Jamee's death, some 20 of the gang's members came to Kary's house. While Jamee was alive, she had never allowed gang members in her house, but this once she decided to make an exception.

The young men who gathered in her living room were, she says, very 53 respectful. "They said that even though Jamee wasn't actively involved with them at the time, he was still a member of their family, and they wanted to offer financial support," Kary recalls. The boys contributed about $400 toward funeral costs.

"After they spoke," Kary says, "I said to them, 'I don't like what you do out 54 there on the streets, but I want to tell you something from my heart. You say Jamee was a member of your family. That makes you a member of my family, too, because Jamee was my son. I'm asking you a favor as family members. I don't want any colors at the funeral. I don't want rags, and I don't want trouble.'" To a person, Kary says, the young men honored her requests, and since the funeral they have been eager to help in any way they can.

In the aftermath of Jamee's death, Kary feels lost. Her youngest son, 55 11-year-old Lewis, had decided just before his brother's death to go live with his father in Louisiana. "He did not want to be involved on the streets with the gangs and the colors and the drugs. He was scared. He didn't want to go to junior high school here," Kary recalls. While Kary supports Lewis' decision, she is lonely. "I feel so empty inside," she says. "I can't remember when I last felt my heart beat inside my chest. The only thing I can feel in my whole body is my head because it hurts all the time."

In her lowest moments, Kary takes some solace in a poem Jamee wrote for 56 her while he was incarcerated after his cocaine arrest. She included the poem, which Jamee had entitled "If You Only Knew," in the program for Jamee's funeral.

I sit here on my bunk
And don't know what to do
My life just caught up in a mess
Because I was a fool
I sometimes wonder to myself
With my heart just full of pain
Boy when I get out of this place
My life won't be the same
I'm sorry for all the pain I caused
For you as well as them
I promise you, and I'll try my best
To not do wrong again
Every night and every day
I always think of you
I just sit here thinking but
If you only knew

Dedicated to my Mom
I love you

QUESTIONS FOR CRITICAL READING, THINKING, DISCUSSION, AND WRITING

Analyzing Content and Technique

1. What is the main point the article is making? Where is this located? Is this an effective place-ment? Explain.
2. What is the stereotype of a "gang parent"? What evidence does the writer provide to show this is not true?
3. Why should mothers not be blamed for their sons' joining a gang? How can they become part of the solution? List all the things a parent can do to make a difference.
4. Examine the three mothers depicted in the article. In what ways are they the same? In what ways are they unique? Did you discover something that surprised you as you read their sto-ries?
5. What did each mother do to try to stop her son from being part of a gang? What were the results? What generalizations can you draw from looking at the three cases?
6. Describe the tone of the article. What does this indicate about the writer's attitude to her sub-ject, the gang mothers? About the audience she is addressing? Pick out images and words that support your answer.

Collaborative Activity

As a group, go to the library and locate another article, essay, poem, or story about gang vio-lence. Discuss the piece with your group. What is its focus? Where is it located? Which commu-nities does it deal with? What is the main point the writer is making? What is its tone? Now for-mulate a list in which you compare and contrast the piece you chose with Horton's article.

Making Connections

1. Horton includes in her article a poem written by a gang member, dedicated to his mother. Taking into account what you have learned from the article as well as any research you did for the collaborative activity above, write a piece from the point of view of a "gang mother." This could be an essay, or a letter or poem addressed to a son (or daughter, for female gangs are not uncommon), explaining the mother's situation and emotions as well as changes she wishes for.

2. Write a problem-solution essay in which you discuss ways in which young men and women can be discouraged from joining gangs. You may draw on your own experience, observation, and outside reading, as well as points from Horton's article. Pay particular attention to using examples and quotations.

Before reading selection 17, write about an encounter you have had with a culture different from your own. What were some of the differences you noted? Was the encounter a positive or negative experience? Why?

Beyond Manzanar: A Personal View of Asian American Womanhood

JEANNE WAKATSUKI HOUSTON

Jeanne Wakatsuki Houston (1935–) grew up in California, where at the age of seven she was interned with her family in a camp near Death Valley for three years. She studied at California State University in San Jose, where she met her husband, the writer James D. Houston. Together they wrote *Farewell to Manzanar*, a record of her experiences in the internment camp. The selection here is reprinted from the collection of essays, *Beyond Manzanar: And Other Views of Asian American Womanhood*.

1

*M*y mother married for love. This was rare among Japanese immigrants living in America during that time—1915. Most were men who had to send for wives from their provinces in Japan via the *Baishakunin* or matchmaker, who exchanged photographs for the prospective couple and made the arrangements. This is not to say that love did not develop or occur among these couples. What is significant about this "Picture Bride" phenomenon is that the reasons for marriage were not love and affection, as is the case for the dominant culture in America. Marriages were arranged to perpetuate the family.

My mother was 18 and living in Spokane, Washington, when she met and fell in love with my father, a student ten years older than herself. She had been promised to someone else, a steady, hard-working farmer and friend of her family. In absolute defiance of her tradition and training, to be dutifully obedient to the authority of parents, she ran away with my father. Thus, their marriage became the first step towards assimilation into American culture; romantic love

Source: From *Beyond Manzanar: And Other Views of Asian American Womanhood*, Capra Press, 1985. Reprinted by permission of the author.

had intertwined itself among the responsibilities which defined their roles as hus-band/father, wife/mother. Perhaps it was this love, unexhibited but pervasive, which softened the sharp facts of the inequities in their relationship, in her acqui-escence to his needs and demands. In my more immature years I could not understand how she could tolerate his volatile temperament, his arrogance and obsession with dignity, and his "kingly" presence in the home. I was in my teens then, not fully assimilated, but trying desperately to be as American as Doris Day. My parents did not behave like the parents of my Caucasian friends, and this was embarrassing for me.

Mama worked very hard. She would garden, cook, care for us when we were ill, and after the war she even went to work in the fish cannery to supple-ment the family income, which was minimal at the time. I felt sorry for her. I remember one day when I was 6 years old watching her scrub clothes, my arms barely reaching over the bathtub's edge, and she on her knees, rubbing soapy shirts against a tin washboard. I watched her silent and sweat-streaked face, her hair greying wispily around her temples. I filled with terror as I envisioned her dying because she worked too hard. I started to cry. 3

She only laughed when I told her my fears and said, "I like to wash clothes. It gives me time to think of other things in my head." She tapped her forehead. "Besides, I'm not a washerwoman. This is just a chore. I'm your mother." 4

I did not understand the weight of her explanation to me then. Being mother was not only enough for her, it was a prized identity. It meant she had a family, and in her world—her peers and community almost exclusively of Japan-ese descent—the family was supreme in its hierarchy of values. Thus, the chores and duties which she inherited as Japanese wife and mother were not her identity as such; they were just a means to accomplish the end, which was to keep her family intact, happy and well. She never confused her tasks with who she was. 5

This concept of the inner self, which I have begun only recently to under-stand as a result of my attempts to rediscover my Japanese "roots," allowed her to form her own image, distinct from the one in the exterior world. This ability to create a psychological privacy, inherited from a people who for centuries have had to create their own internal "space" in an overpopulated island, gave her the freedom, of which she was so deprived in her role as Japanese wife and mother. This was her way to survive . . . and to succeed. She did both with grace and with love. I think of the many people I know today (myself included) who have become so obsessed with freedom and independence. We resent our family, our jobs, our relationships . . . any responsibilities that seem to inhibit our mobility. I have so many more choices than my mother had, so much more external inde-pendence; yet, it was not until recently that I realized mobility and time do not mean freedom. The freedom is *within* me. I must *feel* free to be free. 6

I believe my mother was a fulfilled person. She had ten children who loved her devotedly. Even after ten years since her passing, I can truthfully say not a day passes that I do not think of her, not with grief, but with love and gratitude. What Japanese mother could be a failure when even after death her children do not abandon her? This brings to mind a comment made to me by a Japanese American friend on American values and the family. "We abandon each other 7 when we need each other the most," he said. "We abandon the young and the old. We send our young to nursery schools as early as we can get them in . . . just when they need our love and presence more than any time in their lives. We send our old and sickly to institutions to die alone. Where is our love responsibility? Where is that feeling of responsibility for each other that the family instills? Where is the family?"

There was a time when I would not declare my love for her. Not until I was in college did I realize my Caucasian peers seemed to have a different attitude toward their mothers than I did. Or, at least, they talked about them differently. During my Freshman year I took the required General Psychology course and was exposed for the first time to Freud and Jung, as were most of my classmates. I was stunned to hear them discuss their mothers so impersonally and often with great hostility. It seemed everyone had something negative to say about their "domineering, materialistic, guilt-evoking, aggressive" mothers. I did not understand then that these utterings were merely a way of asserting independence, of striking out at the one authority in their lives that emotionally held them to the "nest." What was clear to me was that mother and motherhood were not "sacred" to them in the same way it was to me. They celebrated Mother's Day, which we never did, yet I heard such resentment surrounding that day, I used to wonder why it was celebrated.

Years later I was keenly reminded again of that period in my life. I was working as the Student Activities Coordinator at one of the colleges at the University of California in Santa Cruz. Among my duties was the responsibility for room assignments and changes. One day, a Chicano student came into my office requesting a room change. He was clearly agitated. I offered to act as mediator or counselor if there was a misunderstanding with his roommate. Reluctantly, he said, "I don't know about these Anglos. My roommate talks so badly about his mother. He calls her a bitch. This hurts me very much. I love my mother. I know she is sacrificing for me, crawling on her hands and knees in the strawberry fields of Delano so I can come to the University. I'm afraid I will hurt him if I have to keep rooming with him." I had felt my throat tighten and my eyes fill with tears, empathizing with him. I was touched by his love and loyalty, his willingness to overtly challenge an attitude so acceptable within the dominant culture and so unacceptable within his.

The word "sacrifice," spoken by my Caucasian friends in reference to their mothers, always carried connotations of guilt and manipulative martyrdom. It did not carry that taint for me or for the Mexican student. In fact, I have found that most of my friends from other ethnic minority backgrounds will readily say, if it is so, that they knew their mothers sacrificed their own comforts, or worked so that they could go to school or have a graduation suit . . . no guilt implied, just a recognition and acceptance of it with gratitude.

I think that Japanese women of my mother's generation who were mothers were fortunate because their role was highly valued by their society . . . their society being the community of other Japanese immigrants. The family and community prized her role, and when she fulfilled that role, she prized herself. She not only knew her worth, she *felt* her significance. There was no celebration of

"Mother's Day," but there was no question that *Oka-san* was respected and loved by her culture.

Her role as wife to my father is not as clear cut in my memory. Whereas her world in the home, in the immediate Japanese community, did not differ much from the society in which she and her mother were raised, my father's world was very different. He had to earn a living for his family in an environment both alien and hostile to him. My mother, already inherently prepared to subordinate herself in their relationship, knew this and zealously sought for ways to elevate his position in the family. He had to absorb the humiliations "out there"; she would absorb them at home. After all, was he not doing this for his family, protecting her, acting as the buffer between herself and that alien *hakujin* world?

She served him . . . with grace and naturalness. I conjure up the image of her calm, smooth face, her alert brown eyes scanning his stockings for holes as she carefully laid them and his underwear out at the foot of their bed. She did this faithfully every morning I can remember when he was at home. He was always served first at meals. She cooked special things for him and sat next to him at the table, vigilantly aware of his needs, handing him the condiments and pouring his tea before he could ask. She drew his bath and massaged him and laid his clothes out when he dressed up. As I was growing up I accepted these rituals to be the natural expressions of a wife's love for her husband. There was no question in my mind that my mother loved my father; that is why she served him. This attitude, that to serve meant to love, became an integral part of my psychological make-up and a source for confusion when I later began to relate to men.

There was also no question in my mind that my father was absolute authority in their relationship and in his relationship to his children. During and after the Second World War, when his dreams and economic situation had hit bottom, and he was too old to start over again as he had already done several times, he raged at his wife and family and drank. His frustration toward the society that rejected and humiliated him caused him to turn on his own and on himself. I never understood how she so patiently endured him during those times. But she never abandoned him, understanding as I did not, the reasons for his anguish, for his sense of failure.

Even though respect for him diminished then, I always felt that he was very powerful and that he dominated her with this power. As they grew older and inevitable thoughts of their passing entered my mind, I worried that she would be lost if he died before her. When that sad day arrived I learned what is meant by the Asian philosophical truism "softness is strength." I had taken my gravely ill father, along with my mother, to see his doctor. The doctor informed me privately that we should take him to the hospital where he would be comfortable, as he could not live more than 10 days.

It was raining. I numbly drove the car toward the hospital, straining to see through the blurred windshields and my own tears. My mother was not crying. "Riku," he said, weakly. He never called her Riku . . . always "Mama." "Don't leave me. Stay with me at the hospital. They won't know how to cook for me . . . or how to care for me." She patted his hand. "You've been a good wife. You've always been the strong one."

Not wanting him to tire, I tried to quiet him. He sat up bolt-like and roared 17
like a lion. "Shut up!" I quaked at his forcefulness, but felt some comfort in
knowing he could still "save face" and be the final authority to his children, even
at death's door. My mother's quiet strength filled the car as she gently stroked his
forehead. Without tears or panic she assured him she would stay with him until
the end.

He died that afternoon a few hours after he entered the hospital. For the 18
ten years afterward that my mother lived, she never once appeared lost or rud-
derless, as I feared she would be with him gone. Hadn't he been the center of her
life? Hadn't the forms in their relationship, the rituals of their roles all affirmed
his power over her? No. She had been the strong one. The structure had been
created for him; but it was her essence that had sustained it.

2

The memories surrounding my awareness of being female seem to fall into 19
two categories: those of the period before the war, when the family made up my
world, and those after the war when I entered puberty, and my world expanded
to include the ways and values of my Caucasian peers. I did not think about my
Asian-ness and how it influenced my self-image as a female, until I married.

In remembering myself as a small child, I find it hard to separate myself 20
from the entity of the family. I was too young to be given "duties" according to
my sex, and I was unaware that this was the organizational basis for the operating of the family. I took it for granted that everyone just did what had to be done
to keep things running smoothly. My five older sisters helped my mother with
domestic duties, and my four older brothers helped my father in the fishing business. What I vaguely recall about the sensibility surrounding our sex differences
was that my sisters and I all liked to please our brothers. Moreso, we tried to
attract positive attention from Papa. A smile or affectionate pat from him was like
a gift from heaven. Somehow, we never felt this way about Mama. We took her
love for granted. But there was something special about Papa.

I never identified this specialness as being one of the blessings of maleness. 21
After all, I played with my brother Kiyo, two years older than myself, and I never
felt there was anything special about him. I could even make him cry. My older
brothers were fun-loving, boisterous and very kind to me, especially when I made
them laugh with my imitations of Carmen Miranda dancing and Bonnie Baker
singing "Oh, Johnny." But Papa was different. His specialness was that he was the
authority, not that he was a male.

After the war, my world drastically changed. The family had disintegrated, 22
my father no longer "Godlike" despite my mother's attempt to sustain that pre-
war image of him. I was spending most of my time with my new Caucasian
friends and learning new values that clashed with the values of my parents. It was
also time that I assumed duties in the home that the girls were supposed to do
. . . like cooking, cleaning the house, washing and ironing clothes. I remember
washing and ironing my brother's shirts, careful to press the collars correctly, trying not to displease them. I cannot ever remember my brothers performing

domestic chores while I lived at home. Yet, even though they may not have been working "out there," as the men were supposed to do, I did not resent it. It would have embarrassed me to see my brothers doing the dishes. Their reciprocation came in a different way.

They were very protective of me and made me feel good and important for 23 being a female. If my brother Ray had extra money, he would sometimes buy me a sexy sweater like my Caucasian friends wore that Mama wouldn't buy for me. My brothers taught me to ride a bicycle, to drive a car, took me to my first dance, and proudly introduced me to their friends.

Although the family had changed, my identity as a female within it did not 24 differ much from my older sisters who grew up before the war. The males and females supported each other but for different reasons. No longer was the survival of the family as a group our primary objective; we cooperated to help each other survive "out there" in the complicated world that had weakened Papa.

My brothers encouraged me to run for school office, to try out for 25 majorette and song leader, and to run for Queen of various festivities. They were proud that I was breaking social barriers still closed to them. It was acceptable for an Oriental male to excel academically and in sports. But to gain recognition socially in a society that had been fed the stereotyped model of the Asian male as cook, houseboy or crazed *kamikaze* pilot, was almost impossible. The more alluring myth of mystery and exotica that surrounds the Oriental female made it easier, though no less spiritually painful, for me.

Whenever I succeeded in the *hakujin* world, my brothers were supportive, 26 whereas, Papa would be disdainful, undermined by my obvious capitulation to the ways of the West. I wanted to be like my Caucasian friends. Not only did I want to look like them, I wanted to act like them. I tried hard to be outgoing and socially aggressive, and to act confidently like my girl friends. At home I was careful not to show these personality traits to my father. For him it was bad enough that I did not even look very Japanese; I was too big, and I walked too assertively. My breasts were large, and besides that I showed them off with those sweaters the *hakujin* girls wore! My behavior at home was never calm and serene, but I still tried to be as Japanese as I could around my father.

As I passed puberty and grew more interested in boys, I soon became aware 27 that an Oriental female evoked a certain kind of interest from males. I was still too young to understand how or why an Oriental female fascinated Caucasian men, and of course, far too young to see then that it was a form of "not seeing," of stereotyping. My brothers would warn me, "Don't trust the *hakujin* boys. They only want one thing. They'll treat you like a servant and expect you to wait on them hand and foot. They don't know how to be nice to you." My brothers never dated Caucasian girls. In fact, I never really dated Caucasian boys until I went to college. In high school, I used to sneak out to dances and parties where I would meet them. I wouldn't even dare to think what Papa would do if he knew I was seeing *hakujin* boys.

What my brothers were saying was that I should not act towards Caucasian 28 males as I did towards them. I must not "wait on them" or allow them to think I would, because they wouldn't understand. In other words, be a Japanese female around Japanese men and act *hakujin* around Caucasian men. This double identity within a "double standard" resulted not only in a confusion for me of my role or roles as female, but also in who or what I was racially. With the admonitions of my brothers lurking deep in my consciousness, I would try to be aggressive, assertive and "come on strong" towards Caucasian men. I mustn't let them think I was submissive, passive and all-giving like Madame Butterfly. With Asian males I would tone down my natural enthusiasm and settle into patterns instilled in me through the models of my mother and my sisters. I was not comfortable in either role.

I found I was more physically attracted to Caucasian men. Although T.V. and film were not nearly as pervasive as they are now, we still had an abundance of movie magazines and movies from which to garner our idols for crushes and fantasy. For years I was madly in love with Lon McCallister and Alan Ladd. Bruce Lee and O.J. Simpson were absent from the idol-making media. Asian men became like "family" to me; they were my brothers. Of course, no one was like my father. He was so powerful. The only men who might possess some of that power were those whose control and dominance over his life diminished his. Those would be the men who interested me.

Although I was attracted to males who looked like someone in a Coca-Cola ad, I yearned for the expressions of their potency to be like that of Japanese men, like that of my father: unpredictable, dominant, and brilliant—yet sensitive and poetic. I wanted a blond Samurai.

When I met my blond Samurai I was surprised to see how readily my mother accepted the idea of our getting married. My father had passed away, but I was still concerned about her reaction. All of my married brothers and sisters had married Japanese American mates. I would be the first to marry a Caucasian. "He's a strong man and will protect you. I'm all for it," she said. Her main concern for me was survival. Knowing that my world was the world of the *hakujin*, she wanted me to be protected, even if it meant marriage to one. It was 1957, and inter-racial couples were a rare sight to see. She felt that my husband-to-be was strong because he was acting against the norms of his culture, perhaps even against his parents' wishes. From her vantage point, where family and group opinion outweighed the individual's, this willingness to oppose them was truly a show of strength.

When we first married I wondered if I should lay out his socks and underwear every morning like my mother used to do. But then my brother's warning not to be subservient to Caucasian men or they will take advantage would float up from the past. So I compromised and laid them out sporadically, whenever I thought to do it . . . which grew less and less often as the years passed. (Now my husband is lucky if *he* can even find a clean pair of socks in the house!) His first reaction to this wifely gesture was to be uncomfortably pleased. Then he was puzzled by its sporadic occurrence, which did not seem to coincide with an act of apology, or because I wanted something. On the days when I felt I should be a good Japanese wife, I did it. On other days, when I felt American and assertive, I did not.

When my mother visited us, as she often did when she was alive, I had to be on good behavior, much to my husband's pleasure and surprise. I would jump up from the table to fill his empty water glass (that is, if she hadn't beat me to it) or butter his roll. If I didn't notice that his plate needed refilling, she would kick me under the table and reprimand me with a disapproving look. Needless to say, we never had mother-in-law problems. He would often ask with hope in his voice, "When is your mother coming to visit?"

Despite the fact that early in our marriage we had become aware of the "images" we had married and were trying to relate to each other as the real people we were, he still hoped deep in his heart that I was his *Cho-Cho san,* his saronged, exotic Dorothy Lamour. And I still saw him as my golden Samurai, wielding his sword of justice and integrity, slaying the dragons that prevented my acceptance as an equal human being in his world, now mine.   34

My mother dutifully served my father throughout their marriage. I never felt she resented it. I served my brothers and father and did not resent it. I was made to feel not only important for performing duties of my role, but absolutely integral for the functioning of the family. I realized a very basic difference in attitude between Japanese and American culture towards serving another. In my family, to serve another could be uplifting, a gracious gesture that elevated oneself. For many white Americans it seems that serving another is degrading, an indication of dependency or weakness in character, or a low place in the social ladder. To be ardently considerate is to be "self-effacing" or apologetic.   35

My father used to say, "Serving humanity is the greatest virtue. Giving service of yourself is more worthy than selling the service or goods of another." He would prefer that we be maids in someone's home, serving someone well, than be a salesgirl where our function would be to exchange someone else's goods, handling money. Perhaps it was his way to rationalize and give pride to the occupations open to us as Orientals. Nevertheless, his words have stayed with me, giving me spiritual sustenance at times when I perceived that my willingness to give was misconstrued to be a need to be liked or an act of manipulation to get something.   36

I was talking about this subject with an Asian American woman friend, recently widowed, whose husband had also been Asian American. He had been a prominent surgeon, highly thought of in the community where we live. She is 42, third generation Chinese, born in San Francisco in 1935, articulate, intelligent and a professional therapist for educationally handicapped children. She "confessed" of her reticence to let her Caucasian friends know she served her husband. "There is such a stereotyped view that is laid on us. They just don't understand *why* we do what we do!"   37

She told me of an incident when she remarked to a Caucasian friend that she polished her husband's shoes. Her friend turned on her in mock fury and said, "Don't you dare let my husband know you do that!" My friend said she felt ashamed, humiliated, that she had somehow betrayed this woman by her seeming subordination to her husband.   38

"I served him in many ways," she said. "I did it because even though he was a graduate of Stanford and professionally successful, he drove himself to work harder and longer to compete because he felt he was handicapped by being Chinese. You know our Asian men, the ones raised with values from the old country,   39 are not equipped to compete like white American men. They are not conditioned to be outwardly aggressive and competitive. It was agony for my husband, and I knew he was out there doing it for us, so I tried to make it easier for him at home." As I looked at her I could see her compassion, and for a flickering moment I saw my mother. A generation had passed, but some things had not changed that much.

My husband and I often joke that the reason we have stayed married for so long is that we continually mystify each other with responses and attitudes that are plainly due to our different backgrounds. For years I frustrated him with unpredictable silences and accusative looks. I felt a great reluctance to tell him what I wanted or what needed to be done in the home. I was inwardly furious that I was being put into the position of having to *tell* him what to do. I felt my femaleness, in the Japanese sense, was being degraded. I did not want to be the authority. That would be humiliating for him and for me. He, on the other hand, considering the home to be under my dominion, in the American sense, did not dare to impose on me what he thought I wanted. He wanted me to tell him or make a list, like his parents did in his home.

Entertaining socially was also confusing. Up to recent times, I still hesitated to sit at one head of our rectangular dining table when my husband sat at the other end. It seemed right to be seated next to him, helping him serve the food. Sometimes I did it anyway, but only with our close friends who didn't misunderstand my physical placement to be psychological subservience.

At dinner parties I always used to serve the men first until I noticed the women glaring at me. I became self-conscious about it and would try to remember to serve the ladies first. Sometimes I would forget and automatically turn to a man. I would catch myself abruptly, dropping a bowl of soup all over him. Then I would have to serve him first anyway, as an apologetic gesture. My unconscious Japanese instinct still managed to get what it wanted!

Now I just entertain according to how I feel that day. If my Japanese sensibility is stronger I act accordingly and feel comfortable. If I feel like going all-American I can do that too, and feel comfortable. I have come to accept the cultural hybridness of my personality, to recognize it as strength and not weakness. Because I am neither culturally pure Japanese nor pure American does not mean I am less of a person. It means I have been enriched with the heritage of both.

As I look back on my marriage and try to compare it to the marriage of my parents, it seems ludicrous to do so . . . like comparing a sailboat to a jet airliner; both get you there, but one depends on the natural element of wind and the other on technological expertise. What does emerge as a basic difference is directly related to the Japanese concept of cooperation for group survival and the American value of competition for the survival of individualism. My Japanese family cooperated to survive economically and spiritually. Although sibling rivalry was subtly present, it was never allowed the ferocity of expression we allow our children. I see our children compete with each other. I have felt my husband and I compete with each other . . . not always in obvious ways such as professional recognition or in the comparison of role responsibilities, but in attitudes towards self-fulfillment. "I love you more than you love me," or "My doing nothing is more boring than your doing nothing."

Competition does provide some challenge and excitement in life. Yet carried   45
to extremes in personal relationships, it can become destructive. How can you fully trust someone you are in competition with? And when trust breaks down, isolation and alienation set in.

I find that another basic difference is between my mother and myself in how   46
we relate to sons. I try very consciously not to indulge my son, as my mother had indulged my brothers. My natural inclination is to do this. So I try to restrain it. In fact, I find myself being harder on him, afraid that my constrained Japanese training to please the male might surface, crippling instead of equipping him for future relationships with females who may not be of my background, hampering his emotional survival in the competitive, independent world he will face when he leaves the nest.

How my present attitudes will affect my children in later years remains to   47
be seen. My world is radically different from my mother's world, and all indications point to an even wider difference in our world from our children's. Whereas my family's and part of my struggle were racially based, I do not foresee a similar struggle for our children. Their biracialness is, indeed, a factor in their identity and self-image, but I feel their struggle will be more to sustain human dignity in a world rapidly dehumanizing itself with mechanization and technology. My hope is they have inherited a strong will to survive, that essential trait which ethnic minorities in this country have sharply honed.

3

In searching for remarks to conclude this paper, I find myself hearkening   48
again to imagined words of advice from my parents. My mother would say, "Love yourself. Nurture your children and your family with love and emotional support. Accept change if it means protecting your loved ones."

My father would say, "We are all brothers. Brother must not be pitted   49
against brother; race must not be pitted against race. We do not raise ourselves at the expense of others. Through cooperation we advance together as human beings."

I see the yin and the yang of their sensibilities and acknowledge how the   50
combination of them has formed my own. Thus, I close with these words, "In this game of life, we are only as good as our partner . . . our partner being the other in a male-female relationship, or a race or ethnic group co-existing with a dominant culture. The best game is when partners are equal, in top form, sharing their diversities, and enriching their experience. Dominating a partner only weakens the game, unbalancing it, lessening its vigor and quality. It is my hope in these changing times that the rules for the game will improve, encouraging understanding, and thus, acceptance and respect for all partners."

QUESTIONS FOR CRITICAL READING, THINKING, DISCUSSION, AND WRITING

Analyzing Content and Technique

1. What does the "Manzanar" of the title refer to? Briefly describe the historical event: What happened and what effects did it have on Houston's family?
2. Houston states that her mother was her most influential role model. How has she supported this throughout her essay?
3. Analyze Houston's attitude toward her father. In what ways is it complicated? How does she present his relationship with her mother? Examining the evidence she provides, do you think she has evaluated it correctly?
4. What is Houston's attitude toward Asian men as she is growing up? Why? What is her attitude toward Caucasian men? Why? How do her views change after her marriage?
5. Analyze the conflicts faced by Houston as a result of living in two cultures. How does she resolve some of them? Evaluate the solutions she finds.

Collaborative Activity

Have each person in the group do a brief clustering exercise with the word "mother," in which they examine how they feel toward their mothers, and why. Share the clusters with the group. Look for commonalities as well as differences. Based on your findings, what generalizations can you draw, as a group, about parent-child relationships in our culture today?

Making Connections

1. Looking back at the collaborative activity above, write an essay in which you compare the Japanese parent-child relationship as Houston presents it to the parent-child relationship in your culture. What similarities and differences emerge? What values are indicated by these? How deeply are the relationships influenced by ethnicity and the time period you are examining?
2. In paragraph 7, Houston uses the words of a friend to comment on American family values: "We abandon each other when we need each other the most. . . . We abandon the young and the old." Keeping in mind that there are always exceptions, would you agree that this is an accurate depiction of family trends in America today? Do different ethnic groups have different trends? Write an essay clarifying your opinion, giving specific examples from Houston's essay and your own experience and reading.

18

Think about the most important female figure in your life. How, if at all, was she related to you? Why was she special? Sprint write for five minutes about any memories that come to mind as you think of her.

Nani

ALBERTO RIOS

Born in Nogales, Arizona, on the Mexican border, to an English mother and a Mexican father, Alberto Rios grew up speaking only English and did not discover his Mexican heritage until much later. He is a writer of poetry, stories, and plays. His books include *Five Indiscretions, Teodoro Luna's Two Kisses, The Iguana Killer,* and *Whispering to Fool the Wind,* from which this selection is taken.

Sitting at her table, she serves
the sopa de arroz to me
instinctively, and I watch her,
the absolute *mamá,* and eat words
I might have had to say more   5
out of embarrassment. To speak,
now-foreign words I used to speak,
too, dribble down her mouth as she serves
me albóndigas. No more
than a third are easy to me.   10
By the stove she does something with words
and looks at me only with her
back. I am full. I tell her
I taste the mint, and watch her speak
smiles at the stove. All my words   15
make her smile. Nani never serves
herself, she only watches me
with her skin, her hair. I ask for more.

I watch the mamá warming more
tortillas for me. I watch her   20
fingers in the flame for me.

Near her mouth, I see a wrinkle speak
of a man whose body serves
the ants like she serves me, then more words
about this and that, flowing more   25
easily from these other mouths. Each serves
as a tremendous string around her,
holding her together. They speak
Nani was this and that to me
and I wonder just how much of me   30
will die with her, what were the words
I could have been, was. Her insides speak
through a hundred wrinkles, now, more
than she can bear, steel around her,
shouting, then, What is this thing she serves?   35

She asks me if I want more.
I own no words to stop her.
Even before I speak, she serves.

QUESTIONS FOR CRITICAL READING, THINKING, DISCUSSION, AND WRITING

Analyzing Content and Technique

1. Analyze the character of Nani. How does the writer feel toward her? In what ways is the set-ting for this poem well chosen?
2. Why does the writer call her "the absolute *mamá*"? What associations does this image hold for you?
3. Analyze the role of language in the relationship between the grandmother and grandson. In what ways does it weaken the relationship? How does it strengthen it?
4. Pick out unusual and original images used by Rios. How might a prose writer have communi-cated the same ideas? What do the images add to the poem?
5. Why does the writer use Spanish words in the poem? What might this tell you of his purpose, or his expectations of his audience?

Collaborative Activity

Have each member of the group bring a poem about a family member that touched them in a particular, positive way. Read the poems aloud, explaining what you liked about each. Have group members comment on each other's poems. Choose one poem from the group to read to the class.

Making Connections

1. Rios's poem addresses the issue of all that we can learn about our cultures and ourselves if we observe or listen to members of an earlier generation. Write an essay about such a per-son who has touched your life or the life of someone you know well. Some points to consider

are: the circumstances of this person's life, his or her values, and how this person has helped shape a sense of identity for you (or someone you know).

2. As you look at Rios's poem, which situates the grandmother in the kitchen, cooking and serving, think of the places and activities you associate with various family members you know. Why? In what way are these places symbolic of their personalities and, perhaps, values? Write an essay in which you analyze one or two family members by describing and explaining the activities you associate most closely with them.

Think about the role your father has played in your life. Do you know your father well? Did work take him away from family life often? Did you resent that? If a father has been absent from your life, examine the reasons why.

A New Breed of Fathers (Student Essay)

Kirill Dmitriev

*I*n the last fifty years we have witnessed many dramatic changes in almost all aspects of American society. No segment of society has undergone greater change than the family. While much research has been devoted to the alteration of the woman's role in the home, considerably less attention has been focused on the equally important subject of the change in men's attitudes toward the family and especially toward parenting.

Growing numbers of men are now seeking a more significant parenting role. In fact the changing face of the American male has been so dramatic that it is hard to believe that only two to three decades ago—perhaps even less in some cases—his behavior was guided by a number of negative masculine stereotypes.

At that time the man was seen as "the financial provider and woman as the primary caregiver at home" (Rice 1). Men were supposed to express love for their children not by staying with them or showing them physical affection, but by working hard and providing them with a stable home, a good education and plenty of food to eat and clothes to wear (Kushner 92). It was the woman's job to provide the children with the time and attention they were unable to get from their work-driven fathers.

For many hard working fathers of the time, success was the key word that proved their worth as human beings. Everything had to take second place to success. Ambition and competition led even men with the strongest family ties to sacrifice family for careers. In the competitive male race to the top, nobody dared to be the first to leave the office to go home. Many men had no inkling of their failure as family members until the plight of their families left them no choice.

An example of this is provided by Alan Silverstein's novel *Mom Kills Kids and Self.* In this book, the key male figure does not realize what kind of a father he has been until he returns from work one day to find that his wife has killed their two sons and herself. In half-crazed shock, the man looks back on his life,

Source: Student essay reprinted by permission.

only then seeing how obsessed he had been with his career. He says, "All right, let's make up for lost time. Who says it's too late?" (Silverstein 280). In the gruesome scene that follows, he tries to play catch with his dead son.

Alan Silverstein is doubtless making an exaggerated statement with his book. Yet he is not all wrong when he claims that "a familiar newspaper headline has suddenly become the case history of all" (Silverstein 4). Many fathers who read this book had to admit that it struck close to home. The book helped them realize how tyrannically their lives had been shaped by a society which, as Harold Kushner points out, seems to believe that

- Doing something that makes money is more valuable than doing something that shapes people's souls.
  - Working with numbers is more valuable than working with human beings
  - Dealing with adults is more valuable than dealing with children (Kushner 92).

The impact of these beliefs on men can be described by what some psychologists call the "Thank God It's Monday" syndrome, the quite pervasive male attitude that weekends at home are an interruption of their "real" life.

The few rare men who did prefer to spend time with children were neither understood nor appreciated by society. In his book *A Choice of Heroes,* Mark Gerzon mentions a young man who was devoted to working with disabled preschool children. However, after graduation when he started looking for jobs, he realized that his occupation "brought him perilously close to the division of the sexes." From the comments and looks he received, he felt that other men were questioning him and looking down at him, wondering if he could "make it" in a "real" job (Gerzon 201). Ultimately, the pressure of a society that believed "a man who would rather talk about first steps than first downs cannot be quite normal" (Larson 2) proved to be too much for this young man, leading him to change careers.

Kyle Pruett from Yale University's Child Study Center cites another case from the time when he studied a group of families where the fathers were the primary caregivers. He recalls that a priest paid a visit to one of the fathers because he thought something had gone wrong with the man's life. His assumption—like that of most people—was that "normal" fathers do not nurture infants, that human males are biologically destined to be remote and uncaring toward infants (Gerzon 91).

But is this assumption true? Three psychologists have conducted studies showing us that male rhesus monkeys, known for their indifferent attitude toward infants, can be caring fathers. In each case month-old rhesus monkeys were taken away from their mothers and placed in a cage with adult males. The psychologists saw a dramatic change in the males' behavior. Indifference disappeared and the fathers played with the infants as intimately and as often as did their female counterparts (Gerzon 205). It is hard to avoid the conclusion that if such a relatively inflexible creature as a male rhesus monkey has a substantial nurturing potential, human males must have it too.

Yet it was not until the 1970s that evidence was presented that a father-infant bond did exist—if only men would let it. Studies showed that fathers who were involved in the birth of their children were later more involved in their care. These studies also showed that by the age of four weeks the infants responded differently to their fathers than to people outside of the family (Larson 92).

Since then changes in the role of the American father have started to catch   11
up with the other profound changes in today's society, breaking through the old stereotypes. A significant increase in the number of double-income families has transformed the traditional responsibilities of husband and wife. Both men and women no longer feel they have to hold on as rigidly to their prescribed duties of being the breadwinner and the caregiver.

As a consequence, more and more men have realized that a family is no less   12
important than work and have started to seek a more balanced life. Even some top executives have decided to sacrifice their careers for the sake of their children. In 1990, Peter Lynch, former head of Fidelity Magellan, one of the nation's largest and most successful stock mutual funds, resigned at the age of forty-six to spend more time with his family. Before making this decision, he had been working eighty hours a week for thirteen years. In 1992, the New York police commissioner quit the nation's largest police force to care for his sick wife and the children she could no longer look after. Also in 1992, Brandon Tartikoff, head of Paramount Pictures, announced his resignation. The forty-one-year-old executive said that it was impossible for him to put into his job the enormous amounts of time it required while his nine-year-old daughter was recuperating from a critical car crash injury. The possibility that similar decisions would have been made three or four decades ago by men in similar positions is highly unlikely (Rice, E 1).

These cases are not just related to a few CEOs who have the financial lux-   13
ury to quit working. They illustrate an important trait of contemporary American society. As Eric Larson demonstrates in his article, the number of middle-class fathers who have decided to spend more time with their families continues to grow. And these fathers are proud of their decision. "Here I am, a needed part of this family, taking an active role in my child's growing up," says a coffee shop owner trying to walk his six-month-old son to sleep. "I'm trying to get in as much time as I can so that when I get older I won't have to say, 'Gee, I wish I'd spent more time with the kids,'" explains a Chrysler assembly-line worker (Larson 95).

From the examples above one can conclude that the new American father   14
enjoys being with his family more than ever before. He makes it a point to give his children the love and attention he lacked from his own father. He is determined that his children will not grow up to say, in the words of the folk song, "Of all the people I love, I know my father the least well."

WORKS CITED

GERZON, MARK. *A Choice of Heroes*. Boston: Houghton Mifflin, 1984.

KUSHNER, HAROLD. "Make More Family Time." *Redbook* 174 (1992): 92–94.

LARSON, ERIC. "The New Father." *Parents Magazine* 66 (1991): 90–95.

RICE, VALERIE. "U.S. Working Men Opting to Spend More Time at Home." *San Jose Mercury News* 31 Oct. 1992, E 1.

SILVERSTEIN, ALAN. *Mom Kills Kids and Self*. New York: Macmillan, 1979.

STRUCTURE, STRATEGY, SUGGESTION

1. What is the thesis of the essay? Where is it placed? Is the placement effective? Come up with another way of introducing the thesis.
2. Create a brief outline of the essay. Into how many major sections can it be divided? What is the main rhetorical mode of the essay?
3. Where does the writer effectively use the rhetorical mode of illustration? How does this strengthen his thesis?
4. Evaluate the writer's use of sources. What kind has he used? For what audiences were they intended? For what audience is his essay intended? What other kinds of research source might he have consulted?
5. Compare the tone of this essay to one of the personal essays in this book. In what way is it different? What are its strengths? What does it lack that the personal essay might have? Which do you prefer and why?
6. Write a research essay, using either print media, films, or interviews, on some other change (or growing trend) that has been observed in the American family in the last three or four decades. Your essay should indicate whether you consider it a positive or negative trend.

SYNTHESIS *Part Two*

1. Having looked at the ideas and examples offered by the writers in this unit, write an essay on the different ways in which the family contributes to our development as human beings. Some points you might consider are: In what positive or negative ways does family affect us? What kinds of things do we learn from our families? In the family unit, who has the greatest influence on children, and does this differ from culture to culture? Which elements of the family are culture-specific and which are universal? Support your answers with specific situations taken from the readings.

2. Marriage, and the steps leading up to it, can differ immensely from culture to culture. "Finding a Wife" and "Pom's Engagement" provide us with a clear example of this. Analyze the two betrothal processes they depict and compare the strengths and weaknesses of each system.

3. "Teenagers in Crisis," "Mothers, Sons and the Gangs," and "Beyond Manzanar" portray several kinds of relationships between teenagers and their mothers, each leading to a number of complex results. Compare and contrast two or three of these relationships, examining in particular the causes which give them their unique shape.

4. Look through the book to find other essays on family roles as they are depicted on television. Write an essay on what a study of such shows can teach us about social trends, and how accurate our understanding would be. Give examples from the text as well as your own observation.

5. "Variations on a Theme" and "Nani" deal with the varied roles that grandparents may play in a family. This issue is also a major focus of "The Last of the Kiowas" (Part Three). Write an essay explaining your view of the role(s) of grandparents in America today. Do they play a significant part in the family? Should they? What is the attitude of the other members in the family toward them? What may be some problems with involving grandparents in the family? You may use relevant points brought up by the writers in this book as well as your own sources, including portraits of grandparents in movies and on television.

PART THREE

What We Hold Within

SELECTIONS IN PART THREE

Part 3: Introduction

O|ur first exposure to the concept of heritage might begin on a simple material level, with heirlooms—objects that have gained a special emotional and symbolic value as they traveled through the years that brought them to us: a mother's wedding necklace, a grandfather's Bible or Koran, a great-aunt's dinner dishes. But we soon realize that heritage is much more than heirlooms. It also resides in genetics—the shape of our eyes or mouth; the way we move or talk or perform a daily task, echoing a parent or, mysteriously, some ancestor we never knew. And ultimately, heritage goes far beyond the boundaries of family, embracing entire communities, or perhaps even nations and races. It colors our tastes and customs, shapes our rituals and beliefs, informs our sense of self and the relationship we have with the universe.

Our cultural inheritance comes to us from many sources—family practices, bedtime stories, food, dress, art, media, myths, taboos. Sometimes it seeps into our lives so imperceptibly and intimately that we are unaware of having a cultural tradition at all. This is often the case in the contemporary United States, where many people complain that our lives have an anonymous sameness. But when we begin to analyze our lives—perhaps at points of conflict, loss, or change—we recognize the presence of our heritage (for each of us has one), sometimes surprisingly, in the most mundane of acts.

Much has been said about the value of ritual as an aspect of heritage—the sense of pride it gives us and the security of belonging, of understanding the world in which we are placed and how it defines us as a culture. All these benefits come together in Gene Logsdon's "Amish Economics" (selection 25). But it is not always that simple. N. Scott Momaday's "The Last of the Kiowas" (selection 23) is colored by sorrow and a sense of loss even as it captures with heart-wrenching beauty the way of his people through his memories of his grandmother. Sometimes we view our legacy—at least parts of it—as negative and dangerous and reject it as Maxine Hong Kingston and Keiko Nozoe do, in different ways, in "No Name Woman" (selection 21) and "The Japanese Syndrome" (selection 27).

For many Americans, especially those whose recent ancestors came from other lands, the cultural legacy is even more complex. On one hand, we are pulled by the values of our original culture—the old traditions that seem to speak to something in our blood. On the other hand, there is the vibrant polyglot life we face in this country, the rainbow shimmer of new and exciting ideas and values that beckon to us. We must compare and contrast, weigh and choose. Sometimes this causes tension between the generations, or fear and a retreat into an unreal past, as in Bharati Mukherjee's "An Indian Family in New York" (selection 26). And sometimes, one hopes, it leads to understanding, acceptance, and mutual enrichment, as implied in Robert Levine and Ellen Wolff's essay, "Social Time" (selection 22).

Heritage is not only something from the past that we carry inside us. As Randall Majors's "America's Emerging Gay Culture" (selectin 24) and Phyllis Rose's "Shopping and Other Spiritual Adventures" (selection 20) illustrate, consciously or otherwise, we are constantly creating traditions and symbols for those who follow. Thus heritage becomes a fabric we weave, even as we are woven into it, and ultimately we must take responsibility for the pattern of which we are a part.

20

PREREADING ACTIVITY

Before you read selection 20, write about your own attitude toward shopping. What are some reasons why you shop? Do you enjoy shopping, or do you detest it? How is your attitude typical of, or different from, the attitude prevalent in your culture?

Shopping and Other Spiritual Adventures in America Today

PHYLLIS ROSE

Phyllis Rose (1942–) has published book reviews and essays in *The Nation, The Atlantic, The Washington Post,* and *The New York Times.* She has taught at Yale, Harvard, and Berkeley, and is currently a professor at Wesleyan University. She is the author of *Parallel Lives,* a biography of Virginia Woolf; and *Jazz Cleopatra.* She has been awarded a Rockefeller and a Guggenheim fellowship. The selection here first appeared in the *Times.*

Last year a new Waldbaum's Food Mart opened in the shopping 1
mall on Route 66. It belongs to the new generation of superdupermarkets open twenty-four hours that have computerized checkout. I went to see the place as soon as it opened and I was impressed. There was trail mix in Lucite bins. There was freshly made pasta. There were coffee beans, four kinds of tahini, ten kinds of herb teas, raw shrimp in shells and cooked shelled shrimp, fresh-squeezed orange juice. Every sophistication known to the big city, even goat's cheese covered with ash, was now available in Middletown, Conn. People raced from the warehouse aisle to the bagel bin to the coffee beans to the fresh fish market, exclaiming at all the new things. Many of us felt elevated, graced, complimented by the presence of this food palace in our town.

This is the wonderful egalitarianism of American business. Was it Andy 2
Warhol who said that the nice thing about Coke is, no can is any better or worse than any other? Some people may find it dull to cross the country and find the same chain stores with the same merchandise from coast to coast, but it means that my town is as good as yours, my shopping mall as important as yours, equally filled with wonders.

Source: From *Never Say Good-Bye* by Phyllis Rose. Copyright © 1991 by Phyllis Rose. Used by permission of Doubleday, a division of Bantam Doubleday Dell Publishing Group, Inc.

Imagine what people ate during the winter as little as seventy-five years ago. 3
They ate food that was local, long-lasting, and dull, like acorn squash, turnips,
and cabbage. Walk into an American supermarket in February and the world lies
before you: grapes, melons, artichokes, fennel, lettuce, peppers, pistachios, dates,
even strawberries, to say nothing of ice cream. Have you ever considered what a
triumph of civilization it is to be able to buy a pound of chicken livers? If you
lived on a farm and had to kill a chicken when you wanted to eat one, you wouldn't
ever accumulate a pound of chicken livers.

Another wonder of Middletown is Caldor, the discount department store. 4
Here is man's plenty: tennis racquets, panty hose, luggage, glassware, records,
toothpaste. Timex watches, Cadbury's chocolate, corn poppers, hair dryers,
warm-up suits, car wax, light bulbs, television sets. All good quality at low prices
with exchanges cheerfully made on defective goods. There are worse rules to live
by. I feel good about America whenever I walk into this store, which is almost
every mid-winter Sunday afternoon, when life elsewhere has closed down. I go to
Caldor the way English people go to pubs: out of sociability. To get away from
my house. To widen my horizons. For culture's sake. Caldor provides me too
with a welcome sense of seasonal change. When the first outdoor grills and lawn
furniture appear there, it's as exciting a sign of spring as the first crocus or robin.

Someone told me about a Soviet emigré who practices English by declaim- 5
ing, at random, sentences that catch his fancy. One of his favorites is, "Fifty percent off all items today only." Refugees from Communist countries appreciate our
supermarkets and discount department stores for the wonders they are. An Eastern European scientist visiting Middletown wept when she first saw the meat
counter at Waldbaum's. On the other hand, before her year in America was up,
her pleasure turned sour. She wanted everything she saw. Her approach to consumer goods was insufficiently abstract, too materialistic. We Americans are
beyond a simple, possessive materialism. We're used to abundance and the possibility of possessing things. The things, and the possibility of possessing them, will
still be there next week, next year. So today we can walk the aisles calmly.

It is a misunderstanding of the American retail store to think we go there 6
necessarily to buy. Some of us shop. There's a difference. Shopping has many purposes, the least interesting of which is to acquire new articles. We shop to cheer
ourselves up. We shop to practice decision-making. We shop to be useful and productive members of our class and society. We shop to remind ourselves how much
is available to us. We shop to remind ourselves how much is to be striven for. We
shop to assert our superiority to the material objects that spread themselves
before us.

Shopping's function as a form of therapy is widely appreciated. You don't 7
really need, let's say, another sweater. You need the feeling of power that comes
with buying or not buying it. You need the feeling that someone wants something you have—even if it's just your money. To get the benefit of shopping, you
needn't actually purchase the sweater, any more than you have to marry every
man you flirt with. In fact, window-shopping, like flirting, can be more reward-
ing, the same high without the distressing commitment, the material encum-
brance. The purest form of shopping is provided by garage sales. A connoisseur

goes out with no goal in mind, open to whatever may come his or her way, secure that it will cost very little. Minimum expense, maximum experience. Perfect shopping.

I try to think of the opposite, a kind of shopping in which the object is all-important, the pleasure of shopping at a minimum. For example, the purchase of blue jeans. I buy new blue jeans as seldom as possible because the experience is so humiliating. For every pair that looks good on me, fifteen look grotesque. But even shopping for blue jeans at Bob's Surplus on Main Street—no frills, bare-bones shopping—is an event in the life of the spirit. Once again I have to come to terms with the fact that I will never look good in Levi's. Much as I want to be mainstream, I never will be.   8

In fact, I'm doubly an oddball, neither Misses nor Junior, but Misses Petite. I look in the mirror, I acknowledge the disparity between myself and the ideal, I resign myself to making the best of it: I will buy the Lee's Misses Petite. Shopping is a time of reflection, assessment, spiritual self-discipline.   9

It is appropriate, I think, that Bob's Surplus has a communal dressing room. I used to shop only in places where I could count on a private dressing room with a mirror inside. My impulse then was to hide my weaknesses. Now I believe in sharing them. There are other women in the dressing room at Bob's Surplus trying on blue jeans who look as bad as I do. We take comfort from one another. Sometimes a woman will ask me which of two items looks better. I always give a definite answer. It's the least I can do. I figure we are all in this together, and I emerge from the dressing room not only with a new pair of jeans but with a renewed sense of belonging to a human community.   10

When a Solzhenitsyn rants about American materialism, I have to look at my digital Timex and check what year this is. Materialism? Like conformism, a hot moral issue of the fifties, but not now. How to spread the goods, maybe. Whether the goods are the Good, no. Solzhenitsyn, like the visiting scientist who wept at the beauty of Waldbaum's meat counter but came to covet everything she saw, takes American materialism too materialistically. He doesn't see its spiritual side. Caldor, Waldbaum's, Bob's Surplus—these, perhaps, are our cathedrals.   11

QUESTIONS FOR CRITICAL READING, THINKING, DISCUSSION, AND WRITING

Analyzing Content and Technique

1. Why is the writer impressed by Waldbaum's Food Mart?
2. Explain the phrase "the wonderful egalitarianism of American business." What are the pros and cons of this egalitarianism?
3. Why does the writer enjoy visiting Caldor's department store?
4. "It is a misunderstanding of the American retail store to think we go there necessarily to buy," Rose says. What are her reasons for shopping?
5. In paragraph 6, Rose uses repetition in several sentences. Why?

6. In paragraph 7 (which begins, "Shopping's function as a form of therapy . . ."), Rose examines the relationship between shopping and buying by drawing an analogy. What is the analogy? Is it effective? Why or why not?
7. Analyze the tone of Rose's piece. How does it help her make her point? Toward which kind of audience is it aimed? What drawback might the use of such a tone have?

Collaborative Activity

Have the group approach the issue of shopping from the other angle, that of the seller. Imagine you are, collectively, about to open a store. What kind would you choose? Where would you locate it? How would you stock and decorate it? Which kind of shopper do you wish to attract? What dangers might you have to watch out for? After discussing these and related issues, write a collaborative paragraph describing the store and explaining the reasons for the choices made by the group.

Making Connections

1. Choose a daily activity that, like shopping, is often viewed negatively (watching television, commuting, eating at a fast food chain, and so forth). Write an essay in which you observe the activity from an unusual angle and persuade the reader of its hidden benefits. You may choose any kind of tone that is appropriate to the purpose of the essay.
2. In this selection, Rose hints that there may be many kinds of shoppers, each with his or her behavior patterns and goals. Write a classification essay in which you divide the kinds of shoppers you have perceived into categories, differentiating each carefully and giving specific examples. Your tone may be serious, humorous, or satiric.

Before you read selection 21, write about a story that a parent or a relative has told you—one that has a moral or teaches a lesson. What cultural values are implied in the story?

No Name Woman

MAXINE HONG KINGSTON

Maxine Hong Kingston (1940–) is a Chinese American who grew up in California. Her poems, short stories, and essays have appeared in magazines such as *The New Yorker, Iowa Review,* and *Ms.* Among her books are *Tripmaster Monkey, China Men,* and the autobiographical *The Woman Warrior,* which won a National Book Critics Circle Award in 1976, and from which the selection here is taken. Hong Kingston has been awarded an NEA fellowship and a Guggenheim fellowship and teaches at the University of California at Berkeley.

"You must not tell anyone," my mother said, "what I am about to 1 tell you. In China your father had a sister who killed herself. She jumped into the family well. We say that your father has all brothers because it is as if she had never been born.

"In 1924 just a few days after our village celebrated seventeen hurry-up 2 weddings—to make sure that every young man who went 'out on the road' would responsibly come home—your father and his brothers and your grandfather and his brothers and your aunt's new husband sailed for America, the Gold Mountain. It was your grandfather's last trip. Those lucky enough to get contracts waved good-bye from the decks. They fed and guarded the stowaways and helped them off in Cuba, New York, Bali, Hawaii. 'We'll meet in California next year,' they said. All of them sent money home.

"I remember looking at your aunt one day when she and I were dressing; I 3 had not noticed before that she had such a protruding melon of a stomach. But I did not think, 'She's pregnant,' until she began to look like other pregnant women, her shirt pulling and the white tops of her black pants showing. She

Source: From *The Woman Warrior* by Maxine Hong Kingston. Copyright © 1975, 1976 by Maxine Hong Kingston. Reprinted by permission of Alfred A. Knopf, Inc.

could not have been pregnant, you see, because her husband had been gone for years. No one said anything. We did not discuss it. In early summer she was ready to have the child, long after the time when it could have been possible.

"The village had also been counting. On the night the baby was to be born 4 the villagers raided our house. Some were crying. Like a great saw, teeth strung with lights, files of people walked zigzag across our land, tearing the rice. Their lanterns doubled in the disturbed black water, which drained away through the broken bunds. As the villagers closed in, we could see that some of them, probably men and women we knew well, wore white masks. The people with long hair hung it over their faces. Women with short hair made it stand up on end. Some had tied white bands around their foreheads, arms, and legs.

"At first they threw mud and rocks at the house. Then they threw eggs and 5 began slaughtering our stock. We could hear the animals scream their deaths— the roosters, the pigs, a last great roar from the ox. Familiar wild heads flared in our night windows; the villagers encircled us. Some of the faces stopped to peer at us, their eyes rushing like searchlights. The hands flattened against the panes, framed heads, and left red prints.

"The villagers broke in the front and the back doors at the same time, even 6 though we had not locked the doors against them. Their knives dripped with the blood of our animals. They smeared blood on the doors and walls. One woman swung a chicken, whose throat she had slit, splattering blood in red arcs about her. We stood together in the middle of the house, in the family hall with the pictures and tables of the ancestors around us, and looked straight ahead.

"At that time the house had only two wings. When the men came back, we 7 would build two more to enclose our courtyard and a third one to begin a second courtyard. The villagers pushed through both wings, even your grandparents' rooms, to find your aunt's, which was also mine until the men returned. From this room a new wing for one of the younger families would grow. They ripped up her clothes and shoes and broke her combs, grinding them underfoot. They tore her work from the loom. They scattered the cooking fire and rolled the new weaving into it. We could hear them in the kitchen breaking our bowls and banging the pots. They overturned the great waist-high earthenware jugs; duck eggs, pickled fruits, vegetables burst out and mixed in acrid torrents. The old woman from the next field swept a broom through the air and loosed the spirits-of-the-broom over our heads. 'Pig.' 'Ghost.' 'Pig,' they sobbed and scolded while they ruined our house.

"When they left, they took sugar and oranges to bless themselves. They cut 8 pieces from the dead animals. Some of them took bowls that were not broken and clothes that were not torn. Afterward we swept up the rice and sewed it back up into sacks. But the smells from the spilled preserves lasted. Your aunt gave birth in the pigsty that night. The next morning when I went for the water, I found her and the baby plugging up the family well.

"Don't let your father know that I told you. He denies her. Now that you 9 have started to menstruate, what happened to her could happen to you. Don't humiliate us. You wouldn't like to be forgotten as if you had never been born. The villagers are watchful."

Whenever she had to warn us about life, my mother told stories that ran like 10 this one, a story to grow up on. She tested our strength to establish realities. Those in the emigrant generations who could not reassert brute survival died young and far from home. Those of us in the first American generations have had to figure out how the invisible world the emigrants built around our childhoods fit in solid America.

The emigrants confused the gods by diverting their curses, misleading them 11 with crooked streets and false names. They must try to confuse their offspring as well, who, I suppose, threaten them in similar ways—always trying to get things straight, always trying to name the unspeakable. The Chinese I know hide their names; sojourners take new names when their lives change and guard their real names with silence.

Chinese-Americans, when you try to understand what things in you are 12 Chinese, how do you separate what is peculiar to childhood, to poverty, insanities, one family, your mother who marked your growing with stories, from what is Chinese? What is Chinese tradition and what is the movies?

If I want to learn what clothes my aunt wore, whether flashy or ordinary, I 13 would have to begin, "Remember Father's drowned-in-the-well sister?" I cannot ask that. My mother has told me once and for all the useful parts. She will add nothing unless powered by Necessity, a riverbank that guides her life. She plants vegetable gardens rather than lawns; she carries the odd-shaped tomatoes home from the fields and eats food left for the gods.

Whenever we did frivolous things, we used up energy; we flew high kites. 14 We children came up off the ground over the melting cones our parents brought home from work and the American movie on New Year's Day—*Oh, You Beautiful Doll* with Betty Grable one year, and *She Wore a Yellow Ribbon* with John Wayne another year. After the one carnival ride each, we paid in guilt; our tired father counted his change on the dark walk home.

Adultery is extravagance. Could people who hatch their own chicks and eat 15 the embryos and the heads for delicacies and boil the feet in vinegar for party food, leaving only the gravel, eating even the gizzard lining—could such people engender a prodigal aunt? To be a woman, to have a daughter in starvation time was a waste enough. My aunt could not have been the lone romantic who gave up everything for sex. Women in the old China did not choose. Some man had commanded her to lie with him and be his secret evil. I wonder whether he masked himself when he joined the raid on the family.

Perhaps she encountered him in the fields or on the mountain where the 16 daughters-in-law collected fuel. Or perhaps he first noticed her in the marketplace. He was not a stranger because the village housed no strangers. She had to have dealings with him other than sex. Perhaps he worked an adjoining field, or he sold her the cloth for the dress she sewed and wore. His demand must have surprised, then terrified her. She obeyed him; she always did as she was told.

When the family found a young man in the next village to be her husband, 17 she stood tractably beside the best rooster, his proxy, and promised before they met that she would be his forever. She was lucky that he was her age and she would be the first wife, an advantage secure now. The night she first saw him, he had sex with her. Then he left for America. She had almost forgotten what he looked like. When she tried to envision him, she only saw the black and white face in the group photograph the men had had taken before leaving.

The other man was not, after all, much different from her husband. They both gave orders: she followed. "If you tell your family, I'll beat you. I'll kill you. Be here again next week." No one talked sex, ever. And she might have separated the rapes from the rest of living if only she did not have to buy her oil from him or gather wood in the same forest. I want her fear to have lasted just as long as rape lasted so that the fear could have been contained. No drawn-out fear. But women at sex hazarded birth and hence lifetimes. The fear did not stop but permeated everywhere. She told the man, "I think I'm pregnant." He organized the raid against her.

On nights when my mother and father talked about their life back home, sometimes they mentioned an "outcast table" whose business they still seemed to be settling, their voices tight. In a commensal tradition, where food is precious, the powerful older people made wrongdoers eat alone. Instead of letting them start separate new lives like the Japanese, who could become samurais and geishas, the Chinese family, faces averted but eyes glowering sideways, hung on to the offenders and fed them leftovers. My aunt must have lived in the same house as my parents and eaten at an outcast table. My mother spoke about the raid as if she had seen it, when she and my aunt, a daughter-in-law to a different household, should not have been living together at all. Daughters-in-law lived with their husbands' parents, not their own; a synonym for marriage in Chinese is "taking a daughter-in-law." Her husband's parents could have sold her, mortgaged her, stoned her. But they had sent her back to her own mother and father, a mysterious act hinting at disgraces not told me. Perhaps they had thrown her out to deflect the avengers.

She was the only daughter; her four brothers went with her father, husband, and uncles "out on the road" and for some years became western men. When the goods were divided among the family, three of the brothers took land, and the youngest, my father, chose an education. After my grandparents gave their daughter away to her husband's family, they had dispensed all the adventure and all the property. They expected her alone to keep the traditional ways, which her brothers, now among the barbarians, could fumble without detection. The heavy, deep-rooted women were to maintain the past against the flood, safe for returning. But the rare urge west had fixed upon our family, and so my aunt crossed boundaries not delineated in space.

The work of preservation demands that the feelings playing about in one's guts not be turned into action. Just watch their passing like cherry blossoms. But perhaps my aunt, my forerunner, caught in a slow life, let dreams grow and fade and after some months or years went toward what persisted. Fear at the enormities of the forbidden kept her desires delicate, wire and bone. She looked at a man because she liked the way the hair was tucked behind his ears, or she liked the question-mark line of a long torso curving at the shoulder and straight at the hip. For warm eyes or a soft voice or a slow walk—that's all—a few hairs, a line, a brightness, a sound, a pace, she gave up family. She offered us up for a charm that vanished with tiredness, a pigtail that didn't toss when the wind died. Why, the wrong lighting could erase the dearest thing about him.

It could very well have been, however, that my aunt did not take subtle ²² enjoyment of her friend, but, a wild woman, kept rollicking company. Imagining her free with sex doesn't fit, though. I don't know any woman like that, or men either. Unless I see her life branching into mine, she gives me no ancestral help.

To sustain her being in love, she often worked at herself in the mirror, ²³ guessing at the colors and shapes that would interest him, changing them frequently in order to hit on the right combination. She wanted him to look back.

On a farm near the sea, a woman who tended her appearance reaped a rep- ²⁴ utation for eccentricity. All the married women blunt-cut their hair in flaps about their ears or pulled it back in tight buns. No nonsense. Neither style blew easily into heart-catching tangles. And at their weddings they displayed themselves in their long hair for the last time. "It brushed the backs of my knees," my mother tells us. "It was braided, and even so, it brushed the backs of my knees."

At the mirror my aunt combed individuality into her bob. A bun could have ²⁵ been contrived to escape into black streamers blowing in the wind or in quiet wisps about her face, but only the older women in our picture album wear buns. She brushed her hair back from her forehead, tucking the flaps behind her ears. She looped a piece of thread, knotted into a circle between her index fingers and thumbs, and ran the double strand across her forehead. When she closed her fingers as if she were making a pair of shadow geese bite, the string twisted together catching the little hairs. Then she pulled the thread away from her skin, ripping the hairs out neatly, her eyes watering from the needles of pain. Opening her fingers, she cleaned the thread, then rolled it along her hairline and the tops of her eyebrows. My mother did the same to me and my sisters and herself. I used to believe that the expression "caught by the short hairs" meant a captive held with a depilatory string. It especially hurt at the temples, but my mother said we were lucky we didn't have to have our feet bound when we were seven. Sisters used to sit on their beds and cry together, she said, as their mothers or their slaves removed the bandages for a few minutes each night and let the blood gush back into their veins. I hope that the man my aunt loved appreciated a smooth brow, that he wasn't just a tits-and-ass man.

Once my aunt found a freckle on her chin, at a spot that the almanac said ²⁶ predestined her for unhappiness. She dug it out with a hot needle and washed the wound with peroxide.

More attention to her looks than these pulling of hairs and pickings at spots ²⁷ would have caused gossip among the villagers. They owned work clothes and good clothes, and they wore good clothes for feasting the new seasons. But since a woman combing her hair hexes beginnings, my aunt rarely found an occasion to look her best. Women looked like great sea snails—the corded wood, babies, and laundry they carried were the whorls on their backs. The Chinese did not admire a bent back; goddesses and warriors stood straight. Still there must have been a marvelous freeing of beauty when a worker laid down her burden and stretched and arched.

Such commonplace loveliness, however, was not enough for my aunt. She ₂₈ dreamed of a lover for the fifteen days of New Year's, the time for families to exchange visits, money, and food. She plied her secret comb. And sure enough she cursed the year, the family, the village, and herself.

Even as her hair lured her imminent lover, many other men looked at her. ₂₉ Uncles, cousins, nephews, brothers would have looked, too, had they been home between journeys. Perhaps they had already been restraining their curiosity, and they left, fearful that their glances, like a field of nesting birds, might be startled and caught. Poverty hurt, and that was their first reason for leaving. But another, final reason for leaving the crowded house was the never-said.

She may have been unusually beloved, the precious only daughter, spoiled ₃₀ and mirror gazing because of the affection the family lavished on her. When her husband left, they welcomed the chance to take her back from the in-laws; she could live like the little daughter for just a while longer. There are stories that my grandfather was different from other people, "crazy ever since the little Jap bayoneted him in the head." He used to put his naked penis on the dinner table, laughing. And one day he brought home a baby girl, wrapped up inside his brown western-style greatcoat. He had traded one of his sons, probably my father, the youngest, for her. My grandmother made him trade back. When he finally got a daughter of his own, he doted on her. They must have all loved her, except perhaps my father, the only brother who never went back to China, having once been traded for a girl.

Brothers and sisters, newly men and women, had to efface their sexual color ₃₁ and present plain miens. Disturbing hair and eyes, a smile like no other threatened the ideal of five generations living under one roof. To focus blurs, people shouted face to face and yelled from room to room. The immigrants I know have loud voices, unmodulated to American tones even after years away from the village where they called their friendships out across the fields. I have not been able to stop my mother's screams in public libraries or over telephones. Walking erect (knees straight, toes pointed forward, not pigeon-toed, which is Chinese-feminine) and speaking in an inaudible voice, I have tried to turn myself American-feminine. Chinese communication was loud, public. Only sick people had to whisper. But at the dinner table, where the family members came nearest one another, no one could talk, not the outcasts nor any eaters. Every word that falls from the mouth is a coin lost. Silently they gave and accepted food with both hands. A preoccupied child who took his bowl with one hand got a sideways glare. A complete moment of total attention is due everyone alike. Children and lovers have no singularity here, but my aunt used a secret voice, a separate attentiveness.

She kept the man's name to herself throughout her labor and dying; she did ₃₂ not accuse him that he be punished with her. To save her inseminator's name she gave silent birth.

He may have been somebody in her own household, but intercourse with a ₃₃ man outside the family would have been no less abhorrent. All the village were kinsmen, and the titles shouted in loud country voices never let kinship be forgotten. Any man within visiting distance would have been neutralized as a lover—"brother," "younger brother," "older brother"—one hundred and fifteen relationship titles. Parents researched birth charts probably not so much to assure good fortune as to circumvent incest in a population that has but one hundred surnames. Everybody has eight million relatives. How useless then sexual mannerisms, how dangerous.

As it came from an atavism deeper than fear, I used to add "brother" 34 silently to boys' names. It hexed the boys, who would or would not ask me to dance, and made them less scary and as familiar and deserving of benevolence as girls.

But, of course, I hexed myself also—no dates. I should have stood up, both 35 arms waving, and shouted out across libraries, "Hey, you! Love me back." I had no idea, though, how to make attraction selective, how to control its direction and magnitude. If I made myself American-pretty so that the five or six Chinese boys in the class fell in love with me, everyone else—the Caucasian, Negro, and Japanese boys—would too. Sisterliness, dignified and honorable, made much more sense.

Attraction eludes control so stubbornly that whole societies designed to 36 organize relationships among people cannot keep order, not even when they bind people to one another from childhood and raise them together. Among the very poor and the wealthy, brothers married their adopted sisters, like doves. Our family allowed some romance, paying adult brides' prices and providing dowries so that their sons and daughters could marry strangers. Marriage promises to turn strangers into friendly relatives—a nation of siblings.

In the village structure, spirits shimmered among the live creatures, bal- 37 anced and held in equilibrium by time and land. But one human being flaring up into violence could open up a black hole, a maelstrom that pulled in the sky. The frightened villagers, who depended on one another to maintain the real, went to my aunt to show her a personal, physical representation of the break she had made in the "roundness." Misallying couples snapped off the future, which was to be embodied in true offspring. The villagers punished her for acting as if she could have a private life, secret and apart from them.

If my aunt had betrayed the family at a time of large grain yields and peace, 38 when many boys were born, and wings were being built on many houses, perhaps she might have escaped such severe punishment. But the men—hungry, greedy, tired of planting in dry soil, cuckolded—had had to leave the village in order to send food-money home. There were ghost plagues, bandit plagues, wars with the Japanese, floods. My Chinese brother and sister had died of an unknown sickness. Adultery, perhaps only a mistake during good times, became a crime when the village needed food.

The round moon cakes and round doorways, the round tables of graduated 39 size that fit one roundness inside another, round windows and rice bowls—these talismen had lost their power to warn this family of the law: a family must be whole, faithfully keeping the descent line by having sons to feed the old and the dead, who in turn look after the family. The villagers came to show my aunt and her lover-in-hiding a broken house. The villagers were speeding up the circling of events because she was too shortsighted to see that her infidelity had already harmed the village, that waves of consequences would return unpredictably, sometimes in disguise, as now, to hurt her. This roundness had to be made coin-sized so that she would see its circumference: punish her at the birth of her baby. Awaken her to the inexorable. People who refused fatalism because they could invent small resources insisted on culpability. Deny accidents and wrest fault from the stars.

After the villagers left, their lanterns now scattering in various directions 40 toward home, the family broke their silence and cursed her. "Aiaa, we're going to die. Death is coming. Death is coming. Look what you've done. You've killed us. Ghost! Dead ghost! Ghost! You've never been born." She ran out into the fields, far enough from the house so that she could no longer hear their voices, and pressed herself against the earth, her own land no more. When she felt the birth coming, she thought that she had been hurt. Her body seized together. "They've hurt me too much," she thought. "This is gall, and it will kill me." Her forehead and knees against the earth, her body convulsed and then released her onto her back. The black well of sky and stars went out and out and out forever; her body and her complexity seemed to disappear. She was one of the stars, a bright dot in blackness, without home, without a companion, in eternal cold and silence. An agoraphobia rose in her, speeding higher and higher, bigger and bigger; she would not be able to contain it; there would be no end to fear.

Flayed, unprotected against space, she felt pain return, focusing her body. 41 This pain chilled her—a cold, steady kind of surface pain. Inside, spasmodically, the other pain, the pain of the child, heated her. For hours she lay on the ground, alternately body and space. Sometimes a vision of normal comfort obliterated reality: she saw the family in the evening gambling at the dinner table, the young people massaging their elders' backs. She saw them congratulating one another, high joy on the mornings the rice shoots came up. When these pictures burst, the stars drew yet further apart. Black space opened.

She got to her feet to fight better and remembered that old-fashioned 42 women gave birth in their pigsties to fool the jealous, pain-dealing gods, who do not snatch piglets. Before the next spasms could stop her, she ran to the pigsty, each step a rushing out into emptiness. She climbed over the fence and knelt in the dirt. It was good to have a fence enclosing her, a tribal person alone.

Laboring, this woman who had carried her child as a foreign growth that 43 sickened her every day, expelled it at last. She reached down to touch the hot, wet, moving mass, surely smaller than anything human, and could feel that it was human after all—fingers, toes, nails, nose. She pulled it up on to her belly, and it lay curled there, butt in the air, feet precisely tucked one under the other. She opened her loose shirt and buttoned the child inside. After resting, it squirmed and thrashed and she pushed it up to her breast. It turned its head this way and that until it found her nipple. There, it made little snuffling noises. She clenched her teeth at its preciousness, lovely as a young calf, a piglet, a little dog.

She may have gone to the pigsty as a last act of responsibility: she would 44 protect this child as she had protected its father. It would look after her soul, leaving supplies on her grave. But how would this tiny child without family find her grave when there would be no marker for her anywhere, neither in the earth nor the family hall? No one would give her a family hall name. She had taken the child with her into the wastes. At its birth the two of them had felt the same raw pain of separation, a wound that only the family pressing tight could close. A child with no descent line would not soften her life but only trail after her, ghost-like, begging her to give it purpose. At dawn the villagers on their way to the fields would stand around the fence and look.

Full of milk, the little ghost slept. When it awoke, she hardened her breasts 45 against the milk that crying loosens. Toward morning she picked up the baby and walked to the well.

Carrying the baby to the well shows loving. Otherwise abandon it. Turn its 46 face into the mud. Mothers who love their children take them along. It was prob-ably a girl; there is some hope of forgiveness for boys.

"Don't tell anyone you had an aunt. Your father does not want to hear her 47 name. She has never been born." I have believed that sex was unspeakable and words so strong and fathers so frail that "aunt" would do my father mysterious harm. I have thought that my family, having settled among immigrants who had also been their neighbors in the ancestral land, needed to clean their name, and a wrong word would incite the kinspeople even here. But there is more to this silence: they want me to participate in her punishment. And I have.

In the twenty years since I heard this story I have not asked for details nor 48 said my aunt's name; I do not know it. People who can comfort the dead can also chase after them to hurt them further—a reverse ancestor worship. The real pun-ishment was not the raid swiftly inflicted by the villagers, but the family's delib-erately forgetting her. Her betrayal so maddened them, they saw to it that she would suffer forever, even after death. Always hungry, always needing, she would have to beg food from other ghosts, snatch and steal it from those whose living descendants give them gifts. She would have to fight the ghosts massed at cross-roads for the buns a few thoughtful citizens leave to decoy her away from village and home so that the ancestral spirits could feast unharassed. At peace, they could act like gods, not ghosts, their descent lines providing them with paper suits and dresses, spirit money, paper houses, paper automobiles, chicken, meat, and rice into eternity—essences delivered up in smoke and flames, steam and incense ris-ing from each rice bowl. In an attempt to make the Chinese care for people out-side the family, Chairman Mao encourages us now to give our paper replicas to the spirits of outstanding soldiers and workers, no matter whose ancestors they may be. My aunt remains forever hungry. Goods are not distributed evenly among the dead.

My aunt haunts me—her ghost drawn to me because now, after fifty years 49 of neglect, I alone devote pages of paper to her, though not origamied into houses and clothes. I do not think she always means me well. I am telling on her, and she was a spite suicide, drowning herself in the drinking water. The Chinese are always very frightened of the drowned one, whose weeping ghost, wet hair hanging and skin bloated, waits silently by the water to pull down a substitute.

QUESTIONS FOR CRITICAL READING, THINKING, DISCUSSION, AND WRITING

Analyzing Content and Technique

1. Why is the house where the narrator's aunt lives raided by the villagers?
2. Analyze the character of the aunt as imagined by the narrator, paying special attention to the contradictory aspects. What enables the narrator to possess these contradictory ideas about her aunt? Discuss what the writer is saying about the power of the imagination through these contradictory portrayals.
3. Why does the narrator's aunt have no name? How does the narrator feel about this, and about her aunt's suicide?
4. How did the Chinese attempt to control sexual relationships in China? How do they do this in the United States?
5. Why does the narrator find it difficult to understand the traditions and customs of China? Which customs does she find particularly difficult to live with?
6. Throughout selection 21, the narrator reinforces the idea that she really does not know much about her aunt. Where does she do this? How is she able to keep our interest in spite of her lack of knowledge? What does this lack of knowledge, coming out of a silence that has been imposed on the women in the family, say about her culture?

Collaborative Activity

Have each member of the group take on the role of one of the characters mentioned in the excerpt—the narrator's mother, the narrator, one of the villagers, the absent husband, and so forth—and write a paragraph about how he or she felt upon hearing of the aunt's death. Read the paragraphs to the group and discuss them, analyzing the different social values inherent in each response.

Making Connections

1. The No Name Woman of the title has a powerful influence on the narrator even though she has never met her. Why? Write an essay in which you explore the reasons for the narrator's obsession with her aunt and examine the ways in which she has affected the narrator's thinking and actions.
2. In many parts of the excerpt, the narrator seems to be in conflict with her heritage, especially in terms of the roles it prescribes for men and women and the sexuality allowed to each. How do you feel about the customs and taboos she depicts? Why? Write an essay in which you analyze them and explain your attitude toward them, carefully keeping in mind the context out of which these customs arise.

22

PREREADING ACTIVITY

Before you read selection 22, write about how important or unimportant punctuality is for you. Do you always try to do things on time? How do you react if someone else is late? Do other people of your cultural background share your attitude toward punctuality?

Social Time: The Heartbeat of Culture

ROBERT LEVINE AND ELLEN WOLFF

Robert Levine is a professor of psychology at the University of California at Irvine. He has taught in many countries. Ellen Wolff is a free-lance writer. This selection first appeared in *Psychology Today*.

"*If a man does not keep pace with his companions, perhaps it is because* 1
he hears a different drummer." This thought by Thoreau strikes a chord in so many people that it has become part of our language. We use the phrase "the beat of a different drummer" to explain any pace of life unlike our own. Such colorful vagueness reveals how informal our rules of time really are. The world over, children simply "pick up" their society's time concepts as they mature. No dictionary clearly defines the meaning of "early" or "late" for them or for strangers who stumble over the maddening incongruities between the time sense they bring with them and the one they face in a new land.

I learned this firsthand, a few years ago, and the resulting culture shock led 2
me halfway around the world to find answers. It seemed clear that time "talks." But what is it telling us?

My journey started shortly after I accepted an appointment as visiting pro- 3
fessor of psychology at the federal university in Niterói, Brazil, a midsized city across the bay from Rio de Janeiro. As I left home for my first day of class, I asked someone the time. It was 9:05 A.M., which allowed me time to relax and look around the campus before my 10 o'clock lecture. After what I judged to be half an hour, I glanced at a clock I was passing. It said 10:20! In panic, I broke for the classroom, followed by gentle calls of "Hola, professor" and "Tudo bem, professor?" from unhurried students, many of whom, I later realized, were my own. I arrived breathless to find an empty room.

154

Frantically, I asked a passerby the time. "Nine forty-five" was the answer. 4
No, that couldn't be. I asked someone else. "Nine fifty-five." Another said:
"Exactly 9:43." The clock in a nearby office read 3:15. I had learned my first lesson about Brazilians: Their time pieces are consistently inaccurate. And nobody
minds.

My class was scheduled from 10 until noon. Many students came late, some 5
very late. Several arrived after 10:30. A few showed up closer to 11. Two came
after that. All of the latecomers wore the relaxed smiles that I came, later, to
enjoy. Each one said hello, and although a few apologized briefly, none seemed
terribly concerned about lateness. They assumed that I understood.

The idea of Brazilians arriving late was not a great shock. I had heard about 6
"mãnha," the Portuguese equivalent of "mañana" in Spanish. This term, meaning "tomorrow" or, "the morning," stereotypes the Brazilian who puts off the
business of today until tomorrow. The real surprise came at noon that first day,
when the end of class arrived.

Back home in California, I never need to look at a clock to know when the 7
class hour is ending. The shuffling of books is accompanied by strained expressions that say plaintively, "I'm starving. . . . I've got to go to the bathroom.
. . . I'm going to suffocate if you keep us one more second." (The pain usually
becomes unbearable at two minutes to the hour in undergraduate classes and five
minutes before the close of graduate classes.)

When noon arrived in my first Brazilian class, only a few students left imme- 8
diately. Others slowly drifted out during the next 15 minutes, and some continued asking me questions long after that. When several remaining students kicked
off their shoes at 12:30, I went into my own "starving/bathroom/suffocation"
routine.

I could not, in all honesty, attribute their lingering to my superb teaching 9
style. I had just spent two hours lecturing on statistics in halting Portuguese.
Apparently, for many of my students, staying late was simply of no more importance than arriving late in the first place. As I observed this casual approach in
infinite variations during the year, I learned that the "mãnha" stereotype over-
simplified the real Anglo/Brazilian differences in conceptions of time. Research
revealed a more complex picture.

With the assistance of colleagues Laurie West and Harry Reis, I compared 10
the time sense of 91 male and female students in Niterói with that of 107 similar
students at California State University in Fresno. The universities are similar in
academic quality and size, and the cities are both secondary metropolitan centers
with populations of about 350,000.

We asked students about their perceptions of time in several situations, such 11
as what they would consider late or early for a hypothetical lunch appointment
with a friend. The average Brazilian student defined lateness for lunch as 33½
minutes after the scheduled time, compared to only 19 minutes for the Fresno
students. But Brazilians also allowed an average of about 54 minutes before
they'd consider someone early, while the Fresno students drew the line at 24.

Are Brazilians simply more flexible in their concepts of time and punctual- 12
ity? And how does this relate to the stereotype of the apathetic, fatalistic and irre-

sponsible Latin temperament? When we asked students to give typical reasons for lateness, the Brazilians were less likely to attribute it to a lack of caring than the North Americans were. Instead, they pointed to unforeseen circumstances that the person couldn't control. Because they seemed less inclined to feel personally responsible for being late, they also expressed less regret for their own lateness and blamed others less when they were late.

We found similar differences in how students from the two countries char- 13 acterized people who were late for appointments. Unlike their North American counterparts, the Brazilian students believed that a person who is consistently late is probably more successful than one who is consistently on time. They seemed to accept the idea that someone of status is expected to arrive late. Lack of punctuality is a badge of success.

Even within our own country, of course, ideas of time and punctuality vary 14 considerably from place to place. Different regions and even cities have their own distinct rhythms and rules. Seemingly simple words like "now," snapped out by an impatient New Yorker, and "later," said by a relaxed Californian, suggest a world of difference. Despite our familiarity with these homegrown differences in tempo, problems with time present a major stumbling block to Americans abroad. Peace Corps volunteers told researchers James Spradley of Macalester College and Mark Phillips of the University of Washington that their greatest difficulties with other people, after language problems, were the general pace of life and the punctuality of others. Formal "clock time" may be a standard on which the world agrees, but "social time," the heartbeat of society, is something else again.

How a country paces its social life is a mystery to most outsiders, one that 15 we're just beginning to unravel. Twenty-six years ago, anthropologist Edward Hall noted in *The Silent Language* that informal patterns of time "are seldom, if ever, made explicit. They exist in the air around us. They are either familiar and comfortable, or unfamiliar and wrong." When we realize we are out of step, we often blame the people around us to make ourselves feel better.

Appreciating cultural differences in time sense becomes increasingly impor- 16 tant as modern communications put more and more people in daily contact. If we are to avoid misreading issues that involve time perceptions, we need to understand better our own cultural biases and those of others.

When people of different cultures interact, the potential for misunderstand- 17 ing exists on many levels. For example, members of Arab and Latin cultures usually stand much closer when they are speaking to people than we usually do in the United States, a fact we frequently misinterpret as aggression or disrespect. Similarly, we assign personality traits to groups with a pace of life that is markedly faster or slower than our own. We build ideas of national character, for example, around the traditional Swiss and German ability to "make the trains run on time." Westerners like ourselves define punctuality using precise measures of time: 5 minutes, 15 minutes, an hour. But according to Hall, in many Mediterranean Arab cultures there are only three sets of time: no time at all, now (which is of varying duration) and forever (too long). Because of this, Americans often find difficulty in getting Arabs to distinguish between waiting a long time and a very long time.

According to historian Will Durant, "No man in a hurry is quite civilized." 18 What do our time judgments say about our attitude toward life? How can a

North American, coming from a land of digital precision, relate to a North African who may consider a clock "the devil's mill"?

Each language has a vocabulary of time that does not always survive translation. When we translated our questionnaires into Portuguese for my Brazilian students, we found that English distinctions of time were not readily articulated in their language. Several of our questions concerned how long the respondent would wait for someone to arrive, as compared with when they hoped for arrival or actually expected the person would come. In Portuguese, the verbs "to wait for," "to hope for" and "to expect" are all translated as "esperar." We had to add further words of explanation to make the distinction clear to the Brazilian students. 19

To avoid these language problems, my Fresno colleague Kathy Bartlett and I decided to clock the pace of life in other countries by using as little language as possible. We looked directly at three basic indicators of time: the accuracy of a country's bank clocks, the speed at which pedestrians walked and the average time it took a postal clerk to sell us a single stamp. In six countries on three continents, we made observations in both the nation's largest urban area and a medium-sized city: Japan (Tokyo and Sendai), Taiwan (Taipei and Tainan), Indonesia (Jakarta and Solo), Italy (Rome and Florence), England (London and Bristol) and the United States (New York City and Rochester). 20

What we wanted to know was: Can we speak of a unitary concept called "pace of life"? What we've learned suggests that we can. There appears to be a very strong relationship (see chart below) between the accuracy of clock time, walking speed and postal efficiency across the countries we studied. 21

We checked 15 clocks in each city, selecting them at random in downtown banks and comparing the time they showed with that reported by the local telephone company. In Japan, which leads the way in accuracy, the clocks averaged just over half a minute early or late. Indonesian clocks, the least accurate, were more than three minutes off the mark. 22

I will be interested to see how the digital-information age will affect our perceptions of time. In the United States today, we are reminded of the exact hour of the day more than ever, through little symphonies of beeps emanating from people's digital watches. As they become the norm, I fear our sense of precision may take an absurd twist. The other day, when I asked for the time, a student looked at his watch and replied, "Three twelve and eighteen seconds." 23

The Pace of Life in Six Countries

	Accuracy of bank clocks	Walking speed	Post office speed
Japan	1	1	1
United States	2	3	2
England	4	2	3
Italy	5	4	6
Taiwan	3	5	4
Indonesia	6	6	5

Numbers (1 is the top value) indicate the comparative rankings of each country for each indicator of time sense.

"'Will you walk a little faster?' said a whiting to a snail. 'There's a porpoise 24
close behind us, and he's treading on my tail.'"

So goes the rhyme from *Alice in Wonderland*, which also gave us that 25
famous symbol of haste, the White Rabbit. He came to mind often as we measured the walking speeds in our experimental cities. We clocked how long it
took pedestrians to walk 100 feet along a main downtown street during business
hours on clear days. To eliminate the effects of socializing, we observed only
people walking alone, timing at least 100 in each city. We found, once again, that
the Japanese led the way, averaging just 20.7 seconds to cover the distance. The
English nosed out the Americans for second place—21.6 to 22.5 seconds—and
the Indonesians again trailed the pack, sauntering along at 27.2 seconds. As you
might guess, speed was greater in the larger city of each nation than in its
smaller one.

Our final measurement, the average time it took postal clerks to sell one 26
stamp, turned out to be less straight-forward than we expected. In each city,
including those in the United States, we presented clerks with a note in the native
language requesting a common-priced stamp—a 20-center in the United States,
for example. They were also handed paper money, equivalent of a $5 bill. In
Indonesia, this procedure led to more than we bargained for.

At the large central post office in Jakarta, I asked for the line to buy stamps 27
and was directed to a group of private vendors sitting outside. Each of them hustled for my business: "Hey, good stamps, mister!" "Best stamps here!" In the
smaller city of Solo, I found a volleyball game in progress when I arrived at the
main post office on Friday afternoon. Business hours, I was told, were over. When
I finally did get there during business hours, the clerk was more interested in discussing relatives in America. Would I like to meet his uncle in Cincinnati? Which
did I like better: California or the United States? Five people behind me in line
waited patiently. Instead of complaining, they began paying attention to our conversation.

When it came to efficiency of service, however, the Indonesians were not 28
the slowest, although they did place far behind the Japanese postal clerks, who
averaged 25 seconds. That distinction went to the Italians, whose infamous postal
service took 47 seconds on the average.

"A man who wastes one hour of time has not discovered the meaning of life. . . ." 29
That was Charles Darwin's belief, and many share it, perhaps at the cost of 30
their health. My colleagues and I have recently begun studying the relationship
between pace of life and well-being. Other researchers have demonstrated that a
chronic sense of urgency is a basic component of the Type A, coronary-prone
personality. We expect that future research will demonstrate that pace of life is
related to rate of heart disease, hypertension, ulcers, suicide, alcoholism, divorce
and other indicators of general psychological and physical well-being.

As you envision tomorrow's international society, do you wonder who will 31
set the pace? Americans eye Japan carefully, because the Japanese are obviously
"ahead of us" in measurable ways. In both countries, speed is frequently confused
with progress. Perhaps looking carefully at the different paces of life around the
world will help us distinguish more accurately between the two qualities. Clues

are everywhere but sometimes hard to distinguish. You have to listen carefully to hear the beat of even your own drummer.

QUESTIONS FOR CRITICAL READING, THINKING, DISCUSSION, AND WRITING

Analyzing Content and Technique

1. How do Brazilians, as opposed to people in the United States, view time? What philosophy of life can you deduce from this?
2. Compare and contrast the classroom behavior of Brazilian students with that of American students. Which do you prefer, and why?
3. What three "basic indicators of time" do Levine and Wolff choose in order to compare the pace of time in different countries? Are the indicators well chosen? Think of two other indicators that you might choose if you were conducting a similar experiment.
4. Paragraph 27 describes an attempt to buy stamps in Solo, Indonesia. What does the incident tell us about the lifestyle of people in this city? How would the scenario be different if this were a post office in your town or city?
5. What is the thesis of the piece and where is it placed? Paraphrase the thesis. How far do you agree with the writers? Why?
6. This essay first appeared in *Psychology Today*, a popular science- and psychology-oriented magazine. Which elements of Levine and Wolff's style indicate that they are writing for a nonacademic audience? List all the things they would have done differently if they had been writing this piece for a scholarly journal.

Collaborative Activity

Formulate a group list of questions you might ask someone that would give you a good indication of how he or she views time. (For example, do you get to appointments on time? Do you always wear a watch? How do you feel when guests arrive late? When you go to a bank for a simple transaction, how long does it take before you begin to get impatient?) Be creative and choose unusual questions. Have each member of the group interview one person outside of class, trying to choose a varied group in terms of age, occupation, race, financial background, and so forth. Report your findings to the class. What conclusions can the class draw from what you learned?

Making Connections

1. Toward the end of the essay, Levine and Wolff quote Darwin: "A man who wastes one hour of time has not discovered the meaning of life." Write an essay responding to this statement. Indicate clearly whether you agree or disagree with it, and why. Support your argument with examples from your own life and culture.
2. Levine and Wolff's essay and Mead and Metraux's essay (in Part Ten) demonstrate that societies have very different attitudes toward abstract concepts such as punctuality and friendship. Write an essay analyzing the attitudes of at least two social groups or cultures toward some concept other than these two (for example, hospitality, possession of material goods, equality of the sexes, obedience to authority, individualism). You should have some familiarity with the concept and the cultures you choose. Use the technique of illustration that Levine and Wolff give us in their essay.

23

Before you read selection 23, write about a person you remember from your childhood years, a person who symbolizes something important about your heritage. Describe this person so that your reader gets a sense of his or her character and lifestyle as well as your own attitude toward him or her.

The Last of the Kiowas

N. SCOTT MOMADAY

N. Scott Momaday (1934–) is a Native American, a Kiowa who grew up on a reservation in Oklahoma. He has a Ph.D. from Stanford University and teaches at the University of Arizona. His first novel, *House Made of Dawn,* won a Pulitzer Prize; his essays, poetry, and book reviews have appeared in magazines such as *The New York Times Book Review* and *National Geographic.* He has been awarded an Academy of American Poets Prize and a Guggenheim Fellowship. This selection is taken from his autobiography, *The Way to Rainy Mountain.*

A single knoll rises out of the plain in Oklahoma, north and west of the Wichita Range. For my people, the Kiowas, it is an old landmark, and they gave it the name Rainy Mountain. The hardest weather in the world is there. Winter brings blizzards, hot tornadic winds arise in the spring, and in summer the prairie is an anvil's edge. The grass turns brittle and brown, and it cracks beneath your feet. There are green belts along the rivers and creeks, linear groves of hickory and pecan, willow and witch hazel. At a distance in July or August the steaming foliage seems almost to writhe in fire. Great green and yellow grasshoppers are everywhere in the tall grass, popping up like corn to sting the flesh, and tortoises crawl about on the red earth, going nowhere in the plenty of time. Loneliness is an aspect of the land. All things in the plain are isolate; there is no confusion of objects in the eye, but *one* hill or *one* tree or *one* man. To look upon that landscape in the early morning, with the sun at your back, is to lose the sense of proportion. Your imagination comes to life, and this, you think, is where Creation was begun.

Source: First published in *The Reporter,* January 23, 1967. Reprinted from *The Way to Rainy Mountain,* © 1969, The University of New Mexico Press.

I returned to Rainy Mountain in July. My grandmother had died in the ₂ spring, and I wanted to be at her grave. She had lived to be very old and at last infirm. Her only living daughter was with her when she died, and I was told that in death her face was that of a child.

I like to think of her as a child. When she was born, the Kiowas were living ₃ the last great moment of their history. For more than a hundred years they had controlled the open range from the Smoky Hill River to the Red, from the head-waters of the Canadian to the fork of the Arkansas and Cimarron. In alliance with the Comanches, they had ruled the whole of the southern Plains. War was their sacred business, and they were among the finest horsemen the world has ever known. But warfare for the Kiowas was preeminently a matter of disposition rather than of survival, and they never understood the grim, unrelenting advance of the U.S. Cavalry. When at last, divided and ill-provisioned, they were driven onto the Staked Plains in the cold rains of autumn, they fell into panic. In Palo Duro Canyon they abandoned their crucial stores to pillage and had nothing then but their lives. In order to save themselves, they surrendered to the soldiers at Fort Sill and were imprisoned in the old stone corral that now stands as a mili-tary museum. My grandmother was spared the humiliation of those high gray walls by eight or ten years, but she must have known from birth the affliction of defeat, the dark brooding of old warriors.

Her name was Aho, and she belonged to the last culture to evolve in North ₄ America. Her forebears came down from the high country in western Montana nearly three centuries ago. They were a mountain people, a mysterious tribe of hunters whose language has never been positively classified in any major group. In the late seventeenth century they began a long migration to the south and east. It was a journey toward the dawn, and it led to a golden age. Along the way the Kiowas were befriended by the Crows, who gave them the culture and reli-gion of the Plains. They acquired horses, and their ancient nomadic spirit was suddenly free of the ground. They acquired Tai-me, the sacred Sun Dance doll, from that moment the object and symbol of their worship, and so shared in the divinity of the sun. Not least, they acquired the sense of destiny, therefore courage and pride. When they entered upon the southern Plains they had been transformed. No longer were they slaves to the simple necessity of survival; they were a lordly and dangerous society of fighters and thieves, hunters and priests of the sun. According to their origin myth, they entered the world through a hol-low log. From one point of view, their migration was the fruit of an old prophecy, for indeed they emerged from a sunless world.

Although my grandmother lived out her long life in the shadow of Rainy ₅ Mountain, the immense landscape of the continental interior lay like memory in her blood. She could tell of the Crows, whom she had never seen, and of the Black Hills, where she had never been. I wanted to see in reality what she had seen more perfectly in the mind's eye, and traveled fifteen hundred miles to begin my pilgrimage.

Yellowstone, it seemed to me, was the top of the world, a region of deep ₆ lakes and dark timber, canyons and waterfalls. But, beautiful as it is, one might have the sense of confinement there. The skyline in all directions is close at hand, the high wall of the woods and deep cleavages of shade. There is a perfect freedom in the mountains, but it belongs to the eagle and the elk, the badger and the bear. The Kiowas reckoned their stature by the distance they could see, and they were bent and blind in the wilderness.

Descending eastward, the highland meadows are a stairway to the plain. In July the inland slope of the Rockies is luxuriant with flax and buckwheat, stonecrop and larkspur. The earth unfolds and the limit of the land recedes. Clusters of trees, and animals grazing far in the distance, cause the vision to reach away and wonder to build upon the mind. The sun follows a longer course in the day, and the sky is immense beyond all comparison. The great billowing clouds that sail upon it are shadows that move upon the grain like water, dividing light. Farther down, in the land of the Crows and Blackfeet, the plain is yellow. Sweet clover takes hold of the hills and bends upon itself to cover and seal the soil. There the Kiowas paused on their way; they had come to the place where they must change their lives. The sun is at home on the plains. Precisely there does it have the certain character of a god. When the Kiowas came to the land of the Crows, they could see the dark lees of the hills at dawn across the Bighorn River, the profusion of light on the grain shelves, the oldest deity ranging after the solstices. Not yet would they veer southward to the caldron of the land that lay below; they must wean their blood from the northern winter and hold the mountains a while longer in their view. They bore Tai-me in procession to the east.

A dark mist lay over the Black Hills, and the land was like iron. At the top of a ridge I caught sight of Devil's Tower upthrust against the gray sky as if in the birth of time the core of the earth had broken through its crust and the motion of the world was begun. There are things in nature that engender an awful quiet in the heart of man; Devil's Tower is one of them. Two centuries ago, because they could not do otherwise, the Kiowas made a legend at the base of the rock. My grandmother said:

> Eight children were there at play, seven sisters and their brother. Suddenly the boy was struck dumb; he trembled and began to run upon his hands and feet. His fingers became claws, and his body was covered with fur. Directly there was a bear where the boy had been. The sisters were terrified; they ran, and the bear after them. They came to the stump of a great tree, and the tree spoke to them. It bade them climb upon it, and as they did so it began to rise into the air. The bear came to kill them, but they were just beyond its reach. It reared against the tree and scored the bark all around with its claws. The seven sisters were borne into the sky, and they became the stars of the Big Dipper.

From that moment, and so long as the legend lives, the Kiowas have kinsmen in the night sky. Whatever they were in the mountains, they could be no more. However tenuous their well-being, however much they had suffered and would suffer again, they had found a way out of the wilderness.

My grandmother had a reverence for the sun, a holy regard that now is all but gone out of mankind. There was a wariness in her, and an ancient awe. She was a Christian in her later years, but she had come a long way about, and she never forgot her birthright. As a child she had been to the Sun Dances; she had taken part in those annual rites, and by them she had learned the restoration of her people in the presence of Tai-me. She was about seven when the last Kiowa Sun Dance was held in 1887 on the Washita River above Rainy Mountain Creek. The buffalo were gone. In order to consummate the ancient sacrifice—to impale the head of a buffalo bull upon the medicine tree—a delegation of old men journeyed into Texas, there to beg and barter for an animal from the Goodnight herd. She was ten when the Kiowas came together for the last time as a living Sun Dance culture. They could find no buffalo; they had to hang an old hide from the sacred tree. Before the dance could begin, a company of soldiers rode out from Fort Sill under orders to disperse the tribe. Forbidden without cause the essential act of their faith, having seen the wild herds slaughtered and left to rot upon the ground, the Kiowas backed away forever from the medicine tree. That was July 20, 1890, at the great bend of the Washita. My grandmother was there. Without bitterness, and for as long as she lived, she bore a vision of deicide.

Now that I can have her only in memory, I see my grandmother in the sev- 10 eral postures that were peculiar to her: standing at the wood stove on a winter morning and turning meat in a great iron skillet; sitting at the south window, bent above her beadwork, and afterwards, when her vision failed, looking down for a long time into the fold of her hands; going out upon a cane, very slowly as she did when the weight of age came upon her; praying. I remember her most often at prayer. She made long, rambling prayers out of suffering and hope, having seen many things. I was never sure that I had the right to hear, so exclusive were they of all mere custom and company. The last time I saw her she prayed standing by the side of her bed at night, naked to the waist, the light of a kerosene lamp moving upon her dark skin. Her long, black hair, always drawn and braided in the day, lay upon her shoulders and against her breasts like a shawl. I do not speak Kiowa, and I never understood her prayers, but there was something inherently sad in the sound, some merest hesitation upon the syllables of sorrow. She began in a high and descending pitch, exhausting her breath to silence; then again and again—and always the same intensity of effort, of something that is, and is not, like urgency in the human voice. Transported so in the dancing light among the shadows of her room, she seemed beyond the reach of time. But that was illusion; I think I knew then that I should not see her again.

Houses are like sentinels in the plain, old keepers of the weather watch. 11 There, in a very little while, wood takes on the appearance of great age. All colors wear soon away in the wind and rain, and then the wood is burned gray and the grain appears and the nails turn red with rust. The windowpanes are black and opaque; you imagine there is nothing within, and indeed there are many ghosts, bones given up to the land. They stand here and there against the sky, and you approach them for a longer time than you expect. They belong in the distance; it is their domain.

Once there was a lot of sound in my grandmother's house, a lot of coming 12 and going, feasting and talk. The summers there were full of excitement and reunion. The Kiowas are a summer people; they abide the cold and keep to themselves, but when the season turns and the land becomes warm and vital they cannot hold still; an old love of going returns upon them. The aged visitors who came to my grandmother's house when I was a child were made of lean and leather, and they bore themselves upright. They wore great black hats and bright ample shirts that shook in the wind. They rubbed fat upon their hair and wound their braids with strips of colored cloth. Some of them painted their faces and carried the scars of old and cherished enmities. They were an old council of warlords, come to remind and be reminded of who they were. Their wives and daughters served them well. The women might indulge themselves; gossip was at once the mark and compensation of their servitude. They made loud and elaborate talk among themselves, full of jest and gesture, fright and false alarm. They went abroad in fringed and flowered shawls, bright beadwork and German silver. They were at home in the kitchen, and they prepared meals that were banquets.

There were frequent prayer meetings, and great nocturnal feasts. When I 13 was a child I played with my cousins outside, where the lamplight fell upon the ground and the singing of the old people rose up around us and carried away into the darkness. There were a lot of good things to eat, a lot of laughter and surprise. And afterwards, when the quiet returned, I lay down with my grandmother and could hear the frogs away by the river and feel the motion of the air.

Now there is a funeral silence in the rooms, the endless wake of some final 14 word. The walls have closed in upon my grandmother's house. When I returned to it in mourning, I saw for the first time in my life how small it was. It was late at night, and there was a white moon, nearly full. I sat for a long time on the stone steps by the kitchen door. From there I could see out across the land; I could see the long row of trees by the creek, the low light upon the rolling plains, and the stars of the Big Dipper. Once I looked at the moon and caught sight of a strange thing. A cricket had perched upon the handrail, only a few inches away from me. My line of vision was such that the creature filled the moon like a fossil. It had gone there, I thought, to live and die, for there, of all places, was its small definition made whole and eternal. A warm wind rose up and purled like the longing within me.

The next morning I awoke at dawn and went out on the dirt road to Rainy 15 Mountain. It was already hot, and the grasshoppers began to fill the air. Still, it was early in the morning, and the birds sang out of the shadows. The long yellow grass on the mountain shone in the bright light, and a scissortail hied above the land. There, where it ought to be, at the end of a long and legendary way, was my grandmother's grave. Here and there on the dark stones were ancestral names. Looking back once, I saw the mountain and came away.

QUESTIONS FOR CRITICAL READING, THINKING, DISCUSSION, AND WRITING

Analyzing Content and Technique

1. What is the immediate reason why Momaday returns to his grandmother's house? What is a larger reason?

2. Trace the movement of the Kiowas from Yellowstone to Rainy Mountain. Analyze some of the things they learn on the way. What might these be symbolic of? Why is it important for the writer to re-enact this journey? Explain the effect of this journey on him.
3. How does Momaday best remember his grandmother? Analyze the scenes in which she appears and create a character sketch of her.
4. What has the grandmother remembered of her own and her tribe's past? By sharing these memories with Momaday, what does she pass on to him?
5. Throughout the piece, animal images are associated with the Kiowas. Analyze these images and explain what they tell us about the characteristics and values of the Kiowas.
6. In this essay, Momaday has used several techniques more commonly found in poetry. One of these is alliteration, the patterned repetition of consonant sounds (for example, in paragraph 12, "full of jest and gesture, fright and false alarm; . . . fringed and flowered shawls, bright beadwork . . ."). Find other examples of alliteration in the essay. What effect does this device have on the reader?

Collaborative Activity

Have group members make a list of older people of their ethnic or cultural background who have had an important influence on the formation of their identity. Each member should choose one person from his or her list and write a paragraph on that person's influence. If there were no such people, the group member should write of the effect of that on his or her life. Share your paragraphs with the group, then choose one the group particularly likes to read aloud to the class.

Making Connections

1. Write an essay comparing the influence of Momaday's grandmother on him with the influence of Hong Kingston's aunt on her in "No Name Woman" (selection 21). What did the grandmother and the aunt teach the narrators about cultural values?
2. Research your own cultural background—your family roots—as Momaday did. You may interview people or use library resources. On the basis of your findings, write an essay discussing where your people came from (you may go back as far as you like), and what lifestyle and values they brought with them.

America's Emerging Gay Culture

RANDALL E. MAJORS

Born in Greenfield, Indiana, Randall E. Majors teaches business at California State University, Hayward. He has written several college textbooks, including *Basic Speech Communication* and *Business Communication*. This selection is taken from *Intercultural Communication*, an anthology edited by Larry Samovar and Richard Porter in 1988.

A gay culture, unique in the history of homosexuality, is emerging in   1
America. Gay people from all walks of life are forging new self-*identity* concepts, discovering new political and social power, and building a revolutionary new life style. As more people "come out," identify themselves as gay, and join with others to work and live as openly gay people, a stronger culture takes shape with each passing year.

There have always been homosexual men and women, but never before has   2
there emerged the notion of a distinct "culture" based on being gay.[1] A useful way to analyze this emerging gay culture is to observe the communication elements by which gay people construct their life styles and social institutions. Lesbians and gay men, hereafter considered together as gay people, are creating a new community in the midst of the American melting pot.[2] They are building social organizations, exercising political power, and solidifying a unique sense of identity—often under repressive and sometimes dangerous conditions. The following essay is an analysis of four major communicative elements of the American gay culture: the gay neighborhood, gay social groups, gay symbols, and gay meeting behavior. These communication behaviors will demonstrate the vibrancy and joy that a new culture offers the American vision of individual freedom and opportunity.

Source: From *Intercultural Communication: A Reader* by Larry Samovar and Richard E. Porter. Reprinted by permission of Gerry L. Coffey, executor of the Estate of Randall E. Majors.

The Gay Neighborhood

Most cultural groups find the need to mark out a home "turf." American social history has many examples of ethnic and social groups who create their own special communities, whether by withdrawing from the larger culture or by forming specialized groups within it. The utopian communities of the Amish or Shakers are examples of the first, and "ghetto" neighborhoods in large urban areas are examples of the latter.

This need to create a group territory fulfills several purposes for gay people. First, a gay person's sense of identity is reinforced if there is a special place that is somehow imbued with "gayness." When a neighborhood becomes the home of many gay people, the ground is created for a feeling of belonging and sharing with others. Signs of gayness, whether overt symbols like rainbow flags or more subtle cues such as merely the presence of other gay people on the street, create the feeling that a certain territory is special to the group and hospitable to the group's unique values.

How do you know when a neighborhood is gay? As with any generality, the rule of thumb is that "enough gay people in a neighborhood and it becomes a gay neighborhood." Rarely do gay people want to paint the streetlamps lavender, but the presence of many more subtle factors gives a gay character to an area. The most subtle cues are the presence of gay people as they take up residence in a district. Word spreads in the group that a certain area is starting to look attractive and open to gay members. There is often a move to "gentrify" older, more affordable sections of a city and build a new neighborhood out of the leftovers from the rush to the suburbs. Gay businesses, those operated by or catering to gay people, often develop once enough clientele is in the area. Social groups and services emerge that are oriented toward the members of the neighborhood. Eventually, the label of "gay neighborhood" is placed on an area, and the transformation is complete. The Castro area in San Francisco, Greenwich Village in New York, New Town in Chicago, the Westheimer district in Houston, and West Hollywood or Silver Lake in Los Angeles are examples of the many emergent gay neighborhoods in cities across America.[3]

A second need fulfilled by the gay neighborhood is the creation of a meeting ground. People can recognize and meet each other more easily when a higher density of population is established. It is not easy to grow up gay in America, gay people often feel "different" because of their sexual orientations. The surrounding heterosexual culture often tries to imprint sexual behaviors and expectations that do not suit gay natures. Because of this pressure, gay people often feel isolated and alienated, and the need for a meeting ground is very important.[4] Merely knowing that there is a specific place where other gay people live and work and play does much to anchor the psychological aspect of gayness in a tangible, physical reality. A gay person's sense of identity is reinforced by knowing that there is a home base, or a safe place where others of a similar persuasion are nearby.

Gay neighborhoods reinforce individual identity by focusing activities and events for members of the group. Celebrations of group unity and pride, demonstrations of group creativity and accomplishment, and services to individual members' needs are more easily developed when centralized. Gay neighborhoods are host to all the outward elements of a community—parades, demonstrations, car washes, basketball games, petition signing, street fairs, and garage sales.

A critical purpose for gay neighborhoods is that of physical and psycho- 8 logical safety. Subcultural groups usually experience some degree of persecution and oppression from the larger surrounding culture. For gay people, physical safety is a very real concern—incidences of homophobic assaults or harassment are common in most American cities.[5] By centralizing gay activities, some safeguards can be mounted, as large numbers of gay people living in proximity create a deterrence to violence. This may be informal awareness of the need to take extra precautions and to be on the alert to help other gay people in distress or in the form of actual street patrols or social groups, such as Community United Against Violence in San Francisco. A sense of psychological safety follows from these physical measures. Group consciousness raising on neighborhood safety and training in safety practices create a sense of group cohesion. The security inspired by the group creates a psychic comfort that offsets the paranoia that can be engendered by alienation and individual isolation.

Another significant result of gay neighborhoods is the political reality of 9 "clout."[6] In the context of American grassroots democracy, a predominantly gay population in an area can lead to political power. The concerns of gay people are taken more seriously by politicians and elected officials representing an area where voters can be registered and mustered into service during elections. In many areas, openly gay politicians represent gay constituencies directly and voice their concerns in ever-widening forums. The impact of this kind of democracy-in-action is felt on other institutions as well: police departments, social welfare agencies, schools, churches, and businesses. When a group centralizes its energy, members can bring pressure to bear on other cultural institutions, asking for and demanding attention to the unique needs of that group. Since American culture has a strong tradition of cultural diversity, gay neighborhoods are effective agents in the larger cultural acceptance of gay people. The gay rights movement, which attempts to secure housing, employment, and legal protection for gay people, finds its greatest support in the sense of community created by gay neighborhoods.

Gay Social Groups

On a smaller level than the neighborhood, specialized groups fulfill the 10 social needs of gay people. The need for affiliation—to make friends, to share recreation, to find life partners, or merely to while away the time—is a strong drive in any group of people. Many gay people suffer from an isolation caused by rejection by other people or by their own fear of being discovered as belonging to an unpopular group. This homophobia leads to difficulty in identifying and meeting other gay people who can help create a sense of dignity and caring. This is particularly true for gay teenagers who have limited opportunities to meet other gay people.[7] Gay social groups serve the important function of helping gay people locate each other so that this affiliation need can be met.

The development of gay social groups depends to a large degree on the number of gay people in an area and the perceived risk factor. In smaller towns and cities, there are often no meeting places, which exacerbates the problem of isolation. In some small towns a single business may be the only publicly known meeting place for gay people within hundreds of miles. In larger cities, however, an elaborate array of bars, clubs, social groups, churches, service agencies, entertainment groups, stores, restaurants, and the like add to the substance of a gay culture. [11]

The gay bar is often the first public gay experience for a gay person, and the gay bar serves as a central focus in gay life for many people. Beyond the personal need of meeting potential relationship partners, the gay bar also serves the functions of entertainment and social activity. Bars offer a wide range of attractions suited to gay people: movies, holiday celebrations, dancing, costume parties, live entertainment, free meals, boutiques, and meeting places for social groups. Uniquely gay forms of entertainment, such as drag shows and disco dancing, were common in gay bars before spreading into the general culture. Bars often become a very central part of a community's social life by sponsoring athletic teams, charities, community services, and other events as well as serving as meeting places. [12]

The centrality of the bar in gay culture has several drawbacks, however. Young gay people are denied entrance because of age restrictions, and there may be few other social outlets for them. A high rate of alcoholism among urban gay males is prominent. With the spread of Acquired Immune Deficiency Syndrome (AIDS), the use of bars for meeting sexual partners has declined dramatically as gay people turn to developing more permanent relationships.[8] [13]

Affiliation needs remain strong despite these dangers, however, and alternative social institutions arise that meet these needs. In large urban areas, where gay culture is more widely developed, social groups include athletic organizations that sponsor teams and tournaments; leisure activity clubs in such areas as country-and-western dance, music, yoga, bridge, hiking, and recreation; religious groups such as Dignity (Roman Catholic), Integrity (Episcopal), and the Metropolitan Community Church (MCC); volunteer agencies such as information and crisis hotlines and charitable organizations; and professional and political groups such as the Golden Gate Business Association of San Francisco or the national lobby group, the Gay Rights Task Force. A directory of groups and services is usually published in urban gay newspapers, and their activities are reported on and promoted actively. Taken together, these groups compose a culture that supports and nourishes a gay person's life. [14]

Gay Symbols

Gay culture is replete with symbols. These artifacts spring up and constantly evolve as gayness moves from being an individual, personal experience into a more complex public phenomenon. All groups express their ideas and values in symbols, and the gay culture, in spite of its relatively brief history, has been quite creative in symbol making. [15]

The most visible category of symbols is in the semantics of gay establish- 16
ment names. Gay bars, bookstores, restaurants, and social groups want to be recognized and patronized by gay people, but they do not want to incur hostility
from the general public. This was particularly true in the past when the threat of
social consequences was greater. In earlier days, gay bars, the only major form of
gay establishment, went by code words such as "blue" or "other"—the Blue Par-
rot, the Blue Goose, the Other Bar, and Another Place.

Since the liberalization of culture after the 1960s, semantics have blossomed 17
in gay place names. The general trend is still to identify the place as gay, either
through affiliation (Our Place or His 'N' Hers), humor (the White Swallow or
Uncle Charley's), high drama (the Elephant Walk or Backstreet), or sexual suggestion (Ripples, Cheeks, or Rocks). Lesbians and gay men differ in this aspect of
their cultures. Lesbian place names often rely upon a more personal or classical
referent (Amanda's Place or the Artemis Cafe), while hypermasculine referents
are commonly used for gay male meeting places (the Ramrod, Ambush, Man-
handlers, the Mine Shaft, the Stud, or Boots). Gay restaurants and non-
pornographic bookstores usually reflect more subdued names, drawing upon clev-
erness or historical associations: Dos Hermanos, Women and Children First,
Diana's, the Oscar Wilde Memorial Bookstore, and Walt Whitman Bookstore.
More commonly, gay establishments employ general naming trends of location,
ownership, or identification of product or service similar to their heterosexual
counterparts. The increasing tendency of businesses to target and cater to gay
markets strengthens the growth and diversity of gay culture.

A second set of gay symbols are those that serve as member-recognition fac- 18
tors. In past ages such nonverbal cues were so popular as to become mythic: the
arched eyebrow of Regency England, the green carnation of Oscar Wilde's day,
and the "green shirt on Thursday" signal of mid-century America. A large reper-
toire of identifying characteristics have arisen in recent years that serve the functions of recognizing other gay people and focusing on particular interests. In the
more sexually promiscuous period of the 1970s, popular identifying symbols were
a ring of keys worn on the belt, either left or right depending upon sexual passivity or aggressiveness, and the use of colored handkerchiefs in a rear pocket coded
to desired types of sexual activity. Political sentiments are commonly expressed
through buttons, such as the "No on 64" campaign against the LaRouche initiative in California in 1986. The pink triangle as a political symbol recalls the persecution and annihilation of gay people in Nazi Germany. The lambda symbol, an
ancient Greek referent, conjures up classical images of gay freedom of expression.
Stud earrings for men are gay symbols in some places, though such adornment has
evolved and is widely used for the expression of general countercultural attitudes.
The rainbow and the unicorn, mythical symbols associated with supernatural
potency, also are common signals of gay enchantment, fairy magic, and spiritual
uniqueness by the more "cosmic" elements of the gay community.

Another set of gay symbols to be aware of are the images of gay people as 19
portrayed in television, film, literature, and advertising. The general heterosexual
culture controls these media forms to a large extent, and the representations of
gay people in those media take on a straight set of expectations and assumptions.

The results are stereotypes that often oversimplify gay people and their values and do not discriminate the subtleties of human variety in gay culture. Since these stereotypes are generally unattractive, they are often the target of protests by gay people. Various authors have addressed the problem of heterosexual bias in the areas of film and literature.[9] As American culture gradually becomes more accepting of and tolerant toward gay people, these media representations become more realistic and sympathetic, but progress in this area is slow.

One hopeful development in the creation of positive gay role models has been the rise of an active gay market for literature. Most large cities have bookstores which stock literature supportive of gay culture. A more positive image for gay people is created through gay characters, heros, and stories that deal with the important issues of family, relationship, and social responsibility. This market is constantly threatened by harsh economic realities, however, and gay literature is not as well developed as it might be.[10]

Advertising probably has done the most to popularize and integrate gay symbols into American culture. Since money making is the goal of advertising, the use of gay symbols has advanced more rapidly in ad media than in the arts. Widely quoted research suggests that gay people, particularly men, have large, disposable incomes, so they become popular target markets for various products: tobacco, body-care products, clothing, alcohol, entertainment, and consumer goods. Typical gay-directed advertising in these product areas includes appeals based upon male bonding, such as are common in tobacco and alcohol sales ads, which are attractive to both straight and gay men since they stimulate the bonding need that is a part of both cultures.

Within gay culture, advertising has made dramatic advances in the past ten years, due to the rise of gay-related businesses and products. Gay advertising appears most obviously in media specifically directed at gay markets, such as gay magazines and newspapers, and in gay neighborhoods. Gay products and services are publicized with many of the same means as are their straight counterparts. Homoerotic art is widely used in clothing and body-care product ads. The male and female body are displayed for their physical and sexual appeal. This eroticizing of the body may be directed at either women or men as a desirable sexual object, and perhaps strikes at a subconscious homosexual potential in all people. Prominent elements of gay advertising are its use of sexuality and the central appeal of hypermasculinization. With the rise of sexual appeals in general advertising through double entendre, sexual punning, subliminal seduction, and erotic art work, it may be that gay advertising is only following suit in its emphasis on sexual appeals. Hugely muscled bodies and perfected masculine beauty adorn most advertising for gay products and services. Ads for greeting cards, billboards for travel service, bars, hotels, restaurants, and clothing stores tingle to the images of Hot 'N' Hunky Hamburgers, Hard On Leather, and the Brothel Hotel or its crosstown rival, the Anxious Arms. Some gay writers criticize this use of advertising as stereotyping and distorting of gay people, and certainly, misconceptions about the diversity in gay culture are more common than understanding. Gay people are far more average and normal than the images that appear in public media would suggest.

Gay Meeting Behavior

The final element of communication in the gay culture discussed here is the 23
vast set of behaviors by which gay people recognize and meet one another. In
more sexually active days before the concern for AIDS, this type of behavior was
commonly called cruising. Currently, promiscuous sexual behavior is far less common than it once was, and cruising has evolved into a more standard meeting
behavior that helps identify potential relationship partners.

Gay people meet each other in various contexts: in public situations, in the 24
workplace, in gay meeting places, and in the social contexts of friends and
acquaintances. Within each context, a different set of behaviors is employed by
which gay people recognize someone else as gay and determine the potential for
establishing a relationship. These behaviors include such nonverbal signaling as
frequency and length of interaction, posture, proximity, eye contact, eye movement and facial gestures, touch, affect displays, and paralinguistic signals.[11] The
constraints of each situation and the personal styles of the communicators create
great differences in the effectiveness and ease with which these behaviors are displayed.

Cruising serves several purposes besides the recognition of other gay peo- 25
ple. Most importantly, cruising is an expression of joy and pride in being gay.
Through cruising, gay people communicate their openness and willingness to
interact. Being gay is often compared to belonging to a universal—though invisible—fraternity or sorority. Gay people are generally friendly and open to meeting other gay people in social contexts because of the common experience of
rejection and isolation they have had growing up. Cruising is the means by which
gay people communicate their gayness and bridge the gap between stranger and
new-found friend.

Cruising has become an integral part of gay culture because it is such a 26
commonplace behavior. Without this interpersonal skill—and newcomers to gay
life often complain of the lack of comfort or ease they have with cruising—a gay
person can be at a distinct disadvantage in finding an easy path into the mainstream of gay culture. While cruising has a distinctly sexual overtone, the sexual
subtext is often a symbolic charade. Often the goals of cruising are no more than
friendship, companionship, or conversation. In this sense, cruising becomes more
an art form or an entertainment. Much as the "art of conversation" was the convention of a more genteel cultural age, gay cruising is the commonly accepted
vehicle of gay social interaction. The sexual element, however, transmitted by
double meaning, clever punning, or blatant nonverbal signals, remains a part of
cruising in even the most innocent of circumstances.

In earlier generations, a common stereotype of gay men focused on the use 27
of exaggerated, dramatic, and effeminate body language—the "limp wrist" image.
Also included in this negative image of gay people was cross-gender dressing,
known as "drag," and a specialized, sexually suggestive argot called "camp."[12]
Some gay people assumed these social roles because that was the picture of "what
it meant to be gay," but by and large these role behaviors were overthrown by the
gay liberation of the 1970s. Gay people became much less locked into these

restraining stereotypes and developed a much broader means of social expression. Currently, no stereotypic behavior would adequately describe gay communication style—it is far too diverse and integrated into mainstream American culture. Cruising evolved from these earlier forms of communication, but as a quintessential gay behavior, cruising has replaced the bitchy camp of an earlier generation of gay people.

The unique factor in gay cruising, and the one that distinguishes it from heterosexual cruising, is the level of practice and refinement the process receives. All cultural groups have means of introduction and meeting, recognition, assessment, and negotiation of a new relationship. In gay culture, however, the "courtship ritual" or friendship ritual of cruising is elaborately refined in its many variants and contexts. While straight people may use similar techniques in relationship formation and development, gay people are uniquely self-conscious in the centrality of these signals to the perpetuation of their culture. There is a sense of adventure and discovery in being "sexual outlaws," and cruising is the shared message of commitment to the gay life style.[13]

Conclusion

These four communication elements of gay culture comprise only a small part of what might be called gay culture. Other elements have been more widely discussed elsewhere: literature, the gay press, religion, politics, art, theater, and relationships. Gay culture is a marvelous and dynamic phenomenon. It is driven and buffeted by the energies of intense feeling and creative effort. Centuries of cultural repression that condemned gay people to disgrace and persecution have been turned upside down in a brief period of history. The results of this turbulence have the potential for either renaissance or cataclysm. The internalized fear and hatred of repression is balanced by the incredible joy and idealism of liberation. Through the celebration of its unique life style, gay culture promises to make a great contribution to the history of sexuality and to the rights of the individual. Whether it will fulfill this promise or succumb to the pressures that any creative attempt must face remains to be seen.

NOTES

1. Several good reviews of "famous homosexuals" include the following: Barbara Grier and Coletta Reid, *Lesbian Lives* (Oakland, Calif.: Diana Press, 1976); Noel I. Garde, *Jonathan to Gide: The Homosexual in History* (New York: Nosbooks, 1969); and A. L. Rowse, *The Homosexual in History* (Metuchen, N.J.: Scarecrow Press, 1975).

2. The relative differences and similarities between gay men and lesbians is a hotly debated issue in the gay/lesbian community. For the purposes of this paper, I have chosen to speak of them as a single unit. For an introduction to this issue, see Celia Kitzinger, *The Social Construction of Lesbianism* (Newbury Park, Calif.: Sage Publications, 1987).

3. An excellent analysis of the role of the Castro in California's gay culture is in Frances FitzGerald, *Cities on a Hill* (New York: Simon and Schuster, 1986). An entertaining source that discusses gay neighborhoods across America is Edmund White, *States of Desire: Travels in Gay America* (New York: E. P. Dutton, 1980).

4. For more information on the problems of gay self-identity, see Don Clark, *(The New) Loving Someone Gay* (Berkeley: Celestial Arts, 1987) and George Weinberg, *Society and the Healthy Homosexual* (New York: Doubleday, 1973).

5. A discussion of violence and its effects on gay people is in Dennis Altman, *The Homosexualization of America: The Americanization of Homosexuality* (New York: St. Martin's Press, 1982), pp. 100–101.

6. For a discussion of emerging gay politics, see Peter Fisher, *The Gay Mystique* (New York: Stein and Day, 1972) and Laud Humphreys, *Out of the Closets: The Sociology of Homosexual Liberation* (Englewood Cliffs, N.J.: Prentice-Hall, 1972).

7. Problems of young gay people are discussed in Mary V. Borhek, *Coming Out to Parents* (New York: Pilgrim Press 1983) and in story form in Mary V. Borhek, *My Son Eric* (New York: Pilgrim Press, 1979) and Aaron Fricke, *Reflections of a Rock Lobster* (New York: Alyson, 1981).

8. Gay relationships are discussed in Betty Berzon, *Permanent Partners: Building Gay and Lesbian Relationships That Last* (New York: E. P. Dutton, 1988) and David P. McWirter and Andrew M. Mattison, *The Male Couple* (Englewood Cliffs, N.J.: Prentice-Hall, 1984).

9. The treatment of gay people in literature is discussed in Barbara Grier, *The Lesbian in Literature* (Iowa City, Iowa: Naiad, 1988); George-Michel Sarotte, *Like a Brother, Like a Lover* (New York: Doubleday, 1978); Ian Young (Ed.), *The Male Homosexual in Literature: A Bibliography* (Metuchen, N.J.: Scarecrow Press, 1975); and Roger Austen, *Playing the Game: The Homosexual Novel in America* (Indianapolis: Bobbs-Merrill Press, 1977). Gay people in films are discussed in Parker Tyler, *Screening the Sexes: Homosexuality in the Movies* (New York: Holt, Rinehart, & Winston, 1972) and Vito Russo, *The Celluloid Closet: Lesbians and Gay Men in American Film* (New York: Harper & Row, 1980).

10. The emergence of positive roles is discussed in Betty Berzon, *Positively Gay* (Los Angeles: Mediamix Associates, 1979).

11. An excellent reference source for more information on gay communication research is Wayne R. Dynes, *Homosexuality: A Research Guide* (New York: Garland, 1987). He covers nonverbal communication in his section on "Social Semiotics," pp. 372 ff.

12. Camp is discussed in Susan Sontag, "Notes on Camp," *Against Interpretation* (New York: Dell, 1969). For a dictionary of antique camp language, see Bruce Rodgers, *The Queen's Vernacular: A Gay Lexicon* (New York: Simon and Schuster, 1972).

13. Altman discusses cruising in *The Homosexualization of America*, p. 176.

QUESTIONS FOR CRITICAL READING, THINKING, DISCUSSION, AND WRITING

Analyzing Content and Technique

1. Why do gay people feel a need to create a group territory? Of the several reasons provided by the writer, which do you consider the most important? Explain.

2. How is the gay social group different from the gay neighborhood in terms of the needs it fulfills? Why is it important to have such social groups?

3. Discuss the institution of the gay bar, enumerating its positive and negative aspects.

4. Analyze the symbols of gay culture. The writer has divided these symbols into several categories. What are these? Pick out from each category an example which you find particularly effective.

5. Why has advertising become interested in using gay symbols? Describe the methods used in gay advertising, comparing and contrasting them with those used by straight advertising.

6. What is the purpose of the essay? Upon what elements or techniques does the writer rely to achieve this purpose? Which parts of the essay interested you most? Evaluate its overall effectiveness.

Collaborative Activity

Have each group member look up and bring to class two advertisements, one gay and one straight, on the same product (for example, clothing, tobacco, alcohol). Discuss, as a group, how these are different or similar. What assumptions underlie each advertisement? Compare the group's conclusions to that provided by the author in paragraph 22.

Making Connections

1. In the opening paragraphs Majors asserts that gay culture today is unique because in earlier times there was never a notion of a distinct "culture" based on being gay. Research this idea to evaluate its accuracy, then write an essay in which you compare gay culture in America today with gay culture in another place and time. Do your findings lead you to agree or disagree with the author?
2. In paragraph 19, the writer states that representations of gay people in television, film, literature, and advertising are often stereotyped and unattractive. The article was first published in 1988. How far is the writer's claim still true? Research the images of gay people in the media and present your conclusions in an essay.

25

What do you know of the Amish? On what is your knowledge or assumptions based? For five minutes, sprint write your impressions of the Amish community. Come back to this activity after reading the selection below and add anything new that you have learned. Did the information presented in the selection surprise you? How?

Amish Economics

GENE LOGSDON

Gene Logsdon is a farmer in Upper Sandusky, Ohio. For over thirty years he has been raising corn, oats, hay, chickens, and sheep and writing on a wide range of issues related to farming. This piece is taken from *At Nature's Pace* (1994), Logsdon's account of Amish life and its positive effects on their farming methods.

The Amish have become a great embarrassment to American 1 agriculture. Many "English" farmers, as the Amish call the rest of us, are in desperate financial straits these days and relatively few are making money. As a result it is fashionable among writers, the clergy, politicians, farm machinery dealers and troubled farm banks to depict the family farmer as a dying breed and to weep great globs of crocodile tears over the coming funeral. All of them seem to forget those small, conservatively-financed family farms that are doing quite well, thank you, of which the premium example is the Amish.

Amish farmers are still making money in these hard times despite (or rather 2 because of) their supposedly outmoded, horse-farming ways. If one of them does get into financial jeopardy, it is most often from listening to the promises of modern agribusiness instead of traditional wisdom. His brethren will usually bail him out. More revealing, the Amish continue to farm profitably not only with an innocent disregard for get-big-or-get-out modern technology, but without participation in direct government subsidies other than those built into market prices, which they can't avoid.

I first learned about the startlingly effective economy of Amish life when I 3 was invited to a barn raising near Wooster, Ohio. A tornado had leveled four barns and acres of prime Amish timber. In just three weeks the downed trees were

Source: Excerpted from *At Nature's Pace* by Gene Logsdon, Pantheon Press, 1994. Reprinted by permission of the author.

sawn into girders, posts, and beams and the four barns rebuilt and filled with live-stock donated by neighbors to replace those killed by the storm. Three weeks. Nor were the barns the usual modern, one-story metal boxes hung on poles. They were huge buildings, three and four stories high, post-and-beam framed, and held together with hand-hewn mortises and tenons. I watched the raising of the last barn in open-mouthed awe. Some 400 Amish men and boys, acting and reacting like a hive of bees in absolute harmony of cooperation, started at sunrise with only a foundation and floor and by noon, *by noon,* had the huge edifice far enough along that you could put hay in it.

A contractor who was watching said it would have taken him and a beefed-up crew all summer to build the barn if, indeed, he could find anyone skilled enough at mortising to do it. He estimated the cost at $100,000. I asked the Amish farmer how much cash he would have in the barn. "About 30,000," he said. And some of that paid out by the Amish church's own insurance arrangements. "We give each other our labor," he explained. "We look forward to raisings. There are so many helping, no one has to work too hard. We get in a good visit." Not the biggest piece of the Rock imaginable carries that kind of insurance.

Not long afterwards, I gave a speech to an organization of farmers concerned with alternative methods of agriculture in which I commiserated at length with the plight of financially depressed farmers. When my talk was over, two Amish men approached me, offering mild criticism. "We have just finished one of our most financially successful years," one of them said. "It is only those farmers who have ignored common sense and tradition who are in trouble." What made his remarks more significant is that he went on to explain that he belonged to a group of Amish that had, as an experiment, temporarily allowed its members to use tractors in the field. He also was making payments on land that he had recently purchased. In other words, he was staring at the same economic gun that's pointed at English farmers and he was still coming out ahead. "But," he said, "I'm going back to horses. They're more profitable."

From then on, I resolved to start cultivating the Amish as assiduously as they cultivated their fields. I had always taken our sorghum to Joe Bontragger's press in the Kenton, Ohio area not far from our farm. We bought bulk foods and angelfood cake at the Peterscheims', and sought advice about operating a woodworking shop at Troyers', but now I expanded my horizons to include eastern Ohio, center of the largest Amish community in the world. When I helped a neighbor haul hay to that area, I received another lesson in Amish economics. If they need to buy extra feed for their livestock, they almost always choose to buy hay and raise the grain rather than vice versa. The price of the hay is partially regained as manure after it passes through the livestock since it allows them to cut down on the amount of fertilizer they need to buy. The greater mass of hay generates a greater mass of manure, adding organic matter to the soil. That is valuable beyond computer calculation. Grain farmers in my area who sold their straw and hay to the Amish were trading their soil fertility for cash of flitting value.

Whenever I got to know an Amish farmer well enough, I asked about farm profits. Always the answer was the same, spoken with careful modesty. Not as good as in the '70s, but still okay. I heard that in 1983, '84, and even '85, when finally the agribusiness magazines admitted that agriculture faced a full-blown crisis.

Eventually, or perhaps inevitably, I took my softball team to Holmes County for a cow-pasture doubleheader with neighborhood Amish players organized by David Kline, Abe Troyer and Dennis Weaver, among others. It was a grand day. We were perhaps a run better than the Amish, but they were twice as adept at dodging piles of manure. Our collected "womenfolk" cheered from the shade. The Amish bishop watched from his buggy behind home plate, sorely tempted, I was told, to join the game but afraid it might seem a bit demeaning to some of his congregation. The games themselves taught two lessons in economy. First, our uniforms of blue and gold cost me more money than I care to talk about. The Amish players, with their traditional denims, broadcloth shirts and straw hats, are always in uniform. Second, some of our player/farmers could not take time off from their high-tech machines to play in the game. The Amish, with their slow, centuries-old methods, had plenty of time. [8]

The games became prelude for discussions about Amish farm economy, since some of our players were farmers also. But long before these post-game discussions took place, Henry Hershberger taught me the deeper truth and wisdom of Amish economy. Hershberger is a bishop in the Schwartzentruber branch of the Amish, the strictest of the many sects. I went to visit Hershberger in 1983 because he had just gotten out of jail, which seemed to me a very curious place for an Amish bishop to be. Hershberger had been in jail because he would not apply for a building permit for his new house. Actually, he told me (in his new house), it was not the permit or building code regulations that got him in trouble with the law. He groped for the unfamiliar English words that would make the meaning clear. Most Amish can't meet certain requirements of the code because of religious convictions. But there is an understanding. The Amish buy the permit, then proceed to violate its rules on details, of lighting and plumbing or whatever, that their religion disallows. The authorities look the other way. [9]

Hershberger had given that practice considerable thought. Not only did it smack of dishonesty but, he realized with the wisdom of 400 years of Amish history that had survived more than one case of creeping totalitarianism, at any time the authorities could decide to enforce the letter of the law. This was particularly worrisome because it would mean greatly increased costs of construction, if indeed some way to get around the religious problem were found. But more importantly, it could mean, with the way the permit business is being handled, that authorities might someday stop Amish from building more houses on their farms. So Hershberger refused to play the game. The bureaucracy was ready to accommodate Hershberger's religion since it is common knowledge that the Amish build excellent houses for themselves—they would be fools not to, of course—but for Hershberger not to offer token obeisance to bureaucracy was unforgivable. That might lead, heaven forbid, to other people questioning the sanctity of the law. [10]

Taken to court, Hershberger was found guilty and given 30 days to pay up and get his permit. He refused. The judge, underestimating the resolve of a Schwartzentruber bishop, fined him $5,000. Hershberger refused to pay. The judge sent him to jail to work off his debt at $20 a day. A great public hue and [11] cry arose. In two weeks Hershberger was set free, still owing the court $4,720. The sheriff was ordered to seize enough property to satisfy the debt. But local auctioneers said they would not cry the sale. No one would haul the livestock. The judge resigned (for other reasons, I was told). Henry Hershberger lives in his new house, at peace, at least for now.

The flood of letters in the Wooster paper over the event became a commu- 12 nity examination of conscience. At first the debate centered on the question of "the law is the law" versus freedom of religion. But slowly the argument got down to the real issue of the permit law: Where does it lead? Who in fact is being protected? Henry Hershberger's contention that building permits can be used to keep housing out of certain areas if the powers on high want it that way is common knowledge: you just make the soil percolation requirement more rigid or start enforcing those already on the books. Nor do building codes guarantee good buildings, as every honest builder will tell you. Codes establish minimum standards which then become ceilings on quality, enabling minimum-standard builders to underbid high-standard builders, encouraging the latter to follow the minimum standards, too. Furthermore, building regulations are rather easily outmaneuvered, glossed over, and bribed away, if the rewards are high enough. Often building codes prevent people from building their own homes for lack of proper certification or a supposedly proper design. Building codes protect not the buyer but the builders, the suppliers of the approved materials, and an army of career regulators. The Amish understand all this. When a culture gives up the knowledge, ability and legality to build its own houses, the people pay. And pay.

But there are even more practical reasons why the Amish economy wants to 13 retain control over its housing. First of all, the Amish home doubles as an Amish church. How many millions of dollars this saves the Amish would be hard to calculate. Amish belief wisely provides for the appointment of ministers by lot. No hierarchy can evolve in Amishland. A minister works his farm like everyone else. That is mainly why the religion so effectively protects the Amish culture of agriculture. Its bishops do not sit in exceedingly well-insulated houses in far-off cities uttering pious pronouncements about the end of family farming.

Secondly, the Amish home doubles as the Amish retirement village and 14 nursing home, thereby saving incalculably more millions of dollars, not to mention the self-respect of the elderly. The Amish do not pay Social Security, nor do they accept it. They know and practice a much better security that requires neither pension nor lifelong savings.

There is an old Amish quiltmaker who lives near Pffeifer's Station, a cross- 15 roads store and village I often frequent. Her immediate family is long gone and she lives now with somewhat distant relatives who, being nearest of kin, are pledged to care for her. Her quarters are a wee bit of a house connected to the main house by a covered walkway. I make up excuses to visit, pretending to be interested in quilts. I have no idea how old she is, other than ancient.

Around her I feel the kind of otherworldly peace I used to feel around nuns 16 before they decided to dress up and hustle about like the rest of us. Her bedroom is just big enough for a bed and quilting frame; her kitchen equally tiny. The boys of the family keep the walkway stacked with firewood for her stove. She has her own little garden. Children play on her doorstep.

She has her privacy but surrounded by living love, not the dutiful profes- 17
sionalism of the old folks' home. And she still earns her way. Quilt buyers come,
adding to her waiting list more quilts than her fingers, now slowed by arthritis,
can ever catch up with. But when she puts down her Bible to dicker over price,
she is as canny a businesswoman as any.

I love that scene. She still lives in the real world. If she were not Amish, she 18
would have languished in some nursing home and no doubt be dead by now—
from sheer boredom if nothing else.

Between the ballgames, sorghum pressings and barnraisings, I have had the 19
chance to observe several Amish households enough to know that there are few
generalities. The Herschbergers of the Schwartzentruber Amish, the Bontraggers
and all who live near Kenton, Ohio, and the Holmes County neighborhood
where we played softball, all represent different economic levels. I do not wish to
say that one is financially better off than another, because I do not know. But
compared to a middle-class English household, the Hershbergers have the fewest
amenities—not even a soft chair, although there is a beautiful, century-old pen-
dulum clock on the wall. The nearby Kenton community is more "advanced"
compared to the Herschbergers'. The Holmes County houses are quite like our
own except for the lack of electricity. These latter houses sport gas appliances,
modem bathrooms, Maytag wringer washers with Honda gasoline motors (the
Amish housewives say Hondas start easier than Briggs & Stratton). Though I saw
none in the homes I visited, some Old Order Amish are allowed to use battery-
operated kitchen mixers and the like—even battery-operated electric typewriters!
Though there is something of a lack of interior decoration as we would call it
(unless you go in for the country-look craze), any middle-class American could
move into one of these Holmes County homes and not feel materially deprived
until habit called for television, radio, or record player.

There are no telephones in the homes, but the Amish use the telephone 20
booths that dot the roadsides. An Amishman views a telephone wire into the
home, like an electric line, as an umbilical cord tying it to dangerous worldly
influences. You will not talk so long or so often at a pay booth down the
road.

Whatever one's view of such fence-straddling religious convictions, they 21
obviously reveal tremendous economizing. In a 1972 study of Illinois Old Order
Amish similar to the Holmes County Amish, conducted by the Center for the
Biology of Natural Systems at Washington University in Saint Louis, Amish
housewives said they spent $10 to $15 a week on food and non-food groceries.
They reported household living expenses from $1,379 for a small, young family
up to $4,700 for a large, better-financed one. My own Amish informants thought
that today, that figure might top out at $8,000 for a large family, including trans-
portation by buggy and occasionally renting a car or riding a bus. A horse and
new buggy cost about $2,000 and last a good bit longer than a $12,000 car.
Throughout the Amish country in eastern Ohio, a vigorous small business has
grown up taxiing Amish around in vans, successfully competing with older private
bus lines that perform the same service at a higher price. Clothing is a low budget item for the Amish as they use long-wearing fabrics and often sew the clothes
themselves. Styles do not change.

Another surprising element in the Amish economy is the busy social life they lead within a day's ride by buggy or bicycle. We could scarcely schedule a softball game because there was always a wedding, a raising, a sale, a quilting, or church and school doings to attend! I can assure the world that the Amish have just as much fun as anyone, at far less than the cost of weekends made for Michelob.

Medical costs are the only expenses the Amish cannot control by their sub-economy. Religion forbids education beyond the early teens so they cannot generate their own doctors and medical facilities, and must pay the same ridiculous rates as the rest of us.

It is in agriculture that the Amish raise economy to a high art. After the ballgames, when talk got around to the hard times in farming today, the Amish said a *good* farmer could still make a good living with a herd of 20 to 25 cows. One of our players countered with mock seriousness: "Don't you know that you need at least 70 cows to make a living these days? Ohio State says so." "Oh my," an Amish dairyman replied, not entirely in jest. "If I could milk 70 cows, I'd be a millionaire." The Amish farmers all agreed that with 20 cows, a farmer could gross $50,000 in a good-weather year, of which "about half" would be net after paying farm expenses including taxes and interest on land debt if any. Deducting $8,000 for family living expenses still leaves a nice nest egg for emergencies, bad years and savings to help offspring get started in farming. Beginning farmers with higher interest payments than normal often work as carpenters or at other jobs on the side. These income estimates agree closely with those in the Washington University study mentioned above and those Wendell Berry reports in *The Gift of Good Land* (*WER* #33, p. 46), a book that demonstrates the sound fiscal foundation of small-scale, traditional farming, even—or especially—in a modern world.

Because my softball players shook their heads in disbelief at these figures, I asked one of the Amish farmers to compare his costs for producing a corn crop of 150 bushels per acre (his excellent yield in '84 and '85) with the 1984 Ohio State budget estimates as published each year by the state extension service. He returned the budget to me by mail with his figures. The first column of figures represents OSU's estimated typical cash grain farmer's cost per acre; the second, the Amish farmer's. I have added footnotes. (See Table on p. 182)

According to Ohio State experts, with the price of corn reckoned at $2.40 a bushel (lower now) a non-Amish farmer would gross $360 per acre against $393 in operating expenses for a net loss of $33 per acre, leading one farmer to comment, "It's a damn good thing I don't have a bigger farm." Meanwhile the Amish would realize a net profit of about $315 per acre. Even if you allow fixed costs in English accounting, Amish farming is better than expert farming by about $150 an acre. Just as important, the Amish seldom sell grain, but feed it to livestock and sell milk, meat, eggs, etc., thus retaining an even greater share of their profit dollar.

I told my Amish source he needed to add the cost of cultivating weeds out of the corn rows. He thought another dollar or two per acre would cover that, with horse cultivating. And, I added, he needed to add the cost of hauling all that manure to the fields. His response was a classic lesson in biological economy. "When I'm hauling manure, should I charge that to cleaning out the barn which

Item	1	2
Variable Costs		
Seed	$24.00	$18.66
Chemical fertilizer	63.00	9.10
Lime	8.00	5.06
Pesticides/herbicides	28.00[1]	2.50
Fuel, grease, oil	19.00	3.00*
Corn drying, fuel, electric	23.00	0.00
Trucking, fuel only	3.00	0.00
Repairs	13.00	.25*
Misc. supplies, utilities, soil tests, small tools, crop insurance, etc.	13.00	.50*
Interest on operating capital	12.00	.00
Fixed Costs		
Labor	9.00	0.00[2]
Machinery charge	50.00	5.00[3]
Land rental charge	110.00	0.00[4]
Management charge	18.00	0.00[5]
Total	$393.00	$44.07

*Estimated.

[1]Herbicide cost can be twice that or more if an application has to be repeated. Dennis Weaver, one of the Amish ballplayers, told me his herbicide cost was $14. "An acre?" I asked. "No," he replied. "Altogether."

[2]The Amish farmer explains that he hires no labor and considers his own as part of the profit, not of the cost.

[3]The Amish farmer said he didn't know exactly how to figure this because his machinery was so old it was "actually gaining in value now." His estimate is probably high. An Amish corn harvester, pulled by horses and powered by a Wisconsin 16HP motor, might cost $3,000 but likely half that. A typical agribusiness corn harvester costs over $100,000.

[4]If you don't rent land, this item is called cost of ownership. The Amishmen say owning the land is a reward, not a cost.

[5]"What does this mean?" the Amishman wrote. "Is this time spent asking experts how to farm?" Again he figures this as part of his salary, not a cost.

keeps the cows healthy, or to fertilizing the field which reduces the fertilizer bill and adds organic matter to the soil, which in turn helps it to use soil nutrients more efficiently and soak up rain better to reduce erosion? How much do you charge for that in your computer? Or maybe I should charge manure hauling to training the young colt in the harness or giving winter exercise to the older horses. Or maybe deduct manure from machinery wear because the ground gets mellower with manure and is easier to work. I don't know how to calculate all that *accurately* on a farm."

The most amazing part of the Amish economy to me is that, contrary to notions cherished by old farm magazine editors who escaped grim childhoods on 1930s farms for softer lives behind desks, the Amish do not work as hard, physically, as I did when my father and I were milking 100 cows with all the modern conveniences in the 1960s. English farmers like to make fun of the Amish for their hair-splitting ways with technology—allowing tractors or engines for stationary power tools but not in the fields. But in addition to keeping the Amish way of life intact, such compromises bring tremendous economy to their farming while lightening the workload. A motor-powered baler or corn harvester, pulled by horses ahead of a forecart, may seem ridiculous to a modern agribusinessman, but it saves thousands of dollars over buying tractors for this work. The reason tractors aren't allowed in the fields is that they would then tempt an Amishman to expand acreage, going into steep debt to do so, and in the process drive other Amish off the land—which is exactly why and how American agriculture got into the trouble engulfing it today.

To satisfy religious restrictions, the Amish have developed many other ingenious ideas to use modern technology in economizing ways. Other farmers should be studying, not belittling, them. When Grade A milk regulations forced electric cooling tanks on dairymen, the Amish adopted diesel motors to generate their own electricity for the milk room, cooler and milk machines. They say it's cheaper than buying electricity and keeps them secure from power outages. Similarly, they operate commercial woodworking and other shops with diesel-powered hydraulic pumps rather than individual electric motors for each tool. Their small woodworking shops, like their printing and publishing houses and a lot of other enterprises, make money where others so often fail.   29

Where Amish are active, countryside and town are full of hustling shops and small businesses, neat homes, solid schools and churches, and scores of roadside stands and cheese factories. East central Ohio even has a small woolen mill, one of the few remaining in the country. Compare this region with the decaying towns and empty farmsteads of the land dominated by large-scale agribusiness. The Amish economy spills out to affect the whole local economy. Some farmers, like Lancie Cleppinger near Mount Vernon, have the great good sense to farm like the Amish, even though they don't live like them. They enjoy profits too. When discussing the problems agribusiness farmers have brought on themselves, Cleppinger just keeps shaking his head and repeating, "What in the world are they thinking?" The Amish sum it up in a sentence: "Don't spend more than you make and life will be good to you." Uncle Deficit should be so wise.   30

QUESTIONS FOR CRITICAL READING, THINKING, DISCUSSION, AND WRITING

Analyzing Content and Technique

1. What is the tone of the opening statement, "The Amish have become a great embarrassment to American agriculture"? Why does the writer say this? How is this related to his thesis?
2. What did the writer learn from observing an Amish barn raising? Discuss the conclusions he draws from the event. How effective is the evidence he provides to support his point? Explain.
3. Why did the Amish bishop choose to build without buying a permit for his house? What long-term effects did he foresee?
4. Discuss the different ways in which the Amish home is so economically viable. What other added benefits does the writer see in the way in which it is set up?

5. Interpret the table of farming costs prepared by the writer. Where do the Amish save the most? How are they able to do this? What underlying cultural values are implied in the difference between "English" and Amish methods? What lessons, according to the writer, can "English" farmers learn from the Amish in this regard? Do you agree?
6. Identify the writer's use of transitional devices to move from one point to another. Pick out one or two you find particularly effective and explain your choice.

Collaborative Activity

As a group, discuss the lifestyle of the Amish. What advantages do you see in it? What disadvantages? Have each group member write down one Amish principle, belief, value, or habit that might help improve his or her lifestyle.

Making Connections

1. Going back to the group activity above, research in greater depth the advantages and disadvantages of the Amish lifestyle. Write a paper in which you weigh these against each other and come up with an overall evaluation of this way of living. How far is it possible, as the author suggests, for us to learn from Amish wisdom?
2. One of the elements the writer admires about Amish culture is that their homes double as retirement villages and nursing homes. Analyze the example of this which he provides. Why is this no longer possible in most other American homes today, although at one time it had been so? When did the change begin, and why? Write a paper in which you discuss your opinion of what happens to the elderly in much of America, giving specific reasons and examples to support your position.

26

PREREADING ACTIVITY

Before you read selection 26, write about the first time you were exposed to a culture different from your own, either directly or through the media. How was this culture different, and how did you feel about it?

An Indian Family in New York

BHARATI MUKHERJEE

Bharati Mukherjee (1940–), originally from India, has lived in Canada and the United States for over thirty years. She teaches at the University of California at Berkeley. Her fiction includes *The Middleman and Other Stories,* a winner of a National Book Critics Circle Award; *The Tiger's Daughter; Wife;* and *Jasmine,* from which this selection is taken. She is also the coauthor, with her husband Clark Blaise, of two nonfiction works, *Days and Nights in Calcutta* and *The Sorrow and the Terror.* Mukherjee has been awarded a Guggenheim Fellowship. The selection occurs at a point in the novel *Jasmine* when the title character, who has entered the country illegally, comes to live with the family of her dead husband's teacher.

*P*rofessorji and his family put me up for five months—and it could 1 have been five years, given the elasticity of the Indian family—just because I was the helpless widow of his favorite student. I was also efficient and uncomplaining, but they would have tolerated a clumsy whiner just as easily.

I want to be fair. Professorji is a generous man. Somehow, the trouble is in 2 me. I had jumped a track. His kind of generosity wasn't good enough for me. It wasn't Prakash's, it wasn't Lillian Gordon's.

The family consisted of his aged parents and his recent bride, Nirmala, a girl 3 of nineteen fresh from a village in the Patiala district. The marriage had been arranged about a year before. She was pretty enough to send a signal to any Indian in Flushing: *He may not look like much over here, but back in India this guy is considered quite a catch.*

In what I already considered "real life," meaning America, he was at least 4 forty, thickening and having to color his hair. He had a new name in New York. Here he was "Dave," not Devinder, and not even Professor, though I never called him anything but Professorji. When he answered the phone, "Dave Vadhera here," even the Vadhera sounded English. It sounded like "David O'Hara."

They had no children. He had avoided marriage until he had saved enough to afford two children, and to educate them in New York. Male or female did not matter, he was a progressive man. They'd been trying, according to Nirmala, who blushingly confided the occasional marital intimacy. I took enough interest in their problem to look and listen for signs of dedicated activity. Perhaps they were more imaginative than I gave them credit for. Nirmala was nineteen: According to my forged passport, I was nineteen too, but I was a widow. She was in the game, I was permanently on the sidelines. Professorji blamed his long hours and back pains. She blamed impurities in the food.

Pleading lab work, Professorji was out of the house by seven o'clock, five days a week. They both came back at six o'clock, harassed and foul-tempered, looking first for snacks and tea, later for a major dinner.

Should anyone ask, I was her "cousin-sister."

Nirmala worked all day in a sari store on our block. Selling upscale fabrics in Flushing indulged her taste for glamour and sophistication. The shop also sold 220-volt appliances, jewelry, and luggage. An adjacent shop under the same Gujarati ownership sold sweets and spices, and rented Hindi movies on cassettes. She was living in a little corner of heaven.

Every night, Nirmala brought home a new Hindi film for the VCR. Showings began promptly at nine o'clock, just after an enormous dinner, and lasted till midnight. They were Bombay's "B" efforts at best, commercial failures and quite a few famous flops, burnished again by the dim light of nostalgia. I could not unroll my sleeping mat until the film was over.

I felt my English was deserting me. During the parents' afternoon naps, I sometimes watched a soap opera. The American channels were otherwise never watched (Professorji's mother said, "There's so much English out there, why do we have to have it in here?"), but for the Saturday-morning Indian shows on cable. Nirmala brought plain saris and salwar-kameez outfits for me from the shop so I wouldn't have to embarrass myself or offend the old people in cast-off American T-shirts. The sari patterns were for much older women, widows.

I could not admit that I had accustomed myself to American clothes. American clothes disguised my widowhood. In a T-shirt and cords, I was taken for a student. In this apartment of artificially maintained Indianness, I wanted to distance myself from everything Indian, everything Jyoti-like. To them, I was a widow who should show a proper modesty of appearance and attitude. If not, it appeared I was competing with Nirmala.

Flushing, with all its immigrant services at hand, frightened me. I, who had every reason to fear America, was intrigued by the city and the land beyond the rivers. The Vadheras, who would soon have saved enough to buy a small apartment building in Astoria, had retired behind ghetto walls.

To date in her year in America, Nirmala had exhausted the available stock of Hindi films on tape and was now renting Urdu films from a Pakistani store.

She faced a grim future of unintelligible Bengali and Karnataka films. Everyone in Flushing seemed to know her craving. Visitors from India left tapes of popular Indian television series, and friends from Flushing were known to drive as far as New Jersey to check out the film holdings in the vast India emporia. They had a bookcase without books, stacked with television shows.

Professorji and Nirmala did not go out at night. "Why waste the money when we have everything here?" And truly they did. They had Indian-food stores in the block, Punjabi newspapers and Hindi film magazines at the corner newsstand, and a movie every night without having to dress up for it. They had a grateful servant who took her pay in food and saris. The parents were long asleep, no need to indulge ritual pleasantries. In the morning, the same film had to be shown again to the parents. Then I walked the rewound cassette back to the rental store.

Professorji's parents, both in their eighties and rather adventurous for their age, demanded constant care. There were thirty-two Indian families in our building of fifty apartments, so specialized as to language, religion, caste, and profession that we did not need to fraternize with anyone but other educated Punjabi-speaking Hindu Jats. There were six families more or less like Professorji's (plus Punjabi-speaking Sikh families who seemed friendly in the elevator and politically tame, though we didn't mingle), and three of the families also had aged parents living in. Every morning, then, it was a matter of escorting the senior Vadheras to other apartments, or else serving tea and fried snacks to elderly visitors.

Sundays the Vadheras allowed themselves free time. We squeezed onto the sofa in the living room and watched videos of Sanjeev Kumar movies or of Amitabh. Or we went to visit with other Punjabi families in sparsely furnished, crowded apartments in the same building and watched their videos. Sundays were our days to eat too much and give in to nostalgia, to take the carom board out of the coat closet, to sit cross-legged on dhurries and matchmake marriages for adolescent cousins or younger siblings. Of course, as a widow, I did not participate. Remarriage was out of the question within the normal community. There were always much older widowers with children to look after who might consider me, and this, I know, was secretly discussed, but my married life and chance at motherhood were safely over.

Professorji's father always lost a little money at poker. Professorji always got a little drunk. When he got drunk he complained that America was killing him. "You want stress," he asked anyone who would listen, "or you want big bank balance?"

The old folks' complaints were familiar ones. In India the groom's mother was absolute tyrant of the household. The young bride would quiver under her commands. But in New York, with a working wife, the mother-in-law was denied her venomous authority. The bent old lady who required my arm to make her way from the television to the bathroom had been harboring hatred and resentment of *her* mother-in-law for sixty-five years. Now that she *finally* had the occasion to vent it, Nirmala wasn't around to receive it. This was the tenor of all the old people's complaints—we have followed our children to America, and look what happens to us! Our sons are selfish. Our daughters want to work and stay thin. All the time, this rush-rush. What to do? There are no grandchildren for us to play with. This country has drained my son of his dum. This country has turned my daughter-in-law into a barren field. If we are doomed to die here, at least let us enjoy the good things of America: friends from our village, plentiful food, VCRs, air conditioning.

I felt myself deteriorating. I had gained so much weight I couldn't get into [19] the cords even when I tried. I couldn't understand the soap operas. I didn't know the answers to game shows. And so I cooked, shopped, and cleaned, tended the old folks, and made conversation with Professorji when he got home.

Professorji was a good man, by his lights, but he didn't seem the same car- [20] ing teacher who, in sleek blue American aerograms only months before, had tempted Prakash, his best engineering student, to leave the petty, luckless world of Jullundhar. Flushing was a neighborhood in Jullundhar. I was spiraling into depression behind the fortress of Punjabiness. Some afternoons when Professorji was out working, and Nirmala was in her shop, and the old Vadheras were snoring through their siestas, I would find myself in the bathroom with the light off, head down on the cold, cracked rim of the sink, sobbing from unnamed, unfulfilled wants. In Flushing I felt immured. An imaginary brick wall topped with barbed wire cut me off from the past and kept me from breaking into the future. I was a prisoner doing unreal time. Without a green card, even a forged one (I knew at least four men in our building who had bought themselves resident alien cards for between two and three thousand dollars), I didn't feel safe going outdoors. If I had a green card, a job, a goal, *happiness* would appear out of the blue.

One Monday—after a particularly boisterous Sunday—Professorji came [21] home around two in the afternoon and caught me crying as he barged into the dark bathroom. He seemed helpless before my grief. I tried to stop my sobbing and swallowing, but the more I tried, the harder the tears came.

Professorji turned on the light, and with it the noisy, hateful fan. "You're [22] like a daughter to me," he said, in his stiff, shy way. "Has anybody been treating you like a servant?"

Disappointments tumbled out of me. I told him I wanted a green card [23] more than anything else in the world, that a green card was freedom.

Professorji put the toilet lid down and sat on it cautiously. He lit a cigarette [24] and held it pinched between thumb and index finger, as my brothers used to. "A green card," he said, "is an expensive but not an impossible proposition. For the rich, such a matter is arranged daily."

"Then arrange it!" I begged. "Please! I'm dying in this limbo." I'd sign any [25] IOU he wanted, at any interest rate he fixed, if he would advance the two or three thousand.

"You?" Professorji smiled. "You think you have enough skills to pay me [26] back so much money within my lifetime?" He suggested I send word to my brothers to see if they could pay him in rupees. "For Prakash's sake," he said, "I'll make this concession. I'll take rupees." He quoted black-market exchange rates that weren't outrageously unfair.

I calculated in my head. Three thousand dollars would come to fifty thou- 27
sand rupees. My brothers were generous, loyal, ingenious men, but they couldn't
get together fifty thousand fixing motor scooters in Hasnapur. I wouldn't
demand it of them. Still, Professorji didn't have to know that.

I glared down at the embarrassed and unhappy man sitting on the toilet lid. 28
"The card is for me, and I shall make the payments." I had to believe that given
a chance I could make the payments.

"And how do you think you'll do that?" he said. He stood up and flushed 29
his cigarette. Then he said, "All right. I shall make all the necessary arrangements.
But this is not something we want to discuss with my wife and parents."

I was so thrown by his quick turnaround that I dropped to my knees and 30
touched his feet to thank him, as I would have done in Hasnapur. He walked
slowly out into the hall, as though my desperation hadn't gone head to head with
his generosity in the tiny bathroom.

Professorji came through, but he was emotionally tight, with Nirmala, with 31
his parents, with me. I was grateful, and I admired him, but I didn't understand
him. He was secretive, he was parsimonious with his affections. I remembered
Prakash's rage against Jagtiani, his depressions, his glee. He told me everything,
took pleasure in my adventures, small as they were. Nirmala had no idea where
her husband worked—he never told her. "What if there's an accident?" I asked,
and she smiled, like a child. "*He* will know," she said, using the pronoun. She had
no idea what he did. He was following an ancient prescription for marital accord:
silence, order, authority. So was she: submission, beauty, innocence.

One day his father cut his head open on the bathtub faucet. I couldn't 32
decide, because I didn't know enough about the old man's immigration status
and medical insurance, if I should rush him by taxi to a hospital or call the emergency squad. Old Mrs. Vadhera was screaming for a doctor, a priest, and her son.
I called Queens College and asked for Professor Vadhera. They asked which
department, and I didn't know. They checked every variant spelling, every
department, and couldn't find him. Try Queensborough College, the woman
suggested. Or LaGuardia Community. I did. Nothing.

Leaving the old woman in charge, I hurried down to Nirmala's sari shop. 33
She was sitting in the back with a Coke, watching an Urdu film. Scurrying
through old papers, she found an address for *him*. The Almighty Him. It was a
street number, not a college.

Flushing was not the downtown of dreams I'd conjured from the aerogram 34
back in Jullundhar. And Professorji was not a professor. He was an importer and
sorter of human hair. The hair came in great bundles from middlemen in villages
as small as Hasnapur all over India. The middlemen shipped the hair in switches.
Every weekday Professorji sat from eight o'clock till six on a kitchen ladder-stool
in a room he rented in the basement of the Khyber Bar BQ measuring and labeling the length and thickness of each separate hair.

Junk hair he sold to wigmakers. Fine hair to instrument makers. Eventually, 35
scientific instruments and the U.S. Defense Department. It was no exaggeration
to say that the security of the free world, in some small way, depended on the hair
of Indian village women. His integrity as a man of science, and as a businessman,

rested on the absolute guarantee that hair from Dave Vadhera met the highest standards and had been personally selected.

As for his father, he said he'd call a doctor friend, an uncertified but still 36 hopeful Delhi doctor working as a technician for a blood bank, who lived three floors down, to come around and bandage the wound. He acted more upset that I'd found him; *found him out.* He suspected that I'd deliberately shamed him, using the excuse of an injured father to pry information out of Nirmala. Now she'd get suspicious if *I* didn't talk about the university and his labs and all his assistants.

I told him not to worry. I would.   37

Actually, he said, he still was a scientist. America hadn't robbed him of his 38 self-respect. "No synthetic material has the human hair's tensile strength. How to gauge humidity without strands?" He picked out a long black hair from the 24-inch tray. "Like this beautiful one. How to read the weather?"

A hair from some peasant's head in Hasnapur could travel across oceans and 39 save an American meteorologist's reputation. Nothing was rooted anymore. Everything was in motion.

"You could sell your hair, if you wanted to. It is eighteen inches at least, I 40 think. We are purchasing Indian ladies' hair only. Indian women are purists, they're cleansing their hair with berries or yogurt only, they're not ruining their hair with shampoos, gels, dyes, and permanents. American women have horrible hair—this I have learned since settling here. Their hair lacks virginity and innocence."

I got the point. He needed to work here, but he didn't have to like it. He 41 had sealed his heart when he'd left home. His real life was in an unlivable land across oceans. He was a ghost, hanging on.

That's when he offered to introduce me to the master forger, another renter 42 in the Khyber basement. He made up a fake bill of sale, my future hair when it was twenty-four inches, for three thousand dollars. He was buying my silence for his shame, and I felt the shame as well.

A week later, I found myself calling Kate Gordon-Feldstein.   43

QUESTIONS FOR CRITICAL READING, THINKING, DISCUSSION, AND WRITING

Analyzing Content and Technique

1. Why does Professorji take the narrator into his home? Why is she not happy there? What changes does she begin to notice in herself while she is living with him?

2. Analyze the relationship between Professorji and his wife, Nirmala. What does it tell us about the traditional roles of husband and wife in Indian society? How does the narrator feel about these roles? Find a passage which summarizes the roles and her attitude toward them.

3. The video movie is an important symbol in this selection. What does it reveal about the characters? What does it indicate about a major theme or idea the writer is trying to convey? Identify another symbol in the selection, and explain what it signifies.

4. What do the old people complain about? What does this indicate about the lives of immigrants and the kinds of problems facing them? How do the characters deal with these problems?
5. In a passage that comes just before this excerpt, the narrator asks herself, "Can wanting be fatal?" In what way does this excerpt answer that question?
6. In what ways, stylistically as well as in terms of conveying ideas, is this selection, an excerpt from a novel, different from an essay? (To answer this, go back to one or two essays you have read in this book and observe how they work.)

Collaborative Activity

As a group, watch a movie (or a scene from a movie), suggested by your instructor, which depicts the lives of immigrants living in the United States. Discuss ways in which these immigrants have held on to their past and ways in which they have changed. Compare their lifestyles and values with those of the family Mukherjee writes about.

Making Connections

1. In this excerpt Mukherjee indicates through imagery and character the negative aspects of living a life isolated from mainstream culture. Do you agree with her that such a life is to be avoided? Write an essay in which you present your opinion based on library research. You may also include your own observations and interviews of immigrants.
2. Selection 26 makes the reader aware that the institution of marriage (and the role of each spouse) differs from culture to culture—and that even within the same culture, many variations are possible. Write an essay examining what marriage means in your culture. Possible questions to address: How do people choose a mate? What is expected of the husband and wife? What are some common problems with marriages? Is any of this changing? Possible sources of information and research are interviews with people—married and single—of different generations, library materials, statistics (regarding divorce, for example), and popular media (such as television shows, films, commercials, and newspaper advertisements).

27

What is a comment you've often heard people make about a behavior pattern supposedly characteristic of your cultural group? (For instance, "Americans talk too loudly.") Describe your feelings about or response to the statement you've cited.

The Japanese Syndrome (Student Essay)

KEIKO NOZOE

"Japanese people never want to make friends with people from other 1
countries," said my host-mother's father to me the other night at a party at her house. "They're always gathering around other Japanese, even when they're away from home."

"I was in Taiwan sometime back," he continued. "One night, I went to a 2
bar. There were some Japanese people there. I asked them to play billiards with me and even offered to buy them drinks. But they wouldn't talk to me, far less join me in a game. On the other hand, the Taiwanese in the bar were much friendlier. Several of them didn't speak English, and I of course didn't speak Taiwanese. But we got along just fine. Somehow we could communicate."

"I'm proud of the fact that I have friends from all over the world," he 3
ended. "But I've never managed to have a Japanese friend. I think the Japanese are the most difficult people to make friends with."

I was quite shocked at this statement, and initially quite upset as well. I have 4
always thought that the Japanese are the politest and friendliest people in the world. But when I analyzed my own behavior, and that of my fellow foreign students, I recognized that there was some truth to what my host-mother's father said. The Japanese do tend to stick to themselves, for a number of reasons. As a result, they do not easily make friends with people of other cultures.

Last spring quarter, my first at an American college, I took an ESL class. 5
The class consisted of students from many countries—Russia, Indonesia, Yugoslavia, Vietnam, Burma, China, etc. There were six Japanese students, including myself, and we became close friends very quickly. I always sat next to another Japanese. When I had questions about the class or the subject matter, I never asked the teacher or my classmates from other countries. I always asked my

Source: Student essay reprinted by permission.

friends, in Japanese. When we had group discussions in class, we always formed our own group. If we were forced by the teacher to join another group, we did not contribute much to the discussion.

Our situation, initially, was no different from that of our other classmates. They, too, were from other countries. For them, too, English was a second language. They, too, found people from their own culture in the class. However, unlike us, they never gathered in a group of their own, excluding the other students. They tried to speak English to each other at every chance they got, and they spoke up about their opinions. Their attitude was positive and outgoing, totally opposite to ours. As a result, they got along better with people. 6

The campus cafeteria was another place where I noticed the tendency of Japanese students to stick together. Every day after class, around 12:30 P.M., I had lunch with my friends. This was a time for almost all the Japanese students on campus to meet. We would occupy a large table and laugh and joke and have a good time. Although we knew we were all here to learn English, we would never speak it on our lunch break. As a result, soon the other students did not want to sit with us, since they could not join in our conversation. They felt that we were purposely creating an unfriendly language barrier between us and them. Many of them were upset with our attitude, and some let us know this quite clearly. 7

There are a number of factors causing this Japanese syndrome. The first is that most Japanese students are very self-conscious about their English-speaking skills, which they feel are inadequate. Most Japanese students in the United States studied English throughout junior high and high school back home. However, our teachers—who were themselves Japanese—did not speak English well. They emphasized grammar and vocabulary, not conversation or listening skills. As a result, when we came to the United States, we felt lost and disappointed. We had thought that because we had studied the language for six or more years and earned good grades, we would have no problems with our classes here. But we discovered that because of our pronunciation, Americans often could not understand what we said! Thus we could not express our ideas. This made us lose much of our self-confidence, especially as we come from a culture that stresses perfection. Even after taking ESL classes, we tended to avoid situations where we would have to talk to non-Japanese people. 8

The role of the student in the Japanese educational system also explains why we are unwilling to speak in learning situations. Japanese students are taught not to talk during class. In fact, few classes in Japan are set up to allow students to discuss class materials and express their opinions. They are supposed to be silent in class and listen carefully to the lecture. The teachers are happier this way. They feel that a student's silence is a mark of respect. That is why it is so hard for a Japanese person to speak up in class or even with a boss. 9

Next, certain differences in racial characteristics add to this problem. The Japanese are not good at talking to people they have just met. Compared with Americans, we are much more reserved. Americans can often converse immediately with strangers on a bus or in a restaurant. This is very uncommon in Japan. For example, when I first rode a bus in the United States, I was surprised to hear people talking to the driver and to the other passengers. Not only were they mak- 10 ing small talk, they were even discussing personal problems, like trouble with a boyfriend or girlfriend, or even divorce! I could not imagine behaving in this way with strangers on an Osaka bus.

Again, unlike most Americans, who are trained to be individualistic, most   11
Japanese have a strong need to belong to a group. This is because Japanese society always emphasizes the value of the group, and the importance of working for the group. Groups exist everywhere—in schools, at work, in neighborhoods. For example, from my elementary school days, I was part of a group of friends. We went everywhere together and did everything together. Everyone I knew belonged to a similar group. If they do not belong to a group, most Japanese tend to feel anxious and isolated. Therefore, as soon as we arrived in the United States, we looked for a group of Japanese students with whom we would feel comfortable, and we stayed with them.

One last explanation for this clustering tendency in Japanese students is that   12
we have always been used to a homogenous society. In Japan, unlike the United States, almost everyone is the same. Japan has the same race, language and culture throughout its four islands. Most people even have the same religion, as there are only two major ones, Buddhism and Christianity. Although there are people of other cultures living in Japan, such as Koreans and Chinese, they are treated as outsiders. We do not try to mix with them. We do not make an effort to make friends with them or talk to them or get to know them. Many Japanese feel uncomfortable with these "foreigners," even if they have been living in the country for generations. Some feel that Japanese culture is superior to the foreigners' cultures. When we come to the United States, many of us bring these attitudes about foreigners with us, and thus we are not comfortable mingling with people of other cultures and customs here.

My host-mother's father's comments have alerted me to a problem that a   13
Japanese person faces in the United States. Having thought about it, I can see how complex the causes of this problem are. But understanding them has made me want to change my behavior patterns. Otherwise I will never be able to speak up and let people know what I think. I will never be able to communicate and learn through friendship with people from other countries, or teach them about Japan. I may go back to Japan without really improving my English skills or increasing my knowledge of other cultures. Then my trip to the United States will have been a wasted opportunity.

STRUCTURE, STRATEGY, SUGGESTION

1. What is the main idea of selection 27? Is there a thesis sentence that states it explicitly?
2. What are the major reasons for the problem Nozoe describes? What writing strategies has she used to develop and support her reasons. Which seems to be the most important reason? Which seems best developed?
3. What technique has Nozoe used in her introduction? Is it a successful introduction? How else might this essay have been introduced?

4. The argument of the essay can be broken down into two parts. Where does the second part begin? What transition (if any) connects the two parts? Are there other transitions?

5. What one element do you consider most effective in this essay? Why? Which element do you feel could be improved? How would you improve it?

6. Write an essay describing a characteristic of your own culture. It can be either a positive or a negative characteristic. Analyze the reasons for its existence. Be sure to give plenty of supporting evidence. Avoid stereotyping and overgeneralization.

SYNTHESIS *Part Three*

1. Several of the authors in Part Three have focused on positive aspects of heritage, some have focused on ways in which heritage may become a burden, and some have presented both aspects. In an essay which draws on the material you have read, analyze the circumstances in which a heritage helps us to grow and the circumstances in which it tends to stifle us.

2. "Amish Economics" and "An Indian Family in New York" give us almost directly opposing viewpoints about cultural communities that keep to themselves. Write an essay comparing and contrasting the viewpoints of the two writers. What is it about the Amish community that makes their "withdrawal" from America a healthy one while Professorji's family gets caught in stagnation and negativity?

3. A number of selections in this section as well as others (such as selection 10) deal with the importance of rituals. Write a paper in which you give your opinion of the importance of rituals. Some questions you might consider are: How do we create rituals? Why are they important? Are there negative aspects to rituals? Which rituals are most easily created? Which are the hardest to carry when moving to a new culture? You may personalize this paper by giving examples of rituals from your life and lives you have observed.

4. Several selections in Part Three ("Amish Economics," "Last of the Kiowas," "Social Time: The Heartbeat of Culture," and "An Indian Family in New York") are about the dynamics that occur when two different cultures or lifestyles meet. In some selections this is seen, as expected, as difficult, confusing, and full of conflict. In some the writers see such a meeting as an exciting learning opportunity. Choose two selections and analyze the problem or opportunity the writer has described in each, focusing especially on what makes the experience positive or negative.

PART FOUR

Places We Call Home

SELECTIONS IN PART FOUR

PART 4: INTRODUCTION

How many of us still live in the house where we were born? Very few, for the lifestyle of the twentieth-century United States is extremely mobile. We move for a variety of reasons—for financial gain, for career opportunities, for higher education, because of family breakups, or just from a sense of adventure, a pioneering spirit. Perhaps because these frequent shifts underline its transience, the concept of home has become more important to us than ever before.

The writers in Part Four demonstrate that people think of "home" in many different ways. Beginning with the microcosmic, home can be a suit of clothes unique to our culture, as in Farley Mowat's "The Perfect House" (selection 30) or a residence that is set up to reflect our values, as in Yi-Fu Tuan's "American Space, Chinese Place" (selection 28). As we move beyond the immediate family to identify with a larger group, home can become a neighborhood, as in Mario Suarez's "El Hoyo" (selection 29); a city, as in Frances FitzGerald's "Gay Freedom Day Parade, San Francisco" (selection 32); or an entire country, as in Cathy Song's "Heaven" (selection 33). As this last piece indicates, home need not even be a physical place actually available to us. It can be an idea, a scent in the air, a certain quality of light that triggers an association. What is important is that it inspires in us a sense of belonging.

If the yin of home lies in this feeling of belonging, the yang of home lies in the pain that occurs when we somehow become estranged from it. Song's poem deals with a Chinese immigrant family dreaming of the perfect homeland in the midst of a hostile Denver slum. James R. Corey (selection 31) shows us that such alienation may unexpectedly occur when we return to the dreamed-of homeland after many years. And Lucretia Dibba (selection 34) mourns the ironic fact that idyllic memories of a past home may lead to feelings of present alienation.

The concept of home may cause new kinds of tensions in a multicultural, multiethnic society. What symbolizes home to one member or one generation of a family might be meaningless to another. The places or memories of places that one person holds dear might be the ones another person shuns. The daily living arrangements vital to one person's comfort might drive his or her roommate crazy. There is no consensus, no sacred central concept of home for us to hold on to and agree with.

Several writers in Part Four illustrate conflicts that arise as a result of this fractured notion of home. Few people would choose to live in Mowat's perfect house. El Hoyo, Suarez's special place, continues to be avoided by mainstream society. Song's narrator and her family face discrimination because their homeland is not the same as that of their neighbors.

The selections in Part Four raise many questions: If cultural values and attitudes toward home and what it means are so different, how can people coexist in harmony? If we can never return home after we have been changed by different lands and cultures, is it better—or at least safer—to remain in one place and not be exposed to other ways of thinking and living? Do neighborhoods characterized by ethnic solidarity unite us and make us stronger, or do they divide us from the rest of the nation? The writers seem to indicate that there are no easy answers, and perhaps no right answers. The only answers that will work for us are those that we fashion for ourselves, like the suits of the Ihalmiut, to fit the shapes of our lives.

28

PREREADING ACTIVITY

Write a letter to a person living in another country, describing your home. Explain, with specific details, important features (such as the family room, the master bedroom, and the Jacuzzi) that indicate a certain lifestyle.

American Space, Chinese Place

YI-FU TUAN

Yi-Fu Tuan (1930–) is from Tianjin, China. He holds graduate degrees in geography from Oxford University, England, and from the University of California at Berkeley and teaches at the University of Wisconsin. Among his books are *Space and Place: The Perspective of Experience* and *Dominance and Affection: The Making of Pets*. Selection 28 was first published in *Harper's Magazine*.

Americans have a sense of space, not of place. Go to an American 1 home in exurbia, and almost the first thing you do is drift toward the picture window. How curious that the first compliment you pay your host inside his house is to say how lovely it is outside his house! He is pleased that you should admire his vistas. The distant horizon is not merely a line separating earth from sky, it is a symbol of the future. The American is not rooted in his place, however lovely: his eyes are drawn by the expanding space to a point on the horizon, which is his future.

By contrast, consider the traditional Chinese home. Blank walls enclose it. 2 Step behind the spirit wall and you are in a courtyard with perhaps a miniature garden around the corner. Once inside the private compound you are wrapped in an ambiance of calm beauty, an ordered world of buildings, pavement, rock, and decorative vegetation. But you have no distant view: nowhere does space open out before you. Raw nature in such a home is experienced only as weather, and the only open space is the sky above. The Chinese is rooted in his place. When he has to leave, it is not for the promised land on the terrestrial horizon, but for another world altogether along the vertical, religious axis of his imagination.

The Chinese tie to place is deeply felt. Wanderlust is an alien sentiment. The 3 Taoist classic *Tao Te Ching* captures the ideal of rootedness in place with these words: "Though there may be another country in the neighborhood so close that they are within sight of each other and the crowing of cocks and barking of dogs in one place can be heard in the other, yet there is no traffic between them; and throughout their lives the two peoples have nothing to do with each other." In theory if not in practice, farmers have ranked high in Chinese society. The reason is not only that they are engaged in the "root" industry of producing food but that, unlike pecuniary merchants, they are tied to the land and do not abandon their country when it is in danger.

Nostalgia is a recurrent theme in Chinese poetry. An American reader of translated Chinese poems may well be taken aback—even put off—by the frequency, as well as the sentimentality of the lament for home. To understand the strength of this sentiment, we need to know that the Chinese desire for stability and rootedness in place is prompted by the constant threat of war, exile, and the natural disasters of flood and drought. Forcible removal makes the Chinese keenly aware of their loss. By contrast, Americans move, for the most part, voluntarily. Their nostalgia for home town is really longing for childhood to which they cannot return: in the meantime the future beckons and the future is "out there," in open space. When we criticize American rootlessness we tend to forget that it is a result of ideals we admire, namely, social mobility and optimism about the future. When we admire Chinese rootedness, we forget that the word "place" means both location in space and position in society: to be tied to place is also to be bound to one's station in life, with little hope of betterment. Space symbolizes hope; place, achievement and stability.

QUESTIONS FOR CRITICAL READING, THINKING, DISCUSSION, AND WRITING

Analyzing Content and Technique

1. The writer begins with a general philosophical and psychological statement about Americans: "Americans have a sense of space, not of place." Explain what he means by this. Do you agree with his ideas? Why or why not? What supporting evidence has the writer provided for his opinion?

2. Which feature of the Chinese home is most obviously different from the American home? How is this symbolic? What underlying cultural values can you discover in this difference?

3. Paragraph 3 (beginning "The Chinese tie to place . . .") deals exclusively with the Chinese temperament. What is the main idea of the paragraph? Write a paragraph on the same topic as it relates to Americans.

4. What sociohistorical reasons does the writer give for Chinese attitudes to place? For American attitudes?

5. What are the strong points of each culture with regard to home? What would you consider the disadvantages of each culture? (Tuan does not discuss this explicitly. Look for implications.)

6. Although this essay raises many thought-provoking issues, it does not always illustrate them with examples. Choose one such area in the essay and add an example of your own to support the writer's point.

Collaborative Activity

Discuss, as a group, the concept of the perfect home. What does your perfect home look like? Which rooms should be the largest? Where should the house be located? How important is the view? Should it be a new house, or one with many memories? Do your findings lead you to agree with Tuan's ideas about the American home? Is there a typical American home with typical features that most people desire?

Making Connections

1. Tuan suggests that a house reflects cultural values, some literally, but many symbolically. Keeping this idea in mind, examine the home of a person from another culture, either someone you have visited or someone you have encountered in a film or a book. In your essay, explain how the architecture and decor of this home reveal important aspects of the culture.
2. How has the American home changed over the last hundred years? Write an essay in which you compare and contrast the home you live in today to the kind of home a person of a similar background or class would have lived in a hundred years ago in this country, examining social and historical events or lifestyle shifts that might have contributed to this change.

29

PREREADING ACTIVITY

Before reading selection 29, take a few minutes to mentally visualize your neighborhood. How do you feel about living here? What kind of atmosphere does it possess? How well does it reflect the personalities and backgrounds of its inhabitants?

El Hoyo

Mario Suarez

Mario Suarez (1925–   ) was born in Tucson, Arizona, and studied at the University of Arizona. A writer of fiction, he has been awarded a Whitney Foundation Fellowship and has had several pieces published in the *Arizona Quarterly*. He brings to his writing his experiences in the Navy and in Brazil, where he lived for some years. But mostly he writes, he says, "for Chicanos about Chicanos." His novels include *A Guy's Worst Enemy*, *The Kiosk*, and *Mex Mecca*.

*F*rom the center of downtown Tucson the ground slopes gently away to Main Street, drops a few feet, and then rolls to the banks of the Santa Cruz River. Here lies the section of the city known as El Hoyo. Why it is called El Hoyo is not very clear. In no sense is it a hole as its name would imply; it is simply the river's immediate valley. Its inhabitants are chicanos who raise hell on Saturday night and listen to Padre Estanislao on Sunday morning. While the term chicano is the short way of saying Mexicano, it is not restricted to the paisanos who came from old Mexico with the territory or the last famine to work for the railroad, labor, sing, and go on relief. Chicano is the easy way of referring to everybody. Pablo Gutíerrez married the Chinese grocer's daughter and now runs a meat department; his sons are chicanos. So are the sons of Killer Jones who threw a fight in Harlem and fled to El Hoyo to marry Cristina Mendez. And so are all of them. However, it is doubtful that all these spiritual sons of Mexico live in El Hoyo because they love each other—many fight and bicker constantly. It is doubtful they live in El Hoyo because of its scenic beauty—it is everything but beautiful. Its houses are simple affairs of unplastered adobe, wood, and abandoned car parts. Its narrow streets are mostly clearings which have, in time,

Source: *Arizona Quarterly*, Summer 1947. Copyright 1947 Arizona Board of Regents. Reprinted by permission.

acquired names. Except for some tall trees which nobody has ever cared to identify, nurse, or destroy, the main things known to grow in the general area are weeds, garbage piles, dark-eyed chavalos, and dogs. And it is doubtful that the chicanos live in El Hoyo because it is safe—many times the Santa Cruz has risen and inundated the area.

In other respects living in El Hoyo has its advantages. If one is born with a weakness for acquiring bills, El Hoyo is where the collectors are less likely to find you. If one has acquired the habit of listening to Octavio Perea's Mexican Hour in the wee hours of the morning with the radio on at full blast, El Hoyo is where you are less likely to be reported to the authorities. Besides, Perea is very popular and sooner or later to everyone "Smoke In The Eyes" is dedicated between the pinto beans and white flour commercials. If one, for any reason whatever, comes on an extended period of hard times, where, if not in El Hoyo, are the neighbors more willing to offer solace? When Teofila Malacara's house burned to the ground with all her belongings and two children, a benevolent gentleman carried through the gesture that made tolerable her burden. He made a list of five hundred names and solicited from each a dollar. At the end of a month he turned over to the tearful but grateful señora one hundred dollars in cold cash and then accompanied her on a short vacation. When the new manager of a local store decided that no more chicanas were to work behind the counters, it was the chicanos of El Hoyo who, on taking their individually small but collectively great buying power elsewhere, drove the manager out and the girls returned to their jobs. When the Mexican Army was en route to Baja California and the chicanos found out that the enlisted men ate only at infrequent intervals, it was El Hoyo's chicanos who crusaded across town with pots of beans and trays of tortillas to meet the train. When someone gets married, celebrating is not restricted to the immediate friends of the couple. Everybody is invited. Anything calls for a celebration and a celebration calls for anything. On Memorial Day there are no less than half a dozen good fights at the Riverside Dance Hall. On Mexican Independence Day more than one flag is sworn allegiance to amid cheers for the queen.

And El Hoyo is something more. It is this something more which brought Felipe Sanchez back from the wars after having killed a score of Vietnamese with his body resembling a patchwork quilt to marry Julia Armijo. It brought Joe Zepeda, a gunner, . . . back to compose boleros. He has a metal plate for a skull. Perhaps El Hoyo is proof that those people exist, and perhaps exist best, who have as yet failed to observe the more popular modes of human conduct. Perhaps the humble appearance of El Hoyo justifies the indifferent shrug of those made aware of its existence. Perhaps El Hoyo's simplicity motivates an occasional chicano to move away from its narrow streets, babbling comadres and shrieking children to deny the bloodwell from which he springs and to claim the blood of a conquistador while his hair is straight and his face beardless. Yet El Hoyo is not an outpost of a few families against the world. It fights for no causes except those which soothe its immediate angers. It laughs and cries with the same amount of passion in times of plenty and of want.

Perhaps El Hoyo, its inhabitants, and its essence can best be explained by telling a bit about a dish called capirotada. Its origin is uncertain. But, according to the time and the circumstance, it is made of old, new or hard bread. It is softened with water and then cooked with peanuts, raisins, onions, cheese, and panocha. It is fired with sherry wine. Then it is served hot, cold, or just "on the weather" as they say in El Hoyo. The Sermeños like it one way, the Garcias another, and the Ortegas still another. While it might differ greatly from one home to another, nevertheless it is still capirotada. And so it is with El Hoyo's chicanos. While being divided from within and from without, like the capirotada, they remain chicanos.

QUESTIONS FOR CRITICAL READING, THINKING, DISCUSSION, AND WRITING

Analyzing Content and Technique

1. Describe the inhabitants of El Hoyo. Who are they? What do they possess in common? How are they different from the people who live in the suburbs? What is the writer's attitude toward them?

2. Suarez uses repetition in several passages in this essay. Locate some of them and analyze their effect. In what other way could Suarez have expressed the same ideas?

3. What are the advantages and disadvantages of living in El Hoyo? In your view, do the advantages outweigh the disadvantages, or vice versa?

4. Paragraph 3 begins, "And El Hoyo is something more." Suarez implies what "something more" is, but does not state it explicitly. What, in your opinion, is this additional quality that the neighborhood possesses?

5. Explain Suarez's attitude toward El Hoyo. Do you think he would like to live here? Why or why not? Would you like to live in a similar neighborhood? Why or why not?

6. This selection includes both specific and general statements. Identify a strong example of each and indicate how it contributes to the overall argumentative structure.

Collaborative Activity

Have group members write a paragraph about their neighbors. How well do they know them? What kind of interactions do they have with them? How friendly are they? Are they happy with these interactions? Discuss the paragraphs. Did most group members have the same kind of experience? What conclusions about neighborhood relationships in America can you draw from this activity?

Making Connections

1. As Suarez indicates, the ideal neighborhood can vary, depending on who you are and where you come from. Describe your concept of the ideal neighborhood. What would you look for in terms of location, atmosphere, culture, entertainment, neighbors, and so forth? Support your ideas with explanations, examples, and descriptions of actual neighborhoods you admire.

2. Using Suarez as a loose model, write an essay describing an ethnic (or otherwise culturally distinct) neighborhood and analyzing what gives it its distinct flavor. You may choose a place that is of your own culture or one you have observed as an outsider. Or you may do library research or conduct interviews to collect your material. Make sure your essay has a clear, strong thesis.

30

The Perfect House

FARLEY MOWAT

Canadian writer Farley Mowat (1921–) is well known for his writings, nonfiction, fiction, and young adult, on endangered animals and peoples. Educated at the University of Toronto, he has won many honors, such as the Mark Twain Award and the Author's Award from the Foundation for the Advancement of Canadian Letters. His books include *People of the Deer, My Discovery of America, Sea of Slaughter,* and two which were made into films: *Woman in the Mists: the Story of Dian Fossey,* and *Never Cry Wolf.*

As I grew to know the People, so my respect for their intelligence   1
and ingenuity increased. Yet it was a long time before I could reconcile my feelings of respect with the poor, shoddy dwelling places that they constructed. As with most Eskimos, the winter homes of the Ihalmiut are the snow-built domes we call igloos. (Igloo in Eskimo means simply "house" and thus an igloo can be built of wood or stone, as well as of snow.) But unlike most other Innuit, the Ihalmiut make snow houses which are cramped, miserable shelters. I think the People acquired the art of igloo construction quite recently in their history and from the coast Eskimos. Certainly they have no love for their igloos, and prefer the skin tents. This preference is related to the problem of fuel.

Any home in the arctic, in winter, requires some fuel if only for cooking.   2
The coast peoples make use of fat lamps, for they have an abundance of fat from the sea mammals they kill, and so they are able to cook in the igloo, and to heat it as well. But the Ihalmiut can ill afford to squander the precious fat of the deer, and they dare to burn only one tiny lamp for light. Willow must serve as fuel, and while willow burns well enough in a tent open at the peak to allow the smoke to

escape, when it is burned in a snow igloo, the choking smoke leaves no place for human occupants.

So snow houses replace the skin tents of the Ihalmiut only when winter has already grown old and the cold has reached the seemingly unbearable extremes of sixty or even seventy degrees below zero. Then the tents are grudgingly abandoned and snow huts built. From that time until spring no fires may burn inside the homes of the People, and such cooking as is attempted must be done outside, in the face of the blizzards and gales.

Yet though tents are preferred to igloos, it is still rather hard to understand why. . . . Great, gaping slits outline each hide on the frame of a tent. Such a home offers hardly more shelter than a thicket of trees, for on the unbroken sweep of the plains the winds blow with such violence that they drive the hard snow through the tents as if the skin walls did not really exist. But the People spend many days and dark nights in these feeble excuses for houses, while the wind rises like a demon of hatred and the cold comes as if it meant to destroy all life in the land.

In these tents there may be a fire; but consider this fire, this smoldering handful of green twigs, dug with infinite labor from under the drifts. It gives heat only for a few inches out from its sullen coals so that it barely suffices to boil a pot of water in an hour or two. The eternal winds pour into the tent and dissipate what little heat the fire can spare from the cook-pots. The fire gives comfort to the Ihalmiut only through its appeal to the eyes.

However, the tent with its wan little fire is a more desirable place than the snow house with no fire at all. At least the man in the tent can have a hot bowl of soup once in a while, but after life in the igloos begins, almost all food must be eaten while it is frozen to the hardness of rocks. Men sometimes take skin bags full of ice into the beds so that they can have water to drink, melted by the heat of their bodies. It is true that some of the People build cook shelters outside the igloos but these snow hearths burn very badly, and then only when it is calm. For the most part the winds prevent any outside cooking at all, and anyway by late winter the willow supply is so deeply buried under the drifts, it is almost impossible for men to procure it.

So you see that the homes of the Ihalmiut in winter are hardly models of comfort. Even when spring comes to the land the improvement in housing conditions is not great. After the tents go up in the spring, the rains begin. During daylight it rains with gray fury and the tents soak up the chill water until the hides hang slackly on their poles while rivulets pour through the tent to drench everything inside. At night, very likely, there will be frost and by dawn everything not under the robes with the sleepers will be frozen stiff.

With the end of the spring rains, the hot sun dries and shrinks the hides until they are drum-taut, but the ordeal is not yet over. Out of the steaming muskegs come the hordes of blood-sucking and flesh-eating flies and these find that the Ihalmiut tents offer no barrier to their invasion. The tents belong equally to the People and to the flies, until midsummer brings an end to the plague, and the hordes vanish.

My high opinion of the People was often clouded when I looked at their homes. I sometimes wondered if the Ihalmiut were as clever and as resourceful as

I thought them to be. I had been too long conditioned to think of home as four walls and a roof, and so the obvious solution of the Ihalmiut housing problem escaped me for nearly a year. It took me that long to realize that the People not only have good homes, but that they have devised the one perfect house.

The tent and the igloo are really only auxiliary shelters. The real home of the Ihalmio is much like that of the turtle, for it is what he carries about on his back. In truth it is the only house that can enable men to survive on the merciless plains of the Barrens. It has central heating from the fat furnace of the body, its walls are insulated to a degree of perfection that we white men have not been able to surpass, or even emulate. It is complete, light in weight, easy to make and easy to keep in repair. It costs nothing, for it is a gift of the land, through the deer. When I consider that house, my opinion of the astuteness of the Ihalmiut is no longer clouded.

Primarily the house consists of two suits of fur, worn one over the other, and each carefully tailored to the owner's dimensions. The inner suit is worn with the hair of the hides facing inward and touching the skin while the outer suit has its hair turned out to the weather. Each suit consists of a pullover parka with a hood, a pair of fur trousers, fur gloves and fur boots. The double motif is extended to the tips of the fingers, to the top of the head, and to the soles of the feet where soft slippers of harehide are worn next to the skin.

The high winter boots may be tied just above the knee so that they leave no entry for the cold blasts of the wind. But full ventilation is provided by the design of the parka. Both inner and outer parkas hang slackly to at least the knees of the wearer, and they are not belted in winter. Cold air does not rise, so that no drafts can move up under the parkas to reach the bare flesh, but the heavy, moisture-laden air from close to the body sinks through the gap between parka and trousers and is carried away. Even in times of great physical exertion, when the Ihalmio sweats freely, he is never in any danger of soaking his clothing and so inviting quick death from frost afterwards. The hides are not in contact with the body at all but are held away from the flesh by the soft resiliency of the deer hairs that line them, and in the space between the tips of the hair and the hide of the parka there is a constantly moving layer of warm air which absorbs all the sweat and carries it off.

Dressed for a day in the winter, the Ihalmio has this protection over all parts of his body, except for a narrow oval in front of his face—and even this is well protected by a long silken fringe of wolverine fur, the one fur to which the moisture of breathing will not adhere and freeze.

In the summer rain, the hide may grow wet, but the layer of air between deerhide and skin does not conduct the water, and so it runs off and is lost while the body stays dry. Then there is the question of weight. Most white men trying to live in the winter arctic load their bodies with at least twenty-five pounds of clothing, while the complete deerskin home of the Innuit weighs about seven pounds. This, of course, makes a great difference in the mobility of the wearers. A man wearing tight-fitting and too bulky clothes is almost as helpless as a man in a diver's suit. But besides their light weight, the Ihalmiut clothes are tailored so that they are slack wherever muscles must work freely beneath them. There is ample space in this house for the occupant to move and to breathe, for there are no partitions and walls to limit his motions, and the man is almost as free in his movements as if he were naked. If he must sleep out, without shelter, and it is fifty below, he has but to draw his arms into his parka, and he sleeps nearly as well as he would in a double-weight eiderdown bag.

This is in winter, but what about summer? I have explained how the porous 15 hide nevertheless acts as a raincoat. Well, it does much more than that. In summer the outer suit is discarded and all clothing pared down to one layer. The house then offers effective insulation against heat entry. It remains surprisingly cool, for it is efficiently ventilated. Also, and not least of its many advantages, it offers the nearest thing to perfect protection against the flies. The hood is pulled up so that it covers the neck and the ears, and the flies find it nearly impossible to get at the skin underneath. But of course the Ihalmiut have long since learned to live with the flies, and they feel none of the hysterical and frustrating rage against them so common with us.

In the case of women's clothing, home has two rooms. The back of the 16 parka has an enlargement, as if it were made to fit a hunchback, and in this space, called the *amaut,* lives the unweaned child of the family. A bundle of remarkably absorbent sphagnum moss goes under his backside and the child sits stark naked, in unrestricted delight, where he can look out on the world and very early in life become familiar with the sights and the moods of his land. He needs no clothing of his own, and as for the moss—in that land there is an unlimited supply of soft sphagnum and it can be replaced in an instant.

When the child is at length forced to vacate this pleasant apartment, 17 probably by the arrival of competition, he is equipped with a one-piece suit of hides which looks not unlike the snow suits our children wear in the winter. Only it is much lighter, more efficient, and much less restricting. This first home of his own is a fine home for the Ihalmio child, and one that his white relatives would envy if they could appreciate its real worth.

This then is the home of the People. It is the gift of the land, but mainly it 18 is the gift of Tuktu.*

QUESTIONS FOR CRITICAL READING, THINKING, DISCUSSION, AND WRITING

Analyzing Content and Technique

1. Find the thesis of the essay. Where is it placed? How is this placement unusual? Give reasons for the writer's choice of placement.
2. Analyze the structure of the essay by writing out a brief outline of the major points. How is the essay organized? How does this help the writer achieve his purpose?
3. What does the writer learn that surprises him? How does it change his preconceptions? What generalization can you make from this experience?
4. Why is the "perfect house" so well suited to the living conditions of the Ihalmiut? How is it better than the white man's inventions? Give specific details.

*The caribou.

5. Throughout the essay, Mowat implies that white men have a particular attitude toward the Eskimos. Explain this, supporting your answer with quotations. What is Mowat's attitude toward them?

Collaborative Activity

As a group, watch a movie or a video that depicts the homes, and lifestyles, of people from a "third world" culture. (Your instructor will be able to suggest titles.) Discuss these homes, examining them carefully for advantages that might not be immediately obvious. Write a collaborative paragraph based on your discussion.

Making Connections

1. As he observes the Ihalmiut, Mowat becomes aware of a change in his thinking process, which he realizes had been "conditioned" in a restrictive manner. Write an essay about another way in which you, or someone you know, have (had) been conditioned by the culture in which you live(d). Analyze the problem caused by this conditioning. How did you become aware of it? What possible solution(s) can you suggest?
2. In this essay, Mowat describes an Eskimo tribe that is still living in accordance with the old ways. This is no longer true of all Eskimos. Write a research paper in which you examine the effect of modernization on the lives of the Eskimos, weighing the advantages and disadvantages.

31

PREREADING ACTIVITY

Before reading selection 31, write about what you think the title means. What are some reasons why such a phenomenon might occur?

Cultural Shock in Reverse

JAMES R. COREY

James Corey (1937–) was brought up on a farm in Montana and has a doctoral degree in American studies from Washington State University. He taught for several years in Saudi Arabia at the University of Petroleum and Minerals, which was designed by King Faisal to encourage young Saudi Arabian men to study in their homeland instead of coming to the west for technical training. Corey has also visited Jordan on a Fulbright scholarship. He now teaches at the New Mexico Institute of Mining and Technology.

When an American university confers a doctoral degree upon a student from an underdeveloped country, it often does so with the expectation that the student will return home and become an instrument of change, of progress in his native land. We educators see the foreign student as a bearer of technological and cultural light from America. We see his future as effecting technological development and putting an end to ignorance, superstition, and other kinds of cultural backwardness.

The student, too, believes in this idea. Anyone who has met and talked with many third-world students knows the zeal with which that dream is held. However, not many American educators have the opportunity to see exactly what becomes of the new Ph.D., to observe what happens to his dream when he tries to realize it at home.

From 1969 to 1977, I taught in a university program in one of the world's most conservative developing countries—Saudi Arabia. I witnessed the return from America of the first significantly large group of Saudi Ph.D.'s. Virtually all of them held the ideal that I described above: to move Saudi Arabia into industrial utopia and out of cultural backwardness.

So far each of these young men has been confronted with the same cruel dilemma: If he wishes to assume a role in the prosperous and challenging area of

Source: *The Chronicle of Higher Education*, April 1979. Reprinted by permission of the author.

technological development, he must give up any plans to tamper directly with the cultural life of the country. In other words, he must buy his future wealth and position at the price of wearing blinders to the cultural problems around him. It is a purchase that produces more and more personal tension, frustration, and bitterness as years go by.

The young Saudi Ph.D. returning home after a lengthy stay in the U.S. 5 experiences something akin to reverse cultural shock. At 28 to 30 years of age, he has often spent up to 10 years—a third of his life—in America. When he steps off the plane in Jeddah or Riyadh or Dhahran, he re-enters an environment that is now foreign to him. Though Saudi Arabia has made progress toward modernity during the 10 years of his absence, it is only as an external mark on the landscape. At her cultural heart, she is as restrictive, as narrow, as apparently ignorant as she ever was when he was a youth.

Cultural traditions that he never questioned as a boy growing up in a 6 squatty, brown village now dismay him by their barbarity and irrationality. He is shocked by the backwardness: His mother and sisters still cannot go out in the streets without covering themselves from head to foot in an ugly, black veil, or *abayah*. His sisters have no choice of whom or when they marry. He himself will marry a girl he has probably never spoken to nor seen. Women he knows will die because their men will not allow male doctors to examine and treat them.

Or consider what the young man faces in the business and legal sectors 7 of the culture. The economic machinery of the country is almost without regulations; it is controlled by men's signatures. The question of what is possible in business is not answered by an examination of commercial codes and regulations, as would be the case in a developed country. Rather, the question of what is possible is directly proportional to a man's standing with those who control the economic machinery. Such a situation is ready-made for exploitation by the unscrupulous. In fact, that is precisely what the young returning Saudi sees: a business environment where paying off the men of influence is the accepted mode of operation, and a legal system that is inadequate to cope with the corruption.

In other areas the situation is just as bad. Deaths attributable to engineer- 8 ing incompetence occur daily. A girls' school collapsed recently, killing a score of youngsters. The highway-accident death rate in Saudi Arabia is appalling.

The problems of corruption and incompetence are the most devastating ills 9 of a developing country, but the returning Ph.D. is almost powerless to do anything about them. He is paralyzed by time-honored cultural patterns. For example, direct criticism is culturally taboo, unless the criticizing is done by the "right" sort of person—but even then the critic may be as likely to suffer cultural ostracism as is the one criticized. A young Saudi who has been tainted by exposure to a foreign culture does not dare to criticize.

To be bothered by payoffs and influence-peddling is to be an exception 10 in the culture. I recall, for example, trying to explain to a group of Saudi students why Vice-President Spiro Agnew was forced out of office. When I explained that Agnew, while governor of Maryland, was alleged to have accepted influence money from various contractors doing business with the state, my audience was unable to comprehend the offense. As one student put it, Why should a man want to be a governor except to use his position for personal financial gain?

As for criticism of incompetence, the critic will constantly confront the argument that the school collapsed or the car accident occurred because it was God's will that it should happen. Death, so the argument goes, is not something attributable to the engineer's or the builder's incompetence; death is the carrying out of God's plan.

Faced with those and similar cultural circumstances, the young idealist has few options. He can throw himself enthusiastically into a money-making area of the country's development, but to do so he must don a mask of cultural conservatism for the sake of the society around him. The mask will include wearing the correct national dress and disdaining foreign clothing styles, trimming his hair and moustache to the proper length and shape, marrying a local girl, speaking Arabic in public, and paying full lip service to the national religion.

But behind the mask he will live a quite different life. Within his own home, he will surround himself with the people and objects of his American life. His friends will be young and either foreigners or foreign-educated Arabs. He will speak English, his second language, almost as frequently as he will his native tongue. He will indulge his tastes for American food, drink, music, and reading material. Most importantly, he will escape from his own culture as often as possible. In fact, he will take as many business and vacation trips to the U.S. as he can possibly arrange.

This dual existence will not be without its adverse effects. I have often observed its results. It produces a tension which for some individuals is intolerable. Many cease to be able to perform productive work because their creative energies become paralyzed. Others discard whatever ideals they once had and become hedonists or alcoholics. A few live in self-imposed exile in the U.S. or elsewhere, waiting for a time when cultural changes will bring the country's technological and cultural advances abreast of each other.

But for most, the mask quickly becomes the true face of the man. Unable to cope for long with the tension of a dual existence, incapable of sustaining a "foreign" identity in his native land, the young Ph.D. simply reaccepts the culture. He allows himself to become an influence peddler and an incompetent. And when the next wave of young idealists arrives, they will find the first group standing in the way of their plan for social reform.

Saudi Arabia is, I am sure, not unique among the developing wealthy nations of the world. The same conditions apply throughout the Arabian peninsula—in Kuwait, Abu Dhabi, Dubai, Qatar, and the emirates of southern Arabia. They also exist in other emerging oil-rich countries—Libya, Algeria, Nigeria, and Iran, for example. It is those countries that are sending increasing numbers of graduate students to the U.S. Thus it may be possible for something to be done in the American universities to prepare these students to cope more effectively with reverse cultural shock.

I can suggest at least three steps.

First, foreign graduate students should not be encouraged to stay on in the   18
U.S. for extended periods. They should return to their home countries for summer vacations at four-year intervals, at a minimum. Two-year intervals would be
even better, given the rapid pace of industrial change in their home countries.
Currently, it is common for foreign students to spend eight or ten or even more
years in the U.S., taking courses the year round. Many universities even urge this
pattern on the students, in an effort to help them overcome language problems
and course deficiencies from their previous educational backgrounds.

Such students are the ones who experience the profoundest shock upon   19
returning home. Certainly, the present level of airline service around the world
should make it easy for nearly all of them to go home for the summer every few
years and see their country's culture first-hand.

Second, professors themselves could do more to help such students cope   20
with their frustrating futures. Too often graduate courses are offered in such a
way as to imply that their content has no relevance to particular cultural, geographical, political, or economic contexts. Subjects are presented as though they
are to be practiced in an ideal world, uninfluenced by outside factors. Fields like
money and banking or highway design or public health—or a hundred others—
do not respond to absolute laws, although they are often taught as if they do.

In fact, the usefulness of such courses to the student is directly proportional   21
to the student's understanding of how *relative* their content is. The foreign student needs to be encouraged to go beyond the American applications of his subjects. He needs to think about money and banking under conditions where all
banking interest is considered usury, about highway engineering where drifting
sand and wandering camels are the main menaces to moving traffic, about public
health where camel's urine is still believed to be the only disinfectant that really
works. The student needs to be encouraged to see his courses in the context of
his native environment, not just in terms in American applications.

Finally, the foreign student needs to realize that American solutions to   22
political problems like corruption and incompetence will not necessarily work
when he gets home. I know several students who have spent a few years in jail
because they apparently forgot that they left American-style freedom behind
when they flew east from Kennedy Airport.

Reverse cultural shock is a real problem for many foreign students. It is time   23
for American universities to undertake measures to counteract its effects. Any
diminishing of the effects of reverse cultural shock will, in the end, benefit all
the parties involved.

QUESTIONS FOR CRITICAL READING, THINKING, DISCUSSION, AND WRITING

Analyzing Content and Technique

1. What expectations are held by the young Saudi Ph.D. who returns home after studying in the
   United States for several years? How are these different from the reality?

2. What cultural traditions dismay him on his return? Why? What had been his reaction to them before he left his country? Why?
3. How does he resolve this problem, and what is its end result?
4. What, according to Corey, are some long-term effects of reverse culture shock on a country's young people?
5. What solutions does Corey suggest for the problem of reverse culture shock? Evaluate them in terms of feasibility. Which of them do you think would be most effective? Why?
6. For whom is Corey writing this essay? What is his purpose? How do you know this? Evaluate how well he achieves this purpose.

Collaborative Activity

Have group members interview people who have come to America from another country. What kind of culture shock did they experience on first arriving here? If they have been back to their country of origin, did they experience reverse culture shock? Write down examples from each person interviewed, then discuss them as a group. Based on your findings, does the group agree with Corey's idea that reverse culture shock is a serious problem that must be addressed?

Making Connections

1. In selection 31, Corey describes how the Saudi graduate is forced to "wear a mask" to survive in his society. Write an essay examining a similar situation in your own society which necessitates or once necessitated such a mask. Describe the mask and explain the social climate that makes or made it necessary. (The example you choose may come from observation, reading, films, or personal experience.)
2. Write an essay comparing the effects of reverse culture shock on the Saudi graduate with the same phenomenon as experienced by someone you know, have interviewed (see Collaborative Activity above), or have read about (this may be a fictional character). You might want to look at Zitkala-Sa's autobiography in Part Five. What similarities and differences do you notice? What is most difficult about each person's situation? What conclusions can be drawn from this study?

32

PREREADING ACTIVITY

Think about the concept of parades. Why are they held? Why might gay people want to hold a parade? How do you feel about the concept of a gay freedom day parade?

Gay Freedom Day Parade, San Francisco

FRANCES FITZGERALD

Frances FitzGerald (1940–) lives in New York and is a journalist and nonfiction writer. Her books include *Fire in the Lake: The Vietnamese and Americans in Vietnam*, and *America Revisited: History Schoolbooks in the Twentieth Century*. This selection is from "The Castro" in her book *Cities on a Hill: A Journey Through Contemporary American Cultures* (1986).

It was one of those days in San Francisco when the weather is so 1 perfect there seems to be no weather. The sun shone out of a cerulean sky lighting the streets to a shadowless intensity. It was a Sunday morning, and the streets were almost empty, so our pickup truck sped uninterrupted up and down the hills, giving those of us in the back a Ferris wheel view of the city. In Pacific Heights the roses were blooming, the hollies were in berry, and enormous clumps of daisies billowed out from under palm trees. On Russian Hill the Victorian houses with their ice-cream-colored facades seemed to reflect this bewilderment of seasons. At the bottom of the hill the skyscrapers of the financial district wheeled through our horizon, and the truck careened through the deserted canyons of the financial district heading for the waterfront.

"Don't worry," said Armistead. "We're on gay time, so the parade won't 2 have started yet."

He was right, of course. Rounding a corner, we came upon a line of 3 stationary floats. The balloons were flying—the lavender, pink and silver bouquets crowding the sky—and the bands were just warming up. People in costumes milled about amid a crowd of young men and women in blue jeans. The Gay Freedom Day Parade had not yet begun.

Our truck nosed itself into the parade lineup behind a group of marchers   4
with signs reading LUTHERANS CONCERNED FOR GAY PEOPLE and a hay
wagon advertising a gay rodeo in Reno, Nevada. Our truck had no sign on it, but
it carried in addition to myself and another journalist, two people well known to
the gay community of the city: the writer and humorist Armistead Maupin and
the professional football player Dave Kopay. In the front seat were Ken Maley
and a couple of other friends of Armistead's.

In a few minutes our part of the parade began to move forward; a country-   5
and-western band struck up somewhere behind us, and a number of men dressed
as cowboys and clowns took their places in and around the hay wagon. A clown
in whiteface with baggy overalls came and walked alongside our truck. I asked
about the rodeo, and he said matter-of-factly, "This is only our second year, so
we don't expect any bulldogging, but we've got a lot of calf ropers, some bronc
riders, and some really wonderful Dale Evans imitations. You've *got* to come."

The clown paused, distracted by the sight of a huge person in velvet robes   6
with ermine trim and red velvet hat to match hurrying along the sidewalk. "Just
who does she think *she* is?" he asked rhetorically. The "Boris Gudunov" personage
was followed by what seemed to be a frowsy middle-aged woman with an
enormous bosom. The woman was wearing a kerchief and a cheap cloth coat, and
she was having some trouble with her high heels—so the red-robed person kept
having to go back to right her and pull her along. "Well, it's certainly not the
Empress," the clown said. "Far too tacky."

The clown drifted off, and I turned to watch a man in a Batman cape and a   7
sequined jockstrap roller-skating by. He had the torso of a dancer, and he moved
with liquid, dreamlike movements, crossing and recrossing the street. He glided
through the Lutheran contingent and then swept through another group of
clergymen carrying large placards of Christ on the cross. At the intersection he
looped around a yellow taxicab filled with young women in T-shirts. The young
women were leaning out of the windows cheering and bouncing about a sign
that read LESBIAN TAXI DRIVERS OF SAN FRANCISCO. One of them, a
slim young woman with long blond hair, I recognized as the taxi driver who had
brought me in from the airport a few weeks before.

Eventually our pickup truck turned onto Market Street, the main   8
thoroughfare of the city, and we had suddenly a view of the whole first half of the
parade—its floats and lines of marchers filling the street in front of us—on its way
to City Hall. The sun was now harsh as a kleig light overhead; it burnished the
streets and set the windows of the skyscrapers on fire. Nearby an elderly Chinese
man with a dog walked along the sidewalk close to the buildings, his head
bowed, his eyes averted from the marchers. A block away a woman in a baggy
coat and kerchief scuttled into a doorway—just in time to avoid the sight of the
transvestite copy of herself hulking down the avenue. Otherwise the sidewalks
and the streets leading off into the downtown were deserted—as empty as if a
neutron bomb had hit, cleaning away the weekday mass of humanity and leaving
the skyscrapers perfectly intact for a new civilization to move in. At this point
there were no spectators; there was no one to watch this horde in its outlandish
costumes march into the city.

That summer—it was 1978—estimates of the gay population of San   9
Francisco ranged from 75,000 to 150,000. If the off-cited figure of 100,000
were correct, this meant that in this city of less than 700,000 people,
approximately one out of every five adults and one out of every three or four
voters was gay. A great proportion of these people—half of them or more—had
moved into the city within the past eight years. And most of these new
immigrants were young, white, and male. There were now some 90 gay bars in
the city and perhaps 150 gay organizations including church groups, social
services, and business associations. There were 9 gay newspapers, 2 foundations,
and 3 Democratic clubs. While the gay men and women had settled all over the
city, they had created an almost exclusive area of gay settlement in the Eureka
Valley, in a neighborhood known as the Castro. The previous year the Castro had
elected a city supervisor, Harvey Milk, who ran as a gay candidate—against 16
opponents including another gay man. Now, quite visibly, this area of settlement
was spreading in all directions: up into the hills above the Castro, down into the
Mission District, and across into the lower Haight Street neighborhood. While
New York and Los Angeles probably had more gay residents, the proportions
were nowhere as high as they were in San Francisco. Possibly the sheer
concentration of gay people in San Francisco had no parallel in history.

At that time most San Franciscans still contrived to ignore the growing gay   10
population in their midst. The local press reported on gay events and on the
growth of the Castro, but most San Franciscans I talked to seemed not to have
noticed these pieces—or they had forgotten them. Small wonder, perhaps, for the
articles were not sensational in any sense. The local reporters seemed to have
gotten quite used to the gay community without ever giving it its due. They now
took certain things for granted. Earlier that year a young journalist from out of
town had gone with the mayor and other city officials to the annual Beaux Arts
Costume Ball. The event had shaken him, but the local newspapers had reported
it as they would a mayoral visit to a Knights of Columbus dinner. It was, after all,
the third year the mayor had gone to a drag ball in the civic auditorium.

The program in my press kit showed that there were 138 contingents in the   11
parade, and that with a few exceptions, such as Straights for Gay Rights and the
San Francisco Commission on the Status of Women, all of them represented gay
organizations of one sort or another. With the program it was possible to sort
these organizations into certain categories: political organizations, human rights
groups, professional associations, social-service organizations, ethnic minority
groups, religious organizations, college groups, out-of-town contingents, such as
the Napa Gay People's Coalition, fraternal organizations, such as those for
transsexuals and bisexuals for gay rights, sports groups, and commercial
enterprises. Perhaps for variety's sake, however, the organizers had chosen to mix
up the categories to some degree, so that the actual order of the parade might
have come from the pages of Claude Lévi-Strauss.[1]

By the time our truck turned onto Market Street, I was in fact too late to see   12
the head of the parade: the Gay American Indian contingent followed by Disabled

---

[1]French anthropologist (1980–   ).

Gay People and Friends, followed by a ninety-piece marching band and the gay political leaders of the city. But leaving my truck to walk along the sidelines where a crowd was now gathering, I was able to make my way up to number forty-one: the Gay Latino Alliance, or GALA, a group of young men dancing down the street to mariachi music. Just behind them was a group representing the gay Jewish synagogue, a rather serious group of people, the men with yarmulkes on carrying a banner with the Star of David. This contingent was closely followed by a Marilyn Monroe look-alike on stilts batting six-inch-long eyelashes and swaying to the music of the disco float just behind her. Farther back there were people in country work clothes with a sign for the Order of Displaced Okies. The Local Lesbian Association Kazoo Marching Band led a number of women's groups, including the San Francisco Women's Center, UC Berkeley Women's Studies, and Dykes on Bikes. This latter group could be easily located, as every time they came to an intersection, the six or seven petite women in tight jeans, men's undershirts, and boots would rev up their motorcycles, bringing loud applause from the crowd. Farther back, behind the Gay Pagans, the Free Beach Activists, the Zimbabwe Medical Drive, and the Alice B. Toklas Democratic Club, came the float that many had been waiting for: the sequined, spangled, and tulle-wrapped chariot of the Council of Grand Dukes and Duchesses of San Francisco. Somewhere in this neighborhood there was a truly unfortunate juxtaposition. The Women Against Violence in Pornography and the Media had taken their proper places in line, but then somehow, perhaps as a result of some confusion in the Society of Janus, elements of the sadomasochistic liberation front had moved in just behind them. The pallid-looking men in uniforms were not dragging chains—the parade organizers had counseled against it—but they were carrying a sign of questionable grammar that read BLACK AND BLUE IS BEAUTIFUL.

At that time—the very height of gay liberation—many Americans believed [13] that the homosexual population of the United States had greatly increased in the past ten or twenty years. And they were willing to explain it. Some said the country was going soft: there was no discipline anymore, and no morality. Others, including a number of gay men, said that the country was finding its ecological balance and creating natural limits to population growth. There was, however, no evidence for the premise—never mind for the theories built upon it. What demographic studies there were showed that male homosexuals had remained a fairly stable percentage of the population since 1948 when the first Kinsey study came out. What had happened since then, but particularly in the past decade, was that homosexuals had assumed much greater visibility. Gay liberation was, more than anything else, a move into consciousness. The movement "created" some homosexuals in that it permitted some people to discover their homosexual feelings and to express them. But its main effect was to bring large numbers of homosexuals out of the closet—and into the consciousness of others. Its secondary effect was to create a great wave of migration into the tolerant cities of the country. All the gay immigrants I talked to said that they had always known they were attracted to the same sex; their decision was not to become a homosexual but to live openly as one and in a gay community. "I lived in Rochester," a young political consultant told me. "I was white, male, and middle class, and I had gone to Harvard. I thought I could do anything I wanted, so I resented having to conceal something as basic as sex. I resented being condemned to repress or ignore my homosexuality and to live in turmoil for the rest of my life. The solution was to move here."

The parade was moving slowly, but the farther we went up Market Street, 14 the more spectators there were. First there was a line of people and then a crowd filling the sidewalks and spilling out into the streets behind. Many of the spectators were young men, and though we had no sign on our truck, it now happened frequently that one of them would call out, "Hey, it's Armistead!" or, "Look, it's Dave Kopay!"

Kopay, tall, broad-shouldered, and lantern-jawed, was not hard to 15 recognize: he looked like a movie version of a football player. A veteran running back, he had played pro ball for eight years with the 49ers, the Lions, the Redskins, the Saints, and the Green Bay Packers. He retired in 1975 and three years later, convinced that rumors of his homosexuality had denied him a coaching job, he decided to come out to a newspaper reporter doing a story on homosexuality in professional sports. The reporter had talked to a number of gay athletes, but only Kopay permitted his name to be used. His gesture created a scandal in the sports world, for while everyone knew there were homosexuals in professional sports, no one wanted the evidence of it. But Kopay became something of a hero among gay men.

Armistead Maupin might have been more difficult to recognize, as he was 16 wearing a lavender-and-yellow hockey jersey with a matching cap pulled down over his bright blue eyes. But in San Francisco he was just as well known as Kopay. A journalist and fiction writer, he was the author of *Tales of the City,* a humorous serial on San Francisco life that had appeared in the *San Francisco Chronicle.* The terrain he mapped in his *Tales* was the world of young single people, gay and straight, who came to San Francisco to change their lives. It was a world he knew well. Maupin, as it happened, came from an aristocratic and ultraconservative North Carolina family. On graduating from the University of North Carolina at Chapel Hill, he had joined the Navy, gone through officers' school, and served a tour of duty in Vietnam. He had then spent another summer in Vietnam as a volunteer building refugee housing with some fellow officers. On his return, President Richard Nixon invited him to the White House and honored him as the very model of patriotic young Republicanism. A year later Maupin left for San Francisco.

Because of his writing but also because of his enormous southern charm, 17 Armistead had become the Gay Personality of San Francisco. The year before he had been master of ceremonies at the gay parade, and he had opened the annual game between the San Francisco Sheriff's Department and the Gay Softball League by throwing out an orange. Once, to demonstrate that nothing is sacred, including *amour-propre,*[2] he turned up in a white rabbit suit to sell jockstraps for a gay charity. The epigraph for his book was a quotation from Oscar Wilde: "It's an odd thing, but anyone who disappears is said to be seen in San Francisco."

---

[2] *amour-propre:* self-esteem or self-respect.

Most of the spectators crowding the sidewalks appeared to be in their twenties or thirties. Dressed California-style in natural fibers and hiking or jogging shoes, both the men and women looked lean, tan, and athletic. Many of the men, now shirtless in the sun, had admirably muscled chests. "Just think," Armistead said, looking out at a row of them sunbathing on a wall, "of all the fortunes spent in bodybuilding equipment." There were some older people, including a group of four women with butch haircuts and lined faces and a couple of men with identical beards and canes, but not very many. And apart from a few glum-looking tourist families, there were hardly any mixed couples or children. To the expert observers on my truck, most of the spectators appeared to be gay. [18]

The majority of San Franciscans could still ignore the growing gay population in their midst in part because the city—in spite of the endless views of self afforded by its hills—was still decentralized, its residential neighborhoods a series of ethnic villages: black, Hispanic, Irish, Italian, and Chinese. Like all the other minorities, the gays had their own neighborhoods and places of entertainment which other San Franciscans circumnavigated as they went from work to home. But then, too, unlike the rest, gay people had no distinguishing marks, no permanent badges of color, class, or accent. Going to work in the downtown, gay people, black or white, men or women, were invisible to others for as long as they wanted to be. Politically speaking, they acted like a highly organized ethnic group—indeed this year (1978) they had persuaded the city government to give the gay parade the same sum it gave ethnic parades for the purpose of encouraging tourism. Yet this minority, being defined by desire alone, materialized only once a year, in June, on Gay Freedom Day. [19]

From time to time during the slow march up Market Street it came to me to see the gay parade as the unfurling of a municipal dream sequence—the clowns, the drag queens, and the men in their leather suits being the fantastic imagery of the city's collective unconscious. Sigmund Freud, after all, had believed that man was born bisexual and that every human being had homosexual desires in some degree. From this perspective it seemed unreasonable that the parade should not include everyone in San Francisco. On the other hand, Freud believed that each individual's inner world was quite unique—individual desires having different qualities or textures, different degrees of intensity and modes of expression. And from this perspective it seemed unreasonable that all these thousands of people should pick up a banner labeled GAY and march with it to City Hall. What made the experience more bewildering still was that to watch the contingents pass by was to watch a confusion of categories something like that of Borges's[3] Chinese list: Dykes on Bikes, California Human Rights Advocates, Sutro Baths, Lesbian Mothers, the Imperial Silver Fox Court. Looking at the costumes—the leather and the tulle—I wondered which were new and which had been worn for decades, even centuries, in the undergrounds of Paris or London. Which were the permanent archetypes of desires, and which merely fashions or the jokes of the young? My friends on the truck would answer with the [20]

[3]Jorge Luis Borges (1899–1986), Argentinian fiction writer.

counterculture koan that everyone—all of us—were in drag. And yet some of these costumes and dream images had settlement patterns in the city. There were in fact four gay centers in San Francisco, each geographically distinct, each containing what appeared to be distinct subcultures or culture parts.

The oldest gay center in the city lay in the Tenderloin—that triangle of [21] sleazy bars and cheap hotels bordered by the business district, the theater district, and Market Street. The Tenderloin, like its counterparts in other cities, was far from exclusively gay. The home of winos and bums, it was the transit station for sailors and other impecunious travelers, and it harbored most of the prostitution, both gay and straight, for the entire city. In the late afternoon female prostitutes, male hustlers, and transvestite whores could be seen performing a complicated street corner ballet as they tried at once to evade the police and sort out their initially undifferentiated customers. In the fifties the district had harbored most of the gay bars in the city—but now only hustler and drag queen bars were left. The Kokpit, owned by a queen called Sweet Lips, had been in operation for about a decade. Now lined with trophies and photographs of countless drag balls, it had become a kind of Toots Shor's of drag San Francisco. A few blocks away there was a bar of a professional and much more highly specialized nature, where six- to seven-foot-tall black transvestites hustled white men in business suits, who were, necessarily, shorter.

Chronologically speaking, Polk Street, or Polk Gulch, was the second gay [22] center of the city. It was the decorators' district, and in the sixties a number of gay bars had moved into the blocks lined with antique shops and furniture stores. Since then it had been the major site of the Halloween festivities. On that one night a year the police stood by, leaving the street to a carnival of witches, clowns, nuns on roller skates, and Jackie Kennedy look-alikes or Patty Hearst look-alikes with toy machine guns. Polk Street was a mixed neighborhood—both gay and straight people lived there, and its restaurants catered to both crowds. Its gay bars were thus not conspicuous except at night when groups of young hustlers stood out on the sidewalks around them. A number of them still catered to the stylish and the well-to-do. They had low lights, expensive furniture, and music by the old favorites: Marlene Dietrich, Noel Coward, and Judy Garland. Even to outsiders their patrons would be recognizable, for Polk Street was still the land of good taste and attitude: the silk scarf so perfectly knotted, the sentimentality, the witty little jab.

A newer gay center lay around Folsom Street in the old warehouse district [23] south of Market. At night Folsom Street was the complement to Polk Street—the raw, as it were, to the cooked—for it was lined with leather bars: the Stud, the Brig, the Ramrod, the Black and Blue. Late at night groups of men in blue jeans, motorcycle jackets, and boots would circle around ranks of Triumphs and Harley-Davidsons, eyeing each other warily. The bars had sawdust on the floors, and men drank beer standing up, shoulder to shoulder, in a din of heavy metal and hard rock. In the Black and Blue some of them wore studded wristbands, studded neckbands, and caps with Nazi insignia; above the bar a huge motorcycle was suspended in a wash of psychedelic lights. On Wednesday nights the Arena bar had a slave auction: men would be stripped almost naked, chained up by men in black masks with whips, prodded, and sold off to the highest bidder. Such was the theater of Folsom Street. The men in leather came from Polk Street and other quiet neighborhoods, the money went to charity, and the "slave" put on a business suit and went to work the next day.

Folsom Street was a night town—the Valley of the Kings, it was called, as opposed to the Valley of the Queens in the Tenderloin and the Valley of the Dolls on Polk Street. But in addition to the leather bars, a variety of gay restaurants, discotheques, bathhouses, and sex clubs had moved into its abandoned warehouses and manufacturing lofts. It was an entertainment place, and few people lived there.

The Castro, by contrast, was a neighborhood. Though first settled by gays—homesteaded, as it were—in the early seventies, it was now the fulcrum of gay life in the city. At first glance it was much like other neighborhoods: a four-block main street with a drugstore, corner groceries, a liquor store, dry cleaners, and a revival movie house whose facade had seen better days. Here and there upscale money was visibly at work: a café advertised Dungeness crab, a store sold expensive glass and tableware, and there were two banks. But there was nothing swish about the Castro. The main street ran off into quiet streets of two- and three-story white-shingle houses; the main haberdashery, The All-American Boy, sold clothes that would have suited a conservative Ivy Leaguer. In fact the neighborhood was like other neighborhoods except that on Saturdays and Sundays you could walk for blocks and see only young men dressed as it were for a hiking expedition. Also the bookstore was a gay bookstore, the health club a gay health club; and behind the shingles hung out on the street there was a gay real-estate brokerage, a gay lawyer's office, and the office of a gay psychiatrist. The bars were, with one exception, gay bars, and one of them, the Twin Peaks bar near Market Street, was, so Armistead told me, the first gay bar in the country to have picture windows on the street.

Armistead and his friends liked to take visitors to the Castro and point out landmarks such as the Twin Peaks. But in fact the only remarkable-looking thing on the street was the crowd of young men. Even at lunchtime on a weekday there would be dozens of good-looking young men crowding the café tables, hanging out at the bars, leaning against doorways, or walking down the streets with their arms around each other. The sexual tension was palpable. "I'd never live here," Armistead said. "Far too intense. You can't go to the laundromat at ten A.M. without the right pair of jeans on." The Castro was the place where most of the young gay men came. Fifty to a hundred thousand came as tourists each summer, and of these, thousands decided to settle, leaving Topeka and Omaha for good. New York and Los Angeles had their Polk Streets and Folsom Districts, but the Castro was unique: it was the first settlement built by gay liberation.

The denizens of the Castro were overwhelmingly male, but occasionally in a crowd of men on the street you would see two or three young women dressed in jeans or jumpsuits. Some gay women lived in the Castro—they considered it safe—and close by there were a few small lesbian settlements in the Haight, the Duboce Triangle and the Mission District. But you could not find these settlements unless you knew where to look, so inconspicuous were they. On one quiet street there was a comfortable neighborhood bar with a jukebox and a pool table; on the walls were framed photographs of the softball team its regulars organized each summer. This was Maud's Study, and the bartender plus all of the customers were women. But there were only five or six lesbian bars in the entire city. There were many more women's organizations, theater groups, social-service organizations, and so on—but there was no female equivalent of the Castro. In Berkeley and north Oakland across the Bay, young political women had taken over some of the big, slightly run-down, shingle houses and started a newspaper, a crafts cooperative, a recording company, and various other enterprises. And there were a number of lesbian farm communes up the coast in northern California. But nowhere did gay women congregate the way gay men did. In the city—feeling themselves vulnerable—they took on protective colorings and melted into the landscape. No one ever knew how many of them there were in San Francisco, as no research money was ever allotted to finding that out. They appeared in large numbers only on Gay Freedom Day.

The front of the parade had long ago reached its terminus at City Hall 28 when our truck pulled into the Civic Center Plaza. A rotunda building like the U.S. Capitol, the San Francisco City Hall looked large and imposing, fronted, as it was, by tree-lined malls and a reflecting pool. At the same time, recently cleaned and bright white against a bright blue sky, it looked like an enormous wedding cake of the sort displayed in old-fashioned Italian bakeries. As we arrived, a tall, handsome woman standing on the dais before its steps was chanting something like a prayer. She was saying:

"In the memory of the recorded nine million women, many of whom were 29 lesbians, who were executed on charges of witchcraft, we invoke the name of the Great Goddess.

"In memory of the uncounted number of gay men who were thrown into 30 the fire as faggots to light the pyres of their sisters, we invoke the name of the Great Goddess, the Mother of all living things."

The speaker, I discovered later, called herself Bayta Podos. She was a 31 secretary and an instructor in women's studies at San Francisco State University. She was also the priestess of a feminist religion that she herself had conceived out of her research into matriarchal or matrilineal societies. She practiced magic and invented rituals to be used on ceremonial occasions. Recently she had closed a feminist conference on violence against women by producing a large wooden sword and instructing the women to meditate upon it, filling it with all their fears and all the anger they felt against the patriarchate. Then she broke the sword in two.

"We invoke you, Great One," she continued. "You whose names have been 32 sung from time beyond time: You who are Inanni, Isis, Ishtar, Anath, Ashtoreth, Amaterasu, Neith, Selket, Turquoise Woman, White Shell Woman, Cihuacotl, Tonantzin, Demeter, Artemis, Earthquake Mother, Kail . . ."

Next to the dais Harvey Milk was standing with a lei of purple orchids 33 around his neck and a bunch of daisies in one hand, giving interviews to a small group of radio and television correspondents. He had already made his speech—a strong one, I was told—denouncing the so-called Briggs Initiative, a proposition on the California ballot which, if passed, would drive all openly gay teachers and all discussions of gay rights out of the public schools. He was now calling for a national gay march on Washington for the following year. Nearby, beside the dais, a woman in a gypsy costume was swinging her child around through the air; a man in a tuxedo with makeup on and long red fingernails strolled past her humming to himself.

In front of the dais a large crowd had assembled—a very large crowd. Indeed, it seemed to me when I looked at it from the top of City Hall steps that I must be looking at all the twenty- to thirty-year-olds in northern California. The young people in front were following the proceedings on the dais enthusiastically. Some were waving banners; others were standing with linked arms, chanting and cheering. Behind them groups of people were lying on the grass, their heads pillowed on backpacks, talking and rolling joints while other groups of young people drifted around them. From the front the crowd looked like an early antiwar demonstration; from the back it looked like the Woodstock nation. Both seemed to be crowds of the sixties returned, only now, both of them were gay. 34

The next day, June 26, 1978, the *San Francisco Chronicle* reported that 240,000 people turned out for the annual Gay Freedom Day Parade. It quoted the police estimate rather than the chamber of commerce estimate of 300,000 made later in the day or the figure of 375,000 quoted by the *Los Angeles Times*. Even the second figure would make the turnout one of the largest in San Francisco's history and would equal nearly half of the adult population of the city. The local press tended to avoid figures leading to such arithmetic. It did not like to advertise that San Francisco had become the gay capital of the country, if not of the world. 35

QUESTIONS FOR CRITICAL READING, THINKING, DISCUSSION, AND WRITING

Analyzing Content and Technique

1. Analyze the tone of the parade and of the essay. Give quotations to support your answer. Is the tone an appropriate one for the writer's purpose? What is the writer's attitude toward her subject?
2. Observe the writer's use of time. In which year does the parade take place? Which parts are written at that time? Identify parts which are written later. Why does the writer do this?
3. Describe the gay centers in San Francisco. How is each one unique?
4. Why has the gay population chosen San Francisco as its "home"? (You will have to examine what the writer implies as well as what she states to fully answer this.) What additional reasons can you find for this phenomenon?
5. What has been the city's response to gay people? Give examples. How is this different from other cities such as New York and Los Angeles which also have large gay populations?
6. Analyze the concluding paragraph. Why does the writer end with this? How does it support her thesis?

Collaborative Activity

Discuss, as a group, parades that you have observed (live or on television) or participated in or come across by chance, here or in another country. What was the purpose of the parade? In what way, if any, did it throw light on the culture of the people involved? In what way, if any, was it reflective of the place where the parade occurred? How did you feel about being there? What over-all impression did you come away with? (Group members who have never experienced a parade will have to read about one or look at a video.) Compile a collaborative list of all the different responses you receive.

Making Connections

1. The kinds of clothing worn by a particular group of people often give us an insight into their concerns, values, and lifestyle. Articles of clothing, or use of colors, may be symbolic as well. Analyze the clothing of the gay population described in this essay, keeping in mind that we are looking at a parade. Do some additional library research on this topic, then write an essay on the types of clothing gay people might wear and what they mean. The purpose of your essay should be to increase the reader's understanding of the gay community.

2. California has been the chosen home not only of the gay population but also of many different communities. Write an essay about such another group, ethnic or otherwise, that came to California for special reasons. (You may choose to write a historical essay on past immigrants to California, or may study current events, or may interview people you know, or may even examine your own life to gather material.) Focus on the sociohistoric causes that led to their choice of California as home.

33

PREREADING ACTIVITY

Write about an ancestral place (a home, a city, a country) that you have never visited, gathering your material by talking to a relative or a friend or by reading about the place. How is this place (as you imagine it) different from your everyday reality?

Heaven

CATHY SONG

Cathy Song (1955–) come om Hawaii, where she attended the University of Hawaii. She holds an M.A. from Boston University and received the Yale Younger Poets Award for her first collection of poems, *Picture Bride*—the story of her Korean grandmother, whose marriage in Hawaii was arranged by photograph. "Heaven" is taken from a new collection, *Frameless Windows, Squares of Light*, and is partly autobiographical. Song lived for a while in Denver (the scene of the poem), has two children, and is deeply interested in her Chinese heritage.

He thinks when we die we'll go to China.
Think of it—a Chinese heaven
where, except for his blond hair,
the part that belongs to his father,
everyone will look like him.
China, that blue flower on the map,   5
bluer than the sea
his hand must span like a bridge
to reach it.
An octave away.   10

I've never seen it.
It's as if I can't sing that far.
But look—
on the map, this black dot.
Here is where we live,   15
on the pancake plains

just east of the Rockies,
on the other side of the clouds.
A mile above the sea,
the air is so thin, you can starve on it.   20
No bamboo trees
But the alpine equivalent,
reedy aspen with light, fluttering leaves.
Did a boy in Guangzhou dream of this
as his last stop?   25

I've heard the trains at night
whistling past our yards,
what we've come to own,
the broken fences, the whiny dog, the rattletrap cars.
It's still the wild west,   30
mean and grubby,
the shootouts and fistfights in the back alley.
With my son the dreamer
and my daughter, who is too young to walk,
I've sat in this spot   35
and wondered why here?
Why in this short life,
this town, this creek they call a river?

He had never planned to stay,
the boy who helped to build   40
the railroads for a dollar a day.
He had always meant to go back.
When did he finally know
that each mile of track led him further away,
that he would die in his sleep,   45
dispossessed,
having seen Gold Mountain,
the icy wind tunneling through it,
these landlocked, makeshift ghost towns?

It must be in the blood,   50
this notion of returning.
It skipped two generations, lay fallow,
the garden an unmarked grave.
On a spring sweater day
it's as if we remember him.   55
I call to the children.
We can see the mountains
shimmering blue above the air.
If you look really hard

says my son the dreamer,
leaning out from the laundry's rigging,
the work shirts fluttering like sails,
you can see all the way to heaven.

60

QUESTIONS FOR CRITICAL READING, THINKING, DISCUSSION, AND WRITING

Analyzing Content and Technique

1. What do we know about the speaker's ancestors and about how she has ended up in Denver?
2. How does the narrator feel about China? How does her son feel? Which details in the poem indicate how they feel about living where they do?
3. Explain the statement in the last stanza (lines 50–51), "It must be in the blood,/ this notion of returning."
4. Identify some examples of figures of speech (simile, metaphor, and so forth) used in the poem. What is their purpose?
5. What is the mood of the poem? How is this conveyed to the reader?
6. State, in your own words, the main idea of the poem.

Making Connections

1. One of the themes of Song's poem is the difficulty immigrants often experience when trying to settle in a new homeland. Write an essay exploring this issue. What are some of the most difficult elements that people from other cultures must adjust to when they come to the United States? Which problems continue to trouble their descendants? Support your thesis with examples from various sources: personal observation, interviews, statistics, etc.
2. Song is trying to recreate a lost "culture" or "home." Write an essay examining her predicament and the methods she uses to recreate what is lost. What additional methods might you use in a similar situation? What is the value of recreating a culture or home?

34

PREREADING ACTIVITY

Write about a time when you lived away from home or visited someone. What was the experience like? What did it make you realize about your home? If you have never been away from home, even for a short trip, interview someone who has and write about his or her experience.

Home (Student Essay)

LUCRETIA DIBBA

1

*H*ome. Why is it that this short word almost always fills us with a sense of comfort and confidence whenever we say it or even think of it? Why is it that we feel insecure and vulnerable when "home" is no longer a part of our everyday lives, when it lies oceans and oceans away? Why is a house not necessarily a home?

2

Six years ago I was living in a home. Now, at age 18, I live in a house in the United States with a family that is not my own. I feel trapped, as though I'm in a prison camp where all my actions and habits are constantly scrutinized. Even in the privacy of my room, I feel exposed. It is as though the very walls and windows are watching me with the eyes of my guardians. Those imaginary eyes, always watchful, always curious—I can't shut them out. They want to wrest my secrets from the core of my being. The only time I can escape from them is when my memory transports me home.

3

I come from Gambia, a tiny country on the western coast of Africa. Because Gambia is so small, nearly all its inhabitants are interrelated. We grew up in an atmosphere of friendship, accepting people of different cultures and customs as part of our everyday life. Certainly this was the case in my family of six, where my mother is a Christian and my father a Moslem. We somehow made it a point to practice both religions at home. Christmas was celebrated with fervor and excitement, and so was Tobaski, a special Moslem festival. It always gave me a sense of pride and joy to see my father accompany my mother to church and share an important part of her life with her. I felt the same emotions when Mother would "help" Father fast on holy days by fasting with him and preparing all the special dishes required for the religious ceremony afterwards. The openness and love

Source: "What Is a Home," student essay reprinted by permission.

they shared and encouraged us to share is one of my most cherished memories of home.

Another thing I appreciate about home is that we were all considered an important and integral part of the family, necessary to the smooth running of the house. My father used to say jokingly that he was the head chef, my mother the manager, my brother the butler, and we girls the chambermaids! I think what he really meant to convey was that we were all working together to produce a happy home. I remember how, even at age 10, I proudly accomplished such tasks as cleaning my room, feeding the goldfish, and watering the potted plants.

In our home there was also a free spirit of communication on which I look back now with longing. Every Saturday, for as far back as I can remember, mother used to hold "house meetings" to discuss any events that had occurred, or any experiences or ideas we might want to share. These took place in my parents' bedroom, on the big, soft bed, all of us sitting cross-legged in a circle, listening to what the others had to say. Even when Father was not there because he had to be at work, we felt his presence and love, and we knew that Mother would fill him in on our concerns. I don't remember many of the topics we discussed, but I do remember the affection and caring which came out of these meetings and which even now holds me in its embrace.

Ironically, the one topic that I *do* remember from those meetings is a matter that I have had great difficulty handling. Somehow we had been talking about living away from home—I don't know why, for there had been no indication of what was to occur in the future—and Mother said, in her gentle, firm voice, "Never feel that the environment you find yourself in, or the people living in it, should change themselves for you. Try to accept them as they are, and be happy. Only then will you feel at home no matter where you go." I've been trying sincerely, Mother. If only I could learn to do it!

But somehow home to me is still the place where each member of the family is treated like a king or queen; where I can entertain as many friends as I want; where I don't have to think of how much water I'm wasting when I feel like taking a long, long shower; where I can cook as much rice as I feel like cooking, even though I know I won't be able to eat it all; where I can "lie in" on holidays until I feel like getting up; where no matter how much of a mess I make or how much trouble I get into, I will still be my parents' "jewel."

And so I cannot feel happy in my new environment, although that isn't the fault of my host family. They are good people, the husband from my hometown in Gambia, the wife from Idaho. Despite the difference in their cultural backgrounds they get along well, not unlike my parents, and have established a routine of sharing chores that works very efficiently. Their house is always immaculately clean, and their well-ordered lives, undisrupted by children, are structured around useful activities such as work, school, and study. They always have time for a friendly comment for me, or for advice that comes out of a genuine desire to be helpful. Yet, if only . . .

If only . . . what? If only sometimes they would leave an unmatched sock lying around, or pile the dirty dishes in the sink overnight, so that I didn't feel as though I had to tiptoe around their perfection, that I had to wipe clean every single item that I touched. If only they would entertain a few friends who laughed too loudly and sometimes drank too much, as my parents did once in a while, so that I, too, could feel free about inviting my friends over. If only they would forget to water the plants or clean out the refrigerator so that I could do it for them. . . . Then maybe I wouldn't feel those eyes on me constantly, assessing my every move, carefully watching this alien being from the "dark continent."

But perhaps there are no eyes lurking behind the doors, no walls with ears.   10 Maybe it is only me, being too sensitive, feeling different from the people around me with their strange habits and accents and their different skin color, making no effort to understand their motives and actions. Maybe it is that, as a result of loneliness and insecurity, I am romanticizing my childhood and clinging to it. Maybe it is the constant comparison of the two worlds, past and present, that is keeping me from being happy today. Maybe it is fear—fear of being faced with the unknown, fear of change, fear that I will forget, that I will betray my past, my heritage.

Whatever it might be, I continue to return for solace to my memories of   11 home. There are only good memories. Anything bad that might have happened has been swept away in the tide of my homesickness. And home remains the one place that radiates wholesomeness, love, understanding and safety. Made magical and unreachable by distance, it is irreplaceable. It will always haunt me and hold me.

STRUCTURE, STRATEGY, SUGGESTION

1. Examine Dibba's current living arrangements. How does she feel about them? Choose one quotation from the text that best sums up her attitude.
2. Analyze the reasons why Dibba feels the way she does about her new environment. Which of these reasons, according to you, is the most important? Explain your choice.
3. What kind of organizing pattern has Dibba used to arrange her reasons? Think of another way of structuring the essay. How would this affect the reader's response?
4. What is the main point of the essay? What, if anything, would you add to the essay to clarify the main point?
5. Analyze Dibba's use of transitions. Where do they occur? What kinds of ideas do they connect? Do they stress similarities or differences? What other transitions might she have used, and where?
6. Dibba's essay is written from the point of view of the visitor. Write an essay from the point of view of the hosts, discussing the difficulties and satisfactions they might encounter. You can support your essay with personal observation and examples or with general reasoning and facts.

SYNTHESIS *Part Four*

1. Part Four presents us with a range of places—from a snowsuit to an entire country—that people have identified as "home." Can you think of other examples of "home"? Write an essay in which you explore how each of these examples helps to expand our definition of "home" in a different way.

2. "El Hoyo" and "Gay Freedom Day Parade, San Francisco" present us with portraits of neighborhoods where a particular group of people congregate. Taking into account the authors' ideas as well as your own opinions on the subject, write an essay in which you present the advantages and disadvantages of living in such neighborhoods.

3. "American Space, Chinese Place" and "The Perfect House," as well as "Amish Economics" in Part Three, indicate that the notion of the perfect home differs widely from culture to culture and community to community. Write an essay in which you examine what is considered to be the ideal home in two or three different cultures or communities. Give specific details where appropriate. What beliefs, values, and lifestyles have contributed to these notions of the perfect house?

4. "Cultural Shock in Reverse," "Heaven," and "Home" depict situations in which people feel alienated and *not* at home. Write a paper in which you identify some of the major causes of such alienation, drawing your material from this text as well as your other reading and experience.

PART FIVE

Ways by Which We Learn

SELECTIONS IN PART FIVE

PART 5: INTRODUCTION

*T*he magical, never-ending process of learning can take place through observation and study, and also through direct experience. Part Five provides us with examples of both kinds of learning. Selections like Ezra Bowen's "Getting Tough" (selection 36), based on the critical analysis of a situation, allow the writer to draw certain conclusions from the evidence examined. Others, like Dick Gregory's "Shame" (selection 37), show us through first person narrative what the author has learned through an immediate encounter. But here too the act of writing, which deepens the learning process, necessitates looking back at the experience and reassessing it.

Writing—and by extension, reading—are central to the learning experience, but learning is certainly not limited to them. As Part Five illustrates, learning can take place under any circumstances. We learn in formal classroom situations, yes, but we learn even more from the daily business of living. And we never know who is going to be our teacher. Sometimes, as expected, it is an educator, as with Gregory, Zitkala-Sa (selection 35) or Santha Rama Rau (selection 38)—although these teachers might be surprised to know what they imprinted on the young minds placed in their care. But sometimes it is a person society does not particularly admire, as in "Barba Nikos" (selection 40) or even someone we generally look down on, like Gregory's wino.

Coming into contact—or conflict—with another culture also provides unique learning opportunities. This is seen in Zitkala-Sa's "The School Days of an Indian Girl," which recounts her experience of being taken from her Native American tribe to be educated at a Quaker missionary school, brilliantly conveying the confusion of a child thrust into a world and a language she does not understand, and her distress at being treated in a way her culture would consider demeaning. This selection also points ironically at the power of the learning process to change us—sometimes in ways we do not want—because when the narrator goes home, she finds herself unable to belong there either. The clash between different worlds is further explored in Liann Sumner's "Discovery" (the student essay, selection 42), which focuses on a journey from the United States to India that exposes the writer to extreme culture shock.

Zitkala-Sa and Sumner remind us that learning is often a painful process, even when the lesson learned may be ultimately valuable to us. This concept is reinforced in "Shame," in which Gregory writes of the humiliation he experienced as an illegitimate child, the memory of which later impels him toward success. In "Getting Tough" the principal Joe Clark uses harsh discipline to keep his problem students in school and out of trouble. And Li-Young Lee's poem (selection 41) teaches us that pain transmuted into art might become a source for some of the deepest, most poignant beauties of our human existence.

35

Write about your earliest memories of being away from home in an environment you found alien and unfriendly. What did you learn from this situation?

The School Days of an Indian Girl

ZITKALA-SA

Zitkala-Sa (1876–1938), also known as Gertrude Bonnin, was of mixed Sioux and white ancestry. Educated at a Quaker missionary school in Indiana and later at Earlham College and at the Boston Conservatory of Music, she became a teacher and violinist as well as an activist for Native American rights. She was the founder of the National Council of American Indians. For many years, she edited the *American Indian Magazine*. Her books include *Old Indian Legends* and *American Indian Stories*. Her autobiographical essays were the first written by a Native American woman without the aid of an editor or interpreter.

The Land of Red Apples

*T*here were eight in our party of bronzed children who were going 1 East with the missionaries. Among us were three young braves, two tall girls, and we three little ones, Judéwin, Thowin, and I.

We had been very impatient to start on our journey to the Red Apple 2 Country, which, we were told, lay a little beyond the great circular horizon of the Western prairie. Under a sky of rosy apples we dreamt of roaming as freely and happily as we had chased the cloud shadows on the Dakota plains. We had anticipated much pleasure from a ride on the iron horse, but the throngs of staring palefaces disturbed and troubled us.

On the train, fair women, with tottering babies on each arm, stopped their 3 haste and scrutinized the children of absent mothers. Large men, with heavy bundles in their hands, halted near by, and riveted their glassy blue eyes upon us.

I sank deep into the corner of my seat, for I resented being watched. 4 Directly in front of me, children who were no larger than I hung themselves upon the backs of their seats, with their bold white faces toward me. Sometimes they

Source: *Atlantic*, February 1900.

took their forefingers out of their mouths and pointed at my moccasined feet. Their mothers, instead of reproving such rude curiosity, looked closely at me, and attracted their children's further notice to my blanket. This embarrassed me, and kept me constantly on the verge of tears.

I sat perfectly still, with my eyes downcast, daring only now and then to shoot long glances around me. Chancing to turn to the window at my side, I was quite breathless upon seeing one familiar object. It was the telegraph pole which strode by at short paces. Very near my mother's dwelling, along the edge of a road thickly bordered with wild sunflowers, some poles like these had been planted by white men. Often I had stopped, on my way down the road, to hold my ear against the pole, and, hearing its low moaning, I used to wonder what the paleface had done to hurt it. Now I sat watching for each pole that glided by to be the last one.

In this way I had forgotten my uncomfortable surroundings, when I heard one of my comrades call out my name. I saw the missionary standing very near, tossing candies and gums into our midst. This amused us all, and we tried to see who could catch the most of the sweet-meats. The missionary's generous distribution of candies was impressed upon my memory by a disastrous result which followed. I had caught more than my share of candies and gums, and soon after our arrival at the school I had a chance to disgrace myself, which, I am ashamed to say, I did.

Though we rode several days inside of the iron horse, I do not recall a single thing about our luncheons.

It was night when we reached the school grounds. The lights from the windows of the large buildings fell upon some of the icicled trees that stood beneath them. We were led toward an open door, where the brightness of the lights within flooded out over the heads of the excited palefaces who blocked the way. My body trembled more from fear than from the snow I trod upon.

Entering the house, I stood close against the wall. The strong glaring light in the large whitewashed room dazzled my eyes. The noisy hurrying of hard shoes upon a bare wooden floor increased the whirring in my ears. My only safety seemed to be in keeping next to the wall. As I was wondering in which direction to escape from all this confusion, two warm hands grasped me firmly, and in the same moment I was tossed high in midair. A rosy-cheeked paleface woman caught me in her arms. I was both frightened and insulted by such trifling. I stared into her eyes, wishing her to let me stand on my own feet, but she jumped me up and down with increasing enthusiasm. My mother had never made a plaything of her wee daughter. Remembering this I began to cry aloud.

They misunderstood the cause of my tears, and placed me at a white table loaded with food. There our party were united again. As I did not hush my crying, one of the older ones whispered to me, "Wait until you are alone in the night."

It was very little I could swallow besides my sobs, that evening.

"Oh, I want my mother and my brother Dawée! I want to go to my aunt!" I pleaded; but the ears of the palefaces could not hear me.

From the table we were taken along an upward incline of wooden boxes, which I learned afterward to call a stairway. At the top was a quiet hall, dimly lighted. Many narrow beds were in one straight line down the entire length of the wall. In them lay sleeping brown faces, which peeped just out of the coverings. I was tucked into bed with one of the tall girls, because she talked to me in my mother tongue and seemed to soothe me.

I had arrived in the wonderful land of rosy skies, but I was not happy, as I had thought I should be. My long travel and the bewildering sights had exhausted me. I fell asleep, heaving deep, tired sobs. My tears were left to dry themselves in streaks, because neither my aunt nor my mother was near to wipe them away.

The Cutting of My Long Hair

The first day in the land of apples was a bitter-cold one; for the snow still covered the ground, and the trees were bare. A large bell rang for breakfast, its loud metallic voice crashing through the belfry overhead and into our sensitive ears. The annoying clatter of shoes on bare floors gave us no peace. The constant clash of harsh noises, with an undercurrent of many voices murmuring an unknown tongue, made a bedlam within which I was securely tied. And though my spirit tore itself in struggling for its lost freedom, all was useless.

A paleface woman, with white hair, came up after us. We were placed in a line of girls who were marching into the dining room. These were Indian girls, in stiff shoes and closely clinging dresses. The small girls wore sleeved aprons and shingled hair. As I walked noiselessly in my soft moccasins, I felt like sinking to the floor, for my blanket had been stripped from my shoulders. I looked hard at the Indian girls, who seemed not to care that they were even more immodestly dressed than I, in their tightly fitting clothes. While we marched in, the boys entered at an opposite door. I watched for the three young braves who came in our party. I spied them in the rear ranks, looking as uncomfortable as I felt.

A small bell was tapped, and each of the pupils drew a chair from under the table. Supposing this act meant they were to be seated, I pulled out mine and at once slipped into it from one side. But when I turned my head, I saw that I was the only one seated, and all the rest at our table remained standing. Just as I began to rise, looking shyly around to see how chairs were to be used, a second bell was sounded. All were seated at last, and I had to crawl back into my chair again. I heard a man's voice at one end of the hall, and I looked around to see him. But all the others hung their heads over their plates. As I glanced at the long chain of tables, I caught the eyes of a paleface woman upon me. Immediately I dropped my eyes, wondering why I was so keenly watched by the strange woman. The man ceased his mutterings, and then a third bell was tapped. Every one picked up his knife and fork and began eating. I began crying instead, for by this time I was afraid to venture anything more.

But this eating by formula was not the hardest trial in that first day. Late in the morning, my friend Judéwin gave me a terrible warning. Judéwin knew a few words of English; and she had overheard the paleface woman talk about cutting our long, heavy hair. Our mothers had taught us that only unskilled warriors who were captured had their hair shingled by the enemy. Among our people, short hair was worn by mourners, and shingled hair by cowards!

We discussed our fate some moments, and when Judéwin said, "We have to submit, because they are strong," I rebelled. ₁₉

"No, I will not submit! I will struggle first!" I answered. ₂₀

I watched my chance, and when no one noticed I disappeared. I crept up the stairs as quietly as I could in my squeaking shoes,—my moccasins had been exchanged for shoes. Along the hall I passed, without knowing whither I was going. Turning aside to an open door, I found a large room with three white beds in it. The windows were covered with dark green curtains, which made the room very dim. Thankful that no one was there, I directed my steps toward the corner farthest from the door. On my hands and knees I crawled under the bed, and cuddled myself in the dark corner. ₂₁

From my hiding place I peered out, shuddering with fear whenever I heard footsteps near by. Though in the hall loud voices were calling my name, and I knew that even Judéwin was searching for me, I did not open my mouth to answer. Then the steps were quickened and the voices became excited. The sounds came nearer and nearer. Women and girls entered the room. I held my breath, and watched them open closet doors and peep behind large trunks. Some one threw up the curtains, and the room was filled with sudden light. What caused them to stoop and look under the bed I do not know. I remember being dragged out, though I resisted by kicking and scratching wildly. In spite of myself, I was carried downstairs and tied fast in a chair. ₂₂

I cried aloud, shaking my head all the while until I felt the cold blades of the scissors against my neck, and heard them gnaw off one of my thick braids. Then I lost my spirit. Since the day I was taken from my mother I had suffered extreme indignities. People had stared at me. I had been tossed about in the air like a wooden puppet. And now my long hair was shingled like a coward's! In my anguish I moaned for my mother, but no one came to comfort me. Not a soul reasoned quietly with me, as my own mother used to do: for now I was only one of many little animals driven by a herder. ₂₃

The Snow Episode

A short time after our arrival we three Dakotas were playing in the snow-drifts. We were all still deaf to the English language, excepting Judéwin, who always heard such puzzling things. One morning we learned through her ears that we were forbidden to fall lengthwise in the snow, as we had been doing, to see our own impressions. However, before many hours we had forgotten the order, and were having great sport in the snow, when a shrill voice called us. Looking up, we saw an imperative hand beckoning us into the house. We shook the snow off ourselves, and started toward the woman as slowly as we dared. ₂₄

Judéwin said: "Now the paleface is angry with us. She is going to punish us for falling into the snow. If she looks straight into your eyes and talks loudly, you must wait until she stops. Then, after a tiny pause, say, 'No.'" The rest of the way we practiced upon the little word "no." ₂₅

As it happened, Thowin was summoned to judgment first. The door shut behind her with a click. ₂₆

Judéwin and I stood silently listening at the keyhole. The paleface woman [27] talked in very severe tones. Her words fell from her lips like crackling embers, and her inflection ran up like the small end of a switch. I understood her voice better than the things she was saying. I was certain we had made her very impatient with us. Judéwin heard enough of the words to realize all too late that she had taught us the wrong reply.

"Oh, poor Thowin!" she gasped, as she put both hands over her ears. [28]

Just then I heard Thowin's tremulous answer, "No." [29]

With an angry exclamation, the woman gave her a hard spanking. Then she [30] stopped to say something. Judéwin said it was this: "Are you going to obey my word the next time?"

Thowin answered again with the only word at her command, "No." [31]

This time the woman meant her blows to smart, for the poor frightened girl [32] shrieked at the top of her voice. In the midst of the whipping the blows ceased abruptly, and the woman asked another question: "Are you going to fall in the snow again?"

Thowin gave her bad password another trial. We heard her say feebly, [33] "No! No!"

With this the woman hid away her half-worn slipper, and led the child out, [34] stroking her black shorn head. Perhaps it occurred to her that brute force is not the solution for such a problem. She did nothing to Judéwin nor to me. She only returned to us our unhappy comrade, and left us alone in the room.

During the first two or three seasons misunderstandings as ridiculous as this [35] one of the snow episode frequently took place, bringing unjustifiable frights and punishments into our little lives.

Within a year I was able to express myself somewhat in broken English. As [36] soon as I comprehended a part of what was said and done, a mischievous spirit of revenge possessed me. One day I was called in from my play for some misconduct. I had disregarded a rule which seemed to me very needlessly binding. I was sent into the kitchen to mash the turnips for dinner. It was noon, and steaming dishes were hastily carried into the dining room. I hated turnips, and their odor which came from the brown jar was offensive to me. With fire in my heart, I took the wooden tool that the paleface woman held out to me. I stood upon a step, and, grasping the handle with both hands, I bent in hot rage over the turnips. I worked my vengeance upon them. All were so busily occupied that no one noticed me. I saw that the turnips were in a pulp, and that further beating could not improve them; but the order was, "Mash these turnips," and mash them I would! I renewed my energy; and as I sent the masher into the bottom of the jar, I felt a satisfying sensation that the weight of my body had gone into it.

Just here a paleface woman came up to my table. As she looked into the jar, [37] she shoved my hands roughly aside. I stood fearless and angry. She placed her red hands upon the rim of the jar. Then she gave one lift and a stride away from the table. But lo! the pulpy contents fell through the crumbled bottom to the floor! She spared me no scolding phrases that I had earned. I did not heed them. I felt triumphant in my revenge, though deep within me I was a wee bit sorry to have broken the jar.

As I sat eating my dinner, and saw that no turnips were served, I whooped 38
in my heart for having once asserted the rebellion within me. . . .

Four Strange Summers

After my first three years of school, I roamed again in the Western country 39
through four strange summers.

During this time I seemed to hang in the heart of chaos, beyond the touch 40
or voice of human aid. My brother, being almost ten years my senior, did not quite
understand my feelings. My mother had never gone inside of a schoolhouse, and
so she was not capable of comforting her daughter who could read and write. Even
nature seemed to have no place for me. I was neither a wee girl nor a tall one; neither a wild Indian nor a tame one. This deplorable situation was the effect of my
brief course in the East, and the unsatisfactory "teenth" in a girl's years.

It was under these trying conditions that, one bright afternoon, as I sat rest- 41
less and unhappy in my mother's cabin, I caught the sound of the spirited step of
my brother's pony on the road which passed by our dwelling. Soon I heard the
wheels of a light buckboard, and Dawée's familiar "Ho!" to his pony. He alighted
upon the bare ground in front of our house. Tying his pony to one of the project-
ing corner logs of the low-roofed cottage, he stepped upon the wooden doorstep.

I met him there with a hurried greeting, and, as I passed by, he looked a 42
quiet "What?" into my eyes.

When he began talking with my mother, I slipped the rope from the pony's 43
bridle. Seizing the reins and bracing my feet against the dashboard, I wheeled
around in an instant. The pony was ever ready to try his speed. Looking backward, I saw Dawée waving his hand to me. I turned with the curve in the road
and disappeared. I followed the winding road which crawled upward between the
bases of little hillocks. Deep water-worn ditches ran parallel on either side. A
strong wind blew against my cheeks and fluttered my sleeves. The pony reached
the top of the highest hill, and began an even race on the level lands. There was
nothing moving within that great circular horizon of the Dakota prairies save the
tall grasses, over which the wind blew and rolled off in long, shadowy waves.

Within this vast wigwam of blue and green I rode reckless and insignifi- 44
cant. It satisfied my small consciousness to see the white foam fly from the
pony's mouth.

Suddenly, out of the earth a coyote came forth at a swinging trot that was 45
taking the cunning thief toward the hills and the village beyond. Upon the
moment's impulse, I gave him a long chase and a wholesome fright. As I turned
away to go back to the village, the wolf sank down upon his haunches for rest,
for it was a hot summer day; and as I drove slowly homeward, I saw his sharp
nose still pointed at me, until I vanished below the margin of the hilltops.

In a little while I came in sight of my mother's house. Dawée stood in the 46
yard, laughing at an old warrior who was pointing his forefinger, and again waving his whole hand, toward the hills. With his blanket drawn over one shoulder,
he talked and motioned excitedly. Dawée turned the old man by the shoulder and
pointed me out to him.

"Oh han!" (Oh yes) the warrior muttered, and went his way. He had ⁴⁷
climbed the top of his favorite barren hill to survey the surrounding prairies,
when he spied my chase after the coyote. His keen eyes recognized the pony and
driver. At once uneasy for my safety, he had come running to my mother's cabin
to give her warning. I did not appreciate his kindly interest, for there was an
unrest gnawing at my heart.

As soon as he went away, I asked Dawée about something else. ⁴⁸

"No, my baby sister. I cannot take you with me to the party to-night," ⁴⁹
he replied. Though I was not far from fifteen, and I felt that before long I
should enjoy all the privileges of my tall cousin, Dawée persisted in calling me
his baby sister.

That moonlight night, I cried in my mother's presence when I heard the ⁵⁰
jolly young people pass by our cottage. They were no more young braves in blankets and eagle plumes, nor Indian maids with prettily painted cheeks. They had
gone three years to school in the East, and had become civilized. The young men
wore the white man's coat and trousers, with bright neckties. The girls wore tight
muslin dresses, with ribbons at neck and waist. At these gatherings they talked
English. I could speak English almost as well as my brother, but I was not properly dressed to be taken along. I had no hat, no ribbons, and no close-fitting
gown. Since my return from school I had thrown away my shoes, and wore again
the soft moccasins.

While Dawée was busily preparing to go I controlled my tears. But when ⁵¹
I heard him bounding away on his pony, I buried my face in my arms and
cried hot tears.

My mother was troubled by my unhappiness. Coming to my side, she ⁵²
offered me the only printed matter we had in our home. It was an Indian Bible,
given her some years ago by a missionary. She tried to console me. "Here, my
child, are the white man's papers. Read a little from them," she said most piously.

I took it from her hand, for her sake; but my enraged spirit felt more like ⁵³
burning the book, which afforded me no help, and was a perfect delusion to my
mother. I did not read it, but laid it unopened on the floor, where I sat on my feet.
The dim yellow light of the braided muslin burning in a small vessel of oil flickered
and sizzled in the awful silent storm which followed my rejection of the Bible.

Now my wrath against the fates consumed my tears before they reached my ⁵⁴
eyes. I sat stony, with a bowed head. My mother threw a shawl over her head and
shoulders, and stepped out into the night.

After an uncertain solitude, I was suddenly aroused by a loud cry piercing ⁵⁵
the night. It was my mother's voice wailing among the barren hills which held the
bones of buried warriors. She called aloud for her brothers' spirits to support her
in her helpless misery. My fingers grew icy cold, as I realized that my unrestrained
tears had betrayed my suffering to her, and she was grieving for me.

Before she returned, though I knew she was on her way, for she had ceased ⁵⁶
her weeping, I extinguished the light, and leaned my head on the window sill.

Many schemes of running away from my surroundings hovered about in my ⁵⁷
mind. A few more moons of such a turmoil drove me away to the Eastern school.
I rode on the white man's iron steed, thinking it would bring me back to my

mother in a few winters, when I should be grown tall, and there would be congenial friends awaiting me. . . .

QUESTIONS FOR CRITICAL READING, THINKING, DISCUSSION, AND WRITING

Analyzing Content and Technique

1. What were Zitkala-Sa's expectations about her journey to "Red Apple Country"? Why did the reality turn out to be so unpleasant?
2. How is the behavior of the "palefaces" different from the way Zitkala-Sa's own people might have acted toward her? What does this indicate about differences between their cultures?
3. What metaphors does Zitkala-Sa use to describe her situation and her feelings? Analyze their significance and the atmosphere they help to create.
4. Based on the evidence provided in this essay, summarize the educational methods and goals of the authorities at the school where Zitkala-Sa finds herself. What are some lessons she "learns" as a result of their policy?
5. Analyze the ironic change that has occurred in Zitkala-Sa by the end of the section titled Four Strange Summers. Why is she so "enraged" by this? What does she imply through this excerpt about education, culture, and alienation?

Collaborative Activity

As a group, sprint write for five minutes on the topic "the worst thing that happened to me at school." Share your writings with each other, discussing what made the experience depicted so negative. Discuss the similarities and differences in the experiences. Did any common themes emerge? Have the group come up with a sentence that summarizes the nature of negative school experiences.

Making Connections

1. Compare Zitkala-Sa's experiences with those of Momaday in Part Three. What do we learn from them about race relationships, attitudes of whites toward Native Americans, and the resulting attitude of Native Americans toward themselves and their heritage?
2. Write a letter to the administrators of Zitkala-Sa's school, evaluating their program and proposing certain educational reforms. In your letter you should indicate your views on what kinds of behavior and what situations enhance the learning process.

36

PREREADING ACTIVITY

Explain the idea of "tough love," with which the selection below begins. Do you agree with it? To what extent? Briefly narrate an incident out of your life or your observation to support your view.

Getting Tough

EZRA BOWEN

Ezra Bowen is an investigative reporter who often writes for *Time,* in which this piece appeared in 1988.

If tough love is your thing, you can find a lot to love about Joe Clark. 1
Bullhorn cradled in one arm, a stack of books and papers resting in the other, the 48-year-old principal of Eastside High in down-at-the-heels Paterson, N.J. (pop. 140,000), charms and bullies his way through the bustling corridors of his ordered domain like an old-time ward boss, relishing every step. He pinches girls on their cheeks, slaps high fives with both boys and girls, greeting most by name. "That a new hairdo, Tanya?" he asks one girl. "I like it. You're looking like a stone fox." "Give me some," he says, dipping his hand into an open bag of corn chips that an admiring boy is holding. "I need the quick energy." Walking through the senior lounge, the principal greets Denise Baker, who has just won a $20,000 scholarship, with some approving Clark doggerel: "If you can conceive it, you can believe it, and you can achieve it." Denise loves it. In fact virtually all the kids seem to revel in the style of the man they privately call "Crazy Joe." More than a few look to him for help: a Hispanic girl approaches to whisper that she needs a winter coat. "I'll get you one," vows the principal, scribbling her name on a pad.

"In this building," Clark proclaims, "everything emanates and ultimates 2
from me. Nothing happens without me." He spots a sign hanging askew over the girls' rest room: "I want that fixed expeditiously," he snaps at a bemused janitor. Attempting to enter a classroom, Clark finds a locked door, rattles the knob; and when the teacher opens, he bluntly orders her to undo the lock. Her response is too slow for Clark: "I said, unlock that door!" he snaps, right in front of her pupils. Clearly, this is a man who believes that if something is wrong, get tough

about it—now. And when the troops do not march smartly to the resident drummer, retribution follows. Smartly.

Clark has proved that time and again since arriving at Eastside in 1982, after 20 years as a teacher and elementary school principal in Paterson. The school, with a student body of 3,200—nearly all black and Hispanic and about a third from families on welfare—was then crawling with pushers, muggers and just about every other species of juvenile thug. Pot smoke blew out of broken windows. Graffiti marred the walls. Doors were damaged. Teachers were afraid to come to work. Clark, a former Army Reserve sergeant, took quick action. He chained doors against pushers and threatened any strays that might leak through with a baseball bat, a 36-in. Willie Mays Big Stick that still rests in a corner of his office. Bellowing through the bullhorn and the school's p.a. system, he banned loitering, mandated keep-to-the-right and keep-moving rules for the corridors, and set up a dress code forbidding hats and any gangish or come-on clothing. Students who got to school late or cut class could expect latrine or graffiti-scrubbing duty. Says Clark: "Discipline is the ultimate tenet of education. Discipline establishes the format, the environment for academic achievement to occur."

Clark's brand of discipline is often harsh. On a single day in his first year, he threw out 300 students for being tardy or absent and, he said, for disrupting the school. "Leeches and parasites," he calls such pupils. Over the next five years he tossed out hundreds more. Faculty members hostile to his vision were dismissed or strongly encouraged to leave. During his six-year tenure some 100 have departed, including a basketball coach who was hustled out by security guards for failing to stand at attention during the singing of the school alma mater. "I expurgated them through a vast variety of methods," says Clark, savoring his idiosyncratic polysyllables. Some people thought that Clark's expurgations had gone too far. In a typically unilateral action, the pugnacious principal last month tossed out 66 "parasitic" students without due process or approval of the school board, insisting that they were "hoodlums, thugs and pathological deviants." The board blew the whistle, charging him with insubordination and threatening him with dismissal.

Almost overnight that local spat found its way onto front pages all across the U.S. The Eastside story—Clark's battle to restore order in his school—became a kind of allegory for all the tribulations, dangers and scattered triumphs of cities large and small, where public education is undergoing its most severe challenge. In a country fed up with kids out of control, Clark seems to represent one effort to return to the law-and-order of a more innocent time. In recent weeks the Paterson principal has found himself not only the subject of network news reports but also a sought-after guest on TV talk shows. CBS's *60 Minutes* has shot a segment on the maverick educator, and Warner Bros. has snapped up the rights to his life story ("six figures," plus a percentage of the net, for Joe), with Sidney Poitier as a possible star. "Isn't it something," Clark beams, "that this little black Newark welfare boy is the most popular man in America right now?" The bat-wielding principal has even caught the eye and ear of the White House. President Reagan has commended Clark as an exemplar of the tough leadership needed in urban schools. In the wake of the board battle, U.S. Secretary of Education William Bennett telephoned to urge Clark to "hang in there." In an even grander gesture of support, Gary Bauer, a former Bennett aide now serving as White House Policy Development Director, offered Eastside's chief a White House post as policy adviser. (Clark turned him down.) Tough leaders like Clark have an important place in the nation's schools, Bennett told the press a few weeks ago. "Sometimes you need Mr. Chips, sometimes you need Dirty Harry."

The attention surrounding Clark has pushed a long-simmering academic   6
debate about urban education into prime time, where it rightly belongs. Two decades of wrenching societal changes in family structure, in drug and alcohol use among teens, in the level of violence in inner cities, plus widespread parental indifference have undermined urban schools. "We have allowed the school situation to disintegrate to the extent that it calls for drastic measures, and therefore, Joe Clark," says Los Angeles Principal George McKenna, who, like Clark, has been singled out for praise by Secretary Bennett. "The ultimate challenge will be whether schools whose students face these pathologies can in fact become more stable and academically successful," says Ernest Boyer, former U.S. Commissioner of Education and President of the Carnegie Foundation for the Advancement of Teaching.

The dire condition of the nation's urban school systems is by now a famil-   7
iar story, but some hard facts and illuminating incidents bear telling:

- In Detroit, high school dropout rates are 41%, with 80% in the worst inner-city districts.
- In St. Louis, 1 of 4 girls in the public schools becomes pregnant before reaching her senior year.
- In Boston schools last year, 55 students were expelled for carrying guns and 2,500 must report to police probation officers for past offenses.
- In Chicago, an open house for the parents of 1,000 pupils at Sherman School drew five mothers and fathers.
- In Texas, the 100 top-ranked school districts spend an average of $5,500 a year per child, while the bottom 100 spend only $1,800. The results are evident in San Antonio's Edgewood district, one of the state's poorest, where 50% of students fall below the national norms in reading and writing.
- In Philadelphia, an administrator describes conditions at an inner-city school: "People coming to class high, not just pupils but teachers as well; filthy bathrooms; gang intimidation; nowhere to hang coats without them being stolen."
- In New York two weeks ago, Principal Edward Morris asked for a transfer from Park West High, where he had clearly lost control of violence-prone students, and where students in the cafeteria stomped a girl so brutally they broke her ribs.

In many schools these realities blend into a panoply of horrors for teachers   8
and administrators. Odette Dunn Harris, principal of William Penn High School in Philadelphia, talks of confiscating crack bags from student pushers in a neighborhood torn by gang wars and racial strife. When she first arrived at the school, "they had riots in the lunchroom. The fire gong used to go off every five minutes, and that was the cue for the kids to break out." Some youngsters still carry knives and guns as casually as pocket combs. One parent assaulted her, and she

notes, "I've had kids say to me, 'I'm going to punch you,' or they call me 'that bald-headed bitch' because of my short hair." At Principal McKenna's Washington Preparatory High in Los Angeles just two weeks ago, three female students, about to cross the street to enter the schoolyard, were wounded in the sudden cross fire of a gang ambush. Says McKenna: "I personally buried six young men last year who had gone to this school, and I do the same thing year after year."

In the face of such grim conditions, Joe Clark has found himself the touchstone of a rekindled national debate about how to put things right in a city schoolhouse gone wrong. In the words of P. Michael Timpane, president of Teachers College at Columbia University: "Joe Clark brings out a lot of broad issues that may not have clear answers." While raising issues, however, Clark has also raised a forest of hackles, for like a lot of people who do things their own way and damn the torpedoes, Clark has stirred up as many critics as admirers. And in the wake of his confrontation with his school board, he has found himself under a drumfire of criticism by other inner-city principals who take issue with his hard-handed style. "If I had to go around with a baseball bat in one hand and a megaphone in the other, I'd sell insurance," blasts Boston Principal Thomas P. O'Neill Jr. (no relation to the former Speaker of the House), who has turned the once troubled Lewenberg middle school into a nationally recognized center of excellence. "Clark's use of force may rid the school of unwanted students," he notes, "but he also may be losing kids who might succeed." Others claim Clark's autocratic approach to discipline suggests that there is a quick solution to complex problems. "He seeds the myth that all we have to do is stop kids from knifing each other," snaps Deborah Meier, who won a $335,000 MacArthur Genius grant for her inspired supervision of Harlem's Central Park East schools. In Los Angeles, McKenna is no less critical. "We want to fix the schools, but you don't do that by seeing the kids as the enemy," he rumbles. "Our role is to rescue and to be responsible," McKenna insists, adding bitterly, "If the students were not poor black children, Joe Clark would not be tolerated." Many civil libertarians join in the criticism. Says Edward Martone, executive director of the New Jersey branch of the American Civil Liberties Union: "If every inner-city principal took the Joe Clark tack, they'd just throw one-third of their student body into the street. At best those kids are going to get minimum-wage jobs. At worst they're going to end up committing crimes and being incarcerated."

On the other hand, many people, both educators and laymen, have rushed to defend Clark. They emphasize that his tough methods are justified by the tough problems he faces. "You cannot use a democratic and collaborative style when crisis is rampant and disorder reigns," insists Kenneth Tewel, a former New York high school principal who now teaches school administration at Queens College. "You need an autocrat to bring things under control." Raymond Gerlik, principal of DeWitt C. Cregier Vocational High in Chicago, thinks Clark did what he had to do. "I sympathize with the guy," he says. "I don't have a bullhorn, but maybe he needed one." William Penn Principal Harris, who managed to purge the gangs from her school, praises Clark's character. "Here is a principal with principles. He is trying to develop strong, independent, law-abiding citizens and is trying to provide the students with a safe, secure place to learn, and for this he is going to be nailed to the wall." Clark's way of sparing no rod nor spoiling any child has touched many other hearts. Supportive letters have poured into his office. A professor's wife from Erie, Pa., tells Clark his philosophy and style are just right; a mother of two from Queens, N.Y., approves of his tough line; and a senior citizen from Olympia, Wash., writes simply, "I wish we had a few more like you." Many of the letters contain money—in amounts from $2 to $100—for Clark's defense fund. This past week brought some big bucks. Jack Berdy, chairman and CEO of On-Line Software, a computer company in Fort Lee, N.J., pledged $1 million in scholarships to Eastside over the next ten years, on the condition that the board resolve its conflict with the principal. "I think dismissal is inappropriate for a man who has brought so much to that school," says Berdy.

Clearly, discussions of Clark's approach to taming the blackboard jungle run 11 high with emotion. Cooler-headed critics—and fans—suggest that the best method of evaluating what he or any other educator has done is to look at the achievements of his students. In Clark's case the record is mixed. No question that he cleaned up the graffiti, kicked out the pushers, restored order. But academic triumphs have been more elusive. While math scores are up 6% during Clark's reign, reading scores have barely budged: they remain in the bottom third of the nation's high school seniors. While a few more students are going to college—211, up from 182 in 1982—Clark has lost considerable ground in the battle against dropouts: when he arrived, Eastside's rate was 13%; now it is 21%. Moreover, as his critics point out, any principal can raise test scores and cut disciplinary problems by tossing out the troublesome low achievers. But this hardly represents a solution to a community's problems. Rather, it just moves those problems from the classroom onto the street, where the dropouts drift into trouble or plain despair. "In many cases the school was the most stabilizing factor in their lives," says Alcena Boozer, head of an outreach program for dropouts in Portland, Ore. "Then that's gone, and nothing's there."

Paterson, like too many other school districts, has no alternative programs 12 for the losers, most of whom simply vanish into a festering underclass of unemployables. Nationally the dropout rate for the past three years has hovered around 1 million—the equivalent of dumping the entire pupil population of New York City, biggest in the U.S., onto the nation's trash heap every year. Very few ever drop back in. Most of the others are lost forever, not only to the school system but to society at large. The battle to prevent those losses has never been more difficult. Old-style pedagogy simply does not work when the climate both inside and outside the schoolhouse is one of paralyzing despair. Inner-city educators speak of a "ghetto mentality," in which very little is expected of students—by parents, teachers and others. Students quickly learn to match those expectations. "Schools knew how to succeed with kids who wanted to succeed," observes President Timpane of Teachers College. "It's only in the past generation that we've had the challenge of trying to succeed with individuals who didn't want to succeed or didn't even want to be in the classroom."

Despite such daunting hurdles, in a few of the roughest districts a handful 13 of schools have managed to become islands of excellence. They did so primarily by establishing high expectations and by getting across the conviction that their kids can and will meet those expectations. No less vital to their success, in almost every case, has been a bold, enduring principal—if not a Joe Clark, then a different kind of strong personality with his or her own talents as manager and leader. The best of these leaders are able to maintain or restore order without abandoning the students who are in trouble. They approach their staffs, students, parents and communities with a cooperative rather than a confrontational style. "Every good school has a good principal," insists William Kristol, chief of staff for Secretary Bennett. "He can set the general tone, the spirit, the ethos if you will, of the school. He can give it a sense of order, enthusiasm for learning and high expectations."

Establishing clear rules is priority No. 1 for many of these principals. Albert [14] Holland, who turned Jeremiah E. Burke High in Boston from one of the city's most dangerous schools into what District Superintendent Charles Gibbons calls an "absolute jewel," began with this set of rules: "In class on time; no hats; no Walkman in school; a student roaming the corridors without a pass is written up immediately and given a warning." His neighbor, Principal O'Neill at Lewenberg, set up equally simple standards. "The first order was to maintain control of the hallways, so we put in quiet, single-filing lines. Students go to their lockers at the beginning of the day. An assignment left in a locker is a missed assignment. Bathroom passes are issued only during the first ten minutes of class." In Chicago, Marva Collins has brought order and learning—and national acclaim—to Westside Preparatory School with her own brand of rules. Chewing gum is out: "If they insist on chewing gum, we have them do a paper on the etymology of the word gum." Any cocky youngster who walks into Westside with a defiant swagger, or wearing gang jewelry, gets special treatment: "I put my arm on their shoulder and say, 'Darling, is your hip broken?' Or, 'You're going to have to take out that earring.'"

The second priority is curriculum, with the teachers to make it work. Maria [15] Tostado, principal of Los Angeles' Garfield High, which twelve years ago had sunk to the brink of losing its accreditation, helps maintain the place as a scholar factory by mixing rules with demanding classes: "We phased out the bonehead courses and put in more advanced, challenging courses." Garfield now boasts 15 advanced-placement teachers in subjects such as calculus and physics. This year 370 students are taking the advanced-placement exams for college credit.

Among the faculty who motivate the high achievers is Jaime Escalante, a [16] math instructor whom Tostado praises as a "teaching genius." He is all of that— a showman, math scholar, father figure and cheerleader. Each Escalante class starts with warm-up music *(We Will Rock You)* and hand clapping as pupils ceremonially drop yesterday's homework into a basket. Advanced-placement students proudly wear T-shirts and satin jackets proclaiming their membership in the elite, college-bound corps. During lectures, Escalante bounces around the room, challenging, explaining, applauding. Tostado remains in awe of her fiery star, to whom she credits much of the school's renaissance: "He calls parents every time someone doesn't show up in class," she says. "He visits parents when they get home from work to get them to sign his contracts pledging hours of extra homework. He spends summers poring over the school records to find recruits for his classes like he was a coach." As a result of such dedication, 70% of last year's graduating class was accepted by colleges—a stunning score for a former gangland satrapy.

At Suitland High in downtrodden Suitland, Md., Principal Joseph Hairston [17] also prizes his teachers, recruited from schools all over the country. He treats them with respect as part of what he calls the "corporate style" and says he wants to "professionalize the workplace." Lately he has been lobbying for across-the-board raises. Hairston believes in discipline (which he prefers to call "reality therapy") and has greatly diversified the curriculum—"from dance to drafting," even to Russian. Under such policies reading scores have soared into the 87th percentile nationally from a dismal 28th. Math scores are up from 60% to 85%. This miracle has been pulled off in a mere year and a half, which, Hairston claims, is plenty of time "if you have an organizational structure, economy and support; if you know what you want to do and how to do it." Last week President Reagan saluted the school's success by paying a visit.

Talented administrators and teachers elsewhere often create special incen- [18] tives to motivate students. At Eastern High in Washington, Ralph Neal, who was named one of the top ten U.S. principals by the National School Safety Center, rewards good grades and attendance records by publishing the information in the Washington *Post* and taking an outstanding youngster to lunch each month at a good Capitol Hill restaurant—where he also fetes his teacher of the month. At Lewenberg in Boston, Principal O'Neill has designed, as a colorful celebration of reading achievements, a twin-tailed Chinese dragon stretching across the entrance to the school's two wings. Students begin each day of the year by reading aloud. And every afternoon, everyone in the school—including secretaries, administrators, security aides and teachers—ends the day by reading silently. Anyone who finishes a novel gets to add a piece of paper to the dragon's tail, with the title of the book and the reader's name. With five months left in the school year, the dragon already stretches about three-quarters of the way down the corridors.

Parent participation is another priority for these bellwether principals. [19] Rubye McClendon, who heads the dazzling, $20 million, virtually all-black magnet school, Benjamin E. Mays High in middle-class southwest Atlanta, put on a special celebration two weeks ago for Martin Luther King Jr. Day, attended by, among others, Atlanta Mayor Andrew Young, whose son goes to the school. Around McClendon, however, Young is just another father who is aware that the principal expects his participation at the school. "Parents are the key to discipline," says McClendon, "and they must know what's going on. We send the syllabus home, and the parents must initial it."

A final point of strategy among principals is to fight the curse of student [20] anonymity in big urban schools. Washington Prep's McKenna is one who believes in person-to-person contact, not only from faculty to student but among the pupils. "The academically advanced should, and at my school do, provide tutoring for the less able," he says. "'Hey, brother, I love you.' That's a stronger philosophy, and there is nothing wimpy about it." He also believes in pressing the flesh in the schoolyard, and some of that flesh is mighty big. In the hallway between fifth and sixth periods, a young giant with a dazzling, ear-to-ear smile engulfs McKenna in a hug and announces he has just been declared academically eligible to play basketball. McKenna grins and admonishes him to keep up his grades. "You hear me, now," he says, shaking his finger at the youngster, who towers over him. Educators wish that charismatic principals like these—and their methods of creating an environment for learning—were the norm in embattled urban schools across America. But they are rare exceptions, unreachable for the majority of America's urban pupils. Says Winifred Green, president of the Southern Coalition for Educational Equality in Jackson, Miss.: "I would move to any city in the country and send my kids to public school if I could pick the school. They are not all even."

A few districts are trying to salvage pupils with alternative opportunities, either inside the schools or outside in other facilities. Two years ago Burke Principal Holland in Boston instituted a program called Lifeline for students who are repeating ninth or tenth grade. Three separate classrooms at Burke house some 45 repeaters, who study three core subjects—English, math and science—for longer than usual periods. They move only among those three rooms, switching classes at intervals different from the rest of the school. "It is a mechanism so that we don't put 19-year-olds in ninth-grade classrooms next to 14-year-olds," says Holland. When the repeaters catch up, they will be moved back into regular classes or sent to alternative programs like Jobs for Youth, which combine work with study. Former Tennessee Governor Lamar Alexander, who has just been named president of the University of Tennessee system, promotes an in-school suspension system that he brought in as Governor as part of his "Better Schools Program" in 1982. Trouble makers booted out of regular classes are sent to designated rooms. There, they must continue to study under the guidance of a disciplinarian like the football coach, or someone else with a touch of intimidation, until they have shaped up for re-entry into regular classes. "This way, getting kicked out is not a free ride," he explains. Alexander, along with Secretary Bennett and others, also believes in allowing youngsters to select their schools. In Memphis, for example, students can pick any school in the city. "Once they have made a choice, you know they want to be there," he says.

In too many cities, however, the choice may be between one dreadful school or another that is mediocre, barely supported by penurious budgets, neglected by parents and politicians, beset by gang rumbles, drug trafficking and other social ills. Says Allan Weinberg, assistant director for reading and English-language arts in Philadelphia: "Schools reflect society. You must always remember that." And American society has left these schools, and the students in them, to struggle on their own.

Clearly, time has run out for such neglect. Says Boston Principal Holland: "Schools can't educate alone. They used to be isolated, but now the problems are so magnified that it takes the family, it takes the school, it takes the community all working together to make education possible." Top educators emphasize that the commitment must be nationwide and backed by consistent Federal Government support. All the wonderful, well-meaning spot programs designed to help underachievers or trouble makers really amount to no more than Band-Aids applied to the lucky few. Fortunately, after proposing cuts in the national education budget in six of its seven years, the Reagan Administration has begun to appreciate the stakes. This year education is one of the few areas where funding will be increased. In his State of the Union address, the President is expected to announce a billion-dollar boost for the 1989 Department of Education budget. The Carnegie Foundation's Boyer believes such federal action comes at the eleventh hour. "This nation cannot survive with any sense of strength or confidence if half our students in urban areas remain economically, socially and civically unprepared," he says, Public education is now on trial in America, and many educators feel that the decade ahead may be the last real chance for the nation's schools. That is, without doubt, the most urgent lesson that Principal Joe Clark can teach.

QUESTIONS FOR CRITICAL READING, THINKING, DISCUSSION, AND WRITING

Analyzing Content and Technique

1. Summarize Joe Clark's policies and beliefs. Evaluate his strategies, identifying their strengths and weaknesses. What is your opinion of McKenna's statement in paragraph 9, "If the students were not poor black children, Joe Clark would not be tolerated"? Explain.
2. What, according to Clark's critics, is the most harmful result of his policies? Do you agree? Explain.
3. Identify some of the strategies used by the other educators mentioned in the article. How are they different in philosophy from Clark's? Which ones do you like the best? Why?
4. Why, according to the writer, are inner-city schools facing unprecedented difficulties today? Can you think of other reasons?
5. How can parents help solve the problem? Point out examples of successful parent interaction from the essay.
6. Why would anonymity lead to student problems? Evaluate the steps being taken to reduce anonymity in inner-city schools.
7. What is the thesis of the essay? Where is it placed? How effective is its placement? Are you convinced of the thesis? Why or why not?

Collaborative Activity

As a group, discuss the writer's purpose. What does he want the reader to feel? To do? What emotions did you experience as you read the article? Did it make you want to take certain actions? What are they? Based on this analysis, do you think the writer has achieved his purpose?

Making Connections

1. What do you imagine Clark might say in self-defense to his critics? Write a letter from him to one of the other inner-city principals in which he explains his viewpoint and his reasons and discusses why he must do things the way he does. Keeping Clark's personality in mind, try to establish his voice in the letter.
2. Do you agree with the writer that American education is in bad shape? Write an essay in which you examine the situation in your school district, using different kinds of supporting evidence, from statistics to student and teacher interviews, to come up with a strong, clear thesis.

37

PREREADING ACTIVITY

Write about one of your early memories of school—a significant incident that left a mark on you. What did you learn from it?

Shame

DICK GREGORY

Dick Gregory (1932–) spent his early years in the slums of St. Louis. He went on to become an outstanding athlete in high school and at Southern Illinois University. Later he became well known as a politically active entertainer involved in the civil rights movement and the antiwar movement of the 1960s. In 1968, he ran for president of the United States as a candidate of the Peace and Freedom Party. His works include *From the Back of the Bus, No More Lies: The Myth and Reality of American History,* and *Dick Gregory's Political Primer.* This selection is from *Nigger,* an autobiography whose coauthor is Robert Lipsyte.

I never learned hate at home, or shame. I had to go to school for 1
that. I was about seven years old when I got my first big lesson. I was in love with a little girl named Helene Tucker, a light-complected little girl with pigtails and nice manners. She was always clean and she was smart in school. I think I went to school then mostly to look at her. I brushed my hair and even got me a little old handkerchief. It was a lady's handkerchief, but I didn't want Helene to see me wipe my nose on my hand. The pipes were frozen again, there was no water in the house, but I washed my socks and shirt every night. I'd get a pot, and go over to Mister Ben's grocery store, and stick my pot down into his soda machine. Scoop out some chopped ice. By evening the ice melted to water for washing. I got sick a lot that winter because the fire would go out at night before the clothes were dry. In the morning I'd put them on, wet or dry, because they were the only clothes I had.

Everybody's got a Helene Tucker, a symbol of everything you want. I loved 2
her for her goodness, her cleanness, her popularity. She'd walk down my street and my brothers and sisters would yell, "Here comes Helene," and I'd rub my tennis sneakers on the back of my pants and wish my hair wasn't so nappy and

the white folks' shirt fit me better. I'd run out on the street. If I knew my place and didn't come too close, she'd wink at me and say hello. That was a good feeling. Sometimes I'd follow her all the way home, and shovel the snow off her walk and try to make friends with her Momma and her aunts. I'd drop money on her stoop late at night on my way back from shining shoes in the taverns. And she had a Daddy, and he had a good job. He was a paper hanger.

I guess I would have gotten over Helene by summertime, but something happened in that classroom that made her face hang in front of me for the next twenty-two years. When I played the drums in high school it was for Helene and when I broke track records in college it was for Helene and when I started standing behind microphones and heard applause I wished Helene could hear it, too. It wasn't until I was twenty-nine years old and married and making money that I finally got her out of my system. Helene was sitting in that classroom when I learned to be ashamed of myself. 3

It was on a Thursday. I was sitting in the back of the room, in a seat with a chalk circle drawn around it. The idiot's seat, the troublemaker's seat. 4

The teacher thought I was stupid. Couldn't spell, couldn't read, couldn't do arithmetic. Just stupid. Teachers were never interested in finding out that you couldn't concentrate because you were so hungry, because you hadn't had any breakfast. All you could think about was noontime, would it ever come? Maybe you could sneak into the cloakroom and steal a bite of some kid's lunch out of a coat pocket. A bite of something. Paste. You can't really make a meal of paste, or put it on bread for a sandwich, but sometimes I'd scoop a few spoonfuls out of the paste jar in the back of the room. Pregnant people get strange tastes. I was pregnant with poverty. Pregnant with dirt and pregnant with smells that made people turn away, pregnant with cold and pregnant with shoes that were never bought for me, pregnant with five other people in my bed and no Daddy in the next room, and pregnant with hunger. Paste doesn't taste too bad when you're hungry. 5

The teacher thought I was a troublemaker. All she saw from the front of the room was a little black boy who squirmed in his idiot's seat and made noises and poked the kids around him. I guess she couldn't see a kid who made noises because he wanted someone to know he was there. 6

It was on a Thursday, the day before the Negro payday. The eagle always flew on Friday. The teacher was asking each student how much his father would give to the Community Chest. On Friday night, each kid would get the money from his father, and on Monday he would bring it to the school. I decided I was going to buy me a Daddy right then. I had money in my pocket from shining shoes and selling papers, and whatever Helene Tucker pledged for her Daddy I was going to top it. And I'd hand the money right in. I wasn't going to wait until Monday to buy me a Daddy. 7

I was shaking, scared to death. The teacher opened her book and started calling out names alphabetically. 8

"Helene Tucker?" 9

"My Daddy said he'd give two dollars and fifty cents." 10

"That's very nice, Helene. Very, very nice indeed." 11

That made me feel pretty good. It wouldn't take too much to top that. I had almost three dollars in dimes and quarters in my pocket. I stuck my hand in my pocket and held onto the money, waiting for her to call my name. But the teacher closed her book after she called everybody else in the class. [12]

I stood up and raised my hand.

"What is it now?" [13]

"You forgot me." [14]

She turned toward the blackboard. "I don't have time to be playing with you, Richard." [15] [16]

"My Daddy said he'd . . ."

"Sit down, Richard, you're disturbing the class." [17]

"My Daddy said he'd give . . . fifteen dollars." [18] [19]

She turned around and looked mad. "We are collecting this money for you and your kind, Richard Gregory. If your Daddy can give fifteen dollars you have no business being on relief." [20]

"I got it right now, I got it right now, my Daddy gave it to me to turn in today, my Daddy said . . ." [21]

"And furthermore," she said, looking right at me, her nostrils getting big and her lips getting thin and her eyes opening wide, "we know you don't have a Daddy." [22]

Helene Tucker turned around, her eyes full of tears. She felt sorry for me. Then I couldn't see her too well because I was crying, too. [23]

"Sit down, Richard." [24]

And I always thought the teacher kind of liked me. She always picked me to wash the blackboard on Friday, after school. That was a big thrill, it made me feel important. If I didn't wash it, come Monday the school might not function right. [25]

"Where are you going, Richard?" [26]

I walked out of school that day, and for a long time I didn't go back very often. There was shame there. [27]

Now there was shame everywhere. It seemed like the whole world had been inside that classroom, everyone had heard what the teacher had said, everyone had turned around and felt sorry for me. There was shame in going to the Worthy Boys Annual Christmas Dinner for you and your kind, because everybody knew what a worthy boy was. Why couldn't they just call it the Boys Annual Dinner, why'd they have to give it a name? There was shame in wearing the brown and orange and white plaid mackinaw the welfare gave to 3,000 boys. Why'd it have to be the same for everybody so when you walked down the street the people could see you were on relief? It was a nice warm mackinaw and it had a hood, and my Momma beat me and called me a little rat when she found out I stuffed it in the bottom of a pail full of garbage way over on Cottage Street. There was shame in running over to Mister Ben's at the end of the day and asking for his rotten peaches, there was shame in asking Mrs. Simmons for a spoonful of sugar, there was shame in running out to meet the relief truck. I hated that truck, full of food for you and your kind. I ran into the house and hid when it came. And then I started to sneak through alleys, to take the long way home so the people going into White's Eat Shop wouldn't see me. Yeah, the whole world heard the teacher that day, we all know you don't have a Daddy. [28]

It lasted for a while, this kind of numbness. I spent a lot of time feeling 29
sorry for myself. And then one day I met this wino in a restaurant. I'd been out
hustling all day, shining shoes, selling newspapers, and I had goo-gobs of money
in my pocket. Bought me a bowl of chili for fifteen cents, and a cheeseburger for
fifteen cents, and a Pepsi for five cents, and a piece of chocolate cake for ten cents.
That was a good meal. I was eating when this old wino came in. I love winos
because they never hurt anyone but themselves.

The old wino sat down at the counter and ordered twenty-six cents worth 30
of food. He ate it like he really enjoyed it. When the owner, Mister Williams,
asked him to pay the check, the old wino didn't lie or go through his pocket like
he suddenly found a hole.

He just said: "Don't have no money." 31

The owner yelled: "Why in hell you come in here and eat my food if you 32
don't have no money? That food cost me money."

Mister Williams jumped over the counter and knocked the wino off his 33
stool and beat him over the head with a pop bottle. Then he stepped back and
watched the wino bleed. Then he kicked him. And he kicked him again.

I looked at the wino with blood all over his face and I went over. "Leave 34
him alone, Mister Williams. I'll pay the twenty-six cents."

The wino got up, slowly, pulling himself up to the stool, then up to the 35
counter, holding on for a minute until his legs stopped shaking so bad. He
looked at me with pure hate. "Keep your twenty-six cents. You don't have to pay,
not now. I just finished paying for it."

He started to walk out, and as he passed me, he reached down and 36
touched my shoulder. "Thanks, sonny, but it's too late now. Why didn't you pay
it before?"

I was pretty sick about that. I waited too long to help another man. 37

QUESTIONS FOR CRITICAL READING, THINKING, DISCUSSION, AND WRITING

Analyzing Content and Technique

1. Analyze the character of the boy as he appears in the first few paragraphs. What changes occur in him as a result of the teacher's comment?
2. Why is Helene Tucker important to him at first? Why does she continue to be important later?
3. How are the two incidents—the classroom episode and the episode with the wino—related? From the way they are presented, deduce the main idea of the piece.
4. It is clear that Gregory feels guilty for not helping the wino in time to save him from being beaten. What is your evaluation of the incident, particularly in terms of Gregory's responsibility?
5. Analyze Gregory's use of repetition as a stylistic device. Identify some effective instances and discuss your response to them. What are some dangers of this technique if the writer is not careful?
6. Analyze the last sentence (paragraph 37). What does it tell us about Gregory's changed perspective and view of himself?

Collaborative Activity

Have each group member take on the role of one of the characters in this excerpt (except that of Gregory). Now write a brief speech to Gregory in the voice of the character you have chosen, discussing how you feel about one of the incidents in the excerpt that involved you. Try to make the voice of the character as authentic as possible. Read your speeches aloud to the group.

Making Connections

1. Compare and contrast the school experiences described by Zitkala-Sa (selection 35) and Dick Gregory. From what you know of their these writers' later lives—and from what they have written—what effect do you think their schooling had on them? (You might want to do some additional reading and research before beginning your essay.)

2. What is Gregory's attitude toward welfare and other similar institutions that exist to help the poor? Do you agree or disagree with him? Write an essay discussing the pros and cons of the effects of welfare on the recipient, taking into account your own opinion as well as Gregory's. Give supporting examples.

38

Freewrite for ten minutes about your first day at a new school or college. What were your impressions of the building, the teachers, the other students? Did you learn anything? Did you have to make adjustments? Were they difficult? After you finish, go through the writing and circle words that indicate emotion. Based on these, how would you classify this experience?

By Any Other Name

SANTHA RAMA RAU

Born in Madras, India, Santha Rama Rau (1923–) has traveled and lived in many countries, including England, South Africa, Japan, and the United States. Her travel books and fiction include *Home to India, Remember the House, The Adventuress,* and *Gifts of Passage* (1951), a collection of autobiographical stories and essays from which this selection is taken.

At the Anglo-Indian day school in Zorinabad to which my sister and I were sent when she was eight and I was five and a half, they changed our names. On the first day of school, a hot, windless morning of a north Indian September, we stood in the headmistress's study and she said, "Now you're the *new* girls. What are your names?"

My sister answered for us. "I am Premila, and she"—nodding in my direction—"is Santha."

The headmistress had been in India, I suppose, fifteen years or so, but she still smiled her helpless inability to cope with Indian names. Her rimless half-glasses glittered, and the precarious bun on the top of her head trembled as she shook her head. "Oh, my dears, those are much too hard for me. Suppose we give you pretty English names. Wouldn't that be more jolly? Let's see, now—Pamela for you, I think." She shrugged in a baffled way at my sister. "That's as close as I can get. And for *you*," she said to me, "how about Cynthia? Isn't that nice?"

My sister was always less easily intimidated than I was, and while she kept a stubborn silence, I said, "Thank you," in a very tiny voice.

We had been sent to that school because my father, among his responsibilities as an officer of the civil service, had a tour of duty to perform in the villages around that steamy little provincial town, where he had his headquarters at that time. He used to make his shorter inspection tours on horseback, and a week before, in the stale heat of a typically postmonsoon day, we had waved good-by to him and a little procession—an assistant, a secretary, two bearers, and the man to look after the bedding rolls and luggage. They rode away through our large garden, still bright green from the rains, and we turned back into the twilight of the house and the sound of fans whispering in every room.

Up to then, my mother had refused to send Premila to school in the 6 British-run establishments of that time, because, she used to say, "you can bury a dog's tail for seven years and it still comes out curly, and you can take a Britisher away from his home for a lifetime and he still remains insular." The examinations and degrees from entirely Indian schools were not, in those days, considered valid. In my case, the question had never come up, and probably never would have come up if Mother's extraordinary good health had not broken down. For the first time in my life, she was not able to continue the lessons she had been giving us every morning. So our Hindi books were put away, the stories of the Lord Krishna as a little boy were left in mid-air, and we were sent to the Anglo-Indian school.

That first day at school is still, when I think of it, a remarkable one. At that 7 age, if one's name is changed, one develops a curious form of dual personality. I remember having a certain detached and disbelieving concern in the actions of "Cynthia," but certainly no responsibility. Accordingly, I followed the thin, erect back of the headmistress down the veranda to my classroom feeling, at most, a passing interest in what was going to happen to me in this strange, new atmosphere of School.

The building was Indian in design, with wide verandas opening onto a 8 central courtyard, but Indian verandas are usually whitewashed, with stone floors. These, in the tradition of British schools, were painted dark brown and had matting on the floors. It gave a feeling of extra intensity to the heat.

I suppose there were about a dozen Indian children in the school—which 9 contained perhaps forty children in all—and four of them were in my class. They were all sitting at the back of the room, and I went to join them. I sat next to a small, solemn girl who didn't smile at me. She had long, glossy-black braids and wore a cotton dress, but she still kept on her Indian jewelry—a gold chain around her neck, thin gold bracelets, and tiny ruby studs in her ears. Like most Indian children, she had a rim of black kohl around her eyes. The cotton dress should have looked strange, but all I could think of was that I should ask my mother if I couldn't wear a dress to school, too, instead of my Indian clothes.

I can't remember too much about the proceedings in class that day, except 10 for the beginning. The teacher pointed to me and asked me to stand up. "Now, dear, tell the class your name."

I said nothing. 11

"Come along," she said, frowning slightly. "What's your name, dear?" 12

"I don't know," I said, finally. 13

The English children in the front of the class—there were about eight or 14 ten of them—giggled and twisted around in their chairs to look at me. I sat down quickly and opened my eyes very wide, hoping in that way to dry them off. The little girl with the braids put out her hand and very lightly touched my arm. She still didn't smile.

Most of that morning I was rather bored. I looked briefly at the children's 15 drawings pinned to the wall, and then concentrated on a lizard clinging to the ledge of the high, barred window behind the teacher's head. Occasionally it would shoot out its long yellow tongue for a fly, and then it would rest, with its eyes closed and its belly palpitating, as though it were swallowing several times quickly. The lessons were mostly concerned with reading and writing and simple numbers—things that my mother had already taught me—and I paid very little attention. The teacher wrote on the easel blackboard words like "bat" and "cat," which seemed babyish to me; only "apple" was new and incomprehensible.

When it was time for the lunch recess, I followed the girl with braids out 16 onto the veranda. There the children from the other classes were assembled. I saw Premila at once and ran over to her, as she had charge of our lunchbox. The children were all opening packages and sitting down to eat sandwiches. Premila and I were the only ones who had Indian food—thin wheat chapatties, some vegetable curry, and a bottle of buttermilk. Premila thrust half of it into my hand and whispered fiercely that I should go and sit with my class, because that was what the others seemed to be doing.

The enormous black eyes of the little Indian girl from my class looked at my 17 food longingly, so I offered her some. But she only shook her head and plowed her way solemnly through her sandwiches.

I was very sleepy after lunch, because at home we always took a siesta. It 18 was usually a pleasant time of day, with the bedroom darkened against the harsh afternoon sun, the drifting off into sleep with the sound of Mother's voice reading a story in one's mind, and, finally, the shrill, fussy voice of the ayah waking one for tea.

At school, we rested for a short time on low, folding cots on the veranda, 19 and then we were expected to play games. During the hot part of the afternoon we played indoors, and after the shadows had begun to lengthen and the slight breeze of the evening had come up we moved outside to the wide courtyard.

I had never really grasped the system of competitive games. At home, 20 whenever we played tag or guessing games, I was always allowed to "win"— "because," Mother used to tell Premila, "she is the youngest, and we have to allow for that." I had often heard her say it, and it seemed quite reasonable to me, but the result was that I had no clear idea of what "winning" meant.

When we played twos-and-threes that afternoon at school, in accordance 21 with my training, I let one of the small English boys catch me, but was naturally rather puzzled when the other children did not return the courtesy. I ran about for what seemed like hours without ever catching anyone, until it was time for school to close. Much later I learned that my attitude was called "not being a good sport," and I stopped allowing myself to be caught, but it was not for years that I really learned the spirit of the thing.

When I saw our car come up to the school gate, I broke away from my 22 classmates and rushed toward it yelling, "Ayah! Ayah!" It seemed like an eternity since I had seen her that morning—a wizened, affectionate figure in her white cotton sari, giving me dozens of urgent and useless instructions on how to be a good girl at school. Premila followed more sedately, and she told me on the way home never to do that again in front of the other children.

When we got home we went straight to Mother's high, white room to have tea with her, and I immediately climbed onto the bed and bounced gently up and down on the springs. Mother asked how we had liked our first day in school. I was so pleased to be home and to have left that peculiar Cynthia behind that I had nothing whatever to say about school, except to ask what "apple" meant. But Premila told Mother about the classes, and added that in her class they had weekly tests to see if they had learned their lessons well.

I asked, "What's a test?"

Premila said, "You're too small to have them. You won't have them in your class for donkey's years." She had learned the expression that day and was using it for the first time. We all laughed enormously at her wit. She also told Mother, in an aside, that we should take sandwiches to school the next day. Not, she said, that *she* minded. But they would be simpler for me to handle.

That whole lovely evening I didn't think about school at all. I sprinted barefoot across the lawns with my favorite playmate, the cook's son, to the stream at the end of the garden. We quarreled in our usual way, waded in the tepid water under the lime trees, and waited for the night to bring out the smell of the jasmine. I listened with fascination to his stories of ghosts and demons, until I was too frightened to cross the garden alone in the semidarkness. The ayah found me, shouted at the cook's son, scolded me, hurried me in to supper—it was an entirely usual, wonderful evening.

It was a week later, the day of Premila's first test, that our lives changed rather abruptly. I was sitting at the back of my class, in my usual inattentive way, only half listening to the teacher. I had started a rather guarded friendship with the girl with the braids, whose name turned out to be Nalini (Nancy, in school). The three other Indian children were already fast friends. Even at that age it was apparent to all of us that friendship with the English or Anglo-Indian children was out of the question. Occasionally, during the class, my new friend and I would draw pictures and show them to each other secretly.

The door opened sharply and Premila marched in. At first, the teacher smiled at her in a kindly and encouraging way and said, "Now, you're little Cynthia's sister?"

Premila didn't even look at her. She stood with her feet planted firmly apart and her shoulders rigid, and addressed herself directly to me. "Get up," she said. "We're going home."

I didn't know what had happened, but I was aware that it was a crisis of some sort. I rose obediently and started to walk toward my sister.

"Bring your pencils and your notebook," she said.

I went back for them, and together we left the room. The teacher started to say something just as Premila closed the door, but we didn't wait to hear what it was.

In complete silence we left the school grounds and started to walk home. Then I asked Premila what the matter was. All she would say was "We're going home for good."

It was a very tiring walk for a child of five and a half, and I dragged along behind Premila with my pencils growing sticky in my hand. I can still remember looking at the dusty hedges, and the tangles of thorns in the ditches by the side of the road, smelling the faint fragrance from the eucalyptus trees and wondering whether we would ever reach home. Occasionally a horse-drawn tonga passed us, and the women, in their pink or green silks, stared at Premila and me trudging along on the side of the road. A few coolies and a line of women carrying baskets of vegetables on their heads smiled at us. But it was nearing the hottest time of day, and the road was almost deserted. I walked more and more slowly, and shouted to Premila, from time to time, "Wait for me!" with increasing peevishness. She spoke to me only once, and that was to tell me to carry my notebook on my head, because of the sun.

When we got to our house the ayah was just taking a tray of lunch into 35 Mother's room. She immediately started a long, worried questioning about what are you children doing back here at this hour of the day.

Mother looked very startled and very concerned, and asked Premila what 36 had happened.

Premila said, "We had our test today, and She made me and the other 37 Indians sit at the back of the room, with a desk between each one."

Mother said, "Why was that, darling?" 38

"She said it was because Indians cheat," Premila added. "So I don't think 39 we should go back to that school."

Mother looked very distant, and was silent a long time. At last she said, "Of 40 course not, darling." She sounded displeased.

We all shared the curry she was having for lunch, and afterward I was sent 41 off to the beautifully familiar bedroom for my siesta. I could hear Mother and Premila talking through the open door.

Mother said, "Do you suppose she understood all that?" 42

Premila said, "I shouldn't think so. She's a baby." 43

Mother said, "Well, I hope it won't bother her." 44

Of course, they were both wrong. I understood it perfectly, and I 45 remember it all very clearly. But I put it happily away, because it had all happened to a girl called Cynthia, and I never was really particularly interested in her.

QUESTIONS FOR CRITICAL READING, THINKING, DISCUSSION, AND WRITING

Analyzing Content and Technique

1. Look up the term "Anglo-Indian." What does it suggest of race relations in India at the time this incident takes place (several decades before Indian independence)?
2. Analyze the character of the headmistress, identifying significant descriptive phrases used by the writer. How is her first interaction with the children symbolic?
3. Describe the writer's family. From the details given about the parents, what can you deduce about their values? How have these values influenced the older daughter, Premila?

4. What is Santha's response to her new name? Why does she tell the class she doesn't know her name? How does she feel at the end of the excerpt?
5. Discuss the reason Premila decides to leave the school for good. What foreshadowings has the writer provided earlier to prepare us for what the teacher tells Premila?
6. Though she is unable to articulate it at the time, the narrator obviously learns something from the incident. What is it? How do you think it affected her future ideas and sense of self?

Collaborative Activity

Examine the essay for details which give us a glimpse of the lives and concepts of the British in India. Make a list of the details you find and analyze what they imply about lifestyle and values. How accurate is the narrator's mother's statement about them in paragraph 6?

Making Connections

1. In an essay, compare Rau's experience of being renamed with Mary Antin's (selection 5). Why do the writers have such different attitudes toward a similar event? Analyze their backgrounds, their situations, and their relationships to the races around them to come up with your answer.
2. Write a letter from the point of view of Santha's mother to the school authorities explaining why she is removing her children from the school. In your letter focus on the problems that exist for Indian children in the school and suggest some changes that need to be made.

39

Write about a disabled person whom you know well or have met. What is your impression of his or her character, goals, hopes, and fears? What similarities do you perceive between him or her and a person who is not disabled?

Footsteps of My Life

HELEN KELLER

Helen Keller (1880–1968), who became blind and deaf as a very young child, was a nationally known lecturer and author. She traveled all over the United States campaigning for improvement in the education and lives of physically handicapped people. Keller was first taught at home (by Anne Sullivan, who is mentioned in this selection) and then went on to study at Radcliffe College, graduating cum laude. Her books include *Helen Keller's Journal*, *Out of the Dark*, *Optimism*, *The Song of the Stone Wall*, *The World I Live In*, and *The Story of My Life*, from which selection 39 is taken.

The most important day I remember in all my life is the one on which my teacher, Anne Mansfield Sullivan, came to me. I am filled with wonder when I consider the immeasurable contrasts between the two lives which it connects. It was the third of March, 1887, three months before I was seven years old. 1

On the afternoon of that eventful day, I stood on the porch, dumb, expectant. I guessed vaguely from my mother's signs and from the hurrying to and fro in the house that something unusual was about to happen, so I went to the door and waited on the steps. The afternoon sun penetrated the mass of honeysuckle that covered the porch, and fell on my upturned face. My fingers lingered almost unconsciously on the familiar leaves and blossoms which had just come forth to greet the sweet southern spring. I did not know what the future held of marvel or surprise for me. Anger and bitterness had preyed upon me continually for weeks and a deep languor had succeeded this passionate struggle. 2

Have you ever been at sea in the dense fog, when it seemed as if a tangible white darkness shut you in, and the great ship, tense and anxious, groped her way toward the shore with plummet and sounding-line, and you waited with beating heart for something to happen? I was like that ship before my education began, only I was without compass or sounding-line, and had no way of knowing how 3

Source: From Helen Keller, *The Story of My Life*, Doubleday, New York, 1954.

near the harbour was. "Light! give me light!" was the wordless cry of my soul, and the light of love shone on me in that very hour.

I felt approaching footsteps. I stretched out my hand as I supposed to my ₄ mother. Some one took it, and I was caught up and held close in the arms of her who had come to reveal all things to me, and, more than all things else, to love me.

The morning after my teacher came she led me into her room and gave me ₅ a doll. The little blind children at the Perkins Institution had sent it and Laura Bridgman had dressed it; but I did not know this until afterward. When I had played with it a little while, Miss Sullivan slowly spelled into my hand the word "d-o-l-l." I was at once interested in this finger play and tried to imitate it. When I finally succeeded in making the letters correctly I was flushed with childish pleasure and pride. Running downstairs to my mother I held up my hand and made the letters for doll. I did not know that I was spelling a word or even that words existed; I was simply making my fingers go in monkey-like imitation. In the days that followed I learned to spell in this uncomprehending way a great many words, among them *pin, hat, cup* and a few verbs like *sit, stand* and *walk.* But my teacher had been with me several weeks before I understood that everything has a name.

One day, while I was playing with my new doll, Miss Sullivan put my big ₆ rag doll into my lap also, spelled "d-o-l-l" and tired to make me understand that "d-o-l-l" applied to both. Earlier in the day we had had a tussle over the words "m-u-g" and "w-a-t-e-r." Miss Sullivan had tired to impress it upon me that "m-u-g" is *mug* and that "w-a-t-e-r" is *water,* but I persisted in confounding the two. In despair she had dropped the subject for the time, only to renew it at the first opportunity. I became impatient at her repeated attempts and, seizing the new doll, I dashed it upon the floor. I was keenly delighted when I felt the fragments of the broken doll at my feet. Neither sorrow nor regret followed my passionate outburst. I had not loved the doll. In the still, dark world in which I lived there was no strong sentiment or tenderness. I felt my teacher sweep the fragments to one side of the hearth, and I had a sense of satisfaction that the cause of my discomfort was removed. She brought me my hat, and I knew I was going out into the warm sunshine. This thought, if a wordless sensation may be called a thought, made me hop and skip with pleasure.

We walked down the path to the well-house, attracted by the fragrance of the ₇ honeysuckle with which it was covered. Some one was drawing water and my teacher placed my hand under the spout. As the cool stream gushed over one hand she spelled into the other the word *water,* first slowly, then rapidly. I stood still, my whole attention fixed upon the motions of her fingers. Suddenly I felt a misty con-sciousness as of something forgotten—a thrill of returning thought; and somehow the mystery of language was revealed to me. I knew then that "w-a-t-e-r" meant the wonderful cool something that was flowing over my hand. That living word awakened my soul, gave it light, hope, joy, set it free! There were barriers still, it is true, but barriers that could in time be swept away.

I left the well-house eager to learn. Everything had a name, and each name ₈ gave birth to a new thought. As we returned to the house every object which I touched seemed to quiver with life. That was because I saw everything with the strange, new sight that had come to me. On entering the door I remembered the doll I had broken. I felt my way to the hearth and picked up the pieces. I tried vainly to put them together. Then my eyes filled with tears; for I realized what I had done, and for the first time I felt repentance and sorrow.

I learned a great many new words that day. I do not remember what they all were; but I do know that *mother, father, sister, teacher* were among them—words that were to make the world blossom for me, "like Aaron's rod, with flowers." It would had been difficult to find a happier child than I was as I lay in my crib at the close of the eventful day and lived over the joys it had brought me, and for the first time longed for a new day to come.

•

I had now the key to all language, and I was eager to learn to use it. Children who hear acquire language without any particular effort; the words that fall from others' lips they catch on the wings, as it were, delightedly, while the little deaf child must trap them by a slow and often painful process. But whatever the process, the result is wonderful. Gradually from naming an object we advance step by step until we have traversed the vast distance between our first stammered syllable and the sweep of thought in a line of Shakespeare.

At first, when my teacher told me about a new thing I asked very few questions. My ideas were vague, and my vocabulary was inadequate; but as my knowledge of things grew, and I learned more and more words, my field of inquiry broadened, and I would return again and again to the same subject, eager for further information. Sometimes a new word revived an image that some earlier experience had engraved on my brain.

I remember the morning that I first asked the meaning of the word, "love." This was before I knew many words. I had found a few early violets in the garden and brought them to my teacher. She tried to kiss me: but at that time I did not like to have any one kiss me except my mother. Miss Sullivan put her arm gently round me and spelled into my hand, "I love Helen."

"What is love?" I asked.

She drew me closer to her and said, "It is here," pointing to my heart, whose beats I was conscious of for the first time. Here words puzzled me very much because I did not then understand anything unless I touched it.

I smelt the violets in her hand and asked, half in words, half in signs, a question which meant, "Is love the sweetness of flowers?"

"No," said my teacher.

Again I thought. The warm sun was shining on us.

"Is this not love?" I asked, pointing in the direction from which the heat came. "Is this not love?"

It seemed to me that there could be nothing more beautiful than the sun, whose warmth makes all things grow. But Miss Sullivan shook her head, and I was greatly puzzled and disappointed. I thought it strange that my teacher could not show me love.

A day or two afterward I was stringing beads of different sizes in symmetrical groups—two large beads, three small ones, and so on. I had made many mistakes, and Miss Sullivan had pointed them out again and again with gentle patience. Finally I noticed a very obvious error in the sequence and for an instant I concentrated my attention on the lesson and tried to think how I should have arranged the beads. Miss Sullivan touched my forehead and spelled with decided emphasis, "Think."

In a flash I knew that the word was the name of the process that was going on in my head. This was my first conscious perception of an abstract idea. 21

For a long time I was still—I was not thinking of the beads in my lap, but trying to find a meaning for "love" in the light of this new idea. The sun had been under a cloud all day, and there had been brief showers; but suddenly the sun broke forth in all its southern splendour. 22

Again I asked my teacher, "Is this not love?" 23

"Love is something like the clouds that were in the sky before the sun came out," she replied. Then in simpler words than these, which at that time I could not have understood, she explained: "You cannot touch the clouds, you know; but you feel the rain and know how glad the flowers and the thirsty earth are to have it after a hot day. You cannot touch love either; but you feel the sweetness that it pours into everything. Without love you would not be happy or want to play." 24

The beautiful truth burst upon my mind—I felt that there were invisible lines stretched between my spirit and the spirits of others. 25

From the beginning of my education Miss Sullivan made it a practice to speak to me as she would speak to any hearing child; the only difference was that she spelled the sentences into my hand instead of speaking them. If I did not know the words and idioms necessary to express my thoughts she supplied them, even suggesting conversation when I was unable to keep up my end of the dialogue. 26

This process was continued for several years; for the deaf child does not learn in a month, or even in two or three years, the numberless idioms and expressions used in the simplest daily intercourse. The little hearing child learns these from constant repetition and imitation. The conversation he hears in his home stimulates his mind and suggests topics and calls forth the spontaneous expression of his own thoughts. This natural exchange of ideas is denied to the deaf child. My teacher, realizing this, determined to supply the kinds of stimulus I lacked. This she did by repeating to me as far as possible, verbatim, what she heard, and by showing me how I could take part in the conversation. But it was a long time before I ventured to take the initiative, and still longer before I could find something appropriate to say at the right time. 27

The deaf and the blind find it very difficult to acquire the amenities of conversation. How much more this difficulty must be augmented in the case of those who are both deaf and blind! They cannot distinguish the tone of the voice or, without assistance, go up and down the gamut of tones that give significance to words; nor can they watch the expression of the speaker's face, and a look is often the very soul of what one says. 28

The next important step in my education was learning to read. 29

As soon as I could spell a few words my teacher gave me slips of cardboard on which were printed words in raised letters. I quickly learned that each printed 30 word stood for an object, an act, or a quality. I had a frame in which I could arrange the words in little sentences; but before I ever put sentences in the frame I used to make them in objects. I found the slips of paper which represented, for example, "doll," "is," "on," "bed," and placed each name on its object; then I put my doll on he bed with the words *is, on, bed* arranged beside the doll, thus making a sentence of words, and at the same time carrying out the idea of the sentence with the things themselves.

One day, Miss Sullivan tells me, I pinned the word *girl* on my pinafore and stood in the wardrobe. On the shelf I arranged the words, *is, in, wardrobe.* Nothing delighted me so much as this game. My teacher and I played it for hours at a time. Often everything in the room was arranged in object sentences. 31

From the printed slip it was but a step to the printed book. I took my "Reader for Beginners" and hunted for the words I knew; when I found them my joy was like that of a game of hide-and-seek. Thus I began to read. Of the time when I began to read connected stories I shall speak later. 32

For a long time I had no regular lessons. Even when I studied most earnestly it seemed more like play than work. Everything Miss Sullivan taught me she illustrated by a beautiful story or a poem. Whenever anything delighted or interested me she talked it over with me just as if she were a little girl herself. What many children think of with dread, as a painful plodding through grammar, hard sums and harder definitions, is today one of my most precious memories. 33

I cannot explain the peculiar sympathy Miss Sullivan had with my pleasures and desires. Perhaps it was the result of long association with the blind. Added to this she had a wonderful faculty for description. She went quickly over uninteresting details, and never nagged me with questions to see if I remembered the day-before-yesterday's lesson. She introduced dry technicalities of science little by little, making every subject so real that I could not help remembering what she taught. 34

We read and studied out of doors, preferring the sunlit woods to the house. All my early lessons have in them the breath of the woods—the fine, resinous odour of pine needles, blended with the perfume of wild grapes. Seated in the gracious shade of a wild tulip tree, I learned to think that everything had a lesson and a suggestion. "The loveliness of things taught me all their use." Indeed, everything that could hum, or buzz, or sing, or bloom, had a part in my education—noisy-throated frogs, katydids and crickets held in my hand until, forgetting their embarrassment, they trilled their reedy note, little downy chickens and wildflowers, the dogwood blossoms, meadow-violets and budding fruit trees. I felt the bursting cotton-bolls and fingered their soft fiber and fuzzy seeds; I felt the low soughing of the wind through the cornstalks, the silky rustling of the long leaves, and the indignant snort of my pony, as we caught him in the pasture and put the bit in his mouth—ah me! how well I remember the spicy, clovery smell of his breath! 35

Sometimes I rose at dawn and stole into the garden while the heavy dew lay on the grass and flowers. Few know what joy it is to feel the roses pressing softly into the hand, or the beautiful motion of the lilies as they sway in the morning breeze. Sometimes I caught an insect in the flower I was plucking, and I felt the 36

faint noise of a pair of wings rubbed together in a sudden terror, as the little creature became aware of a pressure from without.

Another favourite haunt of mine was the orchard, where the fruit ripened   37
early in July. The large, downy peaches would reach themselves into my hand,
and as the joyous breezes flew about the trees the apples tumbled at my feet. Oh,
the delight with which I gathered up the fruit in my pinafore, pressed my face
against the smooth cheeks of the apples, still warm from the sun, and skipped
back to the house!

Our favourite walk was to Keller's Landing, an old tumble-down lumber-   38
wharf on the Tennessee River, used during the Civil War to land soldiers. There
we spent many happy hours and played at learning geography. I built dams of
pebbles, made islands and lakes, and dug river-beds, all for fun, and never
dreamed that I was learning a lesson. I listened with increasing wonder to Miss
Sullivan's descriptions of the great round world with its burning mountains,
buried cities, moving rivers of ice, and many other things as strange. She made
raised maps in clay, so that I could feel the mountain ridges and valleys, and follow with my fingers the devious course of rivers. I liked this, too; but the division
of the earth into zones and poles confused and teased my mind. The illustrative
strings and the orange stick representing the poles seemed so real that even to this
day the mere mention of temperate zone suggests a series of twine circles; and I
believe that if any one should set about it he could convince me that white bears
actually climb the North Pole.

Arithmetic seems to have been the only study I did not like. From the first   39
I was not interested in the science of numbers. Miss Sullivan tried to teach me to
count by stringing beads in groups, and by arranging kindergarten straws I
learned to add and subtract. I never had patience to arrange more than five or six
groups at a time. When I had accomplished this my conscience was at rest for the
day, and I went out quickly to find my playmates.

In this same leisurely manner I studied zoology and botany.   40

Once a gentleman, whose name I have forgotten, sent me a collection of   41
fossils—tiny mollusk shells beautifully marked, and bits of sandstone with the
print of birds' claws, and a lovely fern in bas-relief. These were the keys which
unlocked the treasures of the antediluvian world for me. With trembling fingers I
listened to Miss Sullivan's descriptions of the terrible beasts, with uncouth,
unpronounceable names, which once went tramping through the primeval
forests, tearing down the branches of gigantic trees for food, and died in the dismal swamps of an unknown age. For a long time these strange creatures haunted
my dreams, and this gloomy period formed a somber background to the joyous
Now, filled with sunshine and roses and echoing with the gentle beat of my
pony's hoof.

Another time a beautiful shell was given me, and with a child's surprise and   42
delight I learned how a tiny mollusk had built the lustrous coil for his dwelling
place, and how on still nights, when there is no breeze stirring the waves, the
Nautilus sails on the blue waters of the Indian Ocean in his "ship of pearl." After
I had learned a great many interesting things about the life and habits of the children of the sea—how in the midst of dashing waves the little polyps build the

beautiful coral isles of the Pacific, and the foraminifera have made the chalk-hills of many a land—my teacher read me "The Chambered Nautilus," and showed me that the shell-building process of the mollusks is symbolical of the development of the mind. Just as the wonder-working mantle of the Nautilus changes the material it absorbs from the water and makes it a part of itself, so the bits of knowledge one gathers undergo a similar change and become pearls of thought.

Again, it was the growth of a plant that furnished the text for a lesson. We 43 bought a lily and set it in a sunny window. Very soon the green, pointed buds showed signs of opening. The slender, fingerlike leaves on the outside opened slowly, reluctant, I thought, to reveal the loveliness they hid; once having made a start, however, the opening process went on rapidly, but in order and systematically. There was always one bud larger and more beautiful than the rest, which pushed her outer covering back with more pomp, as if the beauty in soft, silky robes knew that she was the lily-queen by right divine, while her more timid sisters doffed their green hoods shyly, until the whole plant was one nodding bough of loveliness and fragrance.

Once there were eleven tadpoles in a glass globe set in a window full of 44 plants. I remember the eagerness with which I made discoveries about them. It was great fun to plunge my hand into the bowl and feel the tadpoles frisk about, and to let them slip and slide between my fingers. One day a more ambitious fellow leaped beyond the edge of the bowl and fell on the floor, where I found him to all appearance more dead than alive. The only sign of life was a slight wriggling of his tail. But no sooner had he returned to his element than he darted to the bottom, swimming round and round in joyous activity. He had made his leap, he had seen the great world, and was content to stay in his pretty glass house under the big fuchsia tree until he attained the dignity of froghood. Then he went to live in the leafy pool at the end of the garden, where he made the summer nights musical with his quaint love-song.

Thus I learned from life itself. At the beginning I was only a little mass of 45 possibilities. It was my teacher who unfolded and developed them. When she came, everything about me breathed of love and joy and was full of meaning. She has never since let pass an opportunity to point out the beauty that is in everything, nor has she ceased trying in thought and action and example to make my life sweet and useful.

It was my teacher's genius, her quick sympathy, her loving tact which made 46 the first years of my education so beautiful. It was because she seized the right moment to impart knowledge that made it so pleasant and acceptable to me. She realized that a child's mind is like a shallow brook which ripples and dances merrily over the stony course of its education and reflects here a flower, there a bush, yonder a fleecy cloud; and she attempted to guide my mind on its way, knowing that like a brook it should be fed by mountain streams and hidden springs, until it broadened out into a deep river, capable of reflecting in its placid surface, billowy hills, the luminous shadows of trees and the blue heavens, as well as the sweet face of a little flower.

Any teacher can take a child to the classroom, but not every teacher can 47 make him learn. He will not work joyously unless he feels that liberty is his, whether he is busy or at rest; he must feel the flush of victory and the heart-sinking of disappointment before he takes with a will the tasks distasteful to him and resolves to dance his way bravely through a dull routine of textbooks.

My teacher is so near to me that I scarcely think of myself apart from her. ₄₈ How much of my delight in all beautiful things is innate, and how much is due to her influence, I can never tell. I feel that her being is inseparable from my own, and that the footsteps of my life are in hers. All the best of me belongs to her— there is not a talent, or an aspiration or a joy in me that has not been awakened by her loving touch.

QUESTIONS FOR CRITICAL READING, THINKING, DISCUSSION, AND WRITING

Analyzing Content and Technique

1. What analogy does Keller use to explain how she felt as a child before her education began? Do you think it is an appropriate one? How does it help us understand her experience as a deaf and blind individual? Based on this, how would you define the function of analogies?
2. Which incident in Keller's life reveals the mystery of language to her? How? What does she learn?
3. What does Keller particularly appreciate about her teacher?
4. How does Miss Sullivan first answer the child Helen's question, "What is love?" Why does she have difficulty with it? How does she answer the question later? How accurate is her response? What might you have said in her position?
5. Analyze the comparisons Keller makes between the learning process of a deaf-blind child and a hearing-seeing child. What is the tone in which she presents her ideas?
6. What methods does Miss Sullivan adopt to keep Helen interested in her studies? What is her attitude toward Helen's disabilities?
7. Keller writes about studying out of doors (beginning with paragraph 35). What kind of atmosphere does she create in her description of her surroundings? What techniques does she use to make the description powerful?

Collaborative Activity

As a group, conduct library research on how teaching methods for the disabled have changed since Keller's time. Each group in the class should choose one particular disability, physical or cognitive, to study. Focus on one or two specific teaching methods and the related equipment and create a group report to present to the class.

Making Connections

1. Write an essay discussing some of society's attitudes toward disabled people. Points you might consider include these: Have attitudes changed in the last fifty years? If so, how? How do disabled people feel about these attitudes and the behavior they give rise to? What, if anything, would you like to be different? You may want to do some outside reading and interviewing before writing this essay.
2. As we see in Keller's essay, the traditional approach to teaching did not work with her. Her success began when her teacher was able to find an alternative method. What alternative methods of teaching are used in American schools today for learners who are "different"? To explore this topic in an essay, you may either conduct library research or visit an alternative school and interview its staff.

40

Barba Nikos

HARRY MARK PETRAKIS

Harry Mark Petrakis (1923–) is of Greek descent. He was born in St. Louis but has lived most of his life in Chicago. A novelist and writer of short stories, he is fond of describing his own immigrant community. His books include *Collected Stories; Pericles on 31st Street; A Dream of Kings;* and two autobiographical works, *Reflections on a Writer's Life and Work* and *Stelmark: A Family Recollection.*

*T*here was one storekeeper I remember above all others in my youth. 1
It was shortly before I became ill, spending a good portion of my time with a motley group of varied ethnic ancestry. We contended with one another to deride the customs of the old country. On our Saturday forays into neighborhoods beyond our own, to prove we were really Americans, we ate hot dogs and drank Cokes. If a boy didn't have ten cents for this repast he went hungry, for he dared not bring a sandwich from home made of the spiced meats our families ate.

One of our untamed games was to seek out the owner of a pushcart or a 2 store, unmistakably an immigrant, and bedevil him with a chorus of insults and jeers. To prove allegiance to the gang it was necessary to reserve our fiercest malevolence for a storekeeper or peddler belonging to our own ethnic background.

For that reason I led a raid on the small, shabby grocery of old Barba Nikos, 3 a short, sinewy Greek who walked with a slight limp and sported a flaring, handlebar mustache.

We stood outside his store and dared him to come out. When he emerged 4 to do battle, we plucked a few plums and peaches from the baskets on the sidewalk and retreated across the street to eat them while he watched. He waved a fist and hurled epithets at us in ornamental Greek.

Source: Copyright Harry Mark Petrakis, 1983, from *Reflections* (Chicago: Lake View Press, 1983).

Aware that my mettle was being tested, I raised my arm and threw my 　5
halfeaten plum at the old man. My aim was accurate and the plum struck him on
the cheek. He shuddered and put his hand to the stain. He stared at me across
the street, and although I could not see his eyes, I felt them sear my flesh. He
turned and walked silently back into the store. The boys slapped my shoulders in
admiration, but it was a hollow victory that rested like a stone in the pit of my
stomach.

At twilight when we disbanded, I passed the grocery alone on my way 　6
home. There was a small light burning in the store and the shadow of the old
man's body outlined against the glass. Goaded by remorse, I walked to the door
and entered.

The old man moved from behind the narrow wooden counter and stared at 　7
me. I wanted to turn and flee, but by then it was too late. As he motioned for me
to come closer, I braced myself for a curse or a blow.

"You were the one," he said, finally, in a harsh voice. 　8

I nodded mutely. 　9

"Why did you come back?" 　10

I stood there unable to answer. 　11

"What's your name?" 　12

"Haralambos," I said, speaking to him in Greek. 　13

He looked at me in shock. "You are Greek!" he cried. "A Greek boy attack- 　14
ing a Greek grocer!" He stood appalled at the immensity of my crime. "All
right," he said coldly. "You are here because you wish to make amends." His
great mustache bristled in concentration. "Four plums, two peaches," he said.
"That makes a total of 78 cents. Call it 75. Do you have 75 cents, boy?"

I shook my head. 　15

"Then you will work it off," he said. "Fifteen cents an hour into 75 cents 　16
makes"—he paused—"five hours of work. Can you come here Saturday morning?"

"Yes," I said. 　17

"Yes, Barba Nikos," he said sternly. "Show respect." 　18

"Yes, Barba Nikos," I said. 　19

"Saturday morning at eight o'clock," he said. "Now go home and say 　20
thanks in your prayers that I did not loosen your impudent head with a solid
smack on the ear." I needed no further urging and fled.

Saturday morning, still apprehensive, I returned to the store. I began by 　21
sweeping, raising clouds of dust in dark and hidden corners. I washed the windows, whipping the squeegee swiftly up and down the glass in a fever of fear that
some member of the gang would see me. When I finished I hurried back inside.

For the balance of the morning I stacked cans, washed the counter, and 　22
dusted bottles of yellow wine. A few customers entered, and Barba Nikos served
them. A little after twelve o'clock he locked the door so he could eat lunch. He
cut himself a few slices of sausage, tore a large chunk from a loaf of crisp-crusted
bread, and filled a small cup with a dozen black shiny olives floating in brine. He
offered me the cup. I could not help myself and grimaced.

"You are a stupid boy," the old man said. "You are not really Greek, are 　23
you?"

"Yes, I am."   24

"You might be," he admitted grudgingly. "But you do not act Greek. Wrin-   25
kling your nose at these fine olives. Look around this store for a minute. What do
you see?"

"Fruits and vegetables," I said. "Cheese and olives and things like that."   26

He stared at me with a massive scorn. "That's what I mean," he said. "You   27
are a bonehead. You don't understand that a whole nation and a people are in
this store."

I looked uneasily toward the storeroom in the rear, almost expecting some-   28
one to emerge.

"What about olives?" he cut the air with a sweep of his arm. "There are   29
olives of many shapes and colors. Pointed black ones from Kalamata, oval ones
from Amphissa, pickled green olives and sharp tangy yellow ones. Achilles carried
black olives to Troy and after a day of savage battle leading his Myrmidons, he'd
rest and eat cheese and ripe black olives such as these right here. You have heard
of Achilles, boy, haven't you?"

"Yes," I said.   30

"Yes, Barba Nikos."   31

"Yes, Barba Nikos," I said.   32

He motioned at the row of jars filled with varied spices. "There is origanon   33
there and basilikon and daphne and sesame and miantanos, all the marvelous fla-
vorings that we have used in our food for thousands of years. The men of
Marathon carried small packets of these spices into battle, and the scents
reminded them of their homes, their families, and their children."

He rose and tugged his napkin free from around his throat. "Cheese, you   34
said. Cheese! Come closer, boy, and I will educate your abysmal ignorance." He
motioned toward a wooden container on the counter. "That glistening white
delight is feta, made from goat's milk, packed in wooden buckets to retain the flavor. Alexander the Great demanded it on his table with his casks of wine when he
planned his campaigns."

He walked limping from the counter to the window where the piles of   35
tomatoes, celery, and green peppers clustered. "I suppose all you see here are
some random vegetables?" He did not wait for me to answer. "You are dumb
again. These are some of the ingredients that go to make up a Greek salad. Do
you know what a Greek salad really is? A meal in itself, an experience, an emotional involvement. It is created deftly and with grace. First, you place large lettuce leaves in a big, deep bowl." He spread his fingers and moved them slowly,
carefully, as if he were arranging the leaves. "the remainder of the lettuce is shred-
ded and piled in a small mound," he said. "Then comes celery, cucumbers, tomatoes sliced lengthwise, green peppers, origanon, green olives, feta, avocado and
anchovies. At the end you dress it with lemon, vinegar, and pure olive oil, glint-
ing golden in the light."

He finished with a heartfelt sigh and for a moment closed his eyes. Then he   36
opened one eye to mark me with a baleful intensity. "The story goes that Zeus
himself created the recipe and assembled and mixed the ingredients on Mount
Olympus one night when he had invited some of the other gods to dinner."

He turned his back on me and walked slowly again across the store, drag- 37
ging one foot slightly behind him. I looked uneasily at the clock, which showed
that it was a few minutes past one. He turned quickly and startled me. "And
everything else is here," he said loudly. "White beans, lentils, garlic, crisp bread,
kokoretsi, meat balls, mussels and clams." He paused and drew a deep, long
breath. "And the wine," he went on, "wine from Samos, Santorini, and Crete,
retsina and mavrodaphne, a taste almost as old as water . . . and then the fragrant
melons, the pastries, yellow diples and golden loukoumades, the honey custard
galatobouriko. Everything a part of our history, as much a part as the exquisite
sculpture in marble, the bearded warriors, Pan and the oracles at Delphi, and the
nymphs dancing in the shadowed groves under Homer's glittering moon." He
paused, out of breath again, and coughed harshly. "Do you understand now, boy?"

He watched my face for some response and then grunted. We stood silent 38
for a moment until he cocked his head and stared at the clock. "It is time for you
to leave," he motioned brusquely toward the door. "We are square now. Keep it
that way."

I decided the old man was crazy and reached behind the counter for my 39
jacket and cap and started for the door. He called me back. From a box he drew
out several soft, yellow figs that he placed in a piece of paper. "A bonus because
you worked well," he said. "Take them. When you taste them, maybe you will
understand what I have been talking about."

I took the figs and he unlocked the door and I hurried from the store. I 40
looked back once and saw him standing in the doorway, watching me, the
swirling tendrils of food curling like mist about his head.

I ate the figs late that night. I forgot about them until I was in bed and then 41
I rose and took the package from my jacket. I nibbled at one, then ate them all.
They broke apart between my teeth with a tangy nectar, a thick sweetness running like honey across my tongue and into the pockets of my cheeks. In the
morning when I woke, I could still taste and inhale their fragrance.

I never again entered Barba Niko's store. My spell of illness, which began 42
some months later, lasted two years. When I returned to the streets I had forgotten the old man and the grocery. Shortly afterwards my family moved from
the neighborhood.

Some twelve years later, after the war, I drove through the old neighbor- 43
hood and passed the grocery. I stopped the car and for a moment stood before
the store. The windows were stained with dust and grime, the interior bare and
desolate, a store in a decrepit group of stores marked for razing so new structures
could be built.

I have been in many Greek groceries since then and have often bought the 44
feta and Kalamata olives. I have eaten countless Greek salads and have indeed
found them a meal for the gods. On the holidays in our house, my wife and sons
and I sit down to a dinner of steaming, buttered pilaf like my mother used to
make and lemon-egg avgolemono and roast lamb richly seasoned with cloves of
garlic. I drink the red and yellow wines, and for dessert I have come to relish the
delicate pastries coated with honey and powdered sugar. Old Barba Nikos would
have been pleased.

But I have never been able to recapture the halcyon flavor of those figs he ⁴⁵ gave me on that day so long ago, although I have bought figs many times. I have found them pleasant to my tongue, but there is something missing. And to this day I am not sure whether it was the figs or the vision and passion of the old grocer that coated the fruit so sweetly I can still recall their savor and fragrance after almost thirty years.

QUESTIONS FOR CRITICAL READING, THINKING, DISCUSSION, AND WRITING

Analyzing Content and Technique

1. How did gang members have to "prove allegiance"? What conclusions can you draw from this about their values, desires, and fears? Identify another example of "proving allegiance" from the text that illustrates the same tendency.
2. Why does the narrator go back to the store? Where are we given a hint that this is going to occur? Analyze the narrator's character.
3. Analyze the character of Barba Nikos. How is he first presented to us? How does the author cause our impression of him to change?
4. How does food become a major symbol that shifts its meaning throughout the piece? What do specific foods mean to the narrator as a boy? To Barba Nikos? To the narrator as an adult?
5. What does the narrator learn from the encounter? What technique has the author used to let us know this?

Collaborative Activity

Have group members write down an incident in which they were punished for having done something wrong. Did they learn something because of the punishment? As a group, discuss the situations and what was learned. How are the group examples similar to Petrakis's? How are they different?

Making Connections

1. For Petrakis, Barba Nikos's store comes to embody a culture. Choose a place that embodies for you an important aspect of your culture and describe it in a way that clarifies the values it stands for. Be sure to use many concrete examples and, if you can, particular items that act as symbols.
2. One of Petrakis's themes in this selection is the shame one feels about one's ethnicity and how this shame can be transformed into pride. Look through the book to find another writer who presents a similar theme. Write an essay analyzing the causes of such a sense of inferiority and different ways in which it can be overcome, drawing on your own ideas as well as those of the two writers.

41

PREREADING ACTIVITY

Think back on stories told to you, or rhymes or songs sung by friends or family members, that gave you an insight into your culture and identity. Do a clustering exercise exploring what their subjects were. What do you feel you learned from them?

I Ask My Mother to Sing

LI-YOUNG LEE

Li-Young Lee (1957–   ) was born in Jakarta to Chinese parents. Because his father opposed the country's dictatorship, he was imprisoned and later fled to America with his family. Lee lives in Chicago and has taught at Northwestern University and the University of Iowa. His books include *The City in Which I Love You*, which won a Lannan award, and *Rose* (1986), from which this selection is taken.

She begins, and my grandmother joins her.
Mother and daughter sing like young girls.
If my father were alive, he would play
his accordian and sway like a boat.

I've never been in Peking, or the Summer Palace,   5
nor stood on the great Stone Boat to watch
the rain begin on Kuen Ming Lake, the picnickers
running away in the grass.

But I love to hear it sung;
how the waterlilies fill with rain until   10
they overturn, spilling water into water,
then rock back, and fill with more.

Both women have begun to cry.
But neither stops her song.

QUESTIONS FOR CRITICAL READING, THINKING, DISCUSSION, AND WRITING

Analyzing Content and Technique

1. Why does the narrator enjoy hearing about places and events he has never experienced? What does he gain from the song?
2. Why do the women cry? Why do they not stop singing?
3. Though this poem is a brief one, it possesses several themes. Identify some of these.
4. From the image of the father provided, what can you deduce of his personality?
5. Identify an image that runs through the entire poem. How is it transformed by the end? What might it symbolize?
6. What is the tone of the poem? For what kind of audience is Lee writing?

Collaborative Activity

Nature is often the subject of, or an important backdrop to, poetry and song. Have each member of the group bring in a poem or song in which nature plays a significant part and read it aloud. Discuss the role played by nature in each piece. What conclusions can you draw from the discussion about the ways in which nature is important to us?

Making Connections

1. Going back to the collaborative activity above, develop the group discussion into an essay analyzing some of your favorite depictions of nature in poems or songs. Some questions to consider might be: What relationship between humans and nature is indicated in these pieces? Is nature given human characteristics? What kinds of effects does it have on humans? How do the writers feel toward nature? How far is this influenced by their culture? Can you deduce a philosophy from their attitudes?
2. Write an essay analyzing songs, either from your culture or from a culture that you are interested in, that give the listeners a better understanding of the lifestyle, values, and trends of the culture. Narrow your thesis by focusing on a particular kind of song (for example, country western or African American spirituals) that will allow you to explore the topic in depth.

Before reading selection 42, briefly describe a country that you have always been fascinated by but have never traveled to. What aspects of its culture do you find particularly attractive? How did you learn about them?

Discovery (Student Essay)

Liann Sumner

*F*rom San Francisco to Rishikesh was one long nightmarish haul: thirty-two hours of nonstop, mind-numbing stimulus and nerve-jangling noise that we couldn't escape, wedged as we were into our narrow airplane seats. We left before dawn and flew into the next night, following the sun in its path around the globe. The darkness lasted for only a few hours before the harsh light again glinted off the metal wings of the plane into my tired eyes. We reached Delhi at 1:00 in the morning—I'd lost track of what day it was—and the air was thick and moist and unbreathable. Holding onto my husband's and son's hands for dear life, I wondered what I was doing here. I didn't know then that I was beginning an odyssey into India which would change the way I approached life and which would teach me to look below the surface of things and give me a new perception of my own world when I returned to it. 1

Standing on the bus platform at Delhi, I was surrounded by a sea of haunting, hungry brown faces. So many people! They were sleeping on the ground everywhere we turned, cooking over small outdoor fires, even relieving themselves by the side of the road. Many lived out their lives unsheltered except for some corrugated tin for a wall, or a thin blanket or sacking for a bed. I felt overwhelmed by culture shock. Maybe if I could get to our room and wash my face under a spigot of cold water I would feel better, I thought. 2

By late morning it felt like the end of a long, exhausting week. We were only on the first leg of our journey, and already I saw things that I had never even imagined before. There was a dead Brahma bull by the side of the road, with blackbirds tearing at its insides. The water buffaloes that shared a dirt path with us were huge beasts pulling teetering loads of sugar cane. They wove their way around careening, honking buses and pony rickshaws. There was no pattern to the traffic that I could discern: drivers would head straight for an oncoming vehi- 3

Source: Student essay reprinted by permission.

281

cle or pedestrians (us!), blasting their horns and veering away at the last second! It seemed like one big free-for-all with no one in charge.

As the day progressed, I sank into a deep depression. We walked through   4 the village we were staying in, and everything around us was broken or used up, torn or wrecked. We took our grimy clothes to the Dhobi for washing, but when the women scrubbed them on the river rocks and laid them on the banks, I felt uncomfortable. Later, at a little roadside restaurant, I couldn't eat, although I had been ravenous earlier. The smell of burning wood mixed with the odor of open sewers. The restaurant had a dirt floor and a young boy was sweeping a pile of trash in front of our table with a palm frond. Even in the shade, it must have been over 90 degrees. Sitting there drinking a bottle of warm Limca, I felt lost and stranded. Tears filled my eyes, and I couldn't stop them. The familiar world I had known had vanished, replaced by a nightmare. All I could do was sob.

The devastating images kept coming at me. We passed beggars squatting   5 along the roadside: old men whose skin clung to their bones, mothers surrounded by children, thin hands outstretched. Small boys selling trinkets or shining shoes assaulted us for rupees. They would shove their goods into our hands or tug at our clothing, and if we didn't buy what they were selling, they would cry. If we did buy something, a hundred others would swarm around us until we had to break into a run to escape. Soon we had to learn to harden our hearts and ignore them: their need was so huge that we couldn't solve it by ourselves.

As we traveled by bus up the Himalayas to Rishikesh and back, I began to   6 notice a few other things. Once we got used to the pushing and shoving for space, and the crazy way in which the bus drivers swerved along the narrow mountain curves bordered by sheer cliffs, we started to observe the world outside our windows. And it was a fascinating world, with its own fierce beauty. I saw huge monkeys with black faces, cows wearing colorful headdresses, fields of lush green sugar cane, fragrant flowering trees unlike any I'd seen before, mud huts with elaborate patterns painted onto the doorsteps, terraced rice paddies stretching for miles, and anthills more than 3 feet high.

When we stopped in the mountain villages, I was still aware of the squalor   7 and poverty, but I also noticed how resourceful the people were, how they made use of every scrap of whatever was available to them and used it for survival. Even the skinny children frying bread or making chai at the roadside tea stalls—they were survivors, tough as gristle. And how little it took to make them happy! We'd often see them playing, engrossed, with bottle caps or potsherds, or swinging on a gate chanting rhymes. A few times we handed pencils to the children who followed us around, and watched their big eyes light up with surprise and pleasure. And we were impressed by how helpful the people were, how willing to share what little they had. Once there were two little boys traveling by themselves on the bus with us. The other passengers made sure they had enough to eat. When they got roadsick and vomited all over the bus, no one got upset with them. Instead, everyone comforted them and helped clean them up, and when it was time for them to get down, the ticket conductor made sure they were met by relatives.

When we landed in San Francisco a few weeks later, I gazed almost unbe-   8 lievingly at the neatly laid-out highway, the orderly traffic, and the clean, unlittered suburban streets. Although I'd lived here all my life, it was as though I'd never really seen it before. For the first time I appreciated the amount of thought and foresight that went into the grand organization of civic codes that ensure building safety, sewer treatment, and safe water supplies. I appreciated the health regulations that protected us from diseases like the ones I'd seen. For the first time I felt a tangible pride in belonging to a nation that took such good care of me and ran things so efficiently. All my life, I had been blind to luxuries that I had taken for granted. Now I wanted to rush home and pay my taxes and give a loud, joyful cry of "Thank you! Thank you!" And for months afterwards, every time I turned on a warm shower or flushed my toilet or drove a car down a road with signal lights that people obeyed, I marveled at the cooperative human spirit that was responsible for it all and felt a deep comfort, a sense of belonging.

At the same time, I looked at individuals with more perception than before. Perhaps I had learned this in India, where people scrutinized us with a frank and artless curiosity, where everyone was interested in what we did and who we were. But as I looked around me at the people who shared my ordered world, I noticed—again for the first time—a distracted, empty look in their eyes and the stamp of stress on their faces. I saw how they rushed along on their everyday activities with little time for others, how the least breakdown in the system they were used to would annoy them. We were paying a high price for civilization! Although just about all the people I knew had all the food, clothing, and shelter they could want, although they were surrounded by an affluence that would have astounded most Indians, all of this had failed to bring satisfaction or peace to their souls. I thought back to the gentle, caring faces of the Indian people which reflected the serenity of their spirit. In the midst of chaos, they had possessed a tranquillity that eluded us in our perfectly ordered world.

What I discovered on my trip to India has changed the way I view my surroundings. It has brought my life, hitherto a blur of rushing days, into focus. Ironic, isn't it, that I had to go halfway around the world for it!

STRUCTURE, STRATEGY, SUGGESTION

1. What kind of atmosphere is suggested in paragraph 1? How (and where) is this developed in the essay?
2. Find the thesis of the essay. Is it appropriately placed? What transition has Sumner used to introduce the thesis?
3. Where in the essay do major shifts in ideas occur? How are they indicated?
4. Analyze paragraph 9. What is its relationship to paragraph 8? Where in the essay are we given the first hint that the idea in paragraph 9 might be coming up?
5. Which aspects of Sumner's descriptive technique are most effective? Give an example and analyze the way it works.
6. Evaluate the conclusion. How well does it work for you? Why? Write a different kind of conclusion for the essay.
7. Write an essay analyzing a journey which turned out to be an experience that taught you something surprising about yourself. Try to combine explanation with description, as Sumner does.

SYNTHESIS *Part Five*

1. Almost all the selections in Part Five focus on teachers, academic and otherwise, who have taught the writers important lessons of various kinds. While some of the teachers are excellent, some almost destroy their pupils by their actions. Taking into account the ideas presented by the authors, write a paper in which you analyze the qualities that good teachers must possess and the traits that are harmful to the learning process. Support your answer with quotations from the text.

2. "School Days of an Indian Girl" and "By Any Other Name" both depict situations in which the teacher comes from a race which is different from the pupil's and, for various historical and political reasons, looks down on the pupil's culture. Write an essay in which you analyze the effects of such an attitude. What can educators learn from these autobiographies that can be applied to the American classroom today?

3. While selections such as "Shame" and "Barba Nikos" deal with lessons one learns from strangers, "I Ask My Mother to Sing" focuses on what we learn from family. Write a comparison and contrast essay in which you discuss the two kinds of learning experiences. Is there a difference in the kinds of things one learns from family as opposed to strangers? Is it easier or more difficult to learn from family members? You might want to look at some of the selections in Part Two before you come up with answers.

4. Selections such as "Discovery," "Shame," and "I Ask My Mother to Sing" propose that often pain (of various kinds) is a necessary ingredient in the learning process. Do you agree? Write an essay on the importance of pain in teaching us new truths about ourselves and enabling us to see our world in a different way, supporting your thesis with examples from your reading and your experience.

PART SIX

The Imaging
of Ignorance

SELECTIONS IN PART SIX

PART 6: INTRODUCTION

Suspicion. Hostility. Ridicule. Hatred. These are emotions we sometimes encounter when we venture out of the safe cocoon of home into a multicultural society made up of people from backgrounds very different from our own. Worse, these are emotions we ourselves sometimes feel when faced with a confusing diversity of customs, languages, races, and sexual preferences. What causes such prejudice? Is it an insecurity that arises when a different way of living and thinking seems to present a challenge? Is it an age-old need to find, in the "other," a scapegoat we can blame for our troubles? These questions are explored in depth by the writers in Part Six—and the answers they come up with are often unexpected.

Selection 43, Robert Heilbroner's "Don't Let Stereotypes Warp Your Judgments," is an overview of the problem. It alerts us to the fact that we all have a tendency to fall into stereotyping if we are not watchful and do not correct ourselves, and it gives us some excellent reasons why stereotyped thought is as harmful to the thinker as to the victim. Malcolm X presents us with a slightly different angle on this issue in "Hair" (selection 49), in which the young narrator willingly undergoes pain to conform to the mainstream culture's ideal of beauty even though it doesn't fit his racial characteristics.

The other selections in Part Six deal more specifically with actual groups of individuals that have been stereotyped. They illuminate the pain we experience when we are seen not as a person but as a skin color or an eye shape or a sex organ, when only our accents, not our words, are heard. Some selections, like Dwight Okita's "In Response to Executive Order 9066" (selection 47), are written from the viewpoint of the person who has been the object of prejudice. Others, like Andromeda Polhemus's "The Economics of Hate" (selection 50), objectively analyze different minority groups that have suffered at different points in American history.

The authors use a wide range of tones and voices to draw us into their writing and make us empathize with the people they describe. There is, of course, the traditional expository tone, which seeks to persuade us through clear reasoning and nonpersonal examples. This is the tone Heilbroner uses in his essay. Others, such as Susan Jacoby in "Unfair Game" (selection 45) and Vivian Gornick in "Twice an Outsider" (selection 44), bring in powerful personal anecdotes to support their views. Jonathan Kozol (selection 46) uses statistics to shatter the comfortable myth, held by many, that the homeless are shiftless or crazy. Joan Didion uses lush yet pointed description in her essay "Miami: The Cuban Presence" (selection 48) to illustrate the Anglo community's lack of understanding of the Cubans who form such an important part of their city. And some writers prefer to shock us with the unexpected, to hit us with anger laced with humor or sarcasm. Such is Okita's poem, with its deceptively simple narrative tone, or Malcolm X's autobiographical excerpt, which changes its tone at a surprising point in the story.

Each writer in Part Six is dealing with a specific problem affecting one particular group that is distinct from all others. Yet all these writers are united in their feeling that prejudice is unacceptable. They present a range of models for combating prejudice—urbane ridicule, individual anger, organized social movements—and the powerful, concrete ways in which they convey these to us indicate that they have had firsthand experience. They are also united in their belief that prejudice can be overcome, and in their hope that it can be replaced by understanding. Many of them state this directly. Others imply it through the act of writing itself, which helps to remove the ignorance that may ultimately be the source of all prejudice. Their experiences are painful and may

287

shock us: there is no sugar-coating here. But they do show us that alternatives to hatred are possible. They leave us with a clear sense of the depth of the problem of discrimination, a sense that in some way it touches all of us. But they also leave us with the conviction that each of us can do something about it.

43

Don't Let Stereotypes Warp Your Judgments

ROBERT HEILBRONER

Robert Heilbroner (1919–   ) studied at Harvard and teaches economics at the New School for Social Research. His books include *The Future as History* and *An Inquiry into the Human Prospect*. "Don't Let Stereotypes Warp Your Judgments" first appeared in *Reader's Digest*.

*I*s a girl called Gloria apt to be better-looking than one called Bertha? Are criminals more likely to be dark than blond? Can you tell a good deal about someone's personality from hearing his voice briefly over the phone? Can a person's nationality be pretty accurately guessed from his photograph? Does the fact that someone wears glasses imply that he is intelligent?

The answer to all these questions is obviously, "No."

Yet, from all the evidence at hand, most of us believe these things. Ask any college boy if he'd rather take his chances with a Gloria or a Bertha, or ask a college girl if she'd rather blind-date a Richard or a Cuthbert. In fact, you don't have to ask: college students in questionnaires have revealed that names conjure up the same images in their minds as they do in yours—and for as little reason.

Look into the favorite suspects of persons who report "suspicious characters" and you will find a large percentage of them to be "swarthy" or "dark and foreign-looking"—despite the testimony of criminologists that criminals do *not* tend to be dark, foreign or "wild-eyed." Delve into the main asset of a telephone stock swindler and you will find it to be a marvelously confidence-inspiring telephone "personality." And whereas we all think we know what an Italian or a Swede looks like, it is the sad fact that when a group of Nebraska students sought to match faces and nationalities of 15 European countries, they were scored wrong in 93 percent of their identifications. Finally, for all the fact that horn-rimmed glasses have now become the standard television sign of an "intellectual,"

Source: From *Reader's Digest*. Reprinted by permission of the author.

optometrists know that the main thing that distinguishes people with glasses is just bad eyes.

Stereotypes are a kind of gossip about the world, a gossip that makes us pre- judge people before we ever lay eyes on them. Hence it is not surprising that stereotypes have something to do with the dark world of prejudice. Explore most prejudices (note that the word means prejudgment) and you will find a cruel stereotype at the core of each one.

For it is the extraordinary fact that once we have typecast the world, we tend to see people in terms of our standardized pictures. In another demon- stration of the power of stereotypes to affect our vision, a number of Columbia and Barnard students were shown 30 photographs of pretty but unidentified girls, and asked to rate each in terms of "general liking," "intelligence," "beauty" and so on. Two months later, the same group were shown the same photographs, this time with fictitious Irish, Italian, Jewish and "American" names attached to the pictures. Right away the ratings changed. Faces which were now seen as repre- senting a national group went down in looks and still farther down in likability, while the "American" girls suddenly looked decidedly prettier and nicer.

Why is it that we stereotype the world in such irrational and harmful fashion? In part, we begin to typecast people in our childhood years. Early in life, as every parent whose child has watched a TV Western knows, we learn to spot the Good Guys from the Bad Guys. Some years ago, a social psychologist showed very clearly how powerful these stereotypes of childhood vision are. He secretly asked the most popular youngsters in an elementary school to make errors in their morning gym exercises. Afterwards, he asked the class if anyone had noticed any mistakes during gym period. Oh, yes, said the children. But it was the *unpopular* members of the class—the "bad guys"—they remembered as being out of step.

We not only grow up with standardized pictures forming inside of us, but as grown-ups we are constantly having them thrust upon us. Some of them, like the half-joking, half-serious stereotypes of mothers-in-law, or country yokels, or psy- chiatrists, are dinned into us by the stock jokes we hear and repeat. In fact, with- out such stereotypes, there would be a lot fewer jokes. Still other stereotypes are perpetuated by the advertisements we read, the movies we see, the books we read.

And finally, we tend to stereotype because it helps us make sense out of a highly confusing world, a world which William James once described as "one great, blooming, buzzing confusion." It is a curious fact that if we don't *know* what we're looking at, we are often quite literally unable to *see* what we're look- ing at. People who recover their sight after a lifetime of blindness actually cannot at first tell a triangle from a square. A visitor to a factory sees only noisy chaos where the superintendent sees a perfectly synchronized flow of work. As Walter Lippmann has said, "For the most part we do not first see, and then define; we define first, and then we see."

Stereotypes are one way in which we "define" the world in order to see it. They classify the infinite variety of human beings into a convenient handful of "types" towards whom we learn to act in stereotyped fashion. Life would be a wearing process if we had to start from scratch with each and every human contact. Stereotypes economize on our mental effort by covering up the blooming, buzzing confusion with big recognizable cut-outs. They save us the "trouble" of finding out what the world is like—they give it its accustomed look.

Thus the trouble is that stereotypes make us mentally lazy. As S. I. Hayakawa, the authority on semantics, has written: "The danger of stereotypes lies not in their existence, but in the fact that they become for all people some of the time, and for some people all the time, *substitutes for observation*." Worse yet, stereotypes get in the way of our judgment, even when we do observe the world. Someone who has formed rigid preconceptions of all Latins as "excitable," or all teenagers as "wild," doesn't alter his point of view when he meets a calm and deliberate Genoese, or a serious-minded high school student. He brushes them aside as "exceptions that prove the rule." And, of course, if he meets someone true to type, he stands triumphantly vindicated. "They're all like that," he proclaims, having encountered an excited Latin, an ill-behaved adolescent.

Hence, quite aside from the injustice which stereotypes do to others, they impoverish ourselves. A person who lumps the world into simple categories, who type-casts all labor leaders as "racketeers," all businessmen as "reactionaries," all Harvard men as "snobs," and all Frenchmen as "sexy," is in danger of becoming a stereotype himself. He loses his capacity to be himself—which is to say, to see the world in his own absolutely unique, inimitable and independent fashion.

Instead, he votes for the man who fits his standardized picture of what a candidate "should" look like or sound like, buys the goods that someone in his "situation" in life "should" own, lives the life that others define for him. The mark of the stereotype person is that he never surprises us, that we do indeed have him "typed." And no one fits this straitjacket so perfectly as someone whose opinions about *other people* are fixed and inflexible.

Impoverishing as they are, stereotypes are not easy to get rid of. The world we type-cast may be no better than a Grade B movie, but at least we know what to expect of our stock characters. When we let them act for themselves in the strangely unpredictable way that people do act, who knows but that many of our fondest convictions will be proved wrong?

Nor do we suddenly drop our standardized pictures for a blinding vision of the Truth. Sharp swings of ideas about people often just substitute one stereotype for another. The true process of change is a slow one that adds bits and pieces of reality to the pictures in our heads, until gradually they take on some of the blurriness of life itself. Little by little, we learn not that Jews and Negroes and Catholics and Puerto Ricans are "just like everybody else"—for that, too, is a stereotype—but that each and every one of them is unique, special, different and individual. Often we do not even know that we have let a stereotype lapse until we hear someone saying, "all so-and-so's are like such-and-such," and we hear ourselves saying, "Well—maybe."

Can we speed the process along? Of course we can.

First, we can become *aware* of the standardized pictures in our heads, in other peoples' heads, in the world around us.

Second, we can become suspicious of all judgments that we allow excep- 18
tions to "prove." There is no more chastening thought than that in the vast intellectual adventure of science, it takes but one tiny exception to topple a whole
edifice of ideas.

Third, we can learn to be chary of generalizations about people. As F. Scott 19
Fitzgerald once wrote: "Begin with an individual, and before you know it you
have created a type; begin with a type, and you find you have created—nothing."

Most of the time, when we type-cast the world, we are not in fact 20
generalizing about people at all. We are only revealing the embarrassing facts
about the pictures that hang in the gallery of stereotypes in our own heads.

QUESTIONS FOR CRITICAL READING, THINKING, DISCUSSION, AND WRITING

Analyzing Content and Technique

1. How does Heilbroner define stereotypes? Where in the essay does the definition occur? Why doesn't he present it at the very beginning?
2. According to the essay, what are the major causes of stereotyping? Do you agree with Heilbroner's ideas about the causes? Can you identify any other causes?
3. Why does Heilbroner consider stereotypes dangerous? What evidence does he give to support this belief?
4. What can one do to get rid of the habit of stereotyping? What is a common danger that one may encounter in the process of getting rid of stereotypes?
5. Heilbroner uses paragraphs of different lengths—some quite long, some very short. Analyze one long paragraph and one short paragraph that you find effective, and discuss how each works.

Collaborative Activity

As a group, discuss the way in which students are often categorized in groups (for example, nerds, jocks, etc.) and make a list of all the groups you can think of. What image(s) do you associate with each? Write a group description of two or three of these images. How true is the image? How stereotypical?

Making Connections

1. In paragraph 15 Heilbroner states that to think that a member of a minority is "just like everybody else" is also a stereotype. Why does he think this? Do you agree? Write an essay in which you present your own views on this issue, supporting your argument with examples from your reading, observation, and experience.
2. Heilbroner says that stereotypes are often promoted by "the advertisements we read, the movies we see, the books we read" (paragraph 8). Do you agree or disagree? Write an essay supporting your viewpoint by citing at least one advertisement, one movie, and one book.

Consider the title. In what way do you think the writer might be an outsider because she is Jewish? In what way might she be an outsider because she is a woman? Do you agree with her assertion that minorities and women are outsiders in America?

Twice an Outsider: On Being Jewish and a Woman

VIVIAN GORNICK

Vivian Gornick (1935–   ) has taught at several colleges and been a staff writer for *The Village Voice*. Now she works full-time as a free-lance writer. She is particularly interested in women's issues, and her books include *Women in Science* and *Fierce Attachments*. The selection below first appeared in *Tikkun* in 1986.

When I was growing up, the whole world was Jewish. The heroes were Jewish and the villains were Jewish. The landlord, the doctor, the grocer, your best friend, the village idiot, the neighborhood bully: all Jewish. We were working-class and immigrant as well, but that just came with the territory. Essentially, we were Jews on the streets of New York. We learned to be kind, cruel, smart, and feeling in a mixture of language and gesture that was part street slang, part grade-school English, part kitchen Yiddish. We learned about politics and society in much the same way: Down the block were a few Orthodox Jews, up the block a few Zionists, in between a sprinkling of socialists. For the most part, people had no politics at all, only a cautious appetite for the goods of life. It was a small, tight, hyphenated world that we occupied, but I didn't know that; I thought it *was* the world.

One Sunday evening when I was eight years old my parents and I were riding in the back seat of my rich uncle's Buick. We had been out for a drive and now we were back in the Bronx, headed for home. Suddenly, another car sideswiped us. My mother and my aunt shrieked. My uncle swore softly. My father, in whose lap I was sitting, said out the window at the speeding car, "That's all right. Nothing but a bunch of kikes in here." In an instant I knew everything. I knew there was a world beyond our streets, and in that world my

Source: Originally appeared in *New York Times Sunday Magazine,* February 1978. Copyright © 1978 by Susan Jacoby. Reprinted by permission of Georges Borchardt, Inc. for the author.

father was a humiliated man, without power or standing. By extension, we were all vulnerable out there; but *we* didn't matter so much. It was my father, my handsome, gentle father, who mattered. My heart burned for him. I burrowed closer in his lap, pressed myself against his chest. I wanted to warm the place in him that I was sure had grown cold when he called himself a kike.

That was in the middle of the Second World War—*the* watershed event for   3
the men and women of my generation. No matter what your social condition, if you were a child growing up in the early 1940s you entered the decade destined for one kind of life and came out of it headed for another. For those of us who had gone into the war the children of intimidated inner-city Jews, 1945 signified an astonishing change in the atmosphere. The end of the war brought frozen food and nuclear fission, laundromats and anticommunists, Levittown and the breakup of the college quota system. The trolley tracks were torn up, and the streets paved over. Buses took you not only to other parts of the Bronx but into Manhattan as well. When my brother graduated from the Bronx High School of Science in 1947 my father said, "Now you can become a salesman." But my cousin Joey had been a bombardier in the Pacific and was now one of the elite: a returned GI at City College. My brother sat down with my father and explained that even though he was not a genius he had to go to college. It was his right and his obligation. My father stared at his son. Now we were in the new world.

When I was sixteen a girl in the next building had her nose straightened; we   4
all trooped in to see Selma Shapiro lying in state, swathed in bandages from which would emerge a person fit for life beyond the block. Three buildings away a boy went downtown for a job, and on his application he wrote "Arnold Brown" instead of "Arnold Braunowitz." The news swept through the neighborhood like wildfire. A nose job? A name change? What was happening here? It was awful; it was wonderful. It was frightening; it was delicious. Whatever it was, it wasn't stasis. Things felt lively and active. Chutzpah was on the rise, passivity on the wane. We were going to run the gauntlet. That's what it meant to be in the new world. For the first time we could *imagine* ourselves out there.

But who exactly do I mean when I say we? I mean Arnie, not Selma. I mean   5
my brother, not me. I mean the boys, not the girls. My mother stood behind me, pushing me forward. "The girl goes to college, too," she said. And I did. But my going to college would not mean the same thing as my brother's going to college, and we all knew it. For my brother, college meant getting from the Bronx to Manhattan. But for me? From the time I was fourteen I yearned to get out of the Bronx, but get out into *what*? I did not actually imagine myself a working person alone in Manhattan, and nobody else did either. What I did imagine was that I would marry, and that the man I married would get me downtown. He would brave the perils of class and race, and somehow I'd be there alongside him.

The greater chain of social being obtained. Selma straightened her nose so   6
that she could marry upward into the Jewish middle class. Arnie changed his name so that he could wedge himself into the Christian world. It was the boys who would be out there facing down the terrors of the word "kike," not the girls. The boys would run the gauntlet, for themselves and for us. We would be

standing not beside them but behind them, egging them on. And because we knew we'd be behind them we—the girls—never experienced ourselves directly as Jews. I never shivered inside with the fear of being called a kike. I remember that. Somehow I knew that if I were insulted in that way I might feel stunned, but the fear and shame would be once removed. I knew I'd run home to Arnie, and I'd say, "Arnie, they called me a kike," and he'd look miserable, and I'd say, "Do something!" and the whole matter would be out of my hands the minute I said "Do something." It was Arnie who'd have to stand up to the world, search his soul, test his feelings, discover his capacity for courage or action. Not me. And that is why Arnie grew up to become William Paley, and the other boys on the block—the ones who sneered and raged and trembled, who knew they'd have to run that gauntlet, get into that new world like it or not, and were smart and sensitive, and hated and feared and longed for it all—they grew up to become Philip Roth and Woody Allen. Me and Selma? We grew up to become women.

The confusion is historic; the distinction is crucial.   7

Woody Allen is exactly my age. I remember as though it were yesterday   8
listening to Allen's first stand-up comic monologues in the late fifties at the Bitter End Cafe. We were all in our twenties, my friends and I and Allen. It was as though someone on the block had suddenly found it in himself to say to a world beyond the street, "Listen. You wanna know how it is? This is how it is," and with more courage than anxiety he had shaped our experience. This wasn't Milton Berle or Henny Youngman up there, a Borscht Belt comic speaking half Yiddish, half English, all outsiderness. No, this was one of us, describing how it felt to be our age and in our place: on the street, at a party, in the subway, at home in the Bronx or Brooklyn; and then out there, downtown, in the city. Half in, half out.

Philip Roth, of course, cut closer to the bone. His sentence structure   9
deepened the experience, drove home better than Allen could the pain and the excitement, the intelligence and the anguish, the hilarity and the madness of getting so close you could touch it and *still* you weren't inside.

Behind both Allen and Roth stood Saul Bellow, who made the words   10
"manic" and "Jewish" synonymous, whose work glittered with a wild flood of feeling that poured from a river of language, all pent-up brilliance, the intelligence driven to an edge of hysteria that resembled Mel Brooks as much as it did Philip Roth. Although Bellow had been writing since the forties, it was only now in the fifties and sixties that his work and its meaning traveled down from a small community of intellectual readers to the reading populace at large. Here was a street-smart writing Jew who was actually extending the American language, using us—our lives, our idiom—to say something about American life that had not been said before. In the process, he gave us—me and my contemporaries—the equipment to define ourselves, and therefore become ourselves.

These men are on a continuum. From Milton Berle and Mel Brooks to   11
Saul Bellow, Philip Roth, and Woody Allen—the subtle alterations of tone and voice among them constitute a piece of social history, chart a progress of the way Jews felt about themselves in America, embody a fine calibration of rage, resentment, and hunger.

My mother hated Milton Berle, and I understood why—he was hard to ¹²
take. But I laughed against my will, and I knew he was the real thing. To see the
idiom of your life coming back at you, shaped and enlarged by a line of
humorous intelligence as compelling as a poem in the sustained nature of its
thesis and context, was to experience one of life's deepest satisfactions. When that
famous chord of recognition strikes, it is healing—illuminating and healing.

Milton Berle was my first experience of an artist's work applied to the ¹³
grosser materials of my own environment. Berle, operating at a lower level of
genius, was just as sinister as the Marx brothers. It was the wildness of his humor
and the no-holds-barred atmosphere that it generated. Berle was coarse and
vulgar, fast and furious, frightening in the speed of his cunning and his rage. My
mother was repelled. She knew this was Jewish self-hatred at its most vicious.

Mel Brooks was more of the same, only ten years younger, and the ten years ¹⁴
made a difference. A few years ago Brooks reminisced about how, when he began
writing for Sid Caesar, his mother asked him how much money he was making,
and he told her sixty dollars a week. He knew if he told her what he was really
making she'd have a heart attack. "The heart," he said. "It would attack her."
That story was for us: Woody Allen built on it. Brooks—also marked by a Borscht
Belt coarseness that spoke to an uneducated sense of America, a lack of
conversance with the larger culture—was still the shrewd, wild Jew talking, but
his tone was a bit sadder, a bit quieter than Milton Berle's, less defended against
the fears that dominated our lives. The lessened defense was the sign of change.

With Woody Allen, we passed through into a crucial stage of development. ¹⁵
Allen built a persona, an identity, a body of work out of the idea of the mousy
Jew who makes a fool of the gentile rather than of another Jew. This had not
happened before. Its meaning was unmistakable.

The Woody Allen character is obsessed with getting laid. Everyone else does ¹⁶
it; he alone can't do it. Everywhere he goes—in the street, on the subway, at a
party—he gazes mournfully at the golden shiksas all around him, always beyond
reach. It's not a Jewish girl he's trying to get into bed; it's Diane Keaton. The
Jewish girl is Brooklyn; Annie Hall is Manhattan.

And what does sexual success mean? It means everything. It means the ¹⁷
defeat of all that life bitterly withholds, already characterized by the fact that one
has been born a Jew instead of Humphrey Bogart. If Allen can just get that blue-
eyed beauty into bed. He wants it so bad he's going to die of it. He's going to
expire from this hunger right there before your eyes.

The humor turns on Allen's extraordinary ability to mock himself. He's as ¹⁸
brilliant as Charlie Chaplin at making wonderful his own smallness. And he's as
successful as Chaplin at making a hero of the little man, and a fool of the
withholding world in the person of the pretty girl. When Diane Keaton wrings her
hands and moans, "I can't," and Allen blinks like a rabbit and says, "Why? Because
I'm Jewish?"—he accomplishes a minor miracle on the screen. The beautiful
woman is made ridiculous. The golden shiksa has become absurd, inept, incapable:
the insincere and the foolish cut down to size so that Allen can come up to size.

When was the first time I saw it? Which movie was it? I can't remember. I ¹⁹
remember only that at one of them, in the early seventies, I suddenly found

myself listening to the audience laugh hysterically while Allen made a dreadful fool of the girl on the screen, and I realized that he had to make a fool of her, that he would always have to make a fool of her, because she was the foil: the instrument of his unholy deprivation, the exasperating source of life's mean indifference. I said to myself, "This is dis-*gust*-ting," and as I said it I knew I'd been feeling this way all my life: from Milton Berle to Saul Bellow to Woody Allen. I had always laughed, but deep inside I'd frozen up, and now I saw why. Milton Berle with his mother-in-law jokes, Saul Bellow with the mistresses who hold out and the wives who do him in, Mel Brooks and Woody Allen with the girl always and only the carrot at the end of the stick. Every last one of them was trashing women. Using women to savage the withholding world. Using us. Their mothers, their sisters, their wives. To them, we weren't friends or comrades. We weren't even Jews or gentiles. We were just girls.

At that moment I knew that I would never again feel myself more of a Jew than a woman. I had never suffered as men did for being a Jew in a Christian world because, as a Jew, I had not known that I wanted the world. Now, as a woman, I knew I wanted the world and I suffered.

Hannah Arendt, watching the Nazis rise to power in Germany, had denied the meaning of her own Jewishness for a long time. When she acknowledged it, she did so by saying, "When one is attacked as a Jew, one must defend oneself *as a Jew*. Not as a German, not as a world-citizen, not as an upholder of the Rights of Man [emphasis in original]." I read that and I was ready to change the sentences to read, "When one is attacked as a woman, one must defend oneself *as a woman*. Not as a Jew, not as a member of the working class, not as a child of immigrants."

My father had to be Jewish; he had no choice. When he went downtown he heard "kike." I live downtown, and I do not hear "kike." Maybe it's there to be heard and I'm not tuned in, but it can't be there all that much if I don't hear it. I'm out in the world, and this is what I *do* hear:

I walk down the street. A working-class man puts his lips together and makes a sucking noise at me.

I enter a hardware store to purchase a lock. I choose one, and the man behind the counter shakes his head at me. "Women don't know how to use that lock," he says.

I go to a party in a university town. A man asks me what I do. I tell him I'm a journalist. He asks if I run a cooking page. Two minutes later someone asks me not if I have a husband but what my husband does.

I go to another party, a dinner party on New York's Upper West Side. I'm the only woman at the table who is not there as a wife. I speak a few sentences on the subject under discussion. I am not responded to. A minute later my thought is rephrased by one of the men. Two other men immediately address it.

Outsiderness is the daily infliction of social invisibility. From low-grade humiliation to life-threatening aggression, its power lies in the way one is seen, and how that in turn affects the way one sees oneself. When my father heard the word "kike" the life-force within him shriveled. When a man on the street makes animal-like noises at me, or when a man at a dinner table does not hear what I say, the same thing happens to me. This is what makes the heart pound and the head fill with blood. This is how the separation between world and self occurs. This is outsiderness alive in the daily way. It is here, on the issue of being a woman, not a Jew, that I must make my stand and hold my ground.

A few years ago I taught at a state university in a small Western town. One night at a faculty party a member of the department I was working in, a man of modest intelligence, said of another teacher who had aroused strong feeling in the department, "He's a smart Jew crashing about in all directions." I stared at this man, thinking, "How interesting. You *look* civilized." Then I said, quite calmly, "What a quaint phrase. In New York we don't hear ourselves described as smart Jews any more. Is that still current out here?" The man turned dull red, and the exchange was at an end.

A few weeks later at another party I saw this same man engaged in conversation with another member of the department, a woman. I knew this woman, and in my view her gifts of mind and spirit were comparable to the man's. She was not a scholar and he was not a scholar. She was not intellectual and neither was he. They were both hard-working university teachers. I watched the two standing together, talking. The woman gestured widely as she spoke, smiled inordinately, fingered her hair. Her eyes were bright; her tone was eager. She exclaimed; she enthused; she performed. The man stood there, pulling at a pipe, silent, motionless, his body slack, his face immobile, his entire being unreadable except for his eyes and his mouth: in them an expression of mockery and patronage as the woman grew ever more frantic in her need to gain a response. It was clear that the harder she tried, the more secure he felt. At a certain point it became obvious that he was deliberately withholding what he knew she needed. I was watching a ritual exchange of petition and denial predicated on a power structure that in this instance turned wholly on his maleness and her femaleness.

I watched these two for a long time, and as I watched I felt my throat tighten, my arms and legs begin to tingle, a kind of sick feeling spread through my chest and belly. I wanted to put her up against the wall, but I wanted to put him through the wall. I realized I'd been absorbing this kind of thing twenty times a day in this department, in this university, in this town; and it was making me ill.

This daily feeling, this awareness of the subtle ways in institutional life that the most ordinary men accord each other the simplest of recognitions and withhold these recognitions from the equally ordinary women with whom they work, is palpable, and it burns inside every woman who experiences it—whether she is aware of what is happening or has numbed herself to what is happening.

When I hear an anti-Semitic remark I am hurt, I am angered, but I am not frightened. I do not fear for my life or my livelihood or my right to pursue the open expression of my convictions. When I hear a sexist remark I feel all of the above. I feel that stomach-churning rage and pain that tells me that I am in trouble, that I am up against threat and wipeout. I am in the presence of something virulent in the social scheme directed against me not because of what I actually am but because of an immutable condition of birth. Something I might once have experienced as a Jew but today can feel only as a woman.

Bellow, Roth, Allen: These are writers who have had only the taste of their own lives as the stimulus for creative work—and a rich, lively taste it has been: tart and smart, full of bite and wisdom. But these writers were allowed to become so fabulously successful precisely because the stigma of Jewishness was fading even as they were recording it. When Bellow wrote *Herzog,* being Jewish was no longer the open wound it had been when he wrote *The Victim;* and by the time Allen and Roth were coming into their own they were far more integrated into the larger world than their work suggested. Therefore, for Allen or Roth to go on making the golden shiksa the foil, or for Bellow to keep portraying the Jewish intellectual who can't arrive as his foil, is tiresome and unpersuasive. It does not speak to the lives that any of us are now living. Such work strikes no chord of recognition; it strikes only chords of memory and sentiment. The thing about outsiderness is that one feels it in the flesh every day; one feels oneself invisible in the ordinary social way. These are requirements of the condition.

This invisibility once made Jews manic and Blacks murderous. It works on women in a variety of ways:

I leaned across the counter in the hardware store and said to the man who had told me women didn't know how to use the lock I'd chosen, "Would you say that to me if I were Black?" He stared lightly at me for a long moment. Then he nodded. "Gotcha," he said.

To the man at the university party I explained my work in great and careful detail. The man, a sixty-year-old Ivy Leaguer, was frankly puzzled at why I spoke of something fairly simple at such excessive length. I knew this was the first time he had heard what I was *really* saying, and I didn't expect it to sink in. What I did expect was that the next time he heard a woman speak these words, they would begin to take hold.

At the dinner party in New York I made a scene. I brought harmless sociability to an end. I insisted that everyone see that the little social murders committed between men and women were the real subtext of the evening, and that civilized converse was no longer possible unless this underlying truth was addressed. I did this because these were liberal intellectuals. They had heard it all before, many times, and *still* they did not get it. It was as terrible for me to go home that evening with the taste of ashes in my mouth as it was for everyone else—we had all come expecting the warm pleasures of good food and good conversation—but I couldn't have lived with myself that night if I hadn't spoken up. Just as I would have had to speak up if the conversation had suddenly turned politely anti-Semitic. Which it would not have in this company.

The Jewishness inside me is an education. I see more clearly, can think more inventively, because I can think analogously about "them" and "us." That particular knowledge of being one among the many is mine twice over. I have watched masters respond to "them" and "us," and I have learned. I wouldn't have missed being Jewish for the world. It lives in me as a vital subculture, enriching my life as a writer, as an American, and certainly as a woman.

QUESTIONS FOR CRITICAL READING, THINKING, DISCUSSION, AND WRITING

Analyzing Content and Technique

1. Examine the incident in paragraph 2. How does it change the writer's notion of herself and the world?
2. Describe the positive transformation that begins to happen for Jews after 1945. How does it affect the men? Why? How does it affect the women? Why?
3. Analyze the writer's discussion of Woody Allen's achievements. What does she appreciate about him? Explain her reasons. Why is she also angered by him? Explain with an example.
4. Why does the writer feel she is an outsider at the present time? Identify two or three examples she has provided as support. Are these sufficiently convincing for you? Why or why not?
5. What is the thesis of the essay? Where does it appear most clearly? Discuss the placement of the thesis.
6. This writer uses both long and very short paragraphs. Analyze a couple of examples of each and discuss the different effects each kind has on the reader.

Collaborative Activity

Gornick has used a number of allusions in this essay (Levittown, the college quota system, the names of particular writers, and so forth). As a class, make a list of these allusions. The list should then be divided among groups so that each group gets two or three items. Each group should research its allusions and present the findings to the class. After the presentations, the class should discuss the pluses and minuses of using allusions in our writing.

Making Connections

1. Examine Gornick's statement that "outsiderness is the daily infliction of social invisibility" (paragraph 27). What does it mean? Do you agree or disagree? Write an essay in which you define the experience of being an outsider, supported by specific examples and other reading.
2. Write an essay in which you analyze the problems faced by women in America today, narrowing your thesis carefully so that you are able to discuss your chosen segment of this issue in detail. Do you agree with the writer's attitudes on this subject? As you develop your essay, explain clearly why or why not.

Before reading selection 45, write about an experience you (or someone you know) had in which you were treated prejudicially because of your sex. What did the incident indicate to you about the culture in which it occurred?

Unfair Game

SUSAN JACOBY

Susan Jacoby (1946–   ) has been a free-lance writer in the former Soviet Union as well as in the United States. Many of her pieces, published in the *Washington Post* and in *The New York Times,* reflect her interest in women's issues and in education. Her books include *Moscow Conversations, The Friendship Barrier, Inside Soviet Schools,* and *The Possible She.* "Unfair Game" first appeared in *The New York Times.*

*M*y friend and I, two women obviously engrossed in conversation, are sitting at a corner table in the crowded Oak Room of the Plaza at ten o'clock on a Tuesday night. A man materializes and interrupts us with the snappy opening line, "A good woman is hard to find."

We say nothing, hoping he will disappear back into his bottle. But he fancies himself as our genie and asks, "Are you visiting?" Still we say nothing. Finally my friend looks up and says, "We live here." She and I look at each other, the thread of our conversation snapped, our thoughts focused on how to get rid of this intruder. In a minute, if something isn't done, he will scrunch down next to me on the banquette and start offering to buy us drinks.

"Would you leave us alone, please," I say in a loud but reasonably polite voice. He looks slightly offended but goes on with his bright social patter. I become more explicit. "We don't want to talk to you, we didn't ask you over here, and we want to be alone. Go away." This time he directs his full attention to me—and he is mad. "All right, all right, *excuse me.*" He pushes up the corners of his mouth in a Howdy Doody smile. "You ought to try smiling. You might even be pretty if you smiled once in a while."

At last the man leaves. He goes back to his buddy at the bar. I watch them out of the corner of my eye, and he gestures angrily at me for at least fifteen minutes. When he passes our table on the way out of the room, this well-dressed, obviously affluent man mutters, "Good-bye, bitch," under his breath.

Why is this man calling me names? Because I have asserted my right to sit at a table in a public place without being drawn into a sexual flirtation. Because he has been told, in no uncertain terms, that two attractive women prefer each other's company to his.

This sort of experience is an old story to any woman who travels, eats, or drinks—for business or pleasure—without a male escort. In Holiday Inns and at the Plaza, on buses and airplanes, in tourist and first class, a woman is always thought to be looking for a man in addition to whatever else she may be doing. The man who barged in on us at the bar would never have broken into the conversation of two men, and it goes without saying that he wouldn't have imposed himself on a man and a woman who were having a drink. But two women at a table are an entirely different matter. Fair game.

This might be viewed as a relatively small flaw in the order of the universe—something in a class with an airline losing luggage or a computer fouling up a bank statement. Except a computer doesn't foul up your bank account every month and an airline doesn't lose your suitcase every time you fly. But if you are an independent woman, you have to spend a certain amount of energy, day in and day out, in order to go about your business without being bothered by strange men.

On airplanes, I am a close-mouthed traveler. As soon as the "No Smoking" sign is turned off, I usually pull some papers out of my briefcase and start working. Work helps me forget that I am scared of flying. When I am sitting next to a woman, she quickly realizes from my monosyllabic replies that I don't want to chat during the flight. Most men, though, are not content to be ignored.

Once I was flying from New York to San Antonio on a plane that was scheduled to stop in Dallas. My seatmate was an advertising executive who kept questioning me about what I was doing and who remained undiscouraged by my terse replies until I ostentatiously covered myself with a blanket and shut my eyes. When the plane started its descent into Dallas, he made his move.

"You don't really have to get to San Antonio today, do you?"

"Yes."

"Come on, change your ticket. Spend the evening with me here. I'm staying at a wonderful hotel, with a pool, we could go dancing . . ."

"No."

"Well, you can't blame a man for trying."

I do blame a man for trying in this situation—for suggesting that a woman change her work and travel plans to spend a night with a perfect stranger in whom she had displayed no personal interest. The "no personal interest" is crucial; I wouldn't have blamed the man for trying if I had been stroking his cheek and complaining about my dull social life.

There is a nice postscript to this story. Several months later, I was walking my dog in Carl Schurz Park when I ran into my erstwhile seatmate, who was taking a stroll with his wife and children. He recognized me, all right, and was trying to avoid me when I went over and courteously reintroduced myself. I reminded him that we had been on the same flight to Dallas. "Oh yes," he said. "As I recall you were going on to somewhere else." "San Antonio," I said. "I was in a hurry that day."

The code of feminine politeness, instilled in girlhood, is no help in dealing with the unwanted approaches of strange men. Our mothers didn't teach us to tell a man to get lost; they told us to smile and hint that we'd be just delighted to spend time with the gentleman if we didn't have other commitments. The man in the Oak Room bar would not be put off by a demure lowering of eyelids; he had to be told, roughly and loudly, that his presence was a nuisance. 17

Not that I am necessarily against men and women picking each other up in public places. In most instances, a modicum of sensitivity will tell a woman or a man whether someone is open to approaches. 18

Mistakes can easily be corrected by the kind of courtesy so many people have abandoned since the "sexual revolution." One summer evening, I was whiling away a half hour in the outdoor bar of the Stanhope Hotel. I was alone, dressed up, having a drink before going on to meet someone in a restaurant. A man at the next table asked, "If you're not busy, would you like to have a drink with me?" I told him I was sorry but I would be leaving shortly. "Excuse me for disturbing you," he said, turning back to his own drink. Simple courtesy. No insults and no hurt feelings. 19

One friend suggested that I might have avoided the incident in the Oak Room by going to the Palm Court instead. It's true that the Palm Court is a traditional meeting place for unescorted ladies. But I don't like violins when I want to talk. And I wanted to sit in a large, comfortable leather chair. Why should I have to hide among the potted palms to avoid men who think I'm looking for something else? 20

QUESTIONS FOR CRITICAL READING, THINKING, DISCUSSION, AND WRITING

Analyzing Content and Technique

1. Jacoby begins her essay with an incident. What is the point of the incident?
2. What is the thesis of the essay? In this connection, explain the significance of the title.
3. Describe the different methods Jacoby uses to protect herself from unwanted advances. How does she feel about having to use these?
4. Why does Jacoby feel angry about the sexual overtures she describes? Under what circumstances would they be acceptable to her? Do you agree or disagree with her in this respect?
5. What kinds of social conditioning, according to Jacoby, have made matters worse in circumstances like those she describes? From what you know of the writer, infer how she would like women—and men—to be brought up.
6. Why has Jacoby divided the essay into three sections? What part does each of the sections play in her overall argument? Describe another way the essay might have been structured.

Collaborative Activity

In paragraph 17 Jacoby mentions the "code of feminine politeness." Discuss, as a group, what you think this means. Do group members agree that this was the way girls were brought up when they were growing up? Compile a group list of examples that either support or refute Jacoby's argument.

Making Connections

1. Do you agree with Jacoby that people often treat women who are alone in public places differently from men who are alone? Support your viewpoint with reasons and examples from your own observation and draw a conclusion about social values and sex-role expectations.

2. In addition to the examples Jacoby gives us, what are some other stereotypical expectations for males and females? Write an essay exploring the major stereotypes either men or women in your culture have to deal with. You might want to make this a historical study, examining how such stereotypes have changed—or remained the same—over the years.

PREREADING ACTIVITY

Do a clustering exercise based on the phrase "homeless person." What sensory details such as colors, textures, and smells do you associate with the word? What personality traits?

Distancing the Homeless

JONATHAN KOZOL

Jonathan Kozol (1936–) is a writer and social critic deeply concerned with education, especially the education of children. He has been awarded fellowships from the Guggenheim, Ford, and Rockefeller foundations and has won a National Book Award for *Death at an Early Age*. His other books include *Alternative Schools, Prisoners of Silence: Breaking the Bonds of Adult Illiteracy in the United States,* and *Rachel and Her Children: Homeless Families in America.* An earlier version of this essay appeared in *Rachel and Her Children.*

*I*t is commonly believed by many journalists and politicians that the   1
homeless of America are, in large part, former patients of large mental hospitals who were deinstitutionalized in the 1970s—the consequence, it is sometimes said, of misguided liberal opinion, which favored the treatment of such persons in community-based centers. It is argued that this policy, and the subsequent failure of society to build such centers or to provide them in sufficient number, is the primary cause of homelessness in the United States.

Those who work among the homeless do not find that explanation satisfac-   2
tory. While conceding that a certain number of the homeless are, or have been, mentally unwell, they believe that, in the case of most unsheltered people, the primary reason is economic rather than clinical. The cause of homelessness, they say with disarming logic, is the lack of homes and of income with which to rent or acquire them.

They point to the loss of traditional jobs in industry (two million every year   3
since 1980) and to the fact that half of those who are laid off end up in work that pays a poverty-level wage. They point to the parallel growth of poverty in families with children, noting that children, who represent one quarter of our

population, make up forty percent of the poor: since 1968, the number of children in poverty has grown by three million, while welfare benefits to families with children have declined by 35 percent.

And they note, too, that these developments have coincided with a time in which the shortage of low-income housing has intensified as the gentrification of our major cities has accelerated. Half a million units of low-income housing have been lost each year to condominium conversion as well as to arson, demolition, or abandonment. Between 1978 and 1980, median rents climbed 30 percent for people in the lowest income sector, driving many of these families into the streets. After 1980, rents rose at even faster rates. In Boston, between 1982 and 1984, over 80 percent of the housing units renting below three hundred dollars disappeared, while the number of units renting above six hundred dollars nearly tripled.

Hard numbers, in this instance, would appear to be of greater help than psychiatric labels in telling us why so many people become homeless. Eight million American families now pay half or more of their income for rent or a morgage. Six million more, unable to pay rent at all, live doubled up with others. At the same time, federal support for low-income housing dropped from $30 billion (1980) to $9 billion (1986). Under Presidents Ford and Carter, five hundred thousand subsidized private housing units were constructed. By President Reagan's second term, the number had dropped to twenty-five thousand. "We're getting out of the housing business, period," said a deputy assistant secretary of the Department of Housing and Urban Development in 1985.

One year later, the *Washington Post* reported that the number of homeless families in Washington, D.C., had grown by 500 percent over the previous twelve months. In New York City, the waiting list for public housing now contains two hundred thousand names. The waiting is eighteen years.

Why, in the face of these statistics, are we impelled to find a psychiatric explanation for the growth of homelessness in the United States?

A misconception, once it is implanted in the popular imagination, is not easy to uproot, particularly when it serves a useful social role. The notion that the homeless are largely psychotics who belong in institutions, rather than victims of displacement at the hands of enterprising realtors, spares us from the need to offer realistic solutions to the fact of deep and widening extremes of wealth and poverty in the United States. It also enables us to tell ourselves that the despair of homeless people bears no intimate connection to the privileged existence we enjoy—when, for example, we rent or purchase one of those restored townhouses that once provided shelter for people now huddled in the street.

But there may be another reason to assign labels to the destitute. Terming economic victims "psychotic" or "disordered" helps to place them at a distance. It says that they aren't quite like us—and, more important, that we could not be like them. The plight of homeless families is a nightmare. It may not seem natural to try to banish human beings from our midst, but it *is* natural to try to banish nightmares from our minds.

So the rituals of clinical contamination proceed uninterrupted by the eco- 10
nomic facts described above. Research that addresses homelessness as an *injustice*
rather than as a medical *misfortune* does not win the funding of foundations. And
the research which *is* funded, defining the narrowed borders of permissible
debate, diverts our attention from the antecedent to the secondary cause of
homelessness. Thus it is that perfectly ordinary women whom I know in New
York City—people whose depression or anxiety is a realistic consequence of
months and even years in crowded shelters or the streets—are interrogated by
invasive research scholars in an effort to decode their poverty, to find clinical categories for their despair and terror, to identify the secret failing that lies hidden
in their psyche.

Many pregnant women without homes are denied prenatal care because 11
they constantly travel from one shelter to another. Many are anemic. Many
are denied essential dietary supplements by recent federal cuts. As a consequence, some of their children do not live to see their second year of life. Do
these mothers sometimes show signs of stress? Do they appear disorganized,
depressed, disordered? Frequently. They are immobilized by pain, traumatized
by fear. So it is no surprise that when researchers enter the scene to ask them how
they "feel," the resulting reports tell us that the homeless are emotionally
unwell. The reports do not tell us we have *made* these people ill. They do not
tell us that illness is a natural response to intolerable conditions. Nor do they
tell us of the strength and the resilience that so many of these people still retain
despite the miseries they must endure. They set these men and women apart
in capsules labeled "personality disorder" or "psychotic," where they no longer
threaten our complacence.

I visited Haiti not many years ago, when the Duvalier family was still in 12
power. If an American scholar were to have made a psychological study of the
homeless families living in the streets of Port-au-Prince—sleeping amidst rotten
garbage, bathing in open sewers—and if he were to return to the United States
to tell us that the reasons for their destitution were "behavioral problems" or "a
lack of mental health," we would be properly suspicious. Knowledgeable Haitians
would not merely be suspicious. They would be enraged. Even to initiate such
research when economic and political explanations present themselves so starkly
would appear grotesque. It is no less so in the United States.

One of the more influential studies of this nature was carried out in 1985 13
by Ellen Bassuk, a psychiatrist at Harvard University. Drawing upon interviews
with eight homeless parents, Dr. Bassuk contends, according to the *Boston Globe*,
that "90 percent [of these people] have problems other than housing and poverty
that are so acute they would be unable to live successfully on their own." She also
precludes the possibility that illness, where it does exist, may be provoked by destitution. "Our data," she writes, "suggest that mental illness tends to precede
homelessness." She concedes that living in the streets can make a homeless person's mental illness worse; but she insists upon the fact of prior illness.

The executive director of the Massachusetts Commission on Children 14
and Youth believes that Dr. Bassuk's estimate is far too high. The staff of

Massachusetts Human Services Secretary Phillip Johnston believes the appropriate number is closer to 10 percent.

In defending her research, Bassuk challenges such critics by claiming that they do not have data to refute her. This may be true. Advocates for the homeless do not receive funds to defend the sanity of the people they represent. In placing the burden of proof upon them, Dr. Bassuk has created an extraordinary dialectic: How does one prove that people aren't unwell? What homeless mother would consent to enter a procedure that might "prove" her mental health? What overburdened shelter operator would divert scarce funds to such an exercise? It is an unnatural, offensive, and dehumanizing challenge.

Dr. Bassuk's work, however, isn't the issue I want to raise here; the issue is the use or misuse of that work by critics of the poor. For example, in a widely syndicated essay published in 1986, the newspaper columnist Charles Krauthammer argued that the homeless are essentially a deranged segment of the population and that we must find the "political will" to isolate them from society. We must do this, he said, "whether they like it or not." Arguing even against the marginal benefits of homeless shelters, Krauthammer wrote: "There is a better alternative, however, though no one dares speak its name." Krauthammer dares: that better alternative, he said, is "asylum."

One of Mr. Krauthammer's colleagues at the *Washington Post,* the columnist George Will, perceives the homeless as a threat to public cleanliness and argues that they ought to be consigned to places where we need not see them. "It is," he says, "simply a matter of public hygiene" to put them out of sight. Another journalist, Charles Murray, writing from the vantage point of a social Darwinist, recommends the restoration of the almshouses of the 1800s. "Granted Dickensian horror stories about almshouses," he begins, there were nonetheless "good almshouses"; he proposes "a good correctional 'halfway house'" as a proper shelter for a mother and child with no means of self-support.

In the face of such declarations, the voices of those who work with and know the poor are harder to hear.

Manhattan Borough President David Dinkins made the following observation on the basis of a study commissioned in 1986: "No facts support the belief that addiction or behavioral problems occur with more frequency in the homeless family population than in a similar socioeconomic population. Homeless families are not demographically different from other public assistance families when they enter the shelter system. . . . Family homelessness is typically a housing and income problem: the unavailability of affordable housing and the inadequacy of public assistance income."

In a "hypothetical world," write James Wright and Julie Lam of the University of Massachusetts, "where there were no alcoholics, no drug addicts, no mentally ill, no deinstitutionalization, . . . indeed, no personal social pathologies at all, there would still be a formidable homelessness problem, simply because at this stage in American history, there is not enough low-income housing" to accommodate the poor.

New York State's respected commissioner of social services, Cesar Perales, makes the point in fewer words: "Homelessness is less and less a result of personal

failure, and more and more is caused by larger forces. There is no longer affordable housing in New York City for people of poor and modest means."

Even the words of medical practitioners who care for homeless people have   22
been curiously ignored. A study published by the Massachusetts Medical Society, for
instance, has noted that the most frequent illnesses among a sample of the homeless
population, after alcohol and drug use, are trauma (31 percent), upper respiratory
disorders (28 percent), limb disorders (19 percent), mental illness (16 percent), skin
diseases (15 percent), hypertension (14 percent), and neurological illnesses (12 percent). (Excluded from this tabulation are lead poisoning, malnutrition, acute diarrhea, and other illnesses especially common among homeless infants and small children.) Why, we may ask, of all these calamities, does mental illness command so
much political and press attention? The answer may be that the label of mental illness places the destitute outside the sphere of ordinary life. It personalizes an
anguish that is public in its genesis; it individualizes a misery that is both general in
cause and general in application.

The rate of tuberculosis among the homeless is believed to be ten times that   23
of the general population. Asthma, I have learned in countless interviews, is one
of the most common causes of discomfort in the shelters. Compulsive smoking,
exacerbated by the crowding and the tension, is more common in the shelters
than in any place that I have visited except prison. Infected and untreated sores,
scabies, diarrhea, poorly set limbs, protruding elbows, awkwardly distorted wrists,
bleeding gums, impacted teeth, and other untreated dental problems are so common among children in the shelters that one rapidly forgets their presence.
Hunger and emaciation are everywhere. Children as well as adults can bring to
mind the photographs of people found in camps for refugees of war in 1945. But
these miseries bear no stigma, and mental illness does. It conveys a stigma in the
Soviet Union. It conveys a stigma in the United States. In both nations the label
is used, whether as a matter of deliberate policy or not, to isolate and treat as special cases those who, by deed or word or by sheer presence, represent a threat to
national complacence. The two situations are obviously not identical, but they are
enough alike to give Americans reason for concern.

Last summer, some twenty-eight thousand homeless people were afforded   24
shelter by the city of New York. Of this number, twelve thousand were children
and six thousand were parents living together in families. The average child was
six years old, the average parent twenty-seven. A typical homeless family included
a mother with two or three children, but in about one-fifth of these families two
parents were present. Roughly ten thousand single persons, then, made up the
remainder of the population of the city's shelters.

These proportions vary somewhat from one area of the nation to another.   25
In all areas, however, families are the fastest-growing sector of the homeless population, and in the Northeast they are by far the largest sector already. In Massachusetts, three-fourths of the homeless now are families with children; in certain
parts of Massachusetts—Attleboro and Northampton, for example—the proportion reaches ninety percent. Two-thirds of the homeless children studied recently
in Boston were less than five years old.

Of an estimated two to three million homeless people nationwide, about 26 500,000 are dependent children, according to Robert Hayes, counsel to the National Coalition for the Homeless. Including their parents, at least 750,000 homeless people in America are family members.

What is to be made, then, of the supposition that the homeless are primar- 27 ily the former residents of mental hospitals, persons who were carelessly released during the 1970s? Many of them are, to be sure. Among the older men and women in the streets and shelters, as many as one-third (some believe as many as one-half) may be chronically disturbed, and a number of these people were dein-stitutionalized during the 1970s. But in a city like New York, where nearly half the homeless are small children with an average age of six, to operate on the basis of such a supposition makes no sense. Their parents, with an average age of twenty-seven, are not likely to have been hospitalized in the 1970s, either.

Nor is it easy to assume, as was once the case, that single men—those who 28 come closer to fitting the stereotype of the homeless vagrant, the drifting alcoholic of an earlier age—are the former residents of mental hospitals. The age of homeless men has dropped in recent years; many of them are only twenty-one to twenty-eight years old. Fifty percent of homeless men in New York City shel-ters in 1984 were there for the first time. Most had previously had homes and jobs. Many had never before needed public aid.

A frequently cited set of figures tells us that in 1955, the average daily 29 census of nonfederal psychiatric institutions was 677,000, and that by 1984, the number had dropped to 151,000. Subtract the second number from the first, conventional logic tells us, and we have an explanation for the homeless-ness of half a million people. A closer look at the same number offers us a dif-ferent lesson.

The sharpest decline in the average daily census of these institutions 30 occurred prior to 1978, and the largest part of that decline, in fact, appeared at least a decade earlier. From 677,000 in 1955, the census dropped to 378,000 in 1972. The 1974 census was 307,000. In 1976 it was 230,000; in 1977 it was 211,000; and in 1978 it was 190,000. In no year since 1978 has the average daily census dropped by more than 9,000 persons, and in the six-year period from 1978 to 1984, the total decline was 39,000 persons. Compared with a decline of 300,000 from 1955 to 1972, and of nearly 200,000 more from 1972 to 1978, the number is small. But the years since 1980 are the period in which the present homeless crisis surfaced. Only since 1983 have homeless individuals overflowed the shelters.

If the large numbers of the homeless lived in hospitals before they reap- 31 peared in subway stations and in public shelters, we need to ask where they were and what they had been doing from 1972 to 1980. Were they living under bridges? Were they waiting out the decade in the basements of deserted buildings?

No. The bulk of those who had been psychiatric patients and were released 32 from hospitals during the 1960s and early 1970s had been living in the meantime in low-income housing, many in skid-row hotels or boarding houses. Such hous-ing—commonly known as SRO (single-room occupancy) units—was drastically diminished by the gentrification of our cities that began in 1970. Almost 50 percent of SRO housing was replaced by luxury apartments or by office buildings between 1970 and 1980, and the remaining units have been disappearing at even faster rates. As recently as 1986, after New York City had issued a prohibition against conversion of such housing, a well-known developer hired a demolition team to destroy a building in Times Square that had previously been home to indigent people. The demolition took place in the middle of the night. In order to avoid imprisonment, the developer was allowed to make a philanthropic gift to homeless people as a token of atonement. This incident, bizarre as it appears, reminds us that the profit motive for displacement of the poor is very great in every major city. It also indicates a more realistic explanation for the growth of homelessness during the 1980s.

Even for those persons who are ill and were deinstitutionalized during the decades before 1980, the precipitating cause of homelessness in 1987 is not illness but loss of housing. SRO housing, unattractive as it may have been, offered low-cost sanctuaries for the homeless, providing a degree of safety and mutual support for those who lived within them. They were a demeaning version of the community health centers that society had promised; they were the de facto "halfway houses" of the 1970s. For these people too, then—at most half of the homeless single persons in America—the cause of homelessness is lack of housing. 33

A writer in *The New York Times* describes a homeless woman standing on a traffic island in Manhattan. "She was evicted from her small room in the hotel just across the street," and she is determined to get revenge. Until she does, "nothing will move her from that spot. . . . Her argumentativeness and her angry fixation on revenge, along with the apparent absence of hallucinations, mark her as a paranoid." Most physicians, I imagine, would be more reserved in passing judgment with so little evidence, but this author makes his diagnosis without hesitation. "The paranoids of the street," he says, "are among the most difficult to help." 34

Perhaps so. But does it depend on who is offering the help? Is anyone offering to help this woman get back her home? Is it crazy to seek vengeance for being thrown into the street? The absence of anger, some psychiatrists believe, might indicate much greater illness. 35

The same observer sees additional symptoms of pathology ("negative symptoms," he calls them) in the fact that many homeless persons demonstrate a "gross deterioration in their personal hygiene" and grooming, leading to "indifference" and "apathy." Having just identified one woman as unhealthy because she is so far from being "indifferent" as to seek revenge, he now sees apathy as evidence of illness; so consistency is not what we are looking for in this account. But how much less indifferent might the homeless be if those who decide their fate were less indifferent themselves? How might their grooming and hygiene be improved if they were permitted access to a public toilet? 36

In New York City, as in many cities, homeless people are denied the right to wash in public bathrooms, to store their few belongings in a public locker, or, in certain cases, to make use of public toilets altogether. Shaving, cleaning of 37 clothes, and other forms of hygiene are prohibited in the men's room of Grand Central Station. The terminal's three hundred lockers, used in former times by homeless people to secure their goods, were removed in 1986 as "a threat to public safety," according to a study made by the New York City Council.

At one-thirty every morning, homeless people are ejected from the station. [38] Many once attempted to take refuge on the ramp that leads to Forty-second Street because it was protected from the street by wooden doors and thus provided some degree of warmth. But the station management responded to this challenge in two ways. The ramp was mopped with a strong mixture of ammonia to produce a noxious smell, and when the people sleeping there brought cardboard boxes and newspapers to protect them from the fumes, the entrance doors were chained wide open. Temperatures dropped some nights to ten degrees. Having driven these people to the streets, city officials subsequently determined that their willingness to risk exposure to cold weather could be taken as further evidence of mental illness.

At Pennsylvania Station in New York, homeless women are denied the use [39] of toilets. Amtrak police come by and herd them off each hour on the hour. In June 1985, Amtrak officials issued this directive to police: "It is the policy of Amtrak to not allow the homeless and undesirables to remain. . . . Officers are encouraged to eject all undesirables. . . . Now is the time to train and educate them that their presence will not be tolerated as cold weather sets in." In an internal memo, according to CBS, an Amtrak official asked flatly: "Can't we get rid of this trash?"

I have spent many nights in conversation with the women who are huddled [40] in the corridors and near the doorway of the public toilets in Penn Station. Many are young. Most are cogent. Few are dressed in the familiar rags suggested by the term *bag ladies*. Unable to bathe or use the toilets in the station, almost all are in conditions of intolerable physical distress. The sight of clusters of police officers, mostly male, guarding a toilet from use by homeless women speaks volumes about the public conscience of New York.

Where do these women defecate? How do they bathe? What will we do [41] when, in her physical distress, a woman finally disrobes in public and begins to urinate right on the floor? "Gross deterioration," someone will call it, evidence of mental illness. In the course of an impromptu survey in the streets last September, Mayor Koch observed a homeless woman who had soiled her own clothes. Not only was the woman crazy, said the mayor, but those who differed with him on his diagnosis must be crazy, too. "I am the number one social worker in this town—with sanity," said he.

It may be that this woman was psychotic, but the mayor's comment says a [42] great deal more about his sense of revulsion and the moral climate of a decade in which words like these may be applauded than about her mental state.

A young man who had lost his job, then his family, then his home, all in the [43] summer of 1986, spoke with me for several hours in Grand Central Station on the weekend following Thanksgiving. "A year ago," he said, "I never thought that somebody like me would end up in a shelter. Nothing you've ever undergone prepares you. You walk into the place [a shelter on the Bowery]—the smell of sweat and urine hits you like a wall. Unwashed bodies and the look of absolute despair on many, many faces there would make you think you were in Dante's Hell. . . . What you fear is that you will be here forever. You do not know if it is ever going to end. You think to yourself: it is a dream and I will awake. Sometimes I think: it's an experiment. They are watching you to find out how much you can take. . . . I was a pretty stable man. Now I tremble when I meet somebody in the ordinary world. I'm trembling right now. . . . For me, the loss of work and loss of wife had left me rocking. Then the welfare regulations hit me. I began to feel that I would be reduced to trash. . . . Half the people that I know are suffering from chest infections and sleep deprivation. The lack of sleep leaves you debilitated, shaky. You exaggerate your fears. If a psychiatrist came along he'd say that I was crazy. But I was an ordinary man. There was nothing wrong with me. I lost my kids. I lost my home. Now would you say that I was crazy if I told you I was feeling sad?"

"If the plight of homeless adults is the shame of America," writes Fred 44 Hechinger in *The New York Times,* "the lives of homeless children are the nation's crime."

In November 1984, a fact already known to advocates for the homeless was 45 given brief attention by the press. Homeless families, the *New York Times* reported, "mostly mothers and young children, have been sleeping on chairs, counters, and floors of the city's emergency welfare offices." Reacting to such reports, the mayor declared: "The woman is sitting on a chair or on a floor. It is not because we didn't offer her a bed. We provide a shelter for every single person who knocks on our door." On the same day, however, the city reported that in the previous eleven weeks it had been unable to give shelter to 153 families, and in the subsequent year, 1985, the city later reported that about two thousand children slept in welfare offices because of lack of shelter space.

Some eight hundred homeless infants in New York City, reported the 46 National Coalition for the Homeless, "routinely go without sufficient food, cribs, health care, and diapers." The lives of these children "are put at risk," while "high-risk pregnant women" are repeatedly forced to sleep in unsafe "barracks shelters" or welfare offices called Emergency Assistance Units (EAUs). "Coalition monitors, making sporadic random checks, found eight women in their *ninth* month of pregnancy sleeping in EAUs. . . . Two women denied shelter began having labor contractions at the EAU." In one instance, the Legal Aid Society was forced to go to court after a woman lost her child by miscarriage while lying on the floor of a communal bathroom in a shelter which the courts had already declared unfit to house pregnant women.

The coalition also reported numerous cases in which homeless mothers 47 were obliged to choose between purchasing food or diapers for their infants. Federal guidelines issued in 1986 deepened the nutrition crisis faced by mothers in the welfare shelters by counting the high rent paid to the owners of the buildings as a part of family income, rendering their residents ineligible for food stamps. Families I interviewed who had received as much as $150 in food stamps monthly in June 1986 were cut back to $33 before Christmas.

"Now you're hearing all kinds of horror stories," said President Reagan, 48 "about the people that are going to be thrown out in the snow to hunger and

[to] die of cold and so forth. . . . We haven't cut a single budget." But in the four years leading up to 1985, according to the *New Republic,* Aid to Families with Dependent Children had been cut by $4.8 billion, child nutrition programs by $5.2 billion, food stamps by $6.8 billion. The federal government's authority to help low-income families with housing assistance was cut from $30 billion to $11 billion in Reagan's first term. In his fiscal 1986 budget, the president proposed to cut that by an additional 95 percent.

"If even one American child is forced to go to bed hungry at night," the [49] president said on another occasion, "that is a national tragedy. We are too generous a people to allow this." But in the years since the president spoke these words, thousands of poor children in New York alone have gone to bed too sick to sleep and far too weak to rise the next morning to attend a public school. Thousands more have been unable to attend school at all because their homeless status compels them to move repeatedly from one temporary shelter to another. Even in the affluent suburbs outside New York City, hundreds of homeless children are obliged to ride as far as sixty miles twice a day in order to obtain an education in the public schools to which they were originally assigned before their families were displaced. Many of these children get to school too late to eat their breakfast; others are denied lunch at school because of federal cuts in feeding programs.

Many homeless children die—and others suffer brain damage—as a direct [50] consequence of federal cutbacks in prenatal programs, maternal nutrition, and other feeding programs. The parents of one such child shared with me the story of the year in which their child was delivered, lived, and died. The child, weighing just over four pounds at birth, grew deaf and blind soon after, and for these reasons had to stay in the hospital for several months. When he was released on Christmas Eve of 1984, his mother and father had no home. He lived with his parents in the shelters, subways, streets, and welfare offices of New York City for four winter months, and was readmitted to the hospital in time to die in May 1985.

When we met and spoke the following year, the father told me that his wife [51] had contemplated and even attempted suicide after the child's death, while he had entertained the thought of blowing up the welfare offices of New York City. I would tell him that to do so would be illegal and unwise. I would never tell him it was crazy.

"No one will be turned away," says the mayor of New York City, as hun- [52] dreds of young mothers with their infants are turned from the doors of shelters season after season. That may sound to some like denial of reality. "Now you're hearing all these stories," says the president of the United States as he denies that anyone is cold or hungry or unhoused. On another occasion he says that the unsheltered "are homeless, you might say, by choice." That sounds every bit as self deceiving.

The woman standing on the traffic island screaming for revenge until her [53] room has been restored to her sounds relatively healthy by comparison. If three million homeless people did the same, and all at the same time, we might finally be forced to listen.

QUESTIONS FOR CRITICAL READING, THINKING, DISCUSSION, AND WRITING

Analyzing Content and Technique

1. According to Kozol, what are some of the common beliefs about the homeless? Are these accurate or stereotypical? Who holds these beliefs?

2. Why, according to Kozol, do people become homeless? Summarize the arguments he uses to dispute other theories.

3. What evidence does Kozol provide for his idea? Choose one kind of evidence that you find particularly effective and analyze one instance where Kozol uses it well.

4. What are some of the effects of homelessness on children? How does Kozol's description of these effects indicate his feelings?

5. In paragraph 34, Kozol describes a "homeless woman standing on a traffic island in Manhattan" who was observed by a writer for *The New York Times*. What conclusion does the *Times* writer draw about her? On what does he base his opinion? What conclusion does Kozol draw? On what does he base his opinion?

6. Explain, in your own words, the thesis of the essay. Has Kozol convinced you of this thesis? Why or why not?

Collaborative Activity

As a group, research two or three recent magazine or newspaper articles that have been written about the homeless. Have group members choose quotations which struck them as important and relevant from each article. Make a collage in which you put together these quotations, perhaps with pictures or photographs. Each group should display its collage in the classroom so other groups can examine it.

Making Connections

1. In Kozol's essay, we can find several examples of "good" logic (critical thinking based on statistics, clear cause-and-effect relationships, and so forth) and several examples of "bad" logic (hastily drawn conclusions, prejudgments, self-delusion, and so forth). Make a list of each kind. Then, on the basis of these examples, write an essay in which you define "good" and "bad" logic and explain how each can be identified.

2. As Kozol's essay demonstrates, we may often be prejudiced about people who are of our own race but from different economic strata. Write an essay analyzing other examples of "economic" prejudice or stereotyping—that is, prejudice related to the material goods a person or a community possesses—and support your analysis with examples from your own observations.

PREREADING ACTIVITY

Before reading selection 47, write about a time when you (or someone you know) experienced a change in a friendship or some other relationship with a person of another culture or race. What was the cause of this change?

In Response to Executive Order 9066: All Americans of Japanese Descent Must Report to Relocation Centers

DWIGHT OKITA

Dwight Okita (1958–   ) has lived in Chicago most of his life. He went to the University of Illinois and is now an active part of the "performance poetry" scene in Chicago. He writes music and plays as well as poetry. His parents were both sent to relocation camps during World War II.

Dear Sirs:
Of course I'll come. I've packed my galoshes
and three packets of tomato seeds. Janet calls them
"love apples." My father says where we're going
they won't grow.   5

I am a fourteen-year-old girl with bad spelling
and a messy room. If it helps any, I will tell you
I have always felt funny using chopsticks
and my favorite food is hot dogs.
My best friend is a white girl named Denise—   10
we look at boys together. She sat in front of me
all through grade school because of our names:
O'Connor, Ozawa. I know the back of Denise's head very well.
I tell her she's going bald. She tells me I copy on tests.
We're best friends.   15

I saw Denise today in Geography class.
She was sitting on the other side of the room.
"You're trying to start a war," she said, "giving secrets away
to the Enemy, Why can't you keep your big mouth shut?"
I didn't know what to say.
I gave her a packet of tomato seeds
and asked her to plant them for me, told her
when the first tomato ripens
to miss me.

20

QUESTIONS FOR CRITICAL READING, THINKING, DISCUSSION, AND WRITING

Analyzing Content and Technique

1. What is the historical situation which forms the background of this poem?
2. What do we know about the speaker? How do these facts affect our evaluation of the historical context?
3. Describe the tone of the poem. How does the vocabulary strengthen the tone? In what ways is the letter format appropriate for what the poet is trying to achieve?
4. What is the significance of the ending?
5. Analyze the ironies in the poem.
6. What is the purpose of the poem? For what kind of audience is it intended? Do you think the writer achieves his purpose? Why or why not?

Collaborative Activity

What is a poem? What does it do? How is it different from prose nonfiction? From fiction? As a group, explore your ideas on this issue by doing a group clustering exercise with the word "poetry." Now apply your ideas to the poem just read. In what ways is this poem similar to, or different from, your concept of poetry?

Making Connections

1. The white girl Denise in Okita's poem seems to be responding to prejudices toward the Japanese which were fostered by wartime media. Write a research paper on the images and ideas projected by the media at this time, examining actual newspaper articles and editorials. In the conclusion of your paper, evaluate the effect of these articles and editorials.
2. Think of a historical situation or an event in the world or in your community that has moved you or that concerns you closely. Write a letter (prose or poetry) in the voice of someone who is involved in this incident or situation, explaining, overtly or implicitly, how it has affected you.

Miami: The Cuban Presence

JOAN DIDION

Born in Sacramento, Joan Didion (1934–) holds a degree from the University of California at Berkeley and is well known for her award-winning work as a writer and investigative reporter. Her books include *Play It as It Lays*, *Slouching Toward Bethlehem*, *The White Album*, and *Salvador*. This essay first appeared in the *New York Review of Books* in 1987 and became the seed for her book *Miami*.

On the 150th anniversary of the founding of Dade County, in February of 1986, the Miami *Herald* asked four prominent amateurs of local history to name "the ten people and the ten events that had the most impact on the county's history." Each of the four submitted his or her own list of "The Most Influential People in Dade's History," and among the names mentioned were Julia Tuttle ("pioneer businesswoman"), Henry Flagler ("brought the Florida East Coast Railway to Miami"), Alexander Orr, Jr. ("started the research that saved Miami's drinking water from salt"), Everest George Sewell ("publicized the city and fostered its deepwater seaport"). . . . There was Dr. James M. Jackson, an early Miami physician. There was Napoleon Bonaparte Broward, the governor of Florida who initiated the draining of the Everglades. There appeared on three of the four lists the name of the developer of Coral Gables, George Merrick. There appeared on one of the four lists the name of the coach of the Miami Dolphins, Don Shula.

On none of these lists of "The Most Influential People in Dade's History" did the name Fidel Castro appear, nor for that matter did the name of any Cuban, although the presence of Cubans in Dade County did not go entirely unnoted by the *Herald* panel. When it came to naming the Ten Most Important "Events," as opposed to "People," all four panelists mentioned the arrival of the Cubans, but at slightly off angles ("Mariel Boatlift of 1980" was the way one panelist saw it), and as if the arrival had been just another of those isolated disasters or innovations which deflect the course of any growing community, on an approximate par with the other events mentioned, for example the Freeze of 1895, the Hurricane of 1926, the opening of the Dixie Highway, the establishment of Miami International Airport, and the adoption, in 1957, of the metropolitan form of government, "enabling the Dade County Commission to provide urban services to the increasingly populous unincorporated area."

This set of mind, in which the local Cuban community was seen as a civic challenge determinedly met, was not uncommon among Anglos to whom I talked in Miami, many of whom persisted in the related illusions that the city was small, manageable, prosperous in a predictable broadbased way, southern in a progressive Sunbelt way, American, and belonged to them. In fact 43 percent of the population of Dade County was by that time "Hispanic," which meant mostly Cuban. Fifty-six percent of the population of Miami itself was Hispanic. The most visible new buildings on the Miami skyline, the Arquitectonica buildings along Brickell Avenue, were by a firm with a Cuban founder. There were Cubans in the board rooms of the major banks, Cubans in clubs that did not admit Jews or blacks, and four Cubans in the most recent mayoralty campaign, two of whom, Raul Masvidal and Xavier Suarez, had beaten out the incumbent and all other candidates to meet in a runoff, and one of whom, Xavier Suarez, a thirty-six-year-old lawyer who had been brought from Cuba to the United States as a child, was by then mayor of Miami.

The entire tone of the city, the way people looked and talked and met one another, was Cuban. The very image the city had begun presenting of itself, what was then its newfound glamour, its "hotness" (hot colors, hot vice, shady dealings under the palm trees), was that of prerevolutionary Havana, as perceived by Americans. There was even in the way women dressed in Miami a definable Havana look, a more distinct emphasis on the hips and décolletage, more black, more veiling, a generalized flirtatiousness of style not then current in American cities. In the shoe departments at Burdine's and Jordan Marsh there were more platform soles than there might have been in another American city, and fewer displays of the running shoe ethic. I recall being struck, during an afternoon spent at La Liga Contra el Cancer, a prominent exile charity which raises money to help cancer patients, by the appearance of the volunteers who had met that day to stuff envelopes for a benefit. Their hair was sleek, of a slightly other period, immaculate pageboys and French twists. They wore Bruno Magli pumps, and silk and linen dresses of considerable expense. There seemed to be a preference for strictest gray or black, but the effect remained lush, tropical, like a room full of perfectly groomed mangoes.

This was not, in other words, an invisible 56 percent of the population. Even the social notes in *Diario Las Americas* and in *El Herald,* the daily Spanish edition of the *Herald* written and edited for *el exilio,* suggested a dominant culture, one with money to spend and a notable willingness to spend it in public. La Liga Contra el Cancer alone sponsored, in a single year, two benefit dinner dances, one benefit ball, a benefit children's fashion show, a benefit telethon, a benefit exhibition of jewelry, a benefit presentation of Miss Universe contestants, and a benefit showing, with Saks Fifth Avenue and chicken *vol-au-vent*, of the Adolfo (as it happened, a Cuban) fall collection.

One morning *El Herald* would bring news of the gala at the Pavillon of the   6
Amigos Latinamericanos del Museo de Ciencia y Planetarium; another morning, of an upcoming event at the Big Five Club, a Miami club founded by former members of five fashionable clubs in prerevolutionary Havana: a *coctel*, or cocktail party, at which tables would be assigned for yet another gala, the annual "Baile Imperial de las Rosas" of the American Cancer Society, Hispanic Ladies Auxiliary. Some members of the community were honoring Miss America Latina with dinner dancing at the Doral. Some were being honored themselves, at the Spirit of Excellence Awards Dinner at the Omni. Some were said to be enjoying the skiing at Vail; others to prefer Bariloche, in Argentina. Some were reported unable to attend (but sending checks for) the gala at the Pavillon of the Amigos Latinamericanos del Museo de Ciencia y Planetarium because of a scheduling conflict, with *el coctel de* Paula Hawkins.

Fete followed fete, all high visibility. Almost any day it was possible to drive   7
past the limestone arches and fountains which marked the boundaries of Coral Gables and see little girls being photographed in the tiaras and ruffled hoop skirts and maribou-trimmed illusion capes they would wear at their *quinces,* the elaborate fifteenth-birthday parties at which the community's female children come of official age. The favored facial expression for a *quince* photograph was a classic smolder. The favored backdrop was one suggesting Castilian grandeur, which was how the Coral Gables arches happened to figure. Since the idealization of the virgin implicit in the *quince* could exist only in the presence of its natural foil, *machismo,* there was often a brother around, or a boyfriend. There was also a mother, in dark glasses, not only to protect the symbolic virgin but to point out the better angle, the more aristocratic location. The *quinceanera* would pick up her hoop skirts and move as directed, often revealing the scuffed Jellies she had worn that day to school. A few weeks later there she would be, transformed in *Diario Las Americas,* one of the morning battalion of smoldering fifteen-year-olds, each with her arch, her fountain, her borrowed scenery, the gift if not exactly the intention of the late George Merrick, who built the arches when he developed Coral Gables.

Neither the photographs of the Cuban *quinceaneras* nor the notes about   8
the *coctel* at the Big Five were apt to appear in the newspapers read by Miami Anglos, nor, for that matter, was much information at all about the daily life of the Cuban majority. When, in the fall of 1986, Florida International University offered an evening course called "Cuban Miami: A Guide for Non-Cubans," the *Herald* sent a staff writer, who covered the classes as if from a distant beat. "Already I have begun to make some sense out of a culture, that, while it totally surrounds us, has remained inaccessible and alien to me," the *Herald* writer was reporting by the end of the first meeting, and, by the end of the fourth:

What I see day to day in Miami, moving through mostly Anglo corridors of the community, are just small bits and pieces of that other world, the tip of something much larger than I'd imagined. . . . We may frequent the restaurants here, or wander into the occasional festival. But mostly we try to ignore Cuban Miami, even as we rub up against this teeming, incomprehensible presence.

Only thirteen people, including the *Herald* writer, turned up for the first meeting of "Cuban Miami: A Guide for Non-Cubans" (two more appeared at the second meeting, along with a security guard, because of telephone threats prompted by what the *Herald* writer called "somebody's twisted sense of national pride"), an enrollment which suggested a certain willingness among non-Cubans to let Cuban Miami remain just that, Cuban, the "incomprehensible presence." In fact there had come to exist in South Florida two parallel cultures, separate but not exactly equal, a key distinction being that only one of the two, the Cuban, exhibited even a remote interest in the activities of the other. "The American community is not really aware of what is happening in the Cuban community," an exiled banker named Luis Botifoll said in a 1983 *Herald* Sunday magazine piece about ten prominent local Cubans. "We are clannish, but at least we know who is who in the American establishment. They do not." About another of the ten Cubans featured in this piece, Jorge Mas Canosa, the *Herald* had this to say:

> He is an advisor to US Senators, a confidant of federal bureaucrats, a lobbyist for anti-Castro US policies, a near unknown in Miami. When his political group sponsored a luncheon speech in Miami by Secretary of Defense Caspar Weinberger, almost none of the American business leaders attending had ever heard of their Cuban host.

The general direction of this piece, which appeared under the cover line "THE CUBANS: *They're ten of the most powerful men in Miami. Half the population doesn't know it,*" was, as the *Herald* put it,

> to challenge the widespread presumption that Miami's Cubans are not really Americans, that they are a foreign presence here, an exile community that is trying to turn South Florida into North Cuba. . . . The top ten are not separatists; they have achieved success in the most traditional ways. They are the solid, bedrock citizens, hard-working humanitarians who are role models for a community that seems determined to assimilate itself into American society.

This was interesting. It was written by one of the few Cubans then on the *Herald* staff, and yet it described, however unwittingly, the precise angle at which Miami Anglos and Miami Cubans were failing to connect: Miami Anglos were in fact interested in Cubans only to the extent that they could cast them as aspiring immigrants, "determined to assimilate," a "hard-working" minority not different in kind from other groups of resident aliens. (But had I met any Haitians, a number of Anglos asked when I said that I had been talking to Cubans.) Anglos (who were, significantly, referred to within the Cuban community as "Americans") spoke of cross-culturalization, and of what they believed to be a meaningful second-generation preference for hamburgers, and rock-and-roll. They spoke of "diversity," and of Miami's "Hispanic flavor," an approach in which 56 percent of the population was seen as decorative, like the Coral Gables arches.

Fixed as they were on this image of the melting pot, of immigrants fleeing a   12 disruptive revolution to find a place in the American sun, Anglos did not on the whole understand that assimilation would be considered by most Cubans a doubtful goal at best. Nor did many Anglos understand that living in Florida was still at the deepest level construed by Cubans as a temporary condition, an accepted political option shaped by the continuing dream, if no longer the immediate expectation, of a vindicatory return. *El exilio* was for Cubans a ritual, a respected tradition. *La revolución* was also a ritual, a trope fixed in Cuban political rhetoric at least since José Martí, a concept broadly interpreted to mean reform, or progress, or even just change. Ramón Grau San Martín, the president of Cuba during the autumn of 1933 and from 1944 until 1948, had presented himself as a revolutionary, as had his 1948 successor, Carlos Prío. Even Fulgencio Batista had entered Havana life calling for *la revolución,* and had later been accused of betraying it, even as Fidel Castro was now.

This was a process Cuban Miami understood, but Anglo Miami did not,   13 remaining as it did arrestingly innocent of even the most general information about Cuba and Cubans. Miami Anglos for example still had trouble with Cuban names, and Cuban food. When the Cuban novelist Guillermo Cabrera Infante came from London to lecture at Miami-Dade Community College, he was referred to by several Anglo faculty members to whom I spoke as "Infante." Cuban food was widely seen not as a minute variation on that eaten throughout both the Caribbean and the Mediterranean but as "exotic," and full of garlic. A typical Thursday food section of the *Herald* included recipes for Broiled Lemon-Curry Cornish Game Hens, Chicken Tetrazzini, King Cake, Pimiento Cheese, Raisin Sauce for Ham, Sauteed Spiced Peaches, Shrimp Scampi, Easy Beefy Stir-Fry, and four ways to used dried beans ("Those cheap, humble beans that have long sustained the world's poor have become the trendy set's new pet"), none of them Cuban.

This was all consistent, and proceeded from the original construction, that   14 of the exile as an immigration. There was no reason to be curious about Cuban food, because Cuban teenagers preferred hamburgers. There was no reason to get Cuban names right, because they were complicated, and would be simplified by the second generation, or even by the first, "Jorge L. Mas" was the way Jorge Mas Canosa's business card read. "Raul Masvidal" was the way Raul Masvidal y Jury ran for mayor of Miami. There was no reason to know about Cuban history, because history was what immigrants were fleeing.

Even the revolution, the reason for the immigration, could be covered in a   15 few broad strokes: "Batista," "Castro," "26 Julio," this last being the particular broad stroke that inspired the Miami Springs Holiday Inn, on July 26, 1985, the thirty-second anniversary of the day Fidel Castro attacked the Moncada Barracks and so launched his six-year struggle for power in Cuba, to run a bar special on Cuba Libres, thinking to attract local Cubans by commemorating their holiday. "It was a mistake," the manager said, besieged by outraged exiles. "The gentleman who did it is from Minnesota."

There was in fact no reason, in Miami as well as in Minnesota, to know 16 anything at all about Cubans, since Miami Cubans were now, if not Americans, at least aspiring Americans, and worthy of Anglo attention to the exact extent that they were proving themselves, in the *Herald*'s words, "role models for a community that seems determined to assimilate itself into American society"; or, as George Bush put it in a 1986 Miami address to the Cuban American National Foundation, "the most eloquent testimony I know to the basic strength and success of America, as well as to the basic weakness and failure of Communism and Fidel Castro."

The use of this special lens, through which the exiles were seen as a trib- 17 ute to the American system, a point scored in the battle of the ideologies, tended to be encouraged by those outside observers who dropped down from the northeast corridor for a look and a column or two. George Will, in *Newsweek,* saw Miami as "a new installment in the saga of America's absorptive capacity," and Southwest Eighth Street as the place where "these exemplary Americans," the seven Cubans who had been gotten together to brief him, "initiated a columnist to fried bananas and black-bean soup and other Cuban contributions to the tanginess of American life." George Gilder, in *The Wilson Quarterly,* drew pretty much the same lesson from Southwest Eighth Street, finding it "more effervescently thriving than its crushed prototype," by which he seemed to mean Havana. In fact Eighth Street was for George Gilder a street that seemed to "percolate with the forbidden commerce of the dying island to the south . . . the Refrescos Cawy, the Competidora and El Cuño cigarettes, the *guayaberas,* the Latin music pulsing from the storefronts, the pyramids of mangoes and tubers, gourds and plantains, the iced coconuts served with a straw, the new theaters showing the latest anti-Castro comedies."

There was nothing on this list, with the possible exception of the "anti- 18 Castro comedies," that could not most days be found on Southwest Eighth Street, but the list was also a fantasy, and a particularly *gringo* fantasy, one in which Miami Cubans, who came from a culture which had represented western civilization in this hemisphere since before there was a United States of America, appeared exclusively as vendors of plantains, their native music "pulsing" behind them. There was in any such view of Miami Cubans an extraordinary element of condescension, and it was the very condescension shared by Miami Anglos, who were inclined to reduce the particular liveliness and sophistication of local Cuban life to a matter of shrines on the lawn and love potions in the *botanicas,* the primitive exotica of the tourist's Caribbean.

Cubans were perceived as most satisfactory when they appeared most fully 19 to share the aspirations and manners of middle-class Americans, at the same time adding "color" to the city on appropriate occasions, for example at their *quinces* (the *quinces* were one aspect of Cuban life almost invariably mentioned by Anglos, who tended to present them as evidence of Cuban extravagance, i.e., Cuban irresponsibility, or childishness), or on the day of the annual Calle Ocho Festival, when they could, according to the *Herald,* "samba" in the streets and stir up a paella for two thousand (ten cooks, two thousand mussels, two hundred and twenty pounds of lobster, and four hundred and forty pounds of rice), using rowboat oars as spoons. Cubans were perceived as least satisfactory when they "acted clannish," "kept to themselves," "had their own ways," and, two frequent flash points, "spoke Spanish when they didn't need to" and "got political"; complaints, each of them, which suggested an Anglo view of what Cubans should be at significant odds with what Cubans were.

This question of language was curious. The sound of spoken Spanish was [20] common in Miami, but it was also common in Los Angeles, and Houston, and even in the cities of the Northeast. What was unusual about Spanish in Miami was not that it was so often spoken, but that it was so often heard: In, say, Los Angeles, Spanish remained a language only barely registered by the Anglo population, part of the ambient noise, the language spoken by the people who worked in the car wash and came to trim the trees and cleared the tables in restaurants. In Miami Spanish was spoken by the people who ate in the restaurants, the people who owned the cars and the trees, which made, on the socio-auditory scale, a considerable difference. Exiles who felt isolated or declassed by language in New York or Los Angeles thrived in Miami. An entrepreneur who spoke no English could still, in Miami, buy, sell, negotiate, leverage assets, float bonds, and, if he were so inclined, attend galas twice a week, in black tie. "I have been after the *Herald* ten times to do a story about millionaires in Miami who do not speak more than two words in English," one prominent exile told me. "'Yes' and 'no.' Those are the two words. They come here with five dollars in their pockets and without speaking another word of English they are millionaires."

The truculence a millionaire who spoke only two words of English might [21] provoke among the less resourceful native citizens of a nominally American city was predictable, and manifested itself rather directly. In 1980, the year of Mariel, Dade County voters had approved a referendum requiring that county business be conducted exclusively in English. Notwithstanding the fact that this legislation was necessarily amended to exclude emergency medical and certain other services, and notwithstanding even the fact that many local meetings continued to be conducted in that unbroken alternation of Spanish and English which had become the local patois ("I will be in Boston on Sunday and *desafortunadamente yo tengo un compromiso en* Boston *qu no puedo romper y yo no podre estar con Vds.,*" read the minutes of a 1984 Miami City Commission meeting I had occasion to look up. "*En espiritu, estaré, pero* the other members of the commission I am sure are invited . . ."),[1] the very existence of this referendum, was seen by many as ground regained, a point made. By 1985 a St. Petersburg optometrist named Robert Melby was launching his third attempt in four years to have English declared the official language of the state of Florida, as it would be in 1986 of California. "I don't know why our legislators here are so, how should I put it?— spineless," Robert Melby complained about those South Florida politicians who knew how to count. "No one down here seems to want to run with the issue."

---

[1]I will be in Boston on Sunday and unfortunately I have an appointment in Boston that I can't break and I won't be able to be with you. In spirit, I will be, but the other members of the commission I am sure are invited. . . ."

Even among those Anglos who distanced themselves from such efforts, 22
Anglos who did not perceive themselves as economically or socially threatened
by Cubans, there remained considerable uneasiness on the matter of language,
perhaps because the inability or the disinclination to speak English tended to
undermine their conviction that assimilation was an ideal universally shared by
those who were to be assimilated. This uneasiness had for example shown up
repeatedly during the 1985 mayoralty campaign, surfacing at odd but apparently
irrepressible angles. The winner of that contest, Xavier Suarez, who was born in
Cuba but educated in the United States, a graduate of Harvard Law, was
reported in a wire service story to speak, an apparently unexpected accomplishment, "flawless English."

A less prominent Cuban candidate for mayor that year had unsettled 23
reporters at a televised "meet the candidates" forum by answering in Spanish the
questions they asked in English. "For all I or my dumbstruck colleagues knew,"
the *Herald* political editor complained in print after the event, "he was reciting
his high school's alma mater or the Ten Commandments over and over again.
The only thing I understood was the occasional *Cubanos vota Cubano* he tossed
in." It was noted by another *Herald* columnist that of the leading candidates,
only one, Raul Masvidal, had a listed telephone number, but: ". . . if you call
Masvidal's 661-0259 number on Kiaora Street in Coconut Grove—during the
day, anyway—you'd better speak Spanish. I spoke to two women there, and
neither spoke enough English to answer the question of whether it was the
candidate's number."

On the morning this last item came to my attention in the *Herald* I studied 24
it for some time. Raul Masvidal was at that time the chairman of the board of the
Miami Savings Bank and the Miami Savings Corporation. He was a former
chairman of the Biscayne Bank, and a minority stockholder in the M Bank, of
which he had been a founder. He was a member of the Board of Regents for the
state university system of Florida. He had paid $600,000 for the house on Kiaora
Street in Coconut Grove, buying it specifically because he needed to be a Miami
resident (Coconut Grove is part of the city of Miami) in order to run for mayor,
and he had sold his previous house, in the incorporated city of Coral Gables, for
$1,100,000.

The Spanish words required to find out whether the number listed for the 25
house on Kiaora Street was in fact the candidate's number would have been
roughly these: "*¿Es la casa de Raul Masvidal?*" The answer might have been "*Si,*"
or the answer might have been "*No.*" It seemed to me that there must be very
few people working on daily newspapers along the southern borders of the
United States who would consider this exchange entirely out of reach, and fewer
still who would not accept it as a commonplace of American domestic life that
daytime telephone calls to middle-class urban households will frequently be
answered by women who speak Spanish.

Something else was at work in this item, a real resistance, a balkiness, a 26
coded version of the same message Dade County voters had sent when they
decreed that their business be done only in English: WILL THE LAST AMERICAN TO
LEAVE MIAMI PLEASE BRING THE FLAG, the famous bumper stickers had read the

year of Mariel. "It was the last American stronghold in Dade County," the owner of the Gator Kicks Longneck Saloon, out where Southwest Eighth Street runs into the Everglades, had said after he closed the place for good the night of Super Bowl Sunday, 1986. "Fortunately or unfortunately, I'm not alone in my inability," a *Herald* columnist named Charles Whited had written a week or so later, in a column about not speaking Spanish. "A good many Americans have left Miami because they want to live someplace where everybody speaks one language: theirs." In this context the call to the house on Kiaora Street in Coconut Grove which did or did not belong to Raul Masvidal appeared not as a statement of literal fact but as shorthand, a glove thrown down, a stand, a cry from the heart of a beleaguered raj.

QUESTIONS FOR CRITICAL READING, THINKING, DISCUSSION, AND WRITING

Analyzing Content and Technique

1. What is the thesis of the essay? Where is it most explicitly discussed?
2. Describe the "tone" of Miami. In what ways is it Cuban? Why, in spite of its visibility, does the Anglo population pay the Cuban population little attention?
3. Why does Didion consider the Cuban reporter's piece in the *Herald* (paragraph 10) about Cuban immigrants inaccurate? Summarize her view of who the Cuban immigrants are, what they want, and how far they are willing or not willing to assimilate into America.
4. Define the concept of exile as the Cuban sees it. How is this different from the idea of immigration? Of being a refugee?
5. How are the Cubans in Miami different from other immigrants living in the United States? How far do politicians in Washington realize this? Pick out and analyze examples on this issue provided by Didion.
6. For whom is Didion writing this essay? How do we know this? What is her purpose?

Collaborative Activity

Have group members conduct informal interviews with people who have lived in America for at least two generations (that is, neither they nor their parents were immigrants). Ask questions to ascertain how they feel about immigrants, how aware they are of immigrants in their community, and how they perceive the role of these immigrants. Write a collaborative paragraph in which you incorporate your findings.

Making Connections

1. Write a paper in which you research the historical events, which Didion alludes to in this essay, that led to the Cuban exodus. Focus on information which expands our understanding of the Cubans in Miami.
2. One of the issues Didion discusses in this essay is the drive to make English the official language of certain states. How do you feel about this issue? Write an essay in which you examine the arguments presented by those who are for this change as well as those who are against it. What is your ultimate opinion on this issue?

PREREADING ACTIVITY

Write about a "look" (clothing, hair, and so forth) that you or a friend adopted while in high school. Describe the fashion and its symbolic significance.

Hair

MALCOLM X

Malcolm X (1925–1965) was born in Nebraska. He was originally named Malcolm Little, but he changed his name when he joined the Black Muslims, a militant group in which he advanced to a position of leadership. Because of differences in policy, he later established a separate organization of his own; soon after that, he was assassinated at a public meeting. Selection 49 is from an early chapter of *The Autobiography of Malcolm X,* which he wrote in conjunction with Alex Haley. "Conking" refers to straightening curly hair.

Shorty soon decided that my hair was finally long enough to be conked. He had promised to school me in how to beat the barbershop's three-and four-dollar price by making up congolene, and then conking ourselves.

I took the little list of ingredients he had printed out for me, and went to a grocery store, where I got a can of Red Devil lye, two eggs, and two medium-sized white potatoes. Then at a drugstore near the poolroom, I asked for a large jar of vaseline, a large bar of soap, a large-toothed comb and a fine-toothed comb, one of those rubber hoses with a metal spray-head, a rubber apron and a pair of gloves.

"Going to lay on that first conk?" the drugstore man asked me. I proudly told him, grinning, "Right!"

Shorty paid six dollars a week for a room in his cousin's shabby apartment. His cousin wasn't at home. "It's like the pad's mine, he spends so much time with his woman," Shorty said, "Now, you watch me—"

He peeled the potatoes and thin-sliced them into a quart-sized Mason fruit jar, then started stirring them with a wooden spoon as he gradually poured in a little over half the can of lye. "Never use a metal spoon; the lye will turn it black," he told me.

A jelly-like, starchy-looking glop resulted from the lye and potatoes, and Shorty broke in the two eggs, stirring real fast—his own conk and dark face bent down close. The congolene turned pale-yellowish. "Feel the jar," Shorty said. I cupped my hand against the outside, and snatched it away. "Damn right, it's hot, that's the lye," he said. "So you know it's going to burn when I comb it in—it burns *bad*. But the longer you can stand it, the straighter the hair."

He made me sit down, and he tied the string of the new rubber apron tightly around my neck, and combed up my bush of hair. Then, from the big vaseline jar, he took a handful and massaged it hard all through my hair and into the scalp. He also thickly vaselined my neck, ears and forehead. "When I get to washing out your head, be sure to tell me anywhere you feel any little stinging," Shorty warned me, washing his hands, then pulling on the rubber gloves, and tying on his own rubber apron. "You always got to remember that any congolene left in burns a sore into your head."

The congolene just felt warm when Shorty started combing it in. But then my head caught fire.

I gritted my teeth and tried to pull the sides of the kitchen table together. The comb felt as if it was raking my skin off.

My eyes watered, my nose was running. I couldn't stand it any longer; I bolted to the washbasin. I was cursing Shorty with every name I could think of when he got the spray going and started soap-lathering my head.

He lathered and spray-rinsed, lathered and spray-rinsed, maybe ten or twelve times, each time gradually closing the hot-water faucet, until the rinse was cold, and that helped some.

"You feel any stinging spots?"

"No," I managed to say. My knees were trembling.

"Sit back down, then. I think we got it all out okay."

The flame came back as Shorty, with a thick towel, started drying my head, rubbing hard. *"Easy, man, easy"* I kept shouting.

"The first time's always worst. You get used to it better before long. You took it real good, homeboy. You got a good conk."

When Shorty let me stand up and see in the mirror, my hair hung down in limp, damp strings. My scalp still flamed, but not as badly; I could bear it. He draped the towel around my shoulders, over my rubber apron, and began again vaselining my hair.

I could feel him combing, straight back, first the big comb, then the fine-tooth one.

Then, he was using a razor, very delicately, on the back of my neck. Then, finally, shaping the sideburns.

My first view in the mirror blotted out the hurting. I'd seen some pretty conks, but when it's the first time, on your *own* head, the transformation, after the lifetime of kinks, is staggering.

The mirror reflected Shorty behind me. We both were grinning and sweating. And on top of my head was this thick, smooth sheen of shining red hair—real red—as straight as any white man's.

How ridiculous I was! Stupid enough to stand there simply lost in admira- 22
tion of my hair now looking "white," reflected in the mirror in Shorty's room. I
vowed that I'd never again be without a conk, and I never was for many years.

This was my first really big step toward self-degradation: when I endured all 23
of that pain, literally burning my flesh to have it look like a white man's hair. I
had joined that multitude of Negro men and women in America who are brain-
washed into believing that the black people are "inferior"—and white people
"superior"—that they will even violate and mutilate their God-created bodies to
try to look "pretty" by white standards.

QUESTIONS FOR CRITICAL READING, THINKING, DISCUSSION, AND WRITING

Analyzing Content and Technique

1. Why did Malcolm X want a conk? Why does he give us such a detailed description of the pain
   involved in conking?
2. What can we deduce about the characters of the two teenagers? What conclusions can we
   draw about the society in which they live?
3. Where in the selection does the narrator's voice change? What transition is taking place? What
   is the difference in tone and intention between the beginning and the end?
4. Analyze paragraphs 8 to 11. Although they are on the same topic, why has Malcolm X divided
   them into several short paragraphs? How would the effect be different if they were combined?
5. Where has Malcolm X placed the thesis of the essay? What is his intention in placing it there?
   Where else could he have placed it? What would have been lost in that case?
6. What is the tone of the essay? Pick out words and phrases that contribute to the tone. Is the
   tone appropriate for the intended audience? Who is the intended audience? How do we know
   this?

Collaborative Activity

Going back to the prereading activity, discuss, as a group, fashions or "looks" that were popular
while you were in high school. Make a group list of these. Which fashions did you adopt? Were
there some you did not adopt? Why? How did your action affect your self-image?

Making Connections

1. What is Malcolm X saying about the human desire to conform and how it affects our identity?
   Do you agree or disagree with him? Write an essay expressing your own opinion and supporting it with examples from your reading and your experience.
2. What is the difference between the self-image of the teenager Malcolm and that of the adult
   Malcolm? Find two or three other writers in this book who show a similar change in self-
   perception and growth in understanding. Write an essay discussing and connecting their
   insights.

50

PREREADING ACTIVITY
Examine the title. What does it indicate about the causes of racism? Make a list of some other causes of racism that you have observed.

The Economics of Hate (Student Essay)

ANDROMEDA POLHEMUS

Why has racism become such an integral part of our society in America? What has caused prejudice and hate instead of the "melting pot" or the American mosaic we hoped for? Many different forces have created the ongoing distrust between races in America. One such reason, which is linked to or explains many others, is the fear of economic competition. It is when times get hard that we see the most bitter outbursts of racial hatred. "People tend to be more hostile toward others when they feel their security is threatened; thus many social scientists conclude that economic competition and conflict breed prejudice. Certainly a great amount of evidence shows that negative stereotyping, prejudice, and discrimination increase strongly whenever competition for a limited number of jobs increases" (Parrillo 81). So the threat to jobs has been a major influence throughout time in creating racial prejudice in America.

If we examine American history we will see that the struggle for jobs has been a cause of racism from the Germans in the East to the Chinese railroad workers in the West. We hear the same story again and again, prejudice rising when the "natives" realize there is competition in the job market. This is not to say that differing religions, varying traditions, and distinct moral codes had nothing to do with negative sentiments. But these things were more clearly perceived in a people who were "stealing" jobs. The immigrants were no longer seen as newcomers to be ignored or left alone. Now they were opponents. As examples of this tendency, so that we may look in depth, let us focus on the Irish in the East, the Blacks in the South, and the Japanese on the West Coast. Here we have three very different and culturally diverse groups, but all three experienced racism and the resulting discrimination from white America because they threatened jobs.

In the 1840s and 1850s the Irish immigrants began flooding into the East Coast cities like no group of immigrants before them ever had. They were fleeing

Source: Student essay reprinted by permission.

the potato famine, and they came in such numbers as to make up one quarter to one third of the populations in cities like New York, Philadelphia, and Boston (Fallows, 31–37). Because they arrived in such large numbers, they obviously posed a threat to the job market, and thus many stereotypes and negative images became associated with the Irish. When they began coming to New York, "Competition for jobs brought out the 'No Irish Need Apply' signs" (Fallows 33). The fear of competition for work led the "natives" to put pressure on the employers not to hire Irish. They also spread around stereotypes of the Irish being uneducated drunks who were "emotionally unstable and morally primitive" (Parrillo 69) to make them appear undesirable as employees so that they would be given the hardest, lowest-paying jobs.

The results of such racism reached far and wide. Since most of the Irish ⁴ were peasants and therefore unskilled laborers, this discrimination forced them that much easier into manual labor. They became miners, industrial workers, carters, porters, and domestic help. Because of the prejudice against them, they turned inward to depend only on their own community, thus perpetuating racism in both directions. They became a "majority minority group" taking on the lowest jobs, neither understanding nor wishing to deal with the dominant culture. The prejudices initiated by the original competition for jobs lingered on even after the actual economic situation had changed, and in places like Philadelphia, "Church burnings and Know-Nothing riots reflected the Protestant native's growing fear of Catholicism and of competition for jobs at lower occupational levels" (Fallows 35).

Ironically, once the Irish had settled in and had become, because of their ⁵ numbers, an important and powerful minority, they identified with those who had oppressed them. They regarded more recent immigrants as threats and did what they could to keep them out of the work force. "At the close of the Civil War, for example, the Irish, German, and Welsh Pennsylvania coal miners complained of newer immigrants who were endangering their jobs" (Fallows 57–58). The Irish, who by this time had gained political strength through unions, particularly resented those brought in to ruin their strikes such as the Polish, Italians, and French Canadians (Fallows 58). They were also strongly opposed to Abolition because they feared the competition in the work place from the freed slaves.

The double role of the Irish as both the victim and instigators of racist ⁶ prejudice demonstrates two valuable lessons. First, that it is often not the upper classes but those closest to the minority economically, and therefore competing for the same jobs, who have the strongest prejudices. And secondly, that the cycle of racism is self-perpetuating and that it is often forced into being by the economic struggle for jobs.

The freed African Americans suffered from racism from other minorities as ⁷ well as from the dominant class. Because of slavery they entered the occupational arena later than many immigrants. Untrained in skilled labor, they too were forced to look for the same manual jobs the Irish had taken, but in many parts of the country their oppressors were different. "Since the passage of civil rights laws on employment in the twentieth century, researchers have consistently detected the strongest anti-black prejudice among whites who are closest to blacks on the socioeconomic ladder" (Parrillo 82). In this case it was the poor southern whites who now had to vie for jobs against the blacks. Often this was where the core of racial hatred in the South lay.

It is interesting to note that there was less prejudice and no required 8 segregation in the South when the slaves were originally emancipated as opposed to when the poorer whites realized that these newly freed people were applying for the same jobs. "As the Negroes invaded the new mining and industrial towns of the uplands in greater numbers, and the hill-country whites were driven into more frequent and closer association with them, and as the two races were brought into rivalry for subsistence wages in the cotton fields, mines, and wharves, the lower-class white man's demand for Jim Crow laws became more insistent" (Williamson 51).

Anxiety over job security, therefore, played a major part in installing 9 segregation laws. There was definitely already strong racist sentiment in the southern states, but the legalization of these ideas made them a continuing part of the culture. The law had come about more because of fear of economic threat than plain disgust of interacting with blacks. The disgust came later, after the installation of the laws justified such behavior. Even the Ku Klux Klan has definite roots in "protecting" jobs for whites. Originally "the Klan concentrated on maintaining white supremacy by intimidating white employers as well as black workers" (Parillo 369), thus "saving" jobs for lower class whites. As Williamson states, "Economic, social, and political frustrations thus generated aggressiveness among the great mass of whites [and] the Negro became the scapegoat for these aggressions" (Williamson 53).

Because of the Jim Crow segregation laws, many blacks moved out of the 10 South, heading north to find better fortune. But this meant new competition for jobs in the areas to which they moved. As mentioned earlier, the Irish in Boston "were particularly distressed at the prospect of having to compete for a marginal existence with freed slaves" (Fallows 37). This was a sentiment echoed throughout the country and caused many of the labor unions, which had worked *for* the discriminated-against before, to oppose the African Americans. Particularly "the labor unions in the North organized against the blacks" (Parrillo 367) in order to protect all of the other immigrants who had flooded the region earlier. This meant that, as well as discrimination by the majority, strong racist currents began to flow between minorities. We can still see the effects of these today.

This same vicious economic competition is what allowed the population of 11 the West Coast to support discriminatory laws against Asians and eventually the Japanese internment during World War II. The Japanese began emigrating to America in the late 1860s and settled mostly on the West Coast where prejudice already existed against the Chinese railroad workers. The white Americans did not take the time to discern between Asians and initially lumped the Japanese into the same disfavored category. "Hostility from union members, who resented the Asians' willingness to work for lower wages and under poor conditions, produced the inevitable clashes" (Parrillo 286). Because of this resentment the unions in the West organized against Asians the way northern unions had against blacks. As a result the Japanese were pushed out of industrial jobs and gravitated toward the marginal area of agriculture. Most of the Japanese ended up being employed in farming because of "the limitations imposed on them by the racism of the period which restricted their opportunities in other sectors of the economy" (O'Brien and Fugita, 38).

But ironically the Japanese, many of them having come from rural backgrounds, were very successful at agriculture. This led to an even greater resentment. The Californian farmers, fearing for their livelihood, became extremely hate-filled and racist toward the Japanese. These farmers pushed hard, as the threatened whites in the South had, for laws to support their racism and protect their jobs. Alien Land Laws swept throughout the western states prohibiting the Japanese, who could not become naturalized citizens, from owning land. But once again this racist move did not have the desired impact. The children of immigrants who were born in the United States were automatically citizens, and the land could be owned by them. This allowed the Japanese to find a way around the Alien Laws and to continue to be successful.

Because the various laws passed had not fully served their purpose, to wipe out Japanese competition, many of the white Americans directly affected by the competition were immediately supportive of the evacuation and relocation of the Japanese Americans when this was suggested after Pearl Harbor. They were not looking at the Japanese as fellow humans (a common occurrence in racism), or aware of what internment conditions were like, but were only concerned with the fact that this would "eliminate" the competition. Many of them were openly jubilant that this would provide them with the opportunity to buy Japanese farms or small businesses at low prices as a result of the evacuation.

Through the histories of these three minority groups in the United States, we see the strong influence economic competition has had in creating prejudice across America. It may have seemed at first glance that these were separate or isolated events, or even that people did not want to work alongside of different ethnic groups *because* they were racist. But through these histories we can see that racism was the effect, not the cause of the dilemma. We also see how the prejudices which originally arose due to economic fears became institutionalized by laws, and accepted as reasons to hate in their own right.

Some of us would like to think we have left such tendencies behind, but unfortunately this same feeling of economic threat is still a major cause of racism today, both within our country and internationally. Within the inner cities the African Americans feel threatened by the influx of Koreans and so outbreaks of violent acts and derogatory songs against Koreans have ensued. More Korean establishments were destroyed than white ones in the riots that occurred in the aftermath of the Rodney King incident in Los Angeles. And on the international scene Japan-bashing has become very acceptable even in highly respected American magazines in the last five years. The Japanese economy began rising while we started a recession and many people felt we were losing business and jobs to Japan. An upswing in anti-Japanese sentiment occurred almost immediately. Once again the threat to jobs in America has produced racism.

Thus it is particularly important for us in America today to study the causes [16] of racism, learn from its history, and work against our tendency toward it consciously. We are a multiethnic, interdependent community living in an increasingly global world, and in spite of what white supremacists might think, this is not going to change. If we are to live in harmony, without which long-term economic prosperity cannot occur for any of us, we must reteach our country about ethnic relations.

BIBLIOGRAPHY

FALLOWS, MARJORIE R. *Irish Americans: Identity and Assimilation.* Englewood Cliffs, N.J.: Prentice-Hall, 1979.

KITIANO, HARRY. *Japanese Americans: The Evolution of a Subculture.* Englewood Cliffs: Prentice-Hall, 1976.

O'BRIEN, DAVID, and STEPHEN FUGITA. *The Japanese American Experience.* Bloomington and Indianapolis: Indiana University Press, 1991.

PARILLO, VINCENT N. *Strangers to These Shores.* New York: Macmillan, 1994.

WILLIAMSON, JOEL. *The Origins of Segregation.* Lexington: Heath, 1968.

STRUCTURE, STRATEGY, SUGGESTION

1. What is Polhemus's thesis? Where is it placed? Where is it reinforced? How has she narrowed it down?
2. Examine the kinds of evidence Polhemus offers us. How has she organized them? Are they sufficiently convincing? Why or why not?
3. Take a paragraph that strikes you as particularly effective and analyze the structure. What forms its core?
4. Study the body paragraphs of this essay and identify the topic sentences. Where in the paragraph do they usually occur? Where might they have been placed? What does the placement tell us about the writer's style and purpose?
5. Define the tone of the essay. What is it trying to persuade the reader of? What other technique might the writer have used to persuade the reader?
6. Write an essay in which you trace the history of prejudice faced by a minority group either in the United States or elsewhere in the world. In your essay analyze the causes for the prejudice, its effects, or both.

SYNTHESIS *Part Six*

1. The writers in Part Six indicate that we stereotype people in many ways. Analyze three of the readings in this section, classifying the different types of prejudice that are portrayed. From your study, what have you learned of the nature of prejudice?

2. Compare the reactions of the speaker of "In Response to Executive Order 9066" with those of another narrator or speaker in Part Six who experiences discrimination. In your essay, discuss the pros and cons of each response, what the speaker or narrator is trying to achieve, and how far he or she is successful.

3. "Twice an Outsider" and "Hair" discuss how painful the problem of prejudice becomes when it is internalized—that is, when members of the group which is discriminated against begin to see themselves and each other in the negative light in which they have been imaged. Examine the situations portrayed by these writers and discuss the effects of this self-reflexive prejudice as compared to that directed at other people.

4. The selections in Part Six point out the problem of prejudice but also present us with several ways in which to battle it. Write an essay in which you analyze these "solutions," focusing particularly on those which you found unusual, unconventional, and unexpected. Overall, what did you learn from Part Six that you feel might help you deal with situations in daily life?

Words That Shape Us

SELECTIONS IN PART SEVEN

Part 7: Introduction

From the time we are old enough to understand the meanings of the apparently random noises that emerge from the human mouth, we are influenced—for better or for worse—by language. We claim—and rightly—that language is one of the major elements that set us off from other species, even those that communicate by using sounds. We use language for a variety of complex purposes. But, ironically, not all our uses of language are positive; nor do all of them serve to advance communication between individuals or groups. Some uses of language, the reasons behind them, and the effect they have on society and the individual are explored by the writers in Part Seven.

The first essay here, Gordon Allport's "Linguistic Factors in Prejudice" (selection 51), analyzes the psychology behind using negative labels to define people. Allport's ideas, based on careful research, enhance our understanding of many of the other selections in Part Seven, especially Gloria Naylor's essay, "Mommy, What Does 'Nigger' Mean?" (selection 52), which illustrates, through personal example, the many nuances possible in a single, loaded word. Naylor also shows how, in order to defend ourselves, we can reappropriate the same words that have been used to hurt us.

Naylor illustrates how the African American community can use the same word as speakers from mainstream society to communicate something very different. This idea is carried further in Leslie Marmon Silko's "Language and Literature from a Pueblo Indian Perspective" (selection 57), in which she states that the Pueblo peoples have a completely non-English approach to expressing a thought and telling a story.

Two essays that argue on opposite sides of an issue concerning language—and the politics associated with it—are Richard Rodriguez's "Aria" (selection 53) and James Fallows's "Viva Bilingualism" (selection 54). Rodriguez and Fallows, too, consider the question of learning the language of mainstream society as opposed to keeping one's ethnic language and the cultural pride that goes along with it. They give us an opportunity to exercise critical thinking as we weigh their very different arguments and persuasive techniques.

"Breaking Silence" (selection 56) by Janice Mirikitani goes back to the fundamental power of language to change our lives. In this poem, the act of speaking out achieves a miracle that transforms the muted, victimized individuals of the speaker's community into "a rainforest of color and noise."

Together, the writers in this section remind us, in their anguish and their triumph, of the importance of reading, writing, and recording speech, something that today's television-oriented society sometimes forgets. Together they warn us that we must watch the words we use or that we allow to be used, for we can never predict how they might affect another human. Perhaps their work will inspire us to be more careful speakers and writers.

51

PREREADING ACTIVITY

Before reading selection 51, write about what the label "communist" means to you. What images are associated with it in your mind? What historic incidents does it make you think of? Now compare your piece with an encyclopedia entry for the term. What did you discover?

Linguistic Factors in Prejudice

GORDON ALLPORT

Gordon Allport (1897–1967) received his Ph.D. in psychology from Harvard University, specializing in social ethics and prejudice. Except for a few brief teaching assignments at a college in Istanbul and at Dartmouth College, he taught at Harvard all his life. He published more than 200 articles, and among his numerous books are *The Psychology of Radio, Waiting for the Lord,* and *The Nature of Prejudice,* from which this essay is taken.

Without words we should scarcely be able to form categories at all. 1 A dog perhaps forms rudimentary generalizations, such as small-boys-are-to-be-avoided—but this concept runs its course on the conditioned reflex level, and does not become the object of thought as such. In order to hold a generalization in mind for reflection and recall, for identification and for action, we need to fix it in words. Without words our world would be, as William James said, an "empirical sand-heap."

Nouns That Cut Slices

In the empirical world of human beings there are some two and a half bil- 2 lion grains of sand corresponding to our category "the human race." We cannot possibly deal with so many separate entities in our thought, nor can we individualize even among the hundreds whom we encounter in our daily round. We must group them, form clusters. We welcome, therefore, the names that help us to perform the clustering.

Source: From Gordon W. Allport, *The Nature of Prejudice,* © 1979 by Addison-Wesley Publishing Company, Inc. Reprinted by permission of the publisher.

The most important property of a noun is that it brings many grains of sand into a single pail, disregarding the fact that the same grains might have fitted just as appropriately into another pail. To state the matter technically, a noun *abstracts* from a concrete reality some one feature and assembles different concrete realities only with respect to this one feature. The very act of classifying forces us to overlook all other features, many of which might offer a sounder basis than the rubric we select. Irving Lee gives the following example:

> I knew a man who had lost the use of both eyes. He was called a "blind man." He could also be called an expert typist, a conscientious worker, a good student, a careful listener, a man who wanted a job. But he couldn't get a job in the department store order room where employees sat and typed orders which came over the telephone. The personnel man was impatient to get the interview over. "But you're a blind man," he kept saying, and one could almost feel his silent assumption that somehow the incapacity in one aspect made the man incapable in every other. So blinded by the label was the interviewer that he could not be persuaded to look beyond it.[1]

Some labels, such as "blind man," are exceedingly salient and powerful. They tend to prevent alternative classification, or even cross-classification. Ethnic labels are often of this type, particularly if they refer to some highly visible feature, e.g., Negro, Oriental. They resemble the labels that point to some outstanding incapacity—*feeble-minded, cripple, blind man.* Let us call such symbols "labels of primary potency." These symbols act like shrieking sirens, deafening us to all finer discriminations that we might otherwise perceive. Even though the blindness of one man and the darkness of pigmentation of another may be defining attributes for some purposes, they are irrelevant and "noisy" for others.

Most people are unaware of this basic law of language—that every label applied to a given person refers properly only to one aspect of his nature. You may correctly say that a certain man is *human, a philanthropist, a Chinese, a physician, an athlete.* A given person may be all of these; but the chances are that *Chinese* stands out in your mind as the symbol of primary potency. Yet neither this nor any other classificatory label can refer to the whole of a man's nature. (Only his proper name can do so.)

Thus each label we use, especially those of primary potency, distracts our attention from concrete reality. The living, breathing, complex individual—the ultimate unit of human nature—is lost to sight. As in the figure, the label magnifies one attribute out of all proportion to its true significance, and masks other important attributes of the individual.

. . . [A] category, once formed with the aid of a symbol of primary potency, tends to attract more attributes than it should. The category labeled *Chinese* comes to signify not only ethnic membership but also reticence, impassivity, poverty, treachery. To be sure, . . . there may be genuine ethnic-linked traits, making for a certain *probability* that the member of an ethnic stock may have these attributes. But our cognitive process is not cautious. The labeled category, as we have seen, includes indiscriminately the defining attribute, probable attributes, and wholly fanciful, nonexistent attributes.

Even proper names—which ought to invite us to look at the individual per-   8
son—may act like symbols of primary potency, especially if they arouse ethnic
associations. Mr. Greenberg is a person, but since his name is Jewish, it activates
in the hearer his entire category of Jews-as-a-whole. An ingenious experiment
performed by Razran shows this point clearly, and at the same time demonstrates
how a proper name, acting like an ethnic symbol, may bring with it an avalanche
of stereotypes.[2]

Thirty photographs of college girls were shown on a screen to 150 students.   9
The subjects rated the girls on a scale from one to five for *beauty, intelligence,
character, ambition, general likability.* Two months later the same subjects were
asked to rate the same photographs and fifteen additional ones (introduced to
complicate the memory factor). This time five of the original photographs were
given Jewish surnames (Cohen, Kantor, etc.), five Italian (Valenti, etc.), and five
Irish (O'Brien, etc.); and the remaining girls were given names chosen from the
signers of the Declaration of Independence and from the Social Register (Davis,
Adams, Clark, etc.).

When Jewish names were attached to photographs there occurred the fol-   10
lowing changes in ratings:

decrease in liking
decrease in character
decrease in beauty
increase in intelligence
increase in ambition

For those photographs given Italian names there occurred:

decrease in liking
decrease in character
decrease in beauty
decrease in intelligence

Thus a mere proper name leads to prejudgments of personal attributes. The individual is fitted to the prejudiced ethnic category, and not judged in his own right.

While the Irish names also brought about depreciated judgment, the depre-   11
ciation was not as great as in the case of the Jews and Italians. The falling of likability of the "Jewish girls" was twice as great as for "Italians" and five times as
great as for "Irish." We note, however, that the "Jewish" photographs caused
higher ratings in *intelligence* and in *ambition*. Not all stereotypes of out-groups
are unfavorable.

The anthropologist, Margaret Mead, has suggested that labels of primary   12
potency lose some of their force when they are changed from nouns into adjectives.
To speak of a Negro soldier, a Catholic teacher, or a Jewish artist calls attention to
the fact that some other group classifications are just as legitimate as the racial or
religious. If George Johnson is spoken of not only as a Negro but also as a *soldier,*
we have at least two attributes to know him by, and two are more accurate than

one. To depict him truly as an individual, of course, we should have to name many more attributes. It is a useful suggestion that we designate ethnic and religious membership where possible with *adjectives* rather than with *nouns*.

Emotionally Toned Labels

Many categories have two kinds of labels—one less emotional and one more emotional. Ask yourself how you feel, and what thoughts you have, when you read the words *school teacher*, and then *school marm*. Certainly the second phrase calls up something more strict, more ridiculous, more disagreeable than the former. Here are four innocent letters: m-a-r-m. But they make us shudder a bit, laugh a bit, and scorn a bit. They call up an image of a spare, humorless, irritable old maid. They do not tell us that she is an individual human being with sorrows and troubles of her own. They force her instantly into a rejective category. [13]

In the ethnic sphere even plain labels such as Negro, Italian, Jew, Catholic, Irish-American, French-Canadian may have emotional tone for a reason that we shall soon explain. But they all have their higher key equivalents: nigger, wop, kike, papist, harp, cannuck. When these labels are employed we can be almost certain that the speaker *intends* not only to characterize the person's membership, but also to disparage and reject him. [14]

Quite apart from the insulting intent that lies behind the use of certain labels, there is also an inherent ("physiognomic") handicap in many terms designating ethnic membership. For example, the proper names characteristic of certain ethnic memberships strike us as absurd. (We compare them, of course, with what is familiar and therefore "right.") Chinese names are short and silly; Polish names intrinsically difficult and outlandish. Unfamiliar dialects strike us as ludicrous. Foreign dress (which, of course, is a visual ethnic symbol) seems unnecessarily queer. [15]

But of all these "physiognomic" handicaps the reference to color, clearly implied in certain symbols, is the greatest. The word Negro comes from the Latin *niger*, meaning black. In point of fact, no Negro has a black complexion, but by comparison with other blonder stocks, he has come to be known as a "black man." Unfortunately *black* in the English language is a word having a preponderance of sinister connotations: the outlook is black, blackball, blackguard, blackhearted, black death, blacklist, blackmail, Black Hand. In his novel *Moby Dick*, Herman Melville considers at length the remarkably morbid connotations of black and the remarkably virtuous connotations of white. [16]

Nor is the ominous flavor of black confined to the English language. A cross-cultural study reveals that the semantic significance of black is more or less universally the same. Among certain Siberian tribes, members of a privileged clan call themselves "white bones," and refer to all others as "black bones." Even among Uganda Negroes there is some evidence for a white god at the apex of the theocratic hierarchy; certain it is that a white cloth, signifying purity, is used to ward off evil spirits and disease.[3] [17]

There is thus an implied value-judgment in the very concept of *white race* and *black race*. One might also study the numerous unpleasant connotations of *yellow*, and their possible bearing on our conception of the people of the Orient. [18]

Such reasoning should not be carried too far, since there are undoubtedly, 19
in various contexts, pleasant associations with both black and yellow. Black velvet
is agreeable, so too are chocolate and coffee. Yellow tulips are well liked; the sun
and moon are radiantly yellow. Yet it is true that "color" words are used with
chauvinistic overtones more than most people realize. There is certainly condescension indicated in many familiar phrases: dark as a nigger's pocket, darktown
strutters, white hope (a term originated when a white contender was sought
against the Negro heavyweight champion, Jack Johnson), the white man's burden, the yellow peril, black boy. Scores of everyday phrases are stamped with the
flavor of prejudice, whether the user knows it or not.[4]

We spoke of the fact that even the most proper and sedate labels for minor- 20
ity groups sometimes seem to exude a negative flavor. In many contexts and situations the very terms *French-Canadian, Mexican,* or *Jew,* correct and nonmali-
cious though they are, sound a bit opprobrious. The reason is that they are labels
of social deviants. Especially in a culture where uniformity is prized, the name of
any deviant carries with it *ipso facto* a negative value-judgment. Words like
insane, alcoholic, pervert are presumably neutral designations of a human condition, but they are more: they are finger-pointings at deviance. Minority groups
are deviants, and for this reason, from the very outset, the most innocent labels
in many situations imply a shading of disrepute. When we wish to highlight the
deviance and denigrate it still further we use words of a higher emotional key:
crackpot, soak, pansy, greaser, Okie, nigger, harp, kike.

Members of minority groups are often understandably sensitive to names 21
given them. Not only do they object to deliberately insulting epithets, but sometimes see evil intent where none exists. Often the word Negro is spelled with a
small *n*, occasionally as a studied insult, more often from ignorance. (The term is
not cognate with white, which is not capitalized, but rather with Caucasian,
which is.) Terms like "mulatto" or "octoroon" cause hard feeling because of the
condescension with which they have often been used in the past. Sex differentia-
tions are objectionable, since they seem doubly to emphasize ethnic difference:
why speak of Jewess and not of Protestantess, or of Negress and not of whitess?
Similar overemphasis is implied in terms like Chinaman or Scotchman; why not
American man? Grounds for misunderstanding lie in the fact that minority group
members are sensitive to such shadings, while majority members may employ
them unthinkingly.

The Communist Label

Until we label an out-group it does not clearly exist in our minds. Take the 22
curiously vague situation that we often meet when a person wishes to locate
responsibility on the shoulders of some out-group whose nature he cannot specify.
In such a case he usually employs the pronoun "they" without an antecedent.
"Why don't they make these sidewalks wider?" "I hear they are going to build a
factory in this town and hire a lot of foreigners." "I won't pay this tax bill; they can
just whistle for their money." If asked "who?" the speaker is likely to grow confused and embarrassed. The common use of the orphaned pronoun *they* teaches us

that people often want and need to designate out-groups (usually for the purpose of venting hostility) even when they have no clear conception of the out-group in question. And so long as the target of wrath remains vague and ill-defined specific prejudice cannot crystallize around it. To have enemies we need labels.

Until relatively recently—strange as it may seem—there was no agreed-upon symbol for *communist*. The word, of course, existed but it had no special emotional connotation, and did not designate a public enemy. Even when, after World War I, there was a growing feeling of economic and social menace in this country, there was no agreement as to the actual source of the menace. 23

A content analysis of the *Boston Herald* for the year 1920 turned up the following list of labels. Each was used in a context implying some threat. Hysteria had overspread the country, as it did after World War II. Someone must be responsible for the postwar malaise, rising prices, uncertainty. There must be a villain. But in 1920 the villain was impartially designated by reporters and editorial writers with the following symbols: 24

> alien, agitator, anarchist, apostle of bomb and torch, Bolshevik, communist, communist laborite, conspirator, emissary of false promise, extremist, foreigner, hyphenated-American, incendiary, IWW, parlor anarchist, parlor pink, parlor socialist, plotter, radical, red, revolutionary, Russian agitator, socialist, Soviet, syndicalist, traitor, undesirable.

From this excited array we note that the *need* for an enemy (someone to serve as a focus for discontent and jitters) was considerably more apparent than the precise *identity* of the enemy. At any rate, there was no clearly agreed upon label. Perhaps partly for this reason the hysteria abated. Since no clear category of "communism" existed there was no true focus for the hostility. 25

But following World War II this collection of vaguely interchangeable labels became fewer in number and more commonly agreed upon. The out-group menace came to be designated almost always as *communist* or *red*. In 1920 the threat, lacking a clear label, was vague; after 1945 both symbol and thing became more definite. Not that people knew precisely what they meant when they said "communist," but with the aid of the term they were at least able to point consistently to *something* that inspired fear. The term developed the power of signifying menace and led to various repressive measures against anyone to whom the label was rightly or wrongly attached. 26

Logically, the label should apply to specifiable defining attributes, such as members of the Communist Party, or people whose allegiance is with the Russian system, or followers, historically, of Karl Marx. But the label came in for far more extensive use. 27

What seems to have happened is approximately as follows. Having suffered through a period of war and being acutely aware of devastating revolutions abroad, it is natural that most people should be upset, dreading to lose their possessions, annoyed by high taxes, seeing customary moral and religious values threatened, and dreading worse disasters to come. Seeking an explanation for this unrest, a single identifiable enemy is wanted. It is not enough to designate "Russia" or some other distant land. Nor is it satisfactory to fix blame on "changing social conditions." What 28 is needed is a human agent . . . near at hand: someone in Washington, someone in our schools, in our factories, in our neighborhood. If we *feel* an immediate threat, we reason, there must be a near-lying danger. It is, we conclude, communism, not only in Russia but also in America, at our doorstep, in our government, in our churches, in our colleges, in our neighborhood.

Are we saying that hostility toward communism is prejudice? Not neces-   29
sarily. There are certainly phases of the dispute wherein realistic social conflict is involved. American values (e.g., respect for the person) and totalitarian values as represented in Soviet practice are intrinsically at odds. A realistic opposition in some form will occur. Prejudice enters only when the defining attributes of "communist" grow imprecise, when anyone who favors any form of social change is called a communist. People who fear social change are the ones most likely to affix the label to any persons or practices that seem to them threatening.

For them the category is undifferentiated. It includes books, movies,   30
preachers, teachers who utter what for them are uncongenial thoughts. If evil befalls—perhaps forest fires or a factory explosion—it is due to communist saboteurs. The category becomes monopolistic, covering almost anything that is uncongenial. On the floor of the House of Representatives in 1946, Representative Rankin called James Roosevelt a communist. Congressman Outland replied with psychological acumen, "Apparently everyone who disagrees with Mr. Rankin is a communist."

When differentiated thinking is at a low ebb—as it is in times of social   31
crises—there is a magnification of two-valued logic. Things are perceived as either inside or outside a moral order. What is outside is likely to be called "communist." Correspondingly—and here is where damage is done—whatever is called communist (however erroneously) is immediately cast outside the moral order.

This associative mechanism places enormous power in the hands of a dem-   32
agogue. For several years Senator McCarthy managed to discredit many citizens who thought differently from himself by the simple device of calling them communists. Few people were able to see through this trick and many reputations were ruined. But the famous senator has no monopoly on the device. As reported in the *Boston Herald* on November 1, 1946, Representative Joseph Martin, Republican leader in the House, ended his election campaign against his Democratic opponent by saying, "The people will vote tomorrow between chaos, confusion, bankruptcy, state socialism or communism, and the preservation of our American life, with all its freedom and its opportunities." Such an array of emotional labels placed his opponent outside the accepted moral order. Martin was re-elected.

•

Not everyone, of course, is taken in. Demagogy, when it goes too far, meets with   33
ridicule. Elizabeth Dilling's book, *The Red Network*, was so exaggerated in its two-valued logic that it was shrugged off by many people with a smile. One reader remarked, "Apparently if you step off the sidewalk with your left foot you're a communist." But it is not easy in times of social strain and hysteria to keep one's balance, and to resist the tendency of a verbal symbol to manufacture large and fanciful categories of prejudiced thinking.

Verbal Realism and Symbol Phobia

Most individuals rebel at being labeled, especially if the label is uncompli- [34] mentary. Very few are willing to be called *fascistic, socialistic,* or *anti-Semitic.* Unsavory labels may apply to others; but not to us.

An illustration of the craving that people have to attach favorable symbols [35] to themselves is seen in the community where white people banded together to force out a Negro family that had moved in. They called themselves "Neighborly Endeavor" and chose as their motto the Golden Rule. One of the first acts of this symbol-sanctified band was to sue the man who sold property to Negroes. They then flooded the house which another Negro couple planned to occupy. Such were the acts performed under the banner of the Golden Rule.

Studies made by Stagner[5] and by Hartmann[6] show that a person's political [36] attitudes may in fact entitle him to be called a fascist or a socialist, and yet he will emphatically repudiate the unsavory label, and fail to endorse any movement or candidate that overtly accepts them. In short, there is a *symbol phobia* that corresponds to *symbol realism.* We are more inclined to the former when we ourselves are concerned, though we are much less critical when epithets of "fascist," "communist," "blind man," "school marm" are applied to others.

When symbols provoke strong emotions they are sometimes regarded no [37] longer as symbols, but as actual things. The expressions "son of a bitch" and "liar" are in our culture frequently regarded as "fighting words." Softer and more subtle expressions of contempt may be accepted. But in these particular cases, the epithet itself must be "taken back." We certainly do not change our opponent's attitude by making him take back a word, but it seems somehow important that the word itself be eradicated.

Such verbal realism may reach extreme lengths. [38]

The City Council of Cambridge, Massachusetts, unanimously passed a resolution (December, 1939) making it illegal "to possess, harbor, sequester, introduce or transport, within the city limits, any book, map, magazine, newspaper, pamphlet, handbill or circular containing the words Lenin or Leningrad."[7]

Such naiveté in confusing language with reality is hard to comprehend unless we recall that word-magic plays an appreciable part in human thinking. The following examples, like the one preceding, are taken from Hayakawa.

The Malagasy soldier must eschew kidneys, because in the Malagasy language the word for kidney is the same as that for "shot"; so shot he would certainly be if he ate a kidney.

In May, 1937, a state senator of New York bitterly opposed a bill for the control of syphilis because "the innocence of children might be corrupted by a widespread use of the term. . . . This particular word creates a shudder in every decent woman and decent man."

This tendency to reify words underscores the close cohesion that exists [39] between category and symbol. Just the mention of "communist," "Negro," "Jew," "England," "Democrats," will send some people into a panic of fear or a frenzy of anger. Who can say whether it is the word or the thing that annoys them? The label is an intrinsic part of any monopolistic category. Hence to liberate a person from ethnic or political prejudice it is necessary at the same time to liberate him from word fetishism. This fact is well known to students of general semantics who tell us that prejudice is due in large part to verbal realism and to symbol phobia. Therefore any program for the reduction of prejudice must include a large measure of semantic therapy.

NOTES AND REFERENCES

1. I. J. Lee. How do you talk about people? *Freedom Pamphlet.* New York: Anti-Defamation League, 1950, 15.
2. G. Razran. Ethnic dislikes and stereotypes: A laboratory study. *Journal of Abnormal and Social Psychology,* 1950, *45,* 7–27.
3. C. E. Osgood. The nature and measurement of meaning. *Psychological Bulletin,* 1952, 49, 226.
4. L. L. Brown. Words and white chauvinism. *Masses and Mainstream,* 1950, *3,* 3–11. See also: *Prejudice Won't Hide! A Guide for Developing a Language of Equality.* San Francisco: California Federation for Civic Unity, 1950.
5. R. Stagner. Fascist attitudes: An exploratory study. *Journal of Social Psychology,* 1936, *7,* 309–319; Fascist attitudes: their determining conditions, *ibid.,* 438–454.
6. G. Hartmann. The contradiction between the feeling-tone of political party names and public response to their platforms. *Journal of Social Psychology,* 1936, *7,* 336–357.
7. S. I. Hayakawa. *Language in Action.* New York: Harcourt, Brace, 1941, 29.

QUESTIONS FOR CRITICAL READING, THINKING, DISCUSSION, AND WRITING

Analyzing Content and Technique

1. According to Allport, why do we use labels? What are their advantages and disadvantages?
2. What conclusion does he draw from the results of the experiment with the photographs of college women who are randomly given ethnic surnames? Do you agree with his conclusion?
3. In the section "Emotionally Toned Labels" (starting at paragraph 13), Allport discusses the prejudice associated with linguistic references to color. Explain this.
4. What reasons does Allport give to explain the fact that the label "communist" became such an emotionally powerful, negative symbol?
5. Define the terms "verbal realism" and "symbol phobia" as Allport uses them. Give an example of each from the essay.

Collaborative Activity

As a group, study paragraph 21. What is the main point Allport is making here? Does the group agree with the idea? Discuss examples contributed by group members that support, refute, or alter Allport's argument.

Making Connections

1. Write an essay classifying the different kinds of linguistic prejudice discussed by Allport. For each kind, give examples from his essay as well as from your own experience and from other pieces you have read (including the selections in Part Seven).

2. At the conclusion of his essay, Allport claims that "any program for the reduction of prejudice must include a large measure of semantic therapy." Write an essay evaluating Allport's arguments and indicating whether you agree or disagree with him. Be sure to define "semantic therapy" and give examples of it, both from the text and from your own experience and observation.

52

PREREADING ACTIVITY

Think about some uncomplimentary epithets you have used, or heard others use, or have been subjected to, that describe a particular group of people. What kind of connotations did they have? How did using them or being subjected to them make you feel?

Mommy, What Does "Nigger" Mean?

GLORIA NAYLOR

Gloria Naylor (1950–   ) has a M.A. in African American studies from Yale University and writes for *The New York Times*. She has been a visiting professor at several institutions, including Princeton University and Boston University. Her essays have appeared in periodicals such as *Southern Review, Ms.,* and *Essence;* she won an American Book Award for her first novel, *The Women of Brewster Place*. Selection 52, sometimes titled "A Question of Language," was first published by *The New York Times*.

*L*anguage is the subject. It is the written form with which I've man-   1
aged to keep the wolf away from the door and, in diaries, to keep my sanity. In spite of this, I consider the written word inferior to the spoken, and much of the frustration experienced by novelists is the awareness that whatever we manage to capture in even the most transcendent passages falls far short of the richness of life. Dialogue achieves its power in the dynamics of a fleeting moment of sight, sound, smell and touch.

I'm not going to enter the debate here about whether it is language that   2
shapes reality or vice versa. That battle is doomed to be waged whenever we seek intermittent reprieve from the chicken and egg dispute. I will simply take the position that the spoken word, like the written word, amounts to a nonsensical arrangement of sounds or letters without a consensus that assigns "meaning." And building from the meanings of what we hear, we order reality. Words themselves are innocuous; it is the consensus that gives them true power.

I remember the first time I heard the word nigger. In my third-grade class,   3
our math tests were being passed down the rows, and as I handed the papers to

a little boy in back of me, I remarked that once again he had received a much lower mark than I did. He snatched his test from me and spit out that word. Had he called me a nymphomaniac or a necrophiliac, I couldn't have been more puzzled. I didn't know what a nigger was, but I knew that whatever it meant, it was something he shouldn't have called me. This was verified when I raised my hand, and in a loud voice repeated what he had said and watched the teacher scold him for using a "bad" word. I was later to go home and ask the inevitable question that every black parent must face—"Mommy, what does 'nigger' mean?"

And what exactly did it mean? Thinking back, I realize that this could not have been the first time the word was used in my presence. I was part of a large extended family that had migrated from the rural South after World War II and formed a close-knit network that gravitated around my maternal grandparents. Their ground-floor apartment in one of the buildings they owned in Harlem was a weekend mecca for my immediate family, along with countless aunts, uncles and cousins who brought along assorted friends. It was a bustling and open house with assorted neighbors and tenants popping in and out to exchange bits of gossip, pick up an old quarrel or referee the ongoing checkers game in which my grandmother cheated shamelessly. They were all there to let down their hair and put up their feet after a week of labor in the factories, laundries and shipyards of New York.

Amid the clamor, which could reach deafening proportions—two or three conversations going on simultaneously, punctuated by the sound of a baby's crying somewhere in the back rooms or out on the street—there was still a rigid set of rules about what was said and how. Older children were sent out of the living room when it was time to get into the juicy details about "you-know-who" up on the third floor who had gone and gotten herself "p-r-e-g-n-a-n-t!" But my parents, knowing that I could spell well beyond my years, always demanded that I follow the others out to play. Beyond sexual misconduct and death, everything else was considered harmless for our young ears. And so among the anecdotes of the triumphs and disappointments in the various workings of their lives, the word nigger was used in my presence, but it was set within contexts and inflections that caused it to register in my mind as something else.

In the singular, the word was always applied to a man who had distinguished himself in some situation that brought their approval for his strength, intelligence or drive:

"Did Johnny *really* do that?"

"I'm telling you, that nigger pulled in $6,000 of overtime last year. Said he got enough for a down payment on a house."

When used with a possessive adjective by a woman—"my nigger"—it became a term of endearment for husband or boyfriend. But it could be more than just a term applied to a man. In their mouths it became the pure essence of manhood—a disembodied force that channeled their past history of struggle and present survival against the odds into a victorious statement of being: "Yeah, that old foreman found out quick enough—you don't mess with a nigger."

In the plural, it became a description of some group within the community that had overstepped the bounds of decency as my family defined it: Parents who neglected their children, a drunken couple who fought in public, people who simply refused to look for work, those with excessively dirty mouths or unkempt households were all "trifling niggers." This particular circle could forgive hard times, unemployment, the occasional bout of depression—they had gone through all of that themselves—but the unforgivable sin was a lack of self-respect.

A woman could never be a "nigger" in the singular, with its connotation of 11 confirming worth. The noun girl was its closest equivalent in that sense, but only when used in direct address and regardless of the gender doing the addressing. "Girl" was a token of respect for a woman. The one-syllable word was drawn out to sound like three in recognition of the extra ounce of wit, nerve or daring that the woman had shown in the situation under discussion.

"G-i-r-l, stop. You mean you said that to his face?"   12

But if the word was used in a third-person reference or shortened so that it 13 almost snapped out of the mouth, it always involved some element of communal disapproval. And age became an important factor in these exchanges. It was only between individuals of the same generation, or from an older person to a younger (but never the other way around), that "girl" would be considered a compliment.

I don't agree with the argument that use of the word nigger at this social 14 stratum of the black community was an internalization of racism. The dynamics were the exact opposite: the people in my grandmother's living room took a word that whites used to signify worthlessness or degradation and rendered it impotent. Gathering there together, they transformed "nigger" to signify the varied and complex human beings they knew themselves to be. If the word was to disappear totally from the mouths of even the most liberal of white society, no one in that room was naïve enough to believe it would disappear from white minds. Meeting the word head-on, they proved it had absolutely nothing to do with the way they were determined to live their lives.

So there must have been dozens of times that the word "nigger" was spo- 15 ken in front of me before I reached the third grade. But I didn't "hear" it until it was said by a small pair of lips that had already learned it could be a way to humiliate me. That was the word I went home and asked my mother about. And since she knew that I had to grow up in America, she took me in her lap and explained.

QUESTIONS FOR CRITICAL READING, THINKING, DISCUSSION, AND WRITING

Analyzing Content and Technique

1. Naylor raises an important issue (though she does not develop it) when she wonders whether language shapes reality or vice versa. Explain your ideas on this subject.

2. What does Naylor mean when she states, "Words themselves are innocuous; it is the consensus that gives them true power"? Give an example of your own to support her point.

3. What are some of the differences in the way the term "nigger" is used by black and white communities? What are some differences between the plural and singular forms of the term?

4. Naylor gives us some usages of the word "girl." What are these? What other connotations of the word have you come across?
5. According to Naylor, why has the black community adopted the term "nigger"? Do you agree with her explanation? Why or why not?
6. Identify the difference between the first section (paragraphs 1 and 2) and the main body of the essay. How is the last section (paragraphs 14 and 15) different from both of these? Discuss the tone of each of these sections.

Collaborative Activity

Look back on question 2 under Analyzing Content and Technique. Have group members come up with words in the English language that currently hold negative connotations but did not originally do so. Take one of these words and research its background. What caused it to change its meaning?

Making Connections

1. At the end of Naylor's article, we learn that as a child who was humiliated at school, Naylor asked her mother to explain the word "nigger." From the point of view of Naylor's mother, write an essay or a letter explaining what she might have said to her daughter. (You may want to do some research on African American history or literature before starting this assignment.)
2. Choose a word (as Naylor does) which people often use to describe a group that you identify with—racially, ethnically, professionally, or otherwise. Write an essay explaining its connotations and effects, using observation, interviews, and personal experience to support your points.

53

PREREADING ACTIVITY

Sprint write for five minutes about a time when you were exposed to a language different from the one you spoke at home. Describe the situation (at school? while traveling? at work? on moving to a different country?) and your reaction to it.

Aria: A Memoir of a Bilingual Childhood

RICHARD RODRIGUEZ

Richard Rodriguez (1944–   ) is a Mexican American who grew up in California. He received his B.A. from Stanford and graduate degrees from Columbia and the University of California at Berkeley. He is currently an educational consultant and a freelance writer whose work has appeared in *Harper's, Saturday Review, American Scholar,* and *The New York Times.* He has been awarded a Fulbright Fellowship and a National Endowment for the Humanities Fellowship. Selection 53, in a slightly different version, can be found in his autobiography, *Hunger of Memory: The Education of Richard Rodriguez.*

I remember, to start with, that day in Sacramento, in a California   1
now nearly thirty years past, when I first entered a classroom—able to understand about fifty stray English words. The third of four children, I had been preceded by my older brother and sister to a neighborhood Roman Catholic school. But neither of them had revealed very much about their classroom experiences. They left each morning and returned each afternoon, always together, speaking Spanish as they climbed the five steps to the porch. And their mysterious books, wrapped in brown shopping-bag paper, remained on the table next to the door, closed firmly behind them.

An accident of geography sent me to a school where all my classmates were   2
white and many were the children of doctors and lawyers and business executives. On that first day of school, my classmates must certainly have been uneasy to find themselves apart from their families, in the first institution of their lives. But I was astonished. I was fated to be the "problem student" in class.

Source: Reprinted by permission of Georges Borchardt Inc. Copyright © 1980 by Richard Rodriguez. First published in *The American Scholar.*

The nun said, in a friendly but oddly impersonal voice: "Boys and girls, this   3
is Richard Rodriguez." (I heard her sound it out: *Rich-heard Road-ree-guess.*) It
was the first time I had heard anyone say my name in English. "Richard," the nun
repeated more slowly, writing my name down in her book. Quickly I turned to
see my mother's face dissolve in a watery blur behind the pebbled-glass door.

Now, many years later, I hear of something called "bilingual educa-   4
tion"—a scheme proposed in the late 1960s by Hispanic-American social
activists, later endorsed by a congressional vote. It is a program that seeks to
permit non-English-speaking children (many from lower-class homes) to use
their "family language" as the language of school. Such, at least, is the aim its
supporters announce. I hear them, and am forced to say no: It is not possible
for a child, any child, ever to use his family's language in school. Not to
understand this is to misunderstand the public uses of schooling and to trivialize the nature of intimate life.

Memory teaches me what I know of these matters. The boy reminds the   5
adult. I was a bilingual child, but of a certain kind: "socially disadvantaged," the
son of working-class parents, both Mexican immigrants.

In the early years of my boyhood, my parents coped very well in America.   6
My father had steady work. My mother managed at home. They were nobody's
victims. When we moved to a house many blocks from the Mexican-American
section of town, they were not intimidated by those two or three neighbors who
initially tried to make us unwelcome. ("Keep your brats away from my sidewalk!") But despite all they achieved, or perhaps because they had so much to
achieve, they lacked any deep feeling of ease, of belonging in public. They
regarded the people at work or in crowds as being very distant from us. Those
were the others, *los gringos.* That term was interchangeable in their speech with
another, even more telling: *los americanos.*

I grew up in a house where the only regular guests were my relations. On   7
a certain day, enormous families of relatives would visit us, and there would be
so many people that the noise and the bodies would spill out to the backyard
and onto the front porch. Then for weeks no one would come. (If the doorbell
rang, it was usually a salesman.) Our house stood apart—gaudy yellow in a row
of white bungalows. We were the people with the noisy dog, the people who
raised chickens. We were the foreigners on the block. A few neighbors would
smile and wave at us. We waved back. But until I was seven years old, I did not
know the name of the old couple living next door or the names of the kids living across the street.

In public, my father and mother spoke a hesitant, accented, and not always   8
grammatical English. And then they would have to strain, their bodies tense, to
catch the sense of what was rapidly said by *los gringos.* At home, they returned to
Spanish. The language of their Mexican past sounded in counterpoint to the English spoken in public. The words would come quickly, with ease. Conveyed
through those sounds was the pleasing, soothing, consoling reminder that one
was at home.

During those years when I was first learning to speak, my mother and father   9
addressed me only in Spanish; in Spanish I learned to reply. By contrast, English
(inglés) was the language I came to associate with gringos, rarely heard in the
house. I learned my first words of English overhearing my parents speaking to
strangers. At six years of age, I knew just enough words for my mother to trust
me on errands to stores one block away—but no more.

I was then a listening child, careful to hear the very different sounds of   10
Spanish and English. Wide-eyed with hearing, I'd listen to sounds more than to
words. First, there were English (gringo) sounds. So many words still were
unknown to me that when the butcher or the lady at the drugstore said something, exotic polysyllabic sounds would bloom in the midst of their sentences.
Often the speech of people in public seemed to me very loud, booming with confidence. The man behind the counter would literally ask, "What can I do for
you?" But by being so firm and clear, the sound of his voice said that he was a
gringo; he belonged in public society. There were also the high, nasal notes of
middle-class American speech—which I rarely am conscious of hearing today
because I hear them so often, but could not stop hearing when I was a boy.
Crowds at Safeway or at bus stops were noisy with the birdlike sounds of *los gringos*. I'd move away from them all—all the chirping chatter above me.

My own sounds I was unable to hear, but I knew that I spoke English   11
poorly. My words could not extend to form complete thoughts. And the words I
did speak I didn't know well enough to make distinct sounds. (Listeners would
usually lower their heads to hear better what I was trying to say.) But it was one
thing for *me* to speak English with difficulty; it was more troubling to hear my
parents speaking in public: their high-whining vowels and guttural consonants;
their sentences that got stuck with "eh" and "ah" sounds; the confused syntax;
the hesitant rhythm of sounds so different from the way gringos spoke. I'd
notice, moreover, that my parents' voices were softer than those of gringos we
would meet.

I am tempted to say now that none of this mattered. (In adulthood I am   12
embarrassed by childhood fears.) And, in a way, it didn't matter very much that
my parents could not speak English with ease. Their linguistic difficulties had no
serious consequences. My mother and father made themselves understood at the
county hospital clinic and at government offices. And yet, in another way, it mattered very much. It was unsettling to hear my parents struggle with English.
Hearing them, I'd grow nervous, and my clutching trust in their protection and
power would be weakened.

There were many times like the night at a brightly lit gasoline station (a   13
blaring white memory) when I stood uneasily hearing my father talk to a teenage
attendant. I do not recall what they were saying, but I cannot forget the sounds
my father made as he spoke. At one point his words slid together to form one
long word—sounds as confused as the threads of blue and green oil in the pud-
dle next to my shoes. His voice rushed through what he had left to say. Toward
the end, he reached falsetto notes, appealing to his listener's understanding. I
looked away at the lights of passing automobiles. I tried not to hear any more.
But I heard only too well the attendant's reply, his calm, easy tones. Shortly after-

ward, headed for home, I shivered when my father put his hand on my shoulder. The very first chance that I got, I evaded his grasp and ran on ahead into the dark, skipping with feigned boyish exuberance.

But then there was Spanish: *español,* the language rarely heard away from 14 the house; *español,* the language which seemed to me therefore a private language, my family's language. To hear its sounds was to feel myself specially recognized as one of the family, apart from *los otros.* ["the others"]. A simple remark, an inconsequential comment could convey that assurance. My parents would say something to me and I would feel embraced by the sounds of their words. Those sounds said: *I am speaking with ease in Spanish. I am addressing you in words I never use with* los gringos. *I recognize you as someone special, close, like no one outside. You belong with us. In the family. Ricardo.*

At the age of six, well past the time when most middle-class children no 15 longer notice the difference between sounds uttered at home and words spoken in public, I had a different experience. I lived in a world compounded of sounds. I was a child longer than most. I lived in a magical world, surrounded by sounds both pleasing and fearful. I shared with my family a language enchantingly private—different from that used in the city around us.

Just opening or closing the screen door behind me was an important expe- 16 rience. I'd rarely leave home all alone or without feeling reluctance. Walking down the sidewalk, under the canopy of tall trees, I'd warily notice the (suddenly) silent neighborhood kids who stood warily watching me. Nervously, I'd arrive at the grocery store to hear there the sounds of the gringo, reminding me that in this so-big world I was a foreigner. But if leaving home was never routine, neither was coming back. Walking toward our house, climbing the steps from the sidewalk, in summer when the front door was open, I'd hear voices beyond the screen door talking in Spanish. For a second or two I'd stay, linger there listening. Smiling, I'd hear my mother call out, saying in Spanish, "Is that you, Richard?" Those were her words, but all the while her sounds would assure me: *You are home now. Come closer inside. With us.* "*Sí,*" I'd reply.

Once more inside the house, I would resume my place in the family. The 17 sounds would grow harder to hear. Once more at home, I would grow less conscious of them. It required, however, no more than the blurt of the doorbell to alert me all over again to listen to sounds. The house would turn instantly quiet while my mother went to the door. I'd hear her hard English sounds. I'd wait to hear her voice turn to soft-sounding Spanish, which assured me, as surely as did the clicking tongue of the lock on the door, that the stranger was gone.

Plainly it is not healthy to hear such sounds so often. It is not healthy to dis- 18 tinguish public from private sounds so easily. I remained cloistered by sounds, timid and shy in public, too dependent on the voices at home. And yet I was a very happy child when I was at home. I remember many nights when my father would come back from work, and I'd hear him call out to my mother in Spanish, sounding relieved. In Spanish, his voice would sound the light and free notes that he never could manage in English. Some nights I'd jump up just hearing his voice. My brother and I would come running into the room where he was with our mother. Our laughing (so deep was the pleasure!) became screaming. Like others who feel the pain of public alienation, we transformed the knowledge of our public separateness into a consoling reminder of our intimacy. Excited, our voices joined in a celebration of sounds. *We are speaking now the way we never speak out in public—we are together,* the sounds told me. Some nights no one seemed willing to loosen the hold that sounds had on us. At dinner we invented new words that sounded Spanish, but made sense only to us. We pieced together new words by taking, say, an English verb and giving it Spanish endings. My mother's instructions at bedtime would be lacquered with mock-urgent tones. Or a word like *sí,* sounded in several notes, would convey added measures of feeling. Tongues lingered around the edges of words, especially fat vowels. And we happily sounded that military drum roll, the twirling roar of the Spanish *r.* Family language, my family's sounds: the voices of my parents and sisters and brother. Their voices insisting: *You belong here. We are family members. Related. Special to one another. Listen!* Voices singing and sighing, rising and straining, then surging, teeming with pleasure which burst syllables into fragments of laughter. At times it seemed there was steady quiet only when, from another room, the rustling whispers of my parents faded and I edged closer to sleep.

Supporters of bilingual education imply today that students like me miss a great deal by not being taught in their family's language. What they seem not to recognize is that, as a socially disadvantaged child, I regarded Spanish as a private language. It was a ghetto language that deepened and strengthened my feeling of public separateness. What I needed to learn in school was that I had the right, and the obligation, to speak the public language. The odd truth is that my first-grade classmates could have become bilingual, in the conventional sense of the word, more easily than I. Had they been taught early (as upper middle-class children often are taught) a "second language" like Spanish or French, they could have regarded it simply as another public language. In my case, such bilingualism could not have been so quickly achieved. What I did not believe was that I could speak a single public language. 19

Without question, it would have pleased me to have heard my teachers address me in Spanish when I entered the classroom. I would have felt much less afraid. I would have imagined that my instructors were somehow "related" to me; I would indeed have heard their Spanish as my family's language. I would have trusted them and responded with ease. But I would have delayed—postponed for how long?—having to learn the language of public society. I would have evaded—and for how long?—learning the great lesson of school: that I had a public identity. 20

Fortunately, my teachers were unsentimental about their responsibility. What they understood was that I needed to speak public English. So their voices would search me out, asking me questions. Each time I heard them I'd look up in surprise to see a nun's face frowning at me. I'd mumble, not really meaning to answer. The nun would persist. "Richard, stand up. Don't look at the floor. Speak up. Speak to the entire class, not just to me!" But I couldn't believe English could be my language to use. (In part, I did not want to believe it.) I continued to mumble. I resisted the teacher's demands. (Did I somehow suspect that once 21

I learned this public language my family life would be changed?) Silent, waiting for the bell to sound, I remained dazed, diffident, afraid.

Because I wrongly imagined that English was intrinsically a public language 22 and Spanish was intrinsically private, I easily noted the difference between classroom language and the language of home. At school, words were directed to a general audience of listeners. ("Boys and girls . . . ") Words were meaningfully ordered. And the point was not self-expression alone, but to make oneself understood by many others. The teacher quizzed: "Boys and girls, why do we use that word in this sentence? Could we think of a better word to use there? Would the sentence change its meaning if the words were differently arranged? Isn't there a better way of saying much the same thing?" (I couldn't say. I wouldn't try to say.)

Three months passed. Five. A half year. Unsmiling, ever watchful, my teach- 23 ers noted my silence. They began to connect my behavior with the slow progress my brother and sisters were making. Until, one Saturday morning, three nuns arrived at the house to talk to our parents. Stiffly they sat on the blue living-room sofa. From the doorway of another room, spying on the visitors, I noted the incongruity, the clash of two worlds, the faces and voices of school intruding upon the familiar setting of home. I overheard one voice gently wondering, "Do your children speak only Spanish at home, Mrs. Rodriguez?" While another voice added, "That Richard especially seems so timid and shy."

That Rich-heard!   24

With great tact, the visitors continued, "Is it possible for you and your hus- 25 band to encourage your children to practice their English when they are home?" Of course my parents complied. What would they not do for their children's well-being? And how could they question the Church's authority which those women represented? In an instant they agreed to give up the language (the sounds) which had revealed and accentuated our family's closeness. The moment after the visitors left, the change was observed. "*Ahora* ['now'], speak to us only *en inglés* ['in English']," my father and mother told us.

At first, it seemed a kind of game. After dinner each night, the family gath- 26 ered together to practice "our" English. It was still then *inglés*, a language foreign to us, so we felt drawn to it as strangers. Laughing, we would try to define words we could not pronounce. We played with strange English sounds, often over-anglicizing our pronunciations. And we filled the smiling gaps of our sentences with familiar Spanish sounds. But that was cheating, somebody shouted, and everyone laughed.

In school, meanwhile, like my brother and sisters, I was required to attend 27 a daily tutoring session. I needed a full year of this special work. I also needed my teachers to keep my attention from straying in class by calling out, *"Rich-heard!"*—their English voices slowly loosening the ties to my other name, with its three notes, *Ri-car-do.* Most of all, I needed to hear my mother and father speak to me in a moment of seriousness in "broken"—suddenly heartbreaking—English. This scene was inevitable. One Saturday morning I entered the kitchen where my parents were talking, but I did not realize that they were talking in Spanish until, the moment they saw me, their voices changed and they began speaking English. The gringo sounds they uttered startled me. Pushed me away.

In that moment of trivial misunderstanding and profound insight, I felt my throat twisted by unsounded grief. I simply turned and left the room. But I had no place to escape to where I could grieve in Spanish. My brother and sisters were speaking English in another part of the house.

Again and again in the days following, as I grew increasingly angry, I was 28 obliged to hear my mother and father encouraging me: "Speak to us *en inglés.*" Only then did I determine to learn classroom English. Thus, sometime afterward it happened: one day in school, I raised my hand to volunteer an answer to a question. I spoke out in a loud voice and I did not think it remarkable when the entire class understood. That day I moved very far from being the disadvantaged child I had been only days earlier. Taken hold at last was the belief, the calming assurance, that I *belonged* in public.

Shortly after, I stopped hearing the high, troubling sounds of *los gringos*. A 29 more and more confident speaker of English, I didn't listen to how strangers sounded when they talked to me. With so many English-speaking people around me, I no longer heard American accents. Conversations quickened. Listening to persons whose voices sounded eccentrically pitched, I might note their sounds for a few seconds, but then I'd concentrate on what they were saying. Now when I heard someone's tone of voice—angry or questioning or sarcastic or happy or sad—I didn't distinguish it from the words it expressed. Sound and word were thus tightly wedded. At the end of each day I was often bemused, and always relieved, to realize how "soundless," though crowded with words, my day in public had been. An eight-year-old boy, I finally came to accept what had been technically true since my birth: I was an American citizen.

But diminished by then was the special feeling of closeness at home. Gone 30 was the desperate, urgent, intense feeling of being at home among those with whom I felt intimate. Our family remained a loving family, but one greatly changed. We were no longer so close, no longer bound tightly together by the knowledge of our separateness from *los gringos*. Neither my older brother nor my sisters rushed home after school any more. Nor did I. When I arrived home, often there would be neighborhood kids in the house. Or the house would be empty of sounds.

Following the dramatic Americanization of their children, even my parents 31 grew more publicly confident—especially my mother. First she learned the names of all the people on the block. Then she decided we needed to have a telephone in our house. My father, for his part, continued to use the word gringo, but it was no longer charged with bitterness or distrust. Stripped of any emotional content, the word simply became a name for those Americans not of Hispanic descent. Hearing him, sometimes, I wasn't sure if he was pronouncing the Spanish word *gringo*, or saying gringo in English.

There was a new silence at home. As we children learned more and more 32 English, we shared fewer and fewer words with our parents. Sentences needed to be spoken slowly when one of us addressed our mother or father. Often the parent wouldn't understand. The child would need to repeat himself. Still the parent misunderstood. The young voice, frustrated, would end up saying, "Never mind"—the subject was closed. Dinners would be noisy with the clinking of knives and forks against dishes. My mother would smile softly between her remarks; my father, at the other end of the table, would chew and chew his food while he stared over the heads of his children.

My mother! My father! After English became my primary language, I no longer knew what words to use in addressing my parents. The old Spanish words (those tender accents of sound) I had earlier used—*mamá* and *papá*—I couldn't use any more. They would have been all-too-painful reminders of how much had changed in my life. On the other hand, the words I heard neighborhood kids call their parents seemed equally unsatisfactory. "Mother" and "father," "ma," "papa," "pa," "dad," "pop" (how I hated the all-American sound of that last word)—all these I felt were unsuitable terms of address for *my* parents. As a result, I never used them at home. Whenever I'd speak to my parents, I would try to get their attention by looking at them. In public conversations, I'd refer to them as my "parents" or my "mother" and "father."

My mother and father, for their part, responded differently, as their children spoke to them less. My mother grew restless, seemed troubled and anxious at the scarceness of words exchanged in the house. She would question me about my day when I came home from school. She smiled at my small talk. She pried at the edges of my sentences to get me to say something more. ("What . . . ?") She'd join conversations she overheard, but her intrusions often stopped her children's talking. By contrast, my father seemed to grow reconciled to the new quiet. Though his English somewhat improved, he tended more and more to retire into silence. At dinner he spoke very little. One night his children and even his wife helplessly giggled at his garbled English pronunciation of the Catholic "Grace Before Meals." Thereafter he made his wife recite the prayer at the start of each meal, even on formal occasions when there were guests in the house.

Hers became the public voice of the family. On official business it was she, not my father, who would usually talk to strangers on the phone or in stores. We children grew so accustomed to his silence that years later we would routinely refer to his "shyness." (My mother often tried to explain: both of his parents died when he was eight. He was raised by an uncle who treated him as little more than a menial servant. He was never encouraged to speak. He grew up alone—a man of few words.) But I realized my father was not shy whenever I'd watch him speaking Spanish with relatives. Using Spanish, he was quickly effusive. Especially when talking with other men, his voice would spark, flicker, flare alive with varied sounds. In Spanish he expressed ideas and feelings he rarely revealed when speaking English. With firm Spanish sounds he conveyed a confidence and authority that English would never allow him.

The silence at home, however, was not simply the result of fewer words passing between parents and children. More profound for me was the silence created by my inattention to sounds. At about the time I no longer bothered to listen with care to the sounds of English in public, I grew careless about listening to the sounds made by the family when they spoke. Most of the time I would hear someone speaking at home and didn't distinguish his sounds from the words people uttered in public. I didn't even pay much attention to my parents' accented and ungrammatical speech—at least not at home. Only when I was with them in public would I become alert to their accents. But even then their sounds caused me less and less concern. For I was growing increasingly confident of my own public identity.

I would have been happier about my public success had I not recalled, 37 sometimes, what it had been like earlier, when my family conveyed its intimacy through a set of conveniently private sounds. Sometimes in public, hearing a stranger, I'd hark back to my lost past. A Mexican farm worker approached me one day downtown. He wanted directions to some place. "*Hijito* ['little boy, little son'], . . ." he said. And his voice stirred old longings. Another time I was standing beside my mother in the visiting room of a Carmelite convent, before the dense screen which rendered the nuns shadowy figures. I heard several of them speaking Spanish in their busy, singsong, overlapping voices, assuring my mother that, yes, yes, we were remembered, all our family was remembered, in their prayers. Those voices echoed faraway family sounds. Another day a dark-faced old woman touched my shoulder lightly to steady herself as she boarded a bus. She murmured something to me I couldn't quite comprehend. Her Spanish voice came near, like the face of a never-before-seen relative in the instant before I was kissed. That voice, like so many of the Spanish voices I'd hear in public, recalled the golden age of my childhood.

Bilingual educators say today that children lose a degree of "individuality" 38 by becoming assimilated into public society. (Bilingual schooling is a program popularized in the seventies, that decade when middle-class "ethnics" began to resist the process of assimilation—the "American melting pot.") But the bilingualists oversimplify when they scorn the value and necessity of assimilation. They do not seem to realize that a person is individualized in two ways. So they do not realize that, while one suffers a diminished sense of *private* individuality by being assimilated into public society, such assimilation makes possible the achievement of *public* individuality.

Simplistically again, the bilingualists insist that a student should be reminded 39 of his difference from others in mass society, of his "heritage." But they equate mere separateness with individuality. The fact is that only in private—with intimates—is separateness from the crowd a prerequisite for individuality; an intimate "tells" me that I am unique, unlike all others, apart from the crowd. In public, by contrast, full individuality is achieved, paradoxically, by those who are able to consider themselves members of the crowd. Thus it happened for me. Only when I was able to think of myself as an American, no longer an alien in gringo society, could I seek the rights and opportunities necessary for full public individuality. The social and political advantages I enjoy as a man began on the day I came to believe that my name is indeed *Rich-heard Road-ree-guess*. It is true that my public society today is often impersonal; in fact, my public society is usually mass society. But despite the anonymity of the crowd, and despite the fact that the individuality I achieve in public is often tenuous—because it depends on my being one in a crowd—I celebrate the day I acquired my new name. Those middle-class ethnics who scorn assimilation seem to me filled with decadent self-pity, obsessed by the burden of public life. Dangerously, they romanticize public separateness and trivialize the dilemma of those who are truly socially disadvantaged.

If I rehearse here the changes in my private life after my Americanization, it is finally to emphasize a public gain. The loss implies the gain. The house I returned to each afternoon was quiet. Intimate sounds no longer greeted me at the door. Inside there were other noises. The telephone rang. Neighborhood kids ran past the door of the bedroom where I was reading my schoolbooks—covered with brown shopping-bag paper. Once I learned the public language, it would never again be easy for me to hear intimate family voices. More and more of my day was spent hearing words, not sounds. But that may only be a way of saying that on the day I raised my hand in class and spoke loudly to an entire roomful of faces, my childhood started to end. 40

I grew up the victim of a disconcerting confusion. As I became fluent in English, I could no longer speak Spanish with confidence. I continued to understand spoken Spanish, and in high school I learned how to read and write Spanish. But for many years I could not pronounce it. A powerful guilt blocked my spoken words; an essential glue was missing whenever I would try to connect words to form sentences. I would be unable to break a barrier of sound, to speak freely. I would speak, or try to speak, Spanish, and I would manage to utter halting, hiccuping sounds which betrayed my unease. (Even today I speak Spanish very slowly, at best.) 41

When relatives and Spanish-speaking friends of my parents came to the house, my brother and sisters would usually manage to say a few words before being excused. I never managed so gracefully. Each time I'd hear myself addressed in Spanish, I couldn't respond with any success. I'd know the words I wanted to say, but I couldn't say them. I would try to speak, but everything I said seemed to me horribly anglicized. My mouth wouldn't form the sounds right. My jaw would tremble. After a phrase or two, I'd stutter, cough up a warm, silvery sound, and stop. 42

My listeners were surprised to hear me. They'd lower their heads to grasp better what I was trying to say. They would repeat their questions in gentle, affectionate voices. But then I would answer in English. No, no, they would say, we want you to speak to us in Spanish *("en español")*. But I couldn't do it. Then they would call me *pocho*. Sometimes playfully, teasing, using the tender diminutive— *mi pochito*. Sometimes not so playfully but mockingly, *pocho*. (A Spanish dictionary defines that word as an adjective meaning "colorless" or "bland." But I heard it as a noun, naming the Mexican-American who, in becoming an American, forgets his native society.) *"¡Pocho!"* my mother's best friend muttered, shaking her head. And my mother laughed, somewhere behind me. She said that her children didn't want to practice "our Spanish" after they started going to school. My mother's smiling voice made me suspect that the lady who faced me was not really angry at me. But searching her face, I couldn't find the hint of a smile. 43

Embarrassed, my parents would often need to explain their children's inability to speak fluent Spanish during those years. My mother encountered the 44

wrath of her brother, her only brother, when he came up from Mexico one summer with his family and saw his nieces and nephews for the very first time. After
listening to me, he looked away and said what a disgrace it was that my siblings
and I couldn't speak Spanish, *"su propria idioma."* ("their own language"). He
made that remark to my mother, but I noticed that he stared at my father.

One other visitor from those years I clearly remember: a long-time friend of   45
my father from San Francisco who came to stay with us for several days in late
August. He took great interest in me after he realized that I couldn't answer his
questions in Spanish. He would grab me, as I started to leave the kitchen. He
would ask me something. Usually he wouldn't bother to wait for my mumbled
response. Knowingly, he'd murmur, *"¿Ay pocho, pocho, dónde vas?"* ("Pocho, where
are you going?"). And he would press his thumbs into the upper part of my arms,
making me squirm with pain. Dumbly I'd stand there, waiting for his wife to notice
us and call him off with a benign smile. I'd giggle, hoping to deflate the tension
between us, pretending that I hadn't seen the glittering scorn in his glance.

I recount such incidents only because they suggest the fierce power that   46
Spanish had over many people I met at home, how strongly Spanish was associated with closeness. Most of those people who called me a *pocho* could have spoken English to me, but many wouldn't. They seemed to think that Spanish was
the only language we could use among ourselves, that Spanish alone permitted
our association. (Such persons are always vulnerable to the ghetto merchant and
the politician who have learned the value of speaking their clients' "family language" so as to gain immediate trust.) For my part, I felt that by learning English I had somehow committed a sin of betrayal. But betrayal against whom? Not
exactly against the visitors to the house. Rather, I felt I had betrayed my immediate family. I knew that my parents had encouraged me to learn English. I knew
that I had turned to English with angry reluctance. But once I spoke English
with ease, I came to feel guilty. I sensed that I had broken the spell of intimacy
which had once held the family so close together. It was this original sin against
my family that I recalled whenever anyone addressed me in Spanish and I
responded, confounded.

Yet even during those years of guilt, I was coming to grasp certain consoling   47
truths about language and intimacy—truths that I learned gradually. Once, I
remember playing with a friend in the backyard when my grandmother appeared
at the window. Her face was stern with suspicion when she saw the boy (the *gringo*
boy) I was with. She called out to me in Spanish, sounding the whistle of her
ancient breath. My companion looked up and watched her intently as she lowered
the window and moved (still visible) behind the light curtain, watching us both.
He wanted to know what she had said. I started to tell him, to translate her Spanish words into English. The problem was, however, that though I knew how to
translate exactly what she had told me, I realized that any translation would distort
the deepest meaning of her message; it had been directed only to me. This message
of intimacy could never be translated because it did not lie in the actual words she
had used but passed through them. So any translation would have seemed wrong;
the words would have been stripped of an essential meaning. Finally I decided not
to tell my friend anything—just that I didn't hear all she had said.

This insight was unfolded in time. As I made more and more friends out- 48
side my house, I began to recognize intimate messages spoken in English in a
close friend's confidential tone or secretive whisper. Even more remarkable were
those instances when, apparently for no special reason, I'd become conscious of
the fact that my companion was speaking *only to me.* I'd marvel then, just hearing his voice. It was a stunning event to be able to break through the barrier of
public silence, to be able to hear the voice of the other, to realize that it was
directed just to me. After such moments of intimacy outside the house, I began
to trust what I heard intimately conveyed through my family's English. Voices at
home at last punctured sad confusion. I'd hear myself addressed as an intimate—
in English. Such moments were never as raucous with sound as in past times,
when we had used our "private" Spanish. (Our English-sounding house was
never to be as noisy as our Spanish-sounding house had been.) Intimate moments
were usually moments of soft sound. My mother would be ironing in the dining
room while I did my homework nearby. She would look over at me, smile, and
her voice sounded to tell me that I was her son. *Richard.*

Intimacy thus continued at home; intimacy was not stilled by English. 49
Though there were fewer occasions for it—a change in my life that I would never
forget—there were also times when I sensed the deep truth about language and
intimacy: *Intimacy is not created by a particular language; it is created by intimates.* Thus the great change in my life was not linguistic but social. If, after
becoming a successful student, I no longer heard intimate voices as often as I had
earlier, it was not because I spoke English instead of Spanish. It was because I
spoke public language for most of my day. I moved easily at last, a citizen in a
crowded city of words.

As a man I spend most of my day in public, in a world largely devoid of 50
speech sounds. So I am quickly attracted by the glamorous quality of certain alien
voices. I still am gripped with excitement when someone passes me on the street,
speaking in Spanish. I have not moved beyond the range of the nostalgic pull of
those sounds. And there is something very compelling about the sounds of lower-
class blacks. Of all the accented versions of English that I hear in public, I hear
theirs most intently. The Japanese tourist stops me downtown to ask me a question and I inch my way past his accent to concentrate on what he is saying. The
eastern European immigrant in the neighborhood delicatessen speaks to me and,
again, I do not pay much attention to his sounds, nor to the Texas accent of one
of my neighbors or the Chicago accent of the woman who lives in the apartment
below me. But when the ghetto black teenagers get on the city bus, I hear them.
Their sounds in my society are the sounds of the outsider. Their voices annoy me
for being so loud—so self-sufficient and unconcerned by my presence, but for the
same reason they are glamorous: a romantic gesture against public acceptance.
And as I listen to their shouted laughter, I realize my own quietness. I feel envious of them—envious of their brazen intimacy.

I warn myself away from such envy, however. Overhearing those teenagers, 51
I think of the black political activists who lately have argued in favor of using
black English in public schools—an argument that varies only slightly from that

of foreign-language bilingualists. I have heard "radical" linguists make the point that black English is a complex and intricate version of English. And I do not doubt it. But neither do I think that black English should be a language of public instruction. What makes it inappropriate in classrooms is not something in the language itself but, rather, what lower-class speakers make of it. Just as Spanish would have been a dangerous language for me to have used at the start of my education, so black English would be a dangerous language to use in the schooling of teenagers for whom it reinforces feelings of public separateness.

This seems to me an obvious point to make, and yet it must be said. In 52 recent years there have been many attempts to make the language of the alien a public language. "Bilingual education, two ways to understand . . ." television and radio commercials glibly announce. Proponents of bilingual education are careful to say that above all they want every student to acquire a good education. Their argument goes something like this: Children permitted to use their family language will not be so alienated and will be better able to match the progress of English-speaking students in the crucial first months of schooling. Increasingly confident of their ability, such children will be more inclined to apply themselves to their studies in the future. But then the bilingualists also claim another very different goal. They say that children who use their family language in school will retain a sense of their ethnic heritage and their family ties. Thus the supporters of bilingual education want it both ways. They propose bilingual schooling as a way of helping students acquire the classroom skills crucial for public success. But they likewise insist that bilingual instruction will give students a sense of their identity apart from the English-speaking public.

Behind this scheme gleams a bright promise for the alien child: one can 53 become a public person while still remaining a private person. Who would not want to believe such an appealing idea? Who can be surprised that the scheme has the support of so many middle-class ethnic Americans? If the barrio or ghetto child can retain his separateness even while being publicly educated, then it is almost possible to believe that no private cost need be paid for public success. This is the consolation offered by any of the number of current bilingual programs. Consider, for example, the bilingual voter's ballot. In some American cities one can cast a ballot printed in several languages. Such a document implies that it is possible for one to exercise that most public of rights—the right to vote—while still keeping oneself apart, unassimilated in public life.

It is not enough to say that such schemes are foolish and certainly doomed. 54 Middle-class supporters of public bilingualism toy with the confusion of those Americans who cannot speak standard English as well as they do. Moreover, bilingual enthusiasts sin against intimacy. A Hispanic-American tells me, "I will never give up my family language," and he clutches a group of words as though they were the source of his family ties. He credits to language what he should credit to family members. This is a convenient mistake, for as long as he holds on to certain familiar words, he can ignore how much else has actually changed in his life.

It has happened before. In earlier decades, persons ambitious for social 55 mobility, and newly successful, similarly seized upon certain "family words." Workingmen attempting to gain political power, for example, took to calling one another "brother." The word as they used it, however, could never resemble the word (the sound) "brother" exchanged by two people in intimate greeting. The context of its public delivery made it at best a metaphor; with repetition it was only a vague echo of the intimate sound. Context forced the change. Context could not be overruled. Context will always protect the realm of the intimate from public misuse. Today middle-class white Americans continue to prove the importance of context as they try to ignore it. They seize upon idioms of the black ghetto, but their attempt to appropriate such expressions invariably changes the meaning. As it becomes a public expression, the ghetto idiom loses its sound, its message of public separateness and strident intimacy. With public repetition it becomes a series of words, increasingly lifeless.

The mystery of intimate utterance remains. The communication of intimacy passes through the word and enlivens its sound, but it cannot be held by the word. It cannot be retained or ever quoted because it is too fluid. It depends not on words but on persons.

My grandmother! She stood among my other relations mocking me when I no longer spoke Spanish. *Pocho,* she said. But then it made no difference. She'd laugh, and our relationship continued because language was never its source. She was a woman in her eighties during the first decade of my life—a mysterious woman to me, my only living grandparent, a woman of Mexico in a long black dress that reached down to her shoes. She was the one relative of mine who spoke no word of English. She had no interest in gringo society and remained completely aloof from the public. She was protected by her daughters, protected even by me when we went to Safeway together and I needed to act as her translator. An eccentric woman. Hard. Soft.

When my family visited my aunt's house in San Francisco, my grandmother would search for me among my many cousins. When she found me, she'd chase them away. Pinching her granddaughters, she would warn them away from me. Then she'd take me to her room, where she had prepared for my coming. There would be a chair next to the bed, a dusty jellied candy nearby, and a copy of *Life en Español* for me to examine. "There," she'd say. And I'd sit content, a boy of eight. *Pocho,* her favorite. I'd sift through the pictures of earthquake-destroyed Latin-American cities and blonde-wigged Mexican movie stars. And all the while I'd listen to the sound of my grandmother's voice. She'd pace around the room, telling me stories of her life. Her past. They were stories so familiar that I couldn't remember when I'd heard them for the first time. I'd look up sometimes to listen. Other times she'd look over at me, but she never expected a response. Sometimes I'd smile or nod. (I understood exactly what she was saying.) But it never seemed to matter to her one way or the other. It was enough that I was there. The words she spoke were almost irrelevant to that fact. We were content. And the great mystery remained: intimate utterance.

I learn nothing about language and intimacy listening to those social activists who propose using one's family language in public life. I learn much more simply by listening to songs on a radio, or hearing a great voice at the opera, or overhearing the woman downstairs at an open window singing to herself. Singers celebrate the human voice. Their lyrics are words, but, animated by voice, those words are subsumed into sounds. (This suggests a central truth about language: all words are capable of becoming sounds as we fill them with the "music" of our life.) With excitement I hear the words yielding their enormous power to sound, even though their meaning is never totally obliterated. In most songs, the drama or tension results from the way that the singer moves between words (sense) and notes (song). At one moment the song simply "says" something; at another moment the voice stretches out the words and moves to the realm of pure sound. Most songs are about love: lost love, celebrations of loving, pleas. By simply being occasions when sounds soar through words, however, songs put me in mind of the most intimate moments of life.

Finally, among all types of music, I find songs created by lyric poets most compelling. On no other public occasion is sound so important for me. Written poems on a page seem at first glance a mere collection of words. And yet, without musical accompaniment, the poet leads me to hear the sounds of the words that I read. As song, a poem moves between the levels of sound and sense, never limited to one realm or the other. As a public artifact, the poem can never offer truly intimate sound, but it helps me to recall the intimate times of my life. As I read in my room, I grow deeply conscious of being alone, sounding my voice in search of another. The poem serves, then, as a memory device; it forces remembrance. And it refreshes; it reminds me of the possibility of escaping public words, the possibility that awaits me in intimate meetings. 60

The child reminds the adult: to seek intimate sounds is to seek the company of intimates. I do not expect to hear those sounds in public. I would dishonor those I have loved, and those I love now, to claim anything else. I would dishonor our intimacy by holding on to a particular language and calling it my family language. Intimacy cannot be trapped within words; it passes through words. It passes. Intimates leave the room. Doors close. Faces move away from the window. Time passes, and voices recede into the dark. Death finally quiets the voice. There is no way to deny it, no way to stand in the crowd claiming to utter one's family language. 61

The last time I saw my grandmother I was nine years old. I can tell you some of the things she said to me as I stood by her bed, but I cannot quote the message of intimacy she conveyed with her voice. She laughed, holding my hand. Her voice illumined disjointed memories as it passed them again. She remembered her husband—his green eyes, his magic name of Narcissio, his early death. She remembered the farm in Mexico, the eucalyptus trees nearby (their scent, she remembered, like incense). She remembered the family cow, the bell around its neck heard miles away. A dog. She remembered working as a seamstress, how she'd leave her daughters and son for long hours to go into Guadalajara to work. And how my mother would come running toward her in the sun—in her bright yellow dress—on her return. "MMMMAAAAMMMMÁÁÁÁÁ," the old lady mimicked her daughter (my mother) to her daughter's son. She laughed. There was the snap of a cough. An aunt came into the room and told me it was time I should leave. "You can see her tomorrow," she promised. So I kissed my grand- 62 mother's cracked face. And the last thing I saw was her thin, oddly youthful thigh, as my aunt rearranged the sheet on the bed.

At the funeral parlor a few days after, I remember kneeling with my relatives during the rosary. Among their voices I traced, then lost, the sounds of individual aunts in the surge of the common prayer. And I heard at that moment what since I have heard very often—the sound the women in my family make when they are praying in sadness. When I went up to look at my grandmother, I saw her through the haze of a veil draped over the open lid of the casket. Her face looked calm—but distant and unyielding to love. It was not the face I remembered seeing most often. It was the face she made in public when the clerk at Safeway asked her some question and I would need to respond. It was her public face that the mortician had designed with his dubious art. 63

QUESTIONS FOR CRITICAL READING, THINKING, DISCUSSION, AND WRITING

Analyzing Content and Technique

1. What does the boy Richard notice about the English spoken by "los gringos"? How is it different from the English his parents speak? How does his recognition of this difference affect his attitude towards his parents?
2. Rodriguez calls Spanish his "private language," his "family language." Explain, with examples from the text, what he means by this. How does this concept shape his relationship with the mainstream United States?
3. According to Rodriguez, why should schools not provide bilingual education? Do you agree with him? Why or why not? Can you suggest a thrid educational model different from the ones he discusses?
4. Explain what the boy Richard gains as he becomes comfortable with English. What does he lose? Which is more significant, the gain or the loss?
5. Summarize the main ideas of paragraphs 38 and 39. Do you agree with them? Provide an example from your experience or from other reading you have done to support or dispute Rodriguez's views.
6. Who is Rodriguez's intended audience? Pick out one or two passages in the essay that help us identify this audience.

Collaborative Activity

Have group members conduct research on the status of bilingual education in your community. Is it offered in your local school? Is it regarded with general favor or disfavor? Which languages, if any, are offered? Who makes use of, or opposes, these programs? What kind of need in the community does it reflect or fail to address? Do a collaborative presentation to the class based on your findings.

Making Connections

1. For Rodriguez, the world of the family is intrinsically different from the public world, and the two are often in conflict. What is your opinion about this? Choosing examples from your own

and your friends' family life, write an essay developing a clear thesis. Take some of Rodriguez's more important ideas into account.

2. Write an essay, a letter, or a monologue, in the voice of Rodriguez's father, giving his opinions and feelings about the process of his children's education in English, and the resulting change in family dynamics.

54

PREREADING ACTIVITY

Write about your opinion on making bilingual classes available for students from kindergarten through twelfth grade.

Viva Bilingualism

JAMES FALLOWS

James Fallows (1949–   ) has been awarded degrees from Harvard and from Oxford University in England. He has held editorial positions on several magazines such as the *Atlantic Monthly*, the *Washington Monthly*, and the *Texas Monthly*. In the course of his work, he has lived in many countries and has contributed articles to numerous magazines. He was one of President Carter's principal speechwriters. His books include *Who Runs Congress? National Defense*, and *The System*. Selection 54 first appeared in *The New Republic*.

In his classic work of crackpot anthropology, *The Japanese Brain*, Dr. Tadanobu Tsunoda told his Japanese readers not to feel bad about their difficulties learning other languages, especially English. "Isn't it remarkable," he said (I am paraphrasing), "that whenever you meet someone who speaks English really well, he turns out to be a drip?"

The Japanese have their own reasons for seeking such reassurance. Their students learn English exactly the way Americans (used to) learn Latin: through long, boring analyses of antique written passages. Not surprisingly, most of them feel about as comfortable making English conversation as I would if Julius Caesar strolled up for a chat. The few Japanese who do speak good English have generally lived overseas—and to that extent have become less Japanese and, by local standards, more like drips.

Still, for all the peculiar Japaneseness of his sentiment, the spirit of Dr. Tsunoda is alive in America today. It is reflected in the general disdain for bilingualism and bilingual education, and in campaigns like the one on California's ballot last week, sponsored by the group called U.S. English, to declare that English is America's "official" language.

Source: *The New Republic*, November 24, 1986. Reprinted by permission of *The New Republic*, © 1986, The New Republic, Inc.

Yes, yes, everyone needs to learn English. America doesn't want to become   4
Quebec. We have enough other forces pulling us apart that we don't want linguistic divisions too. But is there any reason to get so worked up about today's
Spanish-speaking immigrants, even if they keep learning Spanish while in school?
I will confess that I once shared U.S. English-type fears about Spanish language
separatism. But having spent a long time reporting among immigrants and seeing
how much their children wanted to learn English, I'm not worried anymore.
And, having been out of the country most of the year, I've come to think that
the whole American language scare rests on two bogus and amazingly parochial
assumptions.

The first is a view of bilingualism as a kind of polygamy. That is, according   5
to Western standards it just doesn't work to have two wives. The partners in a
marriage require a certain exclusive commitment from each other. If a man gives
it to one wife, there's not enough left over to give to someone else. Similarly with
language: there's only so much room in a person's brain, and if he speaks one language—let us say Spanish—really well, he'll be all filled up and won't learn English. And if his brain were not a problem, his heart would be, since he can be truly
loyal to only one language. I'm burlesquing the argument a little, but not much.
Why would anyone worry about students taking "maintenance" courses in Spanish, if not for the fear that Spanish would somehow use up the mental and emotional space English should fill?

In the American context, it's easy to see why people might feel this way.   6
Ninety-nine percent of all Americans can happily live their lives speaking and
thinking about no language but English. Foreign-language education has been
falling off, and except in unusual circumstances—wars, mainly—it has never had
much practical reinforcement anyway. When we come across people in the United
States who obviously know a foreign language, the main signal is usually that
their English is so poor.

But suppose that mastering a second language is less like having two wives   7
than like having two children. Maybe there's not really a limit in the brain or
heart, and spreading attention among several languages—like spreading love
among several children—may actually enrich everyone involved. Without going
through all the linguistic arguments showing that bilingualism is possible and natural (one impressive recent summary was *Mirror of Language* by Kenji Hakuta,
published this year) I will merely say that after about five seconds of talking with
someone who really is bilingual, the two-child, rather than two-wife, view comes
to make much more sense.

Everyone has heard about the Scandinavians and Swiss, who grow up in a big   8
swirl of languages and can talk easily to anyone they meet. Their example may seem
too high-toned to be persuasive in connection with today's Spanish-speaking
immigrants, so consider the more down-to-earth illustrations of multilingualism to
be found all over Asia.

Seven years ago, the government of Singapore launched a "Speak Man-   9
darin!" campaign, designed to supplant various southern Chinese dialects with
Mandarin. (This is roughly similar to a "Speak Like Prince Charles!" campaign

being launched in West Virginia.) Since then, competence in Mandarin has gone up—and so has mastery of English. At the beginning of the Speak Mandarin campaign, the pass rate for O-level (high school) exams in English was 41 percent. Now it's 61 percent. During the same period, the O-level pass rate for Mandarin went from 84 percent to 92 percent. The children managed to get better at both languages at once.

Just north of Singapore is Malaysia, another one-time British colony whose main political problem is managing relations among three distinct ethnic groups: Malays, Chinese, and Indians. Each of the groups speaks a different language at home—Malay for the Malays, Cantonese or Hokkien for the Chinese, Tamil for the Indians. But if you put any two Malaysians together in a room, it's almost certain that they'll be able to speak to each other, in either Malay or English, since most people are bilingual and many speak three or more languages. (The Chinese generally speak one or two Chinese dialects, plus English and/or Malay. The Indians speak English or Malay on top of Tamil, and many or most Malays speak English.) Neither Tamil nor the Chinese dialects travel well outside the ethnic group, and Malay doesn't travel anywhere else but Indonesia, so most Malaysians have a strong incentive to learn another language.

I should emphasize that I'm talking about people who in no way fit modern America's idea of a rarefied intellectual elite. They are wizened Chinese shopkeepers, unschooled Indian night guards, grubby Malay food hawkers, in addition to more polished characters who've traveled around the world. Yet somehow they all find room in their brains for more than one language at a time. Is it so implausible that Americans can do the same?

The second antibilingual assumption, rarely stated but clearly there, is that English is some kind of fragile blossom, about to be blown apart by harsh blasts from the Spanish-speaking world. Come on! Never before in world history has a language been as dominant as English is now. In every corner of the world, people realize that their chances to play on the big stage—to make money, have choices, travel—depend on learning English. They don't always succeed, but more and more of them try. In Malaysia, in South China, even in linguophobic Japan, my family's main problem as we travel has been coping with people who spring from behind every lamppost and tofu stand, eager to practice the English they've picked up from the shortwave radio. Malaysia ships out tens of thousands of young people each year for studies in the United States, Australia, and England. Guess what language they have to learn before they go.

It may seem that modern America shamelessly coddles its immigrants, with all those Spanish-language street signs and TV broadcasts and "maintenance" courses, which together reduce the incentive to learn English. Well, I've spent most of this year in a position similar to the immigrants', and it's not as comfortable or satisfactory as it may look. Japan makes many more accommodations to the English language than America does to Spanish. Tokyo has four English-language daily newspapers—more than most American cities—plus several magazines. The major train and subway routes have English signs, most big-city restaurants have English menus, all major hotels have English-speaking staff. Students applying for university admission must pass tests in (written) English. Most shop-keepers, policemen, and passersby can make sense of written-down English mes-sages. Even the Shinkansen, or bullet train, makes its announcements in both Japanese and English—which is comparable to the Eastern shuttle giving each "Please have your fares ready" message in Spanish as well as English. The night-time TV news broadcasts now come in a bilingual version—you push a button on your set to switch from Japanese to English. It is as if the "CBS Evening News" could be simultaneously heard in Spanish.

Does all of this reduce the incentive to learn Japanese, or the feeling of 14 being left out if you don't? Hah! Even though Japanese society is vastly more per-meated by English than American society is by Spanish, each day brings ten thou-sand reminders of what you're missing if you don't know the language. You can't read the mainstream newspapers, can't follow most shows on TV, can't commu-nicate above the "please-give-me-a-ticket-to-Kyoto" level. Without learning the language, you could never hope to win a place as anything but a fringe figure. Some adults nonetheless live out a ghettoized, English-only existence, because Japanese is no cinch, but foreign children raised in Japan pick up the language as the only way to participate.

The incentives for America's newcomers to learn English are even stronger. 15 How are an immigrant's children going to go to any college, get any kind of white-collar job, live anything but a straitened, ghetto existence unless they speak English? When are the SATs, Bruce Springsteen songs, and the David Letterman show going to be in Spanish—or Korean, or Tagalog? If Malaysians and rural Chinese can see that English is their route to a wider world, are Guatemalans and Cubans who've made it to America so much more obtuse? And if they keep up their Spanish at the same time, even through the dreaded "maintenance" courses, why don't we count that as a good thing? It's good for them, in making their lives richer and their minds more flexible, and it's good for the country, in enlarg-ing its ability to deal with the rest of the world.

The adult immigrants themselves don't usually succeed in learning English, 16 any more than my wife and I have become fluent in Japanese. But that has been true of America's immigrants for two hundred years. (The main exception were the Eastern European Jewish immigrants of the early twentieth century, who moved into English faster than Italians, Germans, Poles, or today's Latin Americans.) The Cubans' and Mexicans' children are the ones who learn, as previous immigrants' children have. When someone can find large numbers of children who are being raised in America but don't see English as a necessity, then I'll start to worry.

We don't want to become Quebec—and we're not about to. Quebec, Bel- 17 gium, Sri Lanka, and other places with language problems have old, settled groups who've lived alongside each other, in mutual dislike, for many years—not new groups of immigrants continually being absorbed. We don't need to declare English our official language, because it already is that—as no one knows better than the immigrants and their children. Anywhere else in the world, people would laugh at the idea that English is in any way imperiled. Let's calm down and enjoy the joke too.

QUESTIONS FOR CRITICAL READING, THINKING, DISCUSSION, AND WRITING

Analyzing Content and Technique

1. What, according to Fallows, are the "two bogus and amazingly parochial assumptions" that lead people to oppose bilingualism? Do you agree with him that they are largely invalid? Give reasons.
2. Identify the analogy Fallows uses to describe our ability to learn two languages. What examples does he provide to support his belief in this ability? Discuss whether you find them convincing.
3. Analyze paragraph 13. What is its purpose? How does it fit into the scheme of Fallows's argument?
4. In his conclusion, Fallows asserts, "We don't want to become Quebec—and we're not about to." What reasons does he give for this belief?
5. How do you think Fallows would respond to Rodriguez's argument that monolingual education, leading to assimilation, "makes possible the achievement of public individuality." (Use actual reasons and examples from Fallows's essay.)
6. In what ways does Fallows use the technique of questions? In what ways does the reader respond to this technique?

Collaborative Activity

This essay was written in 1986. Discuss, as a group, how far Fallows's concerns are still valid today. Look up recent bills, proposed laws, and so forth that deal with this issue to find supporting evidence. Summarize your findings in a collaborative paragraph.

Making Connections

1. The essays by Rodriguez (selection 53) and Fallows present two very different stands on bilingualism. Adding your own experience and observation to the information they have provided, write an essay giving your opinion on the value and dangers of bilingualism.
2. Write an imaginary dialogue between Rodriguez and Fallows, in which they discuss bilingualism and the cultural assumptions underlying the issue. Bring in as many of their arguments as you can, using dramatic license as necessary.

55

PREREADING ACTIVITY

Do a clustering exercise around the term AIDS. Now examine the words and phrases you have associated with it. What do they tell you about your attitude toward the disease and those suffering from it?

Ethics and the Language of AIDS

Judith Wilson Ross

Judith Wilson Ross teaches medical ethics to undergraduates and medical students at several institutions. She is the author of several books on the topic of medical ethics and an editor of *Ethical Currents,* a quarterly publication for ethics committees. This selection first appeared in *The Meaning of AIDS: Perspectives from the Humanities* (1989).

If names are not correct, language is not in accordance with the truth of things. If language is not in accordance with the truth of things, affairs cannot be carried on to success.

Confucian Analects, Book XIII

Introduction

AIDS has proven a difficult phenomenon medically, but it is equally problematic from a linguistic perspective. As many writers have commented, the problems that AIDS presents appear new to us because very few remember the great influenza epidemic of 1918–19 and not many have more than dim memories of the pre-1944 fear of tuberculosis or the relatively small polio epidemic of the 1930s and 1940s. For the most part, we have spent our lives in a culture in which infectious disease does not represent a significant threat and thus we had consigned living in fear of life-threatening contagious disease to the pages of history books. New phenomena, however, whether they are new in cultural or in personal history, demand explanations. We need to place them in some context so that we can account for them in our world view. The language that we choose to describe new phenomena displays both the context and the meaning we give to them. In particular, the metaphors we use convey much of the deeper meaning that we attribute to these new events.

Public policy, ethical judgments, and personal choices can all be deeply influenced by the metaphors we have chosen or have grown accustomed to using and hearing others use throughout the last few years. We may talk of facts and objective judgments, but facts can be arranged in many ways to prove many things. They are not as immutable as the scientists would have us believe. Scientific facts past mathematics cannot long exist as independent entities: They are quickly integrated into the linguistic patterns of everyday use where decision making takes place. Everyday language—the jars, as it were, into which these facts are poured—is itself shaped by our perceptual patterns. The metaphors of AIDS—death, sin, crime, war, and civic division—are the shaping perceptions that make the language of AIDS so dangerous.

The Death Metaphor

AIDS is perhaps first of all a metaphor of personified death. The personal account literature is full of references to people who "lost" lovers or friends to AIDS. "AIDS took three people on this street," an acquaintance told me. A young man with AIDS says, "Why did it get me?" In *Life* magazine, "AIDS struck the Burk family"; it "laid their bodies open to lethal infections."[1] Here, AIDS becomes powerful and independent. It goes about choosing its victims, a grim reaper hiding behind ordinary sexual relationships. In *Rolling Stone,* Edmund White uses this metaphor quite specifically: "Gay sex has become equated with death. Behind the friendly smiling face, bronzed and mustachioed, is a skull. . . ."[2] The ubiquitous use of the word *victim* is part of the *AIDS as death* metaphor. Death in our culture is not a kindly God looking to bring his people back into his presence. It is a skeletal figure, stealing people and taking them into the realm of darkness. AIDS is death, out looking for victims.

This image of AIDS as death is reinforced throughout the popular and quasi-academic literature by the unrelenting joining of the word AIDS with the phrase "inevitably/invariably fatal." It is as if one expected a diagnosis of AIDS to lead to instant death. Yet, many people with AIDS live for months and even years and live for the most part outside the hospital. The metaphor of AIDS as death permits us to forget those who have the syndrome. They are dead to us, making it easier to withhold aggressive treatment or financial assistance.

Here, scientific information could help to straighten out our metaphor. From a medical perspective, AIDS is considered to be "invariably fatal" only because it has, historically, been defined that way.[3] When the CDC provided its definition for surveillance purposes, little was known about the natural history of the disease. Now, four years later, it is obvious that AIDS is not an isolated or even disease syndrome. The CDC maintains its definition for the limited purposes of epidemiological surveillance, although it is not accurate for other purposes.[4] The disease is obviously a spectrum disease caused by infection with HTLV-III/LAV. Its effects range from a brief and transient illness, through to generalized lymphadenopathy, to what is called AIDS-Related Complex (ARC), and on to frank or full-blown AIDS. Dr. Robert Gallo, as well as other scientists, has argued for change in this nomenclature.[5] Yet, we cling to AIDS as death, to AIDS as an invariably fatal disease, perhaps because it better fits the drama that we have constructed about the coming of and the meaning of AIDS.

The Punishment Metaphor

The metaphor of AIDS as death leads directly to the metaphor of AIDS as punishment for sin. If Death is about, looking for new victims, then the victim inevitably asks, "Why me? Why was I chosen?" Those who feel threatened also look to find reasons why they may be protected: They ask, "Why not me?" To answer these questions, [people characterize] the disease as the result of something over which [they] have some control, most particularly their own behavior.

Historically, new and threatening events have frequently (some would say invariably) been explained by reference to God's punishment. In the Bible, God repeatedly punishes with disease and with plagues. In Defoe's semifictional account of the 1665 plague, *A Journal of the Plague Year*, he describes the ways in which, at the beginning of the plague, the people looked first to astrologers to explain the plague as a result of astral doings, then to dream interpreters, and finally to preachers who explained it in terms of God's judgment, the "dreadful judgment which hung over their heads."[6]

Fundamentalist ministers have been the most reliable exponents of this version of AIDS as punishment for sin. Thus, the Moral Majority's Jerry Falwell is reputed to have claimed that "AIDS is the wrath of God upon homosexuals."[7] Other fundamentalist ministers have been as forthright in their claims.[8] More ecumenically, the Anglican Dean of Sydney, Australia, is quoted as saying that "gays have blood on their hands."[9] In a secular vein, President Reagan's Pat Buchanan, an ultraconservative, has written that "the poor homosexuals have declared war on nature and now nature is exacting an awful retribution."[10] Although cleansed of religious implications, this is the same view of AIDS as punishment for sin, hut here sin is seen as a violation of the natural law rather than as a violation of God's law. A variation of this metaphor appears in the account of the young man with AIDS who promises his doctor that, if he recovers, he will get a girlfriend.[11] This is sin followed by penance.

It is easy to dismiss this kind of talk as merely the babblings of exceedingly small-minded souls or minds overstressed by illness, and yet the metaphor of AIDS as punishment for sin flourishes as well in academic and liberal forums. AIDS is transmitted sexually and through the blood. Two behaviors statistically account for 90 percent of these transmissions in the U.S.: homosexual intercourse and illegal IV drug use. Both these behaviors are regarded as sinful by many and perhaps most people; gay sex is still illegal in half of the United States, and IV drug use without a prescription is illegal in all states. Because behavior that is regarded as sinful has resulted in exposure to disease, it is easy for the disease to become the punishment for the sin.

Thus, Dr. James L. Fletcher, in an editorial in the *Southern Medical Journal,* cautioned that "a logical conclusion is that AIDS is a self-inflicted disorder for the majority of those who suffer from it. . . . Perhaps, then, homosexuality is not 'alternative' behavior at all, but, as the ancient wisdom of the Bible states, most certainly pathologic." He concludes by suggesting that physicians would do well to seek "reversal treatment" for their gay patients.[12] Similarly, UCLA Medicine Professor Joseph Perloff denies that there is any scapegoating going on with AIDS because "it is not correct to say that nobody is to blame. . . . Ninety percent of all AIDS cases are contracted by either specific sexual acts or specific IV drug abuse. The remaining ten percent—recipients of blood transfusions, children of female AIDS patients, hemophiliacs—may well be regarded as mere 'victims.'"[13]

The overflow of this metaphor is seen in the insistence on "promiscuity" as the source of AIDS contact. Matt Herron, writing in *The Whole Earth Review* in an article that is clearly not intended to be punitive toward gays, nevertheless comments that when "AIDS arrived, . . . the doors of the candy store started to close." Gays, in his account, had been feasting on forbidden fruits and AIDS was a predictable result of this excess. AIDS was not just a disease in this account, nor even *merely* personal punishment for sin. According to Herron, "the teaching of AIDS" is that "[if you] mess around on a grand enough scale, you will begin to disturb human biology itself."[14]

In the general medical literature, writers frequently refer to promiscuity as the source of AIDS, easily confusing a statistical phenomenon with a judgmental one. Even if they were genuinely trying only to indicate that an increased number of sexual partners heightens the risk of having a partner who carries the virus, the choice of the word *promiscuity* is suspect. *Promiscuous* carries with it a moral judgment: It does not simply mean multiple sexual partners. *Promiscuous,* in America's sexual nervousness, very probably means more sexual partners than the speaker currently has, [that is], an inappropriate or morally reprehensible number.[15] Incorporating this word into serious general or medical writing is probably far more effective than Falwell and Buchanan could ever hope to be in driving home the message that AIDS is punishment for sin.

The gay press, too, has writers in this vein. Ned Rorem, writing in the national gay journal *The Advocate,* wonders whether (with respect to AIDS) "some chastisement is at work."[16] Writers who are encouraging reduced numbers of sexual relationships for gay men are now beginning to make a virtue of this reduction, so that monogamy is seen as a morally correct gay life-style. Although monogamy will statistically reduce one's chances of coming in contact with HTLV-III, that in itself is certainly no endorsement of the moral splendor of monogamy or even of its safety, if one's single partner happens to be carrying the virus. Yet, the metaphor of AIDS as punishment for sin makes the virtue of gay monogamy seem a correct analysis.[17]

A final way in which AIDS as punishment for sin is foisted upon us is in the idea of "innocent victims." *Innocence* belongs to the vocabulary of sin. Gay people who never heard of AIDS until they were diagnosed with it are never referred to as *innocent;* nor are IV drug users who met up with HTLV-III entirely to their surprise. *Innocent* victims of AIDS are babies, elderly women, and nuns, all of whom are presumed to have led, for a variety of reasons, blameless lives. This language of "innocent" and, by indirection, "guilty" victims is translated into action in hospitals, in public agencies, and in the news media, where gay men or drug users with AIDS are treated with less sympathy than "innocent" AIDS patients—that is, those who have not sinned on their way to illness, those for whom disease does not represent just desserts.

The Crime and Criminal Metaphor

The AIDS *victim* (guilty or innocent) also belongs to the metaphor of [15] AIDS as crime. It is almost impossible to find an article in the popular press about people with AIDS that does not use the word *victim* several times. When Los Angeles's Archbishop Mahoney announced that the diocese intended to open a hospice for those with AIDS, he could scarcely get through a sentence without talking about "victims." In an interchange that particularly demonstrated the strained use of language, he finally declared, when asked if the hospice would be open only to Catholics, that it would indeed be open to "victims of any faith or belief."[18]

When the person with AIDS is portrayed as a victim, it is because he has [16] had something unexpected done to him [or her, something that is somehow against the law, if only the scientific law as we imaginatively perceive it. Thus, AIDS becomes a supercriminal able to get away with violating the law. It is seen as amazing, Lex Luthor-like, someone who sweeps across the world, striking terror in hearts. *Newsweek* describes AIDS [as] "embark[ing] on an intercontinental killing spree." It becomes a serial killer that "strikes men and women" and "makes deep incursions on heterosexuals."[19] It goes on "a deadly odyssey."[20]

For the *Los Angeles Times,* AIDS becomes a "pathological personality."[21] [17] This language presents a disease that is bigger than life. Its power is awesome and we can only be terrified by it. This kind of image can be used to encourage increased spending (it's so big that you need to spend a lot of money to control it), but it also encourages drastic steps, steps that go outside the ordinary bounds of good sense, good law, and good ethics. Discussions about quarantine usually bring this metaphor into focus. As well, the battle about closing the bathhouses may have been affected by this aspect of the crime/criminal metaphor, because although many acknowledged it to be a drastic action, the action could be justified by the enormity of the "criminal" that was being tracked.

In addition to appearing as a master criminal, AIDS also appears as a new [18] kind of crime. New diseases are easily seen in a crime metaphor exactly because we do not understand them. They then present themselves as puzzles or as mysteries. "An unidentified disease mysteriously focuses on one group."[22] This metaphor feeds directly into our rather trivial fantasies about detective stories and turns physician/scientists into detectives scrambling about, using their superior intellectual abilities to unravel the mystery. It makes "unraveling the secrets of the shifty AIDS virus" the important aspect—not the care of those with the disease. In a recent *New York Times Magazine,* there is a colorful account of the work of four Boston physicians and researchers who are presented as a crackerjack, coordinated and collaborative detective team, out to solve the mystery.[23] The detective story metaphor is widely apparent in the popular press: The *Philadelphia Daily News* warns of a "gay plague baffling medical detectives."[24] "Clues" turn up everywhere. *Medical World News* advises that "mounting evidence suggests that . . . heterosexuals may find themselves tangled in the AIDS web."[25]

The primary problem with this metaphor is that it tends to collapse the *disease* as crime and criminal with the *person who has the disease* as crime and criminal. Thus, whereas *Newsweek* describes AIDS as terrorizing the world, *Life* magazine asserts that "the AIDS *minorities* are beginning to infect the heterosexual, drug-free majority,"[26] and *Weekly World News* moves one step further to have "AIDS *victims* terrorizing everybody" (ital. added).[27]

The War Metaphor

The metaphor of medicine as war is so common that we can perhaps scarcely imagine any other way of talking about how physicians deal with diseases and patients. The physician's job is, after all, to fight disease [using] batteries of tests and . . . an armamentarium of drugs, [giving] orders [to] troops, of course, [who] owe . . . obedience and loyalty. This metaphor developed first in the late 19th century with the discovery of bacteria, which were seen as invaders.[28] HTLV-III infection, as a disease that affects the immune system (with its killer cells that fight off foreign invaders), is particularly surrounded with a scientific vocabulary based on war metaphors. For example, one writer explains that "when the battle against the invading microorganisms is done, . . . T-suppressor cells send out signals to call off the troops." When the AIDS virus appears, it "must first invade a host cell and commandeer some of that cell's DNA material." Eventually, "the body is completely at the mercy of the most commonplace of infectious invaders."[29]

AIDS as a war ("The AIDS Conflict," according to *Newsweek*[30]) is reported much as any other war is. Intrepid *Cosmopolitan* reporter Ralph Gardner, Jr., advises his readers that "if this is a battle that pits man against nature, then nature is pushing back our forces. The news from the front is not good."[31] A dedicated troop rallier, Detroit physician John F. Fennessey does not take such news lying down. He issues a clarion call that "AIDS must be confronted, attacked, and bested by the full, coordinated resources and armamentarium of the medical scientific community. . . . AIDS must and will be confronted and controlled."[32]

Although much of this sounds like no more than bad writing, it is important to remember that the primary element of the war metaphor is the existence of an enemy. AIDS or HTLV-III is, presumably, that enemy. As the crime metaphor permits the person who has the disease to become the criminal, so also does the war metaphor encourage transforming the person housing the enemy into the enemy. Thus, *Medical World News* reports that "an infected person could harbor the virus for 14.9 years."[33] *Life* refers to the 1.3 million Americans who "may be harboring—and passing on—the virus without having symptoms."[34]

Outside of ship anchorage, *harbor* is probably most closely associated with [23] spies and criminals (as in harboring criminals or spies). Harboring suggests that the virus is being hidden knowingly, willingly, and with bad intentions. It does not leave the "infected person" a neutral object. In a war, those who "harbor" the virus are like spies in our midst. Demands for quarantine and isolation of those with AIDS or for labeling and tracking asymptomatic people who are antibody positive are calls to locate the enemy. They are reminiscent of World War II internment policies that we now look back upon with great discomfort. No one believed that *all* Japanese residents were a threat to the country but, because the dangerous ones could not be identified, it seemed appropriate to incarcerate all of them. This decision was supported by the public and, ultimately, by the U.S. Supreme Court, because it occurred in the context of a great war. To the extent that the war metaphor dominates our perceptions of AIDS, we will be more likely to sacrifice people and their rights in the name of protecting society. Edmund White, writing in *Rolling Stone,* argues that "gays are quickly losing basic civil liberties. A real state of siege has been declared."[35] Clearly the war has been declared not on the virus but upon those who carry it.

The war metaphor also gives rise to other elaborations. Susan Sontag has [24] commented that writing about cancer is so dominated by war metaphors that the only thing missing was the body count.[36] Newspaper articles on AIDS now routinely include that body count. The last paragraph of news stories almost invariably gives the absolutely up-to-date numbers of cases and deaths. A scientist calls asymptomatic, antibody-positive individuals "time bomb[s]," because doctors are unsure of when they will "go off," [or] develop [the] disease.[37] AIDS itself is a "time bomb," according to the [Los Angeles] *Times,* because of its financial implications.[38] Bombs loom increasingly large. Several writers, including John Brennan (a *Los Angeles Times* medical columnist), have called for a "Manhattan Project" to fight the "war against AIDS."[39] Brennan even goes so far as to say that creating an AIDS Manhattan Project will produce in a short time the necessary weapons ([that is, the] drugs and vaccines) to win the war, just as the Manhattan Project, in only three years created the atomic bomb, thus "marking the beginning of the use and abuse of nuclear power." The hope of controlling AIDS with something even metaphorically like the atomic bomb is scarcely an encouraging prospect, especially if we must think of it in terms of the abuse of nuclear power. Brennan's statement shows how easily the war metaphor draws one to otherwise unacceptable ideas.

The Metaphor of Otherness: The Divided Community

The most difficult metaphor to illustrate in the language of AIDS may be [25] the most pervasive one. That is the language of otherness, of the divided community. It is heard easily in conversation. Ask half a dozen people what is to be done about the problem of asymptomatic but infectious seropositives and they reliably respond in terms of what "we" must do about "them." The image of AIDS has been carefully sustained as a problem for "them," whoever they may be. Margaret Heckler publicly illustrated this when she announced the availability of the HTLV-III antibody blood test, saying that "we must conquer [AIDS] as well before it . . . threatens the health of our general population."[40] There was considerable distress expressed about this statement, especially from the gay community who thought they were a part of the general public. Nevertheless, the phrase continues to be used when discussing whether AIDS risk groups will change.[41] The speakers seem to believe that they can move the threat of disease further away by casting the high-risk groups out, as if a linguistic distance might provide physical safety.

The persistent recurrence of *leper* and *leprosy* in AIDS discussions and 26 writings is also part of this metaphor. The leper is cast out; he is no longer an integral part of the community. Omnipresent analogies between AIDS and leprosy make it seem acceptable to respond to the newer "plague" in the same way that was acceptable for the older one.

The metaphor of AIDS as otherness permits people to accept lesser treatment 27 for those who belong to that other group than they would demand for themselves. Gardner, for example, points out that "if there was any good news . . . it was only that the great majority of cases (94 percent) remain confined to the four high-risk groups."[42] The idea of otherness is possible only as long as "we" are able to isolate ourselves from linguistic connection with people who have the disease or who are at risk for it. By referring in print to AIDS as a "gay disease" or a "gay plague," those in the straight community are encouraged to think of AIDS as something happening beyond their borders, outside the "general population"—as something happening to people for whom they have no human responsibility. The metaphor of otherness provides comfort to those who use it because it implies that they will be spared harm and responsibility.

Conclusion

In *The Plague,* Camus's penetrating novel of the way in which the residents 28 of the town of Oran, quarantined with bubonic plague, come to grips with their fate, Tarrou tells Dr. Rieux what he thinks must be done. Through the months, he says, "I'd come to realize that all our troubles spring from our failure to use plain, clean-cut language. So I resolved always to speak—and to act—quite clearly, as this was the only way of setting myself on the right track."[43] Susan Sontag, in a much different context, echoes this statement, when she argues that "the most truthful way of regarding illness—and the healthiest way of being ill— is one most purified of, most resistant to, metaphoric thinking."[44]

In Camus's tale, the plague creates community where there had been none: 29 "No longer were there individual destinies; only a collective destiny, made of plague and the emotions shared by all." The metaphors of AIDS, however, work in direct opposition to this sense of community. Crime, sin, war, and the divided policy are all metaphors that oppose a sense of community. They are inherently divisive metaphors that suggest we are not all in this together. But surely we are. There is no question but that ethically one ought not to harm innocent people. But in this situation we are all innocent. Those who are carriers of the HTLV-III virus need to care about and to protect those who are not. Those who have not been exposed also need to care for and to protect those who have. It is not that some of "us" need protection and some of "them" need to sacrifice their rights;

that some belong to death, while others embrace life; that some are righteous and others are sinners; that some are criminals and others their victims; that some are enemies and others loyal and deserving citizens; that some may be cast out, while others are kept securely within. Surely those who have been exposed to AIDS have enough to suffer without being victimized by metaphorical myths.

Disease, especially disease that may lead to death, takes on a dramatic 30 quality in this culture. Drama encourages elevated language. A brief stroll through the *Readers' Guide* listings under AIDS will demonstrate the drama that AIDS has provided for readers in the past few years.[45] It is time, however, to speak plainly. There is too much at stake to permit rhetorical flourish to drive our pens. Again quoting Sontag, "nothing is more punitive than to give a disease a meaning—that meaning being invariably a moral one."[46] AIDS has been permitted and encouraged to carry a moral meaning, but that morality is in our minds, not in the disease. If our ethical Judgments are not to be based on punitiveness and further divisiveness, it is time for us to confront the inner meanings our language betrays and then to rid not only our speaking and writing but also our thinking of these metaphors.

NOTES

1. July 1985, p. 12.
2. Edmund White, "The Story of the Year," *Rolling Stone* 463–64, Dec. 19, 1985/Jan. 2, 1986.
3. Dennis Altman also makes this point: "Although people suffering from ARC can be very sick, relatively few go on to develop the full syndrome and die; one wonders whether the media reaction and resulting hysteria would have been noticeably less had the range of less serious illnesses been included in the conceptualization of AIDS itself from the beginning." *AIDS in the Mind of America,* New York Anchor Press/Doubleday, 1986, p. 36.
4. See also "The Walter Reed Staging Classification for HTLV-III/LAC Infection," *New England Journal of Medicine* 314(2), 1985, pp. 131–32, in which Redfield et al. create a scale/nomenclature for HTLV-III infection: "The clinical presentation of patients with HTLV-III infections can range from asymptomatic (with viremia or antibody or both), through chronic generalized lymphadenopathy, to subclinical and clinical T-cell deficiency."
5. *American Medical News,* Jan. 10, 1986, p. 36. See also David Dassey, "AIDS and Testing for AIDS," *Journal of the American Medical Association* 255 (6), 1986, p. 743.
6. *Journal of the Plague Year,* New Meridien Classic, 1984, p. 36.
7. Falwell has denied this, although several newspaper reporters have insisted that they heard him say it. Altman, op. cit., p. 67.
8. See, for example, Rev. Charles Stanley, president of the Southern Baptist Convention, who has said that "AIDS is God indicating his displeasure toward a sinful life-style." As quoted in *Los Angeles Times,* Jan. 24, 1986, Section 2, p. 5.
9. Altman, op. cit., p. 25.
10. As quoted in *Newsweek,* Aug. 12, 1985, from *New York Post,* May 24 and 25, 1983.
11. See Altman, op. cit., p. 17.
12. *Southern Medical Journal* 77(2), 1984, p. 150.
13. *Los Angeles Times,* Mar. 14, 1986, Section 2, p. 4.
14. Matt Herron, "Living with AIDS," *Whole Earth Review* 48, 1985, p. 52.
15. A recent "Dear Abby" included a letter from a woman who "accepted as due punishment" contracting herpes during a period of "promiscuity." She asks, "What are the facts regarding formerly promiscuous women and AIDS? How many years must I fear retribution for that phase of my life? And how would you define promiscuous?" Abby's reply is that disease isn't punishment but that anyone "who has a sexual relationship with more than one person at a time is promiscuous." *Los Angeles Times,* Mar. 9, 1986, Section 6.

16. *The Advocate,* Sept. 19, 1983.
17. Another variation of AIDS as punishment for sin is expressed by Joan McKenna, a "renegade scientist," who tells gays that "you can't *catch* the deficiencies of an impaired immune system. You have to create them." McKenna teaches "thermobaric therapy," which involves cooling the body's "core temperature." *East/West Journal* 16(1), Jan. 1986, p. 44.
18. *Los Angeles Times,* Feb. 3, 1986, Section 2, p. 1.
19. *Newsweek,* Aug. 12, 1985.
20. *New York Times Magazine,* Feb. 6, 1986, p. 28.
21. *Los Angeles Times,* Nov. 25, 1985, Section 1, p. 2.
22. Herron, op. cit., p. 35.
23. *New York Times Magazine,* Mar. 2, 1986. See also "Disease Detectives Tracking the Killers: The AIDS Hysteria," *Time,* July 1985.
24. Aug. 9, 1982.
25. *Medical World News,* May 13, 1985, p. 11.
26. *Life,* July 1985, p. 12.
27. Nov. 26, 1985, p. 35.
28. Susan Sontag, *Illness as Metaphor,* New York: Vintage Books, 1979, pp. 64–65.
29. Herron, op. cit., p. 46.
30. *Newsweek,* Sept. 23, 1985.
31. Ralph Gardner, Jr., *Cosmopolitan,* Nov. 1984, pp. 150, 155–56.
32. "AIDS Hysteria Counterproductive," reprinted in *American Medical News,* Jan. 17, 1986, p. 4.
33. *Medical World News,* May 13, 1985, p. 11.
34. *Life,* July 1985.
35. White, op. cit., p. 124.
36. Sontag, op. cit., p. 64.
37. *American Medical News,* Nov. 22–29, 1985, p. 28.
38. *Los Angeles Times,* Jan. 12, 1986.
39. *Los Angeles Times,* Oct. 15, 1985, View Section, pp. 1, 3. An Assistant Secretary of Health told President Reagan that AIDS research was the "health equivalent of the Manhattan Project" (*Los Angeles Times,* Dec. 20, 1985, Section 1, p. 2).
40. As quoted in *Journal of the American Medical Association* 253(23), 1985, p. 3377.
41. "IV drug users are most responsible for introducing AIDS into the general population." (Herron, op. cit. p. 7.) "So far, the epidemiological evidence suggests that the disease hasn't yet spread widely in the general population." (C. Marwick, "AIDS Associated Virus Yields Data to Intensifying Scientific Scrutiny," *Journal of the American Medical Association* 254 (20), 1985, p. 2867.) A Washington, D.C., lobbyist is quoted by *American Medical News* as saying "the federal government recognizes that AIDS is a public health crisis that has the potential for infecting the general population." (Jan. 10, 1986, p. 9.)
42. Gardner. op. cit., p. 150.
43. Albert Camus, *The Plague,* Random House, Vintage Books, 1972, p. 236.
44. Sontag, op. cit., pp. 5–6.
45. "Fatal, Incurable, and Spreading," "Battling AIDS," "The Plague Years," "AIDS Neglect," "AIDS Panic," "Public Enemy #1," "Death after Sex," "Homosexual Plague Strikes New Victims," and so forth.
46. Sontag, op. cit., p. 57.

QUESTIONS FOR CRITICAL READING, THINKING, DISCUSSION, AND WRITING

Analyzing Content and Technique

1. What is Ross's thesis? Where is it discussed most clearly? Has it been convincingly argued? Give reasons for your answer.

2. Discuss the purpose of this essay. Who is its intended audience? How do we know this?

3. Examine paragraph 2 and summarize its main point. Do you agree with Ross's idea here? Why or why not?

4. Analyze the different kinds of metaphors discussed by Ross. In each case, why does she feel that the metaphor is harmful?

5. Examine the structure of the essay. Write a paragraph describing the structure and evaluating its effectiveness.

6. Comment on Ross's use of quotations. How well do they support her points? What do they add to or subtract from her style? Explain.

Collaborative Activity

As a group, look again at the different metaphors pointed out by Ross. Which type do you consider most harmful to AIDS patients? Why? Write a brief collaborative paragraph in which you explain the group's opinion.

Making Connections

1. In paragraph 2, Ross argues that "Public policy, ethical judgments, and personal choices can all be deeply influenced by the metaphors we have chosen or have grown accustomed to using and hearing others use." Evaluate her statement in an essay of your own, supporting or refuting her arguments with examples drawn from a field other than AIDS.

2. Ross approaches the problem of AIDS linguistically, but obviously there are many other aspects to this issue. Write an essay in which you examine one of these, doing research and conducting interviews to give your reader sufficient up-to-date information and a clear understanding of the subject. Some topics you might consider are: how AIDS affects the families of patients; what kind of funding is or is not available for AIDS research; and attitudes in the medical community toward AIDS patients.

56

Think about the title. Consider the importance of the action it refers to. Were there times in your own life when you broke silence? What were the effects? How did you feel about your action?

Breaking Silence

JANICE MIRIKITANI

Janice Mirikitani is a poet, activist, and community organizer. She is program director of the Glide Church and Urban Center and has edited a number of anthologies, including *Third World Women* and *Time to Greez! Incantations from the Third World*. Her own books include *Awake in the River* and *Shedding Silence* (1987).

*T*here are miracles that happen
she said.
From silences
in the glass caves of our ears,
from the crippled tongue,   5
from the mute, wet eyelash,
testimonies waiting like winter.
   We were told
that silence was better
golden like our skin,   10
   useful like
go quietly,
   easier like
don't make waves,
expedient like   15
horsetails and deserts.

"Mr. Commissioner . . .
. . . the U.S. Army Signal Corps confiscated
our property . . . it was subjected to vandalism

and ravage. All improvements we had made   20
before our incarceration was stolen
or destroyed . . .
I was coerced into signing documents
giving you authority to take . . .
. . . to take   25
. . . to take."

My mother,
soft like tallow,
her words peeling from her
like slivers   30
of yellow flame,
her testimony
a vat of boiling water
surging through the coldest
bluest vein.   35
   She, when the land labored
with flowers, their scent
flowing into her pores,
had molded her earth
like a woman   40
with soft breasted slopes
yielding silent mornings
and purple noisy birthings,
yellow hay
and tomatoes throbbing   45
like the sea.
   And then
all was hushed for announcements:
   "Take only what you can carry . . ."
We were made to believe   50
our faces betrayed us.
Our bodies were loud
with yellow
screaming flesh
needing to be silenced   55
behind barbed wire.

"Mr. Commissioner . . .
   . . . it seems that we were singled out
from others who were under suspicion.
Our neighbors were of German and Italian   60
descent, some of whom were not citizens . . .
It seems we were singled out . . ."

She had worn her sweat
like lemon leaves
shining from the rough edges of work,   65
removed the mirrors
from her rooms
so she would not be tempted
by vanity.
   Her dreams   70
honed the blade of her plow.
The land,
the building of food was
noisy as the opening of irises.
The sounds of work   75
bolted in barracks . . .
silenced.

"Mr. Commissioner . . .
So when you tell me I must limit testimony
to 5 minutes, when you tell me my time is up,   80
I tell you this:
Pride has kept my lips
pinned by nails
my rage coffined.
But I exhume my past   85
to claim this time.
My youth is buried in Rohwer,
Obachan's ghost visits Amache Gate,
My niece haunts Tule Lake.
Words are better than tears,   90
so I spill them.
I kill this, the silence . . ."

There are miracles that happen,
she said,
and everything is made visible.   95
   We see the cracks and fissures in our soil:
We speak of suicides and intimacies,
of longings lush like wet furrows,
of oceans bearing us toward imagined riches,
of burning humiliations and   100
crimes by the government.
Of self hate and of love that breaks
through silences.
   We are lightning and justice.
   Our souls become transparent like glass   105

revealing tears for war-dead sons
red ashes of Hiroshima
jagged wounds from barbed wire.
　　We must recognize ourselves at last
　　We are a rainforest of color   110
and noise.
　　We hear everything.
　　We are unafraid.
Our Language is beautiful.

QUESTIONS FOR CRITICAL READING, THINKING, DISCUSSION, AND WRITING

Analyzing Content and Technique

1. Discuss the background of the poem. Who is the speaker? What past event is she referring to? What is taking place now in the poem?
2. From the details given, analyze the character of the narrator's mother. How is the daughter different from her?
3. Explain the "miracle" the narrator refers to at the beginning and at the end of the poem. Do you agree with the narrator's word-choice?
4. This poem uses a number of unusual metaphors and similes. Make a list of them. From the list, choose one or two you particularly like and discuss their effect.
5. Who is the poet writing this piece for? Give reasons to support your answer.
6. What is the tone of the poem? Pick out words or phrases that help to establish this tone.

Collaborative Activity

As a group, research Rohwer, Amache Gate, and Tule Lake. Discuss how this knowledge helps you understand the poem better.

Making Connections

1. A line in the poem claims, "Words are better than tears." Examine this statement. Do you agree? When are words better? Are there times when silence is preferable? What function may be served by tears? Write an essay in which you explore the idea of the importance of expressing anger and sorrow through words.
2. The poem indicates that there are important differences between how the Japanese parents (immigrants or first and second generation) acted and how their children are reacting. From this, what conclusions can you draw about how ethnic communities have changed regarding the way in which they view their position and their rights in American society? Write an essay in which you examine one ethnic community closely to support your view.

Think about the acts of storytelling and listening to stories. How important is this in your culture? Who does it and why? Sprint write for five minutes about a storytelling memory that you have. If you have none, write how you feel about that.

Language and Literature from a Pueblo Indian Perspective

LESLIE MARMON SILKO

Leslie Marmon Silko (1948–   ) was born in Albuquerque, New Mexico. She grew up in the Laguna Pueblo reservation in New Mexico and attended the University of New Mexico. She has been awarded a MacArthur Foundation grant and is a teacher and writer of fiction, nonfiction, and poetry. Her books, which draw on her Laguna, Mexican, and white ancestry, include *Ceremony*, *Laguna Woman*, *Almanac of the Dead*, and *Sacred Water*. The selection below first appeared in *English Literature: Opening Up the Canon* (1979).

Where I come from, the words most highly valued are those spoken from the heart, unpremeditated and unrehearsed. Among the Pueblo people, a written speech or statement is highly suspect because the true feelings of the speaker remain hidden as she reads words that are detached from the occasion and the audience. I have intentionally not written a formal paper because I want you to *hear* and to experience English in a structure that follows patterns from the oral tradition. For those of you accustomed to being taken from point A to point B to point C, this presentation may be somewhat difficult to follow. Pueblo expression resembles something like a spider's web—with many little threads radiating from the center, crisscrossing each other. As with the web, the structure emerges as it is made and you must simply listen and trust, as the Pueblo people do, that meaning will be made.

My task is a formidable one: I ask you to set aside a number of basic approaches that you have been using, and probably will continue to use, and instead, to approach language from the Pueblo perspective, one that embraces the whole of creation and the whole of history and time.

Source: Reprinted with the permission of Simon & Schuster from *Yellow Woman and a Beauty of the Spirit* by Leslie Marmon Silko. Copyright © 1996 by Leslie Marmon Silko.

What changes would Pueblo writers make to English as a language for ³
literature? I have some examples of stories in English that I will use to address
this question. At the same time, I would like to explain the importance of
storytelling and how it relates to a Pueblo theory of language.

So, I will begin, appropriately enough, with the Pueblo Creation story, an ⁴
all-inclusive story of how life began. In this story, Tséitsínako, Thought Woman,
by thinking of her sisters, and together with her sisters, thought of everything
that is. In this way, the world was created. Everything in this world was a part of
the original creation; the people at home understood that far away there were
other human beings, also a part of this world. The Creation story even includes a
prophecy, which describes the origin of European and African peoples and also
refers to Asians.

This story, I think, suggests something about why the Pueblo people are ⁵
more concerned with story and communication and less concerned with a
particular language. There are at least six, possibly seven, distinct languages
among the twenty pueblos of the southwestern United States, for example, Zuñi
and Hopi. And from mesa to mesa there are subtle differences in language. But
the particular language being spoken isn't as important as what a speaker is trying
to say, and this emphasis on the story itself stems, I believe, from a view of
narrative particular to the Pueblo and other Native American peoples—that is,
that language *is* story.

I will try to clarify this statement. At Laguna Pueblo, for example, many ⁶
individual words have their own stories. So when one is telling a story, and one
is using words to tell the story, each word that one is speaking has a story of its
own, too. Often the speakers or tellers will go into these word-stories, creating
an elaborate structure of stories-within-stories. This structure, which becomes
very apparent in the actual telling of a story, informs contemporary Pueblo
writing and storytelling as well as the traditional narratives. This perspective on
narrative—of story within story, the idea that one story is only the beginning of
many stories, and the sense that stories never truly end—represents an
important contribution of Native American cultures to the English language.

Many people think of storytelling as something that is done at bedtime, ⁷
that it is something done for small children. But when I use the term *storytelling,*
I'm talking about something much bigger than that. I'm talking about
something that comes out of an experience and an understanding of that original
view of creation—that we are all part of a whole; we do not differentiate or
fragment stories and experiences. In the beginning, Tséitsínako, Thought
Woman, thought of all things, and all of these things are held together as one
holds many things together in a single thought.

So in the telling (and you will hear a few of the dimensions of this telling) ⁸
first of all, as mentioned earlier, the storytelling always includes the audience, the
listeners. In fact, a great deal of the story is believed to be inside the listener; the
storyteller's role is to draw the story out of the listeners. The storytelling
continues from generation to generation.

Basically, the origin story constructs our identity—within this story, we ⁹
know who we are. We are the Lagunas. This is where we come from. We came

this way. We came by this place. And so from the time we are very young, we hear these stories, so that when we go out into the world, when one asks who we are, or where we are from, we immediately know: we are the people who came from the north. We are the people of these stories.

In the Creation story, Antelope says that he will help knock a hole in the   10 earth so that the people can come up, out into the next world. Antelope tries and tries; he uses his hooves, but is unable to break through. It is then that Badger says, "Let me help you." And Badger very patiently uses his claws and digs a way through, bringing the people into the world. When the Badger clan people think of themselves, or when the Antelope people think of themselves, it is as people who are of *this* story, and this is *our* place, and we fit into the very beginning when the people first came, before we began our journey south.

Within the clans there are stories that identify the clan. One moves, then,   11 from the idea of one's identity as a tribal person into clan identity, then to one's identity as a member of an extended family. And it is the notion of "extended family" that has produced a kind of story that some distinguish from other Pueblo stories, though Pueblo people do not. Anthropologists and ethnologists have, for a long time, differentiated the types of stories the Pueblos tell. They tended to elevate the old, sacred, and traditional stories and to brush aside family stories, the family's account of itself. But in Pueblo culture, these family stories are given equal recognition. There is no definite, preset pattern for the way one will hear the stories of one's own family, but it is a very critical part of one's childhood, and the storytelling continues throughout one's life. One will hear stories of importance to the family—sometimes wonderful stories—stories about the time a maternal uncle got the biggest deer that was ever seen and brought it back from the mountains. And so an individual's identity will extend from the identity constructed around the family—"I am from the family of my uncle who brought in this wonderful deer and it was a wonderful hunt."

Family accounts include negative stories, too; perhaps an uncle did   12 something unacceptable. It is very important that one keep track of all these stories—both positive and not so positive—about one's own family and other families. Because even when there is no way around it—old Uncle Pete *did* do a terrible thing—by knowing the stories that originate in other families, one is able to deal with terrible sorts of things that might happen within one's own family. If a member of the family does something that cannot be excused, one always knows stories about similarly inexcusable things done by a member of another family. But this knowledge is not communicated for malicious reasons. It is very important to understand this. Keeping track of all the stories within the community gives us all a certain distance, a useful perspective, that brings incidents down to a level we can deal with. If others have done it before, it cannot be so terrible. If others have endured, so can we.

The stories are always bringing us together, keeping this whole together,   13 keeping this family together, keeping this clan together. "Don't go away, don't isolate yourself, but come here, because we have all had these kinds of experiences." And so there is this constant pulling together to resist the tendency to run or hide or separate oneself during a traumatic emotional experience. This separation not only endangers the group but the individual as well—one does not recover by oneself.

Because storytelling lies at the heart of Pueblo culture, it is absurd to [14] attempt to fix the stories in time. "When did they tell the stories?" or "What time of day does the storytelling take place?"—these questions are nonsensical from a Pueblo perspective, because our storytelling goes on constantly: as some old grandmother puts on the shoes of a child and tells her the story of a little girl who didn't wear her shoes, for instance, or someone comes into the house for coffee to talk with a teenage boy who has just been in a lot of trouble, to reassure him that someone else's son has been in that kind of trouble, too. Storytelling is an ongoing process, working on many different levels.

Here's one story that is often told at a time of individual crisis (and I [15] want to remind you that we make no distinctions between types of story— historical, sacred, plain gossip—because these distinctions are not useful when discussing the Pueblo *experience* of language). There was a young man who, when he came back from the war in Vietnam, had saved up his army pay and bought a beautiful red Volkswagen. He was very proud of it. One night he drove up to a place called the King's Bar right across the reservation line. The bar is notorious for many reasons, particularly for the deep *arroyo* located behind it. The young man ran in to pick up a cold six-pack, but he forgot to put on his emergency brake. And his little red Volkswagen rolled back into the *arroyo* and was all smashed up. He felt very bad about it, but within a few days everybody had come to him with stories about other people who had lost cars and family members to that *arroyo*, for instance, George Day's station wagon, with his mother-in-law and kids inside. So everybody was saying, "Well, at least your mother-in-law and kids weren't in the car when it rolled in," and one can't argue with that kind of story. The story of the young man and his smashed-up Volkswagen was now joined with all the other stories of cars that fell into that *arroyo*.

Now I want to tell you a very beautiful little story. It is a very old story that [16] is sometimes told to people who suffer great family or personal loss. This story was told by my Aunt Susie. She is one of the first generation of people at Laguna who began experimenting with English—who began working to make English speak for us—that is, to speak from the heart. (I come from a family intent on getting the stories told.) As you read the story, I think you will hear that. And here and there, I think, you will also hear the influence of the Indian school at Carlisle, Pennsylvania, where my Aunt Susie was sent (like being sent to prison) for six years.

This scene is set partly in Acoma, partly in Laguna. Waithea was a little girl [17] living in Acoma and one day she said, "Mother, I would like to have some *yashtoah* to eat." *Yashtoah* is the hardened crust of corn mush that curls up. *Yashtoah* literally means "curled up." She said, "I would like to have some *yashtoah*," and her mother said, "My dear little girl, I can't make you any *yashtoah* because we haven't any wood, but if you will go down off the mesa, down below, and pick up some pieces of wood and bring them home, I will make you some *yashtoah*." So Waithea was glad and ran down the precipitous cliff of Acoma mesa. Down below, just as her mother had told her, there were pieces of wood, some curled, some crooked in shape, that she was to pick up and take home. She found just such wood as these.

She brought them home in a little wicker basket. First she called to her mother as she got home, "*Nayah, deeni!* Mother, upstairs!" The Pueblo people always called "upstairs" because long ago their homes were two, three stories, and they entered from the top. She said, "*Deeni!* UPSTAIRS!" and her mother came. The little girl said, "I have brought the wood you wanted me to bring." And she opened her little wicker basket to lay out the pieces of wood but here they were snakes. They were snakes instead of the crooked sticks of wood. And her mother said, "Oh my dear child, you have brought snakes instead!" She said, "Go take them back and put them back just where you got them." And the little girl ran down the mesa again, down below to the flats. And she put those snakes back just where she got them. They were snakes instead and she was very hurt about this and so she said, "I'm not going home. I'm going to *Kawaik,* the beautiful lake place, *Kawaik,* and drown myself in that lake, *byn'yah'nah* [the "west lake"]. I will go there and drown myself." 18

So she started off, and as she passed by the Enchanted Mesa near Acoma she met an old man, very aged, and he saw her running, and he said, "My dear child, where are you going?" "I'm going to *Kawaik* and jump into the lake there." "Why?" "Well, because," she said, "my mother didn't want to make any *yashtoah* for me." The old man said, "Oh, no! You must not go my child. Come with me and I will take you home." He tried to catch her, but she was very light and skipped along. And every time he would try to grab her she would skip faster away from him. 19

The old man was coming home with some wood strapped to his back and tied with yucca. He just let that strap go and let the wood drop. He went as fast as he could up the cliff to the little girl's home. When he got to the place where she lived, he called to her mother. *"Deeni!"* "Come on up!" And he said, "I can't. I just came to bring you a message. Your little daughter is running away. She is going to *Kawaik* to drown herself in the lake there." "Oh my dear little girl!" the mother said. So she busied herself with making the *yashtoah* her little girl liked so much. Corn mush curled at the top. (She must have found enough wood to boil the corn meal and make the *yashtoah.*) 20

While the mush was cooling off, she got the little girl's clothing, her *manta* dress and buckskin moccasins and all her other garments, and put them in a bundle—probably a yucca bag. And she started down as fast as she could on the east side of Acoma. (There used to be a trail there, you know. It's gone now, but it was accessible in those days.) She saw her daughter way at a distance and she kept calling: "Stsamaku! My daughter! Come back! I've got your *yashtoah* for you." But the little girl would not turn. She kept on ahead and she cried: "My mother, my mother, she didn't want me to have any *yashtoah.* So now I'm going to *Kawaik* and drown myself." Her mother heard her cry and said, "My little daughter, come back here!" "No," and she kept a distance away from her. And they came nearer and nearer to the lake. And she could see her daughter now, very plain. "Come back, my daughter! I have your *yashtoah.*" But no, she kept on, and finally she reached the lake and she stood on the edge. 21

She had tied a little feather in her hair, which is traditional (in death they tie 22 this feather on the head). She carried a feather, the little girl did, and she tied it in her hair with a piece of string, right on top of her head she put the feather. Just as her mother was about to reach her, she jumped into the lake. The little feather was whirling around and around in the depths below. Of course the mother was very sad. She went, grieved, back to Acoma and climbed her mesa home. She stood on the edge of the mesa and scattered her daughter's clothing, the little moccasins, the *yashtoah*. She scattered them to the east, to the west, to the north, to the south. And the pieces of clothing and the moccasins and *yashtoah*, all turned into butterflies. And today they say that Acoma has more beautiful butterflies: red ones, white ones, blue ones, yellow ones. They came from this little girl's clothing.[1]

Now this is a story anthropologists would consider very old. The version I 23 have given you is just as Aunt Susie tells it. You can occasionally hear some English she picked up at Carlisle—words like "precipitous." You will also notice that there is a great deal of repetition, and a little reminder about *yashtoah*, and how it is made. There is a remark about the cliff trail at Acoma—that it was once there, but is there no longer. This story may be told at a time of sadness or loss, but within this story many other elements are brought together. Things are not separated out and categorized; all things are brought together. So that the reminder about the *yashtoah* is valuable information that is repeated—a recipe, if you will. The information about the old trail at Acoma reveals that stories are, in a sense, maps, since even to this day there is little information or material about trails that is passed around with writing. In the structure of this story the repetitions are, of course, designed to help you remember. It is repeated again and again, and then it moves on.

The next story I would like to tell is by Simon Ortiz, from Acoma Pueblo. 24 He is a wonderful poet who also works in narrative. One of the things I find very interesting in this short story is that if you listen very closely, you begin to hear what I was talking about in terms of a story never beginning at the beginning, and certainly never ending. As the Hopis sometimes say, "Well, it has gone this far for a while." There is always that implication of a continuing. The other thing I want you to listen for is the many stories within one story. Listen to the kinds of stories contained within the main story—stories that give one a family identity and an individual identity, for example. This story is called "Home Country":

"Well, it's been a while. I think in 1947 was when I left. My husband had been 25 killed in Okinawa some years before. And so I had no more husband. And I had to make a living. O I guess I could have looked for another man but I didn't want to. It looked like the war had made some of them into a bad way anyway. I saw some of them come home like that. They either got drunk or just stayed around a while or couldn't seem to be satisfied anymore with what was there. I guess now that I think about it, that happened to me too although I wasn't in the war not in the Army or even much off the reservation just that several years at the Indian School.

[1]See Leslie Marmon Silko, *Storyteller* (1981).

Well there was that feeling things were changing not only the men the boys, but things were changing.

"One day the home nurse the nurse that came from the Indian health service 26 was at my mother's home my mother was getting near the end real sick and she said that she had been meaning to ask me a question. I said what is the question. And the home nurse said well your mother is getting real sick and after she is no longer around for you to take care of, what will you be doing you and her are the only ones here. And I said I don't know. But I was thinking about it what she said made me think about it. And then the next time she came she said to me Eloise the government is hiring Indians now in the Indian schools to take care of the boys and girls I heard one of the supervisors saying that Indians are hard workers but you have to supervise them a lot and I thought of you well because you've been taking care of your mother real good and you follow all my instructions. She said I thought of you because you're a good Indian girl and you would be the kind of person for that job. I didn't say anything I had not ever really thought about a job but I kept thinking about it.

"Well my mother she died and we buried her up at the old place the cemetery 27 there it's real nice on the east side of the hill where the sun shines warm and the wind doesn't blow too much sand around right there. Well I was sad we were all sad for a while but you know how things are. One of my aunties came over and she advised me and warned me about being too sorry about it and all that she wished me that I would not worry too much about it because old folks they go along pretty soon life is that way and then she said that maybe I ought to take in one of my aunties kids or two because there was a lot of them kids and I was all by myself now. But I was so young and I thought that I might do that you know take care of someone but I had been thinking too of what the home nurse said to me about working. Hardly anybody at our home was working at something like that no woman anyway. And I would have to move away.

"Well I did just that. I remember that day very well. I told my aunties and 28 they were all crying and we all went up to the old highway where the bus to town passed by everyday. I was wearing an old kind of bluish sweater that was kind of big that one of my cousins who was older had got from a white person a tourist one summer in trade for something she had made a real pretty basket. She gave me that and I used to have a picture of me with it on it's kind of real ugly. Yeah that was the day I left wearing a baggy sweater and carrying a suitcase that someone gave me too I think or maybe it was the home nurse there wasn't much in it anyway either. I was scared and everybody seemed to be sad I was so young and skinny then. My aunties said one of them who was real fat you make sure you eat now make your own tortillas drink the milk and stuff like candies is no good she learned that from the nurse. Make sure you got your letter my auntie said. I had it folded into my purse. Yes I had one too a brown one that my husband when he was still alive one time on furlough he brought it on my birthday it was a nice purse and still looked new because I never used it.

"The letter said that I had a job at Keams Canyon the boarding school there 29 but I would have to go to the Agency first for some papers to be filled and that's where I was going first. The Agency. And then they would send me out to Keams Canyon. I didn't even know where it was except that someone of our relatives said that it was near Hopi. My uncles teased me about watching out for the Hopi men and boys don't let them get too close they said well you know how they are and they were pretty strict too about those things and then they were joking and then they were not too and so I said aw they won't get near to me I'm too ugly and I promised I would be careful anyway.

"So we all gathered for a while at my last auntie's house and then the old man my grandfather brought his wagon and horses to the door and we all got in and sat there for a while until my auntie told her father okay father let's go and shook his elbow because the poor old man was old by then and kind of going to sleep all the time you had to talk to him real loud. I had about ten dollars I think that was a lot of money more than it is now you know and when we got to the highway where the Indian road which is just a dirt road goes off the pave road my grandfather reached into his blue jeans and pulled out a silver dollar and put it into my hand. I was so shocked. We were all so shocked. We all looked around at each other we didn't know where the old man had gotten it because we were real poor two of my uncles had to borrow on their accounts at the trading store for the money I had in my purse but there it was a silver dollar so big and shining in my grandfather's hand and then in my hand. 30

"Well I was so shocked and everybody was so shocked that we all started cry-ing right there at the junction of that Indian road and the pave highway I wanted to be a little girl again running after the old man when he hurried with his long legs to the cornfields or went for water down to the river. He was old then and his eye was turned gray and he didn't do much anymore except drive the wagon and chop a little bit of wood but I just held him and I just held him so tightly. 31

"Later on I don't know what happened to the silver dollar it had a date of 1907 on it but I kept it for a long time because I guess I wanted to have it to remember when I left my home country. What I did in between then and now is another story but that's the time I moved away," is what she said.[2] 32

There are a great many parallels between Pueblo experiences and those of African and Caribbean peoples—one is that we have all had the conqueror's language imposed on us. But our experience with English has been somewhat different in that the Bureau of Indian Affairs schools were not interested in teaching us the canon of Western classics. For instance, we never heard of Shakespeare. We were given Dick and Jane, and I can remember reading that the robins were heading south for the winter. It took me a long time to figure out what was going on. I worried for quite a while about our robins in Laguna because they didn't leave in the winter, until I finally realized that all the big textbook companies are up in Boston and *their* robins do go south in the winter. But in a way, this dreadful formal education freed us by encouraging us to maintain our narratives. Whatever literature we were exposed to at school (which was damn little), at home the storytelling, the special regard for telling and bringing together through the telling, was going on constantly. 33

[2]Simon J. Ortiz, *Howbah Indians* (Tucson: Blue Moon Press, 1978).

And as the old people say, "If you can remember the stories, you will be all 34 right. Just remember the stories." When I returned to Laguna Pueblo after attending college, I wondered how the storytelling was continuing (anthropologists say that Laguna Pueblo is one of the more acculturated pueblos), so I visited an English class at Laguna Acoma High School. I knew the students had cassette tape recorders in their lockers and stereos at home, and that they listened to Kiss and Led Zeppelin and were well informed about popular culture in general. I had with me an anthology of short stories by Native American writers, *The Man to Send Rain Clouds.* One story in the book is about the killing of a state policeman in New Mexico by three Acoma Pueblo men in the early 1950s.[3] I asked the students how many had heard this story and steeled myself for the possibility that the anthropologists were right, that the old traditions were indeed dying out and the students would be ignorant of the story. But instead, all but one or two raised their hands—they had heard the story, just as I had heard it when I was young, some in English, some in Laguna.

One of the other advantages that we Pueblos have enjoyed is that we have 35 always been able to stay with the land. Our stories cannot be separated from their geographical locations, from actual physical places on the land. We were not relocated like so many Native American groups who were torn away from their ancestral land. And our stories are so much a part of these places that it is almost impossible for future generations to lose them—there is a story connected with every place, every object in the landscape.

Dennis Brutus has talked about the "yet unborn" as well as "those from the 36 past," and how we are still *all* in *this* place, and language—the storytelling—is our way of passing through or being with them, or being together again. When Aunt Susie told her stories, she would tell a younger child to go open the door so that our esteemed predecessors might bring in their gifts to us. "They are out there," Aunt Susie would say. "Let them come in. They're here, they're here with us *within* the stories."

A few years ago, when Aunt Susie was 106, I paid her a visit, and while I 37 was there she said, "Well, I'll be leaving here soon. I think I'll be leaving here next week, and I will be going over to the Cliff House." She said, "It's going to be real good to get back over there." I was listening, and I was thinking that she must be talking about her house at Paguate Village, just north of Laguna. And she went on, "Well, my mother's sister (and she gave her Indian name) will be there. She has been living there. She will be there and we will be over there, and I will get a chance to write down these stories I've been telling you." Now you must understand, of course, that Aunt Susie's mother's sister, a great storyteller herself, has long since passed over into the land of the dead. But then I realized, too, that Aunt Susie wasn't talking about death the way most of us do. She was talking about "going over" as a journey, a journey that perhaps we can only begin to understand through an appreciation for the boundless capacity of language

[3]See Simon J. Ortiz, "The Killing of a State Cop," in *The Man to Send Rain Clouds,* ed. Kenneth Rosen (New York: Viking Press, 1974), pp. 101–108.

that, through storytelling, brings us together, despite great distances between cultures, despite great distances in time.

QUESTIONS FOR CRITICAL READING, THINKING, DISCUSSION, AND WRITING

Analyzing Content and Technique

1. How, according to the writer, is the structure of Pueblo expression different from that of English? Analyze the analogy she uses to explain this.
2. Examine the creation stories presented by Silko. Why are these important to the Pueblo peoples? What do they learn from them?
3. List the other kinds of stories discussed by Silko. In what additional ways are they important? How do the Pueblo people look at these stories as compared to the anthropologists?
4. Explain what Silko means when she states that a story never begins at the beginning, and certainly never ends. How is this illustrated in the stories she tells in this essay? Give specific examples.
5. What similarity does the writer see between the Pueblo experience and that of the African and Caribbean people? What is the difference?
6. Who is the intended audience for this piece and what is its purpose? Explain with evidence from the text.

Collaborative Activity

As a group, discuss any family stories you have heard. What role have these stories played in your life? How, if at all, have they helped you? Do you see yourself as carrying on similar stories to future generations? Do you see any value in such an activity? Why or why not?

Making Connections

1. As humans we are deeply interested in stories, no matter when and where we live. However, in today's society stories come to us not so much as oral tales but in new and varied forms. In a classification essay, discuss where we get our stories in American culture, and what forms they take. Discuss the advantages and disadvantages of these forms.
2. Write a story of your own, based on a tale you have heard or read from your culture. Try to capture the original flavor of the story, using conversational language where appropriate. As you write this story, think about Silko's claim that non-English languages often have a different way of telling stories or expressing ideas. Does this idea apply to your story?

58

PREREADING ACTIVITY

Before reading selection 58, write about a situation in which you had difficulty communicating with someone close to you. What caused the misunderstandings and the frustrations?

Silence Is a Loud, Loud Language (Student Essay)

Bobbie Su Nadal

Life is the first gift, love the second, and understanding is the third.

Marge Piercy

She calls, says, "Come if you can. We need to talk."   1

"What is it, Mother?" I ask. "Are you sick? Did you hurt yourself?"   2

"Don't be silly. Are you coming or not?"   3

Four days since the phone call, and the taxi blasts from baggage claim into the seam of bumper-to-bumper traffic, squeals onto Century Boulevard, the dark insides of the cab stuttering reflected light like a strobe from the bright billboards that line the street all the way northbound to I-405. It's been years since I've seen my mother, and now I don't know whether to ask the driver to speed up or slow down. Either way, my childhood home will appear soon enough—forty-five minutes at the most, even in this unseasonable rain.   4

•

What is it with mothers and daughters anyway? It's as if my mother and I had been born in separate countries with common borders but alien alphabets. When we try to communicate, somewhere in their formation the words become bent with misunderstanding, turn into a collection of incoherent syllables. Our years together are littered with failed efforts to find a common language.   5

Mother is a woman of hard-honed strength, a woman born to a large German Catholic family on a small Nebraska farm, a family too busy keeping food on the table to have time to talk or listen. Their communication consisted mainly of Franklinesque proverbs, capsulized codes of conduct for the business of living: "Don't put off till tomorrow what you can do today." "If you don't have any-   6

Source: Student Essay reprinted by permission.

thing nice to say, don't say anything at all." That, plus a strict Church doctrine and the Ten Commandments—no one dared question the wisdom of this simple and effective system.

Mother included these codes into our own family's dialect, but in the form 7 of parables, dizzying stories of disasters into which she wove a sequence of tenuously related subjects, half fact, half fiction, peopled with characters I did not know. They are all I remember of our early conversations. I guessed that the tales were supposed to teach me cautionary lessons, but long before I could figure out the point of the story, I would be lost among all those words. I would stare at her in bafflement until she turned away abruptly, exasperated.

As I approached adolescence, matters became worse. No longer willing to 8 listen in helpless confusion, I would challenge her stories and their validity. Through them I felt I was challenging her values and, in essence, the parental authority that I just could not communicate with. Perhaps *this* way I could reach her, I thought, as I rushed headlong into battle. But all that happened was that her stories collapsed into an uncompromising silence.

I began to think I was a genetic mistake, a bald, blank cell that grew dull, 9 an unsilvered mirror incapable of reflection. She could not see herself in me any more than I could see myself in her. We had nothing in common, nothing in our physical appearance, nothing in our personalities, nothing in our basic vocabularies. And so we danced a slow and tortuous dance, out and out into fragmented circles, until our alienation was complete, until all our words, spoken and unspoken, were like dried twigs under our tongues.

Adolescence is a time of pain, but it is also a naive and hopeful time. Surely 10 when I went away to college, I believed, we would be able to start over. It would allow us the distance we needed, the time between our conversations. It would be a forced truce. It would give me the necessary skills to tell her how I felt. And so at college words became my passion. I devoured the great works of literature and memorized the vocabularies of the best orators, trying to find in them a solution to our wordlessness. In my sophomore year, I wrote a poem for Mother, hoping to articulate my deep sense of loss at our verbal impasse:

Mother

my mouth is stuffed
with all this silence
between us. What
should we do with our
wild words, the ones
that bay like dogs
outside our window
at night, that snarl
between the long teeth
of time?
They've grown bloated
over the years, soured

in the dark recesses
of our hearts where
we tried to cage them.
I hear them restless now,
multiplying in packs.
I hear them clatter sharp claws
on our bare floors, hear them
clanging at the gate.

When she received my poem, she called and said, "I didn't know they had   11
wild dogs at school, honey. Don't forget to lock your door."

•

It's still raining. Muddy tracks send slanted streaks running along the back win-   12
dows. I look through them for familiar road signs, see, slashed into the hips of
the San Gabriel mountains, new roads that I could never have imagined possible.
I remember earlier homecomings, riding over the rise and seeing all the lights filling the valley like fireflies. Tonight it is dark, like looking into a decayed tooth.

•

After I started a family of my own, we tried again to close the gap between us.   13
But we could speak only in courtesies. I'd call her once a week to ask if she was
all right. She'd say she was "just fine, thank you." It took all of five minutes to
say everything we could concerning the weather, the neighborhood, the kids, the
house. We sidestepped all controversial or emotionally charged issues. Our language was that of polite conversation—safe, boring, comfortable—but with a dull
ache underneath.

I used to visit her with my children in the fall and summer. Strangely   14
enough, there was an immediate, wonderful connection between my daughter
and mother. It pleased me to see how easy they were with one another, what pure
joy phrased their simple conversations. On the last visit, I handed another poem
to Mother, one that I erased from my computer immediately on my return home
but cannot remove from my own memory today:

At Dusk My Mother

sits in her mother's chair,
works the wicker rocker
and her rosary
at a peaceful pace.
She gazes outside the window
where her granddaughter
who wears her grandmother's chin,
her gold-green eyes,
rides a bike with sturdy legs
under a Chinese pistachio tree which
has burst into flame.

Time leans against

my mother. She feels it
pinch her left hip,
her right elbow,
feels it daily, the way
it chisels circles
around her eyes, her mouth.

The room grows gray.
She gathers the past on her lap
the way she used to
gather children,
presses a string of names
across the beads,
pleads a blessing
for mother, father,
husband of nearly forty years,
all gone now.

She sits and prays,
sits and smiles
at the little girl outside
glowing in the dark.

This time Mother dissolved into tears, turned and hurried into her own   15
room, closing the door.

"What is it, Mother? Did I write something wrong? Was it the part about   16
being old? I'm sorry if I hurt you. Please come out and talk to me."

Hours later she called me in, handed me a sealed envelope that had "Adop-   17
tion Papers" printed across it. She didn't have to say a word. Instinctively, I knew
they were my own. And suddenly, everything fell into place. It wasn't the part
about being old, or the part about her dead loved ones. It was the part that I
thought would make her happy, the part about the physical resemblance between
my daughter and her that finally cut deep enough to expose the secret she had
hidden all this time.

A mix of emotions flooded me: anger for the years of deceit and the   18
wasted efforts at trying to understand her, and relief for what I thought was a
simple answer to all our problems, clicking into place with the precision of a
bullet sliding into its chamber. This finally was cold, clear language: we simply
were not related.

•

We're on the Ventura Freeway at the Coldwater Canyon exit, and before I'm ready,   19
we're at 4545. I nervously pay the driver too much. He leaves me standing in the
mist, jarred by the sharp smell of the wet camphor trees that rim my mother's lot.
The street light is out, but I could have found my way, blindfolded, up the eleven
flagstone stairs to the screened front door that still creaks when I pull it open.

I'm counting the years since our last conversation, that last confrontation.   20
Four. No, longer, much too long.

I think of us, mother and daughter, our wounds from all that emotional 21
rending and ripping, and know this is our last chance. I think of what to say, how
to say it just right. I go over and over each sentence: how it's no longer important to me that we're not blood-related; how she's still my mother, the only one
I'll ever have; how the last few years have taught me what living without her
would be like; how I think we've both been stubborn for too long. . . . Then
the door opens, and there, standing in the smile of the doorway in a cloud of
white hair that frames her face, is Mother.

Where are they now, those fine-tuned words that I thought could change 22
things between us, make everything OK? I can't find them. . . . She holds out
her arms and we fall back into each other's life, cling to each other as though to
life rafts that float easily over all our debris. Somewhere in this sweet silence, so
new to us, more precious than birthright, louder than any spoken word, is forgiveness and healing.

"Mother," I say, "I'm learning to listen to our silence." 23
She says, "Welcome home." 24

STRUCTURE, STRATEGY, SUGGESTION

1. How does Nadal move from the present to the past? Is the method she uses suited to her subject? What other technique could she have used?
2. Find some similes and metaphors that Nadal has used in the prose portion of her essay. How
   do they help to strengthen the points she is presenting?
3. What are some of the reasons why the narrator and the mother are unable to communicate?
   Are there aspects that need further clarification? Pick out examples from the text to support
   your answer.
4. Compare the two poems the narrator writes to her mother. What do they reveal about her
   emotions? What does the mother's response to them reveal about her character? What is the
   effect of combining prose and poetry in the same piece?
5. What realization does the narrator reach by the end of the essay? Are you convinced that the
   relationship between mother and daughter will change? Explain your response.
6. What techniques does Nadal use to make us empathize with the narrator? Evaluate her success.
7. Write an essay exploring the question that Nadal poses at the beginning: "What is it with mothers and daughters anyway?" Some questions you may want to address are: What is the unique
   nature of the bond between mother and daughter? What are some things that might cause conflict between them? What makes communication easy or difficult for them? What are the characteristics of a successful mother-daughter relationship, and do these characteristics vary
   from culture to culture? You may want to add ideas and examples from other writers to your
   own points, drawing on poetry as well as prose.

SYNTHESIS *Part Seven*

1. The writers in this section have opened up several aspects of the complex ways in which we use language and their positive or negative results. Write an essay in which you discuss the power of language to bring us together as well as its power to separate us, defining the circumstances under which each occurs. Support your essay with evidence and ideas from at least three of the readings in Part Seven.

2. In "Language and Literature from a Pueblo Indian Perspective," Silko states that ethnic communities with their own non-English languages have a different way of communicating ideas. Do you think that language is used differently not only by different ethnic communities, but also by males and females? Write an essay in which you examine whether men and women use language differently. You may use the writers in this section to support your view, or you may use outside evidence.

3. "Aria" and "Silence Is a Loud, Loud Language" both deal with the inability of children to communicate with parents, but the causes in each case are different. Write an essay in which you discuss the difficulties of communicating between generations, focusing on what you consider the most important reasons. Take into account the ideas presented in "Aria" and "Silence," and add your own points.

4. The selections by Naylor, Mirikitani, and Ross in this section describe how language can be used to oppress a minority group, but also present linguistic solutions. Write an essay in which you examine the solutions they present, evaluating their effectiveness. You may also present additional solutions.

PART EIGHT

Seeing Ourselves

PART 8: INTRODUCTION

*M*any of the selections in this book focus on how we are viewed by those around us. The viewer might be a member of the family who accepts us with love or approaches us with emotional demands. It could be a teacher or an authority figure with the task of shaping us and furthering our education. Or it could be a person from a different cultural group or social class who examines us with misgivings, perhaps even with fear or hatred. In selections like these, we are made aware of how others feel about us and what they see when they look at us, through their behavior toward us. In Part Eight, however, we will be engaged in a more difficult task: turning the eye inward and looking at ourselves.

How do we define ourselves? The writers in Part Eight show us that there are many ways of doing this. One obvious way is by race. In her autobiographical piece "Graduation" (selection 63), Maya Angelou comes to see that her African American identity, which earlier had made her feel alienated and unhappy, is a fundamental and beautiful part of herself.

But gender is often an inextricable part of our racial identity. In "Where I Come From Is Like This" (selection 59), Paula Gunn Allen illustrates that the life of a Native American woman is very different from that of a Native American man. It makes her approach the world in a unique way, from a female viewpoint she is proud to have inherited from her "foremothers."

Another aspect of identity is class, social and financial. We see this in Sanders's "The Men We Carry in Our Minds" (selection 60), an essay which explains how the writer's upbringing as a male from a working-class background set him apart from the men and women he met in college, and yet made him unusually sensitive to the latter's problems.

Discovering oneself is not always a happy process. Sometimes the identity that appears when we look closely at ourselves—as individuals or as a group—fills us with fear, guilt, anger, or self-loathing. Such is Orwell's case in "Shooting an Elephant" (selection 64) when he sees the true nature of the colonialism he upholds in his position as police chief. This theme is further explored in Jaana Parkkinen's essay "Why They Hated Us" (selection 65), which explodes the myth of the benign British empire with researched evidence. Nawal el-Saadawi's focus is a little different in "Love and Sex in the Life of the Arab" (selection 62), which criticizes the treatment of women in her culture. Nina Easton's "Manufactured Images: How Women Appear in Advertising" (selection 61) looks equally critically at some ways in which we treat women right here in America.

It is not easy to decide who we are, especially when we are told so many contradictory things about ourselves. It may be distressing, too, to admit to ourselves that we are less than perfect, that our actions are not admirable, that we are insecure, apathetic, or unloved. But the writers in Part Eight have done this with an honesty that is difficult not to respond to. They prove to us that even when it is painful and time-consuming, even when it destroys the comfortable myths by which we have lived our lives, seeing ourselves is ultimately worth everything it costs us.

PREREADING ACTIVITY

Before reading selection 59, write about some of the earliest stories you recall being told, sung, or read to you. How did they shape your ideas about the universe and yourself? Who introduced you to them?

Where I Come From Is Like This

PAULA GUNN ALLEN

Paula Gunn Allen (1939–), originally from New Mexico, is part Laguna Pueblo, part Sioux, and part Chicana. Out of this rich and complex heritage came her novel *The Woman Who Owned the Shadows*. Allen is a poet and essayist as well as a novelist and has been widely anthologized. She has taught at various universities, including the University of California at Berkeley and at Los Angeles. The selection here is from the anthology *The Sacred Hoop: Recovering the Feminine in American Indian Traditions*.

I

*M*odern American Indian women, like their non-Indian sisters, are deeply engaged in the struggle to redefine themselves. In their struggle they must reconcile traditional tribal definitions of women with industrial and postindustrial non-Indian definitions. Yet while these definitions seem to be more or less mutually exclusive, Indian women must somehow harmonize and integrate both in their own lives.

An American Indian woman is primarily defined by her tribal identity. In her eyes, her destiny is necessarily that of her people, and her sense of herself as a woman is first and foremost prescribed by her tribe. The definitions of woman's roles are as diverse as tribal cultures in the Americas. In some she is devalued, in others she wields considerable power. In some she is a familial/clan adjunct, in some she is as close to autonomous as her economic circumstances and psychological traits permit. But in no tribal definitions is she perceived in the same way as are women in Western industrial and postindustrial cultures.

Source: From *The Sacred Hoop* by Paula Gunn Allen. Copyright © 1986 by Paula Gunn Allen. Reprinted by permission of Beacon Press.

In the West, few images of women form part of the cultural mythos, and   3
these are largely sexually charged. Among Christians, the Madonna is the female
prototype, and she is portrayed as essentially passive: her contribution is simply
that of birthing. Little else is attributed to her and she certainly possesses few of
the characteristics that are attributed to mythic figures among Indian tribes. This
image is countered (rather than balanced) by the witch-goddess/whore characteristics designed to reinforce cultural beliefs about women, as well as Western
adversarial and dualistic perceptions of reality.

The tribes see women variously, but they do not question the power of fem-   4
ininity. Sometimes they see women as fearful, sometimes peaceful, sometimes
omnipotent and omniscient, but they never portray women as mindless, helpless,
simple, or oppressed. And while the women in a given tribe, clan, or band may be
all these things, the individual woman is provided with a variety of images of women
from the interconnected supernatural, natural, and social worlds she lives in.

As a half-breed American Indian woman, I cast about in my mind for neg-   5
ative images of Indian women, and I find none that are directed to Indian women
alone. The negative images I do have are of Indians in general and in fact are
more often of males than of females. All these images come to me from non-
Indian sources, and they are always balanced by a positive image. My ideas of
womanhood, passed on largely by my mother and grandmothers, Laguna Pueblo
women, are about practicality, strength, reasonableness, intelligence, wit, and
competence. I also remember vividly the women who came to my father's store,
the women who held me and sang to me, the women at Feast Day, at Grab Days,
the women in the kitchen of my Cubero home, the women I grew up with; none
of them appeared weak or helpless, none of them presented herself tentatively. I
remember a certain reserve on those lovely brown faces; I remember the direct
gaze of eyes framed by bright-colored shawls draped over their heads and cascad-
ing down their backs. I remember the clean cotton dresses and carefully pressed
hand-embroidered aprons they always wore; I remember laughter and good food,
especially the sweet bread and the oven bread they gave us. Nowhere in my mind
is there a foolish woman, a dumb woman, a vain woman, or a plastic woman,
though the Indian women I have known have shown a wide range of personal
style and demeanor.

My memory includes the Navajo woman who was badly beaten by her   6
Sioux husband; but I also remember that my grandmother abandoned her Sioux
husband long ago. I recall the stories about the Laguna woman beaten regularly
by her husband in the presence of her children so that the children would not
believe in the strength and power of femininity. And I remember the women who
drank, who got into fights with other women and with the men, and who often
won those battles. I have memories of tired women, partying women, stubborn
women, sullen women, amicable women, selfish women, shy women, and aggressive women. Most of all I remember the women who laugh and scold and sit
uncomplaining in the long sun on feast days and who cook wonderful food on
wood stoves, in beehive mud ovens, and over open fires outdoors.

Among the images of women that come to me from various tribes as well as   7
my own are White Buffalo Woman, who came to the Lakota long ago and brought

them the religion of the Sacred Pipe which they still practice; Tinotzin the goddess who came to Juan Diego to remind him that she still walked the hills of her people and sent him with her message, her demand, and her proof to the Catholic bishop in the city nearby. And from Laguna I take the images of Yellow Woman, Coyote Woman, Grandmother Spider (Spider Old Woman), who brought the light, who gave us weaving and medicine, who gave us life. Among the Keres she is known as Thought Woman who created us all and who keeps us in creation even now. I remember Iyatiku, Earth Woman, Corn Woman, who guides and counsels the people to peace and who welcomes us home when we cast off this coil of flesh as huskers cast off the leaves that wrap the corn. I remember Iyatiku's sister, Sun Woman, who held metals and cattle, pigs and sheep, highways and engines and so many things in her bundle, who went away to the east saying that one day she would return.

II

Since the coming of the Anglo-Europeans beginning in the fifteenth century, the fragile web of identity that long held tribal people secure has gradually been weakened and torn. But the oral tradition has prevented the complete destruction of the web, the ultimate disruption of tribal ways. The oral tradition is vital; it heals itself and the tribal web by adapting to the flow of the present while never relinquishing its connection to the past. Its adaptability has always been required, as many generations have experienced. Certainly the modern American Indian woman bears slight resemblance to her forebears—at least on superficial examination—but she is still a tribal woman in her deepest being. Her tribal sense of relationship to all that is continues to flourish. And though she is at times beset by her knowledge of the enormous gap between the life she lives and the life she was raised to live, and while she adapts her mind and being to the circumstances of her present life, she does so in tribal ways, mending the tears in the web of being from which she takes her existence as she goes. [8]

My mother told me stories all the time, though I often did not recognize them as that. My mother told me stories about cooking and childbearing; she told me stories about menstruation and pregnancy; she told me stories about gods and heroes, about fairies and elves, about goddesses and spirits; she told me stories about the land and the sky, about cats and dogs, about snakes and spiders; she told me stories about climbing trees and exploring the mesas; she told me stories about going to dances and getting married; she told me stories about dressing and undressing, about sleeping and waking; she told me stories about herself, about her mother, about her grandmother. She told me stories about grieving and laughing, about thinking and doing; she told me stories about school and about people; about darning and mending; she told me stories about turquoise and about gold; she told me European stories and Laguna stories; she told me Catholic stories and Presbyterian stories; she told me city stories and country stories; she told me political stories and religious stories. She told me stories about living and stories about dying. And in all of those stories she told me who I was, who I was supposed to be, whom I came from, and who would follow me. In this [9] way she taught me the meaning of the words she said, that all life is a circle and everything has a place within it. That's what she said and what she showed me in the things she did and the way she lives.

Of course, through my formal, white, Christian education, I discovered that other people had stories of their own—about women, about Indians, about fact, about reality—and I was amazed by a number of startling suppositions that others made about tribal customs and beliefs. According to the un-Indian, non-Indian view, for instance, Indians barred menstruating women from ceremonies and indeed segregated them from the rest of the people, consigning them to some space specially designed for them. This showed that Indians considered menstruating women unclean and not fit to enjoy the company of decent (non-menstruating) people, that is, men. I was surprised and confused to hear this because my mother had taught me that white people had strange attitudes toward menstruation: they thought something was bad about it, that it meant you were sick, cursed, sinful, and weak and that you had to be very careful during that time. She taught me that menstruation was a normal occurrence, that I could go swimming or hiking or whatever else I wanted to do during my period. She actively scorned women who took to their beds, who were incapacitated by cramps, who "got the blues." 10

As I struggled to reconcile these very contradictory interpretations of American Indians' traditional beliefs concerning menstruation, I realized that the menstrual taboos were about power, not about sin or filth. My conclusion was later borne out by some tribes' own explanations, which, as you may well imagine, came as quite a relief to me. 11

The truth of the matter as many Indians see it is that women who are at the peak of their fecundity are believed to possess power that throws male power totally out of kilter. They emit such force that, in their presence, any male-owned or -dominated ritual or sacred object cannot do its usual task. For instance, the Lakota say that a menstruating woman anywhere near a yuwipi man, who is a special sort of psychic, spirit-empowered healer, for a day or so before he is to do his ceremony will effectively disempower him. Conversely, among many if not most tribes, important ceremonies cannot be held without the presence of women. Sometimes the ritual woman who empowers the ceremony must be unmarried and virginal so that the power she channels is unalloyed, unweakened by sexual arousal and penetration by a male. Other ceremonies require tumescent women, others the presence of mature women who have borne children, and still others depend for empowerment on postmenopausal women. Women may be segregated from the company of the whole band or village on certain occasions, but on certain occasions men are also segregated. In short, each ritual depends on a certain balance of power, and the positions of women within the phases of womanhood are used by tribal people to empower certain rites. This does not derive from a male-dominant view; it is not a ritual observance imposed on women by men. It derives from a tribal view of reality that distinguishes tribal people from feudal and industrial people. 12

Among the tribes, the occult power of women, inextricably bound to our hormonal life, is thought to be very great; many hold that we possess innately the blood- 13 given power to kill—with a glance, with a step, or with a judicious mixing of menstrual blood into somebody's soup. Medicine women among the Pomo of California cannot practice until they are sufficiently mature; when they are immature, their power is diffuse and is likely to interfere with their practice until time and experience have it under control. So women of the tribes are not especially inclined to see themselves as poor helpless victims of male domination. Even in those tribes where something akin to male domination was present, women are perceived as powerful, socially, physically, and metaphysically. In times past, as in times present, women carried enormous burdens with aplomb. We were far indeed from the "weaker sex," the designation that white aristocratic sisters unhappily earned for us all.

I remember my mother moving furniture all over the house when she wanted   14 it changed. She didn't wait for my father to come home and help—she just went ahead and moved the piano, a huge upright from the old days, the couch, the refrigerator. Nobody had told her she was too weak to do such things. In imitation of her, I would delight in loading trucks at my father's store with cases of pop or fifty-pound sacks of flour. Even when I was quite small I could do it, and it gave me a belief in my own physical strength that advancing middle age can't quite erase. My mother used to tell me about the Acoma Pueblo women she had seen as a child carrying huge ollas (water pots) on their heads as they wound their way up the tortuous stairwell carved into the face of the "Sky City" mesa, a feat I tried to imitate with books and tin buckets. ("Sky City" is the term used by the chamber of commerce for the mother village of Acoma, which is situated atop a high sandstone table mountain.) I was never very successful, but even the attempt reminded me that I was supposed to be strong and balanced to be a proper girl.

Of course, my mother's Laguna people are Keres Indian, reputed to be the   15 last extreme mother-right people on earth. So it is no wonder that I got notably nonwhite notions about the natural strength and prowess of women. Indeed, it is only when I am trying to get non-Indian approval, recognition, or acknowledgment that my "weak sister" emotional and intellectual ploys get the better of my tribal woman's good sense. At such times I forget that I just moved the piano or just wrote a competent paper or just completed a financial transaction satisfactorily or have supported myself and my children for most of my adult life.

Nor is my contradictory behavior atypical. Most Indian women I know are   16 in the same bicultural bind: we vacillate between being dependent and strong, self-reliant and powerless, strongly motivated and hopelessly insecure. We resolve the dilemma in various ways: some of us party all the time; some of us drink to excess; some of us travel and move around a lot; some of us land good jobs and then quit them; some of us engage in violent exchanges; some of us blow our brains out. We act in these destructive ways because we suffer from the societal conflicts caused by having to identify with two hopelessly opposed cultural definitions of women. Through this destructive dissonance we are unhappy prey to the self-disparagement common to, indeed demanded of, Indians living in the United States today. Our situation is caused by the exigencies of a history of invasion, conquest, and colonization whose searing marks are probably ineradicable. A popular bumper sticker on many Indian cars proclaims: "If You're Indian You're In," to which I always find myself adding under my breath, "Trouble."

III

No Indian can grow to any age without being informed that her people [17] were "savages" who interfered with the march of progress pursued by respectable, loving, civilized white people. We are the villains of the scenario when we are mentioned at all. We are absent from much of white history except when we are calmly, rationally, succinctly, and systematically dehumanized. On the few occasions we are noticed in any way other than as howling, bloodthirsty beings, we are acclaimed for our noble quaintness. In this definition, we are exotic curios. Our ancient arts and customs are used to draw tourist money to state coffers, into the pocketbooks and bank accounts of scholars, and into support of the American-in-Disneyland promoters' dream.

As a Roman Catholic child I was treated to bloody tales of how the savage [18] Indians martyred the hapless priests and missionaries who went among them in an attempt to lead them to the one true path. By the time I was through high school I had the idea that Indians were people who had benefited mightily from the advanced knowledge and superior morality of the Anglo-Europeans. At least I had, perforce, that idea to lay beside the other one that derived from my daily experience of Indian life, an idea less dehumanizing and more accurate because it came from my mother and the other Indian people who raised me. That idea was that Indians are a people who don't tell lies, who care for their children and their old people. You never see an Indian orphan, they said. You always know when you're old that someone will take care of you—one of your children will. Then they'd list the old folks who were being taken care of by this child or that. No child is ever considered illegitimate among the Indians, they said. If a girl gets pregnant, the baby is still part of the family, and the mother is too. That's what they said, and they showed me real people who lived according to those principles.

Of course the ravages of colonization have taken their toll; there are [19] orphans in Indian country now, and abandoned, brutalized old folks; there are even illegitimate children, though the very concept still strikes me as absurd. There are battered children and neglected children, and there are battered wives and women who have been raped by Indian men. Proximity to the "civilizing" effects of white Christians has not improved the moral quality of life in Indian country, though each group, Indian and white, explains the situation differently. Nor is there much yet in the oral tradition that can enable us to adapt to these inhuman changes. But a force is growing in that direction, and it is helping Indian women reclaim their lives. Their power, their sense of direction and of self will soon be visible. It is the force of the women who speak and work and write, and it is formidable.

Through all the centuries of war and death and cultural and psychic destruc- [20] tion have endured the women who raise the children and tend the fires, who pass along the tales and the traditions, who weep and bury the dead, who are the dead, and who never forget. There are always the women, who make pots and weave baskets, who fashion clothes and cheer their children on at powwow, who make fry bread and piki bread, and corn soup and chili stew, who dance and sing and remember and hold within their hearts the dream of their ancient peoples—

that one day the woman who thinks will speak to us again, and everywhere there will be peace. Meanwhile we tell the stories of fun and scandal and laugh over all manner of things that happen every day. We watch and we wait.

My great-grandmother told my mother: Never forget you are Indian. And my mother told me the same thing. This, then, is how I have gone about remembering, so that my children will remember too.   21

QUESTIONS FOR CRITICAL READING, THINKING, DISCUSSION, AND WRITING

Analyzing Content and Technique

1. Which images of women from the western tradition does Allen write about? According to her, what do they symbolize? Do you agree or disagree with her? Can you think of other "mythic" images of women from the western tradition?

2. Which images of women from Native American tradition does Allen focus on? What are some of their characteristics? To Allen, what overall sense of womanhood do they give?

3. What role does oral tradition play in tribal culture? Give examples from Allen's essay and from your own cultural experience.

4. What are some of the "startling suppositions" that Allen has found outsiders to make about Native American culture? What, according to her experience and understanding, is the truth? What attitude toward women is implied in this "truth"?

5. Describe the "contradictory behavior" that Allen often sees in herself. Analyze the reasons for this kind of behavior. What larger conclusion can you draw from Allen's examples?

6. According to Allen, what is the "white" view of the effect of colonization on Native Americans? Where does this view come from? Compare this with Allen's own understanding of the matter. Which view are you more convinced by? Explain.

Collaborative Activity

Discuss, as a group, what you were taught at school about Native Americans. What sources did your information come from? What was the focus of these sources? Do you think they gave you sufficient knowledge? Now write a collaborative paragraph about what you have learned from Allen's essay that was new and different from your previous knowledge.

Making Connections

1. Allen states that her purpose in writing is to ensure that her children will know what it is to be Native Americans. What major points does she present about the identity of the Native American woman? In this connection, read a piece by a male writer from a Native American tradition. What additional aspects of the Native American identity are presented in his writing? Write an essay in which you put the ideas of both writers together to create a composite picture of Native American identity.

2. Write an essay clarifying (as Allen has done) what it means to be a person of your culture. You may want to touch on some of the following points: your race, your sex, your role models, some of the stories you grew up with, stereotypical assumptions held by outsiders about your community, and conflicts you experience as you try to live in the present-day United States.

60

PREREADING ACTIVITY

Make a list of what you think society considers male and female responsibilities. Circle the items you disagree with. How far are you in agreement with society's dictates?

The Men We Carry in Our Minds

SCOTT RUSSELL SANDERS

Scott Russell Sanders (1945–   ) teaches at Indiana University and writes for many publications, including the *Chicago Sun-Times*. His writings are of many kinds: fiction, folktales, historical novels, children's books, and essays. They have appeared in magazines such as *North American Review, Omni,* and *Georgia Review.* Sanders has been awarded many fellowships, including one from the National Endowment for the Arts. His recent books include *Stone Country, Bad Man Ballad,* and *The Paradise of Bombs,* from which selection 60 is reprinted.

"*T*his must be a hard time for women," I say to my friend Anneke.   1
"They have so many paths to choose from, and so many voices calling them."

"I think it's a lot harder for men," she replies.   2

"How do you figure that?"   3

"The women I know feel excited, innocent, like crusaders in a just cause.   4
The men I know are eaten up with guilt."

We are sitting at the kitchen table drinking sassafras tea, our hands wrapped   5
around the mugs because this April morning is cool and drizzly. "Like a Dutch
morning," Anneke told me earlier. She is Dutch herself, a writer and midwife and
peacemaker, with the round face and sad eyes of a woman in a Vermeer painting
who might be waiting for the rain to stop, for a door to open. She leans over to
sniff a sprig of lilac, pale lavender, that rises from a vase of cobalt blue.

"Women feel such pressure to be everything, do everything," I say. "Career,   6
kids, art, politics. Have their babies and get back to the office a week later. It's as
if they're trying to overcome a million years' worth of evolution in one lifetime."

"But we help one another. We don't try to lumber on alone, like too many   7
wounded grizzly bears, the way men do." Anneke sips her tea. I gave her the mug
with the owls on it, for wisdom. "And we have this deep-down sense that we're in
the *right*—we've been held back, passed over, used—while men feel they're in the
wrong. Men are the ones who've been discredited, who have to search their souls."

I search my soul. I discover guilty feelings aplenty—toward the poor, the   8
Vietnamese, Native Americans, the whales, an endless list of debts—a guilt in
each case that is as bright and unambiguous as a neon sign. But toward women I
feel something more confused, a snarl of shame, envy, wary tenderness, and
amazement. This muddle troubles me. To hide my unease I say, "You're right, it's
tough being a man these days."

"Don't laugh," Anneke frowns at me, mournful-eyed, through the sassafras   9
steam. "I wouldn't be a man for anything. It's much easier being the victim. All
the victim has to do is break free. The persecutor has to live with his past."

How deep is that past? I find myself wondering after Anneke has left. How   10
much of an inheritance do I have to throw off? Is it just the beliefs I breathed in
as a child? Do I have to scour memory back through father and grandfather?
Through St. Paul? Beyond Stonehenge and into the twilit caves? I'm convinced
the past we must contend with is deeper even than speech. When I think back on
my childhood, on how I learned to see men and women, I have a sense of
ancient, dizzying depths. The back roads of Tennessee and Ohio where I grew up
were probably closer, in their sexual patterns, to the campsites of Stone Age
hunters than to the genderless cities of the future into which we are rushing.

The first men, besides my father, I remember seeing were black convicts and   11
white guards, in the cottonfield across the road from our farm on the outskirts of
Memphis. I must have been three or four. The prisoners wore dingy gray-and-
black zebra suits, heavy as canvas, sodden with sweat. Hatless, stooped, they
chopped weeds in the fierce heat, row after row, breathing the acrid dust of boll-
weevil poison. The overseers wore dazzling white shirts and broad shadowy hats.
The oiled barrels of their shotguns flashed in the sunlight. Their faces in memory
are utterly blank. Of course those men, white and black, have become for me an
emblem of racial hatred. But they have also come to stand for the twin poles of
my early vision of manhood—the brute toiling animal and the boss.

When I was a boy, the men I knew labored with their bodies. They were mar-   12
ginal farmers, just scraping by, or welders, steelworkers, carpenters; they swept
floors, dug ditches, mined coal, or drove trucks, their forearms ropy with muscle;
they trained horses, stoked furnaces, built tires, stood on assembly lines wrestling
parts onto cars and refrigerators. They got up before light, worked all day long whatever the weather, and when they came home at night they looked as though somebody had been whipping them. In the evenings and on weekends they worked on
their own places, tilling gardens that were lumpy with clay, fixing broken-down cars,
hammering on houses that were always too drafty, too leaky, too small.

The bodies of the men I knew were twisted and maimed in ways visible and   13
invisible. The nails of their hands were black and split, the hands tattooed with
scars. Some had lost fingers. Heavy lifting had given many of them finicky backs
and guts weak from hernias. Racing against conveyor belts had given them ulcers.

Their ankles and knees ached from years of standing on concrete. Anyone who had worked for long around machines was hard of hearing. They squinted, and the skin of their faces was creased like the leather of old work gloves. There were times, studying them, when I dreaded growing up. Most of them coughed, from dust or cigarettes, and most of them drank cheap wine or whiskey, so their eyes looked bloodshot and bruised. The fathers of my friends always seemed older than the mothers. Men wore out sooner. Only women lived into old age.

As a boy I also knew another sort of men, who did not sweat and break down like mules. They were soldiers, and so far as I could tell they scarcely worked at all. During my early school years we lived on a military base, an arsenal in Ohio, and every day I saw GIs in the guardshacks, on the stoops of barracks, at the wheels of olive drab Chevrolets. The chief fact of their lives was boredom. Long after I left the Arsenal I came to recognize the sour smell the soldiers gave off as that of souls in limbo. They were all waiting—for wars, for transfers, for leaves, for promotions, for the end of their hitch—like so many braves waiting for the hunt to begin. Unlike the warriors of older tribes, however, they would have no say about when the battle would start or how it would be waged. Their waiting was broken only when they practiced for war. They fired guns at targets, drove tanks across the churned-up fields of the military reservation, set off bombs in the wrecks of old fighter planes. I knew this was all play. But I also felt certain that when the hour for killing arrived, they would kill. When the real shooting started, many of them would die. This was what soldiers were *for,* just as a hammer was for driving nails.

Warriors and toilers: those seemed, in my boyhood vision, to be the chief destinies for men. They weren't the only destinies, as I learned from having a few male teachers, from reading books, and from watching television. But the men on television—the politicians, the astronauts, the generals, the savvy lawyers, the philosophical doctors, the bosses who gave orders to both soldiers and laborers—seemed as remote and unreal to me as the figures in tapestries. I could no more imagine growing up to become one of these cool, potent creatures than I could imagine becoming a prince.

A nearer and more hopeful example was that of my father, who had escaped from a red-dirt farm to a tire factory, and from the assembly line to the front office. Eventually he dressed in a white shirt and tie. He carried himself as if he had been born to work with his mind. But his body, remembering the earlier years of slogging work, began to give out on him in his fifties, and it quit on him entirely before he turned sixty-five. Even such a partial escape from man's fate as he had accomplished did not seem possible for most of the boys I knew. They joined the army, stood in line for jobs in the smoky plants, helped build highways. They were bound to work as their fathers had worked, killing themselves or preparing to kill others.

A scholarship enabled me not only to attend college, a rare enough feat in my circle, but even to study in a university meant for the children of the rich. Here I met for the first time young men who had assumed from birth that they would lead lives of comfort and power. And for the first time I met women who told me that men were guilty of having kept all the joys and privileges of the earth for themselves. I was baffled. What privileges? What joys? I thought about the maimed, dismal lives of most of the men back home. What had they stolen from their wives and daughters? The right to go five days a week, twelve months a year, for thirty or forty years to a steel mill or a coal mine? The right to drop bombs and die in war? The right to feel every leak in the roof, every gap in the fence, every cough in the engine, as a wound they must mend? The right to feel, when the lay-off comes or the plant shuts down, not only afraid but ashamed?

I was slow to understand the deep grievances of women. This was because, as a boy, I had envied them. Before college, the only people I had ever known who were interested in art or music or literature, the only ones who read books, the only ones who ever seemed to enjoy a sense of ease and grace were the mothers and daughters. Like the menfolk, they fretted about money, they scrimped and made-do. But, when the pay stopped coming in, they were not the ones who had failed. Nor did they have to go to war, and that seemed to me a blessed fact. By comparison with the narrow, ironclad days of fathers, there was an expansiveness, I thought, in the days of mothers. They went to see neighbors, to shop in town, to run errands at school, at the library, at church. No doubt, had I looked harder at their lives, I would have envied them less. It was not my fate to become a woman, so it was easier for me to see the graces. Few of them held jobs outside the home, and those who did filled thankless roles as clerks and waitresses. I didn't see, then, what a prison a house could be, since houses seemed to me brighter, handsomer places than any factory. I did not realize—because such things were never spoken of—how often women suffered from men's bullying. I did learn about the wretchedness of abandoned wives, single mothers, widows; but I also learned about the wretchedness of lone men. Even then I could see how exhausting it was for a mother to cater all day to the needs of young children. But if I had been asked, as a boy, to choose between tending a baby and tending a machine, I think I would have chosen the baby. (Having now tended both, I know I would choose the baby.)

So I was baffled when the women at college accused me and my sex of having cornered the world's pleasures. I think something like my bafflement has been felt by other boys (and by girls as well) who grew up in dirt-poor farm country, in mining country, in black ghettos, in Hispanic barrios, in the shadows of factories, in Third World nations—any place where the fate of men is as grim and bleak as the fate of women. Toilers and warriors. I realize now how ancient these identities are, how deep the tug they exert on men, the undertow of a thousand generations. The miseries I saw, as a boy, in the lives of nearly all men I continue to see in the lives of many—the body-breaking toil, the tedium, the call to be tough, the humiliating powerlessness, the battle for a living and for territory.

When the women I met at college thought about the joys and privileges of men, they did not carry in their minds the sort of men I had known in my childhood. They thought of their fathers, who were bankers, physicians, architects, stockbrokers, the big wheels of the big cities. These fathers rode the train to work or drove cars that cost more than any of my childhood houses. They were attended from morning to night by female helpers, wives, and nurses and secretaries. They were never laid off, never short of cash at month's end, never lined up for welfare. These fathers made decisions that mattered. They ran the world.

The daughters of such men wanted to share in this power, this glory. So did 21
I. They yearned for a say over their future, for jobs worthy of their abilities, for
the right to live at peace, unmolested, whole. Yes, I thought, yes yes. The difference between me and these daughters was that they saw me, because of my sex,
as destined from birth to become like their fathers, and therefore as an enemy to
their desires. But I knew better. I wasn't an enemy, in fact or in feeling. I was an
ally. If I had known, then, how to tell them so, would they have believed me?
Would they now?

QUESTIONS FOR CRITICAL READING, THINKING, DISCUSSION, AND WRITING

Analyzing Content and Technique

1. Sanders's friend Anneke tells him that she believes things are harder for men today than for
   women. What does she mean? Do you agree? Why or why not?
2. Do you agree with Sanders that things are harder for women? Evaluate his reasons.
3. Describe the male role models that Sanders has grown up with. What conclusion does he draw
   from them about the destinies of men?
4. How did Sanders view women as he was growing up? How has his vision changed, and how
   has his understanding deepened?
5. Analyze the kind of conflict Sanders faced when he went to college. Why did he experience
   this?
6. Throughout the essay, Sanders compares and contrasts various male roles. With each, he
   offers descriptive details that symbolize an aspect of the men's lifestyles. Choose a few that
   you find particularly effective and explain their significance.

Collaborative Activity

As a group, find the thesis of the essay. Now examine the conclusion. How does it reinforce the
thesis? How effective is it? Write a collaborative conclusion of a different kind for the essay.

Making Connections

1. Who are some of the role models that helped you shape your identity as a man or a woman?
   (These may be people you know, or celebrities, or imaginary characters.) Write an essay
   explaining what they have taught you about your position in society as a male or a female, and
   what they reveal about your culture.
2. Several of the selections in this book deal with the issue that Sanders brings up: Is life tougher
   today for men or for women? Examine the point of view of two or three selections in addition
   to Sanders's, and present your own conclusion.

61

PREREADING ACTIVITY

Consider the title. What pictures does it conjure up in your mind? Do a brainstorming exercise in which you write down three or four different kinds of images that you can think of.

Manufactured Images: How Women Appear in Advertising

NINA EASTON

Nina Easton is a staff writer for the *Los Angeles Times Magazine* and has written for a wide variety of national newspapers and magazines. She is the coauthor of *Reagan Ruling Class* and the author of *Woman Take Charge* (1983), from which the following article was taken.

"The most valuable educational experience a woman can have is one which 1
teaches her to identify and analyze—and resist—the conditions in which she lives,
the morality she has been taught, the false images of herself received from high art
as well as cheap pornography, classic poetry as well as TV commercials."

Adrienne Rich

Ever since the emergence of mass advertising encouraging people to 2
consume—and to keep consuming—Madison Avenue has instilled in women
insecurities and anxiety about their looks, their housekeeping, their relationships,
even their natural body processes. In return, the ad makers have offered products
that promise to relieve those very feelings of inadequacy it nurtured in the first place.

Advertising has taught men contempt for women and women contempt for 3
themselves. It steals a woman's "love of herself as she is and offers it back to her
for the price of a product," writes critic and novelist John Berger.[1]

- How many women feared dishpan hands before Madge warned them about it? 4
- Who worried about "ring-around-the-collar" until the makers of Wisk told 5
  them to? (TV commercial: Woman at a square dance, looking at man's shirt

---

[1]Berger, John, *Ways of Seeing* (Penguin, BBC, London, 1972), p. 134.

exclaims—"Ring around the collar!" Woman with man winces; later she's seen scrubbing wildly.)[2]

- Were "panty lines" a vital issue for women before Underalls? [6]
- What about feminine odor, of which we all now live in deathly fear? (Ad in [7] *TV Guide:* A couple embracing next to the words, "Female Odor is Everyone's Problem.")
- Who was concerned about how their clothes smelled until Downy Fabric Softener [8] warned women they risked losing the respect of their loved ones if they did not?
- Who ever heard of "split ends" before makers of hair conditioners found them [9] to be an effective means of selling their product? And what ever happened to "split ends"? Now, they have been replaced by the quest for "PH balance."
- Who feared pervasive household germs before the 1920s, when Lysol began warn- [10] ing mothers that even "the doorknobs threaten [children] . . . with disease"?[3]

Advertising has manufactured these concerns in two ways. First it has [11] sharply defined the role of a woman based on old-fashioned stereotypes; then it has defined a woman's success by her achievement in those roles. She is depicted, principally, as a homebody. Anyone who watches daytime television is familiar with the frequency with which women are shown as happy housewives, and the rarity of men depicted doing household chores or caring for children.

Advertising, of course, did not create these stereotypes. But it plays a large [12] role in perpetuating them and encouraging women to fulfill them. "Advertising is the worst offender in perpetuating the image of women as sex symbols and an inferior class of human being," concluded the United Nations Commission on the Status of Women. . . .

A Woman's Place

Since the industrial revolution, women have been trained as the purchasing [13] agents and managers of their households. "While women were cultivated as general purchasing managers for the household, the basic definition of *men* in the ads was as bread-winners, wage earners," writes Stuart Ewen.[4]

During the early part of the 20th century, advertisers offered housewives [14] thousands of new products and machines that promised to free them from household drudgery—vacuum cleaners, toasters, electric blenders, can openers, washing machines. But housework remained a full-time job, as women were exhorted to pay attention to minute details in their household. At the end of the day she would still be exhausted. "Rather than viewing the transformation as labor-saving, it is perhaps more useful to view them as labor changing," writes Ewen. . . .

Despite the influx of women into the job market over the past two decades [15] most advertisers have continued to assume that the home is still only a woman's domain. And despite the rise of single men living alone, advertisers still insisted

[2]Cited in "Channeling Children, Sex Stereotypes on Prime Time TV," in *Women on Words and Images* (Princeton, 1975).
[3]Cited in Ewen, Stuart, *Captains of Consciousness* (McGraw-Hill 1976), p. 170.
[4]Ewen, p. 153.

that only women are interested in such things as bathroom cleaners. "I assume that most kitchen products are used by women and that men don't give a damn about them, even bachelors," said one advertising executive. "Since women are the major consumers, the main purpose of such an advertisement is to present a product in an average situation, usually the kitchen, being used by an average type person—the middle class housewife."[5]

He of course neglected to add that advertising has not instilled in men the kinds of fears and anxieties over household cleaning that it has instilled in women. Clean floors and germ free bathrooms have become an obsession for the American housewife.   16

Advertising has defined the successful housewife in this way. To be an accomplished homemaker, she must have polished floors and furniture—no waxy buildup—bright and sweet-smelling laundry, and shining silver. To be a good mother, her cake has to be moist and the family's toilet paper soft.   17

It is not any one ad, or even a pool of ads, that is damaging to women's image. As a 1977 study by the Canadian Advertising Advisory Board explained, "it is the cumulative impact of a whole series of commercials showing household products in use, with women demonstrating the products—often with enthusiasm bordering on ecstasy . . . [that viewers] find incredible, hilarious or insulting."   18

Though household cleanliness is certainly an admirable goal, the study's authors note wryly, "when cleanliness becomes an obsession . . . it reflects a strange set of priorities bordering on emotional ill health." . . .   19

"Fly Me: I'm Barbara"

The second role of a woman in advertising is that of sex-object. In ads aimed at men, sexy young models in skimpy gowns are used as decorative commercial props—for cars, office equipment, stereos, alcohol. *MS.* magazine regularly chastises the worst offenders in its "No Comment" column: the Viking Leisure Products ad with a naked woman stepping into a sauna and copy that reads "Just what you need around the office;" or the scantily clad nymph straddling a man's leg, pulling off his boot, underneath the words, "treat 'em good and they'll treat you good." Are they advertising the boot or the woman?   20

The 1971 Courtney and Lockeretz study found that advertising teaches the public that men regard women primarily as sex objects and are not interested in them as people. With the prevalence of alluring young blonde saying, "take it off, take it all off," and attractive young stewardesses saying, "Fly me, I'm Barbara," in those days, the study's findings are not surprising. Those types of ads, said media analyst Dr. Jean Kilbourne, have a "cumulative unconscious impact" on the public, preaching that "a woman's body is just another piece of merchandise."[6]   21

Women, of course, are offered products to enhance their roles as sex objects. "The first duty of a woman is to attract," said a perfume ad from the   22

---

[5]Packard, Vance. *The Hidden Persuaders* (Pocket Books, New York, 1980), cited on page 237.
[6]ABC interview with Kilbourne on "The Last Word." Other Kilbourne quotes from interview with author, November, 1982.

1920s. "It does not matter how clever or independent you may be, if you fail to influence the men you meet, consciously or unconsciously, you are not fulfilling your fundamental duty as a woman . . ." Advertisements since then have been more subtle but the message is the same. . . .

Changing Times?

Many advertisers are starting to portray women in professional roles and outside the home, while men now change diapers and clean bathrooms and clothes. But have things changed much? 23

"No" is the emphatic answer of Jean Kilbourne. "I've done content analysis [of ads] and it has not changed to the extent we think. Women are still overwhelmingly shown in the home and as sex objects." . . . 24

What are the images the ad makers push? 25

Youth is peddled as compulsory: A man looks distinguished with a little gray around the temples, women look haggard. According to one study only 16 percent of the women shown in television commercials are over 40, while 44 percent of the men shown are over 40.[7] If one were exposed only to the 1,500 advertisements that bombard us each day, one would assume women in America die or go into hiding shortly after age 35. 26

So is thin. Diet soda, diet pills, diet sweeteners, are all directed principally at women. Drink one-calorie Tab, and look like the pert young blonde with colt-like legs in minishorts who trots by men as their heads turn. Now even vitamins are peddled as the perfect complement to a rigorous diet. Often women receive mixed signals: an ad for luscious Sara Lee cake will run into an ad for diet pills or diet soda. This obsession with body weight has produced in women serious inferiority complexes—since few of us can reach that ideal body—and severe eating disorders. At college campuses about 20 percent of the women suffer from serious eating disorders, either anorexia—a neurotic fear of food that leaves women looking like skeletons—or bulimia—the binge-vomit syndrome.[8]. . . 27

Advertisers continue to skillfully prey on women's insecurities. But now they show a sexy business executive instead of a secretary. The Charlie girl is free, independent—and beautiful. The attractive Virginia Slims women flaunt their "liberation." . . . 28

Today women are told how to attract men—not at home but in the business world. Women are taught to use Oil of Olay not only to attract their husbands, but to rise up the corporate ladder. "Would looking younger make you feel more confident at work?" asks the new magazine ads for Oil of Olay (a way of telling women reentering the workforce that they *should* feel insecure about their age). "You know you're good at your job," the ad continues. "Running a household and raising a family gave you the inventiveness and organizational expertise that are necessary in the business world. You're already preparing for 29

---

[7]Butler, Matilda and Paisley, William, *Women and Mass Media* (Human Services Press, New York, 1980), p. 77.
[8]Estimate by Kilbourne.

the next step, going to adult education classes or maybe a company training program to acquire additional skills. But sometimes, when they hire a new coworker fresh out of school, with a bright young face and bright ideas, you wonder if you're moving ahead as rapidly as you should. That's when looking young could well give your confidence a welcome boost."

Attractiveness, ironically, also works against women. They find themselves in a double bind; advertising tells women to be attractive, yet studies show that physical attractiveness handicaps women in the business world because they are more likely to be considered mindless by their male colleagues.[9]

The superwoman image now pushed by advertisers is a good example of how the situation is not really improving, just changing. "You know the superwoman," said marketing research manager Laurie Ashcraft in a recent speech. "She's the one wearing Enjoli who 'brings home the bacon and fries it up in the pan' and waltzes off to an Aviance night . . . The superwoman puts in a full day on the job, she's a model mother, serves three course dinners and hot breakfasts and has time and energy for romance while the children are asleep."[10]

The Power of Suggestion

Suggestiveness, alluring images, rather than claims on the merits of the product itself, are commonly used in selling to women. John Berger writes that advertising "proposes to each one of us that we transform ourselves and our lives by buying something more . . . [it] persuades us of such transformation by showing us people who have apparently been transformed and are, as a result, enviable . . . [ads] are about social relations, not objects; promises not of pleasure but of happiness."[11] . . .

Perfume ads are a good example of how images are used to sell the product: they boldly create images of romantic fantasy worlds—riding a white horse bareback through a field of flowers, warm autumn nights in France, Sophia Loren, tropical islands in the sun. Some are more adventurous. "Her life was more daring than most people's fantasies," says an ad for Isadora perfume. In a Paco Rabanne ad, a photo of a woman, looking like a glamorous James Bond, and a handsome man at her side is clipped with the note: "Robert: I caught up with them at Verfour. The man is definitely Max, her bodyguard. The woman may be Danielle . . . or it may be her damn double again. One of the few things anyone knows about her is that she always wears Calandre." Daring, adventure, romance, all yours for the price of perfume.

By relying on images like these, advertisements can be purposely misleading. "More" cigarettes often does not show the female in its ad smoking a cigarette. Instead she is pursuing a lively and fun single's life, feeding her dog, shopping for houseplants, talking on the phone. Not only is it "More You" but

---

[9]Kilbourne.

[10]Ashcraft, Laurie, speech before National American Marketing Association, February 1982, Mountain Shadows, Arizona.

[11]Berger, p. 131.

"It's beige"—the implication being that the cigarette simply fits in with the lively decor. The reality of someone smoking a cancer-causing cigarette is entirely omitted.

So what? many women ask. Ads don't affect me, I just ignore them.   35

Unfortunately, they do affect us, subtly but powerfully because we are   36
taught these ways of seeing ourselves.

For women consumers, the messages sent by advertising can be debilitating.   37
Bombarded by hundreds of these messages each day—that women are nice to look at but should not be taken seriously—merchants and manufacturers, doctors and lawyers, continue to treat women according to old-fashioned stereotypes: the message is not only that such treatment is okay but that women expect it. As a woman you may find yourself the butt of jokes by auto repairmen, your body sized up by a male loan officer, your questions ignored by your doctor.

"As a consumer what you most want is to be taken seriously," says   38
Kilbourne. "And that is exactly what women are not." And that is exactly what advertising reinforces.

That treatment is compounded by the way in which women are taught by   39
advertising to view themselves. Unable to measure up to the beautiful women or the happy housewives in the ads we see every day, women begin to feel like failures. "It makes us feel incredibly insecure," says Kilbourne.

Because women are told every day that they cannot think for themselves, that   40
they are dependent on men, many women themselves fall into the stereotypical role of the helpless female.

As a result of not only advertising, but also the way women have been   41
trained, they are often less assertive in situations that require a take charge attitude, less likely to challenge an unscrupulous repairman, less likely to ask questions of a lawyer or doctor. There is something "unfeminine" about asserting our rights in the marketplace, about making a fuss about a defective product. So many of us shy away from confrontation, instead letting the people we pay for goods and services bowl us over. We slowly begin to lose control over our own lives.

Today's advertising hurts women as consumers in another way: it impedes   42
our ability to make rational decisions about what we buy. Certainly that is the advertisers' aim. As one ad executive told Vance Packard about the type of research marketers conduct on consumers: "Motivation research is the type of research that seeks to learn what motivates people in making choices. It employs techniques designed to reach the unconscious or subconscious mind because preferences generally are determined by factors of which the individual is not conscious . . . Actually in the buying situation the consumer generally acts emotionally and compulsively, unconsciously reacting to the images and designs which in the subconscious are associated with products."

That technique is particularly effective with women, so they continue to   43
buy and buy, seeking as Berger said, not pleasure but happiness. To advertisers that is perfectly acceptable. Advertising executive Howard Goldstein, producer of advertisements for Jordache jeans (where 10-year-olds are portrayed as sex symbols), says that if a woman or man is sitting at home feeling lousy and wants

to buy a certain cologne or wear certain jeans to make them feel better "that's a positive force."[12]

Experts contacted by Packard disagreed. Said Bernice Allen of Ohio   44
University: "We have no proof that more material goods such as more cars or gadgets have made anyone happier—in fact the evidence seems to point in the opposite direction."[13]

Taking Charge

The first step toward getting out from under the thumb of advertisers is   45
developing a critical eye, knowing what weaknesses the advertiser is attempting to reach in you. When you look at an ad, ask yourself some of these questions, based on guidelines developed by both the National Advertising Review Board and the National Association of Broadcasters, and expanded:

- Are sexual stereotypes perpetuated in the ad?
- Are the women portrayed as stupid, or incapable of making important decisions?
- Does the ad use belittling language toward women (i.e. "bless her heart . . .")?
- Does the ad show a woman waiting on her husband and children?
- Does the ad portray women as more neurotic than men?
- Is there suggestive sexual language about women's role or bodies? (i.e. "turn 'em on with frost and tip . . .")
- Is the woman shown in an alluring, suggestive position?
- Does the ad portray women in a situation that tends to confirm the view that women are the property of men?
- Do I really want and need this product or am I reacting to suggestive images?
- Is the ad suggesting that I can look like the beautiful model in it?
- Does the ad promote the idea that all women have to be slender and "young-looking?"
- Does the ad show working or professional women as sex objects?

If you find an ad particularly offensive, write to the advertiser stating so and   46
telling them that you intend not to buy their product *because* of the ad. Get your friends to write letters too.

QUESTIONS FOR CRITICAL READING, THINKING, DISCUSSION, AND WRITING

Analyzing Content and Technique

1. Examine the epigraph by Adrienne Rich and paraphrase it. Do you agree with it? Why or why not?
2. What is Easton's thesis? Where is it most clearly stated? Discuss the placement of the thesis.
3. Analyze the structure of the essay. Why has Easton divided it into sections? Evaluate the effectiveness of each of the section headings. What did each one lead you to expect?

[12]Interview on "The Last Word" November 23, 1982.
[13]Packard, p. 246.

4. How does Easton counter the women who tell her that advertisements don't affect them because they ignore them? Are you convinced by her argument? Explain.

5. Who is Easton's intended audience? Explain how we know this, quoting one or two passages in support of your answer.

6. Discuss the purpose of this essay. Is the purpose helped by the tone of the essay? Why or why not?

Collaborative Activity

Have each member of the group bring in an advertisement that portrays a woman prominently. Analyze each of these advertisements as a group. Do they support or contradict Easton's argument? Write a collaborative paragraph based on your discussion.

Making Connections

1. A United Nations report that Easton quotes states, "Advertising is the worst offender in perpetuating the image of women as sex symbols and an inferior class of human being." Do you agree? Write an essay in which you compare advertisements with another element of popular culture (movies? songs?) that affects our perception of women negatively, and show the relative influence of each.

2. Imagine you are the advertising executive of a particular company whose products you like and use. Write an essay from the point of view of this person, defending your advertisements. Include actual examples of advertisements (the pictures and words) as well as an analysis of them. You may interview other consumers to find additional support.

PREREADING ACTIVITY

Before reading selection 62, write down what you know (or believe) about the position of men and women in Arab society. On what kind of information are your ideas
based? How do you perceive sex roles among the Arabs as different from what is
prevalent in the United States today?

Love and Sex in the Life of the Arab

Nawal el-Saadawi

Nawal el-Saadawi (1931–) is a novelist, a nonfiction writer, a psychiatrist, and an
advocate of women's rights. Her outspoken views on the oppression of women in
her Arab culture have caused her considerable trouble, including the loss of her
post as director of education in Egypt's Ministry of Health. Her books, which have
been banned in Egypt and several other Arab countries, include *Women and Sex* and
The Hidden Face of Eve: Women in the Arab World, from which this essay is taken.
The essay was translated from the Arabic by the author's husband, Sherif Hetata.

A famous work of art, *A Thousand and One Nights,* has been used by   1
many Western researchers and authors, who describe themselves as "orientalists,"
as a source of material and information for studying the life of the Arab. They
consider that these stories, especially those dealing with love and sexual intrigues,
afford an insight into the understanding of the Arab character, seeing them as
keys with which to open the doors to the "Arab Soul," and as valuable means
towards penetrating the depths, or rather the shallow waters, of the Arab mind
and heart.

Yet anyone with the slightest knowledge of Arab literature knows that the   2
stories related in *A Thousand and One Nights* are only a partial and one-sided
reflection of a very narrow section of Arab society, as it lived and dreamed, loved
and fornicated, intrigued and plundered, more than ten centuries ago. I do not
know very much about the level reached by European civilization at the time, the
state of human affairs in society there, in the sciences and in the arts, but I at least
know enough to be able to say that Arab society had undoubtedly advanced much
further. Many are the scholars, writers and researchers who have made comparisons

Source: First published in English by Zed Books Ltd., London, U.K., and 165 First Avenue, Atlantic
Highlands, N.J. 07716, U.S.A., in 1980. Copyright © Nawal el-Saadawi, 1980.

between the West and the Arab World, only drawing their examples from a period in our history, now more than a thousand years old. One would have to have a very bad memory to forget, in one gigantic leap, what is in terms of time half the number of years which have elapsed since the birth of Christ. How can we depict the contrasts between the Arab character at the time when the people of *A Thousand and One Nights* flew on their magic carpets, and the Western mind of the Victorian era when purity floated like a thick veil over the corrupt and bloated features of a hypocritical society.[1] How much more true and scientific would a comparative study have been of the lifestyles of Arab and European men from the same period, or at least from the Middles Ages when the clergy, who were the male intelligentsia of the time, were busy prompting women accused of sorcery to utter the most obscene sexual epithets, and, under insufferable torture, forcing them to admit to the very crimes which they had been taught to describe?[2]

This picture of the sex-mad Arab fawning on an extensive harem is main- 3 tained with dubious insistence even today. Without exception the films, magazines and newspapers that roll out from the reels of Western producers and the dark-rooms of Western monopolies, depict Arab men as trotting behind the skirts of women, ogling the ample bosoms of seductive blondes, and squandering their money on quenching their thirst for alcohol or sex. Arab women, in their turn, are depicted as twisting and turning in snake-like dances, flaunting their naked bellies and quivering hips, seducing men with the promise of dark passion, playful, secretive and intriguing, a picture drawn from the palaces of *A Thousand and One Nights* and the slave women of the Caliph, Haroun El Raschid.

Is it possible to believe that this distorted image of Arab men and women is 4 representative of their true life and character in the Arab world of today? Personally, I am sure that it is not even representative of men and women living at the time of Haroun El Raschid. Perhaps it has some authenticity as a reflection of certain aspects of the life led by palace rulers and their concubines in those bygone days, but these were only an infinitesimal minority compared to the vast mass of Arabs, who led a harsh and difficult existence with no room for, nor possibility of ever experiencing, the silken cushions, soft flesh and fiery liquids of dissipation. The sexual life of kings and princely rulers, whether in the past or present, in the modern West or more archaic East, to the South of the Earth's equator or to the North, has maintained the same essential pattern, embroidered with a greater or lesser degree of sophistication or refinement, sadism or depravity.

Sweeping judgments, which depict the nature of Arabs in general, and the 5 men of the Arab world in particular, as being obsessed with sex and more inclined to pursue the pleasures of the body than men from other regions or countries, are therefore unfounded and incorrect. Their aim is to contribute to and maintain a distorted image of the Arabs in the minds of people all over the world, to falsify the true colours of their struggle for independence, progress and control over their destinies, and to facilitate the task of conservative, reactionary and imperialist forces that continue to survive and prosper by such means.

I believe that freedom in all its forms, whether sexual, intellectual, social or 6 economic, is a necessity for every man and woman, and for all societies. Nevertheless, I feel that the sexual freedom that has accompanied the evolution of modern capitalist society has been developed very much in a unilateral direction and has not been linked with, or been related to, a parallel development of social and economic freedoms. This sheds some doubt on the real motives behind the consistent and ever increasing campaign calling upon men and women to throw their sexual inhibitions and beliefs overboard. It also jeopardizes the chances of human progress and fulfilment, since a one-sided development that does not take into consideration the totality of life can only lead to new distortions and monstrosities.

This is why there is a growing realization that sexual freedom, as it is 7 preached today in modern capitalist society, has no valid answers or solutions to many of the problems of personal life and human happiness, and that it is only another and perhaps more ingenuous way of making people pay the price of ever expanding consumption, of accumulating profits and of feeding the appetites of monopolistic giants. Another opium to be inhaled and imbibed so that mobilized energies may be dissipated rather than built up into a force of resistance and revolt against all forms of exploitation.

In this respect, Eastern and Arab societies have not differed from the West. 8 Here again it is mainly economic necessity which governs the direction in which values, human morals and norms of sexual behaviour move. The economic imperatives of Arab society required a wide degree of sexual freedom to ensure the provision of large numbers of offspring. Polygamy, as against polyandry, tends to be more prolific as far as children are concerned. Arab society, still primitive and badly equipped to face the vicissitudes and harshness of desert life, suffered from a very high mortality rate, especially among infants and children, which had to be compensated for by correspondingly high birth rates. The economic and military strength of tribes and clans in a society which possessed neither modern tools or machines, nor modern weapons, depended very much on their numbers. In addition, the simple crude existence of desert life and the extreme poverty of nomadic tribes meant that, while the cost of maintaining a child was minimal, the child could play useful roles in meeting the productive needs of the time, being capable of running errands or looking after the camels and sheep.

Wars and battles were an integral part of tribal life and flared up at frequent 9 intervals, and death took a heavy toll of the men. This was particularly the case after Islam started to establish itself and expand. It was natural that this new threat should meet with the resistance of the neighbouring rulers and the older religions entrenched in the surrounding regions, and that the Muslims should be obliged to fight numerous battles before they could succeed in establishing and stabilizing their new State. The result was heavy losses in men and a marked imbalance characterized by a much higher number of women, accentuated by the throngs of women slave prisoners brought back from victorious battles.

The easiest and most natural solution to such a situation was to allow men 10 to marry more than one woman, and in addition to choose from among the women brought back from the wars, or sold in the markets, those whom they considered suitable to be wives, concubines or slaves in their households. Each man did so according to his means, and these means of course varied widely from one man to another. With a superfluity of women, a man would take pride in the number of women he could maintain, and the bigger this number, the more occasion for him to boast about the extensiveness of his female retinue, and about his powers over women, whether in marriage or in love. On the other hand, women would compete for the favours of men and excel in subtle allurements to attract men towards marriage, love and sex.

This was perhaps an additional factor which tended to make Arab women more forward and positive in love and sex, characteristics in clear contrast to the passive attitudes assumed by the vast majority of women living in our modern era. The other factors, mentioned previously, were the matriarchal vestiges which at the time were still strong in Arab society, and the naturalistic attitudes of Islamic teachings which prevented love and sex from being considered sinful as they were by Christianity. On the contrary, Islam described sexual pleasure as one of the attractions of life, one of the delights for those who go to Paradise after death. As a result, Arab women had no hesitation in being positive towards sex, in expressing their desire for men, in exercising their charms, and weaving their net around whoever might be the object of their attentions. Perhaps they were following in the footsteps of their mother, Eve, who had so ably enticed Adam to comply with her wishes and fall victim to *fitna*,[3] with the result that he dropped from the high heavens in which he was confined and landed with his two feet on the solid, rough, but warm and living earth.

For the Arabs the word "woman" invariably evokes the word *fitna*. Arab women combined the qualities of a positive personality and *fitna*, or seductiveness, to such an extent that they became an integral part of the Islamic ethos which has, as one of its cornerstones, the sexual powers of women, and which maintains that their seductiveness can lead to a *fitna* within society. Here the word is used in a related but different sense to mean an uprising, rebellion, conspiracy or anarchy which would upset the existing order of things established by Allah (and which, therefore, is not to be changed). From this arose the conception that life could only follow its normal steady and uninterrupted course, and society could only avoid any potential menace to its stability and structure, or any disruption of the social order, if men continued to satisfy the sexual needs of their women, kept them happy, and protected their honour. If this was not ensured a *fitna* could easily be let loose, since the honour of women would be in doubt, and as a result uneasiness and trouble could erupt at any moment. The virtue of women had to be ensured if peace was to reign among men, not an easy task in view of the *fitna* (seductiveness) of women.

Islam's contribution to the understanding of love, sex and the relations between the sexes has never to my knowledge been correctly assessed and given the consideration it deserves. However, the contradictory aspects inherent in Islamic society are reflected in another dramatically opposed tendency which runs through the body of Islamic teaching, and is a continuation of the rigid, reactionary and conservative reasoning that dominated the concepts and practices of Judaism and Christianity in matters related to sex.

Islam inherited the old image of Eve and of women that depicts them as the close followers and instruments of Satan, the body of women being his abode. A well-known Arab saying maintains that: "Whenever a man and a woman meet together, their third is always Satan." Mahomet the Prophet, despite his love for and understanding of women, warns that: "After I have gone, there will be no greater danger menacing my nation and more liable to create anarchy and trouble than women."[4]

This attitude towards woman was prominent throughout Islamic thought and she always remained a source of danger to man and to society on account of her power of attraction or *fitna*. Man in the face of such seduction was portrayed as helpless, drained of all his capacities to be positive or to resist. Although this was not a new idea, it assumed big proportions in Islamic theology and was buttressed by many *Ahadith* (proverbs and sayings).

Woman was therefore considered by the Arabs as a menace to man and society, and the only way to avoid the harm she could do was to isolate her in the home, where she could have no contact with either one or the other. If for any reason she had to move outside the walls of her prison, all necessary precautions had to be taken so that no one could get a glimpse of her seductiveness. She was therefore enveloped in veils and flowing robes like explosive material which has to be well packed. In some Arab societies, this concern to conceal the body of women went so far that the split-second uncovering of a finger or a toe was considered a potential source of *fitna* in society which might therefore lead to anarchy, uprisings, rebellions and the total destruction of the established order!

Thus it is that Islam confronted its philosophers and theologians with two contradictory, and in terms of logic, mutually exclusive conceptions: (1) Sex is one of the pleasures and attractions of life; (2) To succumb to sex will lead to *fitna* in society—that is crisis, disruption and anarchy.

The only way out of this dilemma, the only path that could reconcile these two conflicting views, was to lay down a system or framework for sex which on the one hand had to avoid *fitna* while on the other would permit abundant reproduction and a good deal of pleasure within the limits of Allah's prescriptions.

The Imam, El Ghazali, explains how the will of Allah and his wisdom are manifested in the fact that he created sexual desire in both men and women. This is expressed in the words of his Prophet when he said: "Marry and multiply." "Since Allah has revealed his secret to us, and has instructed us clearly what to do, refraining from marriage is like refusing to plough the earth, and wasting the seed. It means leaving the useful tools which Allah has created for us idle, and is a crime against the self-evident reasons and obvious aims of the phenomenon of creation, aims written on the sexual organs in Divine handwriting."[5]

For El Ghazali, apart from reproduction, marriage aims at immunity from the Devil, breaking the sharp point of desire, avoiding the dangers of passion, keeping our eyes away from what they should not see, safeguarding the female sexual organs, and following the directives of our Prophet when he said: "He who marries has ensured for himself the fulfilment of half his religion. Let him therefore fear Allah for the other half."[6]

Islamic thought admits the strength and power of sexual desire in women, and in men also. Fayad Ibn Nageeh said that, "if the sexual organ of the man rises up, a third of his religion is lost." One of the rare explanations given to the Prophets' words by Ibn Abbas, Allah's blessing be upon both of them, is that "he who enters into a woman is lost in a twilight" and that "if the male organ rises up, it is an overwhelming catastrophe for once provoked it cannot be resisted by either reason or religion. For this organ is more powerful than all the instruments used by Satan against man." That is why the Prophet, Allah's peace be upon him, said, "I have not seen creatures lacking in mind and religion more capable of overcoming men of reason and wisdom than you [women]."[7] He also warned men: "Do not enter the house of those who have absent ones"—meaning those women whose husbands are away—"for Satan will run out from one of you, like hot blood." And we said, "From you also, O Prophet!" He answered, "And from me also, but Allah has given me his support and so Satan has been subdued."[8]

From the above, it is clear that the Arabs were accustomed to discuss freely 22 with Mahomet and treated him as an ordinary human being like themselves. If he said that Satan ran in their blood, they would riposte that Satan also ran in his blood. Upon which, Mahomet admitted that he was no different from them except in the fact that Allah has come to his rescue and subdued Satan within him. The Arabic word which has been translated into "subdued" is *aslam*, which means "to become a Muslim" (to know peace, to be saved). The meaning of Mahomet's words, therefore, is that his Satan has become a Muslim. Mahomet emphasized the same point when he said: "I have been preferred to Adam in two ways. His wife incited him to disobedience, whereas my wives have helped me to obey. His Satan was a heretic, whereas mine was a Muslim inviting me always to do good."[9]

Islam, therefore, inherited the attitude of Judaism towards Eve, the sinful 23 woman who disobeyed God, and towards sex as related essentially to women, and to Satan. Man, on the other hand, though endowed with an overpowering sexual passion, does not commit sin except if incited to do so by the seductiveness and devilry of woman. He is therefore enjoined to marry and thereby is able to beat back the evils of Satan and the bewitching temptations of women.

Islam encourages men to marry. Mahomet the Prophet of the Muslims, says 24 to them: "Marriage is my law. He who loves my way of life, let him therefore follow my law."[10]

Despite the fact that Islam recognized the existence of sexual passion in 25 both women and men, it placed all its constraints on women, thus forgetting that their sexual desire also was extremely strong. Islam never ignored the deep-seated sexual passion that lies in men, and therefore suggested the solutions that would ensure its satisfaction.

Islamic history, therefore, witnessed men who married hundreds of women. 26 In this connection we may once more quote El Ghazali: "And it was said of Hassan Ibn Ali that he was a great marrier of women, and that he had more than two hundred wives. Sometimes he would marry four at a time, or divorce four at a time and replace them by others." The Prophet Mahomet, Allah's blessings and peace be upon him, said of Hassan Ibn Ali: "You resemble me, and my creativity."[11] The Prophet had once said of himself that he had been given the power of forty men in sex.[12] Ghazali admits that sexual desire in men is very strong and that: "Some natures are overwhelmed by passion and cannot be protected by only one woman. Such men should therefore preferably marry more than one woman and may go up to four."[13]

Some of the close followers of Mahomet (El Sahaba) who led an ascetic life 27 would break their fast by having sexual intercourse before food. At other times they would share a woman's bed before the evening prayer, then do their ablutions and pray. This was in order to empty the heart of everything and so concentrate on the worship of Allah. Thus it was that the secretions of Satan were expelled from the body.

Ghazali carries his thoughts further and says: "Since among Arabs passion is 28 an overpowering aspect of their nature, they have been allowed to marry women slaves if at some time they should fear that this passion will become too heavy a burden for their belief and lead to its destruction. Though it is true that such a marriage could lead to the birth of a child that will be a slave, yet enslaving the child is a lighter offence than the destruction of religious belief." Ghazali evidently believes that religion cannot be preserved from destruction unless men are allowed to marry as many women as they wish, even though in so doing they would be harming the interests of the children.

It is clear that Islam has been very lenient with men in so far as the satis- 29 faction of their sexual desires is concerned. This was true even if it led to the enslavement of children and injustice to innocent creatures or if sought at the expense of a woman slave completely deprived of a wife's normal rights and whose children were destined never to enjoy the rights of a free child born of a free mother.

The inevitable question which arises in the face of these facts is: Why has 30 religion been so lenient towards man? Why did it not demand that he control his sexual passions and limit himself to one wife, just as it demanded of the woman that she limit herself to one husband, even though it had recognized that women's sexual desire was just as powerful, if not more so, as that of men? Why is it that religion was so understanding and helpful where men were concerned, to the extent of sacrificing the interests of the family, the women and even the children, in order to satisfy their desires? Why, in contrast, was it so severe with woman that death could be her penalty if she so much as looked at a man other than her husband?

Islam made marriage the only institution within which sexual intercourse 31 could be morally practised between men and women. Sexual relations, if practised outside this framework, were immediately transformed into an act of sin and corruption. A young man whom society had not endowed with the possibilities of getting married, or buying a woman slave from the market, or providing himself with a concubine, had no way of expending or releasing his pent-up sexual energies. Not even masturbation was permissible.

Ibn Abbas was once asked what he thought of masturbation? He exclaimed: 32 "Ouph, it is indeed bad. I spit on it. To marry a slave woman is better. And to marry a slave woman is preferable to committing adultery." Thus it is that an unmarried youth is torn between three evils. The least of them is to marry a slave woman and have a slave child. The next is masturbation, and the most sinful of all is adultery.[14]

Of these three evils, only the first two were considered permissible. How- 33 ever, the institution of marriage remained very different for men to what it was for women, and the rights accorded to husbands were distinct from those accorded to wives. In fact, it is probably not accurate to use the term "rights of the woman" since a woman under the Islamic system of marriage has no human rights unless we consider that a slave has rights under a slave system. Marriage, in so far as women are concerned, is just like slavery to the slave, or the chains of serfdom to the serf. Ghazali expressed this fact clearly and succinctly when speaking of the rights enjoyed by a husband over his wife: "Perhaps the real answer is that marriage is a form of serfdom. The woman is man's serf and her duty therefore is absolute obedience to the husband in all that he asks of her person."[15] Mahomet himself said: "A woman, who at the moment of death enjoys the full approval of her husband, will find her place in Paradise."[16]

The right enjoyed by a wife in Islam is to receive the same treatment as her husband's other wives. Yet such "justice" is impossible, as the Koran itself has stated: "You will not be able to treat your women equally even if you exert much effort."[17] The Prophet himself preferred some of his wives to others. Some Muslim thinkers opposed polygamous marriage for this reason, and maintained that marriage to more than one woman in Islam was tied to a condition which itself was impossible to fulfil, namely to treat the different wives in exactly the same way and avoid any injustice to one or other of them. A man obviously desires his new wife more than the preceding one(s), otherwise he would not seek to marry her. Justice in this context should mean equality in love, or at least the absence of any tendency to like one wife more and so prefer her to the other(s).[18]

Some Muslim thinkers interpret the two relevant verses of the Koran differently: "Marry as many women as you like, two, three, or four. If you fear not to treat them equally, then marry only one" and "You will not succeed in being just with your women, no matter how careful you are."[19] They consider that justice in this context simply implies providing the women with an equal share of material means for the satisfaction of their needs and that it does not refer to equality in the love and affection borne by the husband for his women.[20]

The question, however, is: What is more important to a woman, or to any human being who respects her dignity and her human qualities, justice in the apportioning of a few piastres,[21] or justice in true love and human treatment? Is marriage a mere commercial transaction by which a woman obtains some money from her husband, or is it a profound exchange of feelings and emotions between a man and a woman?

Even if we were to assume the impossible, and arrive at a situation where the man treats his wives equally, it would not be possible to call this a "right," since the first and foremost criterion of any right is that it should be enjoyed equally by all individuals without distinction or discrimination. If a man marries four wives, even if he treats them equally, it still means that each woman among them has only a quarter of a man, whereas the man has four women. The women here are only equal in the sense that they suffer an equal injustice, just as in bygone days all slaves were "equal" in that sense under the system of slavery. This can in no way be considered equality or justice or rights for women.

The slave and feudal systems came into being in order to serve the interests of the slave and feudal landowners. In the same way, the system of marriage was created to serve the interests of the man against those of the woman and the children.

El Ghazali when speaking of the benefits of marriage for men expresses   39
himself in these words:

> Marriage relieves the mind and heart of the man from the burden of looking after the home, and of being occupied with cooking, sweeping, cleaning utensils and arranging for the necessities of life. If the human being did not possess a passion for living with a mate, he would find it very difficult to have a home to himself, since if obliged to undertake all the tasks of looking after the home, he would find most of his time wasted and would not be able to devote himself to work and to knowledge. A good woman, capable of setting things to rights in the home, is an invaluable aid to religious holiness. If however things go wrong in this area, the heart becomes the seat of anxieties and disturbances, and life is seized with things that chase away its calm. For these reasons Soleiman El Darani has said: "A good wife is not a creation of this world, for in fact she permits you to be occupied with the life of the here-after, and this is so because she looks after the affairs of your home and in addition assuages your passions."[22]

Thus it is that a man cannot devote himself to his religious life, or to knowledge, unless he has a wife who is completely preoccupied with the affairs of his home, with serving him, and feeding him, cleaning his clothes and looking after all his needs. But are we not justified in asking: What about the wife? How can she in turn devote herself to her religious life and the search for knowledge? It is clear that no one has ever thought of the problem from this angle, as if it were a foregone conclusion that women have nothing to do with either religion or knowledge. That their sole function in life is sweeping, cooking, washing clothes and cleaning utensils, and undertaking those tasks that Ghazali has described as a source of trouble and disturbance to the heart, and that chase away the calm of life.

How clear it is that the mind of women and their ambitions, whether in sci-   40
ence or in culture, have been completely dropped from all consideration, so that man can consecrate himself completely to such fields of human activity. He furthermore imposes on woman the troubles and disturbances of the heart and mind that result from being occupied with such domestic tasks, after which she is accused of being stupid and lacking in religious conviction. Woman shoulders all these burdens without receiving any remuneration except the food, clothing and shelter required to keep her alive. Man not only exploits her mind for his own ends by abolishing it, or at least preventing it from developing any potential through science, culture and knowledge, not only does he plunge her whole life into working for him without reward, but he also uses her to satisfy his sexual desires to the extent required by him. It is considered one of her duties, and she must respond to his desires at any time. If she fails to do so, falls ill, refuses, or is prevented by her parents, it is his right to divorce her, and in addition deprive her of alimony.

Among the sacred duties of the wife is complete obedience to the husband.   41
She is not allowed to differ with him, to ask questions, or even to argue certain points. The man on the other hand is not expected to obey his wife. On the con-

trary, it is considered unworthy of a man to do what his wife suggests or asks of him. Omar Ibn El Khattab once said: "Differ with your women and do not do what they ask. Thus you will be blessed. For it is said: Consult them and then act differently." The Prophet advises: "Do not live a slave to your wife." The Muslim religious leader, El Hassan, goes even further when he maintains that: "Whenever a man has started to obey the desires and wishes of his woman, it has ended by Allah throwing him into the fires of Purgatory."[23]

One of the rights of a woman is to be paid a sum of money in the form of a dowry when she is married, and to receive another sum of money as alimony if her husband divorces her. In addition, he is supposed to feed and clothe her, to give her shelter in a home. However, the woman cannot specify any conditions as far as the home she is expected to live in is concerned. It might be a hut made of wood or mud, or a beautiful brick house, depending on the means of the husband. She cannot determine the size of the dowry, or the sum paid to her as alimony, or the food which she is supposed to eat and the clothes she will wear. All these things are decided by the husband according to his assessment of the financial means at his disposal, and how he should spend them.

According to Islamic rules, a woman can ask to be paid for breastfeeding her child.[24] The husband is obliged to pay her for this from his earnings, if the child itself has not some financial resources laid aside for it. If these exist, the payment is made to the mother out of them. The mother is not forced to breastfeed the child if she does not want to, even if pay is offered to her. She can ask to be paid as long as there is no other woman who has voluntarily agreed to breastfeed the child, and to whom the father has no objection. However, if such a woman does exist, the wife no longer has the right to ask for any nursing payment.

Here again it is the husband's will that is crucial, since he can prevent the mother from being paid for nursing her child by finding another woman for this purpose, either on a voluntary basis or for a lower wage.

The mother is also eligible for payment for the rearing of her children, but here again it is the father's prerogative to choose another woman who can offer her services either on a voluntary basis or for less pay.

Such limited rights are almost insignificant, surrounded as they are by impossible conditions and cannot be considered of any real value. On the contrary, they afford the man a possibility of dispensing with the services of the children's mother [as soon as] she makes a request to be paid, thereby in fact obliging her to forego her right to payment for nursing or child-rearing. The vast majority of women, unable to be immune to the tendency for society and families to exaggerate and sanctify the functions of motherhood, cannot but sacrifice themselves for their children and give them everything, including their lives. To sacrifice some minor sum of money is therefore a matter of no consequence.

The exploitation to which a wife and a mother is exposed is evident from the fact that she carries out a number of vital functions without being paid. She is cook, sweeper, cleaner, washerwoman, domestic servant, nurse, governess and teacher to the children, in addition to being an instrument of sexual satisfaction and pleasure to her husband. All this she does free of charge, except for the

expenses of her upkeep, in the form of food, clothing and shelter. She is therefore the lowest paid labourer in existence.

The exploitation of woman is built upon the fact that man pays her the low-   48
est wage known for any category of human beasts of burden. It is he who decides
what she is paid, be it in the form of a few piastres, some food, a dress, or simply
a roof over her head. With this meagre compensation, he can justify the authority he exercises over her. Men exercise their tutelage over women because, as
stated in the Koran, they provide them with the means of livelihood.

Man's lordship over woman is therefore enforced through the meagre   49
piastres he pays her and also through imposing a single husband upon her to
ensure that the piastres he owns are not inherited by the child of another man.
Preserving this inheritance is the motive force behind the severe and rigid laws
which seek to maintain a woman's loyalty to her husband so that no confusion
can affect the line of descent. It is not love between husband and wife which is
sought to be nurtured and cherished by these rules. If it were love between the
couple that was the basis of this search for loyalty between husband and wife,
such loyalty would be required equally from both the woman and the man.
However, since loyalty is sought in the woman alone, by imposing monogamy
on her, whereas the man is permitted to multiply and diversify his sexual relations, it becomes self-evident that conjugal devotion is not a human moral
value, but one of the instruments of social oppression exercised against the
woman to make sure that the succession and inheritance is kept intact. The line
of descent which is sought to be preserved is, of course, that of the man. Thus
adultery on the part of the woman, her betrayal of the nuptial vows sworn to
on the day of marriage, means the immediate destruction of patrilineal descent
and inheritance.

Money is therefore the foundation of morals, or at least of the morals preva-   50
lent where property, exploitation and inheritance are the essence of the economic
system. Yet in religion it is assumed that true morals are dependent rather on
human values. The Koran clearly says: "Neither your wealth, nor your children
can, even if you tread the path of humiliation, bring you close to me." "The highest esteem is given by Allah to those who are the purest."[25]

We have mentioned before that society realized early on the powerful bio-   51
logical and sexual nature of women, which power it compared to that of Satan. It
was therefore inevitable that her loyalty and chastity could only be ensured by
preventing her from having relations with any males apart from her husband and
the men with whom she was forbidden to have sex such as the father, brother,
and paternal or maternal uncles. This is the reason behind the segregation that
arose between men and women, and the outlawing of free intermixing between
them, a segregation put into effect by imprisoning the women within the four
walls of the home. This confinement of women to the home permits the attainment of three inter-related aims: (1) It ensures the loyalty of the woman and pre-
vents her from mixing with strange men; (2) It permits her to devote herself
entirely to the care of her home, husband and children and the aged members of
the family; and (3) It protects men from the dangers inherent in women and their
powers of seduction, which are so potent that when faced by them "men lose

two-thirds of their reason and become incapable of thinking about Allah, science and knowledge."

The Muslim philosophers who so oft proclaim such opinions borrow most of their ideas from the myth of Adam and Eve, seeing woman as a replica of Eve, endowed with powers that are dangerous and destructive to society, to man, and to religion. They believe that civilization has been gradually built up in the struggle against these "female powers," in an attempt to control and suppress them, so as to protect the man and to avoid their minds from being preoccupied with women to the detriment of their duties towards Allah and society.

In order to preserve society and religion from such evils, it was essential to segregate the sexes, and subjugate women by fire and steel when necessary for fire and steel alone can force slaves to submit to unjust laws and systems built on exploitation. Woman's status within marriage is even worse than that of the slave, for woman is exploited both economically and sexually. This apart from the moral, religious and social oppression exercised over her to ensure the maintenance of her double exploitation. Slaves, at least, are partially compensated for the efforts they make in the form of some material reward. But a woman is an unpaid servant to the husband, children and elderly people within the home. And a slave may be liberated by his master to become a free man, and thus enjoy the rights of free men, foremost amongst which is the recognition that he has a brain and religious conviction. But a woman, as long as she remains a woman, has no chance or hope of ever possessing the brain and religious conviction of a man. For women are "lacking in their minds and in their religious faith."

Since men possess more reason and wisdom than women it has become their right, and not that of women, to occupy the positions of ruler, legislator, governor etc. One of the primary conditions in Islam to become a religious or political leader (Imam) or governor (Wali) is to be a "male."[26] Then follow piety, knowledge and competence.

The major ideas on which Islam has based itself in dealing with the question of women and sex can thus be listed as follows:

1. Men should exercise their tutelage over women because they provide for them economically. They are also superior to women as far as reason, wisdom, piety, knowledge and religious conviction are concerned. Authority is the right of men, and obedience the duty of women.

2. Men's energies should be expended in worship, religious activities and in the search for knowledge. This is to be attained by making women devote themselves to serving their men in the home, preparing food and drink, washing, cleaning and caring for the children and elderly.

3. The sexual desires of men should be duly satisfied so that they can concentrate with a clear mind and heart on religious activities, the worship of Allah, the search for knowledge, and the service of society. This also aims to ensure that religion is safeguarded and society preserved from being undermined, or even collapsing. Sexual desire is to be satisfied through marriage, the aims of which are

reproduction and also experience of one of the pleasures promised in Paradise, so that men may be motivated to do good and so be rewarded in the after-life. It is men's uncontested right to fully satisfy their sexual needs by marrying several women, or by taking unto themselves women slaves and concubines. Masturbation however is an evil, and adultery an even greater sin. "Let those who cannot marry remain chaste so that Allah may bestow upon them of His riches. Let he who can marry a woman, who has matured without marriage, take her as a wife. If he cannot, then abstinence is the path."[27]

4.   The seduction of women and their powers of temptation are a danger and a source of destruction. Men must be protected from their seductive powers, and this is ensured by confining them to the home. Man is exposed to annihilation if he succumbs to the temptations of women. In the words of Ibrahim Ebn Adham, "he who is accustomed to the thighs of women will never be a source of anything."[28]

5.   Women are forbidden to leave the home and enter the outside world of men except if an urgent necessity to do this arises, as in illness or death. If a woman goes outside her home she must cover her body completely and not expose her attractions or anything that is liable to seduce a man. Her ornaments should be hidden and her external genital organs preserved intact.

Islam encouraged men to marry and went as far as considering it a religious   56
duty. A familiar Arab saying goes as follows: "Marriage is half of religion." Men were not only asked to marry, but permitted to take several wives, and to have extramarital sexual relations almost at will, by living with concubines or women slaves. They were thus led to boast of the number of women they owned, and to speak with pride of their sexual powers.

The sexual powers of man became a part of the Arab ethos, and within   57
this ethos, were related to manliness and virility. It became a matter for shame if a man was known to be impotent or sexually weak. Obviously, it could only be a woman who would be able to know, and therefore judge, if a man was sexually deficient, and in this resided another source of woman's hidden strength enhancing the dangers she represented. Men therefore had to be protected from her, and society did this by ensuring that her eyes were prevented from seeing anything outside the home—like an animal that becomes blind from being kept in the dark—by covering her face with the thickest of veils, and by obscuring her mind so she would become incapable of discerning the weak from the strong. This is the origin of the greater value attached to a virgin as compared with a woman, when the time comes for her to marry. The virgin knows little or nothing about men and sex, whereas a woman has experience drawn from her past relations with men and from her knowledge of the arts of sex. She can easily discern where lie the weaknesses of a man and where lies his strength. Hence the reduced value attached to a widow or a divorced woman.

Mahomet the Prophet, however, did not comply with these general rules of   58
male conduct in Arab society. He was married fourteen times to women who had been divorced or widowed. The only virgin he married was Aisha. In this respect he was also much more progressive, and much more open-minded than most of

the men of today, who still prefer to marry a virgin and look for the usual blood-stains on the nuptial sheet or cloth. That is why, especially in rural areas, the custom of defloration by the husband's or *daya's* finger is still widespread, and is meant to demonstrate the red evidence of virginity on a white cloth symbolic of purity and an intact family honour.

As we have seen, the status of women and the attitudes towards them changed rapidly after the death of Mahomet. In the very essence of Islam, and in its teachings as practised in the life of the Prophet, women occupied a comparatively high position. But once they were segregated from men and made to live within the precincts of the home, the values of honour, self-respect and pride characteristic of Arab tribal society became closely and almost indissolubly linked to virginity, and to preventing the womenfolk of the family from moving into the outside world. A popular saying among the Palestinians, very common until the middle of the 20th century, goes: "My woman never left our home until the day she was carried out."[29] I remember my mother describing my grandmother and saying that she had only ever moved through the streets on two occasions. The first was when she left her father's house and went to her husband after marriage. And the second when she was carried out of her husband's house to be buried. Both times no part of her body remained uncovered.[30]

Segregation between the world of men and that of women was so strict that a woman who dared to go outside the door of her home was liable to be mal-treated at the hands of men. They might limit themselves to a few rude and insolent glances, or resort to coarse sexual remarks and insults, but very often things would go even further. A man or a boy might stretch out his hand and seize her by the arm or the breast. Sometimes young boys would throw stones at her in the lanes and by-roads of cities and towns, and follow in her footsteps with jeering remarks or sexual insults, in which the organs of her body would be villified in a chorus of loud voices. As a girl I used to be scared of going out into the streets in some of the districts of Cairo during my secondary school days (1943–48). I remember how boys sometimes threw stones at me, or shouted out crude insults as I passed by, such as "Accursed be the cunt of your mother" or "Daughter of the bitch fucked by men." In some Arab countries women have been exposed to physical or moral aggression in the streets simply because their fingers were seen protruding from the sleeves of their dress.[31]

This tendency among males to harm any woman caught crossing the boundaries of her home, and therefore the outer limits of the world prescribed for her by men, or who dares break into and walk through domains reserved for men, proves that they cannot consider her as merely weak and passive. On the contrary, they look upon her as a dangerous aggressor the moment she steps over the frontiers, an aggressor to be punished and made to return immediately to the restrictions of her abode. This attitude bears within itself the proof of woman's strength, a strength from which man seeks to protect himself by all possible means. Not only does he imprison woman within the house, but he also surrounds the male world with all sorts of barricades, stretches of barbed wire, fortifications and even heavy guns.

The female world, on the other hand, is looked upon by men as an area sur- 62
rounded by, and peopled with, obscure and puzzling secrets, filled with all the
dark mystery of sorcery, devilry and the works of Satan. It is a world that a man
may only enter with the greatest caution, and a prayer for Allah's help, Allah who
alone can give us strength and show us the way. Thus it is that the Arab man in
the rural areas of Egypt mutters a string of Allah's names through pursed, fast
moving lips, on entering a house in which there are women: *"Ya Hafez, ya Hafes,
ya Lateef, ya Sattar, ya Rab, ya Satir, ya Karim."* ("O great preserver, almighty
one, God the compassionate, who art alone shielder from all harm, protector
from evil, bountiful and generous.") In some Arab societies the man might add
destour, which is the same word used by peasants to chase away evil spirits or
devils.[32]

Here again we can observe the commonly held idea of a close link between 63
women and devils or evil spirits. It goes back to the story of Eve, and the belief
that she was positive and active where evil is concerned, an instrument of Satan's
machinations. The development of a Sufi theology in Islam, characterized by
renunciation of the world, and meditation and love for Allah—which became a
cult of love in general—allowed women to rise to the level of saints. However, the
number of women saints remained extremely small as compared with men. On
the other hand, where it came to evil spirits 80% of them were popularly considered to be female.[33]

The history of the Arabs shows that the women were undoubtedly much 64
less afraid of the men than the men were of the women. The tragedy of Arab men
however, or rather of most men all over the world, is that they fear woman and
yet desire her. But I think it can be said that Arab men in some periods, especially
in the pre-Islamic and early Islamic eras, were able to overcome their fear of
women to a much greater degree than men in the West. Or perhaps, more precisely, the men's desire for their women was stronger than the inhibitions built
from fear. This is due to the difference in the objective conditions prevailing in
Arab societies as compared to the West, and to the fact, discussed earlier, that
Islam (contrary to Christianity) recognized the validity and legitimacy of sexual
desire.

As a result, sex and love occupied a much more important place in the life 65
of the Arabs, and in their literature and arts. But parallel to this flowering in the
passions which bind men and women together, there was an opposite and almost
equally strong tendency in the teachings of philosophers and men of wisdom, and
in the literary works of writers and poets, that warned against indulging in the
pleasures of sex. Men were abjured not to become "impassioned" with women or
to fall victims to their seductions. One of the famous injunctions of the prominent Arab thinker, Ibn El Mokafa, says: "Know well that one of the things that
can cause the worst of disasters in religion, the greatest exhaustion to the body,
the heaviest strain on the purse, the highest harm to the mind and reason, the
deepest fall in man's chivalry, and the fastest dissipation of his majesty and poise,
is a passion for women."[34]

Ibn Mokafa was no doubt directing his remarks exclusively to those men 66
who possessed "majesty," "poise," and a well garnished purse, since only those

who possessed these trappings could possibly lose them through love of women. Other men, those that constituted the vast majority among the people and who possessed neither majesty, nor poise, nor purse of any kind could not benefit from his advice, or even be in the least concerned with it. They were completely, or almost completely, stripped of all worldly possessions and therefore sometimes even of the means to have just one lawful wife, pay her dowry and keep her children. Such men could not be expected to strut back and forth on the scenes of love and passion.

In Arab society, as in all societies governed by a patriarchal class system where enormous differences exist between various social levels, sex and love, sexual freedom and licence and a life of pleasure were only the lot of a very small minority. The vast majority of men and women were destined to toss and turn on a bed of nails, to be consumed by the flames of sacrifice and to be subjugated by a load of traditions, laws and codes which forbid sex to all except those who can pay its price. [67]

The Arabs, exposed as they were to the shortages and harshness of desert life, to the difficulties and perils of obtaining the bare necessities in a backward and rather savage society, and to the burden of exploitation by their own and surrounding ruling classes, were known for their fortitude, patience, and capacity to stand all kinds of deprivation, whether from food, sex or even water. Yet they were capable, like people in all lands, and at all stages in human development, of finding compensation in other things. This might explain to us why the Arab people were so fond of listening to the stories of *A Thousand and One Nights,* pulsating as they were with the passions of beautiful women and the seductions of sex. This eagerness to listen to, and repeat, what had been told over a thousand nights, aroused a fiery imagination and substituted illusions for what life could not give them in fact. [68]

REFERENCES

1. P. H. Newby, *A Selection from the Arabian Nights,* translated by Sir Richard Burton, Introduction from pp. vii–xvii (Pocket Books, N. T., 1954).
2. Franz G. Alexander and Sheldon T. Selesnick, *The History of Psychiatry,* p. 68.
3. *Fitna,* in Arabic means woman's overpowering seductiveness. It combines the qualities of attraction and mischievousness.
4. Abou Abdallah Mohammed Ismail El Bokhary, *Kitab El Gami El Sahib* (1868), p. 419.
5. Abou Hamid El Ghazali, *Ihya Ouloum El Dine,* Dar El Shaab Publishers (Cairo, 1970), p. 689.
6. *Ibid.,* p. 693.
7. *Ibid.,* p. 695.
8. *Ibid.,* p. 696.
9. *Ibid.,* p. 700.
10. *Ibid.,* p. 683.
11. *Ibid.,* p. 697.
12. Mohammed Ibn Saad, *El Tabakat El Kobra,* Vol. 8, Dar El Tahrir (Cairo, 1970), p. 139.
13. *Ibid.*
14. Abou Hamid, El Ghazali, *Ihy'a Ouloum El Dine,* Dar El Shaab Publishers (Cairo, 1970), p. 697.
15. *Ibid.,* p. 746.
16. *The Koran: Sourat El Nissa'a,* Verse 129.
17. *Ibid.*
18. *El Zamakhshari,* Vol. I, p. 143 and *El Kourtoubi,* Vol. 5, pp. 407–8.

19. *The Koran: Sourat El Nissa'a,* Verses 3 and 129.
20. *El Kourtoubi,* Vol. 5, pp. 20–2; *El Galadine,* Vol. I, p. 27; El Hassas, *Ahkam El Koran.*
21. Egyptian unit of money. One hundred piastres equal one Egyptian pound.
22. Abou Hamid El Ghazali, *Ihya Ouloum El Dine,* p. 699.
23. *Ibid.,* p. 706.
24. Sheikh Mohammed Mahdi Shams El Dine, *Al Islam wa Tanzeem El Waledeya,* Al Ittihad El Aalami Litanzeem El Waledeya. El Maktab El Iklimi Lilshark El Awsat wa Shamal Afrikia 1974, Vol. 2, p. 84.
25. *The Koran: Sourat Sab'a,* Verse 37.
26. *Al Imam Abou Hamid El Ghazali,* Dar El Shaab Publishers (Cairo, 1970), Chapter 3, p. 202.
27. *The Koran: Sourat El Nour,* Verse 33.
28. Abou Hamid El Ghazali, *Ihy'a Ouloum El Dine,* Dar El Shaab Publishers (Cairo, 1970), p. 706.
29. Tewfih Canaan, *Kawaneen Gheir Maktouba Tatahakam fi Makanat El Mara'a El Filistineya (Magalat El Torath, Wal Mogtam'a)* El Takadoum Publishers Al Kouds (Jerusalem), No. 2, 1974, p. 39.
30. My maternal grandmother lived in Cairo (1898–1948). She spent her whole life doing the chores at home and looking after her husband and children. She belonged to a middle class or rather higher middle class family. On the other hand, my paternal grandmother who lived during almost the same period in our village, Kafr Tahla, never knew what it was to wear a veil and used to go out to work in the fields or to buy and sell in the market every day, just as other poor peasant women did.
31. Tewfik Canaan, *Kawaneen Gheir Maktouba Tatahakam fi Makanat El Mara'a,* p. 40.
32. I very often heard the word *destour* repeated by villagers, whether men or women, in gatherings for *zar* (exhortational sessions) when mention was made of evil spirits or devils. One of those present would shout *destour* which means "O God, chase away the evil spirits from our way." The same word is used to clear the way for a man, especially when women are present, and are required to withdraw or to be warned by him that he is about to come in. The word also means the established order, constitution, or constitutional laws.
33. Tewfik Canaan, *El Yanabi'i El Maskouna Wa Shayatin El Ma'a (fi filistine) Magalat El Torath Wal Mogtama,* El Takadam Press (Jerusalem), No. 2, July 1974, p. 38.
34. Ibn El Mokafa, *El Adab El Saghir, Wal Adab El Kebir,* Maktabat El Bayan (Beirut, 1960), p. 127.

QUESTIONS FOR CRITICAL READING, THINKING, DISCUSSION, AND WRITING

Analyzing Content and Technique

1. Which work of literature, according to el-Saadawi, has given the West a mistaken impression of the "Arab soul"? What are some misconceptions it has created? Why are these images inaccurate?

2. What, according to this essay, are the major attitudes in Arab society today about women's sexuality? What is paradoxical about these attitudes?

3. In what ways does the author find the treatment of men and women inequitable? (Give examples from the selection.)

4. How has Islam influenced current attitudes toward women? (Cite appropriate passages from the selection.)

5. What is the writer's purpose? Who is her intended audience? How far do you think she will succeed in reaching them? Explain.

Collaborative Activity

As a group, research the prevalent attitude toward women in a religion other than Islam. Choose one or two passages from a religious text that you consider representative. Write a collaborative paragraph about the group's response to the passage.

Making Connections

1. El-Saadawi takes a close and critical look at the roles of men and women in her society and examines the religious roots of the current attitudes toward the sexes. Study this selection carefully, and then write an essay of your own, analyzing how the roles of men and women in your culture have been influenced by religious ideas or sacred texts. Be sure to give appropriate quotations. If no such influence exists, explain why, and indicate what it tells you about the culture. What has taken the place of religious influence?

2. In this selection, el-Saadawi claims that in her culture a woman is seen as "dangerous and destructive to society." Examine, in an essay, the reasons she gives for this belief. How does she refute them? On the basis of her arguments and her tone, summarize her own attitude toward women and her ideas on how they should be treated.

PREREADING ACTIVITY

Brainstorm about school experiences that made you feel part of a group, in either a positive or a negative way. What kinds of experiences were these? How did they affect your personality? Your sense of self?

Graduation

MAYA ANGELOU

Maya Angelou (1928–)—a writer, dancer, actress, and newspaper correspondent—has lived and traveled in many countries in Europe and Africa. She has written and produced a ten-part television series on the role of African traditions in American life and has directed and starred in several shows, such as *Cabaret for Freedom*. She has been the Northern Coordinator for the Southern Christian Leadership Conference. Her books include the autobiographies *I Know Why the Caged Bird Sings* (from which selection 63 is taken), *Gather Together in My Name* and *Singin' and Swingin' and Gettin' Merry Like Christmas;* and the volumes of poetry, *Just Give Me a Cool Drink of Water 'Fore I Diiie* and *Oh Pray My Wings Are Gonna Fit Me Well.*

The children in Stamps trembled visibly with anticipation. Some 1 adults were excited too, but to be certain the whole young population had come down with graduation epidemic. Large classes were graduating from both the grammar school and the high school. Even those who were years removed from their own day of glorious release were anxious to help with preparations as a kind of dry run. The junior students who were moving into the vacating classes' chairs were tradition-bound to show their talents for leadership and management. They strutted through the school and around the campus exerting pressure on the lower grades. Their authority was so new that occasionally if they pressed a little too hard it had to be overlooked. After all, next term was coming, and it never hurt a sixth grader to have a play sister in the eighth grade, or a tenth-year student to be able to call a twelfth grader Bubba. So all was endured in a spirit of shared understanding. But the graduating classes themselves were the nobility. Like travelers with exotic destinations on their minds, the graduates were remarkably forgetful. They came to school without their books, or tablets or even pencils. Volunteers fell over themselves to secure replacements for the missing equipment. When accepted, the willing workers might or might not be thanked, and it was of no importance to the pregraduation rites. Even teachers were respectful of the now quiet and aging seniors, and tended to speak to them, if not as equals, as beings only slightly lower than themselves. After tests were returned and grades given, the student body, which acted like an extended family, knew who did well, who excelled, and what piteous ones had failed.

Unlike the white high school, Lafayette County Training School distin- 2 guished itself by having neither lawn, nor hedges, nor tennis court, nor climbing ivy. Its two buildings (main classrooms, the grade school and home economics) were set on a dirt hill with no fence to limit either its boundaries or those of bordering farms. There was a large expanse to the left of the school which was used alternately as a baseball diamond or a basketball court. Rusty hoops on the swaying poles represented the permanent recreational equipment, although bats and balls could be borrowed from the P.E. teacher if the borrower was qualified and if the diamond wasn't occupied.

Over this rocky area relieved by a few shady tall persimmon trees the 3 graduating class walked. The girls often held hands and no longer bothered to speak to the lower students. There was a sadness about them, as if this old world was not their home and they were bound for higher ground. The boys, on the other hand, had become more friendly, more outgoing. A decided change from the closed attitude they projected while studying for finals. Now they seemed not ready to give up the old school, the familiar paths and classrooms. Only a small percentage would be continuing on to college—one of the South's A & M (agricultural and mechanical) schools, which trained Negro youths to be carpenters, farmers, handymen, masons, maids, cooks and baby nurses. Their future rode heavily on their shoulders, and blinded them to the collective joy that had pervaded the lives of the boys and girls in the grammar school graduating class.

Parents who could afford it had ordered new shoes and ready-made clothes 4 for themselves from Sears and Roebuck or Montgomery Ward. They also engaged the best seamstresses to make the floating graduating dresses and to cut down secondhand pants which would be pressed to a military slickness for the important event.

Oh, it was important, all right. Whitefolks would attend the ceremony, and 5 two or three would speak of God and home, and the Southern way of life, and Mrs. Parsons, the principal's wife, would play the graduation march while the lower-grade graduates paraded down the aisles and took their seats below the platform. The high school seniors would wait in empty classrooms to make their dramatic entrance.

In the Store I was the person of the moment. The birthday girl. The center. 6 Bailey had graduated the year before, although to do so he had to forfeit all pleasures to make up for his time lost in Baton Rouge.

My class was wearing butter-yellow piqué dresses, and Momma launched 7 out on mine. She smocked the yoke into tiny crisscrossing puckers, then shirred the rest of the bodice. Her dark fingers ducked in and out of the lemony cloth as she embroidered raised daisies around the hem. Before she considered herself finished she had added a crocheted cuff on the puff sleeves, and a pointy crocheted collar.

I was going to be lovely. A walking model of all the various styles of fine 8 hand sewing and it didn't worry me that I was only twelve years old and merely graduating from the eighth grade. Besides, many teachers in Arkansas Negro schools had only that diploma and were licensed to impart wisdom.

The days had become longer and more noticeable. The faded beige of 9 former times had been replaced with strong and sure colors. I began to see my classmates' clothes, their skin tones, and the dust that waved off pussy willows. Clouds that lazed across the sky were objects of great concern to me. Their shiftier shapes might have held a message that in my new happiness and with a little bit of time I'd soon decipher. During that period I looked at the arch of heaven so religiously my neck kept a steady ache. I had taken to smiling more often, and my jaws hurt from the unaccustomed activity. Between the two physical sore spots, I suppose I could have been uncomfortable, but that was not the case. As a member of the winning team (the graduating class of 1940) I had outdistanced unpleasant sensations by miles. I was headed for the freedom of open fields.

Youth and social approval allied themselves with me and we trammeled 10 memories of slights and insults. The wind of our swift passage remodeled my features. Lost tears were pounded to mud and then to dust. Years of withdrawal were brushed aside and left behind, as hanging ropes of parasitic moss.

My work alone had awarded me a top place and I was going to be one of the 11 first called in the graduating ceremonies. On the classroom blackboard, as well as on the bulletin board in the auditorium, there were blue stars and white stars and red stars. No absences, no tardinesses, and my academic work was among the best of the year. I could say the preamble to the Constitution even faster than Bailey. We timed ourselves often: "WethepeopleoftheUnitedStatesinordertoformamore perfectunion . . ." I had memorized the Presidents of the United States from Washington to Roosevelt in chronological as well as alphabetical order.

My hair pleased me too. Gradually the black mass had lengthened and 12 thickened, so that it kept at last to its braided pattern, and I didn't have to yank my scalp off when I tried to comb it.

Louise and I had rehearsed the exercises until we tired out ourselves. Henry 13 Reed was class valedictorian. He was a small, very black boy with hooded eyes, a long, broad nose and an oddly shaped head. I had admired him for years because each term he and I vied for the best grades in our class. Most often he bested me, but instead of being disappointed I was pleased that we shared top places between us. Like many Southern Black children, he lived with his grandmother, who was as strict as Momma and as kind as she knew how to be. He was courteous, respectful and soft-spoken to elders, but on the playground he chose to play the roughest games. I admired him. Anyone, I reckoned, sufficiently afraid or sufficiently dull could be polite. But to be able to operate at a top level with both adults and children was admirable.

His valedictory speech was entitled "To Be or Not to Be." The rigid tenth- 14 grade teacher had helped him write it. He'd been working on the dramatic stresses for months.

The weeks until graduation were filled with heady activities. A group of 15 small children were to be presented in a play about buttercups and daisies and bunny rabbits. They could be heard throughout the building practicing their hops and their little songs that sounded like silver bells. The older girls (nongraduates, or course) were assigned the task of making refreshments for the night's festivities. A tangy scent of ginger, cinnamon, nutmeg and chocolate wafted around the home economics building as the budding cooks made samples for themselves and their teachers.

In every corner of the workshop, axes and saws split fresh timber as the 16 woodshop boys made sets and stage scenery. Only the graduates were left out of the general bustle. We were free to sit in the library at the back of the building or look in quite detachedly, naturally, on the measures being taken for our event.

Even the minister preached on graduation the Sunday before. His subject 17 was, "Let your light so shine that men will see your good works and praise your Father, Who is in Heaven." Although the sermon was purported to be addressed to us, he used the occasion to speak to backsliders, gamblers and general ne'er-do-wells. But since he had called our names at the beginning of the service we were mollified.

Among Negroes the tradition was to give presents to children going only 18 from one grade to another. How much more important this was when the person was graduating at the top of the class. Uncle Willie and Momma had sent away for a Mickey Mouse watch like Bailey's. Louise gave me four embroidered handkerchiefs. (I have her three crocheted doilies.) Mrs. Sneed, the minister's wife, made me an underskirt to wear for graduation, and nearly every customer gave me a nickel or maybe even a dime with the instruction "Keep on moving to higher ground," or some such encouragement.

Amazingly the great day finally dawned and I was out of bed before I knew 19 it. I threw open the back door to see it more clearly, but Momma said, "Sister, come away from that door and put your robe on."

I hoped the memory of that morning would never leave me. Sunlight was 20 itself still young, and the day had none of the insistence maturity would bring it in a few hours. In my robe and barefoot in the backyard, under cover of going to see about my new beans, I gave myself up to the gentle warmth and thanked God that no matter what evil I had done in my life He had allowed me to live to see this day. Somewhere in my fatalism I had expected to die, accidentally, and never have the chance to walk up the stairs in the auditorium and gracefully receive my hard-earned diploma. Out of God's merciful bosom I had won reprieve.

Bailey came out in his robe and gave me a box wrapped in Christmas paper. 21 He said he had saved his money for months to pay for it. It felt like a box of chocolates, but I knew Bailey wouldn't save money to buy candy when we had all we could want under our noses.

He was as proud of the gift as I. It was a soft-leather-bound copy of a 22
collection of poems by Edgar Allan Poe, or, as Bailey and I called him, "Eap." I
turned to "Annabel Lee" and we walked up and down the garden rows, the cool
dirt between our toes, reciting the beautifully sad lines.

Momma made a Sunday breakfast although it was only Friday. After we 23
finished the blessing, I opened my eyes to find the watch on my plate. It was a
dream of a day. Everything went smoothly and to my credit. I didn't have to be
reminded or scolded for anything. Near evening I was too jittery to attend to
chores, so Bailey volunteered to do all before his bath.

Days before, we had made a sign for the Store, and as we turned out the 24
lights Momma hung the cardboard over the doorknob. It read clearly: CLOSED.
GRADUATION.

My dress fitted perfectly and everyone said that I looked like a sunbeam in 25
it. On the hill, going toward the school, Bailey walked behind with Uncle Willie,
who muttered, "Go on, Ju." We wanted him to walk ahead with us because it
embarrassed him to have to walk so slowly. Bailey said he'd let the ladies walk
together, and the men would bring up the rear. We all laughed, nicely.

Little children dashed by out of the dark like fireflies. Their crepe-paper 26
dresses and butterfly wings were not made for running and we heard more than
one rip, dryly, and the regretful "uh uh" that followed.

The school blazed without gaiety. The windows seemed cold and unfriendly 27
from the lower hill. A sense of ill-fated timing crept over me, and if Momma
hadn't reached for my hand I would have drifted back to Bailey and Uncle Willie,
and possibly beyond. She made a few slow jokes about my feet getting cold, and
tugged me along to the now-strange building.

Around the front steps, assurance came back. There were my fellow 28
"greats," the graduating class. Hair brushed back, legs oiled, new dresses and
pressed pleats, fresh pocket handkerchiefs and little handbags, all homesewn. Oh,
we were up to snuff, all right. I joined my comrades and didn't even see my
family go in to find seats in the crowded auditorium.

The school band struck up a march and all classes filed in as had been 29
rehearsed. We stood in front of our seats, as assigned, and on signal from the
choir director, we sat. No sooner had this been accomplished than the band
started to play the national anthem. We rose again and sang the song, after which
we recited the pledge of allegiance. We remained standing for a brief minute
before the choir director and the principal signaled to us, rather desperately I
thought, to take our seats. The command was so unusual that our carefully
rehearsed and smooth-running machine was thrown off. For a full minute we
fumbled for our chairs and bumped into each other awkwardly. Habits change or
solidify under pressure, so in our state of nervous tension we had been ready to
follow our usual assembly pattern: the American national anthem, then the
pledge of allegiance, then the song every Black person I knew called the Negro
National Anthem. All done in the same key, with the same passion and most
often standing on the same foot.

Finding my seat at last, I was overcome with a presentiment of worse things 30
to come. Something unrehearsed, unplanned, was going to happen, and we were

going to be made to look bad. I distinctly remember being explicit in the choice of pronoun. It was "we," the graduating class, the unit, that concerned me then.

The principal welcomed "parents and friends" and asked the Baptist ₃₁ minister to lead us in prayer. His invocation was brief and punchy, and for a second I thought we were getting back on the high road to right action. When the principal came back to the dais, however, his voice had changed. Sounds always affected me profoundly and the principal's voice was one of my favorites. During assembly it melted and lowered weakly into the audience. It had not been in my plan to listen to him, but my curiosity was piqued and I straightened up to give him my attention.

He was talking about Booker T. Washington, our "late great leader," who ₃₂ said we can be as close as the fingers on the hand, etc. . . . Then he said a few vague things about friendship and the friendship of the kindly people to those less fortunate than themselves. With that his voice nearly faded, thin, away. Like a river diminishing to a stream and then to a trickle. But he cleared his throat and said, "Our speaker tonight, who is also our friend, came from Texarkana to deliver the commencement address, but due to the irregularity of the train schedule, he's going to, as they say, 'speak and run.'" He said that we understood and wanted the man to know we were most grateful for the time he was able to give us and then something about how we were willing always to adjust to another's program, and without more ado—"I give you Mr. Edward Donleavy."

Not one but two white men came through the door offstage. The shorter ₃₃ one walked to the speaker's platform, and the tall one moved over to the center seat and sat down. But that was our principal's seat, and already occupied. The dislodged gentleman bounced around for a long breath or two before the Baptist minister gave him his chair, then with more dignity than the situation deserved, the minister walked off the stage.

Donleavy looked at the audience once (on reflection, I'm sure that he ₃₄ wanted only to reassure himself that we were really there), adjusted his glasses and began to read from a sheaf of papers.

He was glad "to be here and to see the work going on just as it was in the ₃₅ other schools."

At the first "Amen" from the audience I willed the offender to immediate ₃₆ death by choking on the word. But Amens and Yes, sir's began to fall around the room like rain on a ragged umbrella.

He told us of the wonderful changes we children in Stamps had in store. ₃₇ The Central School (naturally, the white school was Central) had already been granted improvements that would be in use in the fall. A well-known artist was coming from Little Rock to teach art to them. They were going to have the newest microscopes and chemistry equipment for their laboratory. Mr. Donleavy didn't leave us long in the dark over who made these improvements available to Central High. Nor were we to be ignored in the general betterment scheme he had in mind.

He said that he had pointed out to people at a very high level that one of ₃₈ the first-line football tacklers at Arkansas Agricultural and Mechanical College had graduated from good old Lafayette County Training School. Here fewer

Amens were heard. Those few that did break through lay dully in the air with the heaviness of habit.

He went on to praise us. He went on to say how he had bragged that 39 "one of the best basketball players at Fisk sank his first ball right here at Lafayette County Training School."

The white kids were going to have a chance to become Galileos and 40 Madame Curies and Edisons and Gauguins, and our boys (the girls weren't even in on it) would try to be Jesse Owenses and Joe Louises.

Owens and the Brown Bomber were great heroes in our world, but what 41 school official in the white-goddom of Little Rock had the right to decide that those two men must be our only heroes? Who decided that for Henry Reed to become a scientist he had to work like George Washington Carver, as a boot-black, to buy a lousy microscope? Bailey was obviously always going to be too small to be an athlete, so which concrete angel glued to what county seat had decided that if my brother wanted to become a lawyer he had to first pay penance for his skin by picking cotton and hoeing corn and studying corre-spondence books at night for twenty years?

The man's dead words fell like bricks around the auditorium and too many 42 settled in my belly. Constrained by hard-learned manners I couldn't look behind me, but to my left and right the proud graduating class of 1940 had dropped their heads. Every girl in my row had found something new to do with her handkerchief. Some folded the tiny squares into love knots, some into triangles, but most were wadding them, then pressing them flat on their yellow laps.

On the dais, the ancient tragedy was being replayed. Professor Parsons sat, a 43 sculptor's reject, rigid. His large, heavy body seemed devoid of will or willing-ness, and his eyes said he was no longer with us. The other teachers examined the flag (which was draped stage right) or their notes, or the windows which opened on our now-famous playing diamond.

Graduation, the hush-hush magic time of frills and gifts and congratulations 44 and diplomas, was finished for me before my name was called. The accom-plishment was nothing. The meticulous maps, drawn in three colors of ink, learning and spelling decasyllabic words, memorizing the whole of *The Rape of Lucrece*—it was for nothing. Donleavy had exposed us.

We were maids and farmers, handymen and washerwomen, and anything 45 higher that we aspired to was farcical and presumptuous.

Then I wished that Gabriel Prosser and Nat Turner had killed all whitefolks 46 in their beds and that Abraham Lincoln had been assassinated before the signing of the Emancipation Proclamation, and that Harriet Tubman had been killed by that blow on her head and Christopher Columbus had drowned in the *Santa Maria*.

It was awful to be Negro and have no control over my life. It was brutal to 47 be young and already trained to sit quietly and listen to charges brought against my color with no chance of defense. We should all be dead. I thought I should like to see us all dead, one on top of the other. A pyramid of flesh with the whitefolks on the bottom, as the broad base, then the Indians with their silly tomahawks and teepees and wigwams and treaties, the Negroes with their mops and recipes and cotton sacks and spirituals sticking out of their mouths. The

Dutch children should all stumble in their wooden shoes and break their necks. The French should choke to death on the Louisiana Purchase (1803) while silkworms ate all the Chinese with their stupid pigtails. As a species, we were an abomination. All of us.

Donleavy was running for election, and assured our parents that if he won 48 we could count on having the only colored paved playing field in that part of Arkansas. Also—he never looked up to acknowledge the grunts of acceptance— also, we were bound to get some new equipment for the home economics building and the workshop.

He finished, and since there was no need to give any more than the 49 most perfunctory thank-you's, he nodded to the men on the stage, and the tall white man who was never introduced joined him at the door. They left with the attitude that now they were off to something really important. (The graduation ceremonies at Lafayette County Training School had been a mere preliminary.)

The ugliness they left was palpable. An uninvited guest who wouldn't leave. 50 The choir was summoned and sang a modern arrangement of "Onward, Christian Soldiers," with new words pertaining to graduates seeking their place in the world. But it didn't work. Elouise, the daughter of the Baptist minister, recited "Invictus," and I could have cried at the impertinence of "I am the master of my fate, I am the captain of my soul."

My name had lost its ring of familiarity and I had to be nudged to go and 51 receive my diploma. All my preparations had fled. I neither marched up to the stage like a conquering Amazon, nor did I look in the audience for Bailey's nod of approval. Marguerite Johnson, I heard the name again, my honors were read, there were noises in the audience of appreciation, and I took my place on the stage as rehearsed.

I thought about colors I hated: ecru, puce, lavender, beige and black. 52

There was shuffling and rustling around me, then Henry Reed was 53 giving his valedictory address, "To Be or Not to Be." Hadn't he heard the whitefolks? We couldn't *be*, so the question was a waste of time. Henry's voice came our clear and strong. I feared to look at him. Hadn't he got the message? There was no "nobler in the mind" for Negroes because the world didn't think we had minds, and they let us know it. "Outrageous fortune"? Now, that was a joke. When the ceremony was over I had to tell Henry Reed some things. That is, if I still cared. Not "rub," Henry, "erase." "Ah, there's the erase." Us.

Henry had been a good student in elocution. His voice rose on tides of 54 promise and fell on waves of warnings. The English teacher had helped him to create a sermon winging through Hamlet's soliloquy. To be a man, a doer, a builder, a leader, or to be a tool, an unfunny joke, a crusher of funky toadstools. I marveled that Henry could go through with the speech as if we had a choice.

I had been listening and silently rebutting each sentence with my eyes 55 closed; then there was a hush, which in an audience warns that something unplanned is happening. I looked up and saw Henry Reed, the conservative, the proper, the A student, turn his back to the audience and turn to us (the proud graduating class of 1940) and sing, nearly speaking,

"Lift ev'ry voice and sing
Till earth and heaven ring
Ring with the harmonies of Liberty . . . "

It was the poem written by James Weldon Johnson. It was the music [56] composed by J. Rosamond Johnson. It was the Negro national anthem. Out of habit we were singing it.

Our mothers and fathers stood in the dark hall and joined the hymn of [57] encouragement. A kindergarten teacher led the small children onto the stage and the buttercups and daisies and bunny rabbits marked time and tried to follow:

"Stony the road we trod
Bitter the chastening rod
Felt in the days when hope, unborn, had died
Yet with a steady beat
Have not our weary feet
Come to the place for which our fathers sighed?"

Every child I knew had learned that song with his ABC's and along with [58] "Jesus Loves Me This I Know." But I personally had never heard it before. Never heard the words, despite the thousands of times I had sung them. Never thought they had anything to do with me.

On the other hand, the words of Patrick Henry had made such an [59] impression on me that I had been able to stretch myself tall and trembling and say, "I know not what course others may take, but as for me, give me liberty or give me death."

And now I heard, really for the first time: [60]

"We have come over a way that with tears
has been watered,
We have come, treading our path through
the blood of the slaughtered."

While echoes of the song shivered in the air, Henry Reed bowed his head, [61] said "Thank you," and returned to his place in the line. The tears that slipped down many faces were not wiped away in shame.

We were on top again. As always, again. We survived. The depths had been [62] icy and dark, but now a bright sun spoke to our souls. I was no longer simply a member of the proud graduating class of 1940; I was a proud member of the wonderful, beautiful Negro race.

QUESTIONS FOR CRITICAL READING, THINKING, DISCUSSION, AND WRITING

Analyzing Content and Technique

1. What kind of atmosphere is created in paragraph 1? In paragraph 2? How does this fore-shadow what happens toward the end of the piece?
2. How would you define the attitude of the black community toward graduation? Pick out details that best illustrate this view. Why do you think they have such an attitude?
3. Analyze Donleavy's speech. What are some of the assumptions in the speech? Describe its tone and what it indicates about the kind of person he is. What other details are we given about his character?
4. How does the narrator respond to the speech? Which details indicate that she is not alone in her response? How is the graduating class able to turn this incident around positively?
5. What does the writer learn from this incident about herself and her race? About possible future problems and how to face them? Pick out one or two quotations that best address this issue, and discuss them.
6. Analyze the writer's style and diction, identifying the elements that make it striking.

Collaborative Activity

As a group, discuss the message, or moral, of this piece. Now have group members each sprint write for a few minutes about what they can learn from this piece and apply to their own lives. Read your passages aloud to the group, comparing and contrasting your responses.

Making Connections

1. What were you brought up to believe about education and about the value of education? (Think about the ideas of family members and authority figures outside the family as well as ideas prevalent in your culture—for instance, as seen through the media.) What do you perceive to be the role of education in your life today? How has it shaped your sense of who you are and what you are capable of? Write an essay developing some of these points in an organized manner.
2. In selection 64, a young girl gains a new and different sense of herself. Compare this selection with another one—from any part of the book—that also deals with someone who gains a new vision of himself or herself. Analyze the circumstances that caused this new vision.

64

PREREADING ACTIVITY

Have you (or has someone you know) ever belonged to a minority group that had to interact with a larger community? Describe the experience, explaining the dynamics between the groups.

Shooting an Elephant

GEORGE ORWELL

George Orwell (1903–1950) was born in India. He was sent by his English parents to Eton, a prestigious public school in England. He did not enjoy the experience and returned to India after graduation to work for the Imperial Police. "Shooting an Elephant" recalls an experience he had at that time in Burma. Soon after this, he turned to full-time writing. Among his books are *Down and Out in Paris and London*, which describes his life as an impoverished writer; *Homage to Catalonia*, which deals with his experiences in the Spanish Civil War; and *Animal Farm* and *1984*, two novels which present a stark picture of communism through fantasy and allegory.

In Moulmein, in lower Burma, I was hated by large numbers of   1
people—the only time in my life that I have been important enough for this to happen to me. I was sub-divisional police officer of the town, and in an aimless, petty kind of way anti-European feeling was very bitter. No one had the guts to raise a riot, but if a European woman went through the bazaars alone somebody would probably spit betel juice over her dress. As a police officer I was an obvious target and was baited whenever it seemed safe to do so. When a nimble Burman tripped me up on the football field and the referee (another Burman) looked the other way the crowd yelled with hideous laughter. This happened more than once. In the end, the sneering yellow faces that met me everywhere, the insults hooted after me when I was at a safe distance, got badly on my nerves. The young Buddhist priests were the worst of all. There were several thousands of them in the town and none of them seemed to have anything to do except stand on street corners and jeer at Europeans.

Source: From *Shooting an Elephant and Other Essays* by George Orwell, copyright 1950 by Sonia Brownell Orwell and renewed 1978 by Sonia Pitt-Rivers; reprinted by permission of Harcourt Brace Jovanovich, Inc., the estate of the late Sonia Brownell Orwell, and Martin Secker & Warburg Ltd.

All this was perplexing and upsetting. For at that time I had already made up my mind that imperialism was an evil thing and the sooner I chucked up my job and got out of it the better. Theoretically—and secretly, of course—I was all for the Burmese and all against their oppressors, the British. As for the job I was doing, I hated it more bitterly than I can make clear. In a job like that you see the dirty work of Empire at close quarters. The wretched prisoners huddling in the stinking cages of the lockups, the grey, cowed faces of the long-term convicts, the scarred buttocks of the men who had been flogged with bamboos—all these oppressed me with an intolerable sense of guilt. But I could get nothing into perspective. I was young and ill-educated and I had to think of my problems in the utter silence that is imposed on every Englishman in the East. I did not even know that the British Empire is dying, still less did I know that it is a great deal better than the younger empires that are going to supplant it. All I knew was that I was stuck between my hatred of the Empire I served and my rage against the evil-spirited little beasts who tried to make my job impossible. With one part of my mind I thought of the British Raj as an unbreakable tyranny, as something clamped down, in *saecula saeculorum,* upon the will of prostrate peoples; with another part I thought that the greatest joy in the world would be to drive a bayonet into a Buddhist priest's guts. Feelings like these are the normal by-products of Imperialism; ask any Anglo-Indian official, if you can catch him off duty.

One day something happened which in a roundabout way was enlightening. It was a tiny incident in itself, but it gave me a better glimpse than I had had before of the real nature of imperialism—the real motives for which despotic governments act. Early one morning the sub-inspector at a police station at the other end of town rang me up on the 'phone and said that an elephant was ravaging the bazaar. Would I please come and do something about it? I did not know what I could do, but I wanted to see what was happening and I got on to a pony and started out. I took my rifle, an old .44 Winchester and much too small to kill an elephant, but I thought the noise might be useful *in terrorem*. Various Burmans stopped me on the way and told me about the elephant's doings. It was not, of course, a wild elephant, but a tame one which had gone "must." It had been chained up, as tame elephants always are when their attack of "must" is due, but on the previous night it had broken its chain and escaped. Its mahout, the only person who could manage it when it was in that state, had set out in pursuit, but had taken the wrong direction and was now twelve hours' journey away, and in the morning the elephant had suddenly reappeared in the town. The Burmese population had no weapons and were quite helpless against it. It had already destroyed somebody's bamboo hut, killed a cow and raided some fruit-stalls and devoured the stock; also it had met the municipal rubbish van and, when the driver jumped out and took to his heels, had turned the van over and inflicted violences upon it.

The Burmese sub-inspector and some Indian constables were waiting for me in the quarter where the elephant had been seen. It was a very poor quarter, a labyrinth of squalid bamboo huts, thatched with palm-leaf, winding all over a steep hillside. I remember that it was a cloudy, stuffy morning at the beginning of the rains. We began questioning the people as to where the elephant had gone and, as usual, failed to get any definite information. That is invariably the case in the East; a story always sounds clear enough at a distance, but the nearer you get to the scene of events the vaguer it becomes. Some of the people said that the elephant had gone in one direction, some said that he had gone in another, some professed not even to have heard of any elephant. I had almost made up my mind that the whole story was a pack of lies, when we heard yells a little distance away. There was a loud, scandalized cry of "Go away, child! Go away this instant!" and an old woman with a switch in her hand came round the corner of a hut, violently shooing away a crowd of naked children. Some more women followed, clicking their tongues and exclaiming; evidently there was something that the children ought not to have seen. I rounded the hut and saw a man's dead body sprawling in the mud. He was an Indian, a black Dravidian coolie, almost naked, and he could not have been dead many minutes. The people said that the elephant had come suddenly upon him round the corner of the hut, caught him with its trunk, put its foot on his back and ground him into the earth. This was the rainy season and the ground was soft; and his face had scored a trench a foot deep and a couple of yards long. He was lying on his belly with arms crucified and head sharply twisted to one side. His face was coated with mud, the eyes wide open, the teeth bared and grinning with an expression of unendurable agony. (Never tell me, by the way, that the dead look peaceful. Most of the corpses I have seen looked devilish.) The friction of the great beast's foot had stripped the skin from his back as neatly as one skins a rabbit. As soon as I saw the dead man I sent an orderly to a friend's house nearby to borrow an elephant rifle. I had already sent back the pony, not wanting it to go mad with fright and throw me if it smelt the elephant.

The orderly came back in a few minutes with a rifle and five cartridges, and meanwhile some Burmans had arrived and told us that the elephant was in the paddy fields below, only a few hundred yards away. As I started forward practically the whole population of the quarter flocked out of the houses and followed me. They had seen the rifle and were all shouting excitedly that I was going to shoot the elephant. They had not shown much interest in the elephant when he was merely ravaging their homes, but it was different now that he was going to be shot. It was a bit of fun to them, as it would be to an English crowd; besides they wanted the meat. It made me vaguely uneasy. I had no intention of shooting the elephant—I had merely sent for the rifle to defend myself if necessary—and it is always unnerving to have a crowd following you. I marched down the hill, looking and feeling a fool, with the rifle over my shoulder and an ever-growing army of people jostling at my heels. At the bottom, when you got away from the huts, there was a metalled road and beyond that a miry waste of paddy fields a thousand yards across, not yet ploughed but soggy from the first rains and dotted with coarse grass. The elephant was standing eight yards from the road, his left side towards us. He took not the slightest notice of the crowd's approach. He was tearing up bunches of grass, beating them against his knees to clean them and stuffing them into his mouth.

I had halted on the road. As soon as I saw the elephant I knew with perfect certainty that I ought not to shoot him. It is a serious matter to shoot a working elephant—it is comparable to destroying a huge and costly piece of machinery—

and obviously one ought not to do it if it can possibly be avoided. And at that distance, peacefully eating, the elephant looked no more dangerous than a cow. I thought then and I think now that his attack of "must" was already passing off; in which case he would merely wander harmlessly about until the mahout came back and caught him. Moreover, I did not in the least want to shoot him. I decided that I would watch him for a little while to make sure that he did not turn savage again, and then go home.

But at that moment I glanced round at the crowd that had followed me. It was an immense crowd, two thousand at the least and growing every minute. It blocked the road for a long distance on either side. I looked at the sea of yellow faces above the garish clothes—faces all happy and excited over this bit of fun, all certain that the elephant was going to be shot. They were watching me as they would watch a conjurer about to perform a trick. They did not like me, but with the magical rifle in my hands I was momentarily worth watching. And suddenly I realized that I should have to shoot the elephant after all. The people expected it of me and I had got to do it; I could feel their two thousand wills pressing me forward, irresistibly. And it was at this moment, as I stood there with the rifle in my hands, that I first grasped the hollowness, the futility of the white man's dominion in the East. Here was I, the white man with his gun, standing in front of the unarmed native crowd—seemingly the leading actor of the piece; but in reality I was only an absurd puppet pushed to and fro by the will of those yellow faces behind. I perceived in this moment that when the white man turns tyrant it is his own freedom that he destroys. He becomes a sort of hollow, posing dummy, the conventionalized figure of a sahib. For it is the condition of his rule that he shall spend his life in trying to impress the "natives," and so in every crisis he has got to do what the "natives" expect of him. He wears a mask, and his face grows to fit it. I had got to shoot the elephant. I had committed myself to doing it when I sent for the rifle. A sahib has got to act like a sahib; he has got to appear resolute, to know his own mind and do definite things. To come all that way, rifle in hand, with two thousand people marching at my heels, and then to trail feebly away, having done nothing—no, that was impossible. The crowd would laugh at me. And my whole life, every white man's life in the East, was one long struggle not to be laughed at.

But I did not want to shoot the elephant. I watched him beating his bunch of grass against his knees, with that preoccupied grandmotherly air that elephants have. It seemed to me that it would be murder to shoot him. At that age I was not squeamish about killing animals, but I had never shot an elephant and never wanted to. (Somehow it always seems worse to kill a *large* animal.) Besides, there was the beast's owner to be considered. Alive, the elephant was worth at least a hundred pounds; dead, he would only be worth the value of his tusks, five pounds, possibly. But I had got to act quickly. I turned to some experienced looking Burmans who had been there when we arrived, and asked them how the elephant had been behaving. They all said the same thing: he took no notice of you if you left him alone, but he might charge if you went too close to him.

It was perfectly clear to me what I ought to do. I ought to walk up to within, say, twenty-five yards of the elephant and test his behavior. If he charged, I could shoot; if he took no notice of me, it would be safe to leave him until the mahout came back. But also I knew that I was going to do no such thing. I was a poor shot with a rifle and the ground was soft mud into which one would sink at every step. If the elephant charged and I missed him, I should have about as much chance as a toad under a steam-roller. But even then I was not thinking particularly of my own skin, only of the watchful yellow faces behind. For at that moment, with the crowd watching me, I was not afraid in the ordinary sense, as I would have been if I had been alone. A white man mustn't be frightened in front of "natives"; and so, in general, he isn't frightened. The sole thought in my mind was that if anything went wrong those two thousand Burmans would see me pursued, caught, trampled on and reduced to a grinning corpse like that Indian up the hill. And if that happened it was quite probable that some of them would laugh. That would never do. There was only one alternative. I shoved the cartridges into the magazine and lay down on the road to get a better aim.

The crowd grew very still, and a deep, low, happy sigh, as of people who see 10 the theatre curtain go up at last, breathed from unnumerable throats. They were going to have their bit of fun after all. The rifle was a beautiful German thing with cross-hair sights. I did not then know that in shooting an elephant one would shoot to cut an imaginary bar running from ear-hole to ear-hole. I ought, therefore as the elephant was sideways on, to have aimed straight at his ear hole; actually I aimed several inches in front of this, thinking the brain would be further forward.

When I pulled the trigger I did not hear the bank or feel the kick—one 11 never does when a shot goes home—but I heard the devilish roar of glee that went up from the crowd. In that instant, in too short a time, one would have thought, even for the bullet to get there, a mysterious, terrible change had come over the elephant. He neither stirred nor fell, but every line of his body had altered. He looked suddenly stricken, shrunken, immensely old, as though the frightful impact of the bullet had paralyzed him without knocking him down. At last, after what seemed a long time—it might have been five seconds, I dare say— he sagged flabbily to his knees. His mouth slobbered. An enormous senility seemed to have settled upon him. One could have imagined him thousands of years old. I fired again into the same spot. At the second shot he did not collapse but climbed with desperate slowness to his feet and stood weakly upright, with legs sagging and head drooping. I fired a third time. That was the shot that did for him. You could see the agony of it jolt his whole body and knock the last remnant of strength from his legs. But in falling he seemed for a moment to rise, for as his hind legs collapsed beneath him he seemed to tower upward like a huge rock toppling, his trunk reaching skywards like a tree. He trumpeted, for the first and only time. And then down he came, his belly towards me, with a crash that seemed to shake the ground even where I lay.

I got up. The Burmans were already racing past me across the mud. It was 12 obvious that the elephant would never rise again, but he was not dead. He was breathing very rhythmically with long rattling gasps, his great mound of a side painfully rising and falling. His mouth was wide open—I could see far down into caverns of pale pink throat. I waited a long time for him to die, but his breathing did not weaken. Finally, I fired my two remaining shots into the spot where I thought his heart must be. The thick blood welled out of him like red velvet, but still he did not die. His body did not even jerk when the shots hit him, the tortured breathing continued without a pause. He was dying, very slowly and in great agony, but in some world remote from me where not even a bullet could damage him further. I felt that I had got to put an end to that dreadful noise. It seemed dreadful to see the great beast lying there, powerless to move and yet powerless to die, and not even to be able to finish him. I sent back for my small rifle and poured shot after shot into his heart and down his throat. They seemed to make no impression. The tortured gasps continued as steadily as the ticking of a clock.

In the end I could not stand it any longer and went away. I heard later that 13 it took him half an hour to die. Burmans were bringing dahs and baskets even before I left, and I was told they had stripped his body almost to the bones by the afternoon.

Afterwards, of course, there were endless discussions about the shooting of 14 the elephant. The owner was furious, but he was only an Indian and could do nothing. Besides, legally I had done the right thing, for a mad elephant has to be killed, like a mad dog, if its owner fails to control it. Among the Europeans opinion was divided. The older men said I was right, the younger men said it was a damn shame to shoot an elephant for killing a coolie, because an elephant was worth more than any damn Coringhee coolie. And afterwards I was very glad that the coolie had been killed: it put me legally in the right and it gave me a sufficient pretext for shooting the elephant. I often wondered whether any of the others grasped that I had done it solely to avoid looking a fool.

QUESTIONS FOR CRITICAL READING, THINKING, DISCUSSION, AND WRITING

Analyzing Content and Technique

1. What tone does Orwell set in the first sentence? What is the narrator's attitude toward himself?
2. What is the purpose of paragraphs 1 and 2? What techniques does Orwell use in them to attract the reader's attention?
3. Describe the elephant. (Orwell gives several different descriptions at various points.) How dangerous is it? In what way might it be considered a symbol?
4. Why does the narrator shoot the elephant? How does he feel about his action? Which details imply his emotions most strongly?
5. The shooting of the elephant is presented from the perspectives of several different characters or groups. Who are they? What do their comments and opinions tell us about them and their position in society?
6. What is the thesis of the essay, and where does it occur? Do you think the generalization Orwell draws from this incident is valid? Give reasons to support your opinion.

Collaborative Activity

As a group, make a list of the similes and metaphors used by Orwell. Where do you find most of them? What have they added to his writing? How do they help convince the reader of his thesis?

Making Connections

1. Orwell describes a situation in which group pressure causes an individual to act in a certain way. Write an essay about a similar experience—either personal or observed—and compare it with Orwell's in terms of situation, cause, and effect.

2. In an essay, analyze the effects of colonialism on the colonizer. You may elaborate on some of Orwell's points, but be sure to bring in ideas of your own supported by research.

65

Why They Hated Us: A Study of the Nature of British Imperialism in Orwell's Time (Student Essay)

JAANA PARKKINEN

At the beginning of the twentieth century many Europeans had a 1
glorified and romantic illusion of colonialism. They associated it with luxurious living in tea plantations, afternoon gin and tonics in country clubs, tiger hunting with the local princes and elephant safaris in the jungles. They often left their homes for the overseas colonies in search of an exciting adventure or a huge fortune, or in the hope of converting pagan souls to Christianity and western ideology. But in George Orwell's "Shooting an Elephant" we get a very different picture of colonialism.

As a police officer in British Burma, the young Orwell finds himself in a 2
nightmarish situation stripped of romance and glory. Not only is he appalled by the cruelty and arrogance of the colonial officers, whom he sees as oppressing the indigenous people and leading a segregated life as prisoners of their own prejudice and power. He is also shocked by the hatred he faces from the Burmese. He is distressed by this hatred because he feels he is on the side of the Burmese and against the British, although he cannot articulate this. Yet the Burmese see him only as a representative of a foreign authority they detest and do everything in their power to make his life intolerable. The climax occurs when a Burmese crowd forces him, by sheer wordless pressure, to shoot an elephant he knows to be harmless, showing him, in the process, how he is as entangled as they are in the complicated web of oppression.

What made the relationship between the British and the Burmese so 3
negative? The answer can be found if we look at the historical context of "Shooting an Elephant," which takes place during what is called the period of

Source: Student essay reprinted by permission.

new imperialism (Cohen 23). The British had entered India modestly enough in 1600 as the East India Company, a trading group who had received a charter from Queen Elizabeth I giving them a monopoly on British trade with Asia. The East India Company founded its first colony in 1612 and administered its territories until 1857, when the Indian Mutiny, the first serious rebellion against foreign power, caused India to be set under the direct administration of the British government. This began the period of new imperialism, soon after which, in 1886, the British annexed Burma to India (Lerner 870).

One of the most striking characteristics of the new imperialism was its belligerent ruthlessness. None of the new territories were obtained peacefully. For instance, before the British were able to annex Burma to India, they had to win three wars and overthrow the current Burmese monarch (Aung 233–265). Nor were the new territories governed with diplomacy. Death penalties and brutal punishment policies were commonplace in dealing with native rebels. Orwell's images of "the wretched prisoners huddling in the stinking cages of the lockups, the grey, cowed faces of the long-term convicts, the scarred buttocks of the men who had been flogged with bamboos" (Orwell 270) were merely realistic pictures of everyday life in Burma. British rule was especially violent and unjust immediately after the Third Anglo-Burmese War, during which the Burmese conducted guerrilla warfare against the British army. The rebels and the villages that had aided or hidden them were severely punished, with entire villages being burned and thousands of suspects captured and executed without trial. Many families were uprooted from their homes and relocated, and strangers with pro-British sentiments were appointed as headmen for the new villages (Aung 267).

Burmese hatred of the British stemmed also from the invaders' insensitivity to Burmese sentiment. The fact that Burma was annexed to India alone caused a lot of bitterness. It was an assault to Burmese pride as the two countries had had a long history of strife. Nor had the Burmese forgotten that Indian soldiers, who were part of the official British army by that time, had fought against them during the three Anglo-Burmese wars. Moreover, the Burmese were different from the Indians in race, language, way of life, attitudes and temperament, and particularly religion (Aung 308).

The British lack of knowledge of Buddhism, the official and flourishing religion of Burma, and their unwillingness to learn about it further fueled the hatred against them. They decided to keep religion out of politics, as they had done in India. But whereas in India Hinduism and Islam had been rivals, in Burma Buddhism united the country. The Buddhist monks did not expect much from the British. It would have been enough for the clergy if they had been shown a superficial respect and allowed to keep the religious authority they had enjoyed in independent Burma. But the British ignored and insulted them by not even bothering with simple but important observances such as removing their shoes on entering temples (Aung 300).

The British impact on Burmese economy was also disastrous. As a result of it many peasants were bankrupt and lost their lands and jobs and the entire country became impoverished. Not only did the British export everything they could, from sugar and tobacco to silks and spices that were in great demand in

Europe, they often paid the local growers very little for it (Lerner 564–565). They also forcibly changed the economy of Burma from the barter system to the cash system after the opening of the Suez Canal in 1871, when more rice began to be exported from Burma. The Burmese peasant was both psychologically unprepared for and inexperienced in handling money and thus became an easy prey for foreigners. For example, because the rice trade was flourishing, more land needed to be cleared for rice fields and the peasants needed money to do this. British banks, however, would not grant loans on mortgages of rice fields. The Burmese peasant had to borrow capital from Indian moneylenders at interest rates reaching as high as 120%. The lenders would then foreclose mortgages at the earliest opportunity, causing many peasants to lose their land (Aung 273).

Finally, the attitude of the British did not ease the tension either. Rudyard 8 Kipling has successfully captured this attitude in many of his stories of the British in India, though ironically he does not always see it as a problem. They shouldered "the white man's burden" manfully but lived as far as possible from "native contamination," made no efforts to learn the language or the culture while they drained the land of its wealth, and counted the days till they could return home to retire. Overall, they were suspicious, indifferent and afraid of the people they ruled (Wolpert 93–94).

Given the nature of British colonialism, it is hardly surprising that Orwell was 9 hated by the Burmese. What is a little more surprising is that he did not anticipate the natives' attitude toward the British, especially as he had spent some of his childhood in India. But perhaps his early years in Asia had created in him a deeper than usual sympathy for the indigenous peoples and a belief that surely they would respond to it. Or perhaps, being young and idealistic, he had believed that all he needed to do to be loved was perform his job with courage, honesty and compassion. But standing with his gun in front of the "unarmed native crowd" he finally realizes that the roots of some kinds of hatred reach too deep. That as a white man attempting to rule Asia he will always be alone, not "the leading actor of the piece" but "an absurd puppet pushed to and fro" (Orwell 272), a victim of the same oppression that his countrymen had imposed on the colonies.

BIBLIOGRAPHY

Aung, Maung Htin. *A History of Burma*. New York: Columbia Univ. Press, 1967.

Cohen, Benjamin J. *The Question of Imperialism*. New York: Basic Book, 1973.

Lerner, Robert E., Standish Meacham, and Edward McNall Burns. *Western Civilizations*. 11th ed. New York: Norton, 1988.

Orwell, George. "Shooting an Elephant," in *Multitude: Cross Cultural Readings for Writers*. Ed. C. Divakaruni. New York: McGraw-Hill, 1993.

Wolpert, Stanley. "India," in *The New Encyclopaedia Brittanica*. Macropaedia vol 21. Chicago, 1985.

STRUCTURE, STRATEGY, SUGGESTION

1. Where is the thesis of the essay most clearly stated? What purpose is served by the paragraphs preceding the thesis, particularly the first one? How else might you have begun the essay?

2. Pick out one or two paragraphs you feel to be strong and effective and analyze them. What techniques and rhetorical modes has the writer used to create this effect?
3. Where has the writer placed her topic sentences in general? Why?
4. Analyze the writer's use of research in the essay. How does it help her argument? Do you see any drawbacks? Are there areas you feel should have been looked at more closely?
5. Choose one of the other readings in this section and write a cause-and-effect essay similar to the one that Parkkinen has written here, analyzing the situation depicted by the writer and providing research information that aids our understanding of it. Be sure to stay focused on a strong thesis of your own.

1. In this section we have come across several writers who examine their identities and the forces shaping them. On the basis of what you have learned from their work, write an essay discussing what you consider a healthy self-concept and the ways in which one goes about building it. Support your ideas with quotations from this section.

2. "Where I Come From," "Manufactured Images," and "Love and Sex in the Life of the Arab" all examine ways in which a particular culture creates a particular image of women that leads to particular ways in which they are viewed and treated. Write an essay in which you compare and contrast the different images portrayed by the authors, focusing on one major problem or strength of each.

3. "The Men We Carry in Our Minds" discusses the male heritage of the writer and the effect it has had on his life. Look through the book for one or two other essays that deal with the same theme. Write an essay in which you put together the ideas presented by the writers to come up with your own thesis about the kinds of things men carry, in terms of identity and heritage, from generation to generation.

4. "Graduation" and "Shooting an Elephant" both deal with points in the writers' lives when something happened to change the way they viewed themselves. What were the events? Why did they have this effect on the writers? Write an essay in which you discuss the kinds of events that cause one to re-evaluate one's identity, supporting your answer from your own experience as well as the above readings.

PART NINE

The Uses of
Entertainment

PART 9: INTRODUCTION

O ur favorite pastimes reveal a great deal about who we are, not only as individuals but also as a people. It is, therefore, a mistake to think of entertainment merely as something that diverts us from the more serious business of living. The writers in Part Nine prove that our simplest relaxations—from reading a poem to watching a television show—may reveal amazingly deep and complex aspects of our culture.

Games and the places where they are played can also become cultural symbols. In "Football Red and Baseball Green" (selection 66) Murray Ross shows us how these two sports reveal certain American values. To him, baseball stands for idyllic pastoral values of the past, football for an aggressive leap into the future. And, as he states in his conclusion, only on the playing field can we have both. Another essay that examines place and its effect on the psyche is "Eight Ways of Looking at an Amusement Park" (selection 69), in which Russell Nye examines the many needs fulfilled by this American institution.

What about pastimes that bring us into contact with different kinds of popular or folk or classical art, from watching television to listening to fairy tales to reading poetry? As illustrated by Bruno Bettelheim (selection 71), Pei-ti Feng (selection 72), Donna Woolfolk Cross (selection 68), Laura Coltelli (selection 70), and Diane Goldner (selection 67), these activities can have a profound effect on us. Cross's essay takes a look at modern-day soap operas and the way in which they fashion our values insidiously even as we laugh—or in this case, weep. Goldner holds out the hope that a sitcom might change our perception of youth at risk, and their perception of themselves. Bettelheim points out that the Cinderella tale contains elements which help children mature and deal with everyday terrors. Feng's essay, also on Cinderella, gives a very different, feminist interpretation of the story.

The styles of the selections in Part Nine are particularly striking; the writers seem to have taken a special interest in presenting their arguments artfully. Symbols, analogies, similes, and metaphors abound, intermingled with passages of evocative concrete description that imprint entire selections on our minds, seducing us into participating in the sensuous pleasures that the writers have depicted. Long after we have finished reading these essays and stories, we will taste the crimson sausages and chrome-colored beverages offered to us by the fantasy world of Nye's amusement parks. We will recognize a part of ourselves in the wicked stepmother. And perhaps, when we sit down to watch *Days of Our Lives* or the Big Game, we will see them a little differently.

66

Think about a sport you enjoy watching or participating in. Do a clustering exercise around this sport, in which you jot down all the different reasons you like it. Why does it appeal to your personality? How does it fit your lifestyle?

Football Red and Baseball Green

MURRAY ROSS

Murray Ross (1942–   ) is from Pasadena, California, and was educated at Williams College and the University of California at Berkeley. He is the director of the theater program at the University of Colorado at Colorado Springs, where he also teaches English. He is also the artistic director of Theaterworks, a local theater company. He has published articles on film, drama, and sports. Selection 66 first appeared in the *Chicago Review*.

*E*very Superbowl played in the 1980s rates among the top television   1
draws of the decade—pro football's championship game is right up there on the charts with blockbusters like *Star Wars, Batman,* and the *Rockys.* This revelation is one way of indicating just how popular spectator sports are in this country. Americans, or American men anyway, seem to care about the games they watch as much as the Elizabethans cared about their plays, and I suspect for some of the same reasons. There is, in sport, some of the rudimentary drama found in popular theater: familiar plots, type characters, heroic and comic action spiced with new and unpredictable variations. And common to watching both activities is the sense of participation in a shared tradition and in shared fantasies. If sport exploits these fantasies without significantly transcending them, it seems no less satisfying for all that.

It is my guess that sport spectating involves something more than the vicari-   2
ous pleasures of identifying with athletic prowess. I suspect that each sport contains a fundamental myth which it elaborates for its fans, and that our pleasure in watching such games derives in part from belonging briefly to the mythical world which the game and its players bring to life. I am especially interested in baseball and football because they are so popular and so uniquely *American*; they began here and unlike basketball they have not been widely exported. Thus whatever can be said, mythically, about these games would seem to apply to our culture.

Source: *Chicago Review*, 1971. Reprinted by permission of the author.

Baseball's myth may be the easier to identify since we have a greater histori- 3
cal perspective on the game. It was an instant success during the Industrialization,
and most probably it was a reaction to the squalor, the faster pace, and the dreari-
ness of the new conditions. Baseball was old-fashioned right from the start; it
seems conceived in nostalgia, in the resuscitation of the Jeffersonian dream. It
established an artificial rural environment, one removed from the toil of an urban
life, which spectators could be admitted to and temporarily breathe in. Baseball is
a *pastoral* sport, and I think the game can be best understood as this kind of art.
For baseball does what all good pastoral does—it creates an atmosphere in which
everything exists in harmony.

Consider, for instance, the spatial organization of the game. A kind of con- 4
trolled openness is created by having everything fan out from home plate, and the
crowd sees the game through an arranged perspective that is rarely violated. Visu-
ally this means that the game is always seen as a constant, rather calm whole, and
that the players and the playing field are viewed in relationship to each other. Each
player has a certain position, a special area to tend, and the game often seems to be
as much a dialogue between the fielders and the field as it is a contest between the
players themselves: Will that ball get through the hole? Can that outfielder run
under that fly? As a moral genre, pastoral asserts the virtue of communion with
nature. As a competitive game, baseball asserts that the team which best relates to
the playing field (by hitting the ball in the right places) will win.

Having established its landscape, pastoral art operates to eliminate any ref- 5
erence to that bigger, more disturbing, more real world it has left behind. All
games are to some extent insulated from the outside by having their own rules,
but baseball has a circular structure as well which furthers its comfortable feeling
of self-sufficiency. By this I mean that every motion of extention is also one of
return—a ball hit outside is a *home* run, a full circle. Home—familiar, peaceful,
secure—it is the beginning and end. You must go out but you must come back;
only the completed movement is registered.

Time is a serious threat to any form of pastoral. The genre poses a timeless 6
world of perpetual spring, and it does its best to silence the ticking of clocks which
remind us that in time the green world fades into winter. One's sense of time is
directly related to what happens in it, and baseball is so structured as to stretch out
and ritualize whatever action it contains. Dramatic moments are few, and they are
almost always isolated by the routine texture of normal play. It is certainly a game of
climax and drama, but it is perhaps more a game of repeated and predictable action:
the foul balls, the walks, the pitcher fussing around on the mound, the lazy fly ball
to center field. This is, I think, as it should be, for baseball exists as an alternative to
a world of too much action, struggle, and change. It is a merciful release from a more
grinding and insistent tempo, and its time, as William Carlos Williams suggests,
makes a virtue out of idleness simply by providing it:

> The crowd at the ball game
> is moved uniformly
> by a spirit of uselessness
> Which delights them. . . .

Within this expanded and idle time the baseball fan is at liberty to become   7
a ceremonial participant and a lover of style. Because the action is normalized,
how something is done becomes as important as the action itself. Thus baseball's
most delicate and detailed aspects are often, to the spectator, the most interesting. The pitcher's windup, the anticipatory crouch of the infielders, the quick
waggle of the bat as it poises for the pitch—these subtle miniature movements are
as meaningful as the home runs and the strikeouts. It somehow matters in baseball that all the tiny rituals are observed: The shortstop must kick the dirt and the
umpire must brush the plate with his pocket broom. In a sense baseball is largely
a continuous series of small gestures, and I think it characteristic that the game's
most treasured moment came when Babe Ruth pointed to where he subsequently
hit a home run.

Baseball is a game where the little things mean a lot, and this, together with   8
its clean serenity, its open space, and its ritualized action is enough to place it in
a world of yesterday. Baseball evokes for us a past which may never have been
ours, but which we believe was, and certainly that is enough. In the Second
World War, supposedly, we fought for "Baseball, Mom, and Apple Pie," and considering what baseball means, that phrase is a good one. We fought then for the
right to believe in a green world of tranquility and uninterrupted contentment,
where the little things would count. But now the possibilities of such a world are
more remote, and it seems that while the entertainment of such a dream has an
enduring appeal, it is no longer sufficient for our fantasies. I think this may be
why baseball is no longer our preeminent national pastime, and why its myth is
being replaced by another more appropriate to the new realities (and fantasies) of
our time.

Football, especially professional football, is the embodiment of a newer   9
myth, one which in many respects is opposed to baseball's. The fundamental difference is that football is not a pastoral game; it is a heroic one. Football wants to
convert men into gods; it suggests that magnificence and glory are as desirable as
happiness. Football is designed, therefore, to impress its audience rather differently than baseball.

As a pastoral game, baseball attempts to close the gap between the players   10
and the crowd. It creates the illusion, for instance, that with a lot of hard work,
a little luck, and possibly some extra talent, the average spectator might well be
playing, not watching. For most of us can do a few of the things the ball players
do: catch a pop-up, field a ground ball, and maybe get a hit once in a while. As
a heroic game, football is not concerned with a shared community of near-equals.
It seeks almost the opposite relationship between its spectators and players, one
which stresses the distance between them. We are not allowed to identify directly
with the likes of Jim Brown, the legendary running back for the Cleveland
Browns, any more than we are with Zeus, because to do so would undercut his
stature as something more than human. Pittsburgh's Mean Joe Green, in a classic commercial from the seventies, walks off the battlefield like Achilles, clouded
by combat. A little boy offers him a Coke, reluctantly accepted but enthusiastically drunk, and Green tosses the boy his jersey afterwards—the token of a generous god. Football encourages us to see its players much as the little boy sees

Mean Joe: We look up to them with something approaching awe. For most of us could not begin to imagine ourselves playing their game without risking imminent humiliation. The players are all much bigger and much faster and much stronger than we are, and even as fans we have trouble enough just figuring out what's going on. In baseball what happens is what meets the eye, but in football each play means eleven men acting against eleven other men: It's too much for a single set of eyes to follow. We now are provided with several television commentators to explain the action to us, with the help of the ubiquitous slow-motion instant replay. Even the coaches need their spotters in the stands and their long postgame film analyses to arrive at something like full comprehension of the game they direct and manage.

If football is distanced from its fans by its intricacy and its "superhuman" 11 play, it nonetheless remains an intense spectacle. Baseball, as I have implied, dissolves time and urgency in a green expanse, thereby creating a luxurious and peaceful sense of leisure. As is appropriate to a heroic enterprise, football reverses this procedure and converts space into time. The game is ideally played in an oval stadium, not in a "park," and the difference is the elimination of perspective. This makes football a perfect television game, because even at first hand it offers a flat, perpetually moving foreground (wherever the ball is). The eye in baseball viewing opens up; in football it zeroes in. There is no democratic vista in football, and spectators are not asked to relax, but to concentrate. You are encouraged to watch the drama, not a medley of ubiquitous gestures, and you are constantly reminded that this event is taking place in time. The third element in baseball is the field; in football this element is the clock. Traditionally heroes do reckon with time, and football players are no exceptions. Time in football is wound up inexorably until it reaches the breaking point in the last minutes of a close game. More often than not it is the clock which emerges as the real enemy, and it is the sense of time running out that regularly produces a pitch of tension uncommon in baseball.

A further reason for football's intensity is that the game is played like a war. 12 The idea is to win by going through, around, or over the opposing team and the battle lines, quite literally, are drawn on every play. Violence is somewhere at the heart of the game, and the combat quality is reflected in football's army language ("blitz," "trap," "zone," "bomb," "trenches," etc.). Coaches often sound like generals when they discuss their strategy. Woody Hayes, the former coach of Ohio State, explained his quarterback option play as if it had been conceived in the Pentagon: "You know," he said, "the most effective kind of warfare is siege. You have to attack on broad fronts. And that's all the option is—attacking on a broad front. You know General Sherman ran an option through the South."

Football like war is an arena for action, and like war football leaves little 13 room for personal style. It seems to be a game which projects "character" more than personality, and for the most part football heroes, publicly, are a rather similar lot. They tend to become personifications rather than individuals, and, with certain exceptions, they are easily read emblematically as embodiments of heroic qualities such as "strength," "confidence," "grace," etc.—clichés really, but forceful enough when represented by the play of a Lawrence Taylor, a Joe Montana, or a Jim Rice. Perhaps this simplification of personality results in part from the heroes' total identification with their mission, to the extent that they become more characterized by what they do than by what they intrinsically "are." At any rate football does not make as many allowances for the idiosyncrasies that baseball actually seems to encourage, and as a result there have been few football players as uniquely crazy or human as, say, Casey Stengel or Dizzy Dean.

A further reason for the underdeveloped qualities of football personalities,   14 and one which gets us to the heart of the game's modernity, is that football is very much a game of modern technology. Football's action is largely interaction, and the game's complexity requires that its players mold themselves into a perfectly coordinated unit. The smoothness and precision of play execution are insatiable preoccupations, and most coaches believe that the team which makes the fewest mistakes will be the team that wins. Individual identity thus comes to be associated with the team or unit that one plays for to a much greater extent than in baseball. Darryl Strawberry is mostly Darryl Strawberry, but Dan Hampton is mostly a Chicago Bear. The latter metaphor is a precise one, since football heroes stand out not only because of purely individual acts, but also because they epitomize the action and style of the groups they are connected to. Ideally a football team should be what Camelot was supposed to have been, a group of men who function as equal parts of a larger whole, dependent on each other for total meaning.

The humanized machine as hero is something very new in sport, for in   15 baseball anything approaching a machine has always been suspect. The famous Yankee teams of the fifties were almost flawlessly perfect, yet they never were especially popular. Their admirers took pains to romanticize their precision into something more natural than plain mechanics—Joe DiMaggio, for instance, became the "Yankee Clipper." Even so, most people seemed to want the Brooklyn Dodgers (the "bums") to thrash them in the World Series. One of the most memorable triumphs in recent decades—the victory of the Amazin' Mets in 1969—was memorable precisely because it was the triumph of a random collection of inspired rejects over the superbly skilled, fully integrated, and almost homogenized Baltimore Orioles. In baseball, machinery seems tantamount to villainy, whereas in football this smooth perfection is part of the unexpected integration a championship team must attain.

It is not surprising, really, that we should have a game which asserts the   16 heroic function of a mechanized group, since we have become a country where collective identity is a reality. Yet football's collective pattern is only one aspect of the way in which it seems to echo our contemporary environment. The game, like our society, can be thought of as a cluster of people living under great tension in a state of perpetual flux. The potential for sudden disaster or triumph is as great in football as it is in our own age, and although there is something ludicrous in equating interceptions with assassinations and long passes with moonshots, there is also something valid and appealing in the analogies. It seems to me that football does successfully reflect those salient and common conditions which affect us all, and it does so with the end of making us feel better about them and our lot. For one thing, it makes us feel that something can be released and connected in all this chaos; out of the accumulated pile of bodies something can emerge—a runner breaks into the clear or a pass finds its way to a receiver. To the spectator, plays such as these are human and dazzling. They suggest to the audience what it has hoped for (and been told) all along, that technology is still a tool and not a master. Fans get living proof of this every time a long pass is completed; they appreciate that it is the result of careful planning, perfect integration, and an effective "pattern," but they see too that it is human and that what counts as well is man, his desire, his natural skill, and his "grace under pressure." Football metaphysically yokes heroic action and technology by violence to suggest that they are mutually supportive. It's a doubtful proposition, but given how we live, it has its attractions.

Football, like the space program, is a game in the grand manner. Homer would have chronicled it; Beowulf would have played fullback. Baseball's roots are at least as deep; it's a variation of the Satyr play, it's a feast of fools. But today their mythic resonance has been eroded by commercial success. Like so much else in America, their character has been modified by money.   17

More and more, both baseball and football are being played indoors on rugs in multipurpose spaces. It doesn't make good business sense to play outside where it might rain and snow and do terrible things; it isn't really prudent to play on a natural field that can be destroyed in a single afternoon; and why build a whole stadium or park that's good for only one game? The fans in these stadiums are constantly diverted by huge whiz-bang scoreboards that dominate and describe the action, while the fans at home are constantly being reminded by at least three lively sportscasters of the other games, the other sports, and the other shows that are coming up later on the same stations. Both pro football and pro baseball now play vastly extended seasons, so that the World Series now takes place on chilly October nights and football is well under way before the summer ends. From my point of view all this is regrettable, because these changes tend to remove the games from their intangible but palpable mythic contexts. No longer clearly set in nature, no longer given the chance to breathe and steep in their own special atmospheres, both baseball and football risk becoming demythologized. As fans we seem to participate a little less in mythic ritual these days, while being subjected even more to the statistics, the hype, and the salary disputes that proceed from a jazzed-up, inflated, yet somehow flattened sporting world—a world that looks too much like the one we live in all the time.   18

Still, there is much to be thankful for, and every season seems to bring its own contribution to mythic lore. Some people will think this nonsense, and I must admit there are good reasons for finding both games simply varieties of decadence.   19

In its preoccupation with mechanization, and in its open display of violence, football is the more obvious target for social moralists, but I wonder if this is finally more "corrupt" than the seductive picture of sanctuary and tranquility that baseball has so artfully drawn for us. Almost all sport is vulnerable to such criticism because it is not strictly ethical in intent, and for this reason there will always be room for puritans like the Elizabethan John Stubbes who howled at the "wanton fruits which these cursed pastimes bring forth." As a long-time dedicated fan of almost anything athletic, I confess myself out of sympathy with most of this; which is to say, I guess, that I am vulnerable to those fantasies which these games support, and that I find happiness in the company of people who feel as I do.   20

A final note. It is interesting that the heroic and pastoral conventions which 21 underlie our most popular sports are almost classically opposed. The contrasts are familiar: city versus country, aspirations versus contentment, activity versus peace, and so on. Judging from the rise of professional football, we seem to be slowly relinquishing that unfettered rural vision of ourselves that baseball so beautifully mirrors, and we have come to cast ourselves in a genre more reflective of a nation confronted by constant and unavoidable challenges. Right now, like the Elizabethans, we seem to share both heroic and pastoral yearnings, and we reach out to both. Perhaps these divided needs account in part for the enormous attention we as a nation now give to spectator sports. For sport provides one place where we can have our football and our baseball too.

QUESTIONS FOR CRITICAL READING, THINKING, DISCUSSION, AND WRITING

Analyzing Content and Technique

1. Why, according to Ross, is "sport spectating" such a popular pastime? From the tone of his argument, what kind of audience do you think he is writing for? Players? Sports fans? Others?
2. Ross calls football and baseball uniquely American sports. What reasons does he provide? Do you agree or disagree? Give reasons for your answer.
3. What kind of atmosphere is created during a game of baseball?
4. Does Ross convince the reader that "baseball is a game where the little things mean a lot"? Evaluate the evidence he provides, and add some more of your own.
5. Contrast the "newer myth" of football with that of baseball. What are its major characteristics? Why does it appeal so strongly to present-day Americans? Why, by contrast, does baseball continue to appeal to us?
6. What kinds of allusions to older cultures does Ross make in an effort to explain football and baseball? How do these allusions increase our understanding of these sports?
7. Why is Ross against multipurpose indoor stadiums? Are you convinced by his argument? Explain why or why not.

Collaborative Activity

As a group, examine Ross's statement (paragraph 16) that "we have become a country where collective identity is a reality." How far is this true of the lives of group members? Have each group member come up with an example, personal or observed, that either supports or refutes this comment.

Making Connections

1. Ross makes the point that popular sports tell us something significant about the culture in which they flourish. Choose a sport (other than baseball or football) which you feel is a clear reflection of certain values or attitudes in American culture today, and write an essay explaining what it tells us about our society.
2. Choose a sport that is popular today and trace its historical development. Focus on the changes that have occurred over time and how the sport was adapted to the values of society in each period. (You might need to do some research on this topic.)

Think about the title of this essay, and then about what you consider to be the effects of television on youth today. Do you see television's effects as more positive or negative? Sprint write for five minutes on this topic.

Can TV Help Save Black Youth?

DIANE GOLDNER

Diane Goldner is a freelance writer who originally wrote this essay for *USA Weekend* in 1992.

"*I* had them take down the photos of prizefighters," Bill Cosby says 1 proudly as he points to a picture of two young girls hugging that hangs on a wall of the Upper Manhattan Youth Center. Cosby's guest, Deborah Prothrow-Stith, assistant dean of Harvard University's School of Public Health, nods her approval: Peaceful images are less likely to promote anger than those glorifying violence.

Cosby chomps his cigar and looks pleased. And no wonder. The fictional Harlem youth center is part of the set for his latest TV creation, *Here and Now,* 2 NBC's new Saturday-night series about a graduate student in psychology who works at the center. The student, "A.J." (played by Malcolm-Jamal Warner of *The Cosby Show*), faces down the worst problems of urban America—poverty, violence, gangs, broken homes, disillusionment—one-on-one with kids and their families.

Yes, the comedian who made television history with *The Cosby Show,* the 3 most-watched series ever (at its height in 1986, more than half of the USA's households watching TV on Thursday night were tuned in), now tackles the subject of the nation's disenfranchised kids. And he's doing it in a situation comedy aimed at audiences of all ages.

"It was really the next step," says Cosby, 55, the creator and executive 4 producer of *Here and Now.* In his office at the Kaufman-Astoria studios in the New York City borough of Queens, where the show is taped, he is as animated as when playing *The Cosby Show*'s lovable Cliff Huxtable or appearing in any of his live performances. His eyes roll; his hands wave—he even gets up and struts around the room to act out a character or concept.

Source: "Can TV Help Save Black Youth?" by Diane Goldner as appeared in *USA Weekend,* 1992. Reprinted by permission of the author.

"I want to use this tube," he says, emphatically pointing to a blank TV ⁵ screen on his left, as if it would come alive at his command, "to educate and bring about an awareness of problems. Jesse Jackson thinks 'Keep Hope Alive' is just out there in the ghetto. [But] 'Keep Hope Alive' is in this tube, too."

Cosby's astute companion on the *Here and Now* set, Prothrow-Stith, is the ⁶ author of *Deadly Consequences* (HarperCollins, $25), a book published last year that analyzes the reasons behind teenage violence and puts forth solutions. Prothrow-Stith is a physician and an expert on violence and its prevention, a remarkable voice of hope in a country that felt the rage of last spring's riots in Los Angeles—a country that must confront the despair of the inner-city youths to whom that conflagration spoke. She also is one of Cosby's muses for *Here and Now*.

When Cosby first read *Deadly Consequences*, more than a year ago, he saw ⁷ the problems plaguing the USA's youth in a fresh light, as something that could be changed. "I said: 'Wait a minute—this is a doctor who says there's a form of preventive medicine,'" recalls Cosby, who today wears a fine cotton shirt, dark slacks and a dandy's white hat. "She reacted. [Her ideas] changed the course."

Those ideas are the guiding philosophy behind many *Here and Now* scripts. ⁸ Prothrow-Stith is not paid by the show and does not read the scripts or planned story lines. But Cosby insisted that all of the show's writers read her book. (He still relies on *Cosby* consultant Alvin Poussaint of Harvard and John Bess, who heads the Manhattan Valley Youth Center in Harlem, as paid consultants.)

When *Deadly Consequences* was first released, former U.S. Surgeon General ⁹ C. Everett Koop praised it as a "clear and comprehensive" map "out of the tragic morass" of violence. But it was Cosby who plucked Prothrow-Stith out of academic obscurity and set her in the public arena, inviting her to join him on shows from *Dateline NBC* to *The Maury Povich Show*. *Deadly Consequences*, he says, "states the truth about the violations of youth."

"It was a simple idea," adds the modest Prothrow-Stith, 38, who had her ¹⁰ revelation 14 years ago as a resident doctor at Boston City Hospital. She was stitching up kids who had been stabbed or shot and sending them back onto the streets—often to fight again. She realized then that "we should not just stitch people and send them out."

Prothrow-Stith, the mother of a 13-year-old son and 10-year-old daughter, ¹¹ was seeing firsthand what most Americans learn as a set of statistics: The homicide rate for young black men and boys increased 300 percent from 1950 to 1980; for all Americans, the murder rate was doubled over the past three decades. Murder now is the leading cause of death of young black men and boys. Young blacks succumb to homicide seven times more frequently than young whites. The USA spends $1 billion a year treating gunshot wounds and $60 billion treating violent injuries.

"Every day more than 60 Americans die of homicides," Prothrow-Stith ¹² notes in *Deadly Consequences*. "That means 450 a week, 1900 a month, 23,000 a year. . . . Maybe we should erect a black marble slab and start compiling the names of those whose lives are wasted by violence. In two years we would have a solemn memorial covered with names, just like the Vietnam Veterans Memorial, only this memorial would be different. Very soon the names would spill over, and you would need another memorial and another and another."

Prothrow-Stith, the daughter of solidly middle-class parents, sees this reality 13 every day. She and her husband, a Methodist preacher and activist [for] economic justice in Boston's South End, live in Roxbury, the neighborhood of Boston with the lowest per-capita income and the highest homicide rate. Because she has a teenage son, she says, "it's a personal issue as well as a professional issue."

Violence, she decided, no longer could be tolerated. Her solution: treat 14 violence as a public health issue, like child abuse or drunken driving. Doctors don't just treat the victims of child abuse; they alert social workers to situations that need attention. They don't just treat the victims of car accidents; they lobby for seat-belt laws and stiffer penalties for driving drunk. So why not treat violence, too, as "one piece of a larger picture"?

Prothrow-Stith says that means government financed day care, after-school 15 programs, courses to educate parents and students, health care, and counseling to deal with legitimate anger over unfair situations and to lessen the sources of anger. She also is a strong proponent of gun control. The costs, she estimates, would be "easily" half of what is now spent on prison stays, medical treatment, rehabilitation, lost wages and social decay.

"Somehow, we've convinced [a gang member] that it's easier to do what 16 he's doing than to become a lawyer. . . . Ultimately, the goal is to change the peer pressure so that it is not cool to be in a fight. People are sick of it. They don't want to be around it. They don't want not to enjoy the party because you're fighting. The message is: We're trying to have a society here."

Prothrow-Stith designed a curriculum and began teaching it in public 17 schools. "When I teach I say: 'From your very first cartoon, all the way through *Lethal Weapon*, you're taught that violence is funny, entertaining and successful. It's the way the hero solves things. But it's painful, and it does not solve problems. I am here not only to apologize for what society has done, but also to ask your help in changing this.'" Then she tells her students to make a list of all the things that make them angry. One boy, she recalls, was upset that a friend had been stabbed over the weekend. It took 20 minutes for an ambulance to arrive, even though the hospital was just two minutes away. His friend died.

"I said: 'What can you do? You can beat up the ambulance driver. You can 18 slash the tires. You can beat up the little girl next door. Or you can do nothing, lose your self-esteem, feel bad about yourself, feel bad about your community. You can write a letter to the city. But ultimately . . .' we concluded that the best solution is to get angry and to finish high school and become an ambulance driver and make the drivers more efficient. . . . If I want you to stop doing something, I've got to substitute another behavior."

Prothrow-Stith is enthusiastic about Cosby's application of her ideas to 19 television. "He can make a huge difference. It's impressive and fantastic."

In each episode of *Here and Now,* the A.J. character will confront "some kind 20 of behavior that's a negative," as Cosby puts it, and deal with it positively, *non-violently.* For example, in the first episode, "Cross Roads," A.J. tried to discipline

Randall, whose older brother, Curtis, was the leader of a drug gang. Curtis warned A.J. to lay off. A.J. then refused to discipline Randall and ignored him when he next misbehaved. A hurt Randall then complained to his brother that he was being neglected—which brought Curtis back to menace A.J., four thugs in tow.

"I guess you know what I want," Curtis said.   21

"I hope you want me to get four of my friends so we can shoot some   22 hoops," A.J. answered, defusing the threat with laughter.

Later, A.J. asked: "Curtis, do you care about your brother? Then don't tell   23 me how to do my job." Curtis agreed to back off, and Randall had to acquiesce to discipline like the other kids.

In a future episode, A.J. helps "T," a recovering drug addict, overcome the   24 little voice inside telling him that he's "not worth it." In another episode, counselors help Randall to overcome his fear of a slumber party. It turns out that, terrified of gunshots at night, the boy sleeps with a teddy bear but doesn't want anybody to find out.

But can a sitcom fight junkies and gang wars? Comedy, according to Cosby,   25 makes the audience more open to the subject. Otherwise, they are "gone," he says. "There are two words: 'Serious,' I don't like. 'Honest,' I like. 'This is a serious subject.' No. 'It's a very honest subject.' If you have honesty, you have laughter."

"Even in the worst lives," adds Prothrow-Stith, "there is sugar."   26

"Exactly," says Cosby, who on the strength of his wit climbed out of a   27 "lower lower" economic group in Philadelphia. Now the richest performer in TV, he has said he was similar to some of today's disadvantaged kids in believing that success "happened only to people on the radio."

"Entertainment," he says, "is my elixir to changing [people's] thoughts."   28 By the close of the TV season, he predicts, viewers "who are so blasé about seeing a kid with handcuffs behind his back will know that these are human beings and that there was a life before.

"You know that book *Why Johnny Can't Read?* Well, why did Georgie stab   29 Fred in the foot? Or why did David carry a gun to class? I want people to see the show and understand that these kids they see on the 11 o'clock news—there's more to them than just a simple write-off.

"You hear some kids talk about, 'Hey, did you see him when he leapt over   30 the thing and ran and caught so-and-so?'" Cosby adds, slipping into ghetto rhythm. "I'd like to challenge them to talk with the same enthusiasm about someone who got four A's: 'Did you see how he was studying in the library, man? And he was going around at night and kept a job?' Instead of a drive-by shooting.

"I think we can do it."   31

QUESTIONS FOR CRITICAL READING, THINKING, DISCUSSION, AND WRITING

Analyzing Content and Technique

1. Why does Cosby exchange the photos of prizefighters on the wall of the fictional Harlem Youth Center for that of two young girls hugging? Do you agree with his reasoning? Why or why not?

2. Describe the problem the essay is addressing and evaluate its seriousness, picking out statistics provided in the essay as support.
3. Examine the role played by Prothrow-Stith in dealing with the problem addressed by the essay. What, according to you, is her most valuable contribution? Why?
4. Analyze the two *Here and Now* episodes described in the essay. How effective do you think they would be in changing young people's attitudes? Explain.
5. What does Cosby hope to achieve by the close of the television season? Evaluating what you know of the show and of him, do you think this is a realistic goal? Why? Why is it an important goal?
6. Examine the one-line conclusion to the essay. Is it effective? Why or why not? What would be a more traditional conclusion for the essay?

Collaborative Activity

As a group, examine Prothrow-Stith's statement "Even in the worst lives there is sugar." How do you interpret this statement? Have group members come up with examples that support their understanding of this statement. Write a collaborative paragraph in which you incorporate the examples and express the group's opinions.

Making Connections

1. In this essay Cosby states, "Entertainment is my elixir to changing [people's] thoughts" (paragraph 28). Examine the meaning of this statement, its implication, and the assumptions behind it. How far do you agree with Cosby about the power of entertainment? Write an essay in which you focus on a particular kind of entertainment (not television) and analyze the effect it has on the opinions and attitudes of people. You may use research, personal experience, and interviews to support your thesis.
2. This excerpt is an interview, supported by background material researched by the writer. Using it as a loose model, write an interview essay in which you discuss a person who is involved in an activity or program you feel is of importance in your community. (Community may be interpreted in any way you wish—ethnic community, neighborhood, workplace, and so forth.) Be sure you have a clear, focused thesis and quotations from the person you interview.

Write about a soap opera you are familiar with (or, if you are not familiar with any soap operas, observe one for a day). What values and concerns are apparent in the show?

Sin, Suffer, and Repent

DONNA WOOLFOLK CROSS

Donna Woolfolk Cross (1947–   ) is originally from New York City. She teaches English at Onondaga Community College and writes about language and the media. Her books include *Speaking of Words, Word Abuse: How the Words We Use Abuse Us,* and *Mediaspeak,* from which selection 69 is taken.

Soap operas reverse Tolstoy's famous assertion in Anna Karenina that "Happy families are all alike; every unhappy family is unhappy in its own way." On soaps, every family is unhappy, and each is unhappy in more or less the same way. Marjory Perloff

It is the hope of every advertiser to habituate the housewife to an engrossing narrative whose optimum length is forever and at the same time to saturate all levels of her consciousness with the miracle of a given product, so she will be aware of it all the days of her life and mutter its name in her sleep. James Thurber

In July 1969, when the entire nation was glued to television sets watching the first man walk on the moon, an irate woman called a Wausau, Wisconsin, TV station to complain that her favorite soap opera was not being shown that day and why was that. The station manager replied, "This is probably the most important news story of the century, something you may never again see the equal of." Unimpressed, the lady replied, "Well, I hope they crash."

One can hardly blame her. For weeks, she had been worrying that Audrey might be going blind, that Alice would marry that scoundrel Michael, and that Dr. Hardy might not discover his patient Peter to be his long-lost natural son before the boy died of a brain tumor. Suddenly, in the heat of all these crises, she was cut off from all information about these people and forced to watch the comings and goings of men in rubber suits whom she had never met. It was enough to unhinge anybody.

Dedicated watchers of soap operas often confuse fact with fiction.[1] Sometimes this can be endearing, sometimes ludicrous. During the Senate Watergate hearings (which were broadcast on daytime television), viewers whose favorite soap operas were preempted simply adopted the hearings as substitute soaps. Daniel Shorr reports that the listeners began "telephoning the networks to criticize slow-moving sequences, suggesting script changes and asking for the return of favorite witnesses, like 'that nice John Dean.'"

Stars of soap operas tell hair-raising stories of their encounters with fans suffering from this affliction. Susan Lucci, who plays the promiscuous Erica Kane on "All My Children," tells of a time she was riding in a parade: "We were in a crowd of about 250,000, traveling in an antique open car moving ver-r-ry slowly. At that time in the series I was involved with a character named Nick. Some man broke through, came right up to the car and said to me, 'Why don't you give *me* a little bit of what you've been giving Nick?'" The man hung onto the car, menacingly, until she was rescued by the police. Another time, when she was in church, the reverent silence was broken by a woman's astonished remark, "Oh, my god, Erica prays!" Margaret Mason, who plays the villainous Lisa Anderson in "Days of Our Lives," was accosted by a woman who poured a carton of milk all over her in the supermarket. And once a woman actually tried to force her car off the Ventura Freeway.

Just as viewers come to confuse the actors with their roles, so too they see the soap opera image of life in America as real. The National Institutes of Mental Health reported that a majority of Americans actually adopt what they see in soap operas to handle their own life problems. The images are not only "true to life"; they are a guide for living.

What, then, is the image of life on soap operas? For one thing, marriage is touted as the *ne plus ultra* of a woman's existence. Living together is not a respectable condition and is tolerated only as long as one of the partners (usually the woman) is bucking for eventual marriage. Casual sex is out; only the most despicable villains engage in it: "Diane has no respect for marriage or any of the values we were brought up with. She's a vicious, immoral woman." Occasionally, a woman will speak out against marriage, but it's clear that in her heart of hearts she really wants it. Women who are genuinely not interested in marriage do not appear on soap operas except as occasional caricatures, misguided and immature in their thinking. Reporter Martha McGee appeared on "Ryan's Hope" just long enough to titillate the leading man with remarks like, "I don't know if you're my heart's desire, but you're sexy as hell." Punished for this kind of heretical remark, she was last seen sobbing brokenly in a telephone booth.

No, love and marriage still go together like a horse and carriage in soap operas, though many marriages don't last long enough for the couple to put away all the wedding gifts. As Cornell professor Rose Goldsen says, this is a world of "fly-apart marriages, throwaway husbands, throwaway wives." There is rarely any clear logic behind the dissolution of these relationships; indeed, the TV formula seems to be: the happier the marriage, the more perilous the couple's future. A blissful marriage is the kiss of death: "I just can't believe it about Alice and Steve. I mean, they were the *perfect* couple, the absolute *perfect* couple!"

Most marriages are not pulled apart by internal flaws but by external tam- [8] pering—often by a jealous rival: "C'mon, Peter. Stay for just one more drink. Jan won't mind. And anyway, the night's still young. Isn't it nice to be together all nice and cozy like this?"

Often the wife has willfully brought this state of affairs on herself by com- [9] mitting that most heinous of all offenses: neglecting her man. "NHM" almost always occurs when the woman becomes too wrapped up in her career. Every time Rachel Corey went to New York City for a weekend to further her career as a sculptress, her marriage tottered. At this writing, Ellen Dalton's marriage to Mark appears to be headed for big trouble as a result of her business trip to Chicago:

> ERICA: I warned you, Ellen, not to let your job interfere with your marriage.
> ELLEN: I have tried to do my best for my marriage *and* my job . . . Mark had no right to stomp out of here just now.
> ERICA: Don't you understand? He just couldn't take anymore.
> ELLEN: What do you mean?
> ERICA: It's not just the trip to Chicago that Mark resents. It's your putting your job before having a family.
> ELLEN: I demand the right to be treated as an equal. I don't have to apologize because I don't agree to have a child the minute my husband snaps his fingers. I'm going to Chicago like a big girl and I'm going to do the job I was hired to do. (stalks out the door)
> ERICA: (musing, to herself) Well, I may be old-fashioned, but that's no way to hold onto your man.

Career women do appear frequently on soap operas, but the ones who are [10] romantically successful treat their careers as a kind of sideline. Female cardiologists devote fifteen years of their lives to advanced medical training, then spend most of their time in the hospital coffee shop. One man remarked to a career woman who was about to leave her job, "Oh, Kate, you'll miss working. Those long lunches, those intimate cocktail hours!" Women residents apparently schedule all their medical emergencies before dinnertime, because if they should have to stay late at the hospital, it's the beginning of the end for their marriages. It's interesting to speculate how they might work this out:

> NURSE: Oh my God, Dr. Peterson, the patient's hemorrhaging!
> DR. PETERSON: Sorry, nurse, it'll just have to wait. If I don't get my meat loaf in by a quarter to six, it'll never be ready before my husband gets home.

Husbands, weak-minded souls, cannot be expected to hold out against the [11] advances of any attractive woman, even one for whom they have contempt, if their wives aren't around. Meatloafless, they are very easily seduced. The clear suggestion is that they could hardly have been expected to do otherwise:

"Well, after all, Karen, you weren't around very much during that time. It's not surprising that Michael turned to Pat for a little comfort and understanding."

If, in the brief span of time allotted to them, a couple manage to have intercourse, the woman is certain to become pregnant. Contraception on soap operas is such a sometime thing that even the Pope could scarcely object to it. The birthrate on soaps is eight times as high as the United States birthrate; indeed it's higher than the birthrate of any underdeveloped nation in the world. This rabbitlike reproduction is fraught with peril. One recent study revealed that out of nineteen soap opera pregnancies, eight resulted in miscarriages and three in death for the mother. Rose Goldsen has estimated that the odds are 7 to 10 against any fetus making it to full term, worse if you include getting through the birth canal. Women on soap operas miscarry at the drop of a pin. And, of course, miscarriages are rarely caused by any defect with mother or baby: again, external forces are to blame. Often, miscarriage is brought on by an unappreciative or unfaithful mate. For example, on "Another World," Alice the heroine, suffered a miscarriage when her husband visited his ex-wife Rachel. One woman lost her baby because her husband came home drunk. This plot twist is no doubt particularly appealing to women viewers because of the instant revenge visited upon the transgressing mate. They can fantasize about similar punishment for husbandly malfeasance in their own lives—and about his inevitable guilt and repentance:

HUSBAND: (stonily) Jennifer, these potatoes are too gluey. I can't eat this!
WIFE: (clutches her belly) Oh, no!
HUSBAND: What? What is it?
WIFE: It's the baby! Something's wrong—call the doctor!
HUSBAND: Oh my god, what have I done?
Later, at the hospital:
DOCTOR: I'm sorry, Mr. Henson, but your wife has lost the baby.
HUSBAND: (brokenly) I didn't know, I didn't know. How could I have attacked her potatoes so viciously with her in such a delicate condition!
DOCTOR: Now, now. You musn't blame yourself. We still don't know exactly what causes miscarriages except that they happen for a complicated set of physical and emotional reasons.
HUSBAND: Oh, thank you, Doctor.
DOCTOR: Of course, carping about the potatoes couldn't have *helped*.

Miscarriage is effective as a punishment because it is one of the very worst things that can happen to a woman on a soap opera. In the world of soaps, the one thing every good and worthwhile woman wants is a baby. Soap operas never depict childless women as admirable. These "real people" do not include women like Katharine Hepburn, who once announced that she never wanted to have children because "the first time the kid said no to me, I'd kill it!" Childless women are either to be pitied, if there are physical reasons that prevent them from getting pregnant, or condemned, if they are childless by choice.

Second only to neglecting her man in her hierarchy of female crime is hav-   14
ing an abortion. No admirable character *ever* gets an abortion on a soap opera.
Occasionally, however, a virtuous woman will consider it, usually for one of two
reasons: she doesn't want the man she loves to feel "trapped" into marrying her;
or she has been "violated" by her husband's best friend, a member of the under-
world, or her delivery boy, who may also be her long-lost half brother. But she
always "comes around" in the end, her love for "the new life growing inside me"
conquering her misgivings. If the baby should happen to survive the perilous
journey through the birth canal (illegitimate babies get miscarried at a far higher
rate than legitimate ones), she never has any regrets. Why should she? Babies on
soap operas never drool, spit up, or throw scrambled eggs in their mothers' faces.
Babyhood (and its inevitable counterpart, motherhood) is "sold" to American
women as slickly as soap. Kimberly, of "Ryan's Hope," is so distressed when she
finds out she is pregnant that she runs away from home. She has the baby, pre-
maturely, while alone and unattended on a deserted houseboat. It is a difficult
and dangerous birth. But once the baby is born, Kimberly is all maternal affection. "Where is she?" she shouts. "Why won't they let me see my little girl?" By
the end of the day, she announces, "If anything happens to this baby, I don't
know what I'll do!"

Under the surface of romantic complications, soap operas sell a vision of   15
morality and American family life, of a society where marriage is the highest
good, sex the greatest evil, where babies are worshiped and abortion condemned,
where motherhood is exalted and children ignored. It is a vision of a world
devoid of social conflict. There are hardly any short-order cooks, bus drivers,
mechanics, construction workers, or farmers on soap operas. Blue-collar problems
do not enter these immaculate homes. No one suffers from flat feet or derrière
spread from long hours spent at an unrewarding or frustrating job. The upwardly
mobile professionals who populate soap operas love their work, probably because
they are hardly ever at it—one lawyer clocked in at his office exactly once in three
months. Their problems are those of people with time on their hands to covet the
neighbor's wife, track down villains, betray friends, and enjoy what one observer
has called "the perils of Country Club Place."

It is a world largely devoid of black people and black viewpoints. When   16
black characters do appear, they are doctors or lawyers whose problems, ambitions, and anxieties are identical to those of their white colleagues.[2] Racial discrimination and inequality do not exist, and the black romantic plotlines are indis-
tinguishable from white—though, of course, the two *never* mix. Once, it is true,
in a daring departure from the straight and narrow, "All My Children" showed a
black-white romance which shocked a lot of viewers. But it wasn't really a
romance in the usual sense. At least, it was perfectly clear that black Dr. Nancy
Grant had turned to her white boyfriend Owen solely for comfort after the
breakup of her marriage to black Dr. Frank Grant. They were not—gasp!—sleeping together. Anyway, the whole mess was resolved when Owen considerately
died just minutes after marrying Nancy to save her from disgrace because she was
pregnant with black Dr. Frank Grant's baby. Another experiment with a black-
white flirtation was abruptly ended when the black family moved to another

town. Still another such plotline was resolved when it turned out that the white woman in an interracial relationship was actually a light-skinned black woman who had been "ashamed" of her heritage.

The world of soap operas is without doubt white, upper middle-class—and decidedly small-town. Emerging out of the mists of the American heartland as mysteriously as Brigadoon are towns like Oakdale, Pine Valley, Rosehill. On soap operas, towns never have real-life names like Secaucus or Weedsport. The great American myth of the Good, Clean, Safe Small Town, which some thought had been laid to rest by the likes of Sinclair Lewis and Sherwood Anderson, has been resurrected on the soaps. Only in small towns, the daily message is, can one find true happiness and fulfillment: 17

> CAROL: I've wondered sometimes if you don't get bored living in Oakdale? Living in New York or on the Coast can be so much more exciting.
> SANDY: Excitement is one thing. Real feelings are another.

One half expects her to add, "Oh, Auntie Em, there's no place like home!"

NOTES
1. Contrary to popular belief, soap operas are not the harmless pastime of lonely housewives only. Recent surveys show that many high school and college students, as well as many working and professional people, are addicted to soaps. A sizable chunk of the audience is men. Such well-known people as Sammy Davis, Jr., Van Cliburn, John Connally and Supreme Court Justice Thurgood Marshall admit to being fans of one or more soap operas.
2. "All My Children" has recently introduced a "lower-class" black character—a streetwise teenager named Jesse, who is the despair of his black aunt and uncle, both doctors. It is clear, however, that Jesse's scorn for Establishment values is merely a defense against rejection, and his eventual conversion and admittance to Pine Valley society seems inevitable.

QUESTIONS FOR CRITICAL READING, THINKING, DISCUSSION, AND WRITING

Analyzing Content and Technique

1. What is Cross's first objection to soap operas? What examples does she give? How convincing do you find her examples? Can you add other supporting examples from your experience?
2. What is Cross's second objection to soap operas? Do you agree with it? What evidence does she give to support her opinion?
3. According to Cross, how are women presented on soaps? (Analyze the soap opera's attitude to different female roles.) How are men presented?
4. Cross writes, in paragraph 15, that "soap operas sell a vision of morality and American family life." Is this a positive or negative statement? Give reasons and examples for your answer.
5. Analyze the soap opera's attitude toward minorities. What underlying values and assumptions are indicated by this attitude?
6. Identify two or three examples of humor and exaggeration in Cross's article. Discuss their effect on the reader. How do they help to strengthen Cross's argument?

7. Who is the intended audience for this piece? Explain how you know this, with examples from the text.

Collaborative Activity

As a group, consider how much of what Cross says of soap operas is applicable to television sitcoms. Discuss one or two that group members are familar with, analyzing their portrayal of women. What similarities and differences do you see between these and what Cross says of soaps?

Making Connections

1. Cross asserts that soap operas have a great deal more influence on Americans than we usually believe. What is your opinion? Write an essay based on evidence you have collected by interviewing a broad cross-section of people about their habits with regard to watching soaps, and comparing the values they hold with those found on soaps.
2. Cross's essay illustrates that television shows can often reveal a great deal about a culture. Compare a particular type of television program (such as news, game shows, sitcoms, or crime shows) that is popular in the United States with a similar show (such as a Chinese crime show or a middle eastern news program) in another country. What do the shows tell you about the two cultures? (You may need to do some research before writing this essay.)

PREREADING ACTIVITY

Think back to any visits you have made to an amusement park. What impressions remain in your mind? Do a clustering exercise in which you set down all your impressions, positive or negative, as well as how you feel about the idea of the amusement park. If you have never been to an amusement park, do the exercise imagining what such an experience might be like.

Eight Ways of Looking at an Amusement Park

RUSSELL B. NYE

Russell B. Nye, a freelance writer, originally wrote this piece for the *Journal of Popular Culture* in 1981.

The park is an urban phenomenon, a reaction to the crowded cities of the eighteenth century. Historically it is tied to the Romantic era, which saw nature as a curative, educational force—"God's visible smile," to quote William Cullen Bryant, on mankind. It was no accident that William Penn chose to call his colony "Penn-sylvania," with all the connotations of natural peace and beauty that the Latin word brought from the pastoral tradition.[1]

In 1812 Philadelphia landscaped five acres of the east bank of the Schuylkill River to create the beginnings of Fairmont Park, the birthplace of the American park system. Other city parks were founded over the next few decades in response to the demands of an emergent, prosperous middle class for access to those natural surroundings and open spaces previously available only on the estates of the rich. A third factor in the rise of the public park, particularly during the phenomenal burst of urban population in mid-century, was the desire of reformers to counteract what they believed were the dangerous social effects of city life.

---

[1]Penn in his Philadelphia plan of 1682 in fact set aside five squares as parks, four of which still exist. John Maass, *The Glorious Enterprise: The Centennial Exposition of 1876* (Watkins Glen, N.Y.: Association Press, 1915), pp. 16–18.

Source: "Eight Ways of Looking at an Amusement Park" by Russell B. Nye, as appeared in *The Journal of Popular Culture*, 1981. Reprinted by permission.

The crowded city afforded no chance to be alone with nature or one's self, 3
to ponder questions of life and identity, to learn from God's plants and flowers.
Cities bred suspicion, selfishness, isolation; public parks could provide an effective
antidote. Thus Central Park was designed by Frederick L. Olmsted and Calvert Vaux
in 1858 to furnish New Yorkers a "harmonizing influence" and to "cultivate among
the community loftier and more refined desires." It was to be a passive place without
"boisterous fun and rough sports," a contrast to as well as escape from the city.
Central Park would provide a pattern for many subsequent city parks and was indeed
a precursor of the philosophy that underlay the national park system.[2]

The exposition or "world's fair," a coincidental nineteenth-century develop- 4
ment, introduced another set of factors. Instead of an escape from the city, the
exposition was intended to take advantage of the urban environment for
educational, cultural and especially commercial purposes, reaching as wide an
audience as possible. World's Fairs at London (1851, 1862), Paris (1855, 1867,
1878, 1900) and Vienna (1873) served as models for the first major American
fair, Philadelphia's Exhibition of 1876, which not only commemorated the
nation's Centennial but also exhibited "the arts, manufactures, and products of
soil and mine" to the country and the world. Its purposes, concluded a writer in
1812, were to[3]

> teach knowledge of the markets . . . , form taste and judgment . . . , offer instruc-
> tive insights into creative spheres . . . , and to extend the great civilizing task of
> educating man to be a world citizen.

Its themes were enlightenment, national pride and most of all progress. The
planners of Chicago's Columbia Exposition of 1893 built their project on
Philadelphia's success; chief architect Daniel Burnham envisioned a "White City"
of monumental grandeur to serve as the ideal pattern of what the modern city
could be. The Chicago Fair, unlike Central Park, was not an escape from the city
but an idealization of it—a meeting place for art, uplift, education, social
participation, the good life.[4]

Whatever Burnham's intentions, a substantial part of the Fair's success 5
derived not from its magnificent architecture and hundreds of educational and
artistic exhibits, but from the Midway Plaisance, a mile-long corridor of privately
operated concessions, shops, shows, and games that the Fair's planners included
with—but kept quite separate from—the rest of the exposition. The Midway, as a
contemporary account put it, was "a sideshow pure and simple of halls of
entertainment, pavilions, and gardens." It featured girls—an International Beauty

---

[2]See the discussion in John F. Kasson, *Amusing the Million* (New York: Hill and Wang, 1978), pp.
11–16. Kasson's study of Coney Island is the best treatment of an American amusement park in its
socio-cultural context. One of the most handsomely designed and illustrated studies of a single park
is L. Bush, E. Chukayne, R. Hehr, and R. Hersey, eds., *Euclid Beach Park is Closed for the Season*
(Mentor, Ohio: Amusement Park Books, 1978).
[3]See Maass, *op. cit.* pp. 26–72, 93. The Exhibition contained 249 buildings, 5 1/2 miles of railroad,
153 acres of lawn and flower beds, 20,000 trees and shrubs, and three telegraph systems. It "dazzled
and astounded" Ralph Waldo Emerson but depressed Henry Adams.
[4]See the discussion in Kasson, pp. 17–20.

Show of "forty gaily dressed beauties from forty lands"; Algerian Dancers in their famous Love Dance ("the coarse animal passions of the East"); "sleek odalisques" from the Persian Palace of Eros; three lovely Samoan damsels named Lola, Mela and Feteia—in company with jugglers, sword swallowers, a Chinese joss house, the Hagenbeck Circus, glass blowers, a replica of Kilauea in eruption, and of course the huge wheel designed by George W. Ferris looming over it all.[5] Without denigrating the cultural and educational contributions of the Columbia Exposition, it is not unreasonable to say that the two sights which remained most vividly in the American imagination were the "hootchy kootchy" dance of Fatima in the Turkish Village and the profile of the great Ferris wheel which dominated the landscape.[6] The Midway was energetic, amusing, titillating and plain fun. After that no world's fair could afford to omit a "midway," though it might be called (as in St. Louis) The Pike or (in San Francisco) The Joy Zone. There, in Chicago, lay the germ of the modern amusement park.[7]

Another kind of public entertainment, the county or state fair, also contributed to the creation of the amusement park, although its original purpose was commercial and educational. The first agricultural fair was probably held at Georgetown, D.C., in 1809, followed by an increasing number scattered throughout the East, particularly in New York State and New England. By the close of the century, the fair was an autumn fixture everywhere, a place to display farm machinery and farm products and to serve as an annual gathering place for the rural and small town population. Though exhibits were undoubtedly of first interest at fairs, those who attended expected entertainment—animal shows, acrobats, lectures, slide shows (later movies), horse and automobile races, and rigidly-controlled acts and games. There was almost always a section set aside for merry-go-rounds, rides and concessions that was, in effect, a pleasure park in embryo.

But most certainly the Chicago Fair showed that there was a huge waiting urban market for more Midways, a clientele both available and mobile via railway, streetcar and automobile. There were literally millions of Americans eager to pay for this kind of recreation, people with leisure and money to spend on dancehalls, vaudeville, professional sports, movies, theaters, circuses, carnivals and much else.[8] There were also shrewd men ready to take advantage of them. One, George C. Tilyou, bought and transformed New York's Coney Island in 1895, setting off a wave of similar parks in New York and other urban areas—Sea Lion Park, Steeplechase Park, Luna Park (made out of Sea Lion) and Dreamland. Parks

---

[5]For excellent photographs and descriptions see volume IV of *The Portfolio of Photos of the World's Fair* (Chicago: Household Art Press, 1898).

[6]Chicago's Century of Progress Midway in 1933 featured Sally Rand and her famous fan dance and the Skyride, two 628-foot towers with a rocket car ride at the 200-foot level.

[7]This is not to say that the amusement park is uniquely American. European "pleasure parks" on city outskirts date certainly from the sixteenth century; London's Vauxhall Gardens (1661) and Ranelagh Gardens (1690), Paris' Ruggieri and Tivoli Gardens (later moved to Denmark) date from the eighteenth century. However, none seems to have had direct major influence on the American version.

[8]Dana Tatlin, "Amusing America's Millions," *World's Work* 26 (July 1913), 325–40 is an interesting and insightful survey of the exploding market for public recreation in the period. See also Richard Henry Edwards, *Popular Amusements* (New York: Association Press, 1915).

sprang up across the land, promoted by railroads, inter-urbans, breweries and local entrepreneurs. The years 1900 to 1910, in the words of a contemporary, saw "a hysteria of parks followed by panic."[9] Fortunes were made and lost, parks opened and closed, new rides and concessions tried and abandoned. In 1907 the national capitalization of amusement parks was calculated at over $100,000,000, with predictions of double the sum within the decade.

Alert managers and designers knew what the public wanted and gave it to them. The park was "pleasure to the multitude." It should never be serious, but entertaining, it must be "different from ordinary experience"; it must have "life, action, motion, sensation, shock, swiftness, or else comedy." Those who paid to get in wanted innocent fun, not morality or education—as Frederick Thompson said, they wanted "elaborated child's play." The amusement park, he continued, should be "frankly devoted to fun, the fantastic, the gay, the grotesque."[10]

The modern American amusement park, then, was never a pastoral retreat. It was not a place of quiet self-evaluation but one for participation, noise, jostle, light, color, activity. Tilyou, Thompson and the rest integrated the park into the city by railway, trolley bus and automobile. It was not a flight from urban life but a journey to an intensified version of it, where one mixed with the same city crowds in a different context, "catching," an observer commented, "the full live sense of humanity." An early visitor described it quite accurately as "essentially a place of merriment. . . . There is no other reason for going there."[11] And by enclosing the park and charging admission, operators immediately established control of who entered and what went on inside—creating an engineered environment, carefully planned to manipulate visitors into having fun but also spending money in an orderly, safe and relaxed atmosphere.

1. Thus our first view of the amusement park—as an alternative world to that of our daily lives. The amusement park provides all who come with a chance to be something other than what they are—workers, bosses, fathers, mothers, sons, daughters, anyone with responsibilities or socio-economic functions. The park allows people to operate in a different environment for purposes and rewards quite different from those of the outside workaday world. It is a place where each can set his own easily attainable goals in a known, controllable situation. In this world nothing is done for profit, nothing by necessity. We can beat the weight guesser or win the teddy bear, but in the park's insulated environment we don't have to try to do either, nor does success or failure really matter. We can live in Space World, Frontier Village or Safari Land; take chances without real risk on rides, and in games of skill or chance. In a real sense, within the park we can—for the moment—live in a way we cannot outside it, and at relatively small cost.

2. A second way of looking at an amusement park is related to the first, that is, to see it as fantasy; a stage set, a never-never land where one can walk

---

[9]"Amusing America's Millions," op. cit. 327.

[10]Thompson explained his theories in two remarkable essays, "The Summer Show," *Independent* 62 (June 20, 1907) 1460–62; and "Amusing the Million," *Everybody's Magazine* 19 (Sept 1908), 395–7. See also Edwin Slosson's classic "The Amusement Business," *Independent* 67 (July 21, 1904), pp. 134–38.

[11]Lindsay Denison, "The Biggest Playground in the World," *Munsey's Magazine* 33 (August 1905), pp. 555–61.

out of his own world into a much more interesting one. This of course is one of the oldest attractions of the amusement park and still one of its most powerful. When the visitor arrives at the park's gate, wrote Frederic Thompson,

> His eyes tell him he is in a different world—a dream world, perhaps a nightmare world—where all is bizarre and fantastic—crazier than the craziest part of Paris— gayer and more different from the everyday world. . . . He is prepared to accept all sorts of extravagances—things that elsewhere would be impossible—in perfect faith for the time being.

O. Henry, a constant visitor to Coney Island, loved it for its "breathtaking though safeguarded dip and flight of adventure, the magic carpet that transports you to the realms of fairyland."[12] The park names themselves—Luna, Dreamland, Avalon, and the like—underlined their illusory quality and encouraged the visitor's anticipation. Luna Park gave its customers a wide choice of fantasy worlds, among them a Chinese theater, a Dutch town, a Japanese garden, an Eskimo camp, a tour of Venice and an Indian durbar. The element of fantasy is, of course, still a major element of the modern theme park since Disney pioneered this reemphasis in 1955. Walt Disney World in Florida, for example, forthrightly calls itself "A Magic Kingdom" and offers the public six different lands which (in prose Thompson and his era would have admired)

> capture the spirits of history, fantasy and adventure—with magic. Stroll beneath the soft glow of gaslights in turn-of-the-century Main Street, U.S.A. Sail with a crew of rowdy pirates and explore the tropical rivers of the world in Adventureland. Let a group of zany singing bears entertain you in the Old West atmosphere of Frontier- land. Walk along Liberty Square's cobblestone streets and relive America's struggle for freedom. Greet your favorite childhood storybook characters amidst the happy aura of Fantasyland. And travel to a visionary future of rockets and space journeys in Tomorrowland.

This recent trend in amusement parks, the device of unifying themes, is chiefly the result of the transfer of Hollywood stage-set skills of Illusion, developed over a half-century of movie making, to the park locale. Here, out of sight of the world outside, one may cross the boundaries of space and time to the Old West, the African jungle, early America, or nearly any fantasy land he chooses. "Take a step back in time and ride an authentic Iron Horse," advertises one park, "Transport into the future when you take a voyage to another World." Another invites the customer to an "Enchanted Voyage, an animated journey through a world of make believe," and so do dozens more.[13] What Tilyou and

---

[12]"The Summer Show," *op. cit.* 1461. O. Henry set two of his more sentimental stories at Coney Island: "The Greater Coney" and "Brickdust Row."

[13]A very short list of fantasy lands would include at least six Frontier Towns, several Ghost Towns, Storytowns, Space World, Old Town, Rivertown, several Safari Parks or Trails, Gaslite Village, Main Street, U.S.A., Joyland, Oz City, Mother Goose Park, Dogpatch, Silver Dollar City, Octoberfest, Alice-In-Wonderland, Lion Country, and so on. As of 1975 there were 695 amusement parks, almost all with similar fantasy lands and many with more than one. See *U.S. News and World Report,* July 21, 1975; *Seventeen,* July 1973; and *Holiday,* June-July-August 1975, for reports.

Thompson and the Midway promoters knew would work still does. "From the moment you enter King's Island," the Ohio park's folder says, "a whole new world of fantasy unfolds before your eyes," just as it did at Dreamland two generations ago.[14]

The theatrical element of the park, suggested by the stage set, has been [13] powerfully enhanced by the trend toward "happenings," or playlets, acted out at intervals by employees in costume. Disneyland's parade of story-book characters represented an early phase of this, later theme parks elaborated the idea into what were small but full-scale places and times. The attack on the stage coach, for example, soon became standard fare in Western theme parks. Silver Dollar City, an Old West theme park, had one hundred and three "happenings" daily staged by thirty-three "image characters," among them the town's marshal, doctor, undertaker, mayor, various gunmen, dancehall girls and the like.[15]

The fantasy element of the park is often extended into farce and foolery. [14] Certain games and shows violate our anticipations; they reverse what we expect, take situations and devices out of the normal world and use them absurdly. Things that are harmless and functional in ordinary life take on wild aspects—as in the Hall of Mirrors, the Funhouse, the Oriental Maze, Krazy Kastle and certain games which have long been part of carnival and park attractions. One of the early rides, for example, called The Haunted Swing, placed the visitor in a room which seemed to turn around and upside down while he did not, leaving him with the sensation of spinning around while standing on his head. The Tilt Room, which does exactly that, is an old-time favorite developed around the turn of the century. And who really wants a kewpie doll, or needs a tasselled whip, or carries (outside the park) a pink parasol or a balloon with a silly device? There is also a strong quality of the absurd in some of the rides; there are little cars that don't steer right, floors that spin, sidewalks that jiggle, gusts that blow off hats, mirrors that turn visitors into freaks, strange noises that challenge sanity. What happens is that something that *should* do something suddenly does something quite different; the pleasure comes from the harmless surprise which is itself an essential component of the fantasy the park evokes. We all suspect, at times, that the world is an absurd place, and an amusement park, for a few hours, confirms this without threatening us.

3. A third way of looking at an amusement park is to view it as spectacle, as [15] a unified, harmonious production meant to be *seen* and *heard*. Park planners have always been aware of the importance of the park as a total visual and aural experience that envelops the visitor as he enters and enfolds him until he leaves. The impact is more apparent today, perhaps, than ever before because of the movie set influence. People arrive as separate figures; once inside the gates they merge into and become part of the spectacle. Early designers and operators

---

[14]Dreamland Park in Nara City, Japan, a Disney-land operation, opened in 1960. The first theme park based on television characters seems to have been Bedrock City, Custer, South Dakota (1960) built about the Hanna-Barbera characters The Flintstones. Other Flintstone-theme parks appeared in Holland and Denmark in the sixties.

[15]*Amusement Business,* January 1, 1962, 9.

recognized the necessity of maintaining spatial and architectural unity within the park to emphasize this sense of unified spectacle. Thompson, for example, decided to make Luna Oriental, calling up illusions of the mysterious East; he combined towers, turrets, walls, flags, colors, lights and costumes into one big display with such success that remnants of the Oriental theme are still visible in older amusement parks of today—as in The Arcade of Cedar Point, Ohio, for example.[16]

Thus Lindsay Denison, approaching Coney, saw before him "rising to the sky a thousand glittering towers and minarets, the magically realized dream of poet or painter," a great spectacle of color, activity and excitement. Albert Bigelow Paine, Mark Twain's friend, on leaving Coney Island, looked back as its lights went on in the dusk:

> Tall towers that had grown dim suddenly broke forth in electric outlines and gay rosettes of color, as the living sparks of light travelled hither and thither, until the place was transformed into an enchanted garden, of such a sort as Aladdin never dreamed of.[17]

The contrast of this spectacle with, say, the Chicago or St. Louis fair was deliberate—the exposition style monumental, stately, disciplined; the amusement park a swirl of forms and colors. White City asked for contemplation, Luna for participation. Shapes, sounds, colors and movement combined in one great prospect that drew people into it—"it simply shouted," said one visitor, of "joyousness."

> In cupolas and minarets, in domes and flaunting finials, in myriads of gay bannerets, in the jocund motion of merry-go-rounds, circle swings and wondrous sliding follies, in laughter and shrieks, in the blare of brazen music and the throbbing of tom-toms—it speaks its various language—joyous forever.[18]

4. A fourth way of looking at an amusement part is to consider it as a release from conventional behavior, a place where some of the restraints of daily life may be relaxed. As Tilyou said, visitors can "cut loose from repressions and restrictions, and act pretty much as they feel like acting—since everyone else is doing the same thing." The amusement park, said one analyst in 1907, "was not founded for the culture of decorum, it was founded for the culture of hilarity." "The spirit of the place," he continued, encourages the visitor "to cancel every canon of conventionality, every rubric of discretion," an overstatement but nonetheless a shrewd comment on a traditional component of the park's popularity. But though ordinary rules of behavior might be modified, they were never abandoned. The

---

[16]See Kasson, pp. 66–67, on Luna and Dreamland.

[17]Denison, *op. cit.*, pp. 565–6; and Paine, "The New Coney Island," *Scribner's* 68 (August 1904), pp. 535, 538. Chicago's "White City" was the first to capitalize on the new electric light and other parks were quick to follow. Chicago's 1933 Fair, in memory of 1893, called itself "The City of a Million Lights." On the importance of lighting, see "Painting With Light," *Amusement Business,* May 8, 1965, pp. 20–22.

[18]Rollin Lynde Hartt, "The Amusement Park," *Atlantic Monthly,* Vol. XCXIX (May, 1907), p. 669.

park may be "frisky," wrote Frederic Thompson, "but it knows where to draw the line."[19]

Still, one could—and can—wear funny hats, weird shirts, carry stuffed [18] animals and fancy canes, laugh and shout, and indulge in unusual diets of

> crimson sausages, green corn in the ear, retrospective soft-shell crabs, (*and*) chrome colored beverages . . . which once had bowing acquaintance with oranges and lemons.[20]

A variety of games and contests allowed the client to transcend his inhibitions. A booth that provided baseballs to throw at dishes advertised, "If you can't do it at home, do it here!"[21] While no man in his right mind would dare to impress his girl friend during business hours by striking a post with a maul to ring a bell, he can do it without shame in a park, a fact operators have recognized for generations.

Part of the appeal of the park's unconventionality lay in its pretense of [19] wickedness, its illusion of letting down the bars of propriety, if only a bit. The amusement park postcard, still a standard souvenir, soon became a part of this— "Having a H—of a Time at Lansing Park"; "Don't Bring Your Wife to Pine Point!"; "Look What I Found at Joyland!"—with pictures of girls in bathing suits or men with upraised bottles. Early amusement parks had various devices (and some still do) to blow air jets up women's skirts and rides and games intended to expose legs, thighs and whatever, all within acceptable limits of jocular deviltry. Certain rides were constructed so as to jostle people into physical contact— Love's Journey, Barrel of Fun, The Haunted House, and the traditional Tunnel of Love ("Kiss Her in The Dark!"). The proprietor of one concession called the Foolish House attributed its success to the simple fact that "the men like it because it gives them a chance to hug the girls and the girls like it because it gives them a chance to be hugged," an opinion no doubt equally fitting today.

In the easy environment of the park, the rules of etiquette tend to loosen. [20] Introductions are often dispensed with; one can be interested in another's activities and strike up a conversation with strangers. Families meet and share the day; people find common interests that might extend beyond the park, but need not. Like the dancehall, just then gaining respectability in the cities, the early amusement park provided a meeting place where the young could meet without embarrassment within the sanctioned conventionality of the midway, at the bandstand, or as part of the camaraderie of the boardwalk. "Many come singly,"[22] wrote an observer,

> each lad with an as yet unidentified pompadour in his heart, each lass cherishing a shy anticipation. But how, you ask, shall these youthful strangers be made acquainted? Leave that to them.

[19]Tilyou is quoted by Kasson, 59. The other observer is Hartt, *op. cit.,* 669. Thompson's statement is in "The Summer Show," p. 1612.
[20]Guy Wetmore Carryl, "Marvelous Coney Island," *Munsey's Magazine* 25 (September 1901), p. 814.
[21]H. Rhodes, "City Summer," *Harper's* 131 (June 1915), p. 13.
[22]Hartt, p. 676.

One reason, no doubt, for this sense of "cutting loose" (as Thompson called 21 it) lies in the fact that entrance into the amusement park makes the visitor part of the show—he becomes, in effect, both spectator and performer. Early observers noted how easily people assumed roles without quite realizing it.[23] A woman having her weight guessed or a man at ring-toss is performing and knows it. The group watching is an audience and also knows it; in fact, it may even applaud.

People-watching has long been one of the most obvious participatory 22 elements of park activity, and as each day progresses the merger of spectator and performer becomes quite evident. That those who ride the roller-coaster, for example, are playing roles has long been known to operators and observers—the ritual screamer, the front-seat show-off, the marathon rider, the nerveless cynic, and others. People share rides together, eat together, line up together, play games together; one may for the moment be the center of attention by winning (or losing) a prize or performing in some spectacular way. Thus the park visitor becomes, in a real sense, a part of a collective unit, a partner in the day's play; the rules of social separation are gradually relaxed, as at sporting events and traffic accidents.

5. A fifth way of understanding the amusement park is to consider it as an 23 extension of the backyard outing or family picnic. Early promoters, by altering the atmosphere and character of the old park, practically guaranteed a greatly expanded and much more profitable middle class market. They made it attractive to "respectable funseekers with their families . . . with decent shows, honest prices for food and drink, and some semblance of cleanliness and public order."[24] Frederic Thompson in refurbishing Coney Island, got rid of "the tinhorn gambler, the short-change artist, the gamblers, swindlers, and thugs" to make it, he proudly wrote, "the place where your mother, your sister, and your sweetheart would be comfortable and safe." The change was immediately noticeable and highly profitable. "Everywhere," wrote Paine, "were clean, freshly-clad, well-groomed people and gaily-decked, brightfaced children," an impression borne out by contemporary photographs. Not only was it moral, but also good business. Businessman found[25]

> that decent people have in the aggregate more money to spend than the dissipated even though they spend it more sparingly; that eleven dimes are more than a dollar; and that a show which can take in the whole family pays better than a show to which only one would go.

Parks were shrewdly planned to provide something for everybody in the family at every age group; even those who came without family escort were made to feel somehow they were included in this excursion-like holiday venture.

---

[23]Denison, *op. cit.*, pp. 565–6.

[24]*Ibid.*, p. 558. See especially his contrast of the old and new style parks. Fred F. McClure in 1911 made a survey of commercial recreation in Kansas City, rating each attraction on a "moral worth" scale from 0% to 100%. Kansas City's five amusement parks gained a 71% rating, behind shooting galleries (84% the highest), skating rinks (74%), and theaters (72%). Lowest were "stag shows" (0%), riverboat excursions (7.7%) and dancehalls (23%). Edwards, *Popular Amusements*, pp. 19–20.

[25]"Summer Show," *op. cit.*, 1467; "Amusing the Million," *op. cit.*, 386; *op. cit.*, p. 537; and Slosson, *op. cit.*, 134.

Amusement parks have carefully maintained this family orientation. Walt   24
Disney World advertises "Bring the Whole Family! We have 43 square miles for
you and your family to discover, explore, and enjoy!" Cedar Point calls itself
"Family Fun Capital of the Midwest . . . , the most exciting innovation in
modern family entertainment!" Kings Island, "the perfect one-stop family vacation
resort," promises "fun, adventure, and excitement for every member of the family.
From the smallest toddler to the oldest grandparent." Such emphasis on family
participation is a constant theme in park publicity. "Family," in this context,
implies cleanliness, order, landscaping, no liquor or suggestive shows, a wide mix
of attractions, cheerful and helpful young staff (like the kids next door), and plenty
of free toilets.[26]

The point is to get the whole family into the park and keep it there as long   25
as possible. Operators have been notably successful at this. About one family in
five pays from $4.50 to $9.50 each for entrance to the two dozen major parks,
not including admission to the smaller operations. The big "superparks" keep
customers an average of seven and a half hours, during which time they spend
about $4.50 each over the original admission fee. The reason is clear and
simple—as *United States News and World Report* summarized its study of
amusement parks, it is "wholesome family entertainment at reasonable prices."[27]
One might well underline *family*. A survey conducted in 1972 showed that 58%
of daily attendance at amusement parks derived from family trade, a figure
probably substantially higher today.[28]

6. A sixth way to look at an amusement park is to see it as an adaptation and   26
extension of construction and transportation technology. As Edwin Slosson
perceptively pointed out seventy-five years ago, the park of his day took clever
advantage of two recent technological innovations, structural steel and electric
lights, and of their application to bridge building and skyscraper construction.
Not only park architecture, but the park rides have always been directly indebted
to the kinds of transportation in common use by urban society and industry—the
roller coaster and whip (railroad and streetcar); the Ferris Wheel, seesaw, and its
various mutations (the elevator); the towers and buildings (bridges and office
buildings).[29]

Similarly, the automobile, airplane, motor boat, and space module were   27
quickly adapted to rides in later years—The Dodgem, the Parachute Drop, the

---

[26]Walt Disney World has a 24-hour custodial service; Cedar Point boasts that an empty cigaret pack
will be picked up in five minutes or less. Disney forbids its staff to wear sunglasses since they give the
impression of impersonality. Six Flags emphasizes the importance of the smile—the company song
tells employees, "If you see a frown, you gotta turn it upside down." See *Fortune* (December 1977),
171–2 on staff training programs; see also "Housekeeping at Cedar Point," *Amusement Business,* February 27, 1965, 18–20.
[27]July 2, 1975, 38–40. Also *Newsweek,* July 23, 1973, 42.
[28]*Amusement Business,* January 8, 1972. Sanlando Springs Park in Florida, in fact, experimented with
year-round family memberships in the style of country clubs or golf clubs. "Funtown Atlanta" was
planned on the model of a shopping mall, to make it "an integrated family recreational center." *Ibid.,*
July 3, 1961. On the importance of attracting family trade, see "Is It For You?" *Ibid.,* January 8,
1960, pp. 18–20.
[29]Slosson, *op. cit.,* pp. 135–36.

Rocket Ride, The Jet Whirl, Ride The Rapids, and the like. What park engineers have done since Slosson's time is simply to transfer—quickly, ingeniously, and with shrewd grasp of crowded psychology—the most recent technological innovations into amusement park equivalents. The famous Switchback Railroad, for example, one of the most popular early roller coasters, was actually a real railroad to an abandoned mine, later run through a tunnel to complete the workday analogy. The commercial use and social convenience of this technology in daily life is thus transposed to the non-utilitarian purposes of pleasure, excitement, awe, and counterfeit danger. Going to work on a train, auto, elevated car, or bus day after day is deadly dull; riding a big roller coaster (which is simply an exaggerated version of the daily commuter experience) is anything but. Such famous present-day coasters as Cedar Point's Gemini, Six Flags Over Georgia's Great American Scream Machine or Bob-Lo's Skystreak are actually great big trolley-car rides.[30]

In effect, the amusement park pushed technology beyond rational limits toward parody into the realm of the comic. Small wagons go uphill and downhill at great speed to nowhere; toy autos skitter about and crash without danger or destination; boat-rides down the swirling rapids hardly get the rider wet. The normal technology of transportation and construction in daily life is burlesqued into child's games—sliding on cellar doors, racing coasters down hill, riding bikes no-hands, pumping high on the backyard swing.[31]

7. The illusory or imitative aspect of the amusement park suggests a seventh way of looking at it—as what might be called the riskless risk, a place where one may take chances that are really not chances. The park's basic appeal has long been to provide a sense of imminent danger and the likelihood of disaster without the culmination of either. Early parks specialized in so-called spectacle shows that re-created famous disasters—the Johnstown Flood, the Fall of Pompeii and San Francisco Earthquake were favorites—with great theatrical verisimilitude, creating the thrill but not the tragedy. Parkgoers thus had "a chance to shudder and a chance to be scared out of their wits."[32] For the same reason many parks have featured lion tamers, balloon drops, auto races, wirewalkers, and so on. Just as simulated earthquakes, floods or train wrecks fascinated earlier patrons, so the auto "thrill show" attracted later generations conscious of the dangers of auto travel and street traffic. The original auto "thrill show" appeared in Toledo in 1923; the demolition derby, its carnival-amusement park descendant, was initiated in 1961 in Islip, New York, an interesting adaptation of changing technology to the park's attractions.[33]

---

[30]Gemini, a double-track ride, has a lift height of 125 feet, reaches sixty or more miles per hour, and can handle 52,000 riders per day.

[31]The amusement park ride, in fact, may have developed from the public ice slides of early Russia, adapted by a Frenchman in 1804 to small wagons rolling downhill. The first modern American roller coaster seems to have appeared at Coney Island in 1884. Chicago's Columbian Exposition featured an "Ice Ride" with refrigerated tracks. One may also speculate that some amusement park games and rides may be adaptations of the dollhouse, the treehouse, and the game room.

[32]Denison, *op. cit.,* 340; Hartt, *op. cit.,* pp. 671–72.

[33]*Amusement Business,* July 24, 1961.

A favorite feature of early amusement parks was the fire show (Coney [30] Island's "Fire and Flame" was a pioneer) in which a building was set afire to be extinguished by park firemen with meticulous realism, including screaming women who jumped to death (into safety nets), clouds of smoke, and frequent explosions. Since fire was a constant threat in the city, particularly in tenement districts, the show touched on very real urban experience. The fact that all the performers were trained acrobats and skilled showmen did not detract from the power of the illusion.[34] While disaster shows are still to be seen in some amusement parks, the movies, of course, caught on very early and did them better. Catastrophe is still big box-office; witness *The Poseidon Adventure, Airport 77, The Towering Inferno,* or the recent hit called simply *Disasters.*

The primary appeal of many park rides, like that of the spectacles, was thus [31] predicated on the same "conspicuous joys . . . of vicarious terror and firsthand hair's-breadth escape." Observers of park attractions from that day to this agree on the delightful feeling of fearful anticipation, the dizzying moments of panic and the flattering sense of bravery at having dared an intimidating ride and won out, even if that risk is sham. Riders, too, often remark on the sudden feeling of camaraderie in the group at the finish at having conquered and survived. The scenic railway at Coney Island, for example, had a wooden beam that looked as if it was about to decapitate the riders but just missed—that beam seemed to have stuck in many minds for years after.[35] Designers of park rides still play heavily on this appeal. Although the actual risk is statistically quite minimal, it is a sense of danger which is ingeniously built into them. In fact, one reason that the roller-coaster structure is left unsheathed is that the latticework of open girders (usually of wood) gives a false impression of fragility that heightens the prospective rider's apprehensions. Though engineers are quite capable of designing relatively noiseless cars, they know that the sound of the ride is an integral part of it, and that the rattles, squeaks and thunderous roar of the wheels impart a sense of speed and danger that adds immeasurably to the total effect. The imaginative names given to rides also tend to excite trepidation— Wildcat, Cyclone, Tornado, Blue Racer, Silver Streak, Speed Demon, The Beast—and park advertising strongly reinforces it.[36] Rides continue to constitute the amusement park's major attraction, since they seem to elicit some deep psychological response in everyone—a human need for "the delight of danger and the pleasure of peril," as Edwin Slosson called it. As a modern writer put it, in a superb analysis, to find out why we ride them we need to look inside ourselves:

---

[34]See Hartt's vivid account of such a fire show, p. 673ff., and the effect on spectators of this "coquet with death."

[35]Hartt's detailed analysis of the rides and his reactions (674–5) is worth re-reading. He rode the Scenic Railway, The Flying Airship, and a shoot-the-rapids water ride called Hell Gate.

[36]One of the more ingenious public relations tricks was that devised by Crystal Beach Park in Niagara Falls, Canada, which placed a first-aid station and a trained nurse at the unloading platform of its Cyclone roller coaster.

They go fast. It's like going over the speed limit without the danger and illegality.

They're scary. People like to get scared.

They're fun. They're different, a bit mysterious, almost unnatural.

Some people need coaxing. Others giggle. Some rub their hands in anticipation. The anticipation is half the fun. There's no doubt the anxiety adds to the pleasure, both physical and mental, despite the hand-wringing, the sweaty palms.

At the crest of the hill you open your mouth. It's hard not to. Some people gasp, others scream. You look down. Straight down.

Your body tenses a bit. You look down at your hands and discover someone has painted them white. The car is picking up speed now. Your stomach notes that the bottom of the hill is an awfully long way down.

Then you are up again. A mysterious force wants to lift you off your seat. There are more hills and dips up ahead. More anticipation.

You are screaming. It is a strictly reflex action. Try to hold it in. You can't. Things are flying by awfully fast—track, trees, sky, lights—and your senses have to work overtime to keep up with it all.

When you get out of the car your knees are likely to be weak. Like rubber. Your heart is thumping. Your hands are tingling. Your eyes are refocusing. You remark that it all happened so fast. You think back on it. The experience is a wild blur of sight, sound, feeling. It's exhilarating. Scary. Fun.[37]

8. The eighth way of looking at an amusement park is to view it as the closest approximation of the *total* play experience. It may be the only place in modern life in which all forms of play are represented in a single controlled environment.[38] All human play, as French social psychologist Roger Caillois sees it, may be grouped in four categories:

Competition: contests, both individual and team.

Chance: poker, lotteries, bingo, roulette, parimutuel betting, and the like.

Mimicry: theater, spectacles, movies, television, ceremonies.

Vertigo: swinging, skiing, horseback riding, racing, and other activities which distort sensory stability.[39]

---

[37]Adapted from *The Coaster Enthusiast's Guide to Cedar Point* (Cedar Point, Ohio: Marketing Department, 1978). For an account of the designing and construction of a roller coaster see Jim McHugh, "Anatomy of a Roller Coaster," *Amusement Business*, August 1, 1965, dealing with Riverview Park's Jetstream, built by John Allen of the Philadelphia Toboggan Company.

[38]There are at least six modern theories of play, usefully summarized by Thomas Kando, *Leisure and Popular Culture* (St. Louis: C. V. Mosby Co., 1977), pp. 28–32. The most interesting, however, is that of Roger Caillois, *Man, Play, and Games* (New York: Free Press of Glencoe, 1961), particularly his classification system and his chapter, "Revivals in the Modern World." This portion of the paper is based on his interpretations of fairs, carnivals, parks and circuses.

[39]See Chapter I, "Classification of Games," in Caillois. *Vertigo* is defined as play "designed to distort, mislead, and stimulate confusion, anxiety, nausea, and momentary terror, quickly transformed back into order, at its conclusion." Slosson, *op. cit.*, pp. 136–37, makes precisely the same point, calling it "delightful dizziness."

The amusement park, separated by fences and guards from the outside 33
world, is itself a kind of play field, through whose gates visitors come expecting to
be both spectators and participants. It is a place of action, noise, color and
confusion which people enter only to play, filled with nothing but devices and
situations to help them do so. There are games of competition—all sorts of
shooting and throwing games, weight-guessing, strength-testing devices, and
whole buildings devoted to pinball and other competitive machines. Games of
chance abound—lotteries, spinning fortune wheels, and the ubiquitous bingo
hall. Mimicry, of course, is the entire purpose of the theme park. Many parks also
hire clowns, actors of book characters and animals and other masked or costumed
players to wander the grounds. Vertigo-inducing rides such as whips, Ferris
wheels, swings and slides form the backbone of the park's traditional attractions.
Roller coasters, in particular, combine real speed, simulated danger and sensory
disorder and relief—in two- to three-minute intervals—to produce the most
powerful vertiginous effect of all. Nowhere else in modern life may one put
together in the space of a few hours and with such minor expenditure of money
and energy so complete a play experience.

QUESTIONS FOR CRITICAL READING, THINKING, DISCUSSION, AND WRITING

Analyzing Content and Technique

1. Trace the history of the amusement park. How is its purpose today different from the original
   philosophy behind public parks?
2. List the eight different ways of looking at an amusement park, according to Nye. Analyze the
   way in which he has ordered them. What does this indicate of their relative importance?
3. How does the amusement park offer us "release from conventional behavior" (paragraph 17)?
   Give two or three examples of this from the text. Why might this be attractive to people?
4. Identify the major elements that keep an amusement park from becoming unsafe.
5. Analyze the way in which the writer has structured his paragraphs. Where in general are the
   topic sentences? What effect does this have in terms of reader expectation?
6. Where was this piece originally published? From this information, who do you deduce to be the
   intended audience of the essay? Identify elements within the essay that corroborate your
   deduction. How well does the tone fit this audience?

Collaborative Activity

As a group, discuss the writer's statement that the amusement park has pushed technology
toward parody (paragraph 28). What does he mean? What examples of this has he provided? Does
the group agree that this is how the amusement park uses technology? Have members come up
with other examples of technology in amusement parks today that might point to additional uses
and effects.

Making Connections

1. This essay was written in 1981. How far is the American amusement park today still similar
   to what Nye describes? In what ways is it different? Explore these questions in an essay.

2. Write an essay, loosely based on a structure and concept similar to Nye's, in which you examine another place of entertainment (for example, "Five Ways of Looking at a Football Stadium," "Six Ways of Looking at a Shopping Mall," "Three Ways of Looking at a Bowling Alley"). In your essay, analyze the needs fulfilled and the fantasies created by this place. You may choose any tone you like, serious or humorous, for your piece.

PREREADING ACTIVITY

Think about your own writing process. Make a list of things that come easily to you when writing. Now make a list of things that are difficult or elusive.

An Often Long Journey: An Interview with Joy Harjo

LAURA COLTELLI

Laura Coltelli is the editor of *Winged Words: American Indian Writers Speak Out*. The writer interviewed, Joy Harjo, was born in Tulsa, Oklahoma, in 1951 and is a member of the Creek tribe and a filmmaker, scriptwriter, artist, and poet. Her books include *Secrets from the Center of the World* and *In Mad Love and War*.

LC What does it mean, being an American Indian woman in the 1 United States nowadays?

HARJO To begin, it certainly means you are a survivor. Indian people make 2 up only about one-half of 1 percent of the total population of the United States! It means you carry with you a certain unique perception. And again you are dealing with tribal differences, personal differences, and so on. We are not all alike! Yet, I believe there is a common dream, a common thread between us, mostly unspoken.

I don't believe there are any accidents in why people were born where they 3 were, who they were, or are. There are no accidents. So I realize that being born an American Indian woman in this time and place is with a certain reason, a certain purpose. There are seeds of dreams I hold, and responsibility, that go with being born someone, especially a woman of my tribe, who is also part of this invading other culture, and the larger globe. We in this generation, and the next generation, are dealing with a larger world than the people who went before us— that we know of, because who knows what went down many, many, many years ago that no one remembers. We are dealing with a world consciousness, and have begun to see unity, first with many tribes in the United States and North America with the Pan-Indian movement, and now with tribal people in the rest of the world, Central and South America, Africa, Australian aborigines, and so on. We are not isolated. No one is. What happens here, happens there. But it is on sometimes subtle yet disturbing levels.

LC   Are you active in women's organizations?   4

HARJO   Not really. Sometimes I feel I should be, but it isn't my manner. I   5
participate by doing benefit readings, appearances, taking part when it is useful to do so. I know it is important, and groups are more powerful than one person working alone, but I guess there is no one group that I feel strong enough about to be active in, though I actively take part in many.

LC   Are you suspicious? Of what?   6

HARJO   I've wondered. Maybe it comes from being a mixed-blood in this   7
world. I mean, I feel connected to others, but many women's groups have a majority of white women and I honestly can feel uncomfortable, or even voiceless sometimes. I've lived in and out of both worlds for a long time and have learned how to speak—those groups just affect others that way—with a voicelessness. It's my problem, something I've learned to get over, am learning to overcome, because I am often the only one to speak for many of us in those situations. Sometimes it gets pretty comical, bizarre. When I was on the National Endowment for the Arts literature panel I was often the spokesperson-representative for Indian people, black people, all minority people, including women's, lesbian, and gay groups. It was rather ridiculous and angering at the same time, for we were all considered outside the mainstream of American literature. And it's not true, for often we are closer to the center.

LC   Noni Daylight appears in some of your poems, persona poems. You   8
said, "It's like she was a good friend." Would you comment on that, on the persona in your poems?

HARJO   She began quite some time ago, as a name I gave a real-life woman   9
I couldn't name in a poem. Then she evolved into her own person, took on her own life. And then she left my poems and went into a poem by Barney Bush, a Shawnee poet, and I never saw her again. She never came back!

LC   What about the other stories of women in your poems? Are they true   10
stories?

HARJO   Yes, always on some level. I'm a writer, I like to make up stories, to   11
add to them, often make them larger. The "I" is not always me, but a way I chose to speak the poem. "The Woman Hanging from the Thirteenth Floor" is written around an imaginary woman. You could call her imaginary. But within that space she is real, also. I made a trip to Chicago, oh, about eight years ago, and one of the places I went to while I was there was the Chicago Indian Center. The center was rather bleak, as there wasn't extra money around to buy things to make the place warm, homelike; there were no curtains, nothing like that, but in one room I noticed a rocking chair. It may have been empty, or there may have been someone in it—the image stayed with me. Perhaps it was because the chair was round, and everything else, all around, was square. So, a few years after that trip, the image stayed with me and I would see this woman, rocking and rocking, for her life, and she compelled me to write the poem. And I felt her standing behind me, urging me

on as I wrote, kept looking behind me. When it first appeared, and during the first readings of the poem others would come up after the reading and say, "You know, I know that woman," or "I knew her," or "I heard the story and have a newspaper clipping of it," and the event always had occurred in a different place. And other women are composites of many women I know, or stories I've heard, probably much like a fiction writer would work.

LC   So you became a kind of storyteller?   12

HARJO   In a way, though I am not a good fiction writer, or should I say,   13
have never really tried it, except in terms of screenplays.

LC   "Language identifies the world." You said that the English language is   14
not enough. "It is a male language, not tribal, not spiritual enough."

HARJO   Yes, I said that. I have learned to love the language, or rather, what   15
the language can express. But I have felt bound by the strictness imposed by its male-centeredness, its emphasis on nouns. So, it's also challenging, as a poet, to use it to express tribal, spiritual language, being. But maybe all poets basically are after that, and sometimes it isn't enough and that's when those boundaries become frustrating.

LC   What do you mean by saying English is not enough, English is a male   16
language?

HARJO   Again, maybe it would be that way in any language, the sense of   17
somehow being at a loss for words; [that] could always be the poet's dilemma. The ending of a poem, "Bleed-Through," says it: "There are no words, only sounds / that lead us into the darkest nights / where stars burn into ice / where the dead arise again / to walk in shoes of fire."

LC   Since language has an importance of its own in Indian culture, what's   18
the contribution or influence, just in terms of language, to mainstream American literature?

HARJO   What I think of immediately is the denial, the incredible denial of   19
anything other than that based on the European soul in American literature. Anything else is seen as "foreign," or not consciously integrated into what is called American literature. It could be ethnocentrism backed by a terrible guilt about what happened in this country.

LC   So what's the contribution, just in terms of language, to mainstream   20
American literature?

HARJO   That's a difficult question, one that will take me many months to   21
consider, because I'm always thinking about what I can add to the language, as someone of this background—dreams, and so on. I consider first a certain lyricism, a land-based language.

LC   The spirit of place?   22

HARJO   Yes, the spirit of place recognized, fed, not even paved over,   23
forgotten. Sometimes I feel like specters of forgotten ones roam the literature of some of these American writers who don't understand where they come from, who they are, where they are going. The strongest writers have always been the ones with a well-defined sense of place—I don't mean you have to be a nature writer—I'm thinking of "nonethnic" people, like Flannery O'Connor.

LC   What about imagery?   24

HARJO   Oh sure, imagery. That's definitely a part of it.   25

LC   A new feeling of landscape perhaps?   26

HARJO   Or a knowing of the landscape, as something alive with personality,   27
breathing. Alive with names, alive with events, nonlinear. It's not static and that's
a very important point. The western viewpoint has always been one of the land as
wilderness, something to be afraid of, and conquered because of the fear.

LC   The so-called wilderness.   28

HARJO   Yes, it depends on your viewpoint what wilderness is. For some the   29
city is a wilderness of concrete and steel, made within a labyrinth of mind.

LC   You mentioned before you are not only a poet, but you're a   30
scriptwriter for television and film. How does the process work in translating your
poetical world from one medium to another?

HARJO   Screenwriting is definitely related to poetry. You're dealing again   31
with the translation of emotions into images. There's a similar kind of language
involved. One goal I have, a life goal in terms of the cinema, is to create a film
with a truly tribal vision, viewpoint, in terms of story, camera viewpoints, angles,
everything. It hasn't been done, not on the scale I would like to do it.

LC   What do you think of non-Indian critics of your work and of Indian   32
literature in general?

HARJO   That question could be answered many ways—I mean, there are   33
specific non-Indian critics who get into trying to be Indian, when they don't have
to. What I write, what any of us write, or are after, whether we are Indian,
Chicano, Laotian, is shimmering language, poetry, the same as anyone else who is
writing in whatever language, with whatever sensibilities. Or too often they won't
approach the literature at all, won't read it or speak of it because, again, that guilt
enters in, or that fear that keeps them from entering any place other than what is
most familiar.

As far as the literature goes, I've seen much growth in these last several   34
years, in all of us. We are setting high standards for ourselves, our own standards,
mind you, in terms of what is possible with this language, and with what we have
come to know as artists of this continent.

LC   What writers are important to you?   35

HARJO   I consider first the writers who got me turned on to writing, what   36
writing could do. Because I was rather a late bloomer in this business, I was never
turned on by conventional English-language poetry. These writers include Simon
Ortiz, Leslie Silko, and many black American writers, like June Jordan, later
Audre Lorde and Alice Walker. Also Pablo Neruda, James Wright, Galway
Kinnell, and African writers. I love the work of Amos Tutuola, especially *The
Palm Wine Drunkard*. And there are many others.

LC   Do you see any changes in your work?   37

HARJO   Yes, many. If I didn't see them, didn't see growth, then I wouldn't   38
do it any more. There are leaps between *What Moon Drove Me to This?* and *She
Had Some Horses*, and I expect the leap to be huge between *Horses* and this next
collection I am working on. I feel like I am just now learning how to write a
poem. It has taken me over ten years to get to this point of just beginning.

LC   And what about in terms of technique?   39

HARJO   I'm certainly much more involved with process, inner travel, when   40
I write now than even five years ago. . . .

LC   Would you describe your writing process? I understand that you revise 41
a lot.

HARJO   I begin with the seed of an emotion, a place, and then move from 42
there. It means hours watching the space form in the place in front of the
typewriter, speaking words, listening to them, watching them form, and be crossed
out, on the paper, and so on, and yes, revision. I no longer see the poem as an
ending point, perhaps more the end of a journey, an often long journey that can
begin years earlier, say with the blur of the memory of the sun on someone's cheek,
a certain smell, an ache, and will culminate years later in a poem, sifted through a
point, a lake in my heart through which language must come. That's what I work
with, with my students at the university, opening that place within them of original
language, which I believe must be in everyone, but not everyone can reach it.

LC   You said before that you were speaking with your students about your 43
work as well?

HARJO   I can't separate my work, my writing, from who I am, so of course 44
it comes into the classroom with me in one way or another.

LC   Just a piece of paper with a new poem? 45

HARJO   Oh no, as part of that space I teach out of, a space of intuition 46
made up of everything I know as well as what I don't know, and I've learned in
writing, and in teaching, that it is important to recognize that place, to open
yourself, believing.

QUESTIONS FOR CRITICAL READING, THINKING, DISCUSSION, AND WRITING

Analyzing Content and Technique

1. How does Harjo see her position as an American Indian woman in the United States today? How is her role different from those of earlier generations?
2. Why did Harjo feel uncomfortable when serving on the NEA literary arts panel? How is this related to why she doesn't join women's groups?
3. Why does Harjo call English a "male" language? Evaluate the evidence she provides. This is an unusual way to look at languages. How do you think she would define a "female" language?
4. Discuss the characters in Harjo's poems. On whom are they originally based? What happens to them as Harjo writes? Identify an example of this from the text.
5. Describe the contribution of American Indian writers, in terms of language, to mainstream English literature. How far do you agree with Harjo? Can you think of additional contributions?
6. Examine the questions asked by the interviewer. On the basis of these questions, what would you deduce to be her main concerns? What "message" might she be trying to convey to her readers?

Collaborative Activity

In paragraph 36 Harjo alludes to "what writing could do." Discuss this idea as a group. What are some reasons why we write? What kind of power does writing possess? How might it transform the world? Make a list in which you put together the group's ideas.

Making Connections

1. Look up Harjo's poetry and choose three or four poems which you particularly like. Write an essay in which, on the basis of these poems, you analyze the contribution Harjo has made to American literature.

2. Harjo mentions several times that she feels there is a real difference between "mainstream" and "ethnic" literature in America today. Do you agree? Is it important and valuable to make such distinctions, or is it harmful? Write an essay in which you argue the other side—that is, the similarity between these two literatures—choosing two works from each category to support your thesis.

Why have fairy tales enjoyed such popularity in almost all cultures and times? Before reading selection 73, write down what you consider the reasons for the continued charm of the fairy tale.

"Cinderella": A Story of Sibling Rivalry and Oedipal Conflicts

BRUNO BETTELHEIM

Bruno Bettelheim (1903–1990) was originally from Vienna. He became an American citizen in 1939 and lived in the United States until his death. He taught for many years at the University of Chicago and published articles on psychology in many popular and professional journals. His books include *Love Is Not Enough: The Treatment of Emotionally Disturbed Children; The Informed Heart; Surviving;* and the landmark study *The Uses of Enchantment,* from which selection 73 is excerpted.

*B*y all accounts, "Cinderella" is the best-known fairy tale, and probably also the best-liked. It is quite an old story; when first written down in China during the ninth century A.D., it already had a history. The unrivaled tiny foot size as a mark of extraordinary virtue, distinction, and beauty, and the slipper made of precious material are facets which point to an Eastern, if not necessarily Chinese, origin.[1] The modern hearer does not connect sexual attractiveness and beauty in general with extreme smallness of the foot, as the ancient Chinese did, in accordance with their practice of binding women's feet.

"Cinderella," as we know it, is experienced as a story about the agonies and hopes which form the essential content of sibling rivalry; and about the degraded heroine winning out over her siblings who abused her. Long before Perrault gave "Cinderella" the form in which it is now widely known, "having to live among the ashes" was a symbol of being debased in comparison to one's siblings, irrespective of sex. In Germany, for example, there were stories in which such an ash-boy later becomes king, which parallels Cinderella's fate. "Aschenputtel" is the title of the Brothers Grimm's version of the tale. The term originally designated a lowly, dirty kitchenmaid who must tend to the fireplace ashes.

There are many examples in the German language of how being forced to dwell among the ashes was a symbol not just of degradation, but also of sibling rivalry, and of the sibling who finally surpasses the brother or brothers who have debased him. Martin Luther in his *Table Talks* speaks about Cain as the God-forsaken evildoer who is powerful, while pious Abel is forced to be his ash-brother (*Aschebrüdel*), a mere nothing, subject to Cain; in one of Luther's sermons he says that Esau was forced into the role of Jacob's ash-brother. Cain and Abel, Jacob and Esau are Biblical examples of one brother being suppressed or destroyed by the other.

The fairy tale replaces sibling relations with relations between stepsiblings—perhaps a device to explain and make acceptable an animosity which one wishes would not exist among true siblings. Although sibling rivalry is universal and "natural" in the sense that it is the negative consequence of being a sibling, this same relation also generates equally as much positive feeling between siblings, highlighted in fairy tales such as "Brother and Sister."

No other fairy tale renders so well as the "Cinderella" stories the inner experiences of the young child in the throes of sibling rivalry, when he feels hopelessly outclassed by his brothers and sisters. Cinderella is pushed down and degraded by her stepsisters; her interests are sacrificed to theirs by her (step)mother; she is expected to do the dirtiest work and although she performs it well, she receives no credit for it; only more is demanded of her. This is how the child feels when devastated by the miseries of sibling rivalry. Exaggerated though Cinderella's tribulations and degradations may seem to the adult, the child carried away by sibling rivalry feels, "That's me; that's how they mistreat me, or would want to; that's how little they think of me." And there are moments—often long time periods—when for inner reasons a child feels this way even when his position among his siblings may seem to give him no cause for it.

When a story corresponds to how the child feels deep down—as no realistic narrative is likely to do—it attains an emotional quality of "truth" for the child. The events of "Cinderella" offer him vivid images that give body to his overwhelming but nevertheless often vague and nondescript emotions; so these episodes seem more convincing to him than his life experiences.

The term "sibling rivalry" refers to a most complex constellation of feelings and their causes. With extremely rare exceptions, the emotions aroused in the person subject to sibling rivalry are far out of proportion to what his real situation with his sisters and brothers would justify, seen objectively. While all children at times suffer greatly from sibling rivalry, parents seldom sacrifice one of their children to the others, nor do they condone the other children's persecuting one of them. Difficult as objective judgments are for the young child—nearly impossible when his emotions are aroused—even he in his more rational moments "knows" that he is not treated as badly as Cinderella. But the child often feels mistreated, despite all his "knowledge" to the contrary. That is why he believes in the inherent truth of "Cinderella," and then he also comes to believe in her eventual deliverance and victory. From her triumph he gains the exaggerated hopes for his future which he needs to counteract the extreme misery he experiences when ravaged by sibling rivalry.

Despite the name "sibling rivalry," this miserable passion has only inciden- 8
tally to do with a child's actual brothers and sisters. The real source of it is the
child's feelings about his parents. When a child's older brother or sister is more
competent than he, this arouses only temporary feelings of jealousy. Another
child being given special attention becomes an insult only if the child fears that,
in contrast, he is thought little of by his parents, or feels rejected by them. It is
because of such an anxiety that one or all of a child's sisters or brothers may
become a thorn in his flesh. Fearing that in comparison to them he cannot win
his parents' love and esteem is what inflames sibling rivalry. This is indicated in
stories by the fact that it matters little whether the siblings actually possess greater
competence. The Biblical story of Joseph tells that it is jealousy of parental affection lavished on him which accounts for the destructive behavior of his brothers.
Unlike Cinderella's, Joseph's parent does not participate in degrading him, and,
on the contrary, prefers him to his other children. But Joseph, like Cinderella, is
turned into a slave, and, like her, he miraculously escapes and ends by surpassing
his siblings.

Telling a child who is devastated by sibling rivalry that he will grow up to 9
do as well as his brothers and sisters offers little relief from his present feelings of
dejection. Much as he would like to trust our assurances, most of the time he cannot. A child can see things only with subjective eyes, and comparing himself on
this basis to his siblings, he has no confidence that he, on his own, will someday
be able to fare as well as they. If he could believe more in himself, he would not
feel destroyed by his siblings no matter what they might do to him, since then he
could trust that time would bring about a desired reversal of fortune. But since
the child cannot, on his own, look forward with confidence to some future day
when things will turn out all right for him, he can gain relief only through fantasies of glory—a domination over his siblings—which he hopes will become reality through some fortunate event.

Whatever our position within the family, at certain times in our lives we are 10
beset by sibling rivalry in some form or other. Even an only child feels that other
children have some great advantages over him, and this makes him intensely jealous. Further, he may suffer from the anxious thought that if he did have a sibling, his parents would prefer this other child to him. "Cinderella" is a fairy tale
which makes nearly as strong an appeal to boys as to girls, since children of both
sexes suffer equally from sibling rivalry, and have the same desire to be rescued
from their lowly position and surpass those who seem superior to them.

On the surface, "Cinderella" is as deceptively simple as the story of Little 11
Red Riding Hood, with which it shares greatest popularity. "Cinderella" tells
about the agonies of sibling rivalry, of wishes coming true, of the humble being
elevated, of true merit being recognized even when hidden under rags, of virtue
rewarded and evil punished—a straightforward story. But under this overt
content is concealed a welter of complex and largely unconscious material, which
details of the story allude to just enough to set our unconscious associations
going. This makes a contrast between surface simplicity and underlying complexity which arouses deep interest in the story and explains its appeal to the
millions over centuries. To begin gaining an understanding of these hidden mean-

ings, we have to penetrate behind the obvious sources of sibling rivalry discussed so far.

As mentioned before, if the child could only believe that it is the infirmities [12] of his age which account for his lowly position, he would not have to suffer so wretchedly from sibling rivalry, because he could trust the future to right matters. When he thinks that his degradation is deserved, he feels his plight is utterly hopeless. Djuna Barnes's perceptive statement about fairy tales—that the child knows something about them which he cannot tell (such as that he likes the idea of Little Red Riding Hood and the wolf being in bed together)—could be extended by dividing fairy tales into two groups: one group where the child responds only unconsciously to the inherent truth of the story and thus cannot tell about it; and another large number of tales where the child preconsciously or even consciously knows what the "truth" of the story consists of and thus could tell about it, but does not want to let on that he knows. Some aspects of "Cinderella" fall into the latter category. Many children believe that Cinderella probably deserves her fate at the beginning of the story, as they feel they would, too; but they don't want anyone to know it. Despite this, she is worthy at the end to be exalted, as the child hopes he will be too, irrespective of his earlier shortcomings.

Every child believes at some period of his life—and this is not only at rare [13] moments—that because of his secret wishes, if not also his clandestine actions, he deserves to be degraded, banned from the presence of others, relegated to a netherworld of smut. He fears this may be so, irrespective of how fortunate his situation may be in reality. He hates and fears those others—such as his siblings—whom he believes to be entirely free of similar evilness, and he fears that they or his parents will discover what he is really like, and then demean him as Cinderella was by her family. Because he wants others—most of all, his parents—to believe in his innocence, he is delighted that "everybody" believes in Cinderella's. This is one of the great attractions of this fairy tale. Since people give credence to Cinderella's goodness, they will also believe in his, so the child hopes. And "Cinderella" nourishes this hope, which is one reason it is such a delightful story.

Another aspect which holds large appeal for the child is the vileness of the [14] stepmother and stepsisters. Whatever the shortcomings of a child may be in his own eyes, these pale into insignificance when compared to the stepsisters' and stepmother's falsehood and nastiness. Further, what these stepsisters do to Cinderella justifies whatever nasty thoughts one may have about one's siblings: they are so vile that anything one may wish would happen to them is more than justified. Compared to their behavior, Cinderella is indeed innocent. So the child, on hearing her story, feels he need not feel guilty about his angry thoughts.

On a very different level—and reality considerations coexist easily with fantastic exaggerations in the child's mind—as badly as one's parents or siblings seem [15] to treat one, and much as one thinks one suffers because of it, all this is nothing compared to Cinderella's fate. Her story reminds the child at the same time how lucky he is, and how much worse things could be. (Any anxiety about the latter possibility is relieved, as always in fairy tales, by the happy ending.)

The behavior of a five-and-a-half-year-old girl, as reported by her father, [16] may illustrate how easily a child may feel that she is a "Cinderella." This little girl had a younger sister of whom she was very jealous. The girl was very fond of "Cinderella," since the story offered her material with which to act out her feelings, and because without the story's imagery she would have been hard pressed to comprehend and express them. This little girl had used to dress very neatly and liked pretty clothes, but she became unkempt and dirty. One day when she was asked to fetch some salt, she said as she was doing so, "Why do you treat me like Cinderella?"

Almost speechless, her mother asked her, "Why do you think I treat you like Cinderella?"   17

"Because you make me do all the hardest work in the house!" was the little girl's answer. Having thus drawn her parents into her fantasies, she acted them out more openly, pretending to sweep up all the dirt, etc. She went even further, playing that she prepared her little sister for the ball. But she went the "Cinderella" story one better, based on her unconscious understanding of the contradictory emotions fused into the "Cinderella" role, because at another moment she told her mother and sister, "You shouldn't be jealous of me just because I am the most beautiful in the family."   18

This shows that behind the surface humility of Cinderella lies the conviction of her superiority to mother and sisters, as if she would think: "You can make me do all the dirty work, and I pretend that I am dirty, but within me I know that you treat me this way because you are jealous of me because I am so much better than you." This conviction is supported by the story's ending, which assures every "Cinderella" that eventually she will be discovered by her prince.   19

Why does the child believe deep within himself that Cinderella deserves her dejected state? This question takes us back to the child's state of mind at the end of the oedipal period. Before he is caught in oedipal entanglements, the child is convinced that he is lovable, and loved, if all is well within his family relationships. Psychoanalysis describes this stage of complete satisfaction with oneself as "primary narcissism." During this period the child feels certain that he is the center of the universe, so there is no reason to be jealous of anybody.   20

The oedipal disappointments which come at the end of this developmental stage cast deep shadows of doubt on the child's sense of his worthiness. He feels that if he were really as deserving of love as he had thought, then his parents would never be critical of him or disappoint him. The only explanation for parental criticism the child can think of is that there must be some serious flaw in him which accounts for what he experiences as rejection. If his desires remain unsatisfied and his parents disappoint him, there must be something wrong with him or his desires, or both. He cannot yet accept that reasons other than those residing within him could have an impact on his fate. In his oedipal jealousy, wanting to get rid of the parent of the same sex had seemed the most natural thing in the world, but now the child realizes that he cannot have his own way, and that maybe this is so because the desire was wrong. He is no longer so sure that he is preferred to his siblings, and he begins to suspect that this may be due to the fact that *they* are free of any bad thoughts or wrongdoing such as his.   21

All this happens as the child is gradually subjected to ever more critical attitudes as he is being socialized. He is asked to behave in ways which run counter   22 to his natural desires, and he resents this. Still he must obey, which makes him very angry. This anger is directed against those who make demands, most likely his parents; and this is another reason to wish to get rid of them, and still another reason to feel guilty about such wishes. This is why the child also feels that he deserves to be chastised for his feelings, a punishment he believes he can escape only if nobody learns what he is thinking when he is angry. The feeling of being unworthy to be loved by his parents at a time when his desire for their love is very strong leads to the fear of rejection, even when in reality there is none. This rejection fear compounds the anxiety that others are preferred and also maybe preferable—the root of sibling rivalry.

Some of the child's pervasive feelings of worthlessness have their origin in 23 his experiences during and around toilet training and all other aspects of his education to become clean, neat, and orderly. Much has been said about how children are made to feel dirty and bad because they are not as clean as their parents want or require them to be. As clean as a child may learn to be, he knows that he would much prefer to give free rein to his tendency to be messy, disorderly, and dirty.

At the end of the oedipal period, guilt about desires to be dirty and disor- 24 derly becomes compounded by oedipal guilt, because of the child's desire to replace the parent of the same sex in the love of the other parent. The wish to be the love, if not also the sexual partner, of the parent of the other sex, which at the beginning of the oedipal development seemed natural and "innocent," at the end of the period is repressed as bad. But while this wish as such is repressed, guilt about it and about sexual feelings in general is not, and this makes the child feel dirty and worthless.

Here again, lack of objective knowledge leads the child to think that he is 25 the only bad one in all these respects—the only child who has such desires. It makes every child identify with Cinderella, who is relegated to sit among the cinders. Since the child has such "dirty" wishes, that is where he also belongs, and where he would end up if his parents knew of his desires. This is why every child needs to believe that even if he were thus degraded, eventually he would be rescued from such degradation and experience the most wonderful exaltation—as Cinderella does.

For the child to deal with his feelings of dejection and worthlessness 26 aroused during this time, he desperately needs to gain some grasp on what these feelings of guilt and anxiety are all about. Further, he needs assurance on a conscious and an unconscious level that he will be able to extricate himself from these predicaments. One of the greatest merits of "Cinderella" is that, irrespective of the magic help Cinderella receives, the child understands that essentially it is through her own efforts, and because of the person she is, that Cinderella is able to transcend magnificently her degraded state, despite what appear as insurmountable obstacles. It gives the child confidence that the same will be true for him, because the story relates so well to what has caused both his conscious and his unconscious guilt.

Overtly "Cinderella" tells about sibling rivalry in its most extreme form: the 27 jealousy and enmity of the stepsisters, and Cinderella's sufferings because of it.

The many other psychological issues touched upon in the story are so covertly alluded to that the child does not become consciously aware of them. In his unconscious, however, the child responds to these significant details which refer to matters and experiences from which he consciously has separated himself, but which nevertheless continue to create vast problems for him.

NOTE

1. Artistically made slippers of precious material were reported in Egypt from the third century on. The Roman emperor Diocletian in a decree of A.D. 301 set maximum prices for different kinds of footwear, including slippers made of fine Babylonian leather, dyed purple or scarlet, and gilded slippers for women.

QUESTIONS FOR CRITICAL READING, THINKING, DISCUSSION, AND WRITING

Analyzing Content and Technique

1. Trace the origins of the Cinderella tale. In which cultures has it existed? Which elements of the story have been influenced by these cultures? How do you account for the phenomenon of a common tale of this kind?
2. Analyze the true source of sibling rivalry, according to Bettelheim. How far do you agree with him? Why? How might "Cinderella" help children to deal with sibling rivalry?
3. Explain the term "oedipal conflict." From where does it come? Who popularized the theory? In what ways might it be a product of its culture?
4. Why, according to Bettelheim, might a child relate to Cinderella sitting among the ashes? What statement is he making about a child's psychological makeup? Would this be true of children in different cultures?
5. What is the final lesson taught by "Cinderella" that allows children to gain self-confidence?
6. Describe the tone of the essay. Is it suited to the subject matter? Why or why not? What is the writer's purpose?

Collaborative Activity

As a group, watch a modern film or video rendering of a fairy tale or myth. (Each group in the class should choose a different story.) Next, read an early version of the story. Discuss the themes and lessons stressed by the director of the film or video. How are these similar to, or different from, the original story? Make a brief presentation of your findings to the class.

Making Connections

1. Analyze, in an essay, some fairy-tale characters that you related to, or rejected, as a child. Do you agree with Bettelheim that characters like these help children find a way to express and thus come to terms with troubling emotions? How might they help a child deal with fears?
2. In a well-supported essay, compare a classic fairy tale and a modern children's story reflective of your culture. What are the advantages or disadvantages of each? Which would a child prefer? Which do you prefer? Which would you give a child to read, and why?

Think of a fictional character whom you do not find admirable, even though the author seems to be holding him or her up for admiration. What qualities does this character possess which the author presents positively but to which you react negatively?

"Cinderella": A Tale That Promotes Sexist Values (Student Essay)

PEI-TI FENG

Many people believe that the fairy-tale "Cinderella" is a great help   1
to children because it gives them a sense that life is ultimately good. To girls, especially, the story's message is that their wishes will be fulfilled, and just as Cinderella finds her true love and lives a secure life happily ever after, they will too. Decades ago, this type of unrealistic rags-to-riches story might have pleased many girls, for we were considered inferior to men and as a result had low self-esteem. But today the social structure has undergone tremendous changes so that women have the same rights as men do. We can distinguish ourselves in many different careers and we have many goals for ourselves. No longer are we living for men. We need not construct our happiness only on successful marriages. As a result, a tale like "Cinderella" (written, or collected, not surprisingly, by men like Perrault or the brothers Grimm) is in many ways offensive to the modern woman and inadequate for today's society because it contains many stereotypes of women. These stereotypes, although no longer true of women's reality today, subtly transmit sexist values to children and therefore continue to foster them.

The character of Cinderella is one of the main ways in which this occurs.   2
From the beginning of the story, Cinderella is so kind-hearted, pure, and obedient that she accepts all the meaningless tasks that her stepmother and stepsisters assign her without complaining or even resenting them. She is so weak that she does not stand up for her rights, and her rescue is dependent on fate (the fairy godmother) and the whim of the prince. She is a symbol of all the women who, in years gone by, were suppressed at home and silently accepted this situation. As Madonna Kolbenschlag states in her essay, "A Feminist's View of 'Cinderella,'"

Source: Student essay reprinted by permission.

"The willing acceptance of a condition of worthlessness and her expectation of rescue (as a reward for her virtuous suffering) is a recognizable paradigm of traditional female socialization" (Behrens and Rosen, 564). Although in today's society women are no longer isolated at home and can make major life decisions for themselves, the character of Cinderella continues to give girls the false idea that good (and attractive) women are weak and need to find someone to depend on in order to be happy.

In addition, Cinderella does not even find her true love herself. She is chosen from among hundreds of other girls by her Prince Charming, somewhat like merchandise displayed in front of the Big Buyer. This is a great insult to the humanity of women, and a reflection of times when they were actually (legally) considered the property of men. In the Cinderella story, the deal is controlled only by one person, the prince. What would happen to Cinderella if he were not that charming and she did not like him? Would she still be forced to marry him and continue to perform other meaningless tasks as his wife? I guess so, because the tale indicates that she has no power to control her own life and decide on her own future.

A further problem with the story lies in the fact that the prince chooses Cinderella for her physical appearance, and not for any inner beauty she might possess. He is attracted to her the moment he sees her, and he falls in love with her after dancing with her for a short while. Thus it is not possible that he is enchanted by her kindness, patience, obedience and other traditional womanly virtues. He does not even know her name, a detail which symbolizes that she is not an individual to him, only a gorgeous doll in her gossamer dress and sparkling slippers. Consider the effect of this on impressionable girls who are being taught by the story to pay attention only to how they look on the outside so that they can attract the "right" man, and to ignore the fact that in today's society women can be attractive in many different ways.

Because the first Cinderella story was written in China during the ninth century (by Tuan Cheng-shih), it is very possible that the admirably tiny size of Cinderella's foot originated from the Chinese practice of foot binding. To the Chinese, the tiny foot was a symbol of beauty for two reasons: the woman whose feet had been bound walked with a swing that was considered attractive, and she was unable to walk any distance without someone to help her and thus was largely confined to the home. Cinderella's tiny foot, then, symbolizes helplessness and limitation of activity.

On another level, as Kolbenschlag points out, "the slipper is a symbol of power—with all its accompanying restrictions and demands for conformity" (p. 566). In order to obtain this power, symbolized by marriage to the prince, the stepsisters are willing to conform to whatever society demands of women, symbolized by their hacking off parts of their feet to fit the slipper. Cinderella is luckier—she conforms naturally. Again, what is the message here? That happiness lies only in capturing the man who can provide us with money and authority, and that we should do whatever is necessary to snare him?

Why has "Cinderella" been such a popular story in the past? There are obvious sociological reasons apart from psychological ones. At the time when Perrault and the Grimms wrote their "Cinderella" tales, money was less evenly distributed in society than it is today. Birth was one of the only ways of possessing status and power. Women had almost no chance of making money on their own. Therefore, marrying a rich man was a woman's easiest way—almost her only way—of achieving wealth. Probably every young woman in Perrault's French court had the secret dream that one day she would be chosen by a wealthy, powerful, and handsome "prince," just like Cinderella. Today, on the contrary, owing to far better opportunities and equal rights, women can achieve their goals and accumulate wealth through their own hard work. At the least, they can go out and find work and earn enough to feed themselves. They can take pride and satisfaction in not having to cling to someone else for survival or even success. That is what our dreams and hopes should focus on. Today we need not be Cinderella—we can be the Prince!

I agree that "Cinderella" possesses a great deal of entertainment value. It is 8 always fun to read fantasy stories with impossibly happy endings. But the danger of "Cinderella" is that while it seduces us with its charming tale, it transmits sexist values which have an adverse sociological effect. It gives girls the wrong kind of role models and promotes negative stereotypes—weakness, helplessness, meekness, dependence on males, physical beauty—as desirable virtues. Unless we are careful, therefore, "Cinderella," a fantasy romance of the Middle Ages, may become a tragedy for women of the twentieth century.

BIBLIOGRAPHY
Kolbenschlag, Madonna. "A Feminist's View of 'Cinderella.'" *Writing and Reading across the Curriculum.* 3d ed. Laurence Behrens and Leonard J. Rosen, eds. Boston: Scott Foresman, 1988, pp. 562–568.

STRUCTURE, STRATEGY, SUGGESTION

1. What is the thesis of Feng's essay? Where in the introduction does it occur? Is this placement effective? Why or why not?
2. What is the effect of the quotations Feng uses? What else might she have done with quotations to strengthen her piece further?
3. Analyze the sequence of the points that make up Feng's essay. Why has she ordered them in this way? How else might they be structured?
4. Look back at the points Bettelheim makes about the Cinderella tale (selection 73). Are there points in Feng's essay that are in contradiction to his ideas? Which of the two writers do you agree with more closely? Why? If you agree with parts of each essay, identify these and explain.
5. What is the tone of Feng's essay? Who do you think is the intended audience? How successful is the tone in reaching the audience? What suggestions, if any, would you make about the tone?
6. Write an essay looking critically at a tale or song which is a significant part of your culture but which transmits values you disagree with. Describe these and give reasons for your opinion. Use at least one external source to support your viewpoint.

SYNTHESIS *Part Nine*

1. The selections "Sin, Suffer, and Repent" and "Can TV Help Save Black Youth?" point to the power of television in creating strong impressions and fostering or destroying stereotypes. Examine what each writer has to say about the role of television in creating identities, then write an essay in which you discuss your views on this topic, adding your examples to those used by the writers.

2. Compare and contrast the interview essays "Can TV Help Save Black Youth?" and "An Often Long Journey: An Interview with Joy Harjo." In what ways are the techniques used by them similar? How are they different? On the basis of your examination, what would you say are the particular strengths of interview essays?

3. "Football Red and Baseball Green" and "Eight Ways of Looking at an Amusement Park" explore three of the most popular types of entertainment in American culture today. They indicate that although we may regard entertainment as frivolous, it can be an important cultural aspect of our lives. Write an essay in which you discuss what we learn about the American character from these readings.

524

PART TEN

Our Sameness,
Our Difference

PART 10: INTRODUCTION

arts One through Nine have examined various problems and challenges that arise from diversity. Part Ten, however, concentrates on the benefits of diversity and on how it can enrich us when we make a conscious effort to accept it as an intrinsic part of life.

Dean Barnlund's "Communication in a Global Village" (selection 74) points out the increased need for understanding among different peoples. It suggests several ways in which this may be achieved so that we can become a true global community and not merely a collection of suspicious strangers. Margaret Mead and Rhoda Metraux's "On Friendship" (selection 76) illustrates several of Barnlund's concepts as it examines how the meaning of friendship differs from culture to culture. Mead and Metraux's attitude is one of genuine interest and curiosity as they compare several other European cultures with ours, looking at the best aspects of each and coming to the conclusion that the open attitude of Americans may enable them to embrace other cultures and peoples with relative ease. In "Minor Accidents" (selection 75) Raymonde Carroll focuses on the differences between two cultures—French and American. But she too ultimately claims that under the differences lie interestingly similar values.

A positive approach also marks Karen Kampf's "Crossing Bridges" (selection 81), Craig Wilson's "Mostly Scared" (selection 80), and Mark Singer's "Typical" (selection 79). An unlikely and heartwarming relationship forms between an old black man and his white tutor in Kampf's essay, with the tutor discovering that she learns more from her pupil than he does from her. Wilson's essay analyzes valuable models for coping with prejudice found in Maya Angelou's autobiography, *I Know Why the Caged Bird Sings*. Singer's humorous article is set in a very different milieu, an urbane New York restaurant, and features two multicultural families from dissimilar backgrounds who nevertheless manage to enjoy each other's company and to find various creative methods of communicating.

But what happens when *you* are considered the "other"? When you are regarded as abnormal and shunned by society? Louie Crew's "Thriving as an Outsider" (selection 77) deals with this issue matter-of-factly and without bitterness as he describes the challenge of living openly as a gay man in small-town America. His essay is filled with details and incidents that capture our attention and admiration, and it provides several optimistic and practical solutions to the problem of discrimination.

Two selections in this section focus on the act of asserting one's difference (or accepting someone else's) and its attendant rewards and dangers. "The Cult of Ethnicity" by Arthur Schlesinger, Jr. (Selection 73), cautions us against identifying with our ethnic backgrounds at the cost of our American selves, while "The Real Lesson of L.A.," by Bill Bradley (selection 78), warns us that if we do not take care of the "ethnic" problems of our inner cities, we must all suffer.

The selections in Part Ten are not necessarily bright or happy, nor do they gloss over the complexity of the multicultural experience. Even those that are humorous and optimistic raise thought-provoking issues, and several of the others end in sorrow or in partial loss. Yet ultimately they indicate that the chasms between individuals are largely self-created and can be spanned—and that when we take the trouble to do so, we are transformed by the awareness that, as the poet Benét says in "The Real Lesson of L.A.," *All of these you are/ and each is partly you.*

73

PREREADING ACTIVITY

Respond to the title. What images does the word "cult" conjure up in your mind? What do you think the writer means by the "cult of ethnicity"? Do a brainstorming exercise based on the title that brings out your ideas and attitudes on the subject.

The Cult of Ethnicity, Good and Bad

ARTHUR SCHLESINGER, JR.

Arthur Schlesinger, Jr. (1917–), is a widely known historian and winner of the Pulitzer Prize for his books *The Age of Jackson* and *A Thousand Days: John F. Kennedy in the White House*. Among his many other books are *Is the Cold War Over?* and *The Disuniting of America* (1992), in which he elaborates on the points made in this essay, which was first published in *Time* in 1991.

The history of the world has been in great part the history of the mixing of peoples. Modern communication and transport accelerate mass migrations from one continent to another. Ethnic and racial diversity is more than ever a salient fact of the age.

But what happens when people of different origins, speaking different languages and professing different religions, inhabit the same locality and live under the same political sovereignty? Ethnic and racial conflict—far more than ideological conflict—is the explosive problem of our times.

On every side today ethnicity is breaking up nations. The Soviet Union, India, Yugoslavia, Ethiopia, are all in crisis. Ethnic tensions disturb and divide Sri Lanka, Burma, Indonesia, Iraq, Cyprus, Nigeria, Angola, Lebanon, Guyana, Trinidad—you name it. Even nations as stable and civilized as Britain and France, Belgium and Spain, face growing ethnic troubles. Is there any large multiethnic state that can be made to work?

The answer to that question has been, until recently, the United States. "No other nation," Margaret Thatcher has said, "has so successfully combined people of different races and nations within a single culture." How have Americans succeeded in pulling off this almost unprecedented trick?

528

We have always been a multiethnic country. Hector St. John de Crèvecoeur, who came from France in the eighteenth century, marveled at the astonishing diversity of the settlers—"a mixture of English, Scotch, Irish, French, Dutch, Germans and Swedes . . . this promiscuous breed." He propounded a famous question: "What then is the American, this new man?" And he gave a famous answer: "Here individuals of all nations are melted into a new race of men." *E pluribus unum.*

The United States escaped the divisiveness of a multiethnic society by a brilliant solution: the creation of a brand-new national identity. The point of America was not to preserve old cultures but to forge a new *American* culture. "By an intermixture with our people," President George Washington told Vice President John Adams, immigrants will "get assimilated to our customs, measures and laws: in a word, soon become one people." This was the ideal that a century later Israel Zangwill crystallized in the title of his popular 1908 play *The Melting Pot.* And no institution was more potent in molding Crèvecoeur's "promiscuous breed" into Washington's "one people" than the American public school.

The new American nationality was inescapably English in language, ideas, and institutions. The pot did not melt everybody, not even all the white immigrants; deeply bred racism put black Americans, yellow Americans, red Americans, and brown Americans well outside the pale. Still, the infusion of other stocks, even of nonwhite stocks, and the experience of the New World reconfigured the British legacy and made the United States, as we all know, a very different country from Britain.

In the twentieth century, new immigration laws altered the composition of the American people, and a cult of ethnicity erupted both among non-Anglo whites and among nonwhite minorities. This had many healthy consequences. The American culture at last began to give shamefully overdue recognition to the achievements of groups subordinated and spurned during the high noon of Anglo dominance, and it began to acknowledge the great swirling world beyond Europe. Americans acquired a more complex and invigorating sense of their world—and of themselves.

But, pressed too far, the cult of ethnicity has unhealthy consequences. It gives rise, for example, to the conception of the United States as a nation composed not of individuals making their own choices but of inviolable ethnic and racial groups. It rejects the historic American goals of assimilation and integration. And, in an excess of zeal, well-intentioned people seek to transform our system of education from a means of creating "one people" into a means of promoting, celebrating, and perpetuating separate ethnic origins and identities. The balance is shifting from *unum* to *pluribus.*

That is the issue that lies behind the hullabaloo over "multiculturalism" and "political correctness," the attack on the "Eurocentric" curriculum and the rise of the notion that history and literature should be taught not as disciplines but as therapies whose function is to raise minority self-esteem. Group separatism crystallizes the differences, magnifies tensions, intensifies hostilities. Europe—the unique source of the liberating ideas of democracy, civil liberties, and human rights—is portrayed as the root of all evil, and non-European cultures, their own many crimes deleted, are presented as the means of redemption.

I don't want to sound apocalyptic about these developments. Education is 11
always in ferment, and a good thing, too. The situation in our universities, I am
confident, will soon right itself. But the impact of separatist pressures on our
public schools is more troubling. If a Kleagle of the Ku Klux Klan wanted to
use the schools to disable and handicap black Americans, he could hardly come
up with anything more effective than the "Afrocentric" curriculum. And
if separatist tendencies go unchecked, the result can only be the fragmentation,
resegregation, and tribalization of American life.

I remain optimistic. My impression is that the historic forces driving toward 12
"one people" have not lost their power. The eruption of ethnicity is, I believe, a
rather superficial enthusiasm stirred by romantic ideologues on the one hand and
by unscrupulous con men on the other: self-appointed spokesmen whose claim to
represent their minority groups is carelessly accepted by the media. Most
American-born members of minority groups, white or nonwhite, see themselves
primarily as Americans rather than primarily as members of one or another ethnic
group. A notable indicator today is the rate of intermarriage across ethnic lines,
across religious lines, even (increasingly) across racial lines. "We Americans," said
Theodore Roosevelt, "are children of the crucible."

The growing diversity of the American population makes the quest for 13
unifying ideals and a common culture all the more urgent. In a world savagely
rent by ethnic and racial antagonisms, the United States must continue as an
example of how a highly differentiated society holds itself together.

QUESTIONS FOR CRITICAL READING, THINKING, DISCUSSION, AND WRITING

Analyzing Content and Technique

1. Examine Thatcher's statement (paragraph 4) that "No other nation has so successfully combined people of different races and nations within a single culture." How far do you agree with
   this statement? Explain, giving supporting examples from the essay and from your experience.
2. How, according to the writer, has the United States been able to escape divisiveness? Identify
   two or three quotations he has used to support his points. Which one, among these,
   impressed you the most? Why?
3. Discuss the positives and negatives of the cult of ethnicity. Which aspect does the writer consider more significant? Why? Explain your response to his attitude.
4. Do you agree or disagree with the writer's claim that Americans have one identity? Analyze the
   statement carefully, pointing to ways in which it might be true, as well as ways in which it is not.
5. Consider the meaning of the phrase "the high noon of Anglo dominance" (paragraph 8). What
   does it imply? Do you agree with the author's assumption that such a dominance is a thing of
   the past in America? Explain.
6. For whom is Schlesinger writing this essay? Define his tone. How did you respond to this tone?
   to the underlying attitudes hinted at by his choice of words such as "cult"?

Collaborative Activity

Discuss, as a group, the ethnic background of each member. How much of their ethnic identity
have members retained? In what way? Have each member produce specific examples. Do mem-

bers consider such a retention important? valuable? dangerous? Summarize your discussion in a collaborative essay.

Making Connections

1. Schlesinger tells us that "ethnic and racial conflict . . . is the explosive problem of our times." Do you agree? In an essay, examine the situation in one of the countries mentioned in paragraph 3 or in the United States and analyze the role racial and ethnic conflict plays in its current situation.

2. Think about the final sentence of Schlesinger's essay, "In a world savagely rent by ethnic and racial antagonisms, the United States must continue as an example of how a highly differentiated society holds itself together." What, according to him, is the role the United States must play in the world? How far do you agree with him? Write an essay in which you explore your own ideas of the kind of role the United States should play in the world today, giving specific reasons and examples to support your view.

PREREADING ACTIVITY

Before reading selection 76, list briefly some reasons why communication between people of different cultures may be difficult.

Communication in a Global Village

DEAN BARNLUND

Dean Barnlund (1942–) teaches interpersonal and intercultural communication at San Francisco State University, but his interests also encompass architecture, music, and film. He has traveled around the world five times and has visited more than eighty countries. He is widely known for his articles on anthropology, psychology, sociology, and psychiatry, and his books include *Interpersonal Communication, Communicative Styles of Japanese and Americans,* and *Public and Private Self in Japan and the United States,* from which the selection here is taken.

Nearing Autumn's close.
My neighbor—
How does he live, I wonder?—Bashō

*T*hese lines, written by one of the most cherished of *haiku* poets, express a timeless and universal curiosity in one's fellow man. When they were written, nearly three hundred years ago, the word "neighbor" referred to people very much like one's self—similar in dress, in diet, in custom, in language—who happened to live next door. Today relatively few people are surrounded by neighbors who are cultural replicas of themselves. Tomorrow we can expect to spend most of our lives in the company of neighbors who will speak in a different tongue, seek different values, move at a different pace, and interact according to a different script. Within no longer than a decade or two the probability of spending part of one's life in a foreign culture will exceed the probability a hundred years ago of ever leaving the town in which one was born. As our world is transformed our neighbors increasingly will be people whose life styles contrast sharply with our own.

The technological feasibility of such a global village is no longer in doubt. Only the precise date of its attainment is uncertain. The means already exist: in telecommunication systems linking the world by satellite, in aircraft capable of moving people faster than the speed of sound, in computers which can disgorge facts more rapidly than men can formulate their questions. The methods for bringing people closer physically and electronically are clearly at hand. What is in doubt is whether the erosion of cultural boundaries through technology will bring the realization of a dream or a nightmare. Will a global village be a mere collection or a true community of men? Will its residents be neighbors capable of respecting and utilizing their differences, or clusters of strangers living in ghettos and united only in their antipathies for others?

Can we generate the new cultural attitudes required by our technological virtuosity? History is not very reassuring here. It has taken centuries to learn how to live harmoniously in the family, the tribe, the city state, and the nation. Each new stretching of human sensitivity and loyalty has taken generations to become firmly assimilated in the human psyche. And now we are forced into a quantum leap from the mutual suspicion and hostility that have marked the past relations between peoples into a world in which mutual respect and comprehension are requisite.

Even events of recent decades provide little basis for optimism. Increasing physical proximity has brought no millennium in human relations. If anything, it has appeared to intensify the divisions among people rather than to create a broader intimacy. Every new reduction in physical distance has made us more painfully aware of the psychic distance that divides people and has increased alarm over real or imagined differences. If today people occasionally choke on what seem to be indigestible differences between rich and poor, male and female, specialist and nonspecialist within cultures, what will happen tomorrow when people must assimilate and cope with still greater contrasts in life styles? Wider access to more people will be a doubtful victory if human beings find they have nothing to say to one another or cannot stand to listen to each other.

Time and space have long cushioned intercultural encounters, confining them to touristic exchanges. But this insulation is rapidly wearing thin. In the world of tomorrow we can expect to live—not merely vacation—in societies which seek different values and abide by different codes. There we will be surrounded by foreigners for long periods of time, working with others in the closest possible relationships. If people currently show little tolerance or talent for encounters with alien cultures, how can they learn to deal with constant and inescapable coexistence?

The temptation is to retreat to some pious hope or talismanic formula to carry us into the new age. "Meanwhile," as Edwin Reischauer reminds us, "we fail to do what we ourselves must do if 'one world' is ever to be achieved, and that is to develop the education, the skills and the attitudes that people must acquire if they are to build and maintain such a world. The time is short, and the needs are great. The task faces all human beings. But it is on the shoulders of people living in the strong countries of the world, such as Japan and the United States, that this burden falls with special weight and urgency."[1]

Anyone who has truly struggled to comprehend another person—even those closest and most like himself—will appreciate the immensity of the challenge of intercultural communication. A greater exchange of people between nations, needed as that may be, carries with it no guarantee of increased cultural empathy; experience in other lands often does little but aggravate existing prejudices. Studying guidebooks or memorizing polite phrases similarly fails to explain differences in cultural perspectives. Programs of cultural enrichment, while they contribute to curiosity about other ways of life, do not cultivate the skills to function effectively in the cultures studied. Even concentrated exposure to a foreign language, valuable as it is, provides access to only one of the many codes that regulate daily affairs; human understanding is by no means guaranteed because conversants share the same dictionary. (Within the United States, where people inhabit a common territory and possess a common language, mutuality of meaning among Mexican-Americans, White-Americans, Black-Americans, Indian-Americans—to say nothing of old and young, poor and rich, pro-establishment and anti-establishment cultures—is a sporadic and unreliable occurrence.) Useful as all these measures are for enlarging appreciation of diverse cultures, they fall short of what is needed for a global village to survive.

What seems most critical is to find ways of gaining entrance into the 8 assumptive world of another culture, to identify the norms that govern face-to-face relations, and to equip people to function within a social system that is foreign but no longer incomprehensible. Without this kind of insight people are condemned to remain outsiders no matter how long they live in another country. Its institutions and its customs will be interpreted inevitably from the premises and through the medium of their own culture. Whether they notice something or overlook it, respect or ridicule it, express or conceal their reaction will be dictated by the logic of their own rather than the alien culture.

There are, of course, shelves and shelves of books on the cultures of the 9 world. They cover the history, religion, political thought, music, sculpture, and industry of many nations. And they make fascinating and provocative reading. But only in the vaguest way do they suggest what it is that really distinguishes the behavior of a Samoan, a Congolese, a Japanese or an American. Rarely do the descriptions of a political structure or religious faith explain precisely when and why certain topics are avoided or why specific gestures carry such radically different meanings according to the context in which they appear.

When former President Nixon and former Premier Sato met to discuss a 10 growing problem concerning trade in textiles between Japan and the United States, Premier Sato announced that since they were on such good terms with each other that the deliberations would be "three parts talk and seven parts 'haragei'."[2] Translated literally, "haragei" means to communicate through the belly, that is to feel out intuitively rather than verbally state the precise position of each person.

Subscribing to this strategy—one that governs many interpersonal exchanges 11 in his culture—Premier Sato conveyed without verbal elaboration his comprehension of the plight of American textile firms threatened by accelerating exports of Japanese fabrics to the United States. President Nixon—similarly abiding by norms that govern interaction within his culture—took this comprehension of the American position to mean that new export quotas would be forthcoming shortly.

During the next few weeks both were shocked at the consequences of their 12 meeting: Nixon was infuriated to learn that the new policies he expected were not forthcoming, and Sato was upset to find that he had unwittingly triggered a new wave of hostility toward his country. If prominent officials, surrounded by foreign advisers, can commit such grievous communicative blunders, the plight of the ordinary citizen may be suggested. Such intercultural collisions, forced upon the public consciousness by the grave consequences they carry and the extensive publicity they receive, only hint at the wider and more frequent confusions and hostilities that disrupt the negotiations of lesser officials, business executives, professionals and even visitors in foreign countries.

Every culture expresses its purposes and conducts its affairs through the 13 medium of communication. Cultures exist primarily to create and preserve common systems of symbols by which their members can assign and exchange meanings. Unhappily, the distinctive rules that govern these symbol systems are far from obvious. About some of these codes, such as language, we have extensive knowledge. About others, such as gestures and facial codes, we have only rudimentary knowledge. On many others—rules governing topical appropriateness, customs regulating physical contact, time and space codes, strategies for the management of conflict—we have almost no systematic knowledge. To crash another culture with only the vaguest notion of its underlying dynamics reflects not only a provincial naïveté but a dangerous form of cultural arrogance.

It is differences in meaning, far more than mere differences in vocabulary, 14 that isolate cultures, and that cause them to regard each other as strange or even barbaric. It is not too surprising that many cultures refer to themselves as "The People," relegating all other human beings to a subhuman form of life. To the person who drinks blood, the eating of meat is repulsive. Someone who conveys respect by standing is upset by someone who conveys it by sitting down; both may regard kneeling as absurd. Burying the dead may prompt tears in one society, smiles in another, and dancing in a third. If spitting on the street makes sense to some, it will appear bizarre that others carry their spit in their pocket; neither may quite appreciate someone who spits to express gratitude. The bullfight that constitutes an almost religious ritual for some seems a cruel and inhumane way of destroying a defenseless animal to others. Although staring is acceptable social behavior in some cultures, in others it is a thoughtless invasion of privacy. Privacy, itself, is without universal meaning.

Note that none of these acts involves an insurmountable linguistic challenge. 15 The words that describe these acts—eating, spitting, showing respect, fighting, burying, and staring—are quite translatable into most languages. The issue is more conceptual than linguistic; each society places events in its own cultural frame and it is these frames that bestow the unique meaning and differentiated response they produce.

As we move or are driven toward a global village and increasingly frequent 16 cultural contact, we need more than simply greater factual knowledge of each other. We need, more specifically, to identify what might be called the "rulebooks of meaning" that distinguish one culture from another. For to grasp the way in which other cultures perceive the world, and the assumptions and values that are the foundation of these perceptions, is to gain access to the experience of other human beings. Access to the world view and the communicative style of other cultures may not only enlarge our own way of experiencing the world but enable us to maintain constructive relationships with societies that operate according to a different logic than our own.

To survive, psychologically as well as physically, human beings must inhabit a world that is relatively free of ambiguity and reasonably predictable. Some sort of structure must be placed upon the endless profusion of incoming signals. The infant, born into a world of flashing, hissing, moving images soon learns to adapt by resolving this chaos into toys and tables, dogs and parents. Even adults who have had their vision or hearing restored through surgery describe the world as a frightening and sometimes unbearable experience; only after days of effort are they able to transform blurs and noises into meaningful and therefore manageable experiences.   17

It is commonplace to talk as if the world "has" meaning, to ask what "is" the meaning of a phrase, a gesture, a painting, a contract. Yet when thought about, it is clear that events are devoid of meaning until someone assigns it to them. There is no appropriate response to a bow or a handshake, a shout or a whisper, until it is interpreted. A drop of water and the color red have no meaning, they simply exist. The aim of human perception is to make the world intelligible so that it can be managed successfully; the attribution of meaning is a prerequisite to and preparation for action.[3]   18

People are never passive receivers, merely absorbing events of obvious significance, but are active in assigning meaning to sensation. What any event acquires in the way of meaning appears to reflect a transaction between what is there to be seen or heard, and what the interpreter brings to it in the way of past experience and prevailing motive. Thus the attribution of meaning is always a creative process by which the raw data of sensation are transformed to fit the aims of the observer.   19

The diversity of reactions that can be triggered by a single experience— meeting a stranger, negotiating a contract, attending a textile conference—is immense. Each observer is forced to see it through his or her own eyes, interpret it in the light of his or her own values, fit it to the requirements of his or her own circumstances. As a consequence, every object and message is seen by every observer from a somewhat different perspective. Each person will note some features and neglect others. Each will accept some relations among the facts and deny others. Each will arrive at some conclusion, tentative or certain, as the sounds and forms resolve into a "temple" or "barn," a "compliment" or "insult."   20

Provide a group of people with a set of photographs, even quite simple and ordinary photographs, and note how diverse are the meanings they provoke. Afterward they will recall and forget different pictures; they will also assign quite distinctive meanings to those they do remember. Some will recall the mood of a picture, others the actions; some the appearance and others the attitudes of persons portrayed. Often the observers cannot agree upon even the most "objective" details—the number of people, the precise location and identity of simple objects. A difference in frame of mind—fatigue, hunger, excitement, anger—will change dramatically what they report they have "seen."   21

It should not be surprising that people raised in different families, exposed to different events, praised and punished for different reasons, should come to view the world so differently. As George Kelly has noted, people see the world through templates which force them to construe events in unique ways. These patterns or grids which we fit over the realities of the world are cut from our own experience and values, and they predispose us to certain interpretations. Industrialist and farmer do not see the "same" land; husband and wife do not plan for the "same" child; doctor and patient do not discuss the "same" disease; borrower and creditor do not negotiate the "same" mortgage; daughter and daughter-in-law do not react to the "same" mother.

The world each person creates for himself or herself is a distinctive world, not the same world others occupy. Each fashions from every incident whatever meanings fit his or her own private biases. These biases, taken together, constitute what has been called the "assumptive world of the individual." The world each person gets inside his or her head is the only world he or she knows. And it is this symbolic world, not the real world, that he or she talks about, argues about, laughs about, fights about.

Every communication, interpersonal or intercultural, is a transaction between these private worlds. As people talk they search for symbols that will enable them to share their experience and converge upon a common meaning. This process, often long and sometimes painful, makes it possible finally to reconcile apparent or real differences between them. Various words are used to describe this moment. When it involves an integration of facts or ideas, it is usually called an "agreement"; when it involves sharing a mood or feeling, it is referred as "empathy" or "rapport." But "understanding" is a broad enough term to cover both possibilities; in either case it identifies the achievement of a common meaning.

It would be reasonable to expect that individuals who approach reality similarly might understand each other easily, and laboratory research confirms this conclusion: people with similar perceptual styles attract one another, understand each other better, work more efficiently together and with greater satisfaction than those whose perceptual orientations differ.

It must be emphasized, however, that perceptual orientations, systems of belief, and communicative styles do not exist or operate independently. They overlap and affect each other. They combine in complex ways to determine behavior. What a person says is influenced by what he or she believes and what he or she believes, in turn, by what he or she sees. His or her perceptions and beliefs are themselves partly a product of his or her manner of communicating with others.

People tend to avoid those who challenge their assumptions, who dismiss their beliefs, and who communicate in strange and unintelligible ways. When one reviews history, whether he or she examines crises within or between cultures, he or she finds people have consistently shielded themselves, segregated themselves, even fortified themselves, against wide differences in modes of perception or expression. (In many cases, indeed, have persecuted and conquered the infidel and afterwards substituted their own cultural ways for the offending ones.) Intercultural defensiveness appears to be only a counterpart of interpersonal defensiveness in the face of uncomprehended or incomprehensible differences.

Every culture attempts to create a "universe of discourse" for its members,   28
a way in which people can interpret their experience and convey it to one another.
Without a common system of codifying sensations, life would be absurd and all
efforts to share meanings doomed to failure. This universe of discourse—one of
the most precious of all cultural legacies—is transmitted to each generation in
part consciously and in part unconsciously. Parents and teachers give explicit
instruction in it by praising or criticizing certain ways of dressing, of thinking, of
gesturing, of responding to the acts of others. But the most significant aspects of
any cultural code may be conveyed implicitly, not by rule or lesson but through
modelling behavior. The child is surrounded by others who, through the mere
consistency of their actions as males and females, mothers and fathers, salesclerks
and policemen, display what is appropriate behavior. Thus the grammar of any
culture is sent and received largely unconsciously, making one's own cultural
assumptions and biases difficult to recognize. They seem so obviously right that
they require no explanation.

It is when people nurtured in different psychological worlds meet that differences   29
in cultural perspectives and communicative codes may sabotage efforts to understand one another. Repeated collisions between a foreigner and the members of a
contrasting culture often produce what is called "culture shock." It is a feeling of
helplessness, even of terror or anger, that accompanies working in an alien society. One feels trapped in an absurd and indecipherable nightmare.

It is as if some hostile leprechaun had gotten into the works and as a cosmic   30
caper rewired the connections that hold society together. Not only do the actions of
others no longer make sense, but it is impossible even to express one's own intentions clearly. "Yes" comes out meaning "No." A wave of the hand means "come,"
or it may mean "go." Formality may be regarded as childish, or as a devious form of
flattery. Statements of fact may be heard as statements of conceit. Arriving early, or
arriving late, embarrasses or impresses. "Suggestions" may be treated as "ultima-
tums," or precisely the opposite. Failure to stand at the proper moment, or failure to
sit, may be insulting. The compliment intended to express gratitude instead conveys
a sense of distance. A smile signifies disappointment rather than pleasure.

If the crises that follow such intercultural encounters are sufficiently   31
dramatic or the communicants unusually sensitive, they may recognize the source
of their trouble. If there is patience and constructive intention the confusion can
sometimes be clarified. But more often the foreigner, without knowing it, leaves
behind him or her a trail of frustration, mistrust, and even hatred *of which he or
she is totally unaware*. Neither the foreigner nor his or her associates recognize
that their difficulty springs from sources deep within the rhetoric of their own
societies. Each sees himself or herself as acting in ways that are thoroughly sensible, honest and considerate. And—given the rules governing his own universe of
discourse—each is. Unfortunately, there are few cultural universals, and the
degree of overlap in communicative codes is always less than perfect. Experience
can be transmitted with fidelity only when the unique properties of each code are
recognized and respected, or where the motivation and means exist to bring them
into some sort of alignment.

Cultural norms so completely surround people, so permeate thought and 32 action, that few ever recognize the assumptions on which their lives and their sanity rest. As one observer put it, if birds were suddenly endowed with scientific curiosity they might examine many things, but the sky itself would be overlooked as a suitable subject; if fish were to become curious about the world, it would never occur to them to begin by investigating water. For birds and fish would take the sky and sea for granted, unaware of their profound influence because they comprise the medium for every act. Human beings, in a similar way, occupy a symbolic universe governed by codes that are unconsciously acquired and automatically employed. So much so that they rarely notice that the ways they interpret and talk about events are distinctively different from the ways people conduct their affairs in other cultures.

As long as people remain blind to the sources of their meanings, they are 33 imprisoned within them. These cultural frames of reference are no less confining simply because they cannot be seen or touched. Whether it is an individual neurosis that keeps an individual out of contact with his [or her] neighbors, or a collective neurosis that separates neighbors of different cultures, both are forms of blindness that limit what can be experienced and what can be learned from others.

It would seem that everywhere people would desire to break out of the 34 boundaries of their own experiential worlds. Their ability to react sensitively to a wider spectrum of events and peoples requires an overcoming of such cultural parochialism. But, in fact, few attain this broader vision. Some, of course, have little opportunity for wider cultural experience, though this condition should change as the movement of people accelerates. Others do not try to widen their experience because they prefer the old and familiar, seek from their affairs only further confirmation of the correctness of their own values. Still others recoil from such experiences because they feel it dangerous to probe too deeply into the personal or cultural unconscious. Exposure may reveal how tenuous and arbitrary many cultural norms are; such exposure might force people to acquire new bases for interpreting events. And even for the many who do seek actively to enlarge the variety of human beings with whom they are capable of communicating there are still difficulties.

Cultural myopia persists not merely because of inertia and habit, but 35 chiefly because it is so difficult to overcome. One acquires a personality and a culture in childhood, long before one is capable of comprehending either of them. To survive, each person masters the perceptual orientations, cognitive biases, and communicative habits of his or her own culture. But once mastered, objective assessment of these same processes is awkward since the same mechanisms that are being evaluated must be used in making the evaluations. Once a child learns Japanese or English or Navaho, the categories and grammar of each language predispose him or her to perceive and think in certain ways, and discourage him or her from doing so in other ways. When one attempts to discover why one sees or thinks as one does, one uses the same techniques one is trying to identify. Once one becomes an Indian, an Ibo, or a Frenchman—or even a priest or scientist—it is difficult to extricate oneself from that mooring long enough to find out what one truly is or wants.

Fortunately, there may be a way around this paradox. Or promise of a way ₃₆ around it. It is to expose the culturally distinctive ways various peoples construe events and seek to identify the conventions that connect what is seen with what is thought with what is said. Once this cultural grammar is assimilated and the rules that govern the exchange of meanings are known, they can be shared and learned by those who choose to work and live in alien cultures.

When people within a culture face an insurmountable problem, they turn to ₃₇ friends, neighbors, associates, for help. To them they explain their predicament, often in distinctive personal ways. Through talking it out, however, there often emerge new ways of looking at the problem, fresh incentive to attack it, and alternative solutions to it. This sort of interpersonal exploration is often successful within a culture for people share at least the same communicative style even if they do not agree completely in their perceptions or beliefs.

When people communicate between cultures, where communicative rules as ₃₈ well as the substance of experience differs, the problems multiply. But so, too, do the number of interpretations and alternatives. If it is true that the more people differ the harder it is for them to understand each other, it is equally true that the more they differ the more they have to teach and learn from each other. To do so, of course, there must be mutual respect and sufficient curiosity to overcome the frustrations that occur as they flounder from one misunderstanding to another. Yet the task of coming to grips with differences in communicative styles— between or within cultures—is prerequisite to all other types of mutuality. Without a serious and sustained effort to widen our universe of discourse, no global village can possibly survive.

REFERENCES
1. Reischauer, Edwin. *Man and His Shrinking World*. Tokyo: Asahi Press, 1971, pp. 34–5.
2. Kunihiro, Masao, "U.S.–Japan Communications," in Henry Rosovsky (Ed.), *Discord in the Pacific*, Washington, D.C.: Columbia Books, 1972, p. 167.
3. For a fuller description of the process of assigning and communicating meaning, see Dean Barnlund. "A Transactional Model of Human Communication," in J. Akin and A. Goldberg (Eds.), *Language Behavior*, The Hague: Mouton, 1970.

QUESTIONS FOR CRITICAL READING, THINKING, DISCUSSION, AND WRITING

Analyzing Content and Technique

1. How has the meaning of the term "neighbor" changed, according to Barnlund? What does this indicate about the nature of today's world? What new attitudes does the change require?

2. Why does Barnlund feel that programs of cultural enrichment do not cultivate the skills needed to function effectively in another culture? What does he suggest instead? Do you agree or disagree? Why?

3. Barnlund cites an exchange between Nixon and Sato (paragraphs 10–12). What point does this make about cultural communication?

4. Barnlund states, "It is clear that events are devoid of meaning until someone assigns it to them" (paragraph 18). Explain this statement. Do you agree with it? What illustrations has he provided to support it?
5. Define the term "assumptive world of the individual" (paragraph 23). How does this affect communication between people?
6. Define the term "cultural myopia" (paragraph 35) and evaluate the solutions Barnlund proposes for it.

Collaborative Activity

As a group, look up an international conflict that is currently occurring between two nations, or a civil conflict within a nation. Divide the group into two sections, one to represent each nation or national faction. Have each section discuss the problem from their point of view, explaining why they think it occurred and how they would like it solved. What seems to be at the heart of the conflict? How might communication between the groups be improved? Discuss.

Making Connections

1. Write an essay analyzing the main points Barnlund makes about how individuals see the world and how they try to make sense of it. How far do you agree with his ideas? Give examples from your own experience and observation to support your opinion.
2. In his conclusion, Barnlund states that one must come to grips with "differences in communicative styles" if one is to have a multicultural society. Look at some of the selections in Part Ten which give examples of different communicative styles and write an essay analyzing three or four of these styles, giving specific examples from the text.

PREREADING ACTIVITY

Think of a time when you, or someone you know, accidentally damaged someone else's property. Sprint write for five minutes, describing the incident, the emotions of the people involved, and what was expected of the "guilty party."

Minor Accidents

RAYMONDE CARROLL

Born in Tunisia and educated in France and the United States, Raymonde Carroll is an anthropologist who now teaches Romance languages at Oberlin College. Selection 76 forms a chapter in her book *Cultural Misunderstandings: The French-American Experience* (1988), translated by Carol Volk.

A commercial on American television shows a mother and daughter 1 (twelve or thirteen years old) trying to resolve the problem of a stain on a blouse. The daughter is frantic; her mother promises to do her best to help her. Thanks to a miracle detergent, the blouse is returned to its former beautiful state. In order to understand the depth of the crisis resolved by the detergent in question, one must know that the stained blouse does not belong to the girl on the screen but to her older sister, who lent it to her. The situation is serious enough for the mother to enter the picture, and for us to be relieved (and thankful for the magic detergent) when the blouse, unharmed, is put in its proper place just before the arrival of its owner, who, as it turns out, wants to wear it that very evening. The crisis has been averted; the heroines smile.

Things are not so rosy in the "Dear Abby" column, which millions of 2 Americans read every day in the newspaper. The same problem often appears in many forms: "X borrowed my thingamajig, returned it damaged, and offered neither to replace it nor to repair it. What should I do?"

Are Americans frightened by their older siblings (the first case), or incapable 3 of resolving the slightest problem (the second case)? The list of "adjectives" and of "explanations" can go on, according to one's tastes and culture. What interests me here is the fact that in both "cases" there was a "minor accident." In the first

Source: "Minor Accidents" by Raymonde Carroll, *Cultural Misunderstandings*, trans. by Carol Volk, 1988. Reprinted by permission of the University of Chicago Press and Professor Raymonde Carroll.

case, the "guilty" party knows what to do while in the second the "victim" does not know what to do, which indicates that an expectation was not met.

For a French person, it is likely that both cases would serve as additional [4] proof of the "keen sense of proprietorship characteristic of Americans." But why lend one's property if one feels that way about it? It seems, here again, that the nature of the problem lies elsewhere. Before going any further, however, it would be useful to review a few French cases of "minor accidents." Some of these cases are taken from personal experience. They seemed completely "normal" to the French woman in me but slightly "strange" to the anthropologist in me, who considered them with a voluntarily "foreign" eye.

F (a French woman), her husband, and her daughter, who are preparing [5] to leave a party, are standing in the foyer saying goodbye. As she leaves, F has a "minor accident": while putting on her coat, her hand brushes against a small painting, which, dislodged by the movement, falls to the ground. The lacquered wooden frame breaks, but the damage is reparable. F says to her host, from whom she was just taking leave: "Oh, sorry, I had a little accident." Then, suddenly joking: "But what an idea to put a painting in such a place! My word, you must have done it on purpose!" Not knowing what to do with the little painting which she now has in her hands, she turns it over, probably to examine the damage, and cries out joyously, "Oh, you see, it must have already been broken, since it has been glued." Upon saying this, she points to a piece of sticky paper which appears to have nothing to do with the frame itself. Everyone present clearly sees this, but they all act as if they hadn't noticed, and the host (who is French) hurriedly takes the painting from her and says "Don't worry about it, it's nothing, I'll take care of it." As F attempts to joke some more about the accident, her husband drags her toward the door, saying, "Listen, if you keep this up you'll never be invited here again." Everyone laughs. Exeunt all.

Not once did F offer to have the frame repaired. Rather, it seemed as if all [6] her efforts tended toward minimizing the gravity of the accident by making a joke of it. She thus started recounting another incident: her daughter, when she was still a baby in her mother's arms, had unhooked a signed (she insists) plate from the wall behind her mother, and threw it on the floor. "Well that was a real catastrophe, I didn't know what to do with myself . . ." In other words, the "truly" serious incident, that of the valuable (signed) plate, was the fault of the baby (and at the same time not her fault, since she was a baby?). In comparison, the incident with the frame appears (or should appear?) negligible.

Does the comparison of these two incidents also imply that F is not [7] responsible either? Like the baby? The fact that she did not offer to repair the frame (which would be a recognition of her responsibility) seems to indicate that this is a plausible interpretation of this comparison. Of course, we can say that F was so embarrassed that in the second case, as in the first, she "didn't know what to do with herself" and that joking was a way to hide her embarrassment. But one can just as easily be sorry or embarrassed, and joke around to relax the atmosphere, while at the same time offering to repair the damage.

While at a party at the home of friends of her friends, D, twenty-two years 8
old, Parisian, spills red wine (a full glass) on the carpet. She grabs a small paper
napkin to wipe it up. The friend who had invited her quickly returns from the
kitchen with enough paper towels to really soak up the large quantity of wine;
someone else brings salt. D, while her friend is cleaning, says, "My God, L (the
host) is not going to be happy . . . but can you imagine. . . . That's the trouble
with light-colored carpeting, it's so difficult to clean!" D made an effort, although
insufficient, to repair the damage. But her commentary is strangely similar to that
of F. The "victim" seems to be transformed into the truly responsible party, that is,
into the person who is ultimately responsible for the accident: if the painting hadn't
been placed there . . . if the carpet hadn't been chosen in such a light color . . .

Monsieur T, while visiting his son in the United States, discovers the 9
existence of window shades, which are placed between the window panes and the
curtains in the great majority of American homes and which serve to block out
the sun. These shades are spring-loaded, which allows one to lower or raise them
to any degree at will and thereby to adjust the quantity of light let in. In order to
do this, one must learn to accompany the shade with one's hand, or else it winds
itself up suddenly with a snap. The son demonstrates this for Monsieur T,
insisting particularly on the fact that he must never release the shade and "let it
roll up by itself" (which the French in the United States are endlessly tempted to
do, even if they have been living here for more than twenty years, as I have). The
next day, the son briefly reminds him of his instructions and only succeeds in
exasperating Monsieur T ("Do you think I am a fool?"). A few days later, the son
hears a snap, which sounds like a shot, followed by an exclamation. He runs over
and finds his father in front of the window; as soon as he sees him come in, his
father says, "This is horrible, you'd think you were in the devil's den. My word!
Can't have a weak heart at your place. . . . It's not surprising that Americans all
go to psychiatrists. . . . That gave me a terrible fright, and yet I did exactly as
you said, I don't understand what happened."

L, twenty-eight years old, from the Bordeaux region, shares an apartment 10
with V, approximately the same age, from Normandy. L burns one of her good
saucepans while V is out. Upon V's return, L confesses, apologizes, and, in the
course of her explanation adds, "because, you know, for me, a good saucepan or
a bad saucepan are the same, because I'm not at all materialistic, I don't get
attached to objects." In other words, if this is considered an "accident," it is only
because it is V's nature to regret the loss of a simple saucepan, a mere object.

M, from Midi, lends his projector to S, who returns it, jammed, with these 11
words: "Your projector is strange, it makes a funny noise." S later discovers a slide
which is part of M's collection wedged in the slide mechanism.

S, from the Basque coast, borrows R's car, brings it back the next day, and 12
asks with a sly smile: "Are you sure your car works well? Because it stalled twice.
Once, I was even stuck in the middle of the road because I was trying to turn,
and I was afraid a car would hit me." R, who is S's friend, adds, upon relating to
me this incident: "S is a very nice guy, but he can't drive to save his life."

B, from Paris, returns the typewriter he borrowed from me, and, wearing the 13
mischievous smile of a naughty child who knows he will be excused, tells me, "You

know, your typewriter was very mean to me, it must not like me very much because it was skipping letters constantly. . . . I had to be very careful as I typed."

The preceding examples seem to indicate that French people do not offer 14 to repair things when there has been an accident. Yet this is not the case. Among the cases I collected, offers to repair the damage were just as common as those mentioned above. Thus L, who had already burned V's saucepan, had also, at another time, accidentally broken a hand-crafted pitcher which V had brought back from France. In this case, L, who did indeed understand the sentimental value of pitchers if not the material value of saucepans, offered, or rather promised, to replace the broken object ("I'll buy you one exactly like that"). Over a year later, V tells me, the pitcher had not been replaced, or even mentioned.

This same V, G tells me, borrowed an electronic, programmable calculator 15 to do "a few simple calculations." The calculations were apparently too simple for the delicate mechanism of the instrument because it became "mysteriously" blocked. V offered to share the cost of repairing it with G, thus implying that there must have been something wrong with the machine before she borrowed it (or else she would have offered to pay all the costs). According to G, the cost of repairing it turned out to be so astronomical that he preferred to buy another inexpensive calculator, "just in case." In the meantime, according to G, V never mentioned sharing the costs and never asked for news of the wounded calculator. The last I heard, G and V are still friends.

A variation on this case consists of saying what one would have liked to do, 16 but did not do, to repair an accident. For instance, a white tablecloth which K borrowed from a friend for a holiday meal was irreparably stained. "I thought of buying a tablecloth to replace yours, but I didn't know what you'd like," says K, several years after the accident. The friend asserts that she has never been compensated and that it never put their friendship on the line.

Finally, there are certain cases in which the repair was made. Yet the 17 comments differ depending on whether one talks to the person who caused the "minor accident" and repaired the damage or to the person who was the "victim." I have on occasion heard the former say things such as "I paid a great deal to have a worthless rug cleaned," whereas the latter, whose car was dented and repaired by the friends who had borrowed it made the following comment: "Of course, they paid for the repairs, but now the car is totally ruined."

We might conclude from the preceding examples that the French break 18 everything and repair or replace nothing. Certain French people think so, and, as a result, "do not lend anything to anyone" and "do not ask anything of anyone," because "they never give it back in the state you lent it." As we know from having learned La Fontaine's fables, "Madame Ant is slow to lend/The last thing, this, she suffers from."[1] But there are obviously many French people who do not

---

[1]From "The Ant and the Grasshopper," in *A Hundred Fables from La Fontaine,* trans. Philip Wayne (Doubleday).

hold this attitude, as is proven by the accident cases cited earlier. How then can we interpret the various ways in which the actors treated these accidents? As we have seen, the reactions ranged from playful jokes to reproachful jokes, and from reproachful jokes to disguised accusations. Offers of repairs were not made, made but never followed up on, mentioned as something one had thought of, or else made and followed up on but to no one's satisfaction.

In other words, when I have a "minor accident," it is not really my fault. It [19] is because an object was in a bad place (I might almost say "in my way"), because a carpet was too light to hide stains, because a machine was too delicate to function normally, because to have shades in a house is aberrant, and so on. In fact, I acted in all innocence and nothing would have happened if the others had correctly played their parts. It becomes clear that by joking and "taking things lightly," I place responsibility where it belongs, on the person who committed the error of poorly placing his painting, of choosing an insane color for a carpet, of buying an overly complicated calculator . . . and who, most of all, made the mistake of not sufficiently protecting his possession if he cared about it so much.

By pushing this logic to its extreme, I would say that when entertaining me, [20] X runs the risk of having his good crystal broken if he chooses to use it ("accidents can happen") and that when lending me an object, he should warn me of its fragility. In fact, he should not lend, or put within my reach, an object which is fragile, and certainly not an object about which he cares a great deal. If he does this, X is obviously the one who should assume ultimate responsibility for the accident. Similarly, if I offer to repair or to pay for the damage ("tell me how much I owe you"), I have done my part, I have fulfilled my duty; it is up to X to request the necessary sum when required since I told him I would give it to him. Thus, I force the other to take responsibility for some of my acts, and in doing so I propose or reaffirm a relationship. If X refuses this relationship, he will never again invite me to his house or lend me anything more. And this does happen. But if X accepts the relationship, he reinforces it by placing more value on it than on the damaged object, as valuable as that object may be. Hence the "leave it, it's not important," which erases the accident. And as we more or less tacitly honor the same code, we each have a chance to be both victim and perpetrator of an accident, thus becoming linked to one another and affirming, sometimes against our wishes, the importance of these bonds.

Needless to say, an American would be completely baffled by such conduct. [21] It is, in fact, this type of behavior that provokes the "Dear Abby" letters mentioned at the beginning of this chapter.

An informant described to me the "American general rule" as follows: "If I [22] lend X my car, the minimum I can expect is that, before returning it, he will fill it with more gas than he consumed. If I lend him my car for a fairly long period, he will make a point of returning it to me in a better state than when I lent it to him (washed, waxed, vacuumed, etc.). He will not do this in order to point out my negligence but, in a sense, to repay me for my generosity. He will take responsibility for any necessary repairs, and I will hold him to this (unless it is an old wreck, in which case I would refuse to lend it to him so as to spare him some very predictable, but difficult to attribute, expenses)." Let us then look at some American cases, such as they have been reported to me.

At an elegant dinner, J breaks a crystal glass. She asks the hostess to lend her a glass of the same set, so that she can find a perfect replacement. The hostess honors her request. 23

P, fourteen or fifteen years old, meets a group of friends at D's house. They go to play basketball at the school basketball court and return, tired from the game, to D's house, where his mother serves them lunch. P, drawn without knowing why to a carafe on the buffet, picks up the stopper, which slips from his hands, falls back on the carafe, and chips it. P, confused, apologizes to D's mother for his clumsiness, and without hesitating offers to replace the carafe. P is over forty today, yet he remembers this scene very clearly. He remembers that at the very moment when he offered to replace the carafe he knew that he did not have, but would have to find, the necessary sum, and he also remembers that D's mother left him an escape route ("I'll let you know when I find one"), but not without her having expressed concern and regret over the accident. That is to say, according to him D's mother was willing to be generous, but without diminishing P's responsibility. 24

A dinner with friends. M spills a glass of wine. His wife quickly runs to the kitchen, returns with the necessary products, and sponges up the wine—in short, does everything to repair the accident. M thanks his wife with a look of gratitude and apologizes for his clumsiness. Note: in this case, M's wife has repaired his clumsiness because she forms a couple with him and therefore shares responsibility for the accident, takes responsibility for it as well. This does not preclude the possibility that some couples have "sexist" habits, but it gives the gesture a deeper meaning, as is shown by the fact that the inverse is just as possible: a woman spills some wine and her husband tries to repair the damage. . . . 25

An informal evening. Guests are seated on the carpet, their drinks by their sides. An accident quickly occurs: N spills a glass of tomato juice. The same efforts to clean it, as well and as quickly as possible, are made. N asks if his hosts have a carpet cleaning foam. They respond in the negative. N offers to pay the cost of the cleaning. "Thanks, but don't worry, we'll take care of it, no problem." The difficulty seems to be resolved. Yet later in the evening, on several occasions, N makes allusion to his clumsiness ("Don't give it to me, you know how klutzy I am"; "Oh God, this stain is looking at me"; "I feel so bad, such a beautiful carpet"). 26

A meeting of the members of our block association, held at the house of one of my neighbors. The sofa and chairs are fitted with slip covers, the furniture with cloths to protect the wood, and the table with an oilcloth. Coffee and cake are served in paper cups and on paper plates. Everyone is relaxed, there is no chance of an irreparable accident, everything has been foreseen. 27

Another meeting, at the far more elegant home of one of my colleagues. C, who is about to place his glass of white wine on the coffee table in front of us, stops his gesture halfway and asks our host if the wooden table (modern, elegant) has been treated, "protected." Despite our host's affirmative response, another colleague comes to the rescue and passes C a wooden coaster from a small stack which had been discreetly placed on a table nearby. The glass of cold white wine will leave no trace of its dampness. 28

The recital of cases could go on indefinitely. Those which I have mentioned suffice to illustrate the implicit rules governing American interpersonal exchanges in case of a "minor accident." I will summarize them as follows:

1. If I borrow an object from someone, I have an obligation to return it in the very same state as when it was lent to me. If it is a machine that breaks down in my hands, I must repair it, so as to erase all traces of the mishap. (I don't do this in order to hide the accident, which I must mention in any case, but in order to return the object to its previous condition.)

2. If the damage is irreparable, I must replace the object by an identical one, no matter how much time and searching are required. I can, however, ask the owner of the object where it was purchased. I must not replace it by an "equivalent," which would mean brushing off as unimportant all the reasons for the owner's choice, or the meaning which a certain object has come to have for its owner. Nor can I replace the object by another similar—but more or less expensive—one (a glass for a glass, for example), because in both cases I would be suggesting that all that counts in my eyes is the price of the object.

3. If I have an accident at someone's home, the situation is even more delicate. If I have even slightly damaged a valuable object (an art object or one with sentimental value), I must be grieved by my clumsiness without finding any excuse for myself; I must immediately offer to take the object and to have it repaired (while showing that I know where to go and that I am not going to worsen the damage by leaving the object with nonprofessionals); I must insist on being allowed to do this, if only to relieve my feelings of guilt ("I feel so bad. I wouldn't be able to sleep"). If my host does not wish to signal the end of our relationship, he or she will, out of kindness, allow me to take the object with me, in order to "let me off the hook."

If the accident is of a common sort and not very serious, I must do everything in my power to repair the damage then and there, but I must be careful not to insult my host by offering to replace a common item or to pay the cost of cleaning a tablecloth, for instance, because in doing so I would be suggesting that I do not think he or she has the means to take care of it. In this case, I show that I take the accident seriously by mentioning it several times, by berating myself for my clumsiness, by making fun of myself—in short, by taking total responsibility for the accident.

All this might seem strange, if not "heavy-handed," to a French person. Why make such a fuss? Why put on such an act? Is this yet another example of American "hypocrisy" and "puritanism"?

It is nothing of the kind, of course. On the contrary, although their conduct may be completely different from that of the French people mentioned above (in fact it is exactly opposite), the Americans I have focused on sent a message very similar to that expressed by the French people. Indeed, when I (an American) borrow an object from X, I create or confirm a tie with X (I do not borrow things from just anyone). The care I take with this object will therefore be proportionate to the importance I place on my relationship to the person who lent it to me. Similarly, when I accidentally disturb a home to which I have been invited, my reaction will be interpreted as a conscious commentary on the relationship between my host and myself. If I do everything possible to clean a carpet, it is not for the sake of the endangered carpet (or because my host and I are "materialistic" because we are American) but out of respect for my host. In other words, our relationship does not presuppose that we will "weather difficulties" together (as it does in the French context); it presupposes a tacit pact between the borrower and the lender, the host and the guest, to preserve an equilibrium, without which all relationships of this kind would become impossible. For if I show little concern for something belonging to X which he has put within my reach or at my disposal (thereby trusting me), X has the right to feel wounded, scorned, and to refuse further dealings with me. Meanwhile, the expectation that one will honor this pact is so strong that any avoidance or refusal on my part risks leaving X bewildered, "not knowing what to do," just like the Dear Abby correspondents mentioned earlier. This is, in a sense, because for Americans it is not in the cards that others will behave in ways other than expected (without being criminals, louts, or other types with whom X would not maintain relations).

If my "accident" is really major and X refuses to allow me to free myself, as far as is possible, from my debt, X transforms this bond into a shackle, and I have no reason to maintain a relationship with someone so unconcerned with my feelings. 36

In many circumstances, intercultural misunderstandings spring from the fact that surface resemblances and behavioral similarities conceal profound differences in meaning. It is interesting to see here that the inverse is also true. 37

QUESTIONS FOR CRITICAL READING, THINKING, DISCUSSION, AND WRITING

Analyzing Content and Technique

1. What is the thesis of this essay? Where are we first given a hint of it?
2. Analyze the cases of French responses to accidents (paragraphs 5–16) and summarize the attitude that seems to be indicated by these responses. What do they reveal of cultural values?
3. How is the American response to accidents different? According to the writer, which values are important in American friendships? How would the French interpret the response of Americans to accidents?
4. Examine the writer's statement (paragraph 35) that "although their conduct may be completely different from that of the French people . . . the Americans I have focused on sent a message very similar to that expressed by the French people." What similarities in the two groups does she find? Do you feel she has supplied us with enough proof for us to accept her statement? Explain.
5. Who is the writer's intended audience? How do we deduce this from the text and its tone? Give examples.
6. The writer ends the essay with a very brief, two-sentence conclusion. What are its effects, positive and negative, on the reader? Write a different conclusion for the essay.

Collaborative Activity

As a group, choose one of the cases mentioned in the essay and roleplay it, changing the cultural context (that is, if it is a French situation, make it an American one, and vice versa). After enacting the scene, analyze the differences that appeared in your version. How close was the group's interpretation to Carroll's hypotheses?

Making Connections

1. In several places in the essay, the writer alludes to ways in which the French view Americans. Make a list of the qualities they believe Americans to possess or value, and examine them. Are they mostly positive or negative? In addition, interview one or two persons who were not born in America and ask them for their impressions of the American character. Put these together in an essay in which you explore how Americans appear to people of other countries or cultures.

2. Take one of the cases discussed by the writer and make it cross-cultural—that is, have the "guilty party" belong to one culture, and the "victim" to another. Imagine yourself to be the mediator between the two. In an essay, explain what you would say or do to increase understanding and communication between the two parties.

PREREADING ACTIVITY

Think back on your most meaningful friendships. Describe what you appreciated about them. Were there common elements or patterns in these relationships?

On Friendship

MARGARET MEAD AND RHODA METRAUX

Margaret Mead (1901–1978) grew up in Philadelphia and went to Barnard College and Columbia University. A noted cultural anthropologist, author, and teacher, she began fieldwork in Samoa in her mid-twenties, studying sexual development and family life, which continued to be a major focus of her later work. Her books include *Coming of Age in Samoa, Childhood in Contemporary Cultures, Growing Up in New Guinea,* and *Male and Female.* Rhoda Metraux (1914–), also an anthropologist, collaborated with Mead to produce *A Way of Seeing,* a collection of essays. Selection 77 first appeared in *Redbook,* under the title "Different Lands, Different Friendships."

*F*ew Americans stay put for a lifetime. We move from town to city to   1
suburb, from high school to college in a different state, from a job in one region to a better job elsewhere, from the home where we raise our children to the home where we plan to live in retirement. With each move we are forever making new friends, who become part of our new life at that time.

For many of us the summer is a special time for forming new friendships.   2
Today millions of Americans vacation abroad, and they go not only to see new sights but also—in those places where they do not feel too strange—with the hope of meeting new people. No one really expects a vacation trip to produce a close friend. But surely the beginning of a friendship is possible? Surely in every country people value friendship?

They do. The difficulty when strangers from two countries meet is not a   3
lack of appreciation of friendship, but different expectations about what constitutes friendship and how it comes into being. In those European countries that Americans are most likely to visit, friendship is quite sharply distinguished from

551

other, more casual relations, and is differently related to family life. For a Frenchman, a German or an Englishman friendship is usually more particularized and carries a heavier burden of commitment.

But as we use the word, "friend" can be applied to a wide range of relationships—to someone one has known for a few weeks in a new place, to a close business associate, to a childhood playmate, to a man or woman, to a trusted confidant. There are real differences among these relations for Americans—a friendship may be superficial, casual, situational or deep and enduring. But to a European, who sees only our surface behavior, the differences are not clear. 4

As they see it, people known and accepted temporarily, casually, flow in and out of Americans' homes with little ceremony and often with little personal commitment. They may be parents of the children's friends, house guests of neighbors, members of a committee, business associates from another town or even another country. Coming as a guest into an American home, the European visitor finds no visible landmarks. The atmosphere is relaxed. Most people, old and young, are called by first names. 5

Who, then, is a friend? 6

Even simple translation from one language to another is difficult, "You see," a Frenchman explains, "if I were to say to you in France, 'This is my good friend,' that person would not be as close to me as someone about whom I said only, 'This is my friend.' Anyone about whom I have to say *more* is really less." 7

In France, as in many European countries, friends generally are of the same sex, and friendship is seen as basically a relationship between men. Frenchwomen laugh at the idea that "women can't be friends," but they also admit sometimes that for women "it's a different thing." And many French people doubt the possibility of a friendship between a man and a woman. There is also the kind of relationship within a group—men and women who have worked together for a long time, who may be very close, sharing great loyalty and warmth of feeling. They may call one another *copains*—a word that in English becomes "friends" but has more the feeling of "pals" or "buddies." In French eyes this is not friendship, although two members of such a group may well be friends. 8

For the French, friendship is a one-to-one relationship that demands a keen awareness of the other person's intellect, temperament and particular interests. A friend is someone who draws out your own best qualities, with whom you sparkle and become more of whatever the friendship draws upon. Your political philosophy assumes more depth, appreciation of a play becomes sharper, taste in food or wine is accentuated, enjoyment of a sport is intensified. 9

And French friendships are compartmentalized. A man may play chess with a friend for thirty years without knowing his political opinions, or he may talk politics with him for as long a time without knowing about his personal life. Different friends fill different niches in each person's life. These friendships are not made part of family life. A friend is not expected to spend evenings being nice to children or courteous to a deaf grandmother. These duties, also serious and enjoined, are primarily for relatives. Men who are friends may meet in a café. Intellectual friends may meet in larger groups for evenings of conversation. Working people may meet at the little *bistro* where they drink and talk, far from the 10 family. Marriage does not affect such friendships; wives do not have to be taken into account.

In the past in France, friendships of this kind seldom were open to any but 11
intellectual women. Since most women's lives centered on their homes, their warmest relations with other women often went back to their girlhood. The special relationship of friendship is based on what the French value most—on the mind, on compatibility of outlook, on vivid awareness of some chosen area of life.

Friendship heightens the sense of each person's individuality. Other rela- 12
tionships commanding as great loyalty and devotion have a different meaning. In World War II the first resistance groups formed in Paris were built on the foundation of *les copains*. But significantly, as time went on these little groups, whose lives rested in one another's hands, called themselves "families." Where each had a total responsibility for all, it was kinship ties that provided the model. And even today such ties, crossing every line of class and personal interest, remain binding on the survivors of these small, secret bands.

In Germany, in contrast with France, friendship is much more articulately a 13
matter of feeling. Adolescents, boys and girls, form deeply sentimental attachments, walk and talk together—not so much to polish their wits as to share their hopes and fears and dreams, to form a common front against the world of school and family and to join in a kind of mutual discovery of each other's and their own inner life. Within the family, the closest relationship over a lifetime is between brothers and sisters. Outside the family, men and women find in their closest friends of the same sex the devotion of a sister, the loyalty of a brother. Appropriately, in Germany friends usually are brought into the family. Children call their father's and their mother's friends "uncle" and "aunt." Between French friends, who have chosen each other for the congeniality of their point of view, lively disagreement and sharpness of argument are the breath of life. But for Germans, whose friendships are based on mutuality of feeling, deep disagreement on any subject that matters to both is regarded as a tragedy. Like ties of kinship, ties of friendship are meant to be irrevocably binding. Young Germans who come to the United States have great difficulty in establishing such friendships with Americans. We view friendship more tentatively, subject to changes in intensity as people move, change their jobs, marry, or discover new interests.

English friendships follow still a different pattern. Their basis is shared activ- 14
ity. Activities at different stages of life may be of very different kinds—discovering a common interest in school, serving together in the armed forces, taking part in a foreign mission, staying in the same country house during a crisis. In the midst of the activity, whatever it may be, people fall into step—sometimes two men or two women, sometimes two couples, sometimes three people—and find that they walk or play a game or tell stories or serve on a tiresome and exacting committee with the same easy anticipation of what each will do day by day or in some critical situation. Americans who have made English friends comment that, even years later, "you can take up just where you left off." Meeting after a long interval, friends are like a couple who begin to dance again when the orchestra strikes up after a pause. English friendships are formed outside the family circle, but they are not, as in Germany, contrapuntal to the family nor are they, as in

France, separated from the family. And a break in an English friendship comes not necessarily as a result of some irreconcilable difference of viewpoint or feeling but instead as a result of misjudgment, where one friend seriously misjudges how the other will think or feel or act, so that suddenly they are out of step.

What, then, is friendship? Looking at these different styles, including our own, each of which is related to a whole way of life, are there common elements? There is the recognition that friendship, in contrast with kinship, invokes freedom of choice. A friend is someone who chooses and is chosen. Related to this is the sense each friend gives the other of being a special individual, on whatever grounds this recognition is based. And between friends there is inevitably a kind of equality of give-and-take. These similarities make the bridge between societies possible, and the American's characteristic openness to different styles of relationship makes it possible for him to find new friends abroad with whom he feels at home. 15

QUESTIONS FOR CRITICAL READING, THINKING, DISCUSSION, AND WRITING

Analyzing Content and Technique

1. Where does the thesis of the essay appear? Why do you think the authors placed it there? What is the function of the paragraphs that come before the thesis?
2. What are the major characteristics of American friendships, according to the authors? Do you agree or disagree? Give examples from your own observation and experience to support your answer.
3. What distinguishes French friendships from American friendships? What are some of the advantages of each system?
4. Compare and contrast German and English friendships. What generalizations about national characteristics can you draw from the information given in the essay?
5. Analyze the structure of the essay, making up a brief outline. Which parts are developed in greatest detail? Which parts need more support? To strengthen the sections that need support, add a few points of your own (you might need to do some research or interviewing).
6. Discuss the conclusion. How does it relate to the thesis? From it, what can you deduce about the author's attitude toward cultural differences?

Collaborative Activity

In this essay, although they analyze the subject in depth and provide general examples, the authors have not given us any specific examples involving particular individuals. As a group, discuss where such examples may be added. Choose one of these places and collaboratively write an example. You may make one up, or draw on the experiences of group members. Now discuss how including such an example strengthens the argument.

Making Connections

1. Write an essay analyzing the concept of friendship prevalent in your culture, or a culture that is familiar to you. Compare and contrast it with the concept of friendship in one of the cultures

discussed by Mead and Metraux. Be sure to support your ideas with well-chosen examples, both general and specific.

2. Do you believe that deep and meaningful friendships can be formed between people of different nations and cultures? What difficulties might stand in the way of such friendships? Drawing on Mead and Metraux's ideas as well as your own observations and experience, write an essay in which you explore these questions. You may interview people of different cultures to find supporting evidence for your beliefs.

Have you (or has anyone you know) ever lived in a place where you were regarded as different, an outsider? Write about the experience and explain why you were thought of in this way.

Thriving as an Outsider, Even an Outcast, in Smalltown America

LOUIE CREW

Louie Crew (1936–   ) is a college instructor and an activist for gay rights. He grew up in Alabama and holds degrees from Auburn University and the University of Alabama. He has taught in many parts of the United States and also in China. He is the founder of Integrity, an organization for gay Episcopalians, and many of his essays and poems deal with aspects of the gay experience.

From 1973 to 1979, my spouse and I lived in Fort Valley, a town of 12,000 people, the seat of Peach County, sixty miles northeast of Plains, right in the geographic center of Georgia. I taught English at a local black college and my spouse was variously a nurse, hairdresser, choreographer for the college majorettes, caterer, and fashion designer.

The two of us have often been asked how we survived as a gay, racially integrated couple living openly in that small town. We are still perhaps too close to the Georgia experience and very much caught up in our similar struggles in central Wisconsin to offer a definite explanation, but our tentative conjectures should interest anyone who values the role of the dissident in our democracy.

Survive we did. We even throve before our departure. Professionally, my colleagues and the Regents of the University System of Georgia awarded me tenure, and the Chamber of Commerce awarded my spouse a career medal in cosmetology. Socially, we had friends from the full range of the economic classes in the community. We had attended six farewell parties in our honor before we called a halt to further fetes, especially several planned at too great a sacrifice by some of the poorest folks in the town. Furthermore, I had been away only four months when the college brought me back to address an assembly of Georgia judges, majors, police chiefs, and wardens. We are still called two to three times

Source: Reprinted by permission of the author.

a week by scores of people seeking my spouse's advice on fashion, cooking, or the like.

It was not always so. In 1974 my spouse and I were denied housing which 4 we had "secured" earlier before the realtor saw my spouse's color. HUD documented that the realtor thought that "the black man looked like a criminal." Once the town was up in arms when a bishop accused the two of us of causing a tornado which had hit the town early in 1975, an accusation which appeared on the front page of the newspaper. "This is the voice of God. The town of Fort Valley is harboring Sodomists. Would one expect God to keep silent when homosexuals are tolerated? We remember what He did to Sodom and Gomorrah" (*The Macon Herald,* March 20, 1975: I). A year later my Episcopal vestry asked me to leave the parish, and my own bishop summoned me for discipline for releasing to the national press correspondence related to the vestry's back-room maneuvers. Prompted in part by such officials, the local citizens for years routinely heckled us in public, sometimes threw rocks at our apartment, trained their children to spit on us from their bicycles if we dared to jog, and badgered us with hate calls on an average of six to eight times a week.

One such episode offers a partial clue to the cause of our survival. It was 5 late summer, 1975 or 1976. I was on my motorcycle to post mail at the streetside box just before the one daily pickup at 6:00 P.M. About fifty yards away, fully audible to about seventy pedestrians milling about the court house and other public buildings, a group of police officers, all men, began shouting at me from the steps of their headquarters: "Louise! Faggot! Queer!"

Anyone who has ever tried to ease a motorcycle from a still position with- 6 out revving the engine knows that the feat is impossible: try as I did to avoid the suggestion, I sounded as if I were riding off in a huff. About half-way up the street, I thought to myself, "I'd rather rot in jail than feel the way I do now." I turned around, drove back—the policemen still shouting and laughing—and parked in the lot of the station. When I walked to the steps, only the lone black policeman remained.

"Did you speak to me?" I asked him. 7

"No, sir," he replied emphatically. 8

Inside I badgered the desk sergeant to tell her chief to call me as soon as 9 she could locate him, and I indicated that I would press charges if necessary to prevent a recurrence. I explained that the police misconduct was an open invitation to more violent hoodlums to act out the officers' fantasies with impunity in the dark. Later, I persuaded a black city commissioner and a white one, the latter our grocer and the former our mortician, to threaten the culprits with suspension if ever such misconduct occurred again.

Over a year later, late one Friday after his payday, a black friend of my 10 spouse knocked at our door to offer a share of his Scotch to celebrate his raise— or so he said. Thus primed, he asked me, "You don't recognize me, do you?"

"No," I admitted. 11

"I'm the lone black policeman that day you were heckled. I came by really 12 because I thought you two might want to know what happened inside when Louie stormed up to the sergeant."

"Yes," we said. [13]

"Well, all the guys were crouching behind the partition to keep you from [14] seeing that they were listening. Their eyes bulged when you threatened to bring in the F.B.I. and such. Then when you left, one spoke for all when he said, 'But sissies aren't supposed to do things like that!'"

Ironically, I believe that a major reason for our thriving on our own terms [15] of candor about our relationship has been our commitment to resist the intimidation heaped upon us. For too long lesbians and gay males have unwillingly encouraged abuses against ourselves by serving advance notice to any bullies, be they the barnyard-playground variety, or the Bible-wielding pulpiteers, that we would whimper or run into hiding when confronted with even the threat of exposure. It is easy to confuse sensible nonviolence with cowardly nonresistance.

In my view, violent resistance would be counter-productive, especially for [16] lesbians and gays who are outnumbered 10 to 1 by heterosexuals, according to Kinsey's statistics. Yet our personal experience suggests that special kinds of creative nonviolent resistance are a major source of hope if lesbians and gay males are going to reverse the physical and mental intimidation which is our daily portion in this culture.

Resistance to oppression can be random and spontaneous, as in part was my [17] decision to return to confront the police hecklers, or organized and sustained, as more typically has been the resistance by which my spouse and I have survived. I believe that only organized and sustained resistance offers much hope for long-range change in any community. The random act is too soon forgotten or too easily romanticized.

Once we had committed ourselves to one another, my spouse and I never [18] gave much thought for ourselves to the traditional device most gays have used for survival, the notorious "closet" in which one hides one's identity from all but a select group of friends. In the first place, a black man and a white man integrating a Georgia small town simply cannot be inconspicuous. More importantly, the joint checking account and other equitable economies fundamental to the quality of our marriage are public, not private acts. Our denial of the obvious would have secured closet space only for our suffocation; we would have lied, "We are ashamed and live in secret."

All of our resistance stems from our sense of our own worth, our conviction [19] that we and our kind do not deserve the suffering which heterosexuals continue to encourage or condone for sexual outcasts. Dr. Martin Luther King used to say, "Those who go to the back of the bus, deserve the back of the bus."

Our survival on our own terms has depended very much on our knowing [20] and respecting many of the rules of the system which we resist. We are not simply dissenters, but conscientious ones.

For example, we are both very hard workers. As a controversial person, I [21] know that my professionalism comes under far more scrutiny than that of others. I learned early in my career that I could secure space for my differences by handling routine matters carefully. If one stays on good terms with secretaries, meets all deadlines, and willingly does one's fair share of the busy work of institutions, one is usually already well on the way towards earning collegial space, if not collegial support. In Georgia, I routinely volunteered to be secretary for most committees on which I served, thereby having enormous influence in the final form of the groups' deliberations without monopolizing the forum as most other molders of policy do. My spouse's many talents and sensibilities made him an invaluable advisor and confidante to scores of people in the community. Of course, living as we did in a hairdresser's salon, we knew a great deal more about the rest of the public than that public knew about us.

My spouse and I are fortunate in the fact that we like the enormous amount of work which we do. We are not mere opportunists working hard only as a gimmick to exploit the public for lesbian and gay issues. Both of us worked intensely at our professional assignments long before we were acknowledged dissidents with new excessive pressures to excel. We feel that now we must, however unfairly, be twice as effective as our competitors just to remain employed at all. 22

Our survival has also depended very much on our thorough knowledge of the system, often knowledge more thorough than that of those who would use the system against us. For example, when my bishop summoned me for discipline, I was able to show him that his own canons give him no authority to discipline a lay person except by excommunication. In fact, so hierarchical have the canons of his diocese become, that the only laity who exist worthy of their mention are the few lay persons on vestries. 23

Especially helpful has been our knowledge of communication procedures. For example, when an area minister attacked lesbians and gays on a TV talk show, I requested equal time; so well received was my response that for two more years I was a regular panelist on the talk show, thereby reaching most residents of the entire middle Georgia area as a known gay person, yet one speaking not just to sexual issues, but to a full range of religious and social topics. 24

When I was occasionally denied access to media, as in the parish or diocese or as on campus when gossip flared, I knew the value of candid explanations thoughtfully prepared, xeroxed, and circulated to enough folks to assure that the gossips would have access to the truthful version. For example, the vestry, which acted in secret, was caught by surprise when I sent copies of their hateful letter to most other parishioners, together with a copy of a psalm which I wrote protesting their turning the House of Prayer into a Court House. I also was able to explain that I continued to attend, not in defiance of their withdrawn invitation, but in obedience to the much higher invitation issued to us all by the real head of the Church. In January, 1979, in the first open meeting of the parish since the vestry's letter of unwelcome three years earlier, the entire parish voted to censure the vestry for that action and to extend to me the full welcome which the vestry had tried to deny. Only three voted against censure, all three of them a minority of the vestry being censured. 25

My spouse and I have been very conscious of the risks of our convictions. We have viewed our credentials—my doctorate and his professional licenses—not as badges of comfortable respectability, but as assets to be invested in social change. Dr. King did not sit crying in the Albany jail, "Why don't these folk respect me? How did this happen? What am I doing here?" When my spouse and I have been denied jobs for which we were the most qualified applicants, we have 26 not naively asked how such things could be, nor have we dwelt overly long on self-pity, for we have known in advance the prices we might have to pay, even if to lose our lives. Our realism about danger and risk has helped us to preserve our sanity when everyone about us has seemed insane. I remember the joy which my spouse shared with me over the fact that he had just been fired for his efforts to organize other black nurses to protest their being treated as orderlies by the white managers of a local hospital.

Never, however, have we affirmed the injustices. Finally, we simply cannot   27 be surprised by any evil and are thus less likely to be intimidated by it. Hence, we find ourselves heirs to a special hybrid of courage, a form of courage too often ignored by the heterosexual majority, but widely manifest among sexual outcasts, not the courage of bravado on battlegrounds or sportsfields, but the delicate courage of the lone person who patiently waits out the stupidity of the herd, the cagey courage that has operated many an underground railway station.

Our survival in smalltown America has been helped least, I suspect, by our   28 annoying insistence that potential friends receive us not only in our own right, but also as members of the larger lesbian/gay and black communities of which we are a part. Too many whites and heterosexuals are prepared to single us out as "good queers" or "good niggers," offering us thereby the "rewards" of their friendship only at too great a cost to our integrity. My priest did not whip up the vestry against me the first year we lived openly together. He was perfectly happy to have one of his "clever queers" to dress his wife's hair and the other to help him write his annual report. We became scandalous only when the two of us began to organize the national group of lesbian and gay-male Episcopalians, known as INTEGRITY; then we were no longer just quaint. We threatened his image of himself as the arbiter of community morality, especially as he faced scores of queries from brother priests elsewhere.

Many lesbians and gay males are tamed by dependencies upon carefully   29 selected heterosexual friends with whom they have shared their secret, often never realizing that in themselves alone, they could provide far more affirmation and discover far more strength than is being cultivated by the terms of these "friend-ships." Lesbians and gay males have always been taught to survive on the hetero-sexuals' terms, rarely on one's own terms, and almost never on the terms of a community shared with other lesbians and gay males.

Heterosexuals are often thus the losers. The heterosexual acquaintances   30 close to us early on when we were less visible who dropped us later as our noto-riety spread were in most cases folks of demonstrably much less character strength than those heterosexuals who remained our friends even as we asserted our dif-ference with thoughtful independence.

My spouse and I have never been exclusive nor aspired to move to any   31 ghetto. In December, 1978, on the night the Macon rabbi and I had successfully organized the area's Jews and gays to protest a concert by Anita Bryant, I returned home to watch the videotape of the march on the late news in the com-pany of eight house guests invited by my spouse for a surprise party, not one of them gay (for some strange reason nine out of ten folks are not), not one of them obligated to be at the earlier march, and not one of them uneasy, as most of our acquaintances would have been a few years earlier before we had undertaken this reeducation together.

Folks who work for social change need to be very careful to allow room for it to happen, not to allow realistic appraisals of risks to prevent their cultivation of the very change which they germinate. [32]

Our survival has been helped in no small way by our candor and clarity in response to rumor and gossip, which are among our biggest enemies. On my campus in Georgia, I voluntarily spoke about sexual issues to an average of 50 classes per year outside my discipline. Initially, those encounters sharpened my wits for tougher national forums, but long after I no longer needed these occasions personally for rehearsal, I continued to accept the invitations, thereby reaching a vast majority of the citizens of the small town where we continued to live. I used to enjoy the humor of sharing with such groups facts which would make my day-to-day life more pleasant. For example, I routinely noted that when a male student is shocked at my simple public, "Hello," he would look both ways to see who might have seen him being friendly with the gay professor. By doing this he is telling me and all other knowledgeable folks far more new information about his own body chemistry than he is finding out about mine. More informed male students would reply, "Hello" when greeted. With this method I disarmed the hatefulness of one of their more debilitating weapons of ostracism. [33]

All personal references in public discussions inevitably invade one's privacy, but I have usually found the invasion a small price to pay for the opportunity to educate the public to the fact that the issues which most concern sexual outcasts are not genital, as the casters-out have so lewdly imagined, but issues of justice and simple fairness. [34]

Resistance is ultimately an art which no one masters to perfection. Early in my struggles, I said to a gay colleague living openly in rural Nebraska, "We must stamp on every snake." Wisely he counseled, "Only if you want to get foot poisoning." I often wish I had more of the wisdom mentioned in *Ecclesiastes*, the ability to judge accurately, "The time to speak and the time to refrain from speaking." Much of the time I think it wise to pass public hecklers without acknowledging their taunts, especially when they are cowardly hiding in a crowd. When I have faced bullies head-on, I have tried to do so patiently, disarming them by my own control of the situation. Of course, I am not guaranteed that their violence can thus be aborted every time. [35]

Two major sources of our survival are essentially very private—one, the intense care and love my spouse and I share, and the other, our strong faith in God as Unbounding Love. To these we prefer to make our secular witness, more by what we do than by what we say. [36]

I am not a masochist. I would never choose the hard lot of the sexual outcast in small-town America. Had I the choice to change myself but not the world, I would return as a white male heterosexual city-slicker millionaire, not because whites, males, heterosexuals, city-slickers, and millionaires are better, but because they have it easier. [37]

Yet everyone faces a different choice: accept the world the way you find it, or change it. For year after year I dissented, right in my own neighborhood. [38]

America preserves an ideal of freedom, although it denies freedom in scores 39
of instances. My eighth-grade civics teacher in Alabama did not mention the price
I would have to pay for the freedom of speech she taught me to value. I know
now that the docile and ignorant dislike you fiercely when you speak truth they
prefer not to hear. But I had a good civics class, one that showed me how to
change our government. I rejoice.

Sometimes I think a society's critics must appreciate the society far more 40
than others, for the critics typically take very seriously the society's idle promises
and forgotten dreams. When I occasionally see them, I certainly don't find many
of my heterosexual eighth-grade classmates probing much farther than the issues
of our common Form 1040 headaches and the issues as delivered by the evening
news. Their lives seem often far duller than ours and the main adventures in pioneering they experience come vicariously, through television, the movies, and for
a few, through books. In defining me as a criminal, my society may well have
hidden a major blessing in its curse by forcing me out of lethargy into an ongoing, rigorous questioning of the entire process. Not only do I teach *The Adventures of Huckleberry Finn,* my spouse and I have in an important sense had the
chance to be Huck and Jim fleeing a different form of slavery and injustice in a
very real present.

QUESTIONS FOR CRITICAL READING, THINKING, DISCUSSION, AND WRITING

Analyzing Content and Technique

1. Why does Crew call himself and his partner "dissidents"? What mainstream values are they
   fighting against?
2. What were Crew's early experiences in Fort Valley? What did they reveal about some of the
   town's inhabitants?
3. What methods did Crew and his partner use to fight the negative attitudes they faced? Which
   of their techniques do you consider the most effective? Why?
4. Analyze the relationship between the two men. Which facets of their relationship contributed
   to the success of their resistance?
5. Crew supports his essay with many specific examples. Find one that works especially well for
   you and discuss why it is effective. Analyze its relationship to the thesis.
6. Examine the tone of this essay. Compare it with another piece in Part Ten which has a similar
   theme but a different tone. Discuss why each author has chosen his or her tone. How does
   the tone alert us to the purpose and audience of each piece?
7. Analyze the concluding paragraph and comment on the ideas it presents. How far do you
   agree with them? Explain.

Collaborative Activity

As a group, research the laws of the state in which you live as they relate to gays. What rights
do gays have? What rights do they not have? Discuss the group's response to these rights.

Making Connections

1. Many of the strategies Crew has suggested for social acceptance are not restricted to gays or lesbians. Write an essay discussing which of his strategies could be used successfully by some other minority group you are familiar with. Be sure to give actual instances of difficulties faced by this group before suggesting solutions.
2. Write an essay tracing the history of social attitudes toward gays and lesbians in the United States. How have attitudes changed in the gay and lesbian community and in the mainstream community? What remains the same? What overall conclusion can you draw from the patterns you find? (You will probably need to research this subject.)

Look up the details of the Rodney King incident mentioned in the first paragraph of the essay, if you are not familiar with it. Write a one-paragraph summary of what happened and why.

The Real Lesson of L.A.

BILL BRADLEY

Bill Bradley is a Democratic senator from New Jersey. This article, based on a speech given in the spring of 1992 before the Los Angeles riots occurred, was later expanded and published in *Harper's Magazine* in July 1992.

America has seen two tragedies this past spring: the horrible injustice 1 of the Rodney King verdict and the deplorable violence that subsequently engulfed Los Angeles.

But we will all face a third tragedy if we don't learn the real lesson of this spring. 2 Consider, for example, a teenager who lived in Watts in the 1960s, who saw his neighborhood burned and his friends killed. Politicians came in and said they would restore opportunity, reform the criminal justice system, make the police evenhanded and disciplined, and change the conditions that created the context for the riots.

Now jump forward to 1992. The teenager is forty-five years old, and watches 3 his neighborhood burn again and again sees his friends die. What will this man tell his teenage son about the police, the criminal justice system, the need for hard work, and the prospect of a job? What will he say about his personal safety in the neighborhood or the ability of the political system to help him take control of his life and build a better future?

The needs of our cities are obvious: more jobs, less violence, and stronger 4 families, all in the context of a growing economy that takes everyone to a higher ground. The federal government must commit significant resources to meet the problems of urban America. It is ludicrous for anyone to pretend otherwise.

The fundamental changes, though, won't come from charismatic leaders or 5 from federal bureaucracies. They will come from thousands of "leaders of awareness," in communities across the nation, men and women who will effect lasting change as they champion integrity and humility over self-promotion. But above all, the scape-goating and buck-passing must stop. A sense of urgency must inform our actions. The situation demands a new democratic movement—I call it a conversion, a willingness to convert the outrage of Los Angeles into positive efforts to rebuild our communities.

Conversion must start with the acknowledgment that slavery was America's 6 original sin and race remains our unresolved dilemma. The future of American cities is inextricably bound to the issue of race and ethnicity. By the year 2000, only 57 percent of the people entering the work force in America will be native-born whites. That means that the economic future of the children of white Americans will increasingly depend on the talents of non-white Americans. If we allow this group to fail because of our penny-pinching or our timidity about straight talk, America will become a second-rate power. If this country's minorities succeed, America and all Americans will be enriched. If we don't move ahead and find common ground, we will all be diminished.

In national politics during the last twenty-five years, the issue of race and 7 urban America has been shaped by distortion and silence. Both political parties have contributed to the problem. Republicans have played the race card in a divisive way in order to win votes—remember Willie Horton—and Democrats have suffocated discussion of the self-destructive behavior among parts of the minority population under a cloak of silence and denial. The result is that yet another generation of our children has been lost. We cannot afford to wait any longer. It is time for candor, time for truth, and time for action.

America's cities are poorer, sicker, less educated, and more violent than at 8 any point in my lifetime. The physical problems are obvious: deteriorating schools; aging infrastructure; a diminished manufacturing base; a health care system, short of doctors, that fails to immunize against measles much less educate about AIDS. The jobs have disappeared. The neighborhoods have been gutted. A genuine depression has hit the cities—unemployment, in some areas, matches the levels of the 1930s.

What is less obvious, but equally important, in urban America is the crisis of 9 meaning. Without meaning there can be no hope; without hope there can be no struggle; without struggle there can be no personal betterment. Absence of meaning, influenced by overt and subtle attacks from racist quarters over many years, as well as an increasing pessimism about the possibility of justice, fosters a context for chaos and irresponsibility. Meaning develops from birth. Yet, more than 40 percent of all births in the twenty largest cities of America are to women living alone; among black women, more than 65 percent.

For kids who have no family outside a gang, no connection to religion, no 10 sense of place outside the territory, and no imagination beyond the violence of TV, our claims that government is on their side ring hollow. To them, government is at best incompetent and at worst corrupt. Instead of being rooted in values such as commitment and community service, their desires, like commodities, become rooted in the shallow ground of immediate gratification. TV bombards these kids with messages of conspicuous consumption. They want it now. They become trapped in the quicksands of American materialism, surfeited with images of sex, violence, and drugs.

The physical condition of American cities and the absence of meaning in more and more lives come together at the barrel of a gun. If you were to select one thing that has changed most in cities since the 1960s, it would be fear. Fear covers the streets like a sheet of ice. The number of murders and violent crimes has doubled in the 20 largest cities since 1968. Ninety percent of all violence is committed by males, and they are its predominant victims. Indeed, murder is the leading cause of death for young black males. 11

For African-Americans in cities, violence isn't new. Mothers have sent their children to school through war zones for too many years. What *is* new is the fear among whites of random violence. No place in the city seems safe. Walking the streets seem to be a form of Russian roulette. At its core, this fear is a fear of young black men. Never mind that all black males have to answer for the actions of a few black males. Never mind that Asian-Americans fear both black and white Americans, or that in Miami and Los Angeles, some of the most feared gangs are Latinos and Chinese. Never mind that the ultimate racism was whites ignoring the violence when it wasn't in their neighborhoods, or that black Americans have always feared certain white neighborhoods. 12

Today many white Americans, whether fairly or unfairly, seem to be saying of some black males, "You litter the street and deface the subway, and no one, white or black, says stop. You cut school, threaten a teacher, 'dis' a social worker, and no one, white or black, says stop. You snatch a purse, you crash a concert, break a telephone booth, and no one, white or black, says stop. You rob a store, rape a jogger, shoot a tourist, and when they catch you—if they catch you—you cry racism. And nobody, white or black, says stop." 13

It makes no difference whether this white rap accurately reflects the reality of our cities. Millions of white Americans believe it's true. In a kind of ironic flip of fate, the fear of brutal white oppression experienced for decades in the black community and the seething anger it generated are now mirrored in the fear whites have of random attack from blacks and the growing anger that fear fuels. The white disdain grows when a frightened white politician convenes a commission to investigate charges of racism, and the anger swells when well-known black spokespersons fill the evening news with threats and bombast. 14

Most politicians don't want to confront the reality that causes the fear. But if politicians don't talk about the reality that everyone knows exists, they cannot lead us out of our current crisis. Because very few people of different races have real conversations with each other—when was the last time you had a conversation about race with a person of a different race?—the white vigilante groups and the black spokespersons who appear on television end up being the ones who educate the uneducated about race. The result is that the divide among races in our cities deepens and white Americans become less and less willing to spend the money to ameliorate the cities' condition or to understand that the absence of meaning in the lives of many urban children ultimately threatens the future of their own children. 15

Yet even in this atmosphere of disintegration, the power of the human spirit 16 abides. Heroic families *do* overcome the odds, sometimes working four jobs to send their kids to college. Churches and mosques are peopled by the faithful who *do* practice the power of love. Neighborhood leaders have turned around local schools, organized health clinics, and rehabilitated blocks of housing. These islands of courage and dedication still offer the possibility of local renewal. And our system of government still offers the possibility of national rebirth.

The future of urban America will take one of three paths: abandonment, 17 encirclement, or conversion.

Abandonment will occur if people believe that the creation of suburban 18 America, with its corporate parks and malls—along with the increasing availability of communications technology, which reduces the need for urban proximity— means that the city has outlived its usefulness. Like the small town whose industry leaves, the city will wither and disappear. Massive investment in urban America would be throwing money away, the argument would go, and trying to prevent the decline is futile.

Encirclement will occur if cities become enclaves of the rich surrounded by 19 the poor. Racial and ethnic walls will rise higher. Class lines will be manned by ever-increasing security forces. Deeper divisions will replace communal life, and politics will be played by dividing up a shrinking economic pie into ever smaller ethnic, racial, and religious slices. It will be a kind of *Clockwork Orange* society in which the rich will pay for their security; the middle class, both black and white, will continue to flee as they confront violence; and the poor will be preyed upon at will or will join the army of violent predators. What will be lost by everyone will be freedom, civility, and the chance to build a common future.

Conversion can occur only by winning over all segments of urban life to a 20 new politics of change, empowerment, and common effort. It is as different from the politics of dependency as it is from the politics of greed. Conversion requires listening to the disaffected as well as the powerful. Empowerment requires seizing the moment. It begins with the recognition that all of us advance together or each of us is diminished; that American diversity is not our weakness but our strength; that we will never be able to lead the world by example until we've come to terms with each other and overcome the blight of racial division on our history.

The first concrete step toward conversion is to bring an end to violence in 21 the cities, intervene early in a child's life, reduce child abuse, establish some rules, remain unintimidated, and involve the community in its own salvation. That's what community policing, for example, is about.

The second step is to bolster families in urban America. That effort begins 22 with the recognition that the most important year in a child's life is the first. Fifteen-month houses must be established for women seven months pregnant who want to live the first year of their lives as mothers in a residential program. We must also provide full funding for Head Start and WIC, more generous tax treatment of children, one-year parental leave, tough child support enforcement, and welfare reform that encourages marriage, work, and personal responsibility.

The third step is to create jobs for those who can work—through enterprise 23 zones, the Job Corps, neighborhood reconstruction corps, and investment in the urban infrastructure. It is only through individual empowerment that we can guarantee long-term economic growth. Without economic growth, scapegoats will be sought and racial tensions will heighten. Without growth, hopes will languish.

Ultimately, the key to all this is the political process. It has failed to address 24 our urban prospects because politicians feel accountable mainly to those who vote, and urban America has voted in declining numbers—so politicians have ignored them. Voter registration and active participation remain the critical link.

Stephen Vincent Benét once said about American diversity: "All of these 25 you are / and each is partly you / and none of them is false / and none is wholly true." For those citizens whose ancestors came generations ago there is a need to reaffirm principles—liberty, equality, democracy—even though these principles have always eluded complete fulfillment. The American city has always been the place where these ideas and cultures clashed—sometimes violently. But all people, even those brought here in chattel slavery, are not African or Italian or Polish or Irish or Japanese. They're American.

What we lose when racial or ethnic self-consciousness dominates are 26 tolerance, curiosity, civility—precisely the qualities we need to allow us to live side by side in mutual respect. The fundamental challenge is to understand the suffering of others as well as to share in their joy. To sacrifice that sensitivity on the altar of racial chauvinism is to lose our future. And we *will* lose it unless we move quickly. The American city needs physical rejuvenation, economic opportunity, and moral direction, but above all what it needs is the same thing every small town needs: the willingness to treat a person of any race with the respect you show for a brother or sister, in the belief that together you'll build a better world than you would have ever done alone, a better world in which all Americans stand on common ground.

QUESTIONS FOR CRITICAL READING, THINKING, DISCUSSION, AND WRITING

Analyzing Content and Technique

1. Explain the "third tragedy" which the writer refers to in paragraph 2. Why does the writer think of this as a tragedy? Do you agree with him? Why or why not?
2. Examine the statistic presented by the writer in paragraph 6. How does it aid his argument? Would you have liked to see some other kind of proof in this paragraph? Why or why not?
3. Define the term "crisis of meaning" (paragraph 9) as it relates to urban America. What examples has the writer provided of this? How is it related to the physical problems the writer discusses earlier in the essay?
4. Classify the different kinds of fear present in American society today. Which one does the writer focus on most? Why? Does this surprise you? Explain your response.

5. Discuss the three possibilities for the future of urban America predicted by Bradley. Which do you think we are heading most directly toward? Support your answer with examples from your own observation or experience.

6. List all the "steps" or suggestions for change that Bradley believes will lead to a better urban America. Of these, which does he consider most important? Why? Which do *you* consider most important? Why?

7. Who is Bradley writing this for? What is his purpose? How does this relate to his political position?

Collaborative Activity

As a group, look through recent newspapers for articles or incidents that give you a sense of the state of health of urban America. Pick out one or two that affect the group strongly and make a presentation to the class based on them. Your presentation should compare the group's views on urban America with Bradley's.

Making Connections

1. Research the Watts incident mentioned by Bradley. What were its causes? What happened? What were its results? Write a paper comparing and contrasting it to the Rodney King incident. What conclusions about urban America and race relationships can you draw from the comparison?

2. Write a research paper examining the state of a large urban center close to where you live. What problems does it face? Why? What is being done to solve them? What still needs to be done?

79

PREREADING ACTIVITY

Write about a time when you shared in an activity with a person from another culture whose native language was different from yours. How did you communicate? What was your experience like?

Typical

MARK SINGER

Mark Singer (1947–) was born in Tulsa, Oklahoma, and is a graduate of Yale. He lives in New York and is a staff editor for *The New Yorker*. Selection 81 first appeared in "The Talk of the Town" column in *The New Yorker*.

At the Peking Duck House, on Mott Street, one recent Saturday 1 evening, the Schwartzman family (Papa Fred, Mama Kyoko, sons Harry and Daniel) got together with the Xu family (Papa Jian-Guo, Mama Jun Cai, daughter Ran) for dinner (prawns in garlic sauce, spicy bean curd, Peking duck, mushu pork, sea bass, double-fried pork cutlets, pickled cabbage, and beef with snow peas and bamboo shoots) and conversation (Japanese, Chinese, English, and Yiddish). They shared a big round corner table on the second floor of the restaurant.

The Schwartzmans are one of those typical Manhattan families in which 2 the father, a native of the city who is an entertainment lawyer, has since the birth of his sons (Harry is ten, Daniel is eight) spoken to them only in Yiddish and the mother, a native of Tokyo, has spoken to them only in Japanese. (When Harry grows up, he wants to be "a producer, director, and movie scriptwriter, and also a lawyer, so I won't have to pay a lot of legal fees." Harry gets a kick out of saying this in the presence of his father's clients. Daniel wants to be "a football player, an inventor, or an Air Force pilot." Harry and Daniel learned their English in school.)

The Xus are one of those typical Woodside, Queens, families in which the 3 father is an abstract painter and former set designer for the Shanghai Opera who, in September, 1984, emigrated from the People's Republic of China with forty dollars in his pocket, was bitten by a dog his first night in America, worked as a delivery boy, eventually got discovered by the Carolyn Hill Gallery, in SoHo, and, in time, managed to sell enough of his paintings to send for his wife

Source: From "The Talk of the Town" section of *The New Yorker*, June 15, 1987. © 1987 The New Yorker Magazine, Inc.

and daughter. Four months ago, Mrs. Xu, who is a ballerina, and Ran arrived in America. Ran, eight years old and in the second grade at P.S. 11 in Queens, is the only student in her class whose native tongue is Mandarin. When Ran was four years old, she briefly attended an English-language school in Shanghai. Absorbing the intricacies of English has therefore been less of a challenge for her than it has for her mother. When a Cantonese-speaking waiter materialized, Mr. Xu conferred with his wife in Mandarin, and then, addressing the waiter in English ordered dinner for everyone.

Waiting for the meal to arrive, the Schwartzmans had one of their typical three-way dinner-table conversations. In Japanese, Mrs. Schwartzman asked Harry whether he thought he would like prawns in garlic sauce. In Yiddish, Mr. Schwartzman informed Harry and Daniel that, because dinner with the Xus was a special occasion, it was all right for them to order Coca-Colas. (This was a compromise; Daniel had said he would prefer a beer.) When Daniel slouched in his chair, his father said, *"Daniel, kenst zitzen vi a mensch?"* ("Daniel, can you sit like a human being?"), and Daniel sat upright. When the pancakes for the Peking duck were brought to the table, Harry said that they reminded him of matzos. He also said that his favorite sandwich was one that his mother invented—cream cheese with Japanese codfish roe, on rye or a bagel. (His second-favorite sandwich filling is *natto*, fermented soybean paste, mixed with mustard and soy sauce or with dried seaweed and scallions.) 4

The Schwartzmans became friendly with Mr. Xu two years ago, after meeting him during a reception at Urasenke, a school that teaches the Japanese tea ceremony, on Sixty-ninth Street between Lexington and Third. "When Mr. Xu's wife and daughter arrived in New York, last January, we invited them over for dinner," Fred Schwartzman said. "It was their first meal in an American household—if ours is an American household." Inviting the Schwartzmans to dinner at the Peking Duck House was Mr. Xu's way of reciprocating. 5

During a break between the mu-shu pork and the beef with snow peas and bamboo shoots, Mr. Schwartzman mentioned that Mr. Xu had donated a painting titled "Meditation on the Homeless" to the National Mental Health Association to be auctioned at its big fund-raising gala in Washington in early June, and that Mr. Xu would be a guest of honor. Modestly, Mr. Xu acknowledged that this was true. In a burst of paternal pride, Mr. Schwartzman also mentioned the brilliant term paper Harry had recently written for his fifth-grade class at P.S. 6—ten pages on the types of weaponry used during the Mexican Revolution of 1810. 6

There was a digression into horror movies; Harry and Daniel are tireless Stephen King loyalists. 7

Daniel asked, *"Tate, kennen mir zeben 'Creepshow 2'?"* ("Dad, can we see "'Creepshow 2'?") 8

"Vos is 'Creepshow 2'?" 9

Daniel said that it was a movie that he thought had something to do with black mummies. 10

"Do you appreciate grossness?" Harry asked us. "You should. It's a major part of life." Then he began to read to Ran his favorite passages from the 1987 11 edition of the "Guinness Book of World Records": coffin dimensions for the burial of the fattest person in the world; longest fingernails; smallest waist; most miserly miser; worst possible writing ("The lovely woman-child Kaa was mercilessly chained to the cruel post of the warrior chief Beast with his barbarian tribe now stacking wood at her nubile feet").

Because the restaurant was crowded, it was hard to sustain conversation above the din. At one point, Mr. Xu asked Mr. Schwartzman to repeat something. "Excuse me," Mr. Schwartzman said. "My English is not so good." 12

When Mr. Schwartzman offered a platter of food to Daniel, they had another exchange in Yiddish. 13

"What did you just say to each other?" we asked Daniel. 14

"He asked me if I wanted a pork chop," Daniel said. "And I said, 'No way, José.'" 15

QUESTIONS FOR CRITICAL READING, THINKING, DISCUSSION, AND WRITING

Analyzing Content and Technique

1. Explain the title of this selection. How is the dinner "typical"? How are the families "typical"? What other related ideas does the title imply?
2. How do you feel about the language habits of the Schwartzman family? What values of the parents do these habits reveal? Analyze the language used by the sons. What does it tell us about them?
3. The culinary details mentioned by Singer are significant in several ways. What do they imply about attitude, lifestyle, and philosophy? Compare the food habits and underlying attitude of the characters here with those of some of the characters and narrators in Part Nine, The Uses of Entertainment.
4. Analyze how the narration and description progress. Is the essay organized in a linear way or in some other way? What is the writer's purpose in structuring the piece in this way?
5. Schwartzman begins to refer to his household as an American household but then adds a disclaimer, "if ours is an American household" (paragraph 5). Why does he do this? Would you say that his family is indeed an American family? Give reasons.
6. From the details he stresses, deduce Singer's underlying ideas about culture and communication. Do you agree with them? Why or why not?

Collaborative Activity

Divide your group members into two "families," one a mainstream American family, the other a family that comes from a different culture. Roleplay a dinner scene at a home or restaurant. Imagine the menu and the conversation. What common concerns and interests would you see the families as having? What differences? After this is done, look back and analyze the ideas about culture and communication that are inherent in the scene the group enacted.

Making Connections

1. Both Louie Crew (selection 78) and the families Singer writes about live in a setting where the mainstream culture and lifestyle differ from their own. How do they deal with this in a way that allows them to survive, function, and be happy? Evaluate their methods and explain which ones appeal to you most.

2. Write about a time when you (or someone you know) found yourself in an unfamiliar environment, as Mr. Xu does in Singer's essay. Describe the situation and your feelings, and explain how you behaved. What did your behavior indicate about your attitude? Is there anything you would do differently if you could relive the experience?

80

PREREADING ACTIVITY

Write about a situation you have experienced, observed, or read of in which one community oppressed another. How did the oppressed group handle the situation?

Mostly Scared: Handling Prejudice in I Know Why the Caged Bird Sings

(Student Essay)

CRAIG WILSON

*B*lack or white, rich or poor, every person needs to have a certain 1 amount of self-respect. The breaking of a person's self-esteem is like the cruel, violent breaking of a wild horse. Bridled and broken, the horse goes on living, but joylessly, without the spirit it once had. This is what often occurs in situations of oppression and prejudice, such as the ones depicted in Maya Angelou's autobiography, *I Know Why the Caged Bird Sings*. But what is inspiring about Angelou's book is the fact that though the blacks in the small southern town of Stamps were constantly humiliated and harassed by the whites, who believed them to be inferior human beings, they refused to give up their self-respect. Instead, they discovered ingenious ways of holding on to their humanity and hope, ways that we can all appreciate, no matter what our race or color may be.

Throughout the book, Angelou gives us many examples of prejudice and 2 injustice. One occurs when some white girls come to the family store and taunt Momma, the grandmother that the young Maya loves and reveres. Maya is filled with rage. She cannot understand how Momma can take this abuse, and how she can call the rude girls "Miz" when they are calling her by her first name, a sign of grave disrespect in the black community. She cries as she imagines the terrible things she would like to do to them, such as shooting them with the rifle that hangs in the house. All the while, Momma just stands there humming a song.

At first we might think that Momma is cowardly, or at best a prudent 3 woman with a lot of self-control who knows what kind of trouble she would be in if she retaliated. But when we look at the song she is humming, we realize the source of her strength. She is humming "Bread of Heaven," a song which expresses her reliance on God as her strength. She is at peace with herself because she is with the Lord. As she states elsewhere, "He never give us more than we can

Source: Student essay reprinted by permission.

bear" (p. 132). She is patient because she knows that the trials of this life are temporary and trivial compared with the glory she will have in heaven. This is one way in which many of the blacks in Stamps are able to hold on to their self-respect.

Momma is willing, for the most part, to accept the events of her life as God's will. However, we see a more assertive side of her when she takes Maya, who is suffering from a terrible toothache, to the dentist. The dentist, a white man, refuses to treat Maya, declaring, "I'd rather stick my hand in a dog's mouth than a nigger's" (p. 160). Had Momma been the one in pain, she would probably have accepted his "policy," but like a protective mother bear she stands up to the dentist to help Maya, forcing him to return, with interest, the money he had borrowed from her so that she can take Maya to another dentist. The relish with which she tells Uncle Willie about the event proves that her spirit is still intact. She knows the limits set on her by society, but within those limits she knows who she is and what she can do, and she respects herself.

The black people of Stamps have other ways of combating the prejudice and segregation that faces them all the time. They band together to form a close community, drawing strength from each other and giving each other respect and praise. At events like the annual picnic, the revival, or the children's graduation, they put forth an extra effort to create an atmosphere of festivity, but perhaps the incident that best exemplifies their solidarity is the Joe Louis fight. On that day, they meet at the store, and from the intensity with which they listen to the radio we know that this is not just a sporting event to them. They see in the ring a microcosm of their world. They see black against white, oppressed against oppressor. To them, Joe Louis is a symbol of hope. If he wins, they can be proud of the accomplishments of not just one man but the whole Negro race.

It is this racial identification that helps Maya withstand a major assault on her self-respect at the time of her graduation. The white speaker, Mr. Donleavy, who is supposed to be there to encourage the students, speaks to them condescendingly, implying that they are good for nothing but being chauffeurs and washerwomen, with perhaps a few athletes thrown in. At first Maya is devastated by this and thinks to herself that it is "awful to be a Negro and have no control over my life." But then, as she hears the entire assembly break into the Negro national anthem, her feelings are transformed. As she really listens to the words for the first time, she is inspired by the sufferings and achievements of those who have come before. She realizes that although the blacks have a long way to go, they have come a long way already. She is proud to be a member of the "wonderful, beautiful Negro race" (p. 156).

Another way in which Maya is able to boost her low self-esteem is by finding black women role models to identify with and admire. One of these, obviously, is Momma. It is from Momma that Maya learns values like cleanliness and responsibility, which make her feel better about herself. From Momma, too, she learns to be tenacious and not give up, a quality that aids her later in life when she tries to get a job as a streetcar attendant in San Francisco. From Momma she gets the indomitable spirit that will not allow her white employer, Mrs. Cullinan, to change her name to "Mary" for the sake of convenience. The ingenious revenge she takes on Mrs. Cullinan by breaking her precious dishes echoes Momma's treatment of the dentist.

Another role model for Maya is Mrs. Flowers, the most elegant black   8
woman in Stamps. Mrs. Flowers opens up a new world of possibilities for Maya and makes her think of "people I had never met personally . . . like women in English novels who walked the moors. . . ." (p. 79). Her simple kindness—sharing a few books and cookies with Maya—makes all the difference to the little girl who always thought of herself as ugly and unworthy of love, especially after suffering sexual abuse at the hands of her mother's boyfriend, Mr. Freeman. After the incident with Mrs. Flowers, Maya declares, "I was liked, and what a difference it made. I was respected not as Mrs. Henderson's grandchild or Bailey's sister, but just for being Marguerite Johnson" (p. 85).

Through the books she gives Maya, Mrs. Flowers encourages her imagina-   9
tion and creativity, and this is another way for Maya to cope with oppression and still keep her self-esteem. At first Maya uses her imagination to escape from the harsh reality of her life, dreaming that she is really a blonde princess, or creating a scenario in her mind of Momma beating up the dentist and making him leave town. These are satisfying moments, but temporary. Later, however, when she plays imagination games, "falling into the sky," for example, she finds a more lasting peace within herself. And still later, by writing her autobiography, she celebrates the struggles and triumphs of her community, bringing to life for white readers like myself people we may never have encountered otherwise and thus never learned to admire. By depicting prejudice in all its ugliness, and by showing us that oppressed people are human and worthy of respect, she goes a long way toward reducing prejudice in her readers. For—as Uncle Willie explains to Bailey in answer to his question, "Why do they hate us?"—prejudice comes, most often, out of ignorance and fear: "They don't know us. How can they hate us? They mostly scared" (p. 167).

BIBLIOGRAPHY

Angelou, Maya. *I Know Why the Caged Bird Sings.* New York: Random House, 1969.

STRUCTURE, STRATEGY, SUGGESTION

1. Analyze the introductory paragraph. Evaluate the analogy Wilson has used. Where is the thesis placed? Is this placement effective? Why?

2. Rewrite the introduction, placing the thesis elsewhere and using other techniques (such as an anecdote or a quotation).

3. Make a brief outline of the major points of the essay. Why has Wilson organized them in this manner? (Explain the logic underlying the structure.)

4. Wilson often uses summarized incidents to support his thesis. Find some examples of these in the text. How do they strengthen the essay?

5. Write an essay analyzing a book or film which has given you a glimpse into, and an appreciation of, a culture different from your own. What did you learn from it? Be sure to support your thesis by using quotations and summarized incidents, as Wilson does.

81

PREREADING ACTIVITY

Write about a friendship that you have observed (or experienced) between two people from very different backgrounds. How did the friendship come about? What helped the two to relate to each other?

Crossing Bridges (Student Essay)

KAREN KAMPF

*M*r. Walls was the kind of person I never expected to know. I guess   1
we were lucky to come together the way we did, as student and tutor; any other circumstances which might have brought us into contact elude my imagination. As different as we were (or maybe because of the difference), we enjoyed a mutual admiration that brightened and enriched both our lives.

The first time I met Mr. Walls was at the Menlo Park Library, where we   2
were to have a tutoring session. He was 65 years old and had decided to learn to read. At the time I didn't know why, but I thought it unusual that someone of his age, after having survived the greater part of his life without this skill, would now undertake the task of learning it. Naturally I went into the encounter with a lot of curiosity and a definite bias of admiration for his "gumption." But as I approached him in the library that day, I was taken aback by his appearance. I had known that he was "older" and black, but I hadn't expected to be frightened by him!

Mr. Walls's skin was the color of chocolate pudding, but the texture was not   3
nearly as smooth. It looked as though time had bumped and bruised and blemished it, and it sagged a little on one side of his full face. He wasn't fat, but every part of him seemed thick and sturdy with a kind of quiet, dangerous strength. His nappy hair was sprinkled with grey and peaked in great disheveled crests around his head. His face wore a forbidding grimace, and his body was clothed in a pair of old overalls with the side buttons left open, as if he had forgotten to do them up or didn't know what purpose they served. His shirt was faded and too small for him, so that his knobby wrists stuck out threateningly.

We greeted each other with a nod and a cautious handshake, and then,   4
with much trepidation, I followed him down a flight of stairs to the library basement, where our lessons were to take place. It was a gloomy cement room, and the absence of other people added to my nervousness. I couldn't help thinking

Source: Student essay reprinted by permission.

that this man's appearance inspired about as much trust as that of a hungry, ill-tempered bear.

At some point during that first meeting, he volunteered the information that he had done some boxing in his younger years. He painted a colorful picture of a man who liked to drink and fight and run around with fast women. His eyes twinkled when he talked about his past, but then he announced that it was just that—the past. He didn't drink or fight anymore, he said, and laughed as he added that he was too old to run around. "I use' to," he told me. "I can' no mo. I'se old now." Beneath his devilish sense of humor, I began to sense a desire to assure me of his harmlessness.

From the beginning our biggest problem was verbal communication. To my ears his words sounded as if they belonged to another language, one sprinkled sparingly with English. He dropped vowels and consonants and sometimes whole syllables, and generally garbled the sounds that he did make. Instead of being embarrassed, he would seem impatient, as with a not-too-smart child, when I would say, for the fifth time, "I'm sorry, Mr. Walls, I can't understand what you're saying." But as time went on, I got better at deciphering his speech and at telling him that his diction was incorrect. Mr. Walls became more comfortable, too, and accepted my corrections with a simple dignity. He knew that my intention was not to criticize him but rather to challenge his desire to learn. Between us grew an unspoken understanding that his limited ability to communicate did not reflect on his value as a human being, and our friendship blossomed under the wide umbrella of our respect for each other.

Because of his illiteracy, Mr. Walls had often received poor treatment in the past. At times he would tell me about it. One such episode involved his previous tutor. She had been with him only four months when she left, but despite Mr. Walls's hunger for knowledge, he wasn't disappointed. He described to me how she would hit his hand with her pencil and raise her voice in annoyance every time he read something incorrectly. "She hit me," he said. "I don' lak dat, no. You don' do dat to no one, dat' bad." It made him ashamed and angry, and he wanted to hit her back, but he never did. I didn't say anything to him, but I could really relate to what he said. She reminded me of my kindergarten teacher, a frustrated woman who had left many scars on my childhood consciousness.

We had been meeting twice a week at the library for about a month or so when Mr. Walls asked me to come to his home for his next session. He explained that his wife Macy had recently gone blind and he didn't like leaving her alone. He confessed that he had even quit his job of twenty-five years to stay home and take care of her. It was clear that her sudden disability had shaken him badly and made him newly aware of his love and his dependence on her. Macy had been the one who had read the mail, paid the bills, and recited to him from the Bible. In fact, anything that had required literacy, Macy had handled for him. Now he wanted to be able to do it for her.

From then on, we continued his lessons at his shabby little home in a black neighborhood at the edge of town. In addition to reading and writing, we would have many long talks about life. Mostly these "talks" were stories of his life.

Sometimes he would loosely quote a passage from the Bible and apply it to the story he was telling. His wife, who sat on a nearby couch, would sometimes interject "Amen!" or "That's right!" and he would pause to pat her hand. Although Mr. Walls never moralized, I would come away from our meetings refreshed by his simple views of right and wrong, his intuitive, earthy sense of justice and compassion. I also admired—even envied—the great faith that the couple shared. Amidst the poverty, the drug dealers, and the littered streets full of potholes and the sounds of nightly gunfire, Mr. and Mrs. Walls lived and loved and did their best to find and promote peace and goodness in the world.

Mr. Walls was generally a taciturn man who didn't talk much about his feel- 10
ings, so it came as a surprise to me one day when he told me that he liked me. "You kin'," he said. "People shud be kin' to one a notha'." There was something about the way he said the word "kind" that choked me up. I was surprised to find, after many years, tears in my eyes. I held them back, for I knew that would have embarrassed him. But the emotion of love and fellowship that he evoked stayed with me a long time.

I came away from my encounter with Mr. Walls with a feeling that things 11
were right with the world. This feeling went a long way toward healing my bitter and lonely heart. Many years ago in Sunday school I had been told that we were all brothers and sisters, but my experience of reality had been that the world was full of cold, hard walls that separated me from other people. Now, although I did not sentimentalize or envy the poverty or ignorance in Mr. Walls's life, I did gain a new appreciation and respect for the power of communication between two very different human beings who came from very different social backgrounds. We had started out like citizens of two warring countries—like the Soviet Union and the United States in the past—distant, with huge oceans between us. We didn't even speak the same language or share the same daily experiences. But somehow, our communication grew clear and strong, as if foreshadowing the changes that were beginning to occur on a global scale. His presence in my world had touched a part of me that wanted to believe that all human beings had much to share with each other, that bridges could be built and crossed. Mr. Walls and I had crossed one such bridge together, meeting halfway, and for both of us, it was good.

STRUCTURE, STRATEGY, SUGGESTION

1. Take a look at the first two paragraphs of selection 83. If the essay began with paragraph 2, how and where could the information in paragraph 1 be introduced? What would be the advantage of that kind of structure? What is the advantage of the present structure?
2. Analyze paragraph 3, which provides a vivid physical description. What elements of Kampf's writing help to bring it alive? What other kinds of details might she have added to give us a sense of her first impression of Mr. Walls?
3. Analyze Kampf's use of dialect. What are some advantages and disadvantages of using dialect or foreign vocabulary in an essay? Do you think dialect works well here? Why or why not?

4. What glimpses does Kampf give us of her past life? Write a paragraph developing one of her hints through an incident or example.

5. Compare Kampf's conclusion with some of the other student essays in the book. What elements do the conclusions seem to share? What unique approaches do you see in them?

6. At the end of the essay Kampf states that both she and Mr. Walls gained from their experience. Write an essay from the point of view of Mr. Walls—either in his voice (not necessarily dialect) or your own—indicating what the incident might have meant to him.

SYNTHESIS *Part Ten*

1. "The Cult of Ethnicity," "Thriving as an Outsider," "Mostly Scared," and "The Real Lesson of L.A." discuss the problem of prejudice against minorities. The writers each take a different angle and propose different solutions. Write an essay in which you evaluate their solutions, discussing which ones you are most comfortable with and why. Support your viewpoint with examples from other sources.

2. "Minor Accidents" and "On Friendship" illustrate different attitudes toward friendship in different cultures. Analyzing these, write an essay about possible difficulties or misunderstandings which you feel might arise in cross-cultural relationships. Bring in examples of your own from other cultures that you have studied or are otherwise familiar with.

3. "Typical" and "Crossing Bridges" show us relationships that *do* manage to overcome the barriers of race and class. Write an analytical essay in which you discuss how the individuals depicted in these pieces manage to do this. What additional techniques or attitudes can you think of which might aid cross-cultural relationships? Through examples from your daily experience, the news media, or other books, illustrate how these attitudes work in real-life situations.

4. Many of the selections in this section and elsewhere in the book underline the importance of being able to communicate and relate to others who are different from us, and the dangers of not being able to do so. The writers indicate that this skill is more important today than ever before. Do you agree? Choosing one selection from this section and one from elsewhere in the book, analyze the writers' ideas and add you own views.

Glossary: Terms for Writers

Allegory. Story or set of events that has multiple levels of meaning, a literal level coexisting with a level that is political, religious, and so forth. An extended, systematic metaphor. (*See also* Metaphor.)

Allusion. Brief reference to a person, place, and so forth, in another literary work or to a real-life event, usually for the purpose of comparison or clarification of meaning.

Analogy. Comparison of something, point by point, with something similar.

Audience. Intended readership of a literary work. This often affects the tone of a piece. (*See also* Tone.)

Character. Combination of traits which makes a person unique. Also, people portrayed in literary works are referred to as "characters."

Climax. Crucial moment in a literary work at which the height of suspense is reached, often followed by resolution of a central conflict.

Context. Background, beyond the actual text, that aids in the understanding of a piece. For example, historical context.

Epigraph. Brief quotation from a person or another literary work given at the beginning of a piece. Usually, an epigraph is thematically relevant to what follows.

Figure of speech. *See* Image.

Focus. Angle of vision from which a narrative is presented and characters, and so forth, are viewed. ("Point of view" and "narrative perspective" are used interchangeably with "focus.")

Genre. Traditional literary form for presenting experience in writing. Examples of genres are drama, fiction, and the essay.

Image, imagery. Description, visualization, or representation of something, often through comparison with something else which is more familiar. Images or imagery may involve all the senses. Examples include simile and metaphor. Also called "figure of speech."

Irony. Discrepancy between what appears to be true and what actually is true. Irony may be deliberate or accidental. The term can also refer to a difference between what is expected and what occurs.

Metaphor. Figure of speech in which something is described as, or equated with, something else. For example, "My love is a rose."

Monologue. Long speech by one person. Monologues can occur in prose or poetry.

Mood. Atmosphere of a work, often suggested by setting, vocabulary, and images. (*See also* Tone.)

Myth. Tale or narrative that is shared by a community and attempts to present answers to questions and mysteries regarding human existence. Examples include the creation myths.

Narrator. Person who "tells" or presents a story, poem, essay, and so forth); sometimes called a "speaker." The narrator can be a character in the story or, presumably, the voice of the author. The narrator often sets the tone. (*See also* Tone.)

Onomatopoeia. Imitation in the sound of a word of the sound of the action it is referring to. For example, "Bees buzz."

Overstatement. Presenting something as more important than it really is; sometimes called "hyperbole." Overstatement is the opposite of understatement. (*See also* Understatement.)

Parable. Brief tale with a moral or religious message that can be applied to other situations. A parable is often metaphoric.

Paradox. Apparent contradiction that may hint at a complex, hidden truth.

Personification. Figure of speech that gives human characteristics to inanimate objects. For example, "The rain drummed its fingers on the roof."

Plot. The action of a piece—what occurs, and why.

Point of view. *See* Focus.

Rhyme. In poetry, agreement, at the ends of lines, of vowel and consonant sounds. "Slant rhyme" or "off rhyme" refers to endings whose sounds do not quite match.

Rhythm. In poetry, the flow of stressed and unstressed syllables, pauses, line breaks, stanza breaks, and so forth. In prose, "rhythm" may refer to sentence structure, length of sentences, and larger patterns within the work.

Setting. Location and context within which the action of a literary work takes place. Setting may include time as well as space. Setting influences the tone or atmosphere of a piece.

Simile. Comparison of one item, person, and so forth, with another, using "like" or "as." For example, "My love is like a rose."

Slant rhyme. *See* Rhyme.

Speaker. *See* Narrator.

Stanza. Structural unit into which a poem may be divided. Stanzas are set off from one another by blank spaces. A stanza indicates the rhythm and rhyme structure of a poem.

Symbol. Something standing for, or suggesting, something else that is more complex or greater than itself; for example, a cross. Actions as well as objects can be symbolic. Sometimes symbols are accepted by entire communities (these are public or traditional symbols). Sometimes they exist only in one person's mind (these are private symbols).

Theme. Idea or concept that is of central importance to a literary work. A theme may have to do with some basic human experience (such as death) and our response to it. The interest of a literary work often lies in how the writer has interpreted the theme—that is, in what he or she is saying about it.

Tone. Attitude of a speaker or writer toward a subject. (*See also* Mood.)

Understatement. Rhetorical figure of speech in which something is represented as less important than it really is. Understatement is the opposite of overstatement. (*See also* Overstatement.)

Index

Index of Authors and Titles